CliffsNotes®

TExES™ Math 4–8 (115) and Math 7–12 (235)

Complex Numbers 37
  Basic Concepts of Complex Numbers 37
  Computing with Complex Numbers 38
  Field Properties of the Complex Numbers 39
Part 2 40
  Mathematical Induction 40
  Modular Arithmetic 41
  Matrices 41
    Basic Concepts of Matrices 42
    Operations with Matrices 43
    Determinants 45
  Vectors 47
    Basic Concepts of Vectors 47
    Scalar Multiplication 47
    Addition and Subtraction of Vectors 48

Chapter 2: Patterns and Algebra 49
Part 1 49
  Basic Algebraic Terminology 49
  Polynomials 50
    Performing Operations with Polynomials 50
    Using F.O.I.L. 51
    Special Products 51
    Division of Polynomials 52
    Simplifying Polynomial Expressions 52
    Factoring Polynomials Completely 53
  Rational Expressions 54
  Complex Fractions 56
  One-Variable Linear Equations 56
  One-Variable Inequalities 58
  Transforming Formulas and Two-Variable Equations 58
  One-Variable Absolute Value Equations and Inequalities 59
  Quadratic Equations 60
    Solving Quadratic Equations of the Form $x^2 = C$ 61
    Solving Quadratic Equations by Factoring 62
    Solving Quadratic Equations by Completing the Square 63
    Solving Quadratic Equations by Using the Quadratic Formula . 63
    Solving Equations That Can Be Written in the Form of a Quadratic Equation ... 64
    Solving One-Variable Quadratic Inequalities 64
  Other Common One-Variable Equations 65
    Solving Fractional Equations 65
    Solving Radical Equations 66
    Solving Simple Exponential Equations 67
    Solving Simple Logarithmic Equations 67
  Systems of Equations and Inequalities 68
    Basic Concepts of Systems of Equations 68
    Solving a System of Two Linear Equations by Substitution .. 69
    Solving a System of Two Linear Equations by Elimination ... 69
  Formulas Used in a Two-Dimensional Coordinate Plane 71
  The Equation of a Line 72
  Systems of Two-Variable Linear Inequalities 73
    Graphing Two-Variable Linear Inequalities 73
    Find the Maximum Value of an Equation Subject to Inequality Constraints ... 74
  Algebraic Problem Solving 75
    General Problem-Solving Guidelines 75
    Translating Verbal Relationships 76

CliffsNotes®

TExES™ Math 4–8 (115) and Math 7–12 (235)

by
Sandra Luna McCune, Ph.D.

Houghton Mifflin Harcourt
Boston • New York

About the Author

Sandra Luna McCune, Ph.D., is a former Regents professor in the Department of Elementary Education at Stephen F. Austin State University, where she received the Distinguished Professor Award. She now is a full-time author and consultant.

Author's Acknowledgments

Thanks to everyone on the Editorial Team. I extend gratitude to Greg Tubach for the opportunity to write this book. I offer special thanks to the incomparable duo of Chris Stambaugh and Lynn Northrup and to the ever-meticulous Mary Jane Sterling for their invaluable contributions.

I am grateful to Grace Freedson for being the best agent I could ever imagine.

I thank my precious family—especially my grandchildren Richard, Rose, Jude, Sophie, Josie, Myla, Micah, and Hailey—for their unconditional love and support. I thank my late husband Donice who was my beloved partner, friend, and mentor.

And I thank God for gifting me with a love of mathematics.

Editorial

Executive Editor: Greg Tubach

Senior Editor: Christina Stambaugh

Production Editor: Jennifer Freilach

Copy Editor: Lynn Northrup

Technical Editor: Mary Jane Sterling

Proofreader: Susan Moritz

CliffsNotes® TExES™ Math 4–8 (115) and Math 7–12 (235)

Copyright © 2020 by Houghton Mifflin Harcourt Publishing Company

All rights reserved.

Library of Congress Control Number: 2020935894
ISBN: 978-0-3581-2998-1 (pbk)

Printed in the United States of America
DOO 10 9 8 7 6 5 4 3 2 1

For information about permission to reproduce selections from this book, write to Permissions, Houghton Mifflin Harcourt Publishing Company, 3 Park Avenue, 19th Floor, New York, New York 10016.

www.hmhbooks.com

Note: If you purchased this book without a cover, you should be aware that this book is stolen property. It was reported as "unsold and destroyed" to the publisher, and neither the author nor the publisher has received any payment for this "stripped book."

THE PUBLISHER AND THE AUTHOR MAKE NO REPRESENTATIONS OR WARRANTIES WITH RESPECT TO THE ACCURACY OR COMPLETENESS OF THE CONTENTS OF THIS WORK AND SPECIFICALLY DISCLAIM ALL WARRANTIES, INCLUDING WITHOUT LIMITATION WARRANTIES OF FITNESS FOR A PARTICULAR PURPOSE. NO WARRANTY MAY BE CREATED OR EXTENDED BY SALES OR PROMOTIONAL MATERIALS. THE ADVICE AND STRATEGIES CONTAINED HEREIN MAY NOT BE SUITABLE FOR EVERY SITUATION. THIS WORK IS SOLD WITH THE UNDERSTANDING THAT THE PUBLISHER IS NOT ENGAGED IN RENDERING LEGAL, ACCOUNTING, OR OTHER PROFESSIONAL SERVICES. IF PROFESSIONAL ASSISTANCE IS REQUIRED, THE SERVICES OF A COMPETENT PROFESSIONAL PERSON SHOULD BE SOUGHT. NEITHER THE PUBLISHER NOR THE AUTHOR SHALL BE LIABLE FOR DAMAGES ARISING HEREFROM. THE FACT THAT AN ORGANIZATION OR WEBSITE IS REFERRED TO IN THIS WORK AS A CITATION AND/OR A POTENTIAL SOURCE OF FURTHER INFORMATION DOES NOT MEAN THAT THE AUTHOR OR THE PUBLISHER ENDORSES THE INFORMATION THE ORGANIZATION OR WEBSITE MAY PROVIDE OR RECOMMENDATIONS IT MAY MAKE. FURTHER, READERS SHOULD BE AWARE THAT INTERNET WEBSITES LISTED IN THIS WORK MAY HAVE CHANGED OR DISAPPEARED BETWEEN WHEN THIS WORK WAS WRITTEN AND WHEN IT IS READ.

Trademarks: CliffsNotes, the CliffsNotes logo, Cliffs, CliffsAP, CliffsComplete, CliffsQuickReview, CliffsStudySolver, CliffsTestPrep, CliffsNote-a-Day, cliffsnotes.com, and all related trademarks, logos, and trade dress are trademarks or registered trademarks of Houghton Mifflin Harcourt and/or its affiliates. TExES is a trademark of the Texas Education Agency. All other trademarks are the property of their respective owners. Houghton Mifflin Harcourt is not associated with any product or vendor mentioned in this book.

Table of Contents

Introduction: General Information
   The TExES Mathematics 4–8 Domains and Their Competencies
      Domain I: Number Concepts
      Domain II: Patterns and Algebra
      Domain III: Geometry and Measurement
      Domain IV: Probability and Statistics
      Domain V: Mathematical Processes and Perspectives
      Domain VI: Mathematical Learning, Instruction, and Assessment
   The TExES Mathematics 7–12 Domains and Their Competencies
      Domain I: Number Concepts
      Domain II: Patterns and Algebra
      Domain III: Geometry and Measurement
      Domain IV: Probability and Statistics
      Domain V: Mathematical Processes and Perspectives
      Domain VI: Mathematical Learning, Instruction, and Assessment
   Question Formats
      Multiple-Choice (Select One Answer Choice) Questions
      Multiple-Choice (Select One or More Answer Choices) Questions
   Registration and Policies for the TExES Math Exams
   Passing Score for the TExES Math Exams
   How This CliffsNotes Book Is Organized
   Studying for Your TExES Math Exam
   How to Prepare for the Day of the Test
   What to Do During the Test
   Calculators and the TExES Math Exams

Chapter 1: Number Concepts
   Part 1
      Arithmetic Operations
      Integers
         Subsets of the Integers
         Fundamental Theorem of Arithmetic and Division Algorithm
         Divisibility Rules and Factoring
         Greatest Common Factor and Least Common Multiple
      Rational Numbers
         Fractions
         Decimals
         Percents
      Irrational Numbers
      Real Numbers
      Absolute Value
      Roots and Radicals
      Exponents
      Comparing and Ordering Real Numbers
      Intervals and Interval Notation
      Computing with Real Numbers
         Addition and Subtraction of Real Numbers
         Multiplication and Division of Real Numbers
         Scientific Notation
         Sums, Differences, and Products of Even and Odd Integers
         Sums, Differences, and Products of Rational and Irrational Numbers
         Order of Operations
         Field Properties of the Real Number System

CliffsNotes®

TExES™ Math 4–8 (115) and Math 7–12 (235)

by
Sandra Luna McCune, Ph.D.

Houghton Mifflin Harcourt
Boston • New York

About the Author

Sandra Luna McCune, Ph.D., is a former Regents professor in the Department of Elementary Education at Stephen F. Austin State University, where she received the Distinguished Professor Award. She now is a full-time author and consultant.

Author's Acknowledgments

Thanks to everyone on the Editorial Team. I extend gratitude to Greg Tubach for the opportunity to write this book. I offer special thanks to the incomparable duo of Chris Stambaugh and Lynn Northrup and to the ever-meticulous Mary Jane Sterling for their invaluable contributions.

I am grateful to Grace Freedson for being the best agent I could ever imagine.

I thank my precious family—especially my grandchildren Richard, Rose, Jude, Sophie, Josie, Myla, Micah, and Hailey—for their unconditional love and support. I thank my late husband Donice who was my beloved partner, friend, and mentor.

And I thank God for gifting me with a love of mathematics.

Editorial

Executive Editor: Greg Tubach

Senior Editor: Christina Stambaugh

Production Editor: Jennifer Freilach

Copy Editor: Lynn Northrup

Technical Editor: Mary Jane Sterling

Proofreader: Susan Moritz

CliffsNotes® TExES™ Math 4–8 (115) and Math 7–12 (235)

Copyright © 2020 by Houghton Mifflin Harcourt Publishing Company

All rights reserved.

Library of Congress Control Number: 2020935894
ISBN: 978-0-3581-2998-1 (pbk)

Printed in the United States of America
DOO 10 9 8 7 6 5 4 3 2 1

For information about permission to reproduce selections from this book, write to Permissions, Houghton Mifflin Harcourt Publishing Company, 3 Park Avenue, 19th Floor, New York, New York 10016.

www.hmhbooks.com

Note: If you purchased this book without a cover, you should be aware that this book is stolen property. It was reported as "unsold and destroyed" to the publisher, and neither the author nor the publisher has received any payment for this "stripped book."

THE PUBLISHER AND THE AUTHOR MAKE NO REPRESENTATIONS OR WARRANTIES WITH RESPECT TO THE ACCURACY OR COMPLETENESS OF THE CONTENTS OF THIS WORK AND SPECIFICALLY DISCLAIM ALL WARRANTIES, INCLUDING WITHOUT LIMITATION WARRANTIES OF FITNESS FOR A PARTICULAR PURPOSE. NO WARRANTY MAY BE CREATED OR EXTENDED BY SALES OR PROMOTIONAL MATERIALS. THE ADVICE AND STRATEGIES CONTAINED HEREIN MAY NOT BE SUITABLE FOR EVERY SITUATION. THIS WORK IS SOLD WITH THE UNDERSTANDING THAT THE PUBLISHER IS NOT ENGAGED IN RENDERING LEGAL, ACCOUNTING, OR OTHER PROFESSIONAL SERVICES. IF PROFESSIONAL ASSISTANCE IS REQUIRED, THE SERVICES OF A COMPETENT PROFESSIONAL PERSON SHOULD BE SOUGHT. NEITHER THE PUBLISHER NOR THE AUTHOR SHALL BE LIABLE FOR DAMAGES ARISING HEREFROM. THE FACT THAT AN ORGANIZATION OR WEBSITE IS REFERRED TO IN THIS WORK AS A CITATION AND/OR A POTENTIAL SOURCE OF FURTHER INFORMATION DOES NOT MEAN THAT THE AUTHOR OR THE PUBLISHER ENDORSES THE INFORMATION THE ORGANIZATION OR WEBSITE MAY PROVIDE OR RECOMMENDATIONS IT MAY MAKE. FURTHER, READERS SHOULD BE AWARE THAT INTERNET WEBSITES LISTED IN THIS WORK MAY HAVE CHANGED OR DISAPPEARED BETWEEN WHEN THIS WORK WAS WRITTEN AND WHEN IT IS READ.

Trademarks: CliffsNotes, the CliffsNotes logo, Cliffs, CliffsAP, CliffsComplete, CliffsQuickReview, CliffsStudySolver, CliffsTestPrep, CliffsNote-a-Day, cliffsnotes.com, and all related trademarks, logos, and trade dress are trademarks or registered trademarks of Houghton Mifflin Harcourt and/or its affiliates. TExES is a trademark of the Texas Education Agency. All other trademarks are the property of their respective owners. Houghton Mifflin Harcourt is not associated with any product or vendor mentioned in this book.

Table of Contents

Introduction: General Information 1
   The TExES Mathematics 4–8 Domains and Their Competencies 1
      Domain I: Number Concepts 1
      Domain II: Patterns and Algebra 1
      Domain III: Geometry and Measurement 2
      Domain IV: Probability and Statistics 2
      Domain V: Mathematical Processes and Perspectives 2
      Domain VI: Mathematical Learning, Instruction, and Assessment 2
   The TExES Mathematics 7–12 Domains and Their Competencies 3
      Domain I: Number Concepts 3
      Domain II: Patterns and Algebra 3
      Domain III: Geometry and Measurement 3
      Domain IV: Probability and Statistics 3
      Domain V: Mathematical Processes and Perspectives 4
      Domain VI: Mathematical Learning, Instruction, and Assessment 4
   Question Formats 4
      Multiple-Choice (Select One Answer Choice) Questions 5
      Multiple-Choice (Select One or More Answer Choices) Questions 5
   Registration and Policies for the TExES Math Exams 5
   Passing Score for the TExES Math Exams 6
   How This CliffsNotes Book Is Organized 6
   Studying for Your TExES Math Exam 6
   How to Prepare for the Day of the Test 8
   What to Do During the Test 8
   Calculators and the TExES Math Exams 9

Chapter 1: Number Concepts 11
   Part 1 11
      Arithmetic Operations 11
      Integers 11
         Subsets of the Integers 12
         Fundamental Theorem of Arithmetic and Division Algorithm 12
         Divisibility Rules and Factoring 13
         Greatest Common Factor and Least Common Multiple 14
      Rational Numbers 15
         Fractions 15
         Decimals 18
         Percents 21
      Irrational Numbers 23
      Real Numbers 23
      Absolute Value 24
      Roots and Radicals 26
      Exponents 27
      Comparing and Ordering Real Numbers 29
      Intervals and Interval Notation 30
      Computing with Real Numbers 31
         Addition and Subtraction of Real Numbers 31
         Multiplication and Division of Real Numbers 32
         Scientific Notation 32
         Sums, Differences, and Products of Even and Odd Integers 33
         Sums, Differences, and Products of Rational and Irrational Numbers 34
         Order of Operations 34
         Field Properties of the Real Number System 36

Complex Numbers ... 37
   Basic Concepts of Complex Numbers ... 37
   Computing with Complex Numbers ... 38
   Field Properties of the Complex Numbers ... 39
Part 2 ... 40
   Mathematical Induction ... 40
   Modular Arithmetic ... 41
   Matrices ... 41
      Basic Concepts of Matrices ... 42
      Operations with Matrices ... 43
      Determinants ... 45
   Vectors ... 47
      Basic Concepts of Vectors ... 47
      Scalar Multiplication ... 47
      Addition and Subtraction of Vectors ... 48

Chapter 2: Patterns and Algebra ... 49
Part 1 ... 49
   Basic Algebraic Terminology ... 49
   Polynomials ... 50
      Performing Operations with Polynomials ... 50
      Using F.O.I.L. ... 51
      Special Products ... 51
      Division of Polynomials ... 52
      Simplifying Polynomial Expressions ... 52
      Factoring Polynomials Completely ... 53
   Rational Expressions ... 54
   Complex Fractions ... 56
   One-Variable Linear Equations ... 56
   One-Variable Inequalities ... 58
   Transforming Formulas and Two-Variable Equations ... 58
   One-Variable Absolute Value Equations and Inequalities ... 59
   Quadratic Equations ... 60
      Solving Quadratic Equations of the Form $x^2 = C$ ... 61
      Solving Quadratic Equations by Factoring ... 62
      Solving Quadratic Equations by Completing the Square ... 63
      Solving Quadratic Equations by Using the Quadratic Formula ... 63
      Solving Equations That Can Be Written in the Form of a Quadratic Equation ... 64
      Solving One-Variable Quadratic Inequalities ... 64
   Other Common One-Variable Equations ... 65
      Solving Fractional Equations ... 65
      Solving Radical Equations ... 66
      Solving Simple Exponential Equations ... 67
      Solving Simple Logarithmic Equations ... 67
   Systems of Equations and Inequalities ... 68
      Basic Concepts of Systems of Equations ... 68
      Solving a System of Two Linear Equations by Substitution ... 69
      Solving a System of Two Linear Equations by Elimination ... 69
   Formulas Used in a Two-Dimensional Coordinate Plane ... 71
   The Equation of a Line ... 72
   Systems of Two-Variable Linear Inequalities ... 73
      Graphing Two-Variable Linear Inequalities ... 73
      Find the Maximum Value of an Equation Subject to Inequality Constraints ... 74
   Algebraic Problem Solving ... 75
      General Problem-Solving Guidelines ... 75
      Translating Verbal Relationships ... 76

- Be Methodical with Units ... 76
- Geometry Problems ... 77
- Age Problems ... 78
- Coin Problems ... 79
- Mixture Problems ... 79
- Distance-Rate-Time Problems ... 80
- Average Rate Problems ... 82
- Work Problems ... 82
- Basic Work Problems ... 82
- Quick Solution Method for Two Workers ... 83
- Number Relationships Problems ... 83
- Consecutive Integer Problems ... 84
- Ratio Problems ... 84
- Proportion Problems ... 85
- Basic Percentage Problems ... 85
- Percent Change Problems ... 86
- Simple Interest Problems ... 87
- Compound Interest Problems ... 87
- Direct and Inverse Variation Problems ... 88

Basic Function Concepts ... 88
- Ordered Pairs and Relations ... 88
- *xy*-Coordinate Plane ... 89
- Definition and Representations of a Function ... 89
- Evaluating Functions ... 90

Domain and Range of Functions ... 90

Graphs of Functions ... 91
- Vertical Line Test ... 91
- One-to-One Function and Horizontal Line Test ... 92
- Increasing-Decreasing-Constant Behavior ... 92
- Monotonic Function ... 93
- Extrema ... 93
- Vertical and Horizontal Asymptotes ... 94
- Positive and Negative Behavior ... 95
- Average and Instantaneous Rate of Change ... 95
- Even and Odd Functions ... 97
- Zeros and Intercepts ... 97

Composition and Inverses of Functions ... 98
- Composition of Functions ... 98
- Inverses of Functions ... 99

Features of Common Functions ... 100
- Linear Functions ... 100
- Quadratic Functions ... 102
- Polynomial Functions ... 104
- Rational Functions ... 104
- Square Root Functions ... 105
- Power Functions ... 106
- Piecewise Functions ... 106
- Absolute Value Functions ... 107
- Greatest Integer Functions ... 107
- Exponential Functions ... 108
- Logarithmic Functions ... 108

Transformations ... 109

Modeling with Functions ... 111

Sequences ... 112
- Arithmetic Sequences ... 112
- Geometric Sequences ... 113

Figurate-Number Sequences..113
　　　Recursive Sequences 113
　　　Identifying Patterns for Sequences 114
　Arithmetic and Geometric Series 115
　Introductory Right Triangle Trigonometric Concepts 115
　　　Right Triangle Ratios 116
　　　Trigonometric Ratios of Special Acute Angles..117
　Three Central Calculus Concepts..118
　　　Limits...118
　　　Derivatives 118
　　　Integrals...119
Part 2 119
　Solving General Exponential Equations...119
　Solving General Logarithmic Equations...119
　Matrix Solutions of Systems of Linear Equations 120
　More about Asymptotes 122
　More about Polynomial Functions 124
　Arithmetic of Functions 126
　Trigonometry 127
　　　The Law of Sines and the Law of Cosines 127
　　　The Unit Circle and Trigonometric Functions..129
　　　Trigonometric Functions of Real Numbers 131
　　　Graphs of the Trigonometric Functions...132
　　　Transformations of the Trigonometric Functions 133
　　　Inverse Trigonometric Functions 133
　　　Special Angle Formulas and Identities..134
　　　Trigonometric Equations and Inequalities...135
　Trigonometric Form of a Complex Number..136
　Calculus 137
　　　Limits...137
　　　Derivatives 140
　　　Continuity 143
　　　Analyzing the Behavior of a Function 144
　　　The Mean Value Theorem for Derivatives...147
　　　Integrals...147

Chapter 3: Geometry and Measurement 153
Part 1 153
　Geometry 153
　　　Congruence, Similarity, and Symmetry...153
　　　Angles and Lines...154
　　　Polygons...158
　　　Triangles...159
　　　Quadrilaterals 165
　　　Circles 166
　　　Geometric Transformations...169
　Measurement 178
　　　Dimensional Analysis..178
　　　Perimeter, Area, and Volume..179
　　　Perimeter and Circumference 181
　　　Area 182
　　　Surface Area 184
　　　Volume 186
　　　Precision, Accuracy, and Approximate Error 186

Part 2 187
  Geometry (Continued) 187
    Matrix Representation of Geometric Transformations 187
    Algebraic Representation of Conic Sections 190
    Algebraic Representation of Spheres 193

Chapter 4: Probability and Statistics 195
Part 1 195
  Preliminaries: Counting Techniques 195
    Fundamental Counting Principle 195
    Addition Principle 196
    Permutations 197
    Combinations 198
    Situations Indicating Permutations or Combinations 198
  The Binomial Theorem and Pascal's Triangle 199
    The Binomial Theorem 199
    Pascal's Triangle 200
  Probability 201
    Random Experiments and Sample Spaces 201
    Probability Measures 204
    Random Variables, Probability Distributions, and Expected Value 204
    Events 207
    Combinations of Events 209
    The Addition Rule 211
    Conditional Probability 212
    The Multiplication Rule and Independent and Dependent Events 214
    The Complement Rule 216
    Odds 216
    Frequency Theory of Probability 217
    Geometric Probability 217
  Statistics 217
    Statistical Questions and Types of Data 218
    Graphical Representations of Data 218
    Measures of Central Tendency 225
    Selecting the Most Appropriate Measure of Central Tendency 228
    Percentiles and Quartiles 229
    Measures of Variability 229
    Standard Deviation and Variance 230
    Statistical Inference 236
    Two-Way Frequency Tables of Categorical Data 238
    Investigating Bivariate Data 239
Part 2 244
  Types of Statistical Studies 244
    Survey Studies 244
    Experimental Studies 244
    Observational Studies 245
    Well-Designed Studies 245
  More about Inferential Statistics 246
    The Logic of Hypothesis Testing 246
    Type I and Type II Errors 246

Chapter 5: Mathematical Processes and Perspectives 247
Basic Set Theory 247
  Set Terminology 247
  Set Operations and Venn Diagrams 248

Equivalence Relations..250
Logic...250
   Basic Concepts of Logic...250
   Statements Associated with a Conditional Statement..........................252
   Symbolism Associated with a Conditional Statement...........................252
   Three Basic Proof Techniques for Conditional Statements.....................252
      Direct Proof..253
      Proof by Contradiction (Indirect Proof).................................253
      Proof by Contrapositive...253
   Quantifiers and Negation..254
Logical Reasoning...255

Chapter 6: Mathematical Learning, Instruction, and Assessment 257
Mathematical Learning...257
   Developmentally Appropriate Practice..257
Mathematical Instruction..258
   Planning Mathematical Instruction...258
   Worthwhile Mathematical Tasks...259
   Mathematical Communication..259
   Cooperative Learning in Mathematics Instruction.............................259
   Mathematical Representations and Tools......................................261
   General Guidelines for Mathematical Instruction.............................261
Mathematical Assessment...262
   Purpose of Mathematical Assessment..262
   Traditional Mathematical Assessments..263
   Alternative Mathematical Assessments..263
   Mathematics Homework..264
   Students' Errors..265
   References..265

Definitions and Formulas 267

Chapter 7: TExES Math 4–8 Practice Test 1 269
Answer Key..285
Answer Explanations...287

Chapter 8: TExES Math 4–8 Practice Test 2 305
Answer Key..321
Answer Explanations...323

Chapter 9: TExES Math 7–12 Practice Test 1 341
Answer Key..358
Answer Explanations...360

Chapter 10: TExES Math 7–12 Practice Test 2 377
Answer Key..393
Answer Explanations...395

Appendix A: Simplifying Radicals 417

Appendix B: Long Division of Polynomials 419

Appendix C: Measurement Units and Conversions 420

Introduction

General Information

In Texas, candidates seeking state educator certification must perform satisfactorily on comprehensive exams in their content areas [Texas Administrative Code (TAC), §230.21(a)]. The Texas Education Agency (TEA) developed the Texas Examinations of Educator Standards™ (TExES™) program to effectuate this mandate.

The TExES Mathematics 4–8 (115) test (hereafter, abbreviated as TExES Math 4–8) is designed to assess the mathematical knowledge and skills that entry-level mathematics teachers in grades 4 through 8 need to possess in order to effectively perform their roles as mathematics teachers in Texas schools. Likewise, the TExES Mathematics 7–12 (235) test (hereafter, abbreviated as TExES Math 7–12) is designed to assess the mathematical knowledge and skills that entry-level mathematics teachers in grades 7 through 12 need to possess in order to effectively perform their roles as mathematics teachers in Texas schools.

Both the TExES Math 4–8 and the TExES Math 7–12 consist of 100 selected-response questions. For most of the questions, you choose one correct answer choice from among four options. You record your answer by clicking the radio button corresponding to your answer choice (see "Question Formats" below for a discussion of question formats). No penalty is imposed for wrong answers (i.e., you merely score a zero for that test question). You are given 4 hours and 45 minutes to complete the test. Before you begin the test, you have an additional 15 minutes for a computer-administered testing (CAT) tutorial and compliance agreement. In most circumstances, a teacher candidate cannot retake the test more than four times [Texas Education Code (TEC), §21.048], for a total of five attempts.

The Texas Essential Knowledge and Skills (TEKS) form the core of the subject matter that is assessed on the TExES Math 4–8 and TExES Math 7–12. The content for each of the tests is organized into six broad domains: Number Concepts; Patterns and Algebra; Geometry and Measurement; Probability and Statistics; Mathematical Processes and Perspectives; and Mathematics Learning, Instruction, and Assessment. Each domain is defined by a set of specific competencies and descriptor statements that clarify the knowledge and skills associated with that domain.

The TExES Mathematics 4–8 Domains and Their Competencies

As given in the TExES Math 4–8 preparation manual (www.tx.nesinc.com/content/docs/115PrepManual.pdf), the domains and competencies of the TExES Math 4–8 (and their approximate percentages of the test) are as follows:

Domain I: Number Concepts

(approximately 16 percent of the test)

- Competency 001: *The teacher understands the structure of number systems, the development of a sense of quantity, and the relationship between quantity and symbolic representations.*
- Competency 002: *The teacher understands number operations and computational algorithms.*
- Competency 003: *The teacher understands ideas of number theory and uses numbers to model and solve problems within and outside of mathematics.*

Domain II: Patterns and Algebra

(approximately 21 percent of the test)

- **Competency 004:** *The teacher understands and uses mathematical reasoning to identify, extend, and analyze patterns and understands the relationships among variables, expressions, equations, inequalities, relations, and functions.*
- **Competency 005:** *The teacher understands and uses linear functions to model and solve problems.*
- **Competency 006:** *The teacher understands and uses nonlinear functions and relations to model and solve problems.*
- **Competency 007:** *The teacher uses and understands the conceptual foundations of calculus related to topics in middle school mathematics.*

Domain III: Geometry and Measurement

(approximately 21 percent of the test)

- **Competency 008:** *The teacher understands measurement as a process.*
- **Competency 009:** *The teacher understands the geometric relationships and axiomatic structure of Euclidean geometry.*
- **Competency 010:** *The teacher analyzes the properties of two- and three-dimensional figures.*
- **Competency 011:** *The teacher understands transformational geometry and relates algebra to geometry and trigonometry using the Cartesian coordinate system.*

Domain IV: Probability and Statistics

(approximately 16 percent of the test)

- **Competency 012:** *The teacher understands how to use graphical and numerical techniques to explore data, characterize patterns, and describe departures from patterns.*
- **Competency 013:** *The teacher understands the theory of probability.*
- **Competency 014:** *The teacher understands the relationship among probability theory, sampling, and statistical inference and how statistical inference is used in making and evaluating predictions.*

Domain V: Mathematical Processes and Perspectives

(approximately 10 percent of the test)

- **Competency 015:** *The teacher understands mathematical reasoning and problem solving.*
- **Competency 016:** *The teacher understands mathematical connections within and outside of mathematics and how to communicate mathematical ideas and concepts.*

Domain VI: Mathematical Learning, Instruction, and Assessment

(approximately 16 percent of the test)

- **Competency 017:** *The teacher understands how children learn and develop mathematical skills, procedures, and concepts.*
- **Competency 018:** *The teacher understands how to plan, organize, and implement instruction using knowledge of students, subject matter, and statewide curriculum (Texas Essential Knowledge and Skills [TEKS]) to teach all students to use mathematics.*
- **Competency 019:** *The teacher understands assessment and uses a variety of formal and informal assessment techniques to monitor and guide mathematics instruction and to evaluate student progress.*

The TExES Mathematics 7–12 Domains and Their Competencies

As given in the TExES Math 7–12 preparation manual (www.tx.nesinc.com/content/docs/235PrepManual.pdf), the domains and competencies of the TExES Math 7–12 (and their approximate percentages of the test) are as follows:

Domain I: Number Concepts

(approximately 14 percent of the test)

- Competency 001: *The teacher understands the real number system and its structure, operations, algorithms, and representations.*
- Competency 002: *The teacher understands the complex number system and its structure, operations, algorithms, and representations.*
- Competency 003: *The teacher understands number theory concepts and principles and uses numbers to model and solve problems in a variety of situations.*

Domain II: Patterns and Algebra

(approximately 33 percent of the test)

- Competency 004: *The teacher uses patterns to model and solve problems and formulate conjectures.*
- Competency 005: *The teacher understands attributes of functions, relations, and their graphs.*
- Competency 006: *The teacher understands linear and quadratic functions, analyzes their algebraic and graphical properties, and uses them to model and solve problems.*
- Competency 007: *The teacher understands polynomial, rational, radical, absolute value, and piecewise functions; analyzes their algebraic and graphical properties; and uses them to model and solve problems.*
- Competency 008: *The teacher understands exponential and logarithmic functions, analyzes their algebraic and graphical properties, and uses them to model and solve problems.*
- Competency 009: *The teacher understands trigonometric and circular functions, analyzes their algebraic and graphical properties, and uses them to model and solve problems.*
- Competency 010: *The teacher understands and solves problems using differential and integral calculus.*

Domain III: Geometry and Measurement

(approximately 19 percent of the test)

- Competency 011: *The teacher understands measurement as a process.*
- Competency 012: *The teacher understands geometries, in particular Euclidian geometry, as axiomatic systems.*
- Competency 013: *The teacher understands the results, uses, and applications of Euclidian geometry.*
- Competency 014: *The teacher understands coordinate, transformational, and vector geometry and their connections.*

Domain IV: Probability and Statistics

(approximately 14 percent of the test)

- Competency 015: *The teacher understands how to use appropriate graphical and numerical techniques to explore data, characterize patterns, and describe departures from patterns.*
- Competency 016: *The teacher understands concepts and applications of probability.*

- Competency 017: *The teacher understands the relationships among probability theory, sampling, and statistical inference and how statistical inference is used in making and evaluating predictions.*

Domain V: Mathematical Processes and Perspectives

(approximately 10 percent of the test)

- Competency 018: *The teacher understands mathematical reasoning and problem solving.*
- Competency 019: *The teacher understands mathematical connections both within and outside of mathematics and how to communicate mathematical ideas and concepts.*

Domain VI: Mathematical Learning, Instruction, and Assessment

(approximately 10 percent of the test)

- Competency 020: *The teacher understands how children learn mathematics and plans, organizes, and implements instruction using knowledge of students, subject matter, and statewide curriculum (Texas Essential Knowledge and Skills [TEKS]).*
- Competency 021: *The teacher understands assessment and uses a variety of formal and informal assessment techniques to monitor and guide mathematics instruction and to evaluate student progress.*

Question Formats

By far, the format of most of the questions on your TExES Math exam will be the standard, single-selection multiple-choice question. However, the exam could include other question formats. For a given question, you might be asked to respond as follows:

- Choose one correct answer choice from among four options.
- Select all correct answer choices from a list of options presented.
- Select a response from a drop-down menu.
- Drag and drop an answer choice to an on-screen area where it belongs.
- Fill in a numeric response in an answer box.

If a question is presented to you in an unfamiliar format, read the question carefully. The question will make clear how you are expected to respond.

Below are examples of the two most common question formats you can expect to see on your TExES Math exam: multiple-choice (select one answer) and multiple-choice (select one or more answers).

Read the directions carefully before you answer a question. If a question has answer choices with **radio buttons** (small open circles), then you must select a single answer choice. If a question has answer choices with **checkboxes** (small open squares), then you must select one or more answer choices.

Radio button	○	Multiple-choice question (select one answer choice)
Checkbox	❑	Multiple-choice question (select one or more answer choices)

Note: The practice test questions in this book label each multiple-choice answer choice with a letter for clarity. These letters do not appear on the computer screen when you take the actual test. Instead, you will click on the radio button or checkbox next to the answer(s) you choose.

Multiple-Choice (Select One Answer Choice) Questions

The multiple-choice (select one answer choice) questions require you to choose one correct answer choice from among four options. The correct answer is just one of the answer choices. The use of radio buttons with the answer choices restricts you to one option. The question is scored as incorrect unless you select the one correct choice.

Example

If $xy \neq 0$, then $\dfrac{3}{x} + \dfrac{4}{y} =$

○ $\dfrac{12}{xy}$

○ $\dfrac{7}{x+y}$

○ $\dfrac{7}{xy}$

○ $\dfrac{4x+3y}{xy}$

Multiple-Choice (Select One or More Answer Choices) Questions

The multiple-choice (select one or more answer choices) questions require you to choose ALL of the correct answer choices and *no others* from among a list of options presented. The correct answer might be just one of the answer choices or it could be as many as all of the answer choices. The use of checkboxes with the answer choices enables you to select one or more options. The question is scored as incorrect unless you select all of the correct choices and no others. There is no partial credit.

Example

For which of the following expressions is $a - b$ a factor?

Select all that apply.

☐ $a^2 - b^2$
☐ $a^2 - ab + b^2$
☐ $a^3 - b^3$
☐ $a^3 - 3a^2b + 3ab^2 - b^3$

Registration and Policies for the TExES Math Exams

You can find information about registering for the TExES Math 4–8 or TExES Math 7–12 at www.tx.nesinc.com/PageView.aspx?f=GEN_RegistrationInformation.html. The registration fee in 2020 is $116; the exam must be completed within 170 days of the registration date to avoid forfeiture of the registration fee.

Links for registration policies (e.g., payment policies), testing policies (e.g., test center rules), and score reporting policies (e.g., canceling your scores) can be found at www.tx.nesinc.com/TestView.aspx?f=TXCBT_TestPolicies.html&t=TX160.

Passing Score for the TExES Math Exams

The passing score for either the TExES Math 4–8 or the TExES Math 7–12 is 240 on a scale of 100 to 300. Not all of the 100 questions on the test are used to calculate your score. Your test will likely contain embedded field-test questions that are being considered for possible inclusion in future versions of the test. These questions, whether you answer them correctly or incorrectly, do not count toward your score; however, you will not know which questions are field-test questions. For each scorable question that you answer correctly, you earn 1 raw score point. Your scaled score is based on the percentage of raw score points that you obtain.

How This CliffsNotes Book Is Organized

This CliffsNotes book is composed of an Introduction chapter, six review chapters, and four full-length practice tests (two for TExES Math 4–8 and two for TExES Math 7–12). Chapters 1 through 6 provide review and practice material for the TExES Math 4–8 and TExES Math 7–12. Each review chapter focuses on one of the six domains common to the two tests: Number Concepts; Patterns and Algebra; Geometry and Measurement; Probability and Statistics; Mathematical Processes and Perspectives; and Mathematical Learning, Instruction, and Assessment. These chapters include a thorough review of the knowledge base related to the domain and study strategies for the test.

To accommodate both 4–8 and 7–12 candidates, each of chapters 1 to 4 is divided into two parts. Part 1 provides review material for all candidates who are planning to take a TExES Math exam. Part 2 provides additional content material that goes beyond the eighth-grade level for candidates who are planning to take the TExES Math 7–12 exam. The concepts in chapters 5 and 6 are overarching ideas that are not grade specific, so these chapters are presented as a whole, rather than in two parts.

Chapters 7 and 8 contain two full-length TExES Math 4–8 practice tests, and chapters 9 and 10 contain two full-length TExES Math 7–12 practice tests. The answers to the tests are keyed to the domains, with full explanations of the correct answer choices.

Studying for Your TExES Math Exam

When you read through the domain competencies and descriptor statements of your TExES Math exam, you may feel overwhelmed by the task of preparing for it. Here are some suggestions for developing an effective study program using this CliffsNotes book:

- **To help you organize and budget your time, set up a specific schedule of study sessions.** Set up a regular schedule of study sessions. Try to set aside approximately 3 hours for each session. If you complete one session per day (excluding weekends), it should take you about 4 to 6 weeks to work your way through the review and practice material provided in this book. Of course, if your test date is coming up soon, you might need to lengthen your study time per day.
- **Choose a place for studying that is free of distractions and undue noise so that you can concentrate.** Make sure you have adequate lighting and a room temperature that is comfortable—neither too warm nor too cold. Be sure you have an ample supply of water to keep your body hydrated; you might also want to have some light snacks available. To improve mental alertness, choose snacks that are high in protein and low in carbohydrates. Try to have all the necessary study aids (paper, pen, note cards, and so on) within easy reach, so that you don't have to interrupt your studying to go get something you need. Ask friends not to call you during your study time. Consider logging out of social media accounts and/or placing your phone on silent or "do not disturb" during your study sessions.

- **Don't make excuses.** Studying for your TExES Math exam must be a priority. It will require a substantial investment of your time and a conscientious commitment on your part. Think of it as a job that you must do. In reality, studying for your TExES Math exam is one of the most important jobs you will ever do. The outcome of the test can determine your future career opportunities. Do not avoid studying for it by making excuses or procrastinating.
- **Read through the domains and competencies for the TExES Math exam you are planning to take to get a general picture of what the test covers; then take Practice Test 1 to help you discover your strengths and weaknesses.** Take Practice Test 1 (Chapter 7) if you are a 4–8 math candidate or Practice Test 1 (Chapter 9) if you are a 7–12 math candidate. Work at your own pace without regard to a time limit. After completing and scoring your test, read the answer explanations for all the questions, not just the ones you missed, because you might have gotten some of your correct answers by guessing. Make a list of the domains with which you had the most difficulty. Plan your study program so that you can spend more time on domain topics that your Practice Test 1 results indicate are weak areas for you. For example, if you did very well in number concepts, but poorly in probability and statistics, then you should plan to spend more time studying the review chapter on probability and statistics.
- **Carefully study the review chapters, being sure to concentrate as you go through the material.** Work through the examples and practice problems and make sure you understand them thoroughly. Don't let yourself be diverted by extraneous thoughts or outside distractions. Monitor yourself by making a check mark on a separate sheet of paper when your concentration wanders. Work on reducing the number of check marks you record each study session.
- **Take notes as you study, using your own words to express ideas.** Leave ample room in the left margin so that you can revise or make comments when you review your notes. Extract key ideas and write them in the left margin to use as study cues later. Make flashcards to aid you in memorizing key ideas and keep them with you at all times. When you have spare time, take out the flashcards and go over the information you've recorded on them.
- **Take several brief 2- to 3-minute breaks during your study sessions to give your mind time to absorb the review material you just read.** According to brain research, you remember the first part and last part of something you've read more easily than you remember the middle part. Taking several breaks will allow you to create more beginnings and endings to maximize the amount of material you remember. It is best not to leave your study area during a break. Try stretching or simply closing your eyes for a few minutes.
- **Set aside certain days to review material you have already studied.** This strategy will allow you to reinforce what you have learned and identify topics you may need to restudy.
- **When you complete your first review of material, retake Practice Test 1.** This time use a timer and take the test under the same conditions you expect for the actual test, being sure to adhere to the test time limit of 4 hours and 45 minutes. After completing and scoring your test, again carefully study the answer explanations for *all* the questions. Then, go back and review again any topics in which you performed unsatisfactorily.
- **When you complete your second review of material, take Practice Test 2.** Take Practice Test 2 (Chapter 8) if you are a 4–8 math candidate or Practice Test 2 (Chapter 10) if you are a 7–12 math candidate. Take this test under the same conditions you expect for the actual test, being sure to adhere to the 4 hours and 45 minutes time limit. When you finish taking the test and scoring it, carefully study the answer explanations for *all* the questions. Analyze the results of the practice test and go back and review domain areas in which you are still weak, if needed.
- **Organize a study group, if possible.** A good way to learn and reinforce the material is to discuss it with others. If feasible, set up a regular time to study with one or more classmates or friends. Take turns explaining how to work problems. This strategy will help you not only to clarify your own understanding of the underlying mathematics, but also to discover new insights into how to approach various problems.

After completing your study program, you should find yourself prepared and confident to achieve a passing score on your TExES Math exam.

Introduction: General Information

How to Prepare for the Day of the Test

You can do several things to prepare for the day of the test:

- Know where the test center is located and how to get there.
- Make dependable arrangements to get to the test center in plenty of time and know where to park if you plan to go by car.
- Read "Candidate Rules Agreement for TX Educator Certification Examination Program" (www.tx.nesinc.com/content/docs/CandidateRulesAgreementForTXEducatorCertificationExaminationProgram.pdf) to make sure you know the test center rules.
- Keep all the materials you will need to bring to the test center—especially your admission ticket and two valid, unexpired forms of identification—in a secure place so that you can easily find them on the day of the test.
- Get a good night's rest the night before your test. Avoid taking nonprescription drugs or drinking alcohol the day before the test, as the use of these products might impair your mental faculties on test day.
- On the day of the test, plan to get to the testing center early.
- Dress in comfortable clothing and wear comfortable shoes. Even if it is warm outside, you might want to bring a sweater or sweatshirt to ensure your comfort, depending on the temperature in the testing room.
- Eat a light meal. Select foods that you have found usually give you the most energy and stamina.
- Drink plenty of water to make sure your body remains hydrated during the test for optimal thinking.
- Make a copy of this list and post it in a strategic location. Check it over before you leave for the testing center.

Tip: Go to https://www.youtube.com/watch?v=hIXNdQI2W1g for a video tutorial of what to expect at the test center on test day.

What to Do During the Test

Here are some general test-taking strategies to help maximize your score on the test:

- Before you start the test, take several deep, slow breaths, exhaling slowly while mentally visualizing yourself performing successfully on the test. Do not get upset if you feel nervous. Most of the people taking the test with you will be experiencing some measure of anxiety.
- During the test, follow all the directions, including the oral directions of the test administrator (TA) and the written directions on the computer screen. If you do not understand something in the directions, ask the TA for clarification. The TA will indicate how you are to ask for assistance.
- Move through the test at a steady pace. The test consists of 100 multiple-choice questions. As you begin the test, make a mental note that question 50 is the halfway point. When you get to question 50, check the on-screen timer to see how much time you have left. If less than 2 hours and 22½ minutes remains, you will need to pick up the pace. Otherwise, continue to work as rapidly as you can without being careless, *but do not rush.*
- Try to work the problems in order. However, if a question is taking too much time, use the "Flag for Review" button in the upper right corner of the screen to flag the question as one to come back to, and move on.
- Read each question entirely. Skimming to save time can cause you to misread a question or miss important information. If the question is complex or wordy, restate it in your own words.
- Read all the answer choices before you select an answer. You might find an answer that immediately strikes you as correct, but this determination might have occurred because you jumped to a false conclusion or

made an incorrect assumption. Also, eliminate as many wrong choices as you can. When applicable, estimate the answer to help you decide which answers are unreasonable.

- If you are trying to recall information during the test, close your eyes and try to visualize yourself in your study place. This may trigger your memory.
- Don't read too much into a question. For example, don't presume a geometric figure is drawn accurately or to scale.
- With application problems, always double-check to be sure you are answering the question asked.
- Change an answer only if you have a good reason to do so.
- Refer to the on-screen "Definitions and Formulas" reference material as often as needed.
- Use your calculator wisely. See the section "Calculators and the TExES Math Exams" that follows for a discussion of this topic.
- Remain calm during the test. If you find yourself getting anxious, stop and take several deep, slow breaths and exhale slowly to help you relax. Do not be upset if the person next to you finishes, gets up, and leaves before you do. Keep your mind focused on the task at hand: completing your exam. Trust yourself. You should not expect to know the correct response to every question on the exam. Think only of doing your personal best.
- Before exiting the test, make sure you have marked an answer for every question. Even if you have no clue about the correct answer to a question, make a guess.

Practice these strategies. As you work through the practice tests, consciously use the strategies suggested in this section as preparation for your actual TExES Math exam. Try to reach the point that the strategies are automatic for you.

Tip: Go to http://www.tx.nesinc.com/PageView.aspx?f=HTML_FRAG/GENRB_CBTTutorials.html and click on "Interactive CAT Tutorial" for an interactive TExES CAT tutorial. The tutorial explains and allows you to practice with main features of TExES computer-administered tests, including how to navigate through a test, how to mark answer choices, how to access on-screen reference material, and how to use an on-screen calculator. (Note: The TExES Math 4–8 has an on-screen calculator, but the TExES Math 7–12 does not. See "Calculators and the TExES Math Exams" that follows for further discussion of this topic.)

Calculators and the TExES Math Exams

If you are taking the TExES Math 4–8: An on-screen scientific calculator will be available to you during the test. The calculator button is located in the upper-left corner on the blue toolbar above the question. After you click on the button, you can reposition the calculator by clicking at the top of the calculator window and dragging it to a convenient location on the screen.

This calculator has a keypad and features that are very similar to the TI-30XS MultiView calculator. You can download a 90-day free trial software version of this calculator at https://education.ti.com/en/software/details/en/3E7218FDF3844AFEBA3885B671191CEB/sda-ti-smartview-ti-30x-ti-34-multiview. The free downloadable calculator guidebook is available on the website as well. You should take time to practice using this calculator before you take the TExES Math 4–8. When you use the on-screen calculator while taking the TExES Math 4–8, be sure to evaluate the reasonableness of *all* calculator results.

If you are taking the TExES Math 7–12: You are required to bring your own graphing calculator (but you cannot bring a calculator manual) to use during the exam. Graphing calculators will NOT be provided at the test center. Only the following approved calculator models may be used:

Texas Instruments TI-73
Texas Instruments TI-83

Texas Instruments TI-83 Plus

Texas Instruments TI-83 Plus Silver Edition

Texas Instruments TI-84

Texas Instruments TI-84 Plus

Texas Instruments TI-84 Plus CE

Texas Instruments TI-84 Plus Silver Edition

Texas Instruments TI-Nspire Handheld with the TI-84 Plus Keypad

(Test-takers using the TI-Nspire Handheld must not remove the TI-84 Plus Keypad while testing.)

Your calculator's memory will be cleared by the TA before and after testing. You should back up your calculator's memory, including applications, to an external device before you arrive at the test center. Be sure to put fresh batteries into your calculator before leaving for the test center.

You will benefit greatly from this CliffsNotes book. By using the recommendations provided here as you complete your study program, you will be prepared to walk into the testing room with confidence. Good luck on the test and in your future career as a Texas mathematics teacher!

Chapter 1

Number Concepts

This chapter provides a review of number concepts that are important for you to know, including number systems and their structure, operations, and algorithms, and representations and number theory concepts and principles.

Part 1

Part 1 of this chapter is for all candidates who plan to take a TExES Math exam. Carefully study the review material, being sure to concentrate as you go through it. Work through the examples and practice problems and make sure you understand them thoroughly. When working a practice problem, you should cover up the solution. Then check your answer when you've finished.

Arithmetic Operations

Addition, subtraction, multiplication, and **division** are the four basic arithmetic operations. Each of the operations has special symbolism and terminology associated with it. The following table shows the terminology and symbolism you are expected to know.

Terminology and Symbolism for the Four Basic Arithmetic Operations

Operation	Symbol(s) Used	Names of Parts	Example
Addition	+ (plus sign)	addend + addend = sum	$5 + 9 = 14$
Subtraction	− (minus sign)	minuend − subtrahend = difference	$14 − 5 = 9$
Multiplication	× (times sign)	factor × factor = product	$10 × 6 = 60$
Multiplication	· (raised dot)	factor · factor = product	$10 · 6 = 60$
Multiplication	( )( ) parentheses	(factor)(factor) = product	$(10)(6) = 60$
Division	÷ (division sign)	dividend ÷ divisor = quotient	$60 ÷ 10 = 6$
Division	⟌ (long division symbol)	$\text{divisor} \overline{)\text{dividend}}^{\text{quotient}}$	$10\overline{)60}^{\,6}$
Division	/ (slash or fraction bar)	dividend/divisor = quotient	$60/10 = 6$
Division	stacked fraction bar	$\frac{\text{dividend}}{\text{divisor}} = \text{quotient}$	$\frac{60}{10} = 6$

The examples in the preceding table show that addition and subtraction "undo" each other. Mathematicians express this relationship by saying that addition and subtraction are **inverses** of each other. Similarly, multiplication and division are **inverses** of each other; they "undo" each other, *provided division by 0 is not involved.*

Be *very* careful when division involves zero. Zero can be a dividend; that is, you can divide a nonzero number into zero. However, 0 *cannot* be a divisor, which means that you *cannot* divide by 0. The quotient of any number divided by zero has no meaning; that is, *division by zero is undefined—you can't do it!* Even zero divided by zero is undefined.

Integers

For this topic, you must understand the structure of the integers and their properties.

Subsets of the Integers

The **integers** = {..., –3, –2, –1, 0, 1, 2, 3, ...}.

Note: Read the braces, { }, around the numbers as "The set consisting of." Interpret the three dots, ..., in this context to mean that the pattern continues without end.

The **integers** are either **positive** {1, 2, 3, ...} or **negative** {..., –3, –2, –1}, or **zero**. Negative numbers have a small horizontal line (–) attached to the left of the number. Positive numbers do not need a + sign attached. The number zero is neither positive nor negative. It does not have a sign.

Integers that divide evenly by 2 are **even**. The even integers = {..., –6, –4, –2, 0, 2, 4, 6, ...}. *Tip:* Note that 0 is an even integer.

Integers that do *not* divide evenly by 2 are **odd**. The odd integers = {..., –5, –3, –1, 1, 3, 5, ...}.

The **natural numbers** (or **counting numbers**) = {1, 2, 3, ...}.

The **whole numbers** = {0, 1, 2, 3, ...}.

A **prime number** is an integer greater than 1 that has exactly two distinct factors: itself and 1. The first 10 primes are 2, 3, 5, 7, 11, 13, 17, 19, 23, and 29.

The integers greater than 1 that are *not* prime are the **composite numbers**. The first 10 composites are 4, 6, 8, 9, 10, 12, 14, 15, 16, and 18.

The integer 1 is neither prime nor composite.

Fundamental Theorem of Arithmetic and Division Algorithm

If $ab = n$, where a, b, and n are nonzero integers, then a and b are **factors**, or **divisors**, of n, and n is a **multiple** of a (and of b) and is **divisible** by a (and by b). Here are some useful facts.
- Every integer has a finite number of distinct factors (see "Divisibility Rules and Factoring" below for a formula).
- Every nonzero integer has an infinite number of multiples.
- The number 1 is a factor (or divisor) of every integer, but it is a multiple of only 1 and –1.
- The number 0 is a multiple of every integer, but it is a factor of only 0.

Tip: The terms *factor*, *divisor*, and *divisible* apply only to integers. However, the term *multiple* can be used with any number *x*, as in *nx*, provided *n* is an integer.

Fundamental Theorem of Arithmetic: Every integer greater than or equal to 2 is either a prime or can be factored into a product of primes in one and only one way, except for the order in which the factors appear. The result is the unique **prime factorization** of the integer. For example, the prime factorization of the number 36 is $2 \cdot 2 \cdot 3 \cdot 3 = 2^2 \cdot 3^2$. This representation is the **canonical representation** of 36.

You can use the canonical representation of an integer to find all of its positive factors (or divisors) in a systematic manner. For example, the nine positive factors of 36 are

$1 \cdot 1 = 1$	$1 \cdot 3 = 3$	$1 \cdot 3^2 = 9$
$2 \cdot 1 = 2$	$2 \cdot 3 = 6$	$2 \cdot 3^2 = 18$
$2^2 \cdot 1 = 4$	$2^2 \cdot 3 = 12$	$2^2 \cdot 3^2 = 36$

Division Algorithm: If an integer m is divided by a positive integer d, the result is a unique integer q (the **quotient**) and unique integer r (the **remainder**), where $0 \leq r < d$ and $m = dq + r$. In addition, $r = 0$ if and only if m is a multiple of d.

Here is a practice problem.

> Problem: What are the quotient and remainder when 21 is divided by 5?
> Solution: When 21 is divided by 5, the quotient is 4 and the remainder is 1 because $21 = (5)(4) + 1$.

Note to the reader: In the following discussion of the division algorithm, all variables are nonnegative integers.

The division algorithm theorem simply means that if you divide m by a positive integer d, you get a quotient q and a remainder r, where r is nonnegative and less than d. Consequently, any integer must have either the form dk, $dk + 1$, $dk + 2$, ..., or $dk + (d − 1)$ for a positive integer d. For example, when $d = 2$, every integer has the form $2n$ (even) or $2n + 1$ (odd). This is true because the possible remainders when dividing by 2 are either 0 or 1. Similarly, when $d = 3$, any integer must have either the form $3k$, $3k + 1$, or $3k + 2$. This is true because the possible remainders when dividing by 3 are either 0, 1, or 2.

Here is a practice problem.

> Problem: What are the possible remainders when the square of an integer is divided by 3?
> Solution: Any integer n must be of the form $3k$, $3k + 1$, or $3k + 2$. Then, n^2 must be of the form $(3k)^2 = 9k^2 = 3(3k^2) = 3u$, or $(3k + 1)^2 = 9k^2 + 6k + 1 = 3(3k^2 + 2k) + 1 = 3v + 1$, or $(3k + 2)^2 = 9k^2 + 12k + 4 = 9k^2 + 12k + 3 + 1 = 3(3k^2 + 4k + 1) + 1 = 3w + 1$, where u is the integer $3k^2$, v is the integer $(3k^2 + 2k)$, and w is the integer $(3k^2 + 4k +1)$. Hence, when the square of an integer is divided by 3, the remainder is either 0 or 1.

Divisibility Rules and Factoring

Divisibility rules can help with factoring numbers. You write $a|b$ to mean a divides b evenly or, equivalently, b is **divisible by** a. For example, $3|36$ means 36 is divisible by 3. Therefore, 3 is a factor of 36. The following table shows some common divisibility rules that are helpful to know.

Some Common Divisibility Rules

Divisibility By	Rule	Example
2	The last digit of the number is even.	$2|2,347,854$ because 4 (the last digit) is even.
3	The sum of the number's digits is divisible by 3.	$3|151,515$ because 3 divides $(1 + 5 + 1 + 5 + 1 + 5) = 18$ (the sum of the digits).
4	The last two digits form a number that is divisible by 4.	$4|47,816$ because 4 divides 16 (the number formed by the last two digits).
5	The last digit of the number is 0 or 5.	$5|42,115$ because the last digit is 5.
6	The number is divisible by both 2 and 3.	$6|18,122,124$ because $2|18,122,124$ (the last digit is even) and $3|18,122,124$ (21, the sum of the digits, is divisible by 3).
7	Double the last digit and subtract the product from the number formed by the remaining digits. If the result is a number divisible by 7, the original number is also divisible by 7.	$7|875$ because $(87 - 2 \cdot 5) = (87 - 10) = 77$, which is divisible by 7.
8	The last three digits form a number that is divisible by 8.	$8|55,864$ because 8 divides 864 (the number formed by the last three digits).
9	The sum of the number's digits is divisible by 9.	$9|151,515$ because 9 divides $(1 + 5 + 1 + 5 + 1 + 5) = 18$ (the sum of the digits).
10	The last digit of the number is 0.	$10|66,660$ because the last digit is 0.
11	Alternately add and subtract the digits. If the result is a number divisible by 11, the original number is also divisible by 11.	$11|2,574$ because 11 divides $(2 - 5 + 7 - 4) = 0$ (the alternating sum and difference of the digits).

Here is useful information to know about divisibility and factors.
- If an integer divides evenly into an integer n, then it divides evenly into any multiple of n. For example, 3|36, so 3|13(36) = 468.
- If an integer divides evenly into both of the integers m and n, then it divides evenly into $am + bn$, for any integers a and b. For example, 9|36 and 9|81, so 9|(2 · 36 + 5 · 81); that is, 9|477.
- If the prime factorization of a positive integer z is $p_1^{k_1} p_2^{k_2} \cdots p_n^{k_n}$, where the ps are distinct positive prime numbers and the ks are their corresponding exponents, then the number of positive factors (or divisors) of z is the product $(k_1 + 1)(k_2 + 1) \ldots (k_n + 1)$.

Here is a practice problem.

Problem: Find the number of positive factors of $z = a^3bc^2d^5$, where a, b, c, and d are prime numbers.
Solution: The number of positive factors of $z = a^3bc^2d^5$ is $(3 + 1)(1 + 1)(2 + 1)(5 + 1) = (4)(2)(3)(6) = 144$.

Tip: Recall that if no exponent is written on a variable or number, the exponent is understood to be 1 (for example, $b = b^1$).

Here is a practice problem.

Problem: The number 18 has how many factors (positive and negative)?
Solution: The number of positive factors of 18, which equals $(2)(3^2)$, is $(1 + 1)(2 + 1) = (2)(3) = 6$. Because the negatives of the positive factors are factors of 18 as well, the number of factors of 18 is $2(6) = 12$.

Greatest Common Factor and Least Common Multiple

The **greatest common factor** of two or more numbers is the greatest number that will divide evenly into each of the numbers. It can be obtained by writing the prime factorization of each number and building a product consisting of each factor the *highest* number of times it appears as a *common* factor of the numbers in the set. The greatest common factor of two numbers m and n is denoted gcf (m, n).

Here is a practice problem.

Problem: Find the gcf (24, 36) by using the prime factorization of each number.
Solution: $24 = 2 \cdot 2 \cdot 2 \cdot 3 = 2^3 \cdot 3$ and $36 = 2 \cdot 2 \cdot 3 \cdot 3 = 2^2 \cdot 3^2$. Hence, the gcf (24, 36) = $2^2 \cdot 3 = 12$.

Tip: The gcf of two numbers m and n is also known as their greatest common divisor, denoted gcd (m, n). This terminology is logical because the gcf is the greatest number that will divide evenly into both numbers.

Use the gcf for word problems in which you must find the greatest common number, the greatest common measure, the greatest common size, and so forth that could be used to divide or distribute objects or things evenly from unequal-size sets so that *none are left over*.

Here is a practice problem.

Problem: A high school club has 18 boys and 12 girls as members. For a presentation activity, the club's faculty sponsor wants to evenly divide the boys and girls into groups, so that each group has the same number of boys and the same number of girls as the other groups, and no one is left out. What is the greatest number of groups the sponsor can make?
Solution: The greatest number of groups is the gcf (18, 12), which is 6. Each of the 6 groups will have 5 students in it, 3 boys (18 ÷ 6) and 2 girls (12 ÷ 6). Notice that $5 \times 6 = 30$, which is the total number of student members (18 + 12 = 30).

The **least common multiple** of a set of numbers is the least number that is a multiple of each of the numbers. It can be obtained by writing the prime factorization of each number and building a product consisting of each factor the *most* number of times it appears as a factor in any *one* of the numbers in the set. The least common multiple of two numbers *m* and *n* is denoted lcm (*m*, *n*).

Here is a practice problem.

> Problem: Find the lcm (24, 36) by using the prime factorization of each number.
> Solution: $24 = 2 \cdot 2 \cdot 2 \cdot 3 = 2^3 \cdot 3$ and $36 = 2 \cdot 2 \cdot 3 \cdot 3 = 2^2 \cdot 3^2$. Hence, the lcm (24, 36) = $2^3 \cdot 3^2 = 72$.

Tip: The least common multiple of a set of numbers is the least number that is divisible by each of the numbers in the set.

Use the lcm for application problems in which you must find the minimum common number, the minimum common measure, the minimum common time, and so forth between multiple events or items.

The product of two integers *m* and *n* equals their greatest common factor times their least common multiple; that is, mn = gcf (*m*, *n*) · lcm (*m*, *n*). For example, 24 · 36 = 864, which equals gcf (24, 36) · lcm (24, 36) = 12 · 72 = 864.

Thus, a quick way to compute the lcm of two numbers is to divide their product by their gcf.

Here is a practice problem.

> Problem: At the entrance to a concert, every 75th person gets a coupon for a free music download and every 100th person gets a coupon for an autographed picture of the performer. What is the minimum number of people who must enter for a person to receive both coupons?
> Solution: The minimum number of people is the lcm (75, 100). Find the lcm (75, 100) by dividing their product by their gcf: lcm $(75, 100) = \dfrac{(75)(100)}{\text{gcf}(75,100)} = \dfrac{(75)(100)}{25} = \dfrac{(\overset{3}{\cancel{75}})(100)}{\underset{1}{\cancel{25}}} = 300$. The 300th person will be the first person to receive both coupons.

Rational Numbers

The rational numbers are the numbers that you are familiar with from school and from your everyday experiences with numbers. The rational numbers include the counting numbers, whole numbers, integers, and positive and negative fractions, decimals, and percents.

The **rational numbers** = $\left\{\dfrac{p}{q}, \text{where } p \text{ and } q \text{ are integers with } q \neq 0\right\}$. For example, $\dfrac{3}{4}, -3\left(=\dfrac{-3}{1}\right), -\dfrac{2}{5}, \dfrac{325}{1,000}, \dfrac{15}{7},$ and $-\dfrac{75}{100}$ are rational numbers.

Fractions

A **fraction** $\dfrac{n}{d}$ has three parts, where *n* and *d* are integers, $d \neq 0$. The integer *n* is the **numerator**, the integer *d* is the **denominator**, and the horizontal line between *n* and *d* is the **fraction bar**. Even though it takes two numerical components—the numerator and denominator—to make a fraction, the fraction itself is just one number. Specifically, it is a rational number.

The fraction $\dfrac{n}{d}$ means $n \div d$. ***Remember:*** The denominator of a fraction cannot be zero because division by zero is undefined. *Note:* The fraction $\dfrac{n}{d}$ also is called a **common fraction**.

The **reciprocal** of the fraction $\dfrac{p}{q}$ is the fraction $\dfrac{q}{p}$, provided $p \neq 0$ and $q \neq 0$.

Chapter 1: Number Concepts

A fraction has three signs: the sign of the fraction, the sign of the numerator, and the sign of the denominator. You can change the signs in pairs without changing the value of the fraction. For example, $\frac{3}{4} = -\frac{-3}{4} = -\frac{3}{-4} = \frac{-3}{-4}$.

Fundamental Rule of Fractions: If both the numerator and denominator of a fraction are multiplied (or divided) by the same nonzero number, the value of the fraction is unchanged. The resulting fraction and the original fraction are **equivalent.** Equivalent fractions have the same value. For example, $\frac{3}{4}$ and $\frac{3 \cdot 25}{4 \cdot 25} = \frac{75}{100}$ are equivalent fractions. Similarly, $\frac{24}{36}$ and $\frac{24 \div 12}{36 \div 12} = \frac{2}{3}$ are equivalent fractions.

When a fraction's numerator and denominator have one or more common factors (other than 1), to **reduce** (or **simplify**) the fraction to an equivalent fraction in **lowest terms**, divide the numerator and denominator by their greatest common factor.

Here is a practice problem.

> Problem: Reduce $\frac{75}{100}$ to an equivalent fraction in lowest terms.
>
> Solution: The gcf (75, 100) = 25. Thus, $\frac{75}{100} = \frac{75 \div 25}{100 \div 25} = \frac{3}{4}$.

To write a fraction as an equivalent fraction with a larger denominator, multiply the numerator and denominator by the same whole number (greater than 1).

Here is a practice problem.

> Problem: Write $\frac{2}{3}$ as an equivalent fraction that has a denominator of 36.
>
> Solution: $\frac{2}{3} = \frac{2 \cdot 12}{3 \cdot 12} = \frac{24}{36}$

To write two fractions as equivalent fractions with the same denominator, you can use the least common multiple as the common denominator. In this case, refer to the least common multiple as the **least common denominator (lcd).**

Here is a practice problem.

> Problem: Write $\frac{1}{4}$ and $\frac{2}{3}$ as equivalent fractions with the same least common denominator.
>
> Solution: The lcd (4, 3) = 12; $\frac{1}{4} = \frac{3}{12}$ and $\frac{2}{3} = \frac{8}{12}$.

A **proper fraction** is one in which the numerator is less than the denominator. For example, $\frac{1}{2}, \frac{9}{10}$, and $\frac{24}{36}$ are proper fractions. A **unit fraction** is a proper fraction whose numerator is 1. For example, $\frac{1}{2}, \frac{1}{3}, \frac{1}{4}$, and so on are unit fractions. An **improper fraction** is one in which the numerator is greater than or equal to the denominator. For example, $\frac{3}{2}, \frac{29}{10}$, and $\frac{36}{36}$ are improper fractions. Any improper fraction has a value greater than or equal to 1.

A **mixed number** is the sum of an integer part and a fractional part, written together like these examples: $1\frac{1}{2}, 2\frac{9}{10}$. When you read a mixed number, say the word *and* between the integer and the fraction. For example, $2\frac{9}{10}$ is read as "two and nine-tenths." In a negative mixed number, the negative sign applies to both parts of the mixed number. For example, $-1\frac{1}{2}$ means $-\left(1 + \frac{1}{2}\right) = -\frac{3}{2}$.

To change an improper fraction to a mixed number or to a whole number, divide the numerator by the denominator and write the remainder, if any, like this: $\frac{\text{remainder}}{\text{denominator}}$. For example, $\frac{29}{10} = 10\overline{)29}^{\,2} = 2\frac{9}{10}$. This is true because it is based on the following set of equalities: $\frac{29}{10} = \frac{20}{10} + \frac{9}{10} = 2 + \frac{9}{10} = 2\frac{9}{10}$.

Even though you are allowed to use a calculator when taking your TExES Math exam, you still need to know and understand how to perform computations with fractions. Understanding the process will make it less likely that you will make an error when performing a calculation and will also help you evaluate the reasonableness of the result of your computation.

The following table summarizes rules for addition and subtraction of fractions.

Rules for Addition and Subtraction of Fractions

Operation	Rule	Examples
Addition/Subtraction—Like Denominators	Add/subtract the numerators of the fractions to obtain the numerator of the answer, which is placed over the common denominator. Reduce to lowest terms, if needed.	$\frac{5}{8} + \frac{1}{8} = \frac{5+1}{8} = \frac{6}{8} = \frac{6 \div 2}{8 \div 2} = \frac{3}{4}$; $\frac{5}{8} - \frac{1}{8} = \frac{5-1}{8} = \frac{4}{8} = \frac{4 \div 4}{8 \div 4} = \frac{1}{2}$
Addition/Subtraction—Unlike Denominators	Write the fractions as equivalent fractions with the same least common denominator. Add/subtract the numerators of the fractions to obtain the numerator of the answer, which is placed over the common denominator. Reduce to lowest terms, if needed.	$\frac{1}{4} + \frac{2}{3} = \frac{3}{12} + \frac{8}{12} = \frac{3+8}{12} = \frac{11}{12}$; $\frac{3}{4} - \frac{2}{3} = \frac{9}{12} - \frac{8}{12} = \frac{9-8}{12} = \frac{1}{12}$

The following table summarizes rules for multiplication and division of fractions.

Rules for Multiplication and Division of Fractions

Operation	Rule	Example
Multiplication—Proper Fractions or Improper Fractions	Multiply the numerators to obtain the numerator of the product and multiply the denominators to obtain the denominator of the product. Reduce to lowest terms, if needed.	$\frac{1}{3} \times \frac{3}{4} = \frac{1 \times 3}{3 \times 4} = \frac{3}{12} = \frac{3 \div 3}{12 \div 3} = \frac{1}{4}$
Multiplication—Proper Fraction and Whole Number	Write the whole number as an equivalent fraction with denominator 1 and then multiply as with proper fractions.	$\frac{3}{4} \times 12 = \frac{3}{4} \times \frac{12}{1} = \frac{3 \times 12}{4 \times 1} = \frac{36}{4} = \frac{36 \div 4}{4 \div 4} = \frac{9}{1} = 9$
Multiplication—One or More Mixed Numbers	Change the mixed numbers to improper fractions and then multiply as with proper fractions.	$2\frac{3}{4} \times 1\frac{1}{3} = \frac{11}{4} \times \frac{4}{3} = \frac{11 \times 4}{4 \times 3} = \frac{44}{12} = \frac{44 \div 4}{12 \div 4} = \frac{11}{3}$ or $3\frac{2}{3}$
Division—Proper Fractions or Improper Fractions	Multiply the first fraction by the *reciprocal* of the second fraction.	$\frac{4}{3} \div \frac{1}{2} = \frac{4}{3} \times \frac{2}{1} = \frac{4 \times 2}{3 \times 1} = \frac{8}{3}$ or $2\frac{2}{3}$

continued

Operation	Rule	Example
Division—Whole Number Divisor	Write the whole number as an equivalent fraction with denominator 1 and then multiply the first fraction by the *reciprocal* of the whole number fraction.	$\frac{4}{5} \div 3 = \frac{4}{5} \div \frac{3}{1} = \frac{4}{5} \times \frac{1}{3} = \frac{4 \times 1}{5 \times 3} = \frac{4}{15}$
Division—One or More Mixed Numbers	Change the mixed numbers to improper fractions and then multiply the first fraction by the *reciprocal* of the second fraction.	$2\frac{1}{3} \div 1\frac{1}{2} = \frac{7}{3} \div \frac{3}{2} = \frac{7}{3} \times \frac{2}{3} = \frac{7 \times 2}{3 \times 3} = \frac{14}{9}$ or $1\frac{5}{9}$

Tip: Here is a mnemonic to help you remember division of fractions: "Keep, change, flip," meaning "*Keep* the first fraction, *change* division to multiplication, and then *flip* the second fraction to its reciprocal."

You can make multiplying fractions easier by reducing to lowest terms before any multiplication is performed. Simply divide out factors common to a numerator and denominator (as in reducing) before multiplying. For example,

$$2\frac{3}{4} \times 1\frac{1}{3} = \frac{11}{4} \times \frac{\cancel{4}^{1}}{3} = \frac{11}{3} \text{ or } 3\frac{2}{3}$$

Decimals

Decimals are rational numbers that are written using a base-10 place-value system. The value of a number is based on the placement of the decimal point in the number, as shown below.

Thousands Hundreds Tens Ones **Decimal Point** Tenths Hundredths Thousandths

3, 5 4 7 . 6 1 2

The value of this number is 3 thousands + 5 hundreds + 4 tens + 7 ones + 6 tenths + 1 hundredth + 2 thousandths, which is the same as $3{,}000 + 500 + 40 + 7 + \frac{6}{10} + \frac{1}{100} + \frac{2}{1{,}000}$.

In a decimal number, the number of digits to the right of the decimal point up to and including the final digit is the number of decimal places in the number. For example, a whole number such as 376 has zero decimal places, the number 37.6 has one decimal place, the number 3.76 has two decimal places, and the number 3.760 has three decimal places.

Tip: If no decimal point is shown in a number, the decimal point is understood to be to the immediate right of the rightmost digit.

The decimal equivalent of a rational number either **terminates** in 0s or eventually **repeats** a block of one or more of the same digits.

To obtain the decimal representation of a rational number that is in fractional form, divide the numerator by the denominator. Insert a decimal point in the numerator and zeros to the right of the decimal point to complete the division.

Here is a practice problem.

Problem: Write the decimal representation of $\frac{3}{5}$.

Solution: $\frac{3}{5} = 0.6$ because $5\overline{)3.0}$ with quotient 0.6

In the previous problem, the decimal representation of $\frac{3}{5}$ **terminates** in zeros (eventually has a zero remainder). You needed to insert only one zero after the decimal point for the division to reach a zero remainder. Inserting additional zeros would lead to repeated 0s to the right of 0.6 (like this: 0.6000...).

For some rational numbers, the decimal representation has a **repeating** pattern of one or more digits.

Here is a practice problem.

Problem: Write the decimal representation of $\frac{2}{3}$.

Solution: $\frac{2}{3} = 3\overline{)2.000...}$ with quotient $0.666...$

In the problem above, no matter how long you continue to insert zeros and divide, the 6s in the quotient continue without end. Put a bar over the repeating digit (or digits, when a block of digits repeats) to indicate the repetition. Thus, $\frac{2}{3} = 0.\overline{6}$. Or you can stop the division at some point and write the remainder as a fraction whose denominator is the divisor. For example, carrying the division to two decimal places yields the following:

$$\frac{2}{3} = 0.66\frac{2}{3}$$

Either form is correct. That is, $\frac{2}{3} = 0.\overline{6} = 0.66\frac{2}{3}$.

Tip: It is incorrect to write $\frac{2}{3} = 0.6$ or $\frac{2}{3} = 0.66$. Still, when decimals repeat, they are usually rounded to a specified degree of accuracy. For example, $0.666... \approx 0.67$ when rounded to two decimal places. The symbol "$\approx$" is read "is approximately equal to."

All terminating and repeating decimals are rational numbers. To change a terminating decimal fraction to its equivalent fractional representation, place the digits that are to the right of the decimal point over the power of 10 corresponding to the rightmost place value of the number. Reduce the resulting fraction as needed.

Here is a practice problem.

Problem: Change 0.375 to its equivalent fractional representation.

Solution: $0.375 = \frac{375}{1,000} = \frac{375 \div 125}{1,000 \div 125} = \frac{3}{8}$

Here is a procedure for determining the fractional form of a repeating decimal fraction.

Let $x = 0.4545...$. Determine its fractional form.

Step 1. Multiply both sides of the equation $x = 0.4545...$ by 100 (because two digits repeat).

$$x = 0.4545...$$
$$100 \cdot x = 100(0.4545...)$$
$$100x = 45.4545...$$

Step 2. Subtract the original equation from the new equation.

$$100x = 45.4545\ldots$$
$$-x = -0.4545\ldots$$
$$99x = 45.0000\ldots$$

Step 3. Solve for x by dividing both sides of the resulting equation by the coefficient of x.

$$99x = 45$$
$$\frac{99x}{99} = \frac{45}{99}$$
$$\frac{99x}{99} = \frac{45 \div 9}{99 \div 9}$$
$$x = \frac{5}{11}$$

Thus, $0.4545\ldots = \frac{5}{11}$.

Tip: Notice when you multiply 0.4545... by 100, you can write the product as 45.4545.... You can do this because there are infinitely many 45s to the right of the decimal point, so you can write as many as you please.

You should do your decimal computations with your calculator when you take your TExES Math exam. Just for review, the following table summarizes rules for decimal computations.

Rules for Computations with Decimals

Operation	Rule	Example(s)
Addition/ subtraction	Line up the decimal points vertically. Add/subtract as you would with whole numbers. Place the decimal point in the answer directly under the decimal points in the problem.	$65.3 + 0.34 \rightarrow 65.30$ $\quad$ $65.3 - 0.34 \rightarrow 65.30$ $+0.34$ -0.34 65.64 64.96
Tip: Fill in empty decimal places with zeros.		
Multiplication	Multiply the numbers as whole numbers. Place the decimal point in the proper place in the product. The number of decimal places in the product is the sum of the number of decimal places in the numbers being multiplied. If there are not enough places, insert one or more zeros at the *left* end of the number.	0.002 $0.002 \times 0.0003 \rightarrow \ \underline{\times 0.0003}$ 0.0000006
Division	Rewrite the problem as an equivalent problem with a whole number divisor. Do this by multiplying the divisor and dividend by the power of 10 that makes the divisor a whole number, inserting additional zeros after the dividend, if needed. Divide as with whole numbers. Place the decimal point in the quotient directly above the decimal point in the dividend.	$2.04 \div 0.002 \rightarrow 0.002\overline{)2.040} \rightarrow 0002\overline{)2040.} = 1{,}020$

Chapter 1: Number Concepts

Percents

Percent means "per hundred." The percent sign is a short way to write $\frac{1}{100}$ or 0.01. When you have a percent sign, you can substitute multiplying by $\frac{1}{100}$ or by 0.01 for the percent sign. Thus, 100% is just a special way to write the number 1—because $100\% = 100\left(\frac{1}{100}\right) = \frac{100}{100} = 1$. If you have 100% of something, you have all of it. A percent that is less than 100% is less than 1. When you have less than 100% of something, you have less than all of it. A percent that is greater than 100% is greater than 1. When you have more than 100% of something, you have more than all of it. Here are examples: 100% of $200 is $200; 50% of $200 is $100; and 150% of $200 is $300.

In general, a **percent** expresses a number as an equivalent ratio in which the denominator is 100. For example, $25\% = 25\left(\frac{1}{100}\right) = \frac{25}{100} = 0.25$.

To write a percent as an equivalent fraction, multiply the number immediately to the left of the percent sign by $\frac{1}{100}$. Drop the percent sign because you have replaced it with multiplying by $\frac{1}{100}$. The resulting fraction may then be reduced to lowest terms, if possible.

Here are two practice problems.

    Problem: Write 50% as an equivalent fraction in reduced form.
    Solution: $50\% = 50\left(\frac{1}{100}\right) = \frac{50}{100} = \frac{50 \div 50}{100 \div 50} = \frac{1}{2}$

    Problem: Write 125% as an equivalent fraction in reduced form.
    Solution: $125\% = 125\left(\frac{1}{100}\right) = \frac{125}{100} = \frac{125 \div 25}{100 \div 25} = \frac{5}{4} = 1\frac{1}{4}$

When percents contain decimal fractions, replace the percent sign with multiplying by $\frac{1}{100}$, and then multiply the numerator and denominator by 10, 100, or 1,000, and so on, to remove the decimal in the numerator. Next, reduce the resulting fraction, if possible.

Here is a practice problem.

    Problem: Write 12.5% as an equivalent fraction in reduced form.
    Solution: $12.5\% = 12.5\left(\frac{1}{100}\right) = \frac{12.5}{100} = \frac{12.5 \times 10}{100 \times 10} = \frac{125}{1,000} = \frac{125 \div 125}{1,000 \div 125} = \frac{1}{8}$

If a percent contains a simple common fraction, replace the percent sign with multiplying by $\frac{1}{100}$, and then reduce, if possible.

Here is a practice problem.

    Problem: Write $\frac{1}{2}\%$ as an equivalent fraction in reduced form.
    Solution: $\frac{1}{2}\% = \frac{1}{2}\left(\frac{1}{100}\right) = \frac{1}{200}$

Tip: $\frac{1}{2}\%$ is less than 1%.

When percents contain mixed fractions, change the mixed fraction to an improper fraction, replace the percent sign with multiplying by $\frac{1}{100}$, and then reduce, if possible.

Here is a practice problem.

>Problem: Write $33\frac{1}{3}\%$ as an equivalent fraction in reduced form.
>Solution: $33\frac{1}{3}\% = \frac{100}{3}\left(\frac{1}{100}\right) = \frac{100}{300} = \frac{100 \div 100}{300 \div 100} = \frac{1}{3}$

To write a percent as an equivalent decimal, change it to an equivalent fraction in which the denominator is 100 and then divide by 100. For example, $75\% = \frac{75}{100} = 100\overline{)75.00}^{\,0.75}$. A shortcut for this process is to move the decimal point two places to the left (which is the same as dividing by 100), inserting leftmost zeros as needed, and discard the percent sign.

Here are three practice problems.

>Problem: Write 25% as an equivalent decimal.
>Solution: 25% = 0.25

>Problem: Write 8% as an equivalent decimal.
>Solution: 8% = 0.08

>Problem: Write 200% as an equivalent decimal.
>Solution: 200% = 2.00 = 2

Conversely, to write a decimal in percent form, move the decimal point two places to the right (which is the same as multiplying by 100), inserting rightmost zeros as needed, and attach the percent sign (%) at the end of the resulting number.

Here are three practice problems.

>Problem: Write 0.45 as an equivalent percent.
>Solution: 0.45 = 45%

>Problem: Write 0.125 as an equivalent percent.
>Solution: 0.125 = 12.5%

>Problem: Write 0.0025 as an equivalent percent.
>Solution: 0.0025 = 0.25%

To write a fraction in percent form, first write the fraction as an equivalent decimal by performing the indicated division and then change the resulting decimal to a percent. When the quotient is a repeating decimal, carry the division to two decimal places and then write the remainder as a fraction, like this: $\frac{\text{remainder}}{\text{divisor}}$.

Here are two practice problems.

>Problem: Write $\frac{3}{5}$ as an equivalent percent.
>Solution: $\frac{3}{5} = 0.6 = 60\%$

>Problem: Write $\frac{1}{3}$ as an equivalent percent.
>Solution: $\frac{1}{3} = 0.33\frac{1}{3} = 33\frac{1}{3}\%$

Before you take your TExES Math exam, it would be to your advantage to memorize the following list of common percents with their fraction and decimal equivalents. Make a set of flashcards to carry with you and drill on these when you have spare time.

$100\% = 1.00 = 1$ $33\frac{1}{3}\% = 0.33\frac{1}{3} = \frac{1}{3}$ $20\% = 0.20 = 0.2 = \frac{1}{5}$ $10\% = 0.10 = 0.1 = \frac{1}{10}$

$75\% = 0.75 = \frac{3}{4}$ $66\frac{2}{3}\% = 0.66\frac{2}{3} = \frac{2}{3}$ $40\% = 0.40 = 0.4 = \frac{2}{5}$ $30\% = 0.30 = 0.3 = \frac{3}{10}$

$50\% = 0.50 = 0.5 = \frac{1}{2}$ $60\% = 0.60 = 0.6 = \frac{3}{5}$ $5\% = 0.05 = \frac{1}{20}$

$25\% = 0.25 = \frac{1}{4}$ $80\% = 0.80 = 0.8 = \frac{4}{5}$

Tip: Pay attention to decimals with percent signs. For example, do not confuse 0.25% with 25%. These two percents are not equal: 0.25% = 0.0025, while 25% = 0.25, which is 100 times larger than 0.0025.

Irrational Numbers

Irrational numbers are numbers that *cannot* be written as the ratio of two integers. They have nonterminating, nonrepeating decimal representations. There are infinitely many decimals that are neither terminating nor repeating decimals. For example, 0.343344333444… is such a decimal. Even though you can predict that if the pattern in the digits to the right of the decimal point continues, four 3s followed by four 4s would come next in the decimal representation, the number is not a repeating decimal because a *block of the same digits* does not repeat. Therefore, 0.343344333444… is an irrational number. Other examples of irrational numbers are $\sqrt{6}$ (the square root of 6), $\sqrt[3]{-75}$ (the cube root of –75), e (Euler's number), and π (pi). With these numbers, there is no discernible repeating pattern in the decimal representation. You can use an ellipsis (…) to indicate digits are missing, as shown here.

$$\sqrt{6} = 2.449490\ldots \quad \sqrt[3]{-75} = -4.217163\ldots \quad e = 2.718281\ldots \quad \pi = 3.141593\ldots$$

Tip: Some roots of rational numbers are rational, and others are not. For example, $\sqrt{6}$ is irrational; but $\sqrt{4}$ is 2, a rational number. $\sqrt[3]{-75}$ is irrational; but $\sqrt[3]{-8}$ is –2, a rational number. Furthermore, be cautious with *even* roots of rational numbers. When working with real numbers, be aware that taking the square root, fourth root, eighth root, and so forth of a *negative* number will *not* yield a real number.

For computational purposes, you can only approximate irrational numbers. For example, if you want to use $\sqrt{6}$, $\sqrt[3]{-75}$, e, or π in computations, you can obtain an approximate value for each using a preselected number of decimal places. For example, their decimal representations rounded to two places are as follows:

$$\sqrt{6} \approx 2.45 \quad \sqrt[3]{-75} \approx -4.22 \quad e \approx 2.72 \quad \pi \approx 3.14$$

Tip: Use your calculator to estimate irrational numbers.

However, it is important to remember that if the *exact* value of an irrational root is desired, the radical symbol must be retained. For example, if the area of a square is 6 cm², then the exact length of each side of the square is $\sqrt{6}$ cm. *Note:* See "Roots and Radicals" later in this chapter for an additional discussion of roots.

Real Numbers

The real numbers, denoted R, are made up of all the rational numbers plus all the irrational numbers. The counting numbers, whole numbers, integers, rational numbers, and irrational numbers are all subsets of the real numbers. The relationship of the subsets of the real numbers is illustrated in the following figure. Each set in the figure contains those sets below it to which it is connected.

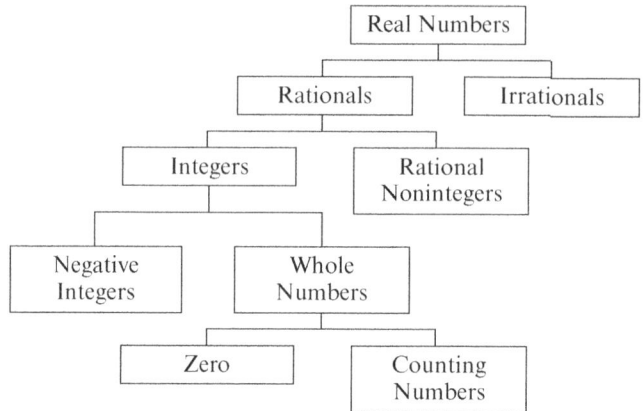

The real numbers can be represented on a number line. Every real number corresponds to a point on the number line, and every point on the number line corresponds to a real number. Positive numbers are located to the right of zero, and negative numbers are to the left of zero. Here are examples.

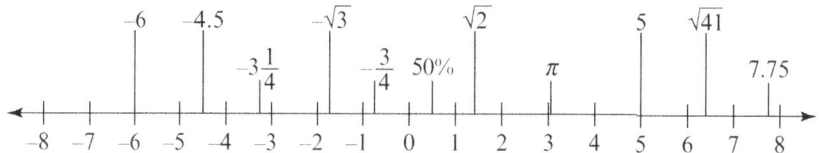

Real numbers are sometimes called **signed numbers** because they are positive, negative, or zero.

Absolute Value

The **absolute value** of a real number is its distance from zero on the number line. The absolute value is indicated by two vertical bars (| |), one on either side of the number. As shown below, |6| = |–6| = 6 because each is 6 units from zero on the number line.

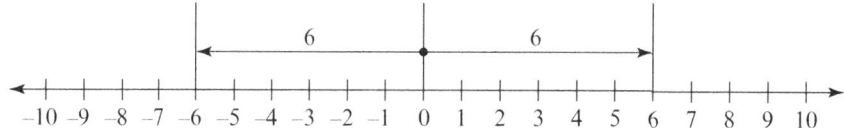

Tip: A number and its opposite have the same absolute value.

Distance always has a *nonnegative* (*positive* or *zero*) value. So, absolute value is always *nonnegative*. The absolute value of zero is zero; and, for any *nonzero* number, the absolute value is positive. This is true whether the nonzero number is positive or negative. Here are examples.

$$|0| = 0 \quad |-15| = 15 \quad \left|\frac{3}{4}\right| = \frac{3}{4} \quad |-4.5| = 4.5 \quad |-100| = 100 \quad |100| = 100$$

As you can see, the absolute values of the numbers in the examples are the values of the numbers with no signs attached. The signs are unnecessary because the absolute value of a number is positive or zero, neither of which needs a sign attached. In simple terms, the absolute value of a number is its size without regard to a positive or negative value.

Obviously, the absolute value of a specific number (one whose numerical value you know and that you could locate on a number line) is just the value of the number with no sign attached. However, when you don't know the numerical value of an unknown number x, its absolute value could be x or it could be x's opposite. Therefore, **absolute value** is defined as follows:

$$\text{For any real number } x, \text{ the absolute value of } x \text{ is } |x| = \begin{cases} x, & \text{if } x \geq 0 \\ -x, & \text{if } x < 0 \end{cases}.$$

The definition says that for a positive number or zero ($x \geq 0$), the absolute value is the same as the number, but for a negative number ($x < 0$), the absolute value is the same as the number's opposite. Remember, $-x$ can be a positive number. Don't be confused by the − symbol to the left of x in the lower portion of the definition. The − symbol to the immediate left of x is the symbol for the operation of **negation.** It tells you to change the sign of the number x. When the number x itself is *nonnegative* (positive or zero), $|x|$ is the *nonnegative* number x; but when the number x is *negative*, $|x|$ is the *positive* number $-x$.

Here is a practice problem.

    Problem: Evaluate $|-8.5| - |3.2| + |-6.4|$.

    Solution: $|-8.5| - |3.2| + |-6.4| = 8.5 - 3.2 + 6.4 = 11.7$

Absolute value has the following properties for all real numbers x and y.

$$|x| \geq 0$$
$$|0| = 0$$
$$|x| = |-x|$$
$$|xy| = |x||y|$$
$$\left|\frac{x}{y}\right| = \frac{|x|}{|y|}, \text{ provided } y \neq 0$$
$$|x+y| \leq |x| + |y|$$
$$\sqrt{x^2} = |x|$$

Here is a practice problem.

    Problem: Evaluate $\left|\frac{-3}{5}\right|$.

    Solution: $\left|\frac{-3}{5}\right| = \frac{|-3|}{|5|} = \frac{3}{5}$

Here are additional properties that are useful to know.

If c is any positive number,

$|x| = c$ if and only if $x = c$ or $x = -c$.

$|x| < c$ if and only if $-c < x < c$ (**conjunction**).

$|x| > c$ if and only if $x < -c$ or $x > c$ (**disjunction**).

Note: Properties involving < and > hold if you replace < with ≤ and > with ≥.

Here are two practice problems.

>Problem: Write $|x| < 2.5$ as a conjunction.
>Solution: $|x| < 2.5$ if and only if $-2.5 < x < 2.5$.
>Problem: Write $|x| \geq \frac{1}{2}$ as a disjunction.
>Solution: $|x| \geq \frac{1}{2}$ if and only if $x \leq -\frac{1}{2}$ or $x \geq \frac{1}{2}$.

See "Absolute Value Functions" in Chapter 2 for an additional discussion of absolute value.

Roots and Radicals

You **square** a number by multiplying the number by itself. The reverse of squaring a number is finding the **square root**. Every positive number has two square roots that are equal in absolute value and opposite in sign. For example, $(5)^2 = 25$ and $(-5)^2 = 25$ implies 5 and –5 are square roots of 25. The positive square root is the **principal square root**. The **square root radical sign** $(\sqrt{\ })$ denotes the principal square root. Thus, $\sqrt{(5)(5)} = \sqrt{25} = 5$ and $\sqrt{(-5)(-5)} = \sqrt{25} = 5$. In general, $\sqrt{x^2} = |x|$. Zero has only one square root, namely 0. The principal square root of 0 is 0.

Tip: The square root radical sign $(\sqrt{\ })$ always returns one number as the answer, and that number is nonnegative (positive or 0). For example, $\sqrt{25} = 5$, not ±5, and $\sqrt{(-5)^2} = |-5| = 5$, not –5.

A number that is an exact square of another number is a **perfect square**. Here is a list of principal square roots of some perfect squares.

$\sqrt{1} = 1 \quad \sqrt{25} = 5 \quad \sqrt{81} = 9 \quad \sqrt{169} = 13 \quad \sqrt{289} = 17$
$\sqrt{4} = 2 \quad \sqrt{36} = 6 \quad \sqrt{100} = 10 \quad \sqrt{196} = 14 \quad \sqrt{400} = 20$
$\sqrt{9} = 3 \quad \sqrt{49} = 7 \quad \sqrt{121} = 11 \quad \sqrt{225} = 15 \quad \sqrt{625} = 25$
$\sqrt{16} = 4 \quad \sqrt{64} = 8 \quad \sqrt{144} = 12 \quad \sqrt{256} = 16$

Tip: If you are dealing only with real numbers, do not try to find square roots of negative numbers because no real number will multiply by itself to give a negative number.

You **cube** a number by using it as a factor three times. The inverse of cubing a number is finding the **cube root**. Every real number has exactly one real cube root, called its **principal cube root**. The **cube root radical sign** $(\sqrt[3]{\ })$ denotes the principal cube root. The small 3 in the radical sign indicates to find the cube root. The principal cube root of a negative number is negative, and the principal cube root of a positive number is positive. For example, $\sqrt[3]{8} = 2$ and $\sqrt[3]{-8} = -2$. The principal cube root of 0 is 0.

A number that is an exact cube of another number is a **perfect cube**. Here is a list of principal cube roots of some positive perfect cubes.

$\sqrt[3]{1} = 1 \quad \sqrt[3]{8} = 2 \quad \sqrt[3]{27} = 3 \quad \sqrt[3]{64} = 4 \quad \sqrt[3]{125} = 5 \quad \sqrt[3]{216} = 6 \quad \sqrt[3]{343} = 7 \quad \sqrt[3]{1,000} = 10$

In general, if $a^n = x$ where n is a positive integer, a is called an ***n*th root** of x, written $a = \sqrt[n]{x}$. In the **radical expression** $\sqrt[n]{x}$, $\sqrt[n]{\ }$ is the **radical sign,** x is the **radicand,** and n is the **index** and indicates which root is desired. If no index is written, it is understood to be 2, and the radical expression indicates the principal square root of the radicand.

Here are some facts about roots.

> A positive real number has exactly one real positive nth root whether n is even or odd.
>
> When n is odd, every real number has exactly one real nth root.
>
> When n is even, the nth root of a negative number is undefined in the real number system.
>
> The nth root of zero is zero, whether n is even or odd.

Here are examples.

$\sqrt{36} = 6 \quad \sqrt[3]{125} = 5 \quad \sqrt[3]{-64} = -4 \quad \sqrt{-64}$ Not a real number $\quad \sqrt[4]{-16}$ Not a real number

Here is a practice problem.

Problem: Evaluate $\sqrt[3]{64} + \sqrt{64} - \sqrt[3]{216} + \sqrt{81}$.
Solution: $\sqrt[3]{64} + \sqrt{64} - \sqrt[3]{216} + \sqrt{81} = 4 + 8 - 6 + 9 = 15$.

Following are rules for radical expressions when x and y are real numbers, m and n are positive integers, and the radical expression denotes a real number.

> $\sqrt[n]{0} = 0 \qquad \sqrt[n]{x^n} = x$ if n is odd $\qquad \sqrt[n]{x^n} = |x|$ if n is even $\qquad \sqrt[n]{x^m} = \left(\sqrt[n]{x}\right)^m \qquad \sqrt[pn]{x^{pm}} = \sqrt[n]{x^m}$
>
> $\left(\sqrt[n]{x}\right)\left(\sqrt[n]{y}\right) = \sqrt[n]{xy} \qquad \dfrac{\sqrt[n]{x}}{\sqrt[n]{y}} = \sqrt[n]{\dfrac{x}{y}}, (y \neq 0) \qquad \sqrt[n]{\sqrt[m]{x}} = \sqrt[mn]{x} \qquad a\left(\sqrt[n]{x}\right) + b\left(\sqrt[n]{x}\right) = (a+b)\left(\sqrt[n]{x}\right)$

These rules form the basis for simplifying radical expressions. (See Appendix A for a discussion of simplifying radicals.)

Here is a practice problem.

Problem: Evaluate $\sqrt[3]{\dfrac{27}{64}} - \sqrt{\dfrac{25}{81}}$.

Solution: $\sqrt[3]{\dfrac{27}{64}} - \sqrt{\dfrac{25}{81}} = \dfrac{\sqrt[3]{27}}{\sqrt[3]{64}} - \dfrac{\sqrt{25}}{\sqrt{81}} = \dfrac{3}{4} - \dfrac{5}{9} = \dfrac{27}{36} - \dfrac{20}{36} = \dfrac{7}{36}$

Exponents

In mathematical expressions, **exponentiation** is indicated by a small raised number, called the **exponent,** written to the upper right of a **base** number or expression. Common types of exponents are summarized in the following table.

Common Types of Exponents

Type of Exponent	Definition	Examples
Positive Integer	If x is any real number and n is a positive integer, then $x^n = \underbrace{x \cdot x \cdot x \cdots x}_{n \text{ factors of } x}$, where x^n is read "x to the nth power" or as "x to the n." *Tip:* The exponent 2 on a number is usually read "squared" rather than "to the second power." Likewise, the exponent 3 is usually read "cubed" rather than "to the third power."	$12^2 = 12 \cdot 12 = 144; (-3)^3 = (-3)(-3)(-3) = -27;$ $2^5 = 2 \cdot 2 \cdot 2 \cdot 2 \cdot 2 = 32$

continued

Chapter 1: Number Concepts

Type of Exponent	Definition	Examples
Zero	For any real number x (except 0), $x^0 = 1$.	$(-128.75)^0 = 1$; $\left(5^{100}\right)^0 = 1$
Positive Rational Number	If x is any real number and m and n are positive integers, then $x^{\frac{1}{n}} = \sqrt[n]{x}$ and $x^{\frac{m}{n}} = \left(\sqrt[n]{x}\right)^m$ or $\sqrt[n]{x^m}$, provided, in all cases, that $x \geq 0$ when n is even.	$16^{\frac{1}{2}} = \sqrt{16} = 4$; $64^{\frac{4}{3}} = \left(\sqrt[3]{64}\right)^4 = (4)^4 = 256$; $(-32)^{\frac{3}{5}} = \left(\sqrt[5]{-32}\right)^3 = (-2)^3 = -8$
Negative Rational Number	If x is any real number (except 0) and m and n are positive integers so that $-n$ and $-\frac{m}{n}$ are negative numbers, then $x^{-n} = \frac{1}{x^n}$. Also, $\frac{1}{x^{-n}} = x^n$, $x^{-\frac{m}{n}} = \frac{1}{x^{\frac{m}{n}}} = \frac{1}{\left(\sqrt[n]{x}\right)^m}$, and $\frac{1}{x^{-\frac{m}{n}}} = x^{\frac{m}{n}} = \left(\sqrt[n]{x}\right)^m$, provided, in all cases, $x > 0$ when n is even.	$5^{-3} = \frac{1}{5^3} = \frac{1}{125}$; $\frac{1}{5^{-3}} = 5^3 = 125$; $(-64)^{-\frac{2}{3}} = \frac{1}{(-64)^{\frac{2}{3}}} = \frac{1}{\left(\sqrt[3]{-64}\right)^2} = \frac{1}{(-4)^2} = \frac{1}{16}$

Here is a practice problem.

Problem: Evaluate $2^6 - 25^{\frac{1}{2}} + 64^{\frac{2}{3}} + (1{,}000)^0$.

Solution: $2^6 - 25^{\frac{1}{2}} + 64^{\frac{2}{3}} + (1{,}000)^0 = 64 - 5 + 16 + 1 = 76$

The following rules for exponents hold.

Rules for Exponents

Rule	Example(s)
$b^m b^n = b^{m+n}$ (product rule)	$2^3 2^4 = 2^{3+4} = 2^7$
$\frac{b^m}{b^n} = b^{m-n} = \frac{1}{b^{n-m}}$, $b \neq 0$ (quotient rule)	$\frac{3^6}{3^2} = 3^{6-2} = 3^4$; $\frac{5^4}{5^7} = 5^{4-7} = \frac{1}{5^{7-4}} = \frac{1}{5^3}$
$\left(b^m\right)^p = b^{mp}$ (power of a power)	$\left(5^3\right)^2 = 5^{3 \cdot 2} = 5^6$
$(ab)^p = a^p b^p$ (power of a product)	$(5 \cdot 2)^3 = 5^3 2^3$
$\left(\frac{a}{b}\right)^p = \frac{a^p}{b^p}$, $b \neq 0$ (power of a quotient)	$\left(\frac{10}{2}\right)^3 = \frac{10^3}{2^3}$ and $\frac{10^3}{2^3} = \left(\frac{10}{2}\right)^3$
$\left(\frac{a}{b}\right)^{-p} = \left(\frac{b}{a}\right)^p$, $a \neq 0, b \neq 0$ (reciprocal rule)	$\left(\frac{3}{4}\right)^{-2} = \left(\frac{4}{3}\right)^2$
$(a+b)^n = \underbrace{(a+b)(a+b)\cdots(a+b)}_{n \text{ times}}$, for n a positive integer (power of a binomial)	$(a+b)^2 = (a+b)(a+b) = a^2 + 2ab + b^2$ *Tip:* Expand the product using rules for multiplying binomials in Chapter 2.
If $a^m = a^n$, then $m = n$, provided $a \neq 1$ (one-to-one property).	$2^x = 2^9$ implies $x = 9$.

Here is a practice problem.

Problem: Evaluate $\frac{5^{200}}{5^{198}} - \left(\frac{1}{4}\right)^{-2}$.

Solution: $\frac{5^{200}}{5^{198}} - \left(\frac{1}{4}\right)^{-2} = 5^{200-198} - \left(\frac{4}{1}\right)^2 = 5^2 - 4^2 = 25 - 16 = 9$.

Here is clarification about exponents.

- The product and quotient rules for exponential expressions can be used only when the exponential expressions have exactly the same base. For example, $x^2 x^3 = x^{2+3} = x^5$ and $\dfrac{x^5}{x^3} = x^{5-3} = x^2$, but $x^2 y^3$ and $\dfrac{x^5}{y^3}$ cannot be simplified further.
- Switching the exponent and base changes the value of the expression. For example, $2^5 \ne 5^2$; $2^5 = 32$, but $5^2 = 25$.
- Exponentiation does not "distribute" over addition (or subtraction). For example, $(3 + 2)^3 \ne 3^3 + 2^3$; $(3 + 2)^3 = 5^3 = 125$, but $3^3 + 2^3 = 27 + 8 = 35$.
- An exponent applies only to the base to which it is attached. For example, $3 \cdot 5^2 \ne 3^2 \cdot 5^2$; $3 \cdot 5^2 = 3 \cdot 25 = 75$, but $3^2 \cdot 5^2 = 9 \cdot 25 = 225$.
- Exponentiation takes precedence over negation. For example, $-5^2 \ne (-5)^2$; $-5^2 = -(5 \cdot 5) = -25$, but $(-5)^2 = -5 \cdot -5 = 25$.
- Use parentheses around the factors for which the exponent applies. For example, $(3 \cdot 5)^2 = 3^2 \cdot 5^2 = 9 \cdot 25 = 225$.
- A negative number raised to an even power yields a positive product. For example, $(-2)^4 = -2 \cdot -2 \cdot -2 \cdot -2 = 16$.
- A negative number raised to an odd power yields a negative product. For example, $(-2)^5 = -2 \cdot -2 \cdot -2 \cdot -2 \cdot -2 = -32$.
- A negative exponent means to write a reciprocal, not to make your answer negative. For example, $2^{-6} = \dfrac{1}{2^6} = \dfrac{1}{64}$, not $-\dfrac{1}{64}$ or -64.
- A nonzero number or mathematical expression raised to the 0 power is 1; that is, (nonzero numerical quantity)^0 = 1.

In general, when you have zero or negative exponents in a mathematical expression, you should rewrite it as an equivalent expression that no longer contains zero or negative exponents. For example,

$$\dfrac{x^3 y^{-4} z^{-1}}{u^0 x^{-2} y^3 z^{-3}} = \dfrac{x^3 x^2 z^3}{1 y^4 y^3 z} = \dfrac{x^5 z^2}{y^7}$$

Be careful with this process. Only exponential expressions that are *factors* can be moved from the numerator to the denominator (or from the denominator to the numerator) of a fraction simply by changing the sign of the exponent. For example,

Do this: $\dfrac{1}{2^{-1} 3^{-1}} = \dfrac{2 \cdot 3}{1} = \dfrac{6}{1} = 6$ and this: $\dfrac{1}{2^{-1} + 3^{-1}} = \dfrac{1}{\dfrac{1}{2} + \dfrac{1}{3}} = \dfrac{1}{\dfrac{5}{6}} = 1\dfrac{1}{5}$, but NOT this: $\dfrac{1}{2^{-1} + 3^{-1}} = \dfrac{2 + 3}{1} = \dfrac{5}{1} = 5$.

Comparing and Ordering Real Numbers

When you are comparing two real numbers, think of their relative locations on the number line. The number that is farther to the right is the greater number. For example, $-3.25 < -0.5$ because, as shown on the number line below, -0.5 lies to the right of -3.25.

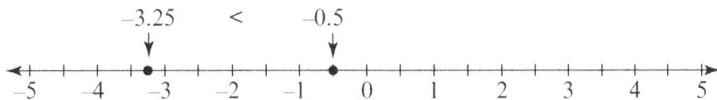

When you compare decimals, compare the digits in each place value from left to right. If the decimals do not have the same number of decimal places, insert or delete zeros after the last digit to the right of the decimal point to make the number of decimal places the same. Remember, inserting or deleting zeros after the last digit to the right of the decimal point (called **trailing zeros**) does not change the value of a decimal. For example, $2.5 = 2.50 = 2.500 = 2.5000$ and so on. Thus, $2.28 < 2.5$ because $2.28 < 2.50$.

When comparing fractions that have the same denominator, compare the numerators. For example, $\frac{7}{8} > \frac{5}{8}$ because 7 > 5.

If the denominators of the fractions are not the same, you can write the fractions as equivalent fractions using a common denominator and then compare the numerators. For example, $\frac{3}{4} < \frac{7}{8}$ because $\frac{6}{8} < \frac{7}{8}$. You also could change each of the fractions to a decimal and then make the comparison. For example, $\frac{3}{4} < \frac{7}{8}$ because 0.750 < 0.875.

Tip: Change fractions to decimals by performing the division on your calculator.

When you are instructed to order a list of numbers, put them in order from least to greatest or from greatest to least, depending on how the question is stated.

Here are some tips for handling situations that might occur in problems that involve comparing and ordering real numbers.

- If both decimals and fractions are involved, change the fractions to decimals, and round them off if they repeat.
- If negative numbers are involved, they will be less than all the positive numbers and 0.
- If percents are involved, change the percents to decimals.
- If the problem contains exponential expressions, evaluate them before making comparisons.
- If you have square roots that are rational numbers, find the square roots before making comparisons.
- If you have irrational square roots, use a calculator to estimate the square roots before comparing them to other numbers.

Here is a practice problem.

Problem: Order the following numbers from least to greatest: $\sqrt{37}, 2^3, \frac{2}{3}, 4.39, -4, \frac{9}{2}$.

Solution: You do not have to proceed in the order the numbers are listed. Clearly, –4 is less than all the other numbers. Estimate $\sqrt{37}$ to be approximately 6.08. Evaluate 2^3 to obtain 8. Change $\frac{2}{3}$ to 0.67 (rounding to 2 places) and $\frac{9}{2}$ to 4.50, which is greater than 4.39. In order from least to greatest, these six numbers are –4, 0.67, 4.39, 4.50, 6.08, and 8. Thus, the final answer is $-4, \frac{2}{3}, 4.39, \frac{9}{2}, \sqrt{37}, 2^3$.

Intervals and Interval Notation

Intervals show sets of numbers on the real number line. **Open intervals** do not include the endpoints. **Closed intervals** include both endpoints. **Half-open** (or half-closed) intervals include only one endpoint. Finite intervals are **bounded intervals**. Intervals that extend indefinitely to the right or left or both are **unbounded intervals**.

To graph an interval on the number line, shade the number line to show the numbers included in the interval. Use a solid circle to indicate an endpoint is included and an open circle to indicate an endpoint is not included. The following table summarizes intervals and interval notation. *Note:* The symbols –∞ (**negative infinity**) and ∞ (**positive infinity**) do not represent real numbers. These symbols are used to convey the unboundedness of intervals that extend indefinitely to the right or left or both.

Interval	Notation and Type	Graph
$x < b$	$(-\infty, b)$, unbounded, open	
$x > a$	(a, ∞), unbounded, open	

Interval	Notation and Type	Graph
$x \leq b$	$(-\infty, b]$, unbounded, half-open	←━━━━━━━━━●→ b
$x \geq a$	$[a, \infty)$, unbounded, half-open	←●━━━━━━━━━→ a
$a < x < b$	(a, b), bounded, open	←○━━━━━○→ a b
$a \leq x < b$	$[a, b)$, bounded, half-open	←●━━━━━○→ a b
$a < x \leq b$	$(a, b]$, bounded, half-open	←○━━━━━●→ a b
$a \leq x \leq b$	$[a, b]$, bounded, closed	←●━━━━━●→ a b

Here are two practice problems.

> Problem: Write an inequality to represent the interval (–5, 8] and state whether the interval is bounded or unbounded.
>
> Solution: The interval (–5, 8] corresponds to the inequality $-5 < x \leq 8$ and is bounded.
>
> Problem: Write an inequality to represent the interval (8, ∞) and state whether the interval is bounded or unbounded.
>
> Solution: The interval (8, ∞) corresponds to the inequality $x > 8$ and is unbounded.

Computing with Real Numbers

For your TExES Math exam, you will need to know how to perform addition, subtraction, multiplication, and division of real numbers. These operations are performed by using the absolute values, which are always positive or zero, of the numbers.

Addition and Subtraction of Real Numbers

For sums and differences of real numbers, use the following rules.

Rules for Addition and Subtraction of Real Numbers

Rule	Examples
Rule 1: The sum of 0 and any number is the number.	$-6 + 0 = -6$; $0 + 5 = 5$
Rule 2: The sum of a number and its opposite is 0.	$-4 + 4 = 0$; $8 + (-8) = 0$
Rule 3: To add two numbers that have the same sign, add their absolute values and keep the same sign.	$4 + 6 = 10$; $-4 + (-6) = -10$
Rule 4: To add two numbers that have opposite signs, subtract the lesser absolute value from the greater absolute value and make the sign of the result the same as the sign of the number with the greater absolute value.	$-5 + 13 = 8$; $4 + (-16) = -12$
Rule 5: To subtract one number from another, add the opposite of the second number to the first.	$28 - (-2) = 28 + (2) = 30$; $-36 - 16 = -36 + (-16) = -52$

Tip: To avoid sign errors when you are performing computations with real numbers, change instances of – – to + and change instances of – + or + – to –. Thereafter, keep a – sign with the number that follows it.

Here is a practice problem.

> Problem: Compute 18 – –20 + –5 – 6.
> Solution: 18 – –20 + –5 – 6 = 18 + 20 – 5 – 6 = 27

The distance between any two numbers on the number line is the absolute value of their difference.

Here is a practice problem.

> Problem: Find the distance between –13 and –8 on the number line.
> Solution: The distance between –13 and –8 is the absolute value of their difference, which equals |–13 – (–8)| = |–13 + 8| = |–5| = 5.

Tip: Absolute value bars act as grouping symbols (like parentheses). Therefore, compute inside the absolute value bars before evaluating the absolute value of a numerical expression.

Multiplication and Division of Real Numbers

For products and quotients of real numbers, use the following rules.

Rules for Multiplication and Division of Real Numbers

Rule	Examples
Rule 1: Zero times any number is 0.	$0 \cdot 8 = 0$; $-7 \cdot 0 = 0$
Rule 2: To multiply two nonzero numbers that have the same sign, multiply their absolute values and keep the product positive.	$2 \cdot 5 = 10$; $-2 \cdot -5 = 10$
Rule 3: To multiply two nonzero numbers that have opposite signs, multiply their absolute values and make the product negative.	$-2 \cdot 5 = -10$; $2 \cdot -5 = -10$
Rule 4: When 0 is one of the factors, the product is always 0; otherwise, products with an even number of negative factors are positive, whereas those with an odd number of negative factors are negative.	$(-2)(6)(0)(-1) = 0$; $(-2)(6)(5)(-1) = 60$; $(-2)(6)(-5)(-1) = -60$
Rule 5: To divide by a nonzero number, follow the same rules for the signs as for multiplication, except divide the absolute values of the numbers instead of multiplying.	$\frac{45}{9} = 5$; $\frac{-15}{5} = -3$; $\frac{50}{-25} = -2$; $\frac{-24}{-6} = 4$
Rule 6: The quotient is 0 when the dividend is 0 and the divisor is a nonzero number.	$\frac{0}{100} = 0$; $\frac{0}{-100} = 0$
Rule 7: The quotient is undefined when the divisor is 0.	$\frac{100}{0}$ is undefined; $\frac{0}{0}$ is undefined

Tip: Unlike addition, for multiplication and division when the signs are the same, it doesn't matter what the common sign is—the product or quotient is positive no matter what. Similarly, unlike addition, for multiplication and division when the signs are different, it doesn't matter which number has the greater absolute value—the product or quotient is negative no matter what.

Scientific Notation

Scientific notation is a way to write very large or very small numbers in a shortened form. Scientific notation helps keep track of the decimal places and makes performing computations with these numbers easier.

Chapter 1: Number Concepts

A number written in scientific notation is written as a product of two factors. The first factor is a number that is greater than or equal to 1, but less than 10. The second factor is a power of 10. The idea is to make a product that will equal the given number. Any decimal number can be written in scientific notation.

Follow these steps to write a number in scientific notation:

Step 1. Move the decimal point to the immediate right of the first *nonzero* digit of the number.

Step 2. Indicate multiplication by the proper power of 10. The exponent for the power of 10 is the number of places you moved the decimal point in Step 1.

- If you moved the decimal point to the *left,* make the exponent positive.
- If you moved the decimal point to the *right,* make the exponent negative.
- If you did not move the decimal point, make the exponent 0.

Here are three practice problems.

Problem: Write 34,000 in scientific notation.
Solution: Written in scientific notation, 34,000 is 3.4×10^4.

Problem: Write 6.5 in scientific notation.
Solution: Written in scientific notation, 6.5 is 6.5×10^0.

Problem: Write 0.00047 in scientific notation.
Solution: Written in scientific notation, 0.00047 is 4.7×10^{-4}.

As long as you make sure your first factor is greater than or equal to 1 and less than 10, you can convert a number written in scientific notation to standard form by performing the indicated multiplication.

Tip: A shortcut for multiplying by 10^n is to move the decimal point *n* places to the right, inserting rightmost zeros after the last nonzero digit as needed.

Here is a practice problem.

Problem: Convert 2.54×10^5 to standard form.
Solution: $2.54 \times 10^5 = 2.54 \times 10,000 = 254,000$

Tip: A shortcut for multiplying by 10^{-n} is to move the decimal point *n* places to the left, inserting leftmost zeros between the first nonzero digit and the decimal point as needed.

Here is a practice problem.

Problem: Convert 1.5×10^{-4} to standard form.
Solution: $1.5 \times 10^{-4} = \dfrac{1.5}{10,000} = 0.00015$

Sums, Differences, and Products of Even and Odd Integers

Here is helpful information to know about sums, differences, and products of even and odd integers.

- The sum or difference of two even integers is even. Examples: $24 + 8 = 32$; $(-30) + (-4) = -34$; $100 - 56 = 44$
- The sum or difference of two odd integers is even. Examples: $27 + 9 = 36$; $(-41) + (-5) = -46$; $95 - 53 = 42$
- The sum or difference of an even integer and an odd integer is odd. Examples: $24 + 7 = 31$; $(-15) + (-4) = -19$; $101 - 70 = 31$
- The product of two even numbers is even. Examples: $(4)(-28) = -112$; $(18)(12) = 216$

Chapter 1: Number Concepts

- The product of two odd numbers is odd. Examples: (5)(3) = 15; (–7)(–13) = 91
- The product of an even integer and an odd integer is even. Examples: (4)(–25) = –100; (18)(3) = 54
- If n is an integer and n^2 is even, then n is even. Examples: If $n^2 = 36$, then $n = 6$ or –6. If $n^2 = 64$, then $n = 8$ or –8.
- If n is an integer and n^2 is odd, then n is odd. Examples: If $n^2 = 81$, then $n = 9$ or –9. If $n^2 = 625$, then $n = 25$ or –25.

Tip: An even integer can be written as 2n, where n is an integer. An odd integer can be written as 2m + 1, where m is an integer.

Sums, Differences, and Products of Rational and Irrational Numbers

Here is helpful information to know about sums, differences, and products of rational and irrational numbers.

- The sum or difference of two rational numbers is rational. Examples: $1.75 + \frac{3}{2} = 3.25$; $-\frac{1}{3} - \left(-\frac{5}{6}\right) = \frac{1}{2}$
- The product of two rational numbers is rational. Examples: $(2.5)(-1.1) = -2.75$; $\left(\frac{3}{4}\right)(90.8) = 68.1$
- The sum or difference of a rational number and an irrational number is irrational. Examples: $\sqrt{2} + 9$; $1\frac{3}{4} - \sqrt{41}$
- The product of a nonzero rational number and an irrational number is irrational. Examples: $(0.5)(\sqrt{2}) = 0.5\sqrt{2}$; $(-1)(-\sqrt{23}) = \sqrt{23}$
- The sum or difference of two irrational numbers can be rational or irrational. Examples: $4\sqrt{5} - 4\sqrt{5} = 0$ (rational); $4\sqrt{5} + 2\sqrt{5} = 6\sqrt{5}$ (irrational)
- The product of two irrational numbers can be rational or irrational. Examples: $(4\sqrt{3})(-5\sqrt{3}) = -60$ (rational); $(7\sqrt{2})(3\sqrt{8}) = 84$ (rational); $(5\sqrt{2})(\sqrt{3}) = 5\sqrt{6}$ (irrational)
- For any positive real number a, $\left(\sqrt[n]{a}\right)^n = a$ and $\sqrt[n]{a^n} = a$. Examples: $\left(\sqrt[4]{81}\right)^4 = 81$ and $\sqrt[5]{2^5} = 2$

Order of Operations

When more than one operation is involved in a numerical expression, you must follow the **order of operations** to evaluate the expression. A commonly used mnemonic is "Please Excuse My Dear Aunt Sally"—abbreviated as PE(MD)(AS). The first letters of the words remind you of the following:

> First, operations enclosed in **P**arentheses (or other grouping symbols, if present)
> Next, **E**xponentiation
> Then, **M**ultiplication and **D**ivision in the order in which they occur from left to right
> Last, **A**ddition and **S**ubtraction in the order in which they occur from left to right

Tip: Note that multiplication does not have to be done before division, or addition before subtraction. You multiply and divide in the order in which these operations occur in the problem. Similarly, you add and subtract in the order in which these operations occur in the problem. That's why there are parentheses around MD and AS in PE(MD)(AS).

Grouping symbols such as parentheses ( ), brackets [ ], and braces { } keep things together that belong together. Fraction bars, absolute value bars, and square root symbols also are grouping symbols. Always do the operations inside grouping symbols FIRST—especially when you have addition and/or subtraction inside the grouping symbols. Otherwise, you might get an incorrect result. When you no longer need the grouping symbols, omit them. Look at this example.

Do this: $(1 + 1)^3 = 2^3 = 8$ (correct answer); NOT this: $(1 + 1)^3 = 1^3 + 1^3 = 1 + 1 = 2$ (wrong answer)

Here are two practice problems.

Problem: Evaluate $90 - 5 \cdot 3^2 + \dfrac{42}{5+2}$.

Solution:
$$90 - 5 \cdot 3^2 + \dfrac{42}{5+2} = 90 - 5 \cdot 3^2 + \dfrac{42}{7} \quad \text{First, compute under the fraction bar.}$$
$$= 90 - 5 \cdot 9 + \dfrac{42}{7} \quad \text{Next, evaluate the exponent.}$$
$$= 90 - 45 + 6 \quad \text{Then, multiply and divide from left to right.}$$
$$= 51 \quad \text{Finally, add and subtract from left to right.}$$

Thus, $90 - 5 \cdot 3^2 + \dfrac{42}{5+2} = 51$.

Problem: Evaluate $-50 + \dfrac{40}{2^3} - 5(4+6)$.

Solution:
$$-50 + \dfrac{40}{2^3} - 5(4+6) = -50 + \dfrac{40}{2^3} - 5(10) \quad \text{First, compute inside parentheses.}$$
$$= -50 + \dfrac{40}{8} - 5(10) \quad \text{Next, evaluate the exponent.}$$
$$= -50 + 5 - 50 \quad \text{Then, multiply and divide from left to right.}$$
$$= -95 \quad \text{Finally, add and subtract from left to right.}$$

Thus, $-50 + \dfrac{40}{2^3} - 5(4+6) = -95$.

Sometimes, you might find it convenient to transform exponential expressions by applying the rules of exponents *before* proceeding through the order of operations.

Here is a practice problem.

Problem: Evaluate $(3 \cdot 10)^2 - \dfrac{5^7}{5^4}$.

Solution:

$$(3 \cdot 10)^2 - \dfrac{5^7}{5^4} = 3^2 \cdot 10^2 - \dfrac{5^7}{5^4} \quad \text{Transform } (3 \cdot 10)^2 \text{ instead of multiplying inside the parentheses first.}$$
$$= 3^2 \cdot 10^2 - 5^3 \quad \text{Transform } \dfrac{5^7}{5^4} \text{ instead of doing the exponentiation first.}$$
$$= 9 \cdot 100 - 125$$
$$= 900 - 125$$
$$= 775$$

Thus, $(3 \cdot 10)^2 - \dfrac{5^7}{5^4} = 775$.

Tip: If you decide to apply the rules of exponents before proceeding through the order of operations, only transform products or quotients, not sums or differences. Otherwise, errors could result.

Field Properties of the Real Number System

The set of real numbers has the following **field properties** under the binary operations of addition and multiplication for all real numbers a, b, and c.

Field Properties

Property	Explanation
Closure property: $a + b$ and ab are real numbers.	The sum or product of any two real numbers is a real number.
Commutative property: $a + b = b + a$ and $ab = ba$.	Switching the order of any two addends or any two factors does not affect the final sum or product.
Associative property: $(a + b) + c = a + (b + c)$ and $(ab)c = a(bc)$.	The way the addends or factors are grouped does not affect the final sum or product.
Additive identity property: There exists a real number, denoted 0, such that $a + 0 = a$ and $0 + a = a$.	This property ensures that zero is a real number and that its sum with any real number is the number.
Multiplicative identity property: There exists a real number, denoted 1, such that $a \cdot 1 = a$ and $1 \cdot a = a$.	This property ensures that 1 is a real number and that its product with any real number is the number.
Additive inverse property: For every real number a, there exists a real number, denoted $-a$, such that $a + (-a) = 0$ and $(-a) + a = 0$.	This property ensures that for every real number, there is another real number, opposite to it in sign, which, when added to the number, gives 0.
Multiplicative inverse property: For every nonzero real number a, there exists a real number, denoted a^{-1}, such that $a \cdot a^{-1} = 1$ and $a^{-1} \cdot a = 1$.	This property ensures that for every real number, *except zero*, there is another real number, which, when multiplied by the number, gives 1.
Distributive property: $a(b + c) = ab + ac$.	When you have a factor times a sum, you can either add first and then multiply, or multiply first and then add. Either way, the answer works out to be the same.
Zero product property: If $ab = 0$, then $a = 0$ or $b = 0$ (or both = 0).	If a product of two factors is zero, then one or both of the factors are zero.

Subtraction and division are defined as follows.

> **Subtraction:** $a - b = a + (-b)$
> **Division:** $a \div b = \dfrac{a}{b} = a \cdot b^{-1} = a \cdot \dfrac{1}{b}$

Note: A **binary operation** is one that is performed on only two numbers at a time to obtain another number.

For your TExES Math exam, be prepared to identify properties of the real numbers used in a calculation.

Here is a practice problem.

> Problem: Which property of the real numbers is used first in the following calculation: $8(215) = 1{,}720$?
> Solution: Since $8(215) = 8(200 + 10 + 5) = 8 \cdot 200 + 8 \cdot 10 + 8 \cdot 5 = 1{,}600 + 80 + 40 = 1{,}720$, the distributive property is used first in the calculation.

On your TExES Math exam, you might be asked whether a defined binary operation has given field properties. Symbols commonly used for defined operations are ⊕, ⊗, *, °, and #.

Here is a practice problem.

> Problem: Consider the operation $\oplus$ defined by $a \oplus b = 2a + 3b$, where the operations on the right side of the equal sign denote the standard arithmetic operations. Is the operation $\oplus$ commutative over the set of real numbers?
>
> Solution: To determine whether $\oplus$ is commutative over the set of real numbers, you should ask the question, "Does $a \oplus b$ equal $b \oplus a$ for all real numbers a and b?" In other words, you need to determine whether $2a + 3b = 2b + 3a$ for all real numbers a and b. Clearly, the answer is no. For example, when $a = 2$ and $b = 5$, $2 \cdot 2 + 3 \cdot 5 = 19$, which is not equal to $2 \cdot 5 + 3 \cdot 2 = 16$. Therefore, the operation $\oplus$ is not commutative over the set of real numbers.

Tip: Even though commutativity (associativity and so on) might hold for some numbers from a given set, if it does not hold for *all* numbers from the set, the operation under consideration is not commutative (associative and so on) over the given set of numbers.

Complex Numbers

For this topic, you must understand the structure of the complex number systems and perform basic operations on numbers in this system.

Basic Concepts of Complex Numbers

The main concepts about complex numbers are the following:

- **Complex numbers** have the **standard form** $a + bi$, where a and b are real numbers and i represents the **imaginary unit** $\sqrt{-1}$.
- The coefficients a and b of a complex number are the **real part** and **imaginary part**, respectively, of the number. *Note:* The imaginary part is b, not bi.
- The square of the imaginary unit is -1; that is, $i^2 = -1$.
- Complex numbers can be defined as ordered pairs (a, b), where a is the real part and b is the imaginary part of the number.
- The real numbers are a subset of the complex numbers, and result when the imaginary part (b) is zero.
- Two complex numbers $a + bi$ and $c + di$ written in standard form are equal to each other if and only if $a = c$ and $b = d$.
- The complex numbers $a + bi$ and $a - bi$ are **complex conjugates** of each other. The product of a complex number and its conjugate is a real number.

The complex numbers can be represented in the complex plane, where the horizontal axis is the **real axis** and the vertical axis is the **imaginary axis**. The complex numbers $z_1 = 2 + i = (2, 1)$, $z_2 = 3 - 2i = (3, -2)$, $z_3 = -3 + 2i = (-3, 2)$, and $z_4 = -2 - 4i = (-2, -4)$ are shown in the complex plane in the following figure.

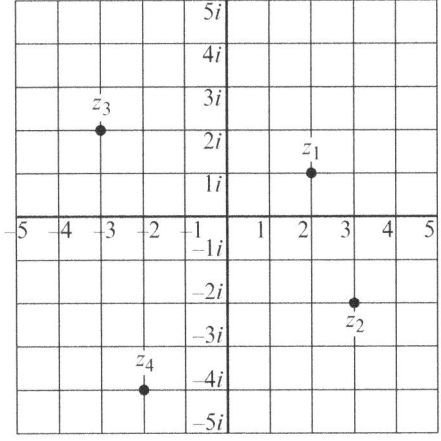

Computing with Complex Numbers

The rules for performing operations with complex numbers follow. Keep in mind that because the coefficients a and b in a complex number $a + bi$ are *real* numbers, the computations involving these real number coefficients must adhere to the rules given in "Computing with Real Numbers" earlier in this chapter.

For sums and differences of complex numbers, use the following rules.

Rule	Example
Rule 1: Addition of two complex numbers: $(a + bi) + (c + di) = (a + c) + (b + d)i$ *Tip:* Add the real parts. Add the imaginary parts.	$(8 + 3i) + (-5 + 7i) = (8 - 5) + (3 + 7)i = 3 + 10i$
Rule 2: Subtraction of two complex numbers: $(a + bi) - (c + di) = (a - c) + (b - d)i$ *Tip:* Subtract the real parts. Subtract the imaginary parts.	$(-5 + 9i) - (2 + 11i) = (-5 - 2) + (9 - 11)i = -7 - 2i$

Here are two practice problems.

Problem: Write the sum of the complex numbers $(5 + 8i)$ and $(7 - 2i)$ in standard form.
Solution: $(5 + 8i) + (7 - 2i) = 12 + 6i$

Problem: Write the difference of the complex numbers $(5 + 8i)$ and $(7 - 2i)$ in standard form.
Solution: $(5 + 8i) - (7 - 2i) = -2 + 10i$

For products of complex numbers, use the following rule.

Rule	Example
Rule 3: Multiplication of two complex numbers: $(a + bi)(c + di) = (ac - bd) + (ad + bc)i$ *Tip:* In practice, to avoid errors, use F.O.I.L. (First terms, Outer terms, Inner terms, and Last terms) to perform the multiplication and simplify using $i^2 = -1$. (See "Polynomials" in Chapter 2 for a review of F.O.I.L.)	$(2 + 3i)(-4 + 5i) = -8 + 10i - 12i + 15i^2 = -8 + 10i - 12i - 15 = -23 - 2i$

Here are two practice problems.

Problem: Write the product of the complex numbers $(2 + 3i)$ and $(4 + i)$ in standard form.
Solution: $(2 + 3i)(4 + i) = 8 + 2i + 12i + 3i^2 = 8 + 14i + 3i^2 = 8 + 14i + 3(-1) = 8 + 14i - 3 = 5 + 14i$

Problem: Find the product of the complex number $(2 + 3i)$ and its conjugate $(2 - 3i)$.
Solution: $(2 + 3i)(2 - 3i) = 4 - 9i^2 = 4 - 9(-1) = 4 + 9 = 13$

For quotients of complex numbers, you have the following rule that makes use of the complex conjugate.

Rule	Example
Rule 4: Division of two complex numbers: $\dfrac{a+bi}{c+di} = \dfrac{(a+bi)}{(c+di)} \cdot \dfrac{(c-di)}{(c-di)} = \dfrac{ac+bd}{c^2+d^2} + \dfrac{bc-ad}{c^2+d^2}i$ *Tip:* Multiply the numerator and denominator by the complex conjugate of the denominator.	$\dfrac{6+5i}{3+4i} = \dfrac{(6+5i)}{(3+4i)} \cdot \dfrac{(3-4i)}{(3-4i)} = \dfrac{18-24i+15i-20i^2}{9-16i^2} = \dfrac{18-24i+15i+20}{9+16}$ $= \dfrac{38-9i}{25} = \dfrac{38}{25} - \dfrac{9}{25}i$

Here is a practice problem.

> Problem: Write the quotient of the complex numbers $(2 + 3i)$ and $(4 - 2i)$ in standard form.
>
> Solution: $\dfrac{2+3i}{4-2i} = \dfrac{(2+3i)(4+2i)}{(4-2i)(4+2i)} = \dfrac{8+4i+12i+6i^2}{16-4i^2} = \dfrac{8+16i-6}{16+4} = \dfrac{2+16i}{20} = \dfrac{1}{10} + \dfrac{4}{5}i$

Tip: When multiplying or dividing complex numbers, it is important to remember that $i^2 = -1$.

Use the definition of multiplication and the fact that $i^2 = -1$ to compute whole number powers of the imaginary unit i. For example, $i^1 = i$; $i^2 = -1$; $i^3 = i \cdot i^2 = i \cdot -1 = -i$; $i^4 = i^2 \cdot i^2 = -1 \cdot -1 = 1$; $i^5 = i \cdot i^4 = i \cdot 1 = i$; $i^6 = i^2 \cdot i^4 = -1 \cdot 1 = -1$; $i^7 = i^3 \cdot i^4 = -i \cdot 1 = -i$; $i^8 = i^4 \cdot i^4 = 1 \cdot 1 = 1$. As you look at this list, you see a pattern of $i, -1, -i, 1, i, -1, -i, 1, \ldots$. This pattern will continue through higher powers of i. In general, $(i^4)^n = 1$ for any integer.

Here is a practice problem.

> Problem: Evaluate i^{103}.
>
> Solution: $i^{103} = (i^4)^{25} i^3 = (1)(-i) = -i$

Field Properties of the Complex Numbers

The set of complex numbers has the following **field properties** under the binary operations of addition and multiplication for all complex numbers $a + bi$, $c + di$, and $e + fi$.

Field Properties of the Complex Numbers

Field Property	Explanation
Closure Property of Addition	$(a + bi) + (c + di) = (a + c) + (b + d)i$ is a complex number.
Closure Property of Multiplication	$(a + bi)(c + di) = (ac - bd) + (ad + bc)i$ is a complex number.
Commutative Property of Addition	$(a + bi) + (c + di) = (c + di) + (a + bi)$
Commutative Property of Multiplication	$(a + bi)(c + di) = (c + di)(a + bi)$
Associative Property of Addition	$[(a + bi) + (c + di)] + (e + fi) = (a + bi) + [(c + di) + (e + fi)]$
Associative Property of Multiplication	$[(a + bi)(c + di)](e + fi) = (a + bi)[(c + di)(e + fi)]$
Additive Identity Property	There exists a complex number, 0, such that $(a + bi) + (0) = a + bi$ and $(0) + (a + bi) = a + bi$.
Multiplicative Identity Property	There exists a complex number, 1, such that $(a + bi)(1) = a + bi$ and $(1)(a + bi) = a + bi$.
Additive Inverse Property	For every complex number $a + bi$, there exists a complex number, $(-a) + (-b)i$, such that $(a + bi) + [(-a) + (-b)i] = 0$ and $[(-a) + (-b)i] + (a + bi) = 0$.
Multiplicative Inverse Property	For every nonzero complex number $a + bi$, there exists a complex number, $\left(\dfrac{a}{a^2+b^2}\right) + \left(\dfrac{-b}{a^2+b^2}\right)i$, such that $(a+bi)\left(\left(\dfrac{a}{a^2+b^2}\right) + \left(\dfrac{-b}{a^2+b^2}\right)i\right) = 1$ and $\left(\left(\dfrac{a}{a^2+b^2}\right) + \left(\dfrac{-b}{a^2+b^2}\right)i\right)(a+bi) = 1$.
Distributive Property	$(a + bi)[(c + di) + (e + fi)] = (a + bi)(c + di) + (a + bi)(e + fi)$.

Note: Proof of each of these properties relies on the corresponding field property for the real numbers.

In general, a system consisting of a set S and two binary operations defined on S is a **field** if the field properties are satisfied for S under the two operations.

Chapter 1: Number Concepts

Part 2

Part 2 of this chapter is for candidates who plan to take the TExES Math 7–12. This review material goes beyond the standards for the TExES Math 4–8.

Mathematical Induction

> **Principle of Mathematical Induction:** Let $S(n)$ be a statement involving the natural number n.
>
> (1) If the statement is true when $n = 1$, and;
>
> (2) whenever the statement is true for $n = k$, then it is also true for $n = k + 1$, then the statement is true for all natural numbers n.

You can use the principle of mathematical induction to prove a wide collection of statements involving the natural numbers. The basic idea of mathematical induction is that to prove that a statement holds for all natural numbers n, you first show that it holds for $n = 1$. Next, you assume the **inductive hypothesis** that the statement is true for $n = k$; and show that the inductive hypothesis implies the statement is also true for $k + 1$.

Tip: You cannot prove that a statement holds for all natural numbers by repeatedly substituting values into the statement and evaluating. This strategy can lead to invalid results.

Here is an example of a proof by mathematical induction.

> Prove $1 + 2 + 3 + \cdots + n = \dfrac{n(n+1)}{2}$.

(1) The statement is true for $n = 1$ because $1 = \dfrac{1(1+1)}{2}$.

(2) Assume the inductive hypothesis that the statement is true for some natural number k. That is, assume

$1 + 2 + 3 + \cdots + k = \dfrac{k(k+1)}{2}$ is true.

Show that the inductive hypothesis implies that the statement is also true for $k + 1$. That is, show that

$1 + 2 + 3 + \cdots + k + (k+1) = \dfrac{(k+1)((k+1)+1)}{2} = \dfrac{(k+1)(k+2)}{2}$ is also true.

By the inductive hypothesis,

$$1 + 2 + 3 + \cdots + k + (k+1) = [1 + 2 + 3 + \cdots + k] + (k+1)$$
$$= \dfrac{k(k+1)}{2} + (k+1)$$
$$= \dfrac{k(k+1)}{2} + \dfrac{2(k+1)}{2}$$
$$= \dfrac{k^2 + k + 2k + 2}{2}$$
$$= \dfrac{k^2 + 3k + 2}{2}$$
$$= \dfrac{(k+1)(k+2)}{2}$$

Thus, the statement is true for $n = k + 1$ whenever it is true for $n = k$. Therefore, by the principle of mathematical induction, the statement $1+2+3+\cdots+n = \dfrac{n(n+1)}{2}$ is true for all natural numbers n.

For your TExES Math exam, make sure you fully understand the process of mathematical induction and when its use is appropriate. The reason you must understand the process is that a question might ask about the process rather than for you to prove a statement.

Modular Arithmetic

Modular arithmetic is a system of arithmetic focused on the remainders obtained when integers are divided by one another. The main concepts about modular arithmetic are the following:

- a is **congruent** to b modulo m, written $a \equiv b \pmod{m}$, if $a - b$ is divisible by m. The number m is the **modulus** of the congruence.
- $a \equiv b \pmod{m}$ if a and b yield the same remainder when divided by m.
- $a \equiv b \pmod{m}$ if $a - b = km$ for some integer k.
- $a \equiv 0 \pmod{m}$ if and only if $a = km$ for some integer k. Thus, $km \equiv 0 \pmod{m}$ for any integers k and m.
- Given $a = mq + r$ with $0 \leq r < m$, then, in arithmetic modulo m, the set of integers $\{0, 1, 2, \ldots, m-1\}$ is the **standard representation** for the integers.
- $a \equiv a \pmod{m}$ for any integers a and m.
- $a \equiv b \pmod{1}$ for any integers a and b.
- If $a \equiv b \pmod{m}$ and $c \equiv d \pmod{m}$, then $(a + c) \equiv (b + d) \pmod{m}$ and $(a - c) \equiv (b - d) \pmod{m}$.
- If $a \equiv b \pmod{m}$ and $c \equiv d \pmod{m}$, then $ac \equiv bd \pmod{m}$.
- If $a \equiv b \pmod{m}$, then $a^n \equiv b^n \pmod{m}$ for any nonnegative integer n.
- All integers that are congruent modulo m can be treated as identical when adding, subtracting, multiplying, or raising to powers. You might informally say that you can jump freely from one to another. You can do this multiple times without concern.

Here are three practice problems.

Problem: What is the standard representation for 26 modulo 3?
Solution: Because the remainder is 2 when 26 is divided by 3, $26 \equiv 2 \pmod{3}$.

Problem: Are 46 and 31 congruent modulo 3? Justify your answer.
Solution: Yes, $46 \equiv 31 \pmod{3}$ because $46 - 31 = 15$, which is divisible by 3.

Problem: What is the remainder when 2019^{2019} is divided by 2018?
Solution: $2019 \equiv 1 \pmod{2018}$; so, $2019^{2019} \equiv 1^{2019} \equiv 1 \pmod{2018}$. Thus, the remainder is 1.

Tip: The preservation of congruencies under addition, subtraction, and multiplication does not extend to division. For example, $10 \equiv 2 \pmod 8$, but $5 \not\equiv 1 \pmod 8$.

Matrices

A **matrix** is a rectangular array of **elements** (usually) enclosed in brackets. The elements of a matrix are real or complex numbers, or expressions representing real or complex numbers. A matrix with m rows and n columns is an $m \times n$ matrix. Matrices are commonly denoted by uppercase letters and their elements by the corresponding lowercase letters, which are subscripted to indicate the location of the elements in the matrix. For a matrix A, the notation a_{ij} denotes the element in the ith row and jth column of the matrix. It is also customary to denote an $m \times n$ matrix A by $\left[a_{ij}\right]_{(m,n)}$ or simply by $\left[a_{ij}\right]$, if the order is clear.

Chapter 1: Number Concepts

Basic Concepts of Matrices

The **order** of a matrix is the number of rows and columns it contains; thus, an $m \times n$ matrix has order $m \times n$. A $1 \times n$ matrix is a **row vector** of order n. An $m \times 1$ matrix is a **column vector** of order m.

Here are two practice problems.

Problem: What is the order of the matrix $\begin{bmatrix} 5 & 0 & 4 \\ 6 & -2 & 9 \end{bmatrix}$?

Solution: $\begin{bmatrix} 5 & 0 & 4 \\ 6 & -2 & 9 \end{bmatrix}$ is a 2×3 matrix.

Problem: What is the order of the matrix $\begin{bmatrix} -1 & 2 \\ 0 & 0 \\ 5 & 4 \end{bmatrix}$?

Solution: $\begin{bmatrix} -1 & 2 \\ 0 & 0 \\ 5 & 4 \end{bmatrix}$ is a 3×2 matrix.

If $m = n$, the matrix is a **square matrix** of order n.

The **main diagonal** of a square matrix of order n is the diagonal of elements $a_{11}, a_{22}, \ldots, a_{nn}$ from the top-left corner to the bottom-right corner of the matrix.

Here is a practice problem.

Problem: What are the elements on the main diagonal of the square matrix $\begin{bmatrix} 1 & 2 & 0 \\ 2 & 0 & -3 \\ 0 & -3 & 5 \end{bmatrix}$?

Solution: The elements on the main diagonal of the square matrix $\begin{bmatrix} 1 & 2 & 0 \\ 2 & 0 & -3 \\ 0 & -3 & 5 \end{bmatrix}$ are 1, 0, and 5.

A **diagonal matrix** is a square matrix whose only nonzero elements are on the main diagonal. A diagonal matrix that has only ones on the main diagonal is an **identity matrix**. The identity matrix of order n is denoted I_n. Here is an example of an identity matrix of order 2.

$$I_2 = \begin{bmatrix} 1 & 0 \\ 0 & 1 \end{bmatrix}$$

A square matrix containing only 0 elements is the zero matrix, denoted 0 (or $0_{n \times n}$).

The **negative of a matrix** $A = [a_{ij}]$ is the matrix $-A = [-a_{ij}]$, whose elements are the negatives of their corresponding elements in A.

Two matrices A and B are **equal** if and only if they have the same order and their corresponding elements are equal. Therefore, if two matrices $A = [a_{ij}]$ and $B = [b_{ij}]$ are equal, then $a_{ij} = b_{ij}$, for $1 \leq i \leq m$ and $1 \leq j \leq n$. For example:

$$\begin{bmatrix} 2 & 8 \\ -7 & 1 \end{bmatrix} = \begin{bmatrix} \sqrt{4} & 2^3 \\ \frac{-21}{3} & 1 \end{bmatrix} \qquad \begin{bmatrix} 1 & 0 & 0 \\ 0 & 1 & 0 \\ 0 & 0 & 1 \end{bmatrix} \neq \begin{bmatrix} 1 & 0 \\ 0 & 1 \end{bmatrix} \qquad \begin{bmatrix} 2 & 4 & 6 \end{bmatrix} \neq \begin{bmatrix} 2 \\ 4 \\ 6 \end{bmatrix}$$

The **transpose** of an $m \times n$ matrix A is an $n \times m$ matrix, denoted A^T (read as "A transpose"), obtained by interchanging the rows and columns of A. *Note:* The transpose of a matrix A is also denoted A'.

Here is a practice problem.

Problem: Given $A = \begin{bmatrix} 5 & 0 & 4 \\ 6 & -2 & 9 \end{bmatrix}$, determine A^T.

Solution: Given $A = \begin{bmatrix} 5 & 0 & 4 \\ 6 & -2 & 9 \end{bmatrix}$, then $A^T = \begin{bmatrix} 5 & 6 \\ 0 & -2 \\ 4 & 9 \end{bmatrix}$.

Operations with Matrices

For this topic, you must be able to perform scalar multiplication and add, subtract, and multiply vectors and matrices and find inverses of matrices.

Scalar Multiplication

A **scalar** is a number or numerical quantity.

The **scalar product**, kA, of an $m \times n$ matrix $A = [a_{ij}]$ and a scalar k is the $m \times n$ matrix $R = kA$, where $[r_{ij}] = [ka_{ij}]$.

Note: Any size matrix can be multiplied by a scalar.

Here is a practice problem.

Problem: Given $A = \begin{bmatrix} 5 & 2 \\ 0 & -1 \end{bmatrix}$, find $3A$.

Solution: $3A = 3\begin{bmatrix} 5 & 2 \\ 0 & -1 \end{bmatrix} = \begin{bmatrix} 15 & 6 \\ 0 & -3 \end{bmatrix}$

Matrix Addition and Subtraction

Two matrices are **conformable for matrix addition or subtraction** if they have the same order. *Note:* Addition or subtraction of matrices with unlike orders is not defined.

The **sum**, $A + B$, of two $m \times n$ matrices $A = [a_{ij}]$ and $B = [b_{ij}]$ is the $m \times n$ matrix $S = A + B$, where $[s_{ij}] = [a_{ij} + b_{ij}]$.

Here is a practice problem.

Problem: Given $A = \begin{bmatrix} 4 & 1 \\ -3 & 6 \end{bmatrix}$ and $B = \begin{bmatrix} 2 & -5 \\ 0 & 3 \end{bmatrix}$, find $A + B$.

Solution: $A + B = \begin{bmatrix} 4 & 1 \\ -3 & 6 \end{bmatrix} + \begin{bmatrix} 2 & -5 \\ 0 & 3 \end{bmatrix} = \begin{bmatrix} 6 & -4 \\ -3 & 9 \end{bmatrix}$

With respect to matrix addition, the *0* matrix is the **additive identity** element and $-A$ is the **additive inverse** for the matrix A. That is, if A and 0 have the same order, then $A + 0 = 0 + A = A$ and $A + -A = -A + A = 0$.

The **difference**, $A - B$, of two matrices is defined to be $A + (-B)$. In practice, to subtract two matrices, subtract corresponding elements of the two matrices.

Here is a practice problem.

Problem: Given $A = \begin{bmatrix} 4 & 1 \\ -3 & 7 \end{bmatrix}$ and $B = \begin{bmatrix} 2 & -5 \\ 0 & 3 \end{bmatrix}$, find $A - B$.

Solution: $A - B = \begin{bmatrix} 4 & 1 \\ -3 & 7 \end{bmatrix} - \begin{bmatrix} 2 & -5 \\ 0 & 3 \end{bmatrix} = \begin{bmatrix} 2 & 6 \\ -3 & 4 \end{bmatrix}$

The Inner Product

The **inner product** (also called the **dot product**), $A \cdot B$, *in that order* of a $1 \times m$ row vector $A = [a_{11}, a_{12}, \ldots a_{1m}]$ and an

$m \times 1$ column vector $B = \begin{bmatrix} b_{11} \\ b_{21} \\ \vdots \\ b_{m1} \end{bmatrix}$, is the scalar $a_{11}b_{11} + a_{12}b_{21} + \ldots + a_{1m}b_{m1}$. Notice that you multiply *row by column*:

Multiply each element of the row times the corresponding element of the column and then sum the products.

Here is a practice problem.

Problem: Find the inner product of $A = \begin{bmatrix} 1 & 0 & 5 & -2 \end{bmatrix}$ and $B = \begin{bmatrix} 3 \\ -1 \\ 0 \\ 4 \end{bmatrix}$.

Solution: $A \cdot B = \begin{bmatrix} 1 & 0 & 5 & -2 \end{bmatrix} \cdot \begin{bmatrix} 3 \\ -1 \\ 0 \\ 4 \end{bmatrix} = 1 \cdot 3 + 0 \cdot (-1) + 5 \cdot 0 + -2 \cdot 4 = -5$

Matrix Multiplication

Two matrices, A and B, are **conformable for matrix multiplication** in the order AB, only if the number of columns of matrix A is equal to the number of rows of matrix B. In the product, AB, we say B is **premultiplied** by A and A is **postmultiplied** by B. *Multiplication of matrices that are not conformable is not defined.*

The **product**, AB, *in that order* of an $m \times k$ matrix $A = [a_{ij}]$ and a $k \times n$ matrix $B = [b_{ij}]$ is the $m \times n$ matrix $C = [c_{ij}] = [a_{i1}b_{1j} + a_{i2}b_{2j} + \cdots + a_{ik}b_{kj}]$, for $1 \le i \le m$ and $1 \le j \le n$. Notice that the element c_{ij} is the inner product of the *i*th row of A and the *j*th column of B.

Here is a practice problem.

Problem: Given $A = \begin{bmatrix} 1 & 5 \\ 3 & -5 \end{bmatrix}$ and $B = \begin{bmatrix} 0 & 4 & 2 \\ -5 & 3 & 1 \end{bmatrix}$, compute AB.

Solution:

$AB = \begin{bmatrix} 1 & 5 \\ 3 & -5 \end{bmatrix} \begin{bmatrix} 0 & 4 & 2 \\ -5 & 3 & 1 \end{bmatrix} = \begin{bmatrix} 1 \cdot 0 + 5 \cdot (-5) & 1 \cdot 4 + 5 \cdot 3 & 1 \cdot 2 + 5 \cdot 1 \\ 3 \cdot 0 + (-5) \cdot (-5) & 3 \cdot 4 + (-5) \cdot 3 & 3 \cdot 2 + (-5) \cdot 1 \end{bmatrix} = \begin{bmatrix} -25 & 19 & 7 \\ 25 & -3 & 1 \end{bmatrix}$

Tip: Because of the distinctive way that matrix multiplication is defined, in general, matrix multiplication is not commutative, not even for square matrices of the same order. Because of this noncommutative feature of matrix arithmetic, you must pay careful attention to the order of the factors in any product of matrices when you are taking your TExES Math exam.

With respect to matrix multiplication, the matrix I is the **multiplicative identity** element; that is, if A is an $m \times n$ matrix, then $AI_n = A$ and $I_m A = A$.

Matrix Inverses

If A is a square matrix of order n and there exists a square matrix B of order n such that $AB = BA = I$, then B is the **inverse** of A. A matrix A that has an inverse is said to be **invertible** (or **nonsingular**). If no such matrix B exists, then A is **singular**.

Not all square matrices have inverses, but when the inverse of a square matrix exists, the inverse is unique and is designated A^{-1}. Thus, $AA^{-1} = A^{-1}A = I$.

The inverse of a 2×2 nonsingular matrix $A = \begin{bmatrix} a_{11} & a_{12} \\ a_{21} & a_{22} \end{bmatrix}$ is given by $A^{-1} = \dfrac{1}{\det(A)} \begin{bmatrix} a_{22} & -a_{12} \\ -a_{21} & a_{11} \end{bmatrix}$,

where $\det(A) = a_{11}a_{22} - a_{12}a_{21} \neq 0$. The scalar $\det(A) = a_{11}a_{22} - a_{12}a_{21}$ is the determinant of A. (See the next section, "Determinants," for an additional discussion of determinants.) The procedure, which works *only* for nonsingular 2×2 matrices, can be stated in four steps:

1. Compute $\det(A) = a_{11}a_{22} - a_{12}a_{21}$.
2. Switch a_{11} and a_{22}.
3. Change the signs of a_{12} and a_{21} (but don't switch them!).
4. Multiply each element by $\dfrac{1}{\det(A)}$.

The reason you must understand the process is that a question might ask about the process rather than for you to find the inverse.

Here is a practice problem.

Problem: Let $A = \begin{bmatrix} 1 & 1 \\ 4 & 2 \end{bmatrix}$, find A^{-1}.

Solution: $A^{-1} = \dfrac{1}{\det(A)} \begin{bmatrix} 2 & -1 \\ -4 & 1 \end{bmatrix} = \dfrac{1}{-2} \cdot \begin{bmatrix} 2 & -1 \\ -4 & 1 \end{bmatrix} = \begin{bmatrix} -1 & \dfrac{1}{2} \\ 2 & -\dfrac{1}{2} \end{bmatrix}$

Note: The matrix $A = \begin{bmatrix} a_{11} & a_{12} \\ a_{21} & a_{22} \end{bmatrix}$ has an inverse if and only if $\det(A) = a_{11}a_{22} - a_{12}a_{21} \neq 0$.

With respect to arithmetic operations, matrices *that contain elements that are complex numbers or real numbers* have some properties in common with the properties of their elements. With respect to the operation of matrix addition, the set of $m \times n$ matrices is closed, commutative, and associative, and has an additive identity and an additive inverse for each $m \times n$ matrix. For the operation of matrix multiplication, certain restrictions on the order of the matrices involved in the multiplication must be met before the operation is defined. For situations in which matrix multiplication is defined, matrix multiplication is closed, associative, has a multiplicative identity, and distributes over addition. In general, matrix multiplication is *not* commutative, nor do there always exist multiplicative inverses.

Tip: Your TI calculator has matrix features that you can use to perform matrix computations. Refer to the calculator guidebook for instructions or search for relevant online videos.

Determinants

For every square matrix A, there is a unique corresponding scalar called the **determinant** of A, denoted $\det(A)$ (or $|a_{ij}|$), which is a well-defined combination of products of the elements of A. *Note:* Only square matrices have determinants.

The determinant of a 2×2 matrix $A = \begin{bmatrix} a_{11} & a_{12} \\ a_{21} & a_{22} \end{bmatrix}$ is $\det(A) = \begin{vmatrix} a_{11} & a_{12} \\ a_{21} & a_{22} \end{vmatrix} = a_{11}a_{22} - a_{12}a_{21}$.

For example, the determinant of $A = \begin{bmatrix} 4 & 2 \\ -2 & 1 \end{bmatrix}$ is $\begin{vmatrix} 4 & 2 \\ -2 & 1 \end{vmatrix} = (4)(1) - 2(-2) = 4 + 4 = 8$.

One way to obtain the determinant of a 3×3 matrix $A = \begin{bmatrix} a_{11} & a_{12} & a_{13} \\ a_{21} & a_{22} & a_{23} \\ a_{31} & a_{32} & a_{33} \end{bmatrix}$ is given by $\det(A) = \begin{vmatrix} a_{11} & a_{12} & a_{13} \\ a_{21} & a_{22} & a_{23} \\ a_{31} & a_{32} & a_{33} \end{vmatrix} =$

$a_{11}\begin{vmatrix} a_{22} & a_{23} \\ a_{32} & a_{33} \end{vmatrix} - a_{12}\begin{vmatrix} a_{21} & a_{23} \\ a_{31} & a_{33} \end{vmatrix} + a_{13}\begin{vmatrix} a_{21} & a_{22} \\ a_{31} & a_{32} \end{vmatrix} = a_{11}(a_{22}a_{33} - a_{23}a_{32}) - a_{12}(a_{21}a_{33} - a_{23}a_{31}) + a_{13}(a_{21}a_{32} - a_{22}a_{31})$.

Tip: A common error in applying this definition is to forget the negative sign on the second term.

This method is by **expansion along the first row** (actually, with some adjustments you can use any row or column). A simple way to identify the elements in the 2×2 determinant that is multiplied by a_{1j} is to do the following: In the 3×3 matrix, cross out the row and column containing a_{1j}. The remaining array of elements are the elements of the determinant.

Here is a practice problem.

Problem: Find the determinant of $B = \begin{bmatrix} 3 & 0 & 4 \\ -1 & 6 & 2 \\ 5 & -3 & 6 \end{bmatrix}$.

Solution:

$\det(B) = \begin{vmatrix} 3 & 0 & 4 \\ -1 & 6 & 2 \\ 5 & -3 & 6 \end{vmatrix} = 3\begin{vmatrix} 6 & 2 \\ -3 & 6 \end{vmatrix} - 0\begin{vmatrix} -1 & 2 \\ 5 & 6 \end{vmatrix} + 4\begin{vmatrix} -1 & 6 \\ 5 & -3 \end{vmatrix} = 3(36+6) - 0(-6-10) + 4(3-30) = 126 - 108 = 18$

Here are some properties of determinants for a given square $n \times n$ matrix A.

- If A has a row or column consisting of only 0s, then $\det(A) = 0$.
- If two rows/columns of A are proportional (that is, one is a scalar multiple of the other), then $\det(A) = 0$.
- $\det(kA) = k^n \det(A)$
- $\det(A) = \det(A^T)$
- If A is a diagonal matrix, then $\det(A) = a_{11}a_{22}\cdots a_{nn}$.
- The matrix A has an inverse if and only if $\det(A) \neq 0$.
- If $\det(A) \neq 0$, then $\det(A^{-1}) = \dfrac{1}{\det(A)}$.
- If the **coefficient matrix** $A = [a_{ij}]$ of the system of n linear equations with n unknowns given by

$$a_{11}x_1 + a_{12}x_2 + \cdots + a_{1n}x_n = c_1$$
$$a_{21}x_1 + a_{22}x_2 + \cdots + a_{2n}x_n = c_2$$
$$\cdots \quad \cdots \quad \cdots \quad \cdots$$
$$a_{n1}x_1 + a_{n2}x_2 + \cdots + a_{nn}x_n = c_n$$

has a nonzero determinant (that is, if $\det(A) \neq 0$), then the system has exactly one solution. If $\det(A) = 0$, then the system might have no solution or infinitely many solutions.
- The effects of performing elementary row operations on a matrix A are the following:
  - If B is a matrix obtained by multiplying a single row/column of A by a scalar k, then $\det(B) = k\det(A)$.
  - If B is a matrix obtained by interchanging exactly two rows/columns of A, then $\det(B) = -\det(A)$.
  - If B is a matrix obtained by multiplying a single row/column of A by a scalar k, and adding the result to another row/column, then $\det(B) = \det(A)$.

Vectors

A **vector** is a quantity that has both a magnitude (or size) and a direction. Two of the most common ways of representing vector quantities in two-dimensional space are by ordered pairs and by directed line segments or "arrows." In this section, the algebraic representation of vectors is by ordered pairs and the geometric representation of vectors is by directed line segments.

Basic Concepts of Vectors

In the geometric representation of a vector, the length of the segment represents the magnitude, and the arrowhead signifies the direction. The notation $\overrightarrow{AB}$ indicates the vector with initial point A and terminal point B. Symbolically, lowercase bold letters denote vectors. The figure below shows the vector $\mathbf{v} = \overrightarrow{AB}$.

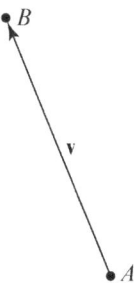

Graphical representation of vectors in a coordinate plane uses some conventions that are important to know. For example, if **v** is a vector whose initial point is at the origin of the rectangular coordinate system and its terminal point has coordinates (v_1, v_2) as shown below, then the vector $\mathbf{v} = (v_1, v_2)$ and v_1 and v_2 are the components of **v**.

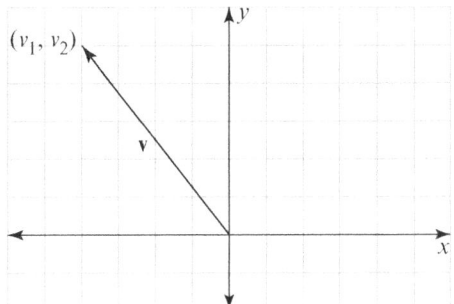

Vectors are equal if they have the same magnitude and direction, regardless of their positions in space.

The **zero vector,** denoted by $\mathbf{0} = (0, 0)$, is a vector with no length. Because it has no length, by convention, it has any direction that it needs to have in a given problem.

The **negative** of a vector $\mathbf{v} = (v_1, v_2)$ is the vector $-\mathbf{v} = (-v_1, -v_2)$ with the same length as **v**, but with opposite direction.

Scalar Multiplication

The multiplication of a vector by a constant is **scalar multiplication.** The product of a vector $\mathbf{v} = (v_1, v_2)$ and a scalar k is the vector $k\mathbf{v} = (kv_1, kv_2)$, whose magnitude is k times the magnitude of **v** and whose direction is the same direction as **v** if $k > 0$, or the opposite direction if $k < 0$.

Clearly, scalar multiplication may alter the magnitude or direction, or both. Multiplying by a scalar with absolute value less than 1 will compress the vector, while multiplying by a scalar with absolute value greater than 1 will stretch the vector. Multiplying by a negative scalar reverses the vector's direction.

Chapter 1: Number Concepts

The following properties hold for vectors **u** and **v** and scalars c and k.

$$1\mathbf{u} = \mathbf{u} \qquad 0\mathbf{u} = \mathbf{0} \qquad (ck)\mathbf{u} = c(k\mathbf{u}) = k(c\mathbf{u})$$
$$(c + k)\mathbf{u} = c\mathbf{u} + k\mathbf{u} \qquad c(\mathbf{u} + \mathbf{v}) = c\mathbf{u} + c\mathbf{v}$$

Here is a practice problem.

Problem: If **v** = (5,−4), express −3**v** in component form.
Solution: −3**v** = (−3 · 5, −3 · −4) = (−15, 12).

Addition and Subtraction of Vectors

Geometrically, the **sum** or **resultant** of two vectors **u** and **v** is a vector **w** = **u** + **v** formed by placing the initial point of **v** on the terminal point of **u** and then joining the initial point of **u** to the terminal point of **v** as shown below.

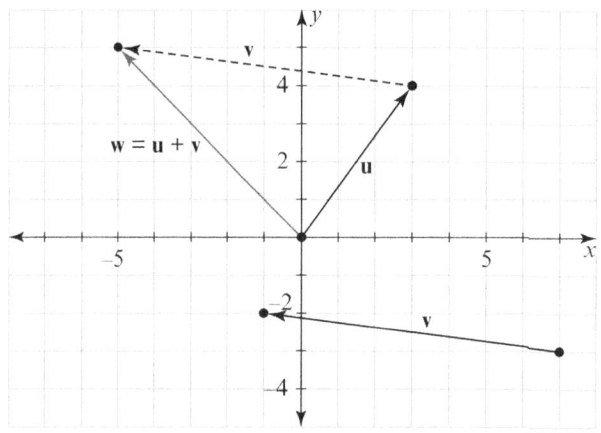

The **difference u − v** of two vectors **u** and **v** is defined to be **u** + (−**v**).

If **u** and **v** are expressed in component form, $\mathbf{u} = (u_1, u_2)$ and $\mathbf{v} = (v_1, v_2)$, then $\mathbf{u} + \mathbf{v} = (u_1 + v_1, u_2 + v_2)$ and $\mathbf{u} - \mathbf{v} = (u_1 - v_1, u_2 - v_2)$.

The following properties hold for vectors **u** and **v**.

$$\mathbf{u} + \mathbf{v} = \mathbf{v} + \mathbf{u} \qquad \mathbf{u} + \mathbf{0} = \mathbf{0} + \mathbf{u} = \mathbf{u}$$
$$\mathbf{u} + (-\mathbf{u}) = (-\mathbf{u}) + \mathbf{u} = \mathbf{0} \qquad \mathbf{u} + (\mathbf{v} + \mathbf{w}) = (\mathbf{u} + \mathbf{v}) + \mathbf{w}$$

Here is a practice problem.

Problem: If **u** = (8,0) and **v** = (5,−4), compute $\frac{1}{2}\mathbf{u} + 3\mathbf{v}$ and express the result in component form.

Solution: $\frac{1}{2}\mathbf{u} + 3\mathbf{v} = (4,0) + (15,-12) = (19,-12)$

Chapter 2

Patterns and Algebra

This chapter provides a review of essential algebraic concepts, including patterns, relations, functions, and algebraic reasoning and analysis, and presents foundational concepts of trigonometry and calculus as well.

Part 1

Part 1 of this chapter is for all candidates who plan to take a TExES Math exam. Carefully study the review material, being sure to concentrate as you go through it. Work through the examples and practice problems and make sure you understand them thoroughly. When working a practice problem, you should cover up the solution. Then check your answer when you've finished.

Basic Algebraic Terminology

A **variable** is a placeholder for a number (or numbers, in some cases) whose value may vary. Symbols (often lowercase or uppercase letters such as $x, y, z, A, B,$ or C) represent variables. The symbol that represents a variable is its name.

A **constant** is a number whose value does not change. For example, all the real and complex numbers are constants. Each has a fixed, definite value.

A **numerical expression** is any constant or combination of two or more constants joined by explicit or implied operational symbols. For example, 100, 3.5, $\frac{3 \cdot 25}{4 \cdot 5}$, 0.75(2,000) + 2,500, and $\pi(6)^2$ are numerical expressions.

An **algebraic expression** is a symbol or combination of symbols that represents a number. Algebraic expressions consist of one or more variables joined by one or more operations with or without constants (explicitly) included. **Juxtaposition** is commonly used to indicate multiplication. That is, when constants and variables or two or more variables (with or without constants) are written side by side, they are products. For example, $7x$ is the result of multiplying 7 and x. Thus, $7 \cdot x = x \cdot 7 = (7)(x) = (7)x = x(7) = 7x$. Similarly, axy means a times x times y. The expressions $7x$, axy, $6x + 3$, $5x^4 + 3x^3 - 12x^2 + 15$, $(a + 5)^2 - 3$, $7abc$, and $\frac{3}{a+3} + \frac{10}{t-25}$ are algebraic expressions.

A **term** is a constant, variable, or product of constants or variables. For example, x, $8ab$, $-9z$, $10xyz$, $x(-6x)$, and 11 are terms. In algebraic expressions, terms are separated by addition.

Here is a practice problem.

> Problem: List the terms of the algebraic expression $6x^4 + 3x^3 - 12x^2 + 15$.
>
> Solution: The algebraic expression $6x^4 + 3x^3 - 12x^2 + 15$ has four terms: $6x^4$, $3x^3$, $-12x^2$, and 15. Note that $-12x^2$, rather than $12x^2$, is a term because, by the definition of subtraction, $6x^4 + 3x^3 - 12x^2 + 15 = 6x^4 + 3x^3 + -12x^2 + 15$.

In the algebraic expression $6x^4 + 3x^3 - 12x^2 + 15$, the terms $6x^4$, $3x^3$, and $-12x^2$ are **variable terms** and 15 is the **constant term** in the expression.

In a term that is a product of two or more factors, the **coefficient** of a factor is the product of the other factors in that term.

Here is a practice problem.

> Problem: What is the coefficient of x in the term $4xy^2$?
> Solution: The coefficient of x in the term $4xy^2$ is $4y^2$.

The numerical factor, or the product of the numerical factors, of a term is its **numerical coefficient.** If no numerical coefficient is explicitly written, then the numerical coefficient is understood to be 1.

Here is a practice problem.

> Problem: What is the numerical coefficient of $(2)(5)xyz$?
>
> Solution: The numerical coefficient of $(2)(5)xyz$ is 10, which is $(2)(5)$.

A **monomial** is a term, such as $6x^4y$, that when simplified is a constant or a product of one or more variables each raised to a nonnegative integer power, with or without an explicit numerical coefficient. The **degree of a monomial** is the sum of the exponents of its variables. The degree of a nonzero constant c is zero because $c = cx^0$ for any constant c. The degree of the monomial 0 is undefined.

Here is a practice problem.

> Problem: What is the degree of the monomial $6x^4y$?
>
> Solution: The degree of the monomial $6x^4y$ is 5.

Like terms are monomial terms that differ only in their numerical coefficients. For example, $6x^4y$ and $-4x^4y$ are like terms; however, $6x^4y$ and $-4xy^4$ are **unlike terms.** All constants are like terms.

A **polynomial** is an algebraic expression composed of one or more monomials. Thus, a **monomial** is a polynomial of exactly one term. A **binomial** is a polynomial of exactly two terms, such as $x + 3$. A **trinomial** is a polynomial of exactly three terms, such as $9x^4 - 24x^2 + 16$. Beyond three terms, polynomials are n-term polynomials.

Polynomials

For this topic, you must know how to perform operations on polynomials and manipulate polynomial expressions.

Performing Operations with Polynomials

The following table summarizes rules for addition and subtraction of polynomials.

Addition and Subtraction of Polynomials

Operation	Rule	Example
Addition	Combine *like* monomial terms by adding their numerical coefficients; use the result as the coefficient of the common variable factor or factors. Simply indicate the sum/difference of *unlike* terms.	$(5x^2 + 10x - 6) + (3x^2 - 2x + 4) = 5x^2 + 10x - 6 + 3x^2 - 2x + 4$ $= 8x^2 + 8x - 2$
Subtraction	Keep the first polynomial, change the sign of every term of the second polynomial, and proceed as in addition.	$(5x^2 + 10x - 6) - (3x^2 - 2x + 4) = 5x^2 + 10x - 6 - 3x^2 + 2x - 4$ $= 2x^2 + 12x - 10$

Tip: When simple parentheses (or brackets or braces) are immediately preceded by a + symbol, they can be removed without changing the signs of the terms within, but if the parentheses are immediately preceded by a – symbol, the sign of *every* term within the grouping must be changed when the parentheses are removed. In the second case, you *mentally* change the – symbol that precedes the parentheses to a + symbol and do not explicitly write the change because + · + = + and + · – = –.

To multiply two polynomials, multiply each term in the first polynomial by each term in the second polynomial and then simplify, as needed. The following table summarizes rules for multiplication of polynomials.

Multiplication of Polynomials

Type of Multiplication	Rule	Example
Monomial by Monomial	Multiply both the numerical coefficients and the variable factors.	$(-5x^2y)(10xy) = -50x^3y^2$
Polynomial by Monomial	Use the distributive property to multiply each term of the polynomial by the monomial.	$2x^2(3x^2 - 5x + 1) = 6x^4 - 10x^3 + 2x^2$
Polynomial by Polynomial	Use the distributive property to multiply each term of the second polynomial by each term of the first polynomial, and then combine like terms.	$(x+2)(x^2 - 2x + 4) = x^3 - 2x^2 + 4x + 2x^2 - 4x + 8$ $= x^3 + 8$
Binomial by Binomial	Use the distributive property to multiply each term of the second binomial by each term of the first binomial, and then combine like terms. (See "Using F.O.I.L." below for an efficient way to multiply two binomials.)	$(2x-3)(x+4) = 2x^2 + 8x - 3x - 12$ $= 2x^2 + 5x - 12$

Using F.O.I.L.

Use F.O.I.L. (First terms, Outer terms, Inner terms, and Last terms) to multiply two binomials. Here is an example.

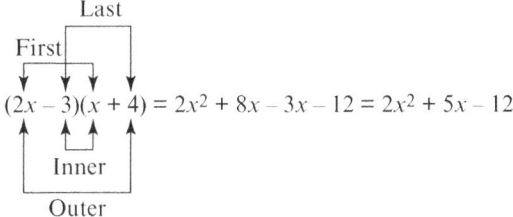

Tip: Remember that when you multiply variable factors, you *add* (not multiply) the exponents of like bases.

Tip: When multiplying polynomials, if possible, arrange the terms of the polynomials in descending or ascending powers of a common variable.

Special Products

Some special products to know for your TExES Math exam are given in the following table.

Special Products

Special Name	Special Product	Example(s)
Perfect Trinomial Squares	$(x + y)^2 = (x + y)(x + y) = x^2 + 2xy + y^2$ $(x - y)^2 = (x - y)(x - y) = x^2 - 2xy + y^2$	$(x + 3)^2 = x^2 + 6x + 9$ $(2x - 5)^2 = 4x^2 - 20x + 25$
Difference of Two Squares	$(x + y)(x - y) = x^2 - y^2$	$(x + 3)(x - 3) = x^2 - 9$
Sum of Two Cubes	$(x + y)(x^2 - xy + y^2) = x^3 + y^3$	$(x + 2)(x^2 - 2x + 4) = x^3 + 8$
Difference of Two Cubes	$(x - y)(x^2 + xy + y^2) = x^3 - y^3$	$(x - 2)(x^2 + 2x + 4) = x^3 - 8$
Perfect Cubes	$(x + y)^3 = x^3 + 3x^2y + 3xy^2 + y^3$ $(x - y)^3 = x^3 - 3x^2y + 3xy^2 - y^3$	$(x + 2)^3 = x^3 + 6x^2 + 12x + 8$ $(x - 2)^3 = x^3 - 6x^2 + 12x - 8$

Tip: It is a common mistake to omit the middle terms when squaring or cubing binomials. The square of a binomial has three terms (a trinomial), and the cube of a binomial has four terms. Just remember that the number of terms is *one more* than the exponent used.

Division of Polynomials

Division of polynomials is analogous to division of real numbers. Because division by 0 is undefined, you must exclude values for the variable or variables that would make the divisor 0. For convenience, you can assume such values are excluded as you review the rules in this section.

The following table summarizes rules for division of polynomials by monomials.

Division by a Monomial

Type of Division	Rule	Example
Monomial by Monomial	Divide the numerical coefficients. Divide the variable factors that have a common base. Leave other variable factors alone. Use the quotient of the numerical coefficients as the coefficient for the answer.	$\dfrac{-50x^3y^2z}{-5x^2y} = 10xyz$
Polynomial by Monomial	Divide each term of the polynomial by the monomial.	$\dfrac{25x^5y^3 + 35x^3y^2 - 10x^2y}{-5x^2y} = \dfrac{25x^5y^3}{-5x^2y} + \dfrac{35x^3y^2}{-5x^2y} + \dfrac{-10x^2y}{-5x^2y}$ $= -5x^3y^2 - 7xy + 2$

Tip: To avoid sign errors when you are doing division of polynomials, keep a – symbol with the number that follows it.

Long division of polynomials is performed like long division in arithmetic. The result is usually written as a mixed expression: quotient + $\dfrac{\text{remainder}}{\text{divisor}}$. See Appendix B for an example of long division of polynomials.

Simplifying Polynomial Expressions

A polynomial expression is **simplified** when all indicated operations have been performed and it contains no uncombined like terms. The **degree of a polynomial** is the same as the greatest of the degrees of its monomial terms after the polynomial has been simplified.

To simplify a polynomial expression, use the following steps:

Steps for Simplifying a Polynomial Expression

1. When grouping symbols are present, perform all operations within grouping symbols, starting with the innermost grouping symbol and working outward.
2. Perform all indicated multiplication, starting with exponentiation, being sure to enclose the product in parentheses if it is to be multiplied by an additional factor.
3. Remove all remaining parentheses and combine like terms using addition or subtraction as indicated.

Tip: Simplifying polynomials follows PE(MD)(AS), which makes sense since the variables in the polynomials represent numbers (see "Order of Operations" in Chapter 1).

Here are two practice problems.

>Problem: Simplify the expression $2 + 4(x + 3y - 10)$.
>Solution: $2 + 4(x + 3y - 10) = 2 + 4x + 12y - 40 = 4x + 12y - 38$

Tip: For the above problem, don't make the mistake of writing $2 + 4(x + 3y - 10)$ as $6(x + 3y - 10)$. Remember, multiplication must be performed before addition (or subtraction) unless grouping symbols indicate otherwise.

>Problem: Simplify the expression $2(x + 3)(x - 3) - (x + 3)^2$.
>Solution: $2(x + 3)(x - 3) - (x + 3)^2 = 2(x^2 - 9) - (x^2 + 6x + 9) = 2x^2 - 18 - x^2 - 6x - 9 = x^2 - 6x - 27$

Tip: Enclosing intermediate products in parentheses helps prevent careless errors.

Factoring Polynomials Completely

Factoring a polynomial completely means writing it as a product of prime polynomial factors. A **prime polynomial** is one whose only factors are itself and 1. Before you can say a polynomial is a prime factor, you must specify the set of numbers that are available as coefficients when you are factoring. For example, over the rationals, the polynomial $x^2 - 3$ is prime; but over the irrationals, $x^2 - 3$ is factorable as $(x + \sqrt{3})(x - \sqrt{3})$.

Similarly, over the real numbers, $x^2 + 4$ is prime; but over the complex numbers, $x^2 + 4$ is factorable as $(x + 2i)(x - 2i)$. Not to worry, you will know over which numbers you are to factor from the context of the problem.

As a general rule, you can safely limit the coefficients of variable terms in polynomials to real numbers. However, when you have polynomial equations, the roots of the equations can be real or complex numbers. A polynomial that cannot be written as a product of two or more polynomial factors is said to be **prime**. To factor a polynomial that is not prime, you must find two or more polynomials whose product is the original polynomial. For example, $(2x - 3)(x + 4)$ is a **factorization** of $2x^2 + 5x - 12$ because $(2x - 3)(x + 4) = 2x^2 + 5x - 12$. The polynomials $(2x - 3)$ and $(x + 4)$ cannot be factored further, so they are **prime polynomial factors** of $2x^2 + 5x - 12$.

When factoring polynomials, proceed systematically as follows.

1. Check for a greatest common monomial factor.
2. If a factor is a binomial, check for
   difference of two squares: $x^2 - y^2 = (x + y)(x - y)$
   sum of two cubes: $x^3 + y^3 = (x + y)(x^2 - xy + y^2)$
   difference of two cubes: $x^3 - y^3 = (x - y)(x^2 + xy + y^2)$
3. If a factor is a trinomial, check for
   general factorable quadratic: $x^2 + (a+b)x + ab = (x+a)(x+b)$
   $acx^2 + (ad+bc)x + bd = (ax+b)(cx+d)$

   perfect trinomial square: $a^2x^2 + 2abxy + b^2y^2 = (ax+by)^2$
   $a^2x^2 - 2abxy + b^2y^2 = (ax-by)^2$
4. If a factor has four terms, try grouping some of the terms together and factoring the groups separately first, and then factoring the entire expression.
5. Write the original polynomial as the product of all the factors obtained.

Tip: After making sure all factors are prime polynomials, check your solution by multiplying the factors to obtain the original polynomial.

Here are four practice problems. Factor over the real numbers unless instructed otherwise.

Problem: Completely factor $x^2 - 3x - 4$.
Solution: $x^2 - 3x - 4 = (x - 4)(x + 1)$

Problem: Completely factor $16a^2b^2 + 4a^2$ over the complex numbers.
Solution: $16a^2b^2 + 4a^2 = 4a^2(4b^2 + 1) = 4a^2(2b + i)(2b - i)$

Problem: Completely factor $80x^3y - 270y^4$.
Solution: $80x^3y - 270y^4 = 10y(8x^3 - 27y^3) = 10y(2x - 3y)(4x^2 + 6xy + 9y^2)$

Problem: Completely factor $3x^4y + 3x^3y - 27x^2y - 27xy$.
Solution: $3x^4y + 3x^3y - 27x^2y - 27xy = 3xy(x^3 + x^2 - 9x - 9) = 3xy[(x^3 + x^2) - (9x + 9)] = 3xy[x^2(x + 1) - 9(x + 1)] = 3xy[(x + 1)(x^2 - 9)] = 3xy[(x + 1)(x + 3)(x - 3)] = 3xy(x + 1)(x + 3)(x - 3)$

Rational Expressions

A **rational expression** is an algebraic fraction in which both the numerator and denominator are polynomials. Values for which the denominator evaluates to 0 are excluded. For example, $\frac{2x}{5}$ (no excluded value); $\frac{5}{2x}$, $(x \neq 0)$; $\frac{x^2 - 4}{x^2 - 3x - 4} = \frac{(x+2)(x-2)}{(x-4)(x+1)}$, $(x \neq 4, x \neq -1)$; and all polynomials (no excluded values) are rational expressions. Hereafter, whenever a rational expression is written, it will be understood that any values for which the expression is undefined are excluded.

To perform computations with algebraic fractions, often you will need to factor the polynomials used in the algebraic fractions. For example, factoring is frequently necessary when reducing algebraic fractions to lowest terms and when finding a common denominator for algebraic fractions. The following table summarizes the process.

Reducing Algebraic Fractions to Lowest Terms

Type of Algebraic Fraction	Rule	Example
$\frac{\text{monomial}}{\text{monomial}}$	Divide numerator and denominator by the greatest common factor of the two monomials.	$\frac{9x^5y^2z}{12x^2y^3} = \frac{3x^2y^2 \cdot 3x^3z}{3x^2y^2 \cdot 4y} = \frac{\cancel{3x^2y^2} \cdot 3x^3z}{\cancel{3x^2y^2} \cdot 4y} = \frac{3x^3z}{4y}$
$\frac{\text{monomial}}{\text{polynomial}}$ or $\frac{\text{polynomial}}{\text{monomial}}$	Factor out the greatest monomial factor, if any, from the polynomial, and then divide numerator and denominator by the greatest common factor.	$\frac{-9x^2y}{12x^3y - 36x^2y - 48xy} = \frac{-9x^2y}{12xy(x^2 - 3x - 4)} = \frac{3xy(-3x)}{3xy(4)(x^2 - 3x - 4)}$ $= \frac{\cancel{3xy}(-3x)}{\cancel{3xy}(4)(x^2 - 3x - 4)} = \frac{-3x}{4(x^2 - 3x - 4)} = -\frac{3x}{4(x - 4)(x + 1)}$ $\frac{12x^3y - 36x^2y - 48xy}{9x^2y} = \frac{12xy(x^2 - 3x - 4)}{3xy(3x)} = \frac{4(x^2 - 3x - 4)}{3x} = \frac{4(x - 4)(x + 1)}{3x}$
$\frac{\text{polynomial}}{\text{polynomial}}$	Factor the polynomials completely, and then divide numerator and denominator by the greatest common factor(s), if any.	$\frac{9x^2y - 9y}{12x^3y - 36x^2y - 48xy} = \frac{9y(x^2 - 1)}{12xy(x^2 - 3x - 4)} = \frac{3y(3)(x+1)(x-1)}{3y(4x)(x+1)(x-4)}$ $= \frac{\cancel{3y}(3)\cancel{(x+1)}(x-1)}{\cancel{3y}(4x)\cancel{(x+1)}(x-4)} = \frac{3(x-1)}{4x(x-4)}$

Tip: When reducing algebraic fractions, make sure you divide by factors only. For example, $\dfrac{x+2}{4}$ cannot be reduced further. Even though 2 is a factor of the denominator, it is not a factor of the numerator—it is a term of the numerator. Remember, divide the numerator and denominator by common factors, not terms.

The following table summarizes computations with algebraic fractions.

Computations with Algebraic Fractions

Operation	Rule	Example
Addition/Subtraction: Like Denominators	Add/subtract the numerators to find the numerator of the answer, which is placed over the common denominator. Simplify and reduce to lowest terms, if needed.	$\dfrac{x+2}{x-3} + \dfrac{2x-11}{x-3} = \dfrac{3x-9}{x-3} = \dfrac{3(x-3)}{x-3} = \dfrac{3}{1} = 3$
	When subtracting, you must change the sign of every term of the numerator of the second fraction.	$\dfrac{5x^2}{3(x+1)} - \dfrac{4x^2+1}{3(x+1)} = \dfrac{5x^2 - 4x^2 - 1}{3(x+1)}$ $= \dfrac{x^2 - 1}{3(x+1)}$ $= \dfrac{\cancel{(x+1)}(x-1)}{3\cancel{(x+1)}}$ $= \dfrac{x-1}{3}$
Addition/Subtraction: Unlike Denominators	Factor each denominator completely. Find the common denominator, which is the product of each prime factor the highest number of times it is a factor in any one denominator. Write each algebraic fraction as an equivalent fraction having the common denominator as a denominator. Add/subtract the numerators to find the numerator of the answer, which is placed over the common denominator. Simplify and reduce to lowest terms, if needed.	$\dfrac{1}{x^2-3x-4} + \dfrac{2}{x^2-1} = \dfrac{1}{(x+1)(x-4)} + \dfrac{2}{(x+1)(x-1)}$ $= \dfrac{1(x-1)}{(x+1)(x-4)(x-1)} + \dfrac{2(x-4)}{(x+1)(x-1)(x-4)}$ $= \dfrac{x-1}{(x+1)(x-4)(x-1)} + \dfrac{2x-8}{(x+1)(x-1)(x-4)}$ $= \dfrac{3x-9}{(x+1)(x-1)(x-4)} = \dfrac{3(x-3)}{(x+1)(x-1)(x-4)}$
Multiplication	Factor all numerators and denominators completely and then divide numerators and denominators by their common factors (as in reducing). The product of the remaining numerator factors is the numerator of the answer, and the product of the remaining denominator factors is the denominator of the answer.	$\dfrac{a^2+4a+4}{a^2+a-2} \cdot \dfrac{a^2-2a+1}{a^2-4} = \dfrac{(a+2)(a+2)}{(a+2)(a-1)} \cdot \dfrac{(a-1)(a-1)}{(a+2)(a-2)}$ $= \dfrac{\cancel{(a+2)}\cancel{(a+2)}}{\cancel{(a+2)}\cancel{(a-1)}} \cdot \dfrac{\cancel{(a-1)}(a-1)}{\cancel{(a+2)}(a-2)}$ $= \dfrac{a-1}{a-2}$

continued

Operation	Rule	Example
Division	Multiply the first algebraic fraction by the reciprocal of the second algebraic fraction.	$\dfrac{a^2+4a+4}{a^2+a-2} \div \dfrac{a^2-4}{a^2-2a+1} = \dfrac{a^2+4a+4}{a^2+a-2} \cdot \dfrac{a^2-2a+1}{a^2-4}$ $= \dfrac{(a+2)(a+2)}{(a+2)(a-1)} \cdot \dfrac{(a-1)(a-1)}{(a+2)(a-2)}$ $= \dfrac{\cancel{(a+2)}\cancel{(a+2)}}{\cancel{(a+2)}\cancel{(a-1)}} \cdot \dfrac{\cancel{(a-1)}(a-1)}{\cancel{(a+2)}(a-2)}$ $= \dfrac{a-1}{a-2}$

Complex Fractions

A **complex fraction** is a fraction that has fractions in its numerator, denominator, or both. You can simplify a complex fraction by multiplying its numerator and denominator by the least common denominator of all the fractions used in its numerator and denominator.

Here is a practice problem.

Problem: Simplify the complex fraction $\dfrac{\frac{1}{x}+\frac{1}{y}}{\frac{1}{x}-\frac{1}{y}}$.

Solution: $\dfrac{\frac{1}{x}+\frac{1}{y}}{\frac{1}{x}-\frac{1}{y}} = \dfrac{xy\left(\frac{1}{x}+\frac{1}{y}\right)}{xy\left(\frac{1}{x}-\frac{1}{y}\right)} = \dfrac{xy \cdot \frac{1}{x} + xy \cdot \frac{1}{y}}{xy \cdot \frac{1}{x} - xy \cdot \frac{1}{y}} = \dfrac{y+x}{y-x}$

One-Variable Linear Equations

An **equation** is a statement that two mathematical expressions are equal. An equation has two sides. Whatever is on the left side of the equal sign is the left side (LS) of the equation, and whatever is on the right side of the equal sign is the right side (RS) of the equation. Equations containing only numerical expressions are either true or false. An equation is true when the LS has the same value as the RS. For example, 1 + 2 = 3 is true, but 1 + 2 = 5 is false. An equation containing one or more variables is an **open sentence.** For example, $x + 2 = 3$ and $x + 2y = 8$ are open sentences. Generally, you can determine whether an open sentence is true or false only after numerical quantities are substituted for the variables in the sentence.

A **one-variable linear equation** has only one variable. The variable has an exponent of 1 (commonly not written, but understood), and no products of variables or variable divisors occur in the equation. A **solution,** or **root,** of a one-variable equation is a number that when substituted for the variable makes the equation true. To determine whether a number is a solution of a one-variable equation, replace the variable with the number and perform all operations indicated on each side of the equation. If the resulting statement is true, the number is a solution of the equation. This process is called **checking** a solution.

The **solution set** of an equation is the set consisting of all the solutions of the equation. **Equivalent equations** are equations that have the same solution set. If the solution set is the set of all possible values of the variable, the equation is an **identity.** For example, $x + 7 = x + 5 + 2$ is an identity because any number substituted for x will make the equation true. Thus, an identity has an infinite number of solutions. If the solution set is empty, the equation has **no solution.** For example, $x + 7 = x + 5$ has no solution because there is no number that will make the equation true. To **solve an equation** means to find its solution set.

A one-variable linear equation can be written in the form $ax + b = 0$, where $a \neq 0$ and b is a constant in the discussion. Unless the equation is an identity or has no solution, the solution set of a one-variable linear equation consists of one number.

When you are solving a one-variable linear equation, the two main actions that will result in equivalent equations are the following:

1. Addition or subtraction of the same quantity to both sides of the equation.
2. Multiplication or division by the same *nonzero* quantity to both sides of the equation.

Tip: It is important to remember that when you are solving an equation, you must never multiply or divide both sides by 0.

The strategy in solving a one-variable linear equation is to proceed through a series of steps until you produce an equivalent equation that has the form variable = solution (or solution = variable). The equal sign in an equation is like a balance point. To keep the equation in balance, what you do to one side of the equation you must do to its other side. You decide what to do by inspecting what has been done to the variable. You undo what's been done until the variable is by itself on one side of the equation only, the variable's coefficient is understood to be 1, and the other side of the equation is a single number all by itself.

To solve a one-variable linear equation, use the following procedure:

Steps for Solving a One-Variable Linear Equation

1. Remove grouping symbols, if any, by applying the distributive property, and then simplify.
2. If the variable appears on both sides of the equation, eliminate the variable from one side of the equation. Undo indicated addition or subtraction to get all terms containing the variable on one side and all other terms on the other side. Then simplify.
3. If a number is added to the variable term, subtract that number from both sides of the equation. If a number is subtracted from the variable term, add that number to both sides of the equation. Then simplify.
4. If necessary, factor the side containing the variable so that one of the factors is the variable.
5. Divide both sides of the equation by the coefficient of the variable. If the coefficient is a fraction, eliminate the fraction by multiplying both sides of the equation by the fraction's reciprocal.

Tip: You should check the solution in the original equation.

Here is a practice problem.

Problem: Solve $\frac{2}{3}x - 45 = -\frac{1}{2}(x + 48)$.

Solution:

$$\frac{2}{3}x - 45 = -\frac{1}{2}(x + 48)$$

$$\frac{2}{3}x - 45 = -\frac{1}{2}x - 24$$

$$\frac{2}{3}x - 45 + \frac{1}{2}x = -\frac{1}{2}x - 24 + \frac{1}{2}x$$

$$\frac{7}{6}x - 45 = -24$$

$$\frac{7}{6}x - 45 + 45 = -24 + 45$$

$$\frac{7}{6}x = 21$$

$$\frac{\cancel{6}}{\cancel{7}} \cdot \frac{\cancel{7}}{\cancel{6}} x = \frac{6}{\cancel{7}} \cdot \cancel{21}^3$$

$$x = 18$$

Of course, as long as you keep the equation in balance, you can modify the equation-solving process based on the particular equation you are trying to solve. For example, if an equation contains fractions, you first might multiply both sides of the equation by the lcm of all the denominators to eliminate fractions from both sides of the equation. You also might do some of the steps mentally to save time. Just always make sure that you are doing the same operation to both sides of the equation, whether or not you show all your work!

Here is a practice problem.

Problem: Solve $\dfrac{x-3}{2} = \dfrac{2x+4}{5}$.

Solution:

$$\dfrac{x-3}{2} = \dfrac{2x+4}{5}$$

$$\dfrac{\cancel{10}^{5}}{1}\left(\dfrac{x-3}{\cancel{2}}\right) = \dfrac{\cancel{10}^{2}}{1}\left(\dfrac{2x+4}{\cancel{5}}\right)$$

$$5x - 15 = 4x + 8$$
$$5x - 4x = 8 + 15$$
$$x = 23$$

One-Variable Inequalities

If you replace the equal sign in a one-variable linear equation with < (less than), > (greater than), ≤ (less than or equal to), or ≥ (greater than or equal to), the result is a **one-variable linear inequality.** The solution sets of one-variable linear inequalities are subsets of the real numbers. (See "Set Terminology" in Chapter 5 for a discussion of the term *subset.*) You can graph the solution set of the inequality on a number line.

You solve an inequality just as you would an equation *except* for one very important difference: If you multiply or divide both sides of the inequality by a *negative* number, you must *reverse* the direction of the inequality.

Here is a practice problem.

Problem: Solve $3x + 5 \geq 5x - 7$.

Solution:

$$3x + 5 \geq 5x - 7$$
$$3x + 5 - 5x \geq 5x - 7 - 5x$$
$$-2x + 5 \geq -7$$
$$-2x + 5 - 5 \geq -7 - 5$$
$$-2x \geq -12$$

$$\dfrac{\cancel{-2}x}{\cancel{-2}} \leq \dfrac{\cancel{-12}^{6}}{\cancel{-2}}$$ (Reverse the direction of the inequality because you divided by a negative number.)

$$x \leq 6$$

Transforming Formulas and Two-Variable Equations

An equation that expresses the relationship between two or more variables is a **formula.** The procedure for solving one-variable linear equations can be used to solve a formula for a specific variable when the value(s) of the other variable(s) are known. The procedure also can be used to solve a formula or literal equation (an equation with no numbers, only letters) for a specific variable in terms of the other variable(s). What you must keep in mind when using the procedure for these purposes is that, when the word *variable* is used, it is referring only to the variable *for which you are solving.* In general, isolate the specific variable of interest and treat all other variable(s) as constants. This is called changing the subject of the formula or literal equation.

Here is a practice problem.

Problem: Solve $C = \frac{5}{9}(F - 32)$ for F.

Solution:

$$C = \frac{5}{9}(F - 32)$$
$$C = \frac{5}{9}F - \frac{160}{9}$$
$$C + \frac{160}{9} = \frac{5}{9}F$$
$$\frac{9}{5}\left(C + \frac{160}{9}\right) = \frac{9}{5} \cdot \frac{5}{9}F$$
$$\frac{9}{5}C + 32 = F$$

Use the procedure for solving one-variable linear equations to solve two-variable equations for one variable in terms of the other variable. For example, use the procedure to transform equations of lines into the form $y = mx + b$, where m and b are constants. (See "The Equation of a Line" later in this chapter for a discussion of this topic.)

Here is a practice problem.

Problem: Write $-2x + 3y = 1$ in the form $y = mx + b$.

Solution:

$$-2x + 3y = 1$$
$$3y = 2x + 1$$
$$y = \frac{2}{3}x + \frac{1}{3}$$

One-Variable Absolute Value Equations and Inequalities

Solve **one-variable absolute value equations** using the procedure for solving one-variable linear equations. To transform one-variable absolute value equations into linear equations, use the following statements:

$|ax + b| = 0$ if and only if $ax + b = 0$.

If c is any positive number, $|ax + b| = c$ if and only if either $ax + b = c$ or $ax + b = -c$.

Tip: Notice that for equations like |ax + b| = c, you must solve *two* linear equations. Don't forget the second equation!

Here are two practice problems.

Problem: Solve $|2x + 6| = 0$.

Solution:

$$|2x + 6| = 0 \text{ implies}$$
$$2x + 6 = 0$$
$$2x = -6$$
$$x = -3$$

Problem: Solve $|2x + 6| = 10$.

Solution:

$$|2x+6| = 10 \text{ implies}$$
$$2x+6 = 10 \text{ or } 2x+6 = -10$$
$$2x = 4 \text{ or } 2x = -16$$
$$x = 2 \text{ or } x = -8$$

Solve **one-variable absolute value inequalities** using the procedure for solving one-variable linear inequalities. To transform one-variable absolute value inequalities into linear inequalities, apply the following statements:

If $c > 0$, $|ax + b| < c$ if and only if $-c < ax + b < c$.

If $c > 0$, $|ax + b| > c$ if and only if either $ax + b < -c$ or $ax + b > c$.

The expression $-c < ax + b < c$ is called a **double inequality** because it is a concise way to express the two inequalities: $-c < ax + b$ and $ax + b < c$.

Note: You can replace $<$ with $\leq$ and $>$ with $\geq$ everywhere in the given inequalities, and the statements will still hold.

Tip: Notice that for absolute value inequalities, you must set up and solve *two* linear inequalities. Don't forget the second inequality! If the inequality symbol is < (or ≤), the connecting word between the two inequalities is "and" (double inequality). If the inequality symbol is > (or ≥), the connecting word is "or."

Here are two practice problems.

Problem: Solve $|2x + 6| < 10$.

Solution: $|2x + 6| < 10$ if and only if $-10 < 2x + 6 < 10$.

Solve this double inequality by applying the techniques for solving inequalities to the two inequalities simultaneously. Focus on isolating the variable in the middle variable expression. Whatever you do to the middle expression, you must do to each of the two expressions on either side, as shown here.

$$-10 < 2x+6 < 10$$
$$-16 < 2x < 4$$
$$-8 < x < 2$$

The solution set for $|2x + 6| < 10$ is $\{x | -8 < x < 2\}$.

Problem: Solve $|2x + 6| > 10$.

Solution: $|2x + 6| > 10$ if and only if either $2x + 6 < -10$ or $2x + 6 > 10$. Solve each of these two linear inequalities as shown here.

$$2x+6 < -10 \qquad 2x+6 > 10$$
$$2x < -16 \qquad 2x > 4$$
$$x < -8 \qquad x > 2$$

The solution set for $|2x + 6| > 10$ is $\{x | x < -8 \text{ or } x > 2\}$.

Quadratic Equations

A **one-variable quadratic equation** is an equation that can be written in the **standard form** $ax^2 + bx + c = 0$, where $a \neq 0$ and a, b, and c are real-valued constants in the discussion. Specifically, ***a*** is the numerical coefficient of x^2, **b** is the numerical coefficient of x, and **c** is the constant coefficient, or simply the constant term. The solutions of a quadratic equation are its **roots.** A quadratic equation may have exactly one real root, exactly two real unequal roots, or exactly two unequal complex roots (and *no* real roots).

Note: Quadratic equations in which *a*, *b*, or *c* is not an element of the real numbers are not covered on your TExES Math exam.

Solving Quadratic Equations of the Form $x^2 = C$

Quadratic equations that can be written in the form $x^2 = C$ have the solution $x = \pm\sqrt{C}$. If the quantity *C* is 0, there is one *real* root that has the value 0; if positive, there are two unequal *real* roots; and if negative, there are two unequal *complex* roots (and no real roots).

Here are three practice problems.

Problem: Solve $3x^2 = 48$.
Solution: First, solve for x^2, then solve for x.

$$3x^2 = 48$$
$$x^2 = 16$$
$$x = \pm\sqrt{16}$$
$$x = \pm 4$$

Problem: Solve $2x^2 - 5 = 25$.
Solution: First, solve for x^2, then solve for x.

$$2x^2 - 5 = 25$$
$$2x^2 = 30$$
$$x^2 = 15$$
$$x = \pm\sqrt{15}$$

Problem: Solve $4x^2 + 9 = 0$.
Solution: First, solve for x^2, then solve for x.

$$4x^2 + 9 = 0$$
$$4x^2 = -9$$
$$x^2 = -\frac{9}{4}$$
$$x = \pm\sqrt{-\frac{9}{4}}$$
$$x = \pm\frac{3}{2}i$$

This process can be extended to quadratic equations when they are rewritten in the form $(x + k)^2 = C$, where *C* is a constant. For such equations, it is evident that $x + k$ must be one of the square roots of *C*. Thus, $(x + k) = \pm\sqrt{C}$.

Here is a practice problem.

> Problem: Solve $(x + 3)^2 = 49$.
> Solution:
> $$(x+3)^2 = 49$$
> $$(x+3) = \pm\sqrt{49}$$
> $$x+3 = \pm 7$$
> $$x+3 = -7 \text{ or } x+3 = 7$$
> $$x = -10 \text{ or } x = 4$$

Solving Quadratic Equations by Factoring

The procedure for solving a quadratic equation by factoring is based on the **property of zero products** for numbers: If the product of two quantities is zero, at least one of the quantities is zero.

To solve a quadratic equation by factoring, use the following procedure:

Steps for Solving a Quadratic Equation by Factoring
1. Express the equation in standard form: $ax^2 + bx + c = 0$.
2. Factor the left side of the equation completely.
3. Set each factor containing the variable equal to zero.
4. Solve each of the resulting linear equations.

Tip: You should check each root by substituting its value into the original equation.

Here is a practice problem.

> Problem: Solve $x(x + 8) = 20$ by factoring.
> Solution:
> $$x(x+8) = 20$$
> $$x^2 + 8x - 20 = 0$$
> $$(x+10)(x-2) = 0$$
> $$x = -10 \text{ or } x = 2$$

Tip: Some beginners start solving $x(x + 8) = 20$ by setting each factor on the left equal to 20. This is incorrect. The property of zero products can only be applied when the product is *zero*, not 20 or any other nonzero number.

Chapter 2: Patterns and Algebra

Solving Quadratic Equations by Completing the Square

To solve a quadratic equation by completing the square, use the following procedure:

Steps for Solving a Quadratic Equation by Completing the Square

1. Express the equation in the form $ax^2 + bx =$ numerical expression.
2. If the coefficient a is not 1, divide each term by a to obtain an equation of the form $x^2 + \dfrac{b}{a}x =$ numerical expression.
3. Add the square of half the coefficient of x to both sides of the equation and then simplify to obtain an equation of the form $x^2 + \dfrac{b}{a}x + \left(\dfrac{b}{2a}\right)^2 = C$, where C is a constant.
4. Factor the perfect trinomial square on the left side of the equation as the square of a binomial so that you have an equation of the form $\left(x + \dfrac{b}{2a}\right)^2 = C$.
5. Recognizing that $x + \dfrac{b}{2a}$ must be one of the square roots of C, write $\left(x + \dfrac{b}{2a}\right) = \pm\sqrt{C}$, being sure to prefix a $\pm$ symbol to the square root of the right side of the equation.
6. Solve each of the resulting two linear equations.

Tip: You should check each root by substituting its value into the original equation.

Here is a practice problem.

Problem: Solve $x(x + 8) = 20$ by completing the square.
Solution:
$$x(x+8) = 20$$
$$x^2 + 8x = 20$$
$$x^2 + 8x + 4^2 = 20 + 4^2$$
$$x^2 + 8x + 16 = 36$$
$$(x+4)^2 = 36$$
$$(x+4) = \pm\sqrt{36}$$
$$x + 4 = \pm 6$$
$$x + 4 = -6 \text{ or } x + 4 = 6$$
$$x = -10 \text{ or } x = 2$$

Note: In most instances, this method would not be an efficient way to solve a quadratic equation on your TExES Math exam. Use factoring or the quadratic formula instead.

Solving Quadratic Equations by Using the Quadratic Formula

To solve a quadratic equation by using the quadratic formula, use the following procedure:

Steps for Solving a Quadratic Equation by Using the Quadratic Formula

1. Express the equation in standard form: $ax^2 + bx + c = 0$.
2. Determine the values of a, b, and c.
3. Substitute into the quadratic formula: $x = \dfrac{-b \pm \sqrt{b^2 + 4ac}}{2a}$.
4. Evaluate and simplify each of the two resulting expressions on the right side of the equation.

Tip: You should check each root by substituting its value into the original equation.

Here is a practice problem.

> Problem: Solve $x(x + 8) = 20$ by using the quadratic formula.
> Solution:
> $$x(x+8) = 20$$
> $$x^2 + 8x - 20 = 0$$
>
> $a = 1, b = 8, c = -20$ (include the $-$ sign).
>
> $$x = \frac{-8 \pm \sqrt{8^2 - 4(1)(-20)}}{2(1)} = \frac{-8 \pm \sqrt{64+80}}{2} = \frac{-8 \pm \sqrt{144}}{2} = \frac{-8 \pm 12}{2}$$
>
> Therefore, $x = \frac{-8-12}{2}$ or $x = \frac{-8+12}{2}$, from which you obtain $x = -10$ or $x = 2$.

Tip: When solving quadratic equations, *never* divide both sides of the equation by the variable or by an expression containing the variable.

The quantity $b^2 - 4ac$ is the **discriminant** of the quadratic equation $ax^2 + bx + c = 0$. The equation has exactly one real root if $b^2 - 4ac = 0$, two real unequal roots if $b^2 - 4ac > 0$, and two complex unequal roots (and no real roots) if $b^2 - 4ac < 0$.

Solving Equations That Can Be Written in the Form of a Quadratic Equation

You can solve equations that are not quadratic equations, but that can be written in the form of a quadratic equation, by using the methods for solving quadratic equations. It naturally follows that equations that can be written so one side is a factorable higher degree polynomial and the other side contains only 0 can be solved by factoring completely, setting each factor equal to 0, and then solving the resulting equations.

Here is a practice problem.

> Problem: Solve $x^4 - 13x^2 + 36 = 0$.
> Solution:
> $$x^4 - 13x^2 + 36 = 0$$
> $$(x^2 - 4)(x^2 - 9) = 0$$
> $$(x+2)(x-2)(x+3)(x-3) = 0$$
> $$x+2 = 0, \ x-2 = 0, \ x+3 = 0, \text{ or } x-3 = 0$$
> $$x = -2, 2, -3, \text{or } 3$$

Solving One-Variable Quadratic Inequalities

Quadratic inequalities have the standard forms $ax^2 + bx + c < 0$, $ax^2 + bx + c > 0$, $ax^2 + bx + c \leq 0$, and $ax^2 + bx + c \geq 0$. The solution sets for quadratic inequalities in standard form are based on the rules for multiplying signed numbers: If two factors have the same sign, their product is positive; if they have opposite signs, their product is negative. To solve a quadratic inequality, put it in standard form with $a > 0$ and apply the following.

> If $ax^2 + bx + c = 0$ has no real roots, $ax^2 + bx + c$ is always positive (and $-ax^2 - bx - c$ is always negative).

If $ax^2 + bx + c = 0$ has exactly one real root, $ax^2 + bx + c$ is 0 at that root and positive everywhere else.

If $ax^2 + bx + c = 0$ has two real roots, $ax^2 + bx + c$ is negative between them, positive to the left of the leftmost root, positive to the right of the rightmost root, and 0 only at its roots.

Here are two practice problems.

Problem: Solve $x^2 + 2x - 24 < 0$.

Solution: $x^2 + 2x - 24 = (x + 6)(x - 4) = 0$ has two real roots, –6 and 4. So $x^2 + 2x - 24$ is negative when $-6 < x < 4$.

Problem: Solve $x^2 + 2x - 24 \geq 0$.

Solution: $x^2 + 2x - 24 = (x + 6)(x - 4) = 0$ has two real roots, –6 and 4. So $x^2 + 2x - 24$ is 0 at –6 and 4 and positive in the intervals $(-\infty, -6)$ and $(4, \infty)$, yielding $x \leq -6$ or $x \geq 4$ as the solution.

Note: If you have a quadratic inequality in which $a < 0$, to put the inequality in standard form with $a > 0$, multiply both sides of the inequality by –1 and reverse the direction of the inequality.

Other Common One-Variable Equations

In this section, you will solve fractional equations, radical equations, and simple exponential and logarithmic equations. *Note:* Solving general exponential and logarithmic equations is presented in Part 2 for candidates who plan to take the TExES Math 7–12.

Solving Fractional Equations

A **fractional equation** is one in which a variable appears in the denominator of one or more terms. For example, $\frac{1}{2} + \frac{1}{x} = \frac{5}{6}$ and $\frac{x-2}{x} = \frac{4}{x(x-2)}$ are fractional equations. Linear equations that have fractional coefficients, such as $\frac{1}{2}x - 6 = 4$, are not fractional equations. Many fractional equations can be transformed into linear or quadratic equations by multiplying both sides of the equation by the lcm of the equation's fractions. However, this action does not necessarily result in an equivalent equation. Check your result against the excluded values for the equation's variable. A result that is an excluded value is rejected. It cannot be in the solution set.

Here is a practice problem.

Problem: Solve $\frac{x-2}{x} = \frac{4}{x(x-2)}$.

Solution:

$$\frac{x-2}{x} = \frac{4}{x(x-2)}$$

Assuming $x \neq 0$ and $x \neq 2$,

$$x(x-2)\left(\frac{x-2}{x}\right) = x(x-2)\left(\frac{4}{x(x-2)}\right)$$

$$(x-2)(x-2) = 4$$

$$x^2 - 4x + 4 = 4$$

$$x^2 - 4x = 0$$

$$x(x-4) = 0$$

$$x = 0 \text{ (reject) or } x = 4$$

Check: The equation $\dfrac{x-2}{x} = \dfrac{4}{x(x-2)}$ has two excluded values; x cannot be 0 or 2. Thus, 0 is rejected, meaning $x = 4$ is the only solution of $\dfrac{x-2}{x} = \dfrac{4}{x(x-2)}$.

Solving Radical Equations

A **radical equation** is one in which the variable appears in a radical. For example, $\sqrt{2x-4}+1=7$ and $x+3 = \sqrt{x+5}+4$ are radical equations. To solve a radical equation that contains only one radical, use the following procedure:

Steps for Solving a One-Radical Equation
1. Get the radical on one side of the equation and all other terms on the other side.
2. Eliminate the radical by raising both sides of the equation to an appropriate power. For square root radicals, square both sides. For cube root radicals, cube both sides, and so forth.
3. Solve the resulting equation.
4. Check for extraneous roots by substituting your obtained value(s) in the original radical equation. Do not skip this step.

Tip: Squaring both sides of an equation (or raising to any even power) can introduce "solutions," called extraneous roots, that did not exist previously. Extraneous roots are not true solutions of the original radical equation and should be rejected as answers.

Here is a practice problem.

Problem: Solve $x+3 = \sqrt{x+5}+4$.
Solution:

$$x+3 = \sqrt{x+5}+4$$
$$x-1 = \sqrt{x+5}$$
$$(x-1)^2 = (\sqrt{x+5})^2$$
$$x^2 - 2x + 1 = x + 5$$
$$x^2 - 3x - 4 = 0$$
$$(x+1)(x-4) = 0$$
$$x = -1 \text{ or } x = 4$$

Check $x = -1$:
$$x+3 = \sqrt{x+5}+4$$
$$(-1)+3 \stackrel{?}{=} \sqrt{(-1)+5}+4$$
$$2 \stackrel{?}{=} \sqrt{4}+4$$
$$2 \stackrel{?}{=} 2+4$$
$$2 \neq 6 \text{ (Reject } x=-1)$$

Check $x = 4$:
$$x+3 = \sqrt{x+5}+4$$
$$(4)+3 \stackrel{?}{=} \sqrt{(4)+5}+4$$
$$7 \stackrel{?}{=} \sqrt{9}+4$$
$$7 \stackrel{?}{=} 3+4$$
$$7 \stackrel{\checkmark}{=} 7$$

Thus, the solution of $x+3 = \sqrt{x+5}+4$ is $x = 4$.

Solving Simple Exponential Equations

An **exponential equation** is one in which the variable appears in an exponent. For example, $5^{2x-1} = 125$ and $2^x = 64$ are exponential equations. Some simple exponential equations can be easily solved by equating exponents of like bases.

Here is a practice problem.

>Problem: Solve $5^{2x-1} = 125$.
>
>Solution:
>
>$$5^{2x-1} = 125$$
>$$5^{2x-1} = 5^3, \text{ which implies}$$
>$$2x - 1 = 3$$
>$$2x = 4$$
>$$x = 2$$

Solving Simple Logarithmic Equations

Logarithms are exponents. If $c = \log_b(a)$, then c is the **exponent** you use on b to get a; that is, $b^c = a$. The number b is the **base** for the logarithm. It must be a positive number and not equal to 1. Here are examples.

>$\log_2(16) = 4$ because 4 is the exponent you use on 2 to get 16; that is, $2^4 = 16$.
>
>$\log_2\left(\dfrac{1}{8}\right) = -3$ because -3 is the exponent you use on 2 to get $\dfrac{1}{8}$; that is, $2^{-3} = \dfrac{1}{8}$.

The **common logarithm** has base 10. Here are examples.

>$\log_{10}(100) = 2$ because 2 is the exponent you use on 10 to get 100; that is, $10^2 = 100$.
>
>$\log_{10}(0.001) = -3$ because -3 is the exponent you use on 10 to get 0.001; that is, $10^{-3} = \dfrac{1}{10^3} = \dfrac{1}{1,000} = 0.001$.

Tip: Generally, if no base is shown on a log, it is assumed to be base 10, the common logarithm.

The **natural logarithm** has the base e, where e is the irrational number whose rational decimal approximation is 2.718281828 (to nine digits). The natural logarithm of a number x is usually written $\ln x$. Here are examples.

>$\ln(e^5) = 5$ because 5 is the exponent you use on e to get e^5; that is, $(e)^5 = e^5$.
>
>$\ln\left(\dfrac{1}{e}\right) = -1$ because -1 is the exponent you use on e to get $\dfrac{1}{e}$; that is, $e^{-1} = \dfrac{1}{e}$.

A **logarithmic equation** is one in which the variable appears in a logarithm. For example, $\log_{10}(x) = -2$ and $\log_2(x - 4) = 5$ are logarithmic equations. Some simple logarithmic equations can be easily solved by writing the logarithmic equation in exponential form and evaluating to determine the value of the variable.

Here is a practice problem.

>Problem: Solve $\log_2(x - 4) = 5$.
>
>Solution: In exponential form, $\log_2(x - 4) = 5$ is equivalent to $2^5 = x - 4$. Thus, $32 = x - 4$, which yields $x = 36$.

Systems of Equations and Inequalities

For this topic, you solve and graph systems of equations and inequalities.

Basic Concepts of Systems of Equations

A set of equations, each with the same set of variables, is called a **system** when the equations in the set are considered simultaneously. The system possesses a **solution** when the equations in the system are all satisfied by at least one set of values of the variables. A system that has a solution is **consistent.** A system that has no solution is **inconsistent.**

A **system of two linear equations in two variables** consists of a pair of linear equations in the same two variables. To **solve a system** of linear equations in two variables means to find all pairs of values for the two variables that make *both* equations true simultaneously. A pair of values—for example, an x value paired with a corresponding y value—is an **ordered pair** and is written as (x, y). An ordered pair that makes an equation true is said to **satisfy** the equation. When an ordered pair makes both equations in a system true, the ordered pair **satisfies** the system. The **solution set** is the collection of all solutions. There are three possibilities: The system has exactly *one solution, no solution,* or *infinitely many solutions.*

Geometrically, the two equations of a system of linear equations in two variables can be represented as lines in the coordinate plane. For the two lines, there are three possibilities that can occur, corresponding to the three possibilities for the solution set. If the system is consistent and has exactly one solution, then the two lines intersect in a unique point in the plane. The ordered pair that corresponds to the point of intersection is the solution to the system. If the system is consistent and has infinitely many solutions, then the two lines are coincident (that is, have all points in common). If the system is inconsistent and has no solutions, then the two lines are parallel in the plane. Here are illustrations.

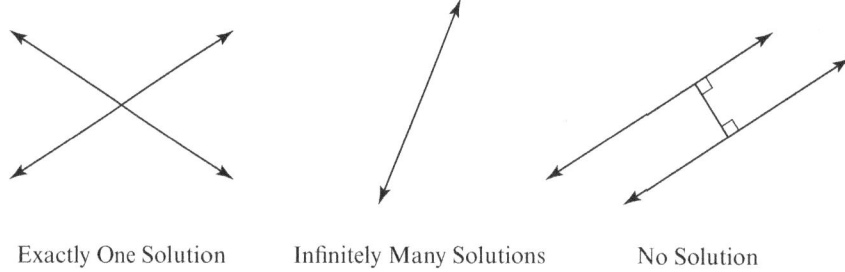

Exactly One Solution   Infinitely Many Solutions   No Solution

Note: See "Basic Function Concepts" later in this chapter for a discussion of the coordinate plane.

A quick way to decide whether a system of two linear equations has exactly one solution, infinitely many solutions, or no solution is to look at ratios of the coefficients of the two equations, where A_1, B_1, and C_1 are the coefficients in the first equation and A_2, B_2, and C_2 are the corresponding coefficients in the second equation.

If $\dfrac{A_1}{A_2} \neq \dfrac{B_1}{B_2}$, the system has exactly one solution; if $\dfrac{A_1}{A_2} = \dfrac{B_1}{B_2} = \dfrac{C_1}{C_2}$, the system has infinitely many solutions; and if $\dfrac{A_1}{A_2} = \dfrac{B_1}{B_2} \neq \dfrac{C_1}{C_2}$, the system has no solution.

Solving a System of Two Linear Equations by Substitution

To solve a system of linear equations by **substitution,** use the following procedure:

Steps for Solving a System of Linear Equations by Substitution

1. Select the simpler equation and solve it for one of the variables in terms of the other. You can solve for either variable. Use your judgment to decide.
2. Using the other given equation, replace the variable solved for in Step 1 with the expression obtained, simplify, and solve for the second variable.
3. Using the simpler equation, substitute the value obtained in Step 2 for the second variable, simplify, and solve for the first variable.

Tip: You should check the solution in the original equations.

Here is a practice problem (for convenience, the equations are numbered).

Problem: Solve the system $\begin{matrix}(1) & x+y=1{,}950 \\ (2) & 9x+6y=13{,}950\end{matrix}$ by the method of substitution.

Solution: Quick check: The system has exactly one solution because $\frac{1}{9} \neq \frac{1}{6}$.

Solve equation (1) for x to obtain $x = 1{,}950 - y$. Substitute this result into equation (2) and solve for y.

$$9x + 6y = 13{,}950$$
$$9(1{,}950 - y) + 6y = 13{,}950$$
$$17{,}550 - 9y + 6y = 13{,}950$$
$$17{,}550 - 3y = 13{,}950$$
$$-3y = -3{,}600$$
$$y = 1{,}200$$

Substituting $y = 1{,}200$ into $x = 1{,}950 - y$ yields $x = 1{,}950 - 1{,}200 = 750$.
The solution is $x = 750$, $y = 1{,}200$.

Solving a System of Two Linear Equations by Elimination

To solve a system of linear equations by **elimination,** use the following procedure:

Steps for Solving a System of Linear Equations by Elimination

1. Write both equations in standard form: $Ax + By = C$.
2. Eliminate one of the variables. If necessary, multiply one or both of the equations by a nonzero constant or constants to make the coefficients of one of the variables sum to zero. You can eliminate either variable. Use your judgment to decide.
3. Add the transformed equations and then solve for the variable that was not eliminated.
4. Substitute the value obtained in Step 3 into one of the original equations, simplify, and solve for the other variable.

Tip: You should check the solution in the original equations.

Here is a practice problem (for convenience, the equations are numbered).

Problem: Solve the system $\begin{array}{l}(1)\ 3y = 2x + 1 \\ (2)\ 3x - 7y = 6\end{array}$ by the method of elimination.

Solution: Write both equations in standard form: $\begin{array}{l}(1)\ -2x + 3y = 1 \\ (2)\ 3x - 7y = 6\end{array}$

Quick check: The system has exactly one solution because $\dfrac{-2}{3} \neq \dfrac{3}{-7}$.

To eliminate x, multiply equation (1) by 3 and equation (2) by 2.

$$\begin{array}{l}-2x + 3y = 1 \\ 3x - 7y = 6\end{array} \text{ implies } \begin{array}{l}3(-2x + 3y) = 3(1) \\ 2(3x - 7y) = 2(6)\end{array} \text{ implies } \begin{array}{l}-6x + 9y = 3 \\ 6x - 14y = 12\end{array}$$

Add the transformed equations and solve for y.

$$\begin{array}{r}-6x + 9y = 3 \\ \underline{6x - 14y = 12} \\ 0 - 5y = 15 \\ y = -3\end{array}$$

Substitute $y = -3$ into equation (1) and solve for x.

$$\begin{array}{r}-2x + 3y = 1 \\ -2x + 3(-3) = 1 \\ -2x - 9 = 1 \\ -2x = 10 \\ x = -5\end{array}$$

The solution is $x = -5$, $y = -3$.

You can extend the procedures for solving a system of two linear equations to systems of three linear equations or more. Proceed systematically, taking two equations at a time. You also can use matrix techniques to solve systems of equations. See "Matrix Solutions of Systems of Linear Equations" in Part 2 of this chapter for a discussion of this topic.

Use the methods in this section to solve systems of equations in two variables when one of the equations is nonlinear.

Here is a practice problem.

Problem: Solve the system $\begin{array}{l}5x - y = 12 \\ 2x^2 + y = 0\end{array}$.

Solution: Observe that the coefficients of y sum to zero. Add the two equations.

$$\begin{array}{r}5x - y = 12 \\ \underline{2x^2 + y = 0} \\ 2x^2 + 5x + 0 = 12\end{array}$$

Solve the resulting quadratic equation.

$$\begin{array}{r}2x^2 + 5x = 12 \\ 2x^2 + 5x - 12 = 0 \\ (2x - 3)(x + 4) = 0 \\ 2x - 3 = 0 \text{ or } x + 4 = 0 \\ 2x = 3 \text{ or } x = -4 \\ x = 1.5 \text{ or } x = -4\end{array}$$

Do not make the mistake of stopping at this point and writing (1.5, −4) as the solution. You have obtained two distinct values for x and now must obtain the corresponding y value for each.

Substitute $x = 1.5$ and $x = -4$ into $5x - y = 12$ to find the corresponding y value for each.

$$5(1.5) - y = 12 \quad \text{or} \quad 5(-4) - y = 12$$
$$-y = 4.5 \quad \text{or} \quad -y = 12$$
$$y = -4.5 \quad \text{or} \quad y = -32$$

Thus, two ordered pairs, (1.5, −4.5) and (−4, −32), satisfy the system $\begin{matrix} 5x - y = 12 \\ 2x^2 + y = 0 \end{matrix}$.

Formulas Used in a Two-Dimensional Coordinate Plane

To find the **slope m of the line** that connects the points (x_1, y_1) and (x_2, y_2) in a coordinate plane, use the following formula:

$$\text{Slope of line} = m = \frac{y_2 - y_1}{x_2 - x_1}, \ (x_1 \neq x_2)$$

Here is a practice problem.

Problem: Find the slope m of the line passing through the points (−1, −5) and (−3, 4).

Solution: $m = \dfrac{y_2 - y_1}{x_2 - x_1} = \dfrac{4 - (-5)}{-3 - (-1)} = \dfrac{4+5}{-3+1} = -\dfrac{9}{2}$

When a line slopes *upward* to the right, its slope is *positive*, and when a line slopes *downward* to the right, its slope is *negative*. All horizontal lines have slope 0. Vertical lines have no slope (it's undefined). If two lines are parallel, their slopes are equal. If two lines are perpendicular, their slopes are negative reciprocals of each other.

Note: See "Features of Common Functions" later in this chapter for an additional discussion of slope.

To find the **distance d between two points** (x_1, y_1) and (x_2, y_2) in a coordinate plane, use the following formula:

$$\text{Distance between two points} = d = \sqrt{(x_2 - x_1)^2 + (y_2 - y_1)^2}$$

The distance d between two points (x_1, y_1) and (x_2, y_2) in a coordinate plane can be interpreted geometrically as the length of the hypotenuse of a right triangle having legs of length $x_2 - x_1$ and $y_2 - y_1$ as illustrated below.

Here is a practice problem.

Problem: Find the distance d between the points (−1, −5) and (−3, 4) in the coordinate plane.

Solution: $d = \sqrt{(x_2 - x_1)^2 + (y_2 - y_1)^2} = \sqrt{(-3-(-1))^2 + (-5-4)^2} = \sqrt{(-2)^2 + (-9)^2} = \sqrt{4 + 81} = \sqrt{85}$

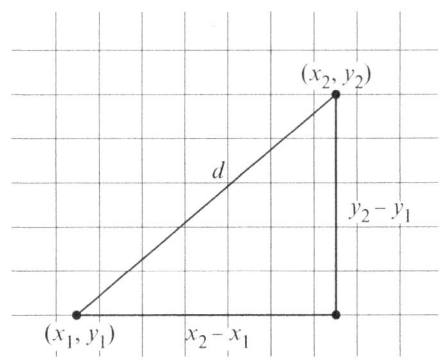

Chapter 2: Patterns and Algebra

To find the **midpoint between two points** (x_1, y_1) and (x_2, y_2) in a coordinate plane, use the following formula:

$$\text{Midpoint between two points} = \left(\frac{x_1 + x_2}{2}, \frac{y_1 + y_2}{2}\right)$$

Here is a practice problem.

Problem: Find the midpoint between the points $(-1, -5)$ and $(-3, 4)$ in the coordinate plane.

Solution: $\text{midpoint} = \left(\frac{x_1 + x_2}{2}, \frac{y_1 + y_2}{2}\right) = \left(\frac{-1-3}{2}, \frac{-5+4}{2}\right) = \left(\frac{-4}{2}, \frac{-1}{2}\right) = \left(-2, -\frac{1}{2}\right)$

Tip: Notice that you add, not subtract, the coordinates in the numerator.

To find the (perpendicular) distance d from point (x_1, y_1) to line $Ax + By + C = 0$, use the following formula:

$$d = \frac{|Ax_1 + By_1 + C|}{\sqrt{A^2 + B^2}}$$

Here is a practice problem.

Problem: Find the distance d from $(-3, 4)$ to the line $y = \frac{6}{5}x + 2$.

Solution: First transform $y = \frac{6}{5}x + 2$ to the form $Ax + By + C = 0$.

$$y = \frac{6}{5}x + 2 \text{ implies}$$
$$5y = 6x + 10 \text{ implies}$$
$$-6x + 5y - 10 = 0$$

Now substitute $x_1 = -3$ and $y_1 = 4$ into the formula for the distance from a point to the line.

$$d = \frac{|Ax_1 + By_1 + C|}{\sqrt{A^2 + B^2}} = \frac{|-6(-3) + 5(4) - 10|}{\sqrt{(-6)^2 + 5^2}} = \frac{|28|}{\sqrt{61}} = \frac{28}{\sqrt{61}}$$

Tip: When substituting values into formulas, enclose in parentheses any negative substituted value to avoid making a sign error.

The Equation of a Line

The equation of a nonvertical line can be determined using one of the following:

- The **slope-intercept form:** $y = mx + b$, where the line determined by the equation has slope $= m$ and y-intercept $= b$
- The **standard form:** $Ax + By = C$, where the line determined by the equation has slope $= -\frac{A}{B}$ and y-intercept $= \frac{C}{B}$, $(B \neq 0)$
- The **point-slope form:** $y - y_1 = m(x - x_1)$, where m is the slope of the line and (x_1, y_1) is a point on the line

Here is a practice problem.

Problem: Find the slope-intercept form of the equation of the line that passes through the points $(-3, 4)$ and $(-5, 2)$.

Solution: The slope of the line is $m = \dfrac{y_2 - y_1}{x_2 - x_1} = \dfrac{2-4}{(-5)-(-3)} = \dfrac{2-4}{-5+3} = \dfrac{-2}{-2} = 1$. Selecting $(-3, 4)$ from the two points and substituting into $y - y_1 = m(x - x_1)$ gives $y - 4 = 1(x - (-3))$ or, equivalently, $y - 4 = x + 3$, which yields the equation $y = x + 7$.

Note: See the previous section, "Formulas Used in a Two-Dimensional Coordinate Plane," for the formula for finding the slope of a line given two points on the line.

Two special cases of linear equations are the equations for horizontal and vertical lines. Horizontal lines have equations of the form $y = k$ ($m = 0$). Vertical lines have equations of the form $x = h$ (undefined slope).

Here is a summary of equations of lines.

Equations of Lines

Slope-intercept form (functional form)	$y = mx + b$
Point-slope form	$y - y_1 = m(x - x_1)$
Standard form	$Ax + By = C$ (A and B not both zero)
Horizontal line	$y = k$ for any constant k
Vertical line (not a function)	$x = h$ for any constant h

Note: Not all authorities agree on the standard form. Some write the standard form as $Ax + By + C = 0$; others designate $y = mx + b$ as the standard form. We do not anticipate that your correct responses on your TExES Math exam will be jeopardized by this inconsistency.

Systems of Two-Variable Linear Inequalities

For this topic, you will graph two-variable linear inequalities and find the maximum (or minimum) value of an equation that is subject to inequality constraints.

Graphing Two-Variable Linear Inequalities

The graph of a two-variable linear inequality, such as $3x + y \leq 5$, $3x - y \geq 1$, and $x - y < 0$, is a half-plane.

To graph a two-variable inequality, use the following procedure:

> **Steps for Graphing a Two-Variable Linear Inequality**
>
> 1. Rewrite the inequality in an equivalent form with only y on the left side of the inequality symbol.
> 2. Graph the linear equation that results when the inequality symbol is replaced with an equal sign. Use a dashed line for $<$ or $>$ inequalities and a solid line for $\leq$ or $\geq$ inequalities. This is the boundary line.
> 3. If the inequality contains $<$ or $\leq$, shade the portion of the plane beneath the line. If the inequality contains $>$ or $\geq$, shade the portion of the plane above the line.

Here is a practice problem.

> Problem: Graph the inequality $3x + y \leq 5$.
>
> Solution: Rewrite the inequality as $y \leq -3x + 5$. Graph $y = -3x + 5$. Make the line a solid line and shade the portion of the plane beneath the line, as shown here.

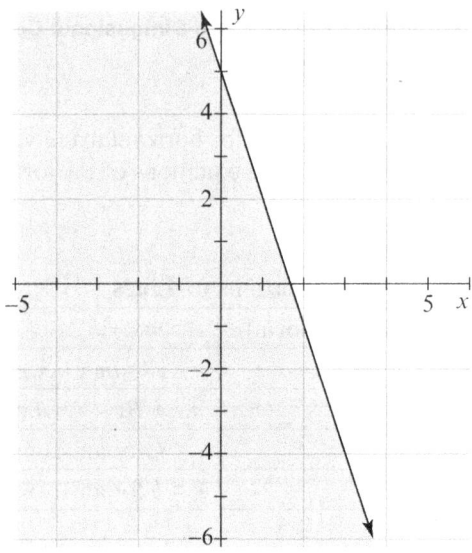

Graph of $y \leq -3x + 5$

Find the Maximum Value of an Equation Subject to Inequality Constraints

Suppose you want to find the maximum value of the equation $z = 2x + 5y$ subject to the following constraints:

$$3x + y \leq 5$$
$$3x - y \geq 1$$
$$x - y \leq 0$$

The general process to find the maximum value of the given equation (called the "optimization" equation) is to graph the set of constraint inequalities to produce a region in the plane that represents their intersections. The maximum value of the equation will occur at one of the corners of the region. To algebraically determine the corner points, find the points of intersection of the boundary lines of the region. In other words, pair the following equations and solve for the intersection of each pair (for convenience, the equations are numbered):

(1) $3x + y = 5$ or, equivalently, $y = -3x + 5$
(2) $3x - y = 1$ or, equivalently, $y = 3x - 1$
(3) $x - y = 0$ or, equivalently, $y = x$

Solve (1) and (2) to obtain the corner point (1, 2). Solve (1) and (3) to obtain the corner point (1.25, 1.25). Solve (2) and (3) to obtain the corner point (0.5, 0.5). See the graph below. The shading is the intersection of the half-planes described by the original inequalities.

Substitute the corner point values into the equation, $z = 2x + 5y$, to find the maximum.

At (1, 2), $z = 2(1) + 5(2) = 12$; at (1.25, 1.25), $z = 2(1.25) + 5(1.25) = 8.75$; and at (0.5, 0.5), $z = 2(0.5) + 5(0.5) = 3.5$.

Subject to the given constraints, the maximum value for $z = 2x + 5y$ is 12.

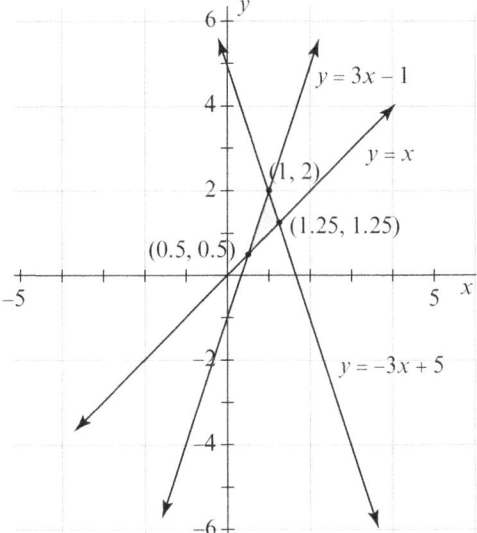

Tip: As this problem demonstrates, you can find the maximum (or minimum) of an equation that is subject to inequality constraints by determining the corner points of the intersection region of the set of constraint inequalities.

Algebraic Problem Solving

You can expect to encounter application problems on your TExES Math exam. This section presents some helpful ideas for algebraically dealing with application problems.

General Problem-Solving Guidelines

Here are some general problem-solving guidelines for solving application problems using algebraic techniques.

Problem-Solving Guidelines

1. **Understand the problem.** Ask yourself: What is the problem asking me to determine? In other words, what is the question? Look for words like *find, determine, what is, how many, how far, how much,* and *what time*. Identify the unknown(s) that will lead to a solution.

2. **Represent unknowns with variable expressions.** Decide how many unknowns are in the problem. If there is one unknown, let the variable represent this unknown quantity. As you represent unknowns, make explicit statements such as "Let $x = \ldots$" so it is clear what each variable represents. Specify the variable's units, if applicable. Sometimes you will have two or more unknowns in a problem. In this case, you can assign the unknowns different variable names. *Tip:* Using the first letter of the name of an unknown as a variable name can be helpful. As another option, you might assign a variable name to one unknown and express the other unknowns in terms of that variable. If a first unknown is described in terms of a second unknown, assign the variable name to the *second* unknown. For example, if a garden's length is 3 meters more than its width, then let w = the garden's width (in meters) and $w + 3$ meters = the garden's length (in meters). *Note:* Whether you use one variable name or two or more variable names, the problem-solving process leads to one-variable linear equations.

> 3. **Write one or more equations that represent the facts in the problem.** Using the variable representations determined in Step 2, write one or more statements of equality that accurately model the relationships in the problem. If units are involved, check that the indicated calculations will result in proper units (see "Be Methodical with Units" below for an additional discussion of this topic). Decide whether making a table or sketching a diagram would be helpful. Try to relate the current problem to problems you have worked in the past. Keep in mind that you will need as many equations as you have variables in order to obtain numerical values for the variables.
> 4. **Solve the equation(s).** Carefully work out your solution. Make sure you copy all information accurately. Write neatly so that you can check over your work. If the answer should have units, check whether your calculations will result in the proper units for the answer. *Tip:* When solving an equation, you might find it convenient to omit the units, given that you have already checked that the answer will have the proper units.
> 5. **Verbalize and assess the solution.** State the solution in words (include units, if applicable). Did you answer the question that was asked? Check your solution in the context of the problem. Does it make sense? Is it reasonable? Are the units correct?

Note: The problem-solving process is systematic, but not rigid. In practice, it seldom occurs in a linear fashion. Not infrequently, you will have to go back to a previous step. As you gain confidence in your problem-solving ability, you might skip steps, or even combine steps. When you work through the practice problems in this section, keep in mind that there are usually multiple ways to solve a problem. You might think of ways to reach the correct solutions other than the ones shown.

Translating Verbal Relationships

The following table summarizes commonly used algebraic symbolism for verbal relationships. The letter x is used in the table to represent an unknown number.

Signal Words or Phrases	Example	Algebraic Symbolism
add, plus, sum of, increased by, added to, more than, greater than, total of, that exceeds	a number that exceeds x by 10	$x + 10$
minus, subtracted from, difference between, less than, decreased by, reduced by, diminished by, fewer than	10 less than x	$x - 10$
times, multiplied by, product of, twice, double, triple, quadruple, fraction of, percent of	twice x	$2x$, $2 \cdot x$, $2(x)$, $(2)(x)$, or $(2)x$
divided by, quotient of, ratio of, for each, x for every, per	ratio of x and 5	$\dfrac{x}{5}$
equals, is, was, are, were, will be, gives, yields, results in, exceeds by	50% of x is 20 more than the quotient of x and 4.	$50\% x = \dfrac{x}{4} + 20$

Tip: Do not put periods at the end of algebraic symbolism for verbal statements.

Be Methodical with Units

Word problems often involve quantities that are specified with units (such as 25 inches, 8.5 pounds, 2 hours, 3 years, 55 miles per hour, $650, and so forth). Such quantities have both a numerical component and a units component. In computations, the units must undergo the same mathematical operations that are performed on the numerical component of the quantity.

Add or subtract units only if they can be expressed as like units. For example, 10 inches + 1 foot = 10 inches + 12 inches = 22 inches. (See Appendix C for a Measurement Units and Conversions table.)

Multiply and divide units whether they are like or unlike. However, the resulting product or quotient must have meaning in the context of the problem. You perform operations on units like you do on numbers.

For example, (5 ft)(8 ft) = 40 ft² and $\left(60 \, \frac{\text{miles}}{\text{hr}}\right)(2.5 \text{ hr}) = \left(60 \, \frac{\text{miles}}{\cancel{\text{hr}}}\right)(2.5 \, \cancel{\text{hr}}) = 150$ miles.

Geometry Problems

Here is a practice problem.

Problem: The length of a rectangular garden is 3 meters more than its width. The garden's perimeter is 54 meters. Find the garden's area.

Solution: The garden is rectangular. You do not know its length or width. You will need the values of both to find the garden's area, so this problem has two unknowns. Let l = the garden's length and w = the garden's width. Its perimeter is 54 meters. The formula for the perimeter of a rectangle is $P = 2l + 2w = 2(l + w)$ and the formula for the area of a rectangle is $A = lw$, where l is the rectangle's length and w is its width. (See "Perimeter, Area, and Volume" in Chapter 3 for common geometric formulas.)

Make a sketch.

Tip: For geometry problems, making a sketch helps you visualize the problem.

Method 1. Use one variable.

The garden's length is described in terms of its width. Let w = the garden's width in meters. Then $l = w + 3$ meters = the garden's length in meters. Write an equation that represents the facts given in the question.

$$2[(w + 3 \text{ meters}) + w] = 54 \text{ meters}$$

Solve the equation, omitting the units for convenience.

$$2[(w+3) + w] = 54$$
$$2[w+3 + w] = 54$$
$$2[2w+3] = 54$$
$$4w+6 = 54$$
$$4w = 48$$
$$w = 12$$
$$w+3 = 15$$

The area of the garden is (12 m)(15 m) = 180 m².

77

Method 2. Use two variables.

Let w = the garden's width in meters and l = the garden's length in meters. Write two equations that represent the facts given in the question.

(1) $l = w + 3$ meters

(2) $2(l + w) = 54$ meters

Simultaneously solve the two equations, omitting the units for convenience.

(1) $l = w + 3$

(2) $2(l + w) = 54$

Using the substitution method, substitute $l = w + 3$ from equation (1) into equation (2) to obtain

$$2[(w + 3) + w] = 54$$

Complete the solution as shown in Method 1.

Make sure you answer the question that was asked. In this question, after you obtain the garden's length and width, you must calculate the garden's area to answer the question.

Note: Hereafter, only one solution method will be shown.

Age Problems

Here is a practice problem.

Problem: Reima is twice as old as Dustin. In 5 years, Reima's age will be 55 years minus Dustin's age. What is Reima's age now?

Solution: You don't know Reima's age or Dustin's age now. Reima's age now is described as "twice as old as Dustin," so designate the variable as Dustin's age now.

Let d = Dustin's age in years now, and $2d$ = Reima's age in years now.

Make a table to organize the information in the question.

When?	Dustin's Age	Reima's Age
Now	d	$2d$
5 years from now	$d + 5$ years	$2d + 5$ years

From the question, you know that Reima's age 5 years from now is 55 years minus Dustin's age 5 years from now. Use the information in the table to set up an equation to match the facts in the question.

$$(2d + 5 \text{ years}) = 55 \text{ years} - (d + 5 \text{ years})$$

Solve the equation, omitting the units for convenience.

$$(2d + 5) = 55 - (d + 5)$$
$$2d + 5 = 55 - d - 5$$
$$2d + 5 = 50 - d$$
$$3d + 5 = 50$$
$$3d = 45$$
$$d = 15$$
$$2d = 30$$

Reima's age now is 30 years.

Make sure you answer the question asked. In this question, after you obtain Dustin's age now, calculate Reima's age now.

Coin Problems

Here is a practice problem.

> Problem: A collection of 250 U.S. quarters and dimes has a total value of $40.00. How many quarters are in the collection?
>
> *Note:* In coin problems, you must assume there are no rare coins with values more than their face values in a collection.
>
> Solution: You don't know the number of quarters or the number of dimes, so use two variables. Let q = the number of quarters and d = the number of dimes. Make a table to organize the information given.
>
> | Denomination | Quarters | Dimes | Total |
> |---|---|---|---|
> | Face Value per Coin | $0.25 | $0.10 | N/A |
> | Number of Coins | q | d | 250 |
> | Value of Coins | $0.25q$ | $0.10d$ | $40.00 |
>
> Use the table to write two equations to represent the facts given. *Remember:* You need two equations when you have two variables.
>
> $$q + d = 250$$
> $$\$0.25q + \$0.10d = \$40.00$$
>
> Solve the system, omitting the units for convenience.
>
> (1) $q + d = 250$
>
> (2) $0.25q + 0.10d = 40.00$
>
> Solve equation (1) for d and substitute the result into equation (2). Then solve for q.
>
> (1) $d = 250 - q$
>
> (2) $0.25q + 0.10(250 - q) = 40.00$
>
> $$0.25q + 0.10(250 - q) = 40$$
> $$0.25q + 25 - 0.10q = 40$$
> $$0.15q + 25 = 40$$
> $$0.15q = 15$$
> $$q = 100$$
>
> There are 100 quarters in the collection.

Mixture Problems

Here is a practice problem.

> Problem: A chemist has a 36% alcohol solution and a 90% alcohol solution. How many milliliters of each should be used to make 1,200 milliliters of a 72% alcohol solution?
>
> Solution: You have two unknowns. Let x = the number of milliliters of the 36% alcohol solution to be used, and let y = the number of milliliters of the 90% alcohol solution to be used.
>
> Make a table to organize the mixture information.
>
> | When? | Percent Alcohol Strength | Number of Milliliters | Amount of Alcohol |
> |---|---|---|---|
> | Before mixing | 36% | x | 36%x |
> | | 90% | y | 90%y |
> | After mixing | 72% | 1,200 | 72%(1,200) |

Use the table to write two equations to represent the facts given.
$$x + y = 1{,}200$$
$$36\%x + 90\%y = 72\%(1{,}200)$$
The amount of alcohol before mixing equals the amount of alcohol after mixing.

Solve the system, changing percents to decimals before proceeding.

(1) $x + y = 1{,}200$

(2) $0.36x + 0.90y = 0.72(1{,}200)$

Solve equation (1) for y and substitute the result into equation (2). Then solve for x.

(1) $y = 1{,}200 - x$

(2) $0.36x + 0.90(1{,}200 - x) = 0.72(1{,}200)$

$$0.36x + 0.90(1{,}200 - x) = 0.72(1{,}200)$$
$$0.36x + 1{,}080 - 0.90x = 864$$
$$-0.54x + 1{,}080 = 864$$
$$-0.54x = -216$$
$$x = 400$$
$$y = 1{,}200 - x = 1{,}200 - 400 = 800$$

Therefore, 400 milliliters of the 36% alcohol solution and 800 milliliters of the 90% alcohol solution should be used to make 1,200 milliliters of a 72% alcohol solution.

Tip: In mixture problems, the "before mixing" amount (or value) of a substance equals the "after mixing" amount (or value) of that substance.

Distance-Rate-Time Problems

The distance, d, a vehicle travels at a uniform rate of speed, r, for a given length of time, t, is $d = rt$.

One Moving Object Problems

Here is a practice problem.

Problem: How many hours will it take for a car traveling at 60 miles per hour to travel 150 miles?

Solution: Let t = the time, in hours; d = 150 miles; and r = 60 miles per hour.

Write an equation that represents the facts: 150 miles = (60 miles per hour)(t).

Solve the equation, omitting the units for convenience.

$$150 = 60t$$
$$\frac{150}{60} = t$$
$$t = 2.5$$

It will take 2.5 hours.

Two Moving Objects Problems

Commonly, in two moving objects problems, three situations occur:

- The two objects travel away from each other in opposite directions, usually at different speeds.
- The two objects travel toward each other in opposite directions, usually at different speeds.
- The two objects travel in the same direction at different speeds, initially separated by a given distance, and the faster vehicle must overtake the slower vehicle.

Using logical reasoning, you can reduce each of these situations to a simple $d = rt$ computation.

Here are three practice problems.

Problem: A car and a truck leave the same location at the same time. The car travels due east at 70 miles per hour. The truck travels due west at 65 miles per hour. If the two vehicles continue to travel at their respective speeds, in how many hours will the two vehicles be 405 miles apart?

Solution: Let $t =$ the time, in hours, it will take for the two vehicles to be 405 miles apart. See the diagram below. *Note:* The two vehicles travel simultaneously for t hours.

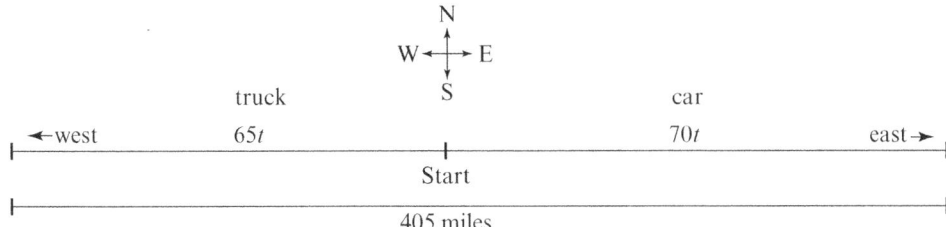

The two vehicles are traveling away from each other in opposite directions. The distance between them is increasing at a combined speed of 70 mph + 65 mph = 135 mph. Therefore, the situation reduces to the equation 405 miles = (135 mph)(t).

Solve the equation, omitting the units for convenience.

$$135t = 405$$
$$t = 3$$

In 3 hours the two vehicles will be 405 miles apart.

Problem: Two walkers, one walking at 3 miles per hour and the other at 2 miles per hour, are 8 miles apart when they begin walking toward each other on the same path. If the two walkers continue to walk at their respective rates, in how many minutes will it take them to reach each other?

Solution: Let $t =$ the time, in hours, it will take for the two walkers to reach each other. *Note:* The two walkers travel simultaneously for t hours.

The two walkers are traveling toward each other in opposite directions. The distance between them is decreasing at a combined rate of 3 mph + 2 mph = 5 mph. Therefore, the situation reduces to the equation 8 miles = (5 mph)(t).

Solve the equation, omitting the units for convenience.

$$5t = 8$$
$$t = 1.6$$

In 1.6 hours, or 96 minutes, the walkers will reach each other.

Problem: A bus leaves a location, traveling at 50 miles per hour. One hour later, a car leaves the same location traveling in the same direction at 70 miles per hour. If the two vehicles continue to travel at their respective speeds, how many hours will it take the car to reach the bus?

Solution: Let $t =$ the time it will take the car to reach the bus. *Note:* After the car leaves the location, the two vehicles travel simultaneously for t hours.

The two vehicles are traveling in the same direction at different speeds, initially separated by a distance of 50 miles (because the bus has traveled 1 hour before the car leaves). The distance between them is decreasing at a rate of 70 mph – 50 mph = 20 mph. Therefore, the situation reduces to the equation 50 miles = (20 mph)(t).

Solve the equation, omitting the units for convenience.

$$20t = 50$$
$$t = 2.5$$

In 2.5 hours, the car will reach the bus.

Average Rate Problems

Here is a practice problem.

Problem: On a trip, a car travels for 1 hour at 65 miles per hour and thereafter for 2 hours at 50 miles per hour. Find the average speed of the car for the trip.

Solution: Let s = the average speed for the trip. The average speed s is the total distance traveled divided by the total time traveled. Thus, $s = \dfrac{(65 \text{ mph})(1 \text{ hour}) + (50 \text{ mph})(2 \text{ hours})}{(1 \text{ hour} + 2 \text{ hours})} = \dfrac{165 \text{ miles}}{3 \text{ hours}} = 55 \text{ mph}$.

Notice that the average speed is not the simple arithmetic average of 65 mph and 50 mph, which is 57.5 mph.

Work Problems

In work problems, the portion of a task completed in a unit time period is the reciprocal of the amount of time it takes to complete the task. For example, if it takes Bresha 4 hours, working alone, to paint a hallway, then the portion of the hallway she can paint in 1 hour, working alone, is $\dfrac{1}{4}$ of the hallway. Additionally, when two or more individuals (machines, devices, entities, etc.) work together, the portion of the work done per unit time by the first individual plus the portion of the work done per unit time by the second individual plus the portion of the work done per unit time by the third individual and so on equals the portion of the work done per unit time when all individuals work together. *Note:* The unit time for the work done must be the same for all, individually and combined.

Basic Work Problems

Here is a practice problem.

Problem: Bresha can paint a hallway in 4 hours working alone. Payton can do the same task in 6 hours working alone. How long (in hours) will it take Bresha and Payton, working together, to paint the hallway?

Solution: Let t = the time it will take Bresha and Payton, working together, to paint the hallway.

Make a table to organize the information given.

Situation	Time (in hours)	Portion of Hallway per Hour
Bresha working alone	4	$\dfrac{1}{4}$
Payton working alone	6	$\dfrac{1}{6}$
Bresha and Payton working together	t	$\dfrac{1}{t}$

Using the table, write a statement of equality based on the following fact:

The portion of the hallway done per hour by Bresha plus the portion of the hallway done per hour by Payton equals the portion of the hallway done per hour by Bresha and Payton working together.

$\dfrac{1}{4}$ of the hallway per hour + $\dfrac{1}{6}$ of the hallway per hour = $\dfrac{1}{t}$ of the hallway per hour

Solve the equation, omitting the units for convenience.

$$\frac{1}{4} + \frac{1}{6} = \frac{1}{t}$$
$$\frac{3}{12} + \frac{2}{12} = \frac{1}{t}$$
$$\frac{5}{12} = \frac{1}{t}$$
$$5t = 12$$
$$t = 2.4$$

The time it will take Bresha and Payton, working together, to paint the hallway is 2.4 hours.

Tip: The time it will take when two or more individuals (or machines, devices, entities, etc.) work together (in a positive way) is always less than the least individual time.

Quick Solution Method for Two Workers

When only two workers are involved in a work problem, you can use a quick solution method.

Here is a practice problem.

Problem: Working alone, machine A can make 500 units of a product in 4 hours. Working alone, machine B can make 500 units of the product in 3 hours. How long will it take both machines, working together, to make 500 units of the product?

Solution: In this problem, you have two machines that will work together to produce 500 units of a product. When you have two "workers" (in this case, the two machines) that can do the same job, a quick way to determine the time it will take them to do it together is to *multiply* their individual times, then divide this product by the *sum* of their individual times. *Tip:* Think "product over sum."

In the problem given, machine A's time working alone is 4 hours, and machine B's time working alone is 3 hours. Omitting units, their time working together is $\frac{(3)(4)}{3+4} = \frac{12}{7} = 1\frac{5}{7}$.

Working together, it will take the two machines $1\frac{5}{7}$ hours (or about 1 hour and 43 minutes) to make 500 units of the product.

Number Relationships Problems

Here is a practice problem.

Problem: One number is 4 times another number. Twice the sum of the two numbers is 85. Find the larger number.

Solution: You are to find the larger of two numbers. This number is unknown. Also unknown is the smaller of the two numbers. Let s = the smaller number and $4s$ = the larger number. Write and solve an equation that represents the facts given.

$$2(s + 4s) = 85$$
$$2s + 8s = 85$$
$$10s = 85$$
$$s = 8.5$$

Find $4s$, the larger number.

$$4s = 4(8.5) = 34$$

The larger number is 34.

Consecutive Integer Problems

Consecutive integers follow one another in order. For consecutive integer problems, let n = the least integer, $n + 1$ = the next integer, and so on.

Here is a practice problem.

Problem: The greatest of four consecutive integers is $-\frac{1}{3}$ times the sum of the other three integers. What is the value of the greatest integer?

Solution: Let n = the first integer (the least one), $n + 1$ = the second integer, $n + 2$ = the third integer, and $n + 3$ = the fourth integer (the greatest one).

Write and solve an equation that represents the facts given.

$$-\frac{1}{3}[(n)+(n+1)+(n+2)] = (n+3)$$
$$-\frac{1}{3}[n+n+1+n+2] = n+3$$
$$-\frac{1}{3}[3n+3] = n+3$$
$$-n-1 = n+3$$
$$-2n = 4$$
$$n = -2$$
$$n+3 = 1$$

The greatest of the four integers is 1.

For consecutive even or odd integers, let n = the first integer, $n + 2$ = the second integer, $n + 4$ = the third integer, and so on.

Tip: If you know the sum of three consecutive integers, the middle integer is the sum divided by 3. For example, if the sum of three consecutive even integers is 102, the middle integer is $\frac{102}{3} = 34$, and the other two even integers are 32 and 36.

Ratio Problems

A **ratio** is the result of a multiplicative comparison of two quantities or measures. You can express the ratio "three to four" in three different forms. You can write the ratio as 3 to 4, 3:4, or $\frac{3}{4}$. The numbers 3 and 4 are the terms of the ratio. On your TExES Math exam, if two quantities are in the ratio a to b and you are given their sum is c, solve $ax + bx = c$ for x, then compute ax or bx—whichever one is needed.

Here is a practice problem.

Problem: The ratio of boys to girls in a group of 35 students is 3 to 4. How many girls are in the group?

Solution: Solve $3x + 4x = 35$.

$$3x + 4x = 35$$
$$7x = 35$$
$$x = 5$$
$$4x = 20$$

There are 20 girls in the group.

Tip: You can extend this strategy to three or more quantities.

Proportion Problems

A **proportion** is a mathematical statement that the values of two ratios are equal. The **terms** of the proportion are the four numbers that make up the two ratios. For example, the proportion $\frac{a}{b} = \frac{c}{d}$ has terms a, b, c, and d. The **fundamental property of proportions** is the following: $\frac{a}{b} = \frac{c}{d}$ if and only if $ad = bc$. In other words, **cross products,** ad and bc, of a proportion are equal. To solve for a missing term of a proportion, find a cross product that results in a numerical value, and then divide by the numerical term you didn't use. For example, in the proportion, $\frac{5}{x} = \frac{2}{13}$, $x = \frac{(5)(13)}{2} = 32.5$.

To solve an application problem that calls for a proportion, find a sentence or phrase that provides information for the left ratio of the proportion. Then find another sentence or phrase that provides information for the right ratio. Next, write and solve the proportion.

Here is a practice problem.

> Problem: On a map, the distance between two cities is 15.5 inches. The scale on the map shows that 0.5 inch represents 20 miles. What is the distance, in miles, between the two cities?
>
> Solution: Let $d =$ the distance, in miles, between the two cities.
>
> Write a proportion that represents the facts given. The first sentence provides information for the left ratio of the proportion (15.5 inches represents d miles on the map). The second sentence provides information for the right ratio (0.5 inch represents 20 miles on the map). Write the proportion.
>
> $$\frac{d}{15.5 \text{ in}} = \frac{20 \text{ miles}}{0.5 \text{ in}}$$
>
> Check to make sure that the units in the left ratio match up with the units in the right ratio. On the left, you have miles in the numerator and inches in the denominator, and on the right, you have miles in the numerator and inches in the denominator as well. If the units in the left and right ratios don't match up, the proportion is incorrect.
>
> Solve the proportion.
>
> $$d = \frac{(15.5 \text{ in})(20 \text{ miles})}{0.5 \text{ in}} = 620 \text{ miles}$$
>
> The distance between the two cities is 620 miles.

Basic Percentage Problems

Basic percentage problems use the formula $P = RB$ (or, equivalently, $RB = P$), where P is the **percentage** (the portion of the whole), R is the **rate** (the quantity with a % sign or the word *percent* attached), and B is the **base** (the whole amount).

Tip: For convenience, when P is unknown, write the formula as $P = RB$, but when B or R is unknown, write the formula as $RB = P$.

Tip: In application problems, a percent without a base is usually meaningless. Be sure to identify the base associated with each percent mentioned in a problem.

Here are three practice problems.

> Problem: Morgaan works at a computer store that pays a commission rate of 3% to employees for all sales. Last week, Morgaan's sales totaled $4,500. What is Morgaan's commission for last week?
>
> Solution: In this problem, Morgaan's commission is P, which is unknown, R is 3%, and B is $4,500. Write and solve an equation that represents the facts, omitting the units for convenience.

Chapter 2: Patterns and Algebra

$$P = RB$$
$$P = 3\%(4,500)$$
$$P = 0.03(4,500)$$
$$P = 135$$

Morgaan's commission for last week is $135.

Problem: A department store offers a 25% discount on all clothing items during a 2-day sale. Karlie got $74.25 off the price of a jacket she purchased during the sale. What was the jacket's original price?

Solution: In this problem, the original price of the jacket is B, which is unknown, R is 25%, and P is $74.25. Write an equation that represents the facts given.

$$RB = P$$
$$25\% B = \$74.25$$

Solve the equation, omitting the units for convenience.

$$25\% B = 74.25$$
$$0.25 B = 74.25$$
$$B = 297$$

The jacket's original price was $297.

Problem: A customer pays a sales tax of $7.60 at a restaurant on a meal that costs $95.00. What is the sales tax rate for the purchase?

Solution: In this problem, the sales tax rate is R, which is unknown, P is $7.60, and B is $95.00. Write and solve an equation that represents the facts, omitting the units for convenience.

$$RB = P$$
$$R(95.00) = 7.60$$
$$95R = 7.60$$
$$R = 0.08$$
$$R = 8\%$$

The sales tax rate is 8%.

Percent Change Problems

To compute percent change (increase or decrease) in the value of an item, use the following formula:

$$\text{Percent Change} = \frac{|\text{New Value} - \text{Old Value}|}{\text{Old Value}} \times 100\%$$

Tip: Always divide by the value that occurred first in time.

Here are two practice problems.

Problem: A collectible toy increased in value from $345 to $414. What is the percent increase in the value of the toy?

Solution: Omitting the units, the percent increase is

$$\frac{|\text{New Value} - \text{Old Value}|}{\text{Old Value}} \times 100\% = \frac{|414 - 345|}{345} \times 100\% = \frac{|69|}{345} \times 100\% = \frac{69}{345} \times 100\% = 0.2 \times 100\% = 20\% \text{ increase}$$

Problem: A necklace decreased in value from $250.00 to $212.50. What is the percent decrease in the value of the necklace?

Solution: Omitting the units, the percent decrease is

$$\frac{|\text{New Value} - \text{Old Value}|}{\text{Old Value}} \times 100\% = \frac{|212.50 - 250.00|}{250.00} \times 100\% = \frac{|-37.50|}{250.00} \times 100\% = \frac{37.50}{250.00} \times 100\%$$

$$= 0.15 \times 100\% = 15\% \text{ decrease}$$

Tip: Percent change, whether it is an increase or a decrease, is *always* positive.

Simple Interest Problems

The simple interest formula is $I = Prt$ (or equivalently, $Prt = I$), where I is the simple interest accumulated on a principal, P, at a simple interest rate, r, per time period for t time periods.

Tip: For the formula $I = Prt$, the interest rate time units must match the time period units.

Here is a practice problem.

Problem: How many years will it take $10,000 invested at 2% annual interest to earn $1,500 in interest?
Note: 2% annual interest = a rate of 2% per year.
Solution: Let t = the time (in years) it will take the investment to earn $1,500 in interest at the given rate. The formula $I = Prt$ applies to the situation in this problem. The time period is t, which is unknown; I is $1,500; P is $10,000; and r is 2% per year.
Write an equation that represents the facts given.

$$I = Prt$$

$$\$1,500 = (\$10,000)\left(\frac{2\%}{\text{yr}}\right)(t)$$

Tip: Put units that follow the word *per* in a denominator.

Solve the equation, omitting the units for convenience.

$$1,500 = (10,000)(2\%)(t)$$
$$1,500 = 200t$$
$$7.5 = t$$

It will take 7.5 years for an investment of $10,000 to earn $1,500 in interest at a rate of 2% per year.

Compound Interest Problems

The compound interest formula is $I = P\left(1 + \frac{r}{n}\right)^{nt} - P$, where I is the interest earned on the principal, P, and on previously earned interest at a compound interest rate, r, which is compounded n times per year for t years.

Here is a practice problem.

Problem: How much interest will be earned on $10,000 invested at 2% annual interest compounded quarterly in 7 years?
Solution: The formula $I = P\left(1 + \frac{r}{n}\right)^{nt} - P$ applies to the situation in this problem. The interest I is unknown, t is 7 years, P is $10,000, r is 2%, and n is 4.
Write an equation that represents the facts given.

$$I = \$10,000\left(1 + \frac{0.02}{4}\right)^{4 \cdot 7} - \$10,000$$

Solve the equation.

$$I = \$10,000\left(1+\frac{0.02}{4}\right)^{4 \cdot 7} - \$10,000 = \$10,000(1.005)^{28} - \$10,000 \approx \$11,498.73 - \$10,000 = \$1,498.73$$

The amount of interest earned on an investment of $10,000 at a rate of 2% annual interest compounded quarterly in 7 years is approximately $1,498.73.

Direct and Inverse Variation Problems

A linear equation of the form $y = kx$, where k is a nonzero constant, expresses a **direct variation** between x and y. The variable y varies directly with the variable x. The ratio of the two variables remains constant. The constant k is the **constant of variation.**

Here is a practice problem.

> Problem: If y varies directly as x, and $x = 24$ when $y = 18$, what is the equation that describes this direct variation?
>
> Solution: Solve $k(24) = 18$ to determine that the constant of variation is $k = \frac{18}{24} = \frac{3}{4}$. Thus, the equation is $y = \frac{3}{4}x$.

An equation of the form $y = \frac{k}{x}$ or $xy = k$, where k is a nonzero constant, expresses an **inverse variation** between x and y. The variable y varies inversely as x, and conversely. The ratio of one variable to the reciprocal of the other is constant.

Here is a practice problem.

> Problem: The time t to travel a fixed distance varies inversely with r, the speed of travel. If it takes Isabel 30 minutes to drive home at 48 miles per hour, what is the equation that describes this inverse variation?
>
> Solution: The units are not the same, so change 30 minutes to $\frac{1}{2}$ hour.
>
> Solve $\frac{1}{2} = \frac{k}{48}$ to determine $k = 24$. Thus, the equation is $t = \frac{24}{r}$.

Basic Function Concepts

For this topic, you must demonstrate an ability to understand attributes of functions and their graphs.

Ordered Pairs and Relations

An **ordered pair** of numbers, denoted (x, y), is a pair of numbers expressed in a specific order so that one number is written first in the ordered pair, and the other number is written second. In the ordered pair (x, y), x is the **first component** (or **x-coordinate**), and y is the **second component** (or **y-coordinate**). Two ordered pairs are equal if and only if they have *exactly* the same components in the same order; that is, $(a, b) = (c, d)$ if and only if $a = c$ and $b = d$. The set consisting of all possible ordered pairs of real numbers is denoted $R \times R$, or simply R^2. A **relation** $\Re$ in R^2 is any subset of R^2. The set consisting of all the first components in the ordered pairs contained in $\Re$ is the **domain** of $\Re$, and the set of all second components is the **range** of $\Re$.

xy-Coordinate Plane

Graphically, R^2 is represented by the **xy-coordinate plane.** Here is an illustration.

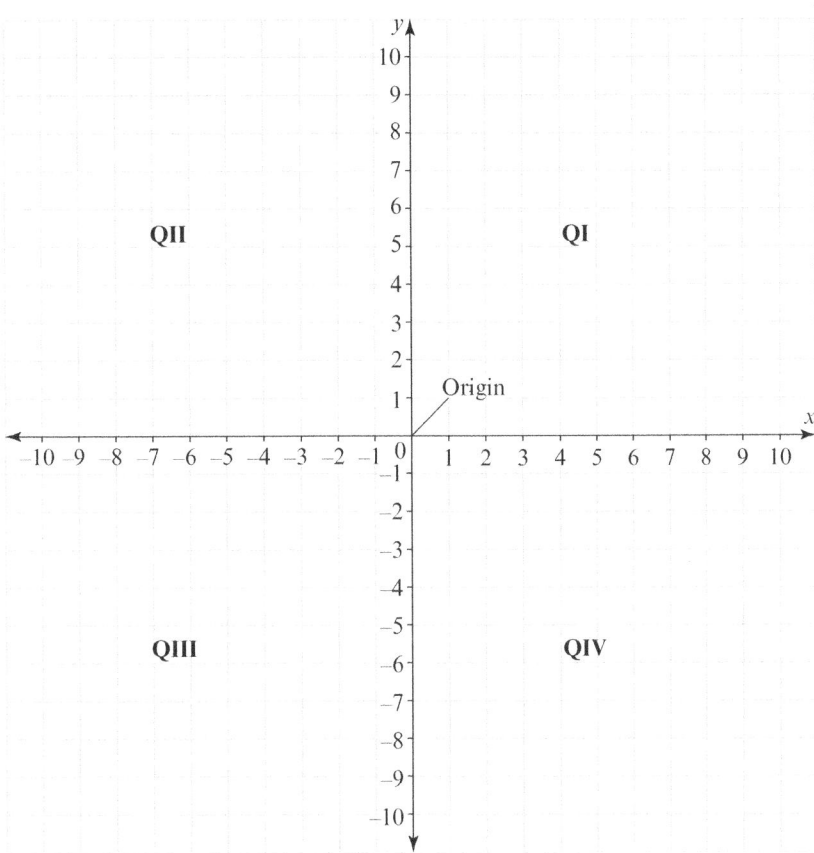

Two intersecting real number lines form the **axes** of the coordinate plane. The **horizontal axis** with positive direction to the right is commonly designated the **x-axis,** and the **vertical axis** with positive direction upward is commonly designated the **y-axis.** Their point of intersection is the **origin.** The axes divide the coordinate plane into four **quadrants.** The Roman numerals I, II, III, and IV name the quadrants. The numbering process starts in the upper-right quadrant and proceeds counterclockwise.

Every ordered pair, (x, y), of real numbers defines a point in the coordinate plane, and every point in the coordinate plane has a location defined by an ordered pair, (x, y), of real numbers. The numbers x and y are the **coordinates** of the point.

Definition and Representations of a Function

A **function** is a set of ordered pairs for which each first component is paired with *one and only one* second component. In other words, a function is a relation in which no two ordered pairs have the same first component but different second components; that is, if (a, b) and (a, d) are ordered pairs in the same function, then $b = d$. Thus, the ordered pairs (1, 2) and (2, 3) can both be elements of the same function, but the ordered pairs (1, 2) and (1, 3) cannot.

Single letters, such as f and g, are commonly used as names for functions. For the function f, the ordered pairs are written $(x, f(x))$ or (x, y), where $y = f(x)$. You read the function notation $f(x)$ as "f of x."

Functions are represented in various ways. If a function consists of a *finite* number of ordered pairs, you can define the function by listing or showing its ordered pairs in a set, in a table, as an arrow diagram, or as a graph in a coordinate plane. You also might define the function by giving a rule or an equation. When the number of ordered pairs is *infinite,* more often than not the function is defined by either an equation or a graph. *Note:* In this book, equations that define functions will use only real numbers as coefficients or constants.

89

In the function defined by $y = f(x)$, x is the **independent variable** and y is the **dependent variable**. The variable y is "dependent" on x in the sense that you substitute a value of x, called an **argument** of f, into $y = f(x)$ to find y, the value of f at x (also called the **image** of x under f). *Note:* The argument of a function is often referred to as its **input**, and its image under f as the **output**.

Two functions f and g are equal, written $f = g$, if and only if their domains are equal and $f(x) = g(x)$ for all x in their common domain. (See "Domain and Range of Functions" below for a discussion of the domain of a function.)

Evaluating Functions

Think of a function as a process f that takes an input number x and produces from it the output number $y = f(x)$. That is, $f(\text{input}) = \text{output}$. Here are examples.

For every input, x, the function defined by $y = 2x + 1$ produces exactly one output, y. When $x = -5$, $y = 2(-5) + 1 = -10 + 1 = -9$; when $x = 3$, $y = 2(3) + 1 = 6 + 1 = 7$; and so forth.

For every input, x, the function defined by $f(x) = x^2$ produces exactly one output, $f(x)$. When $x = -2$, $f(-2) = (-2)^2 = 4$; when $x = 2$, $f(2) = (2)^2 = 4$; and so forth. Notice in this example that the output for the input -2 is the same as the output for the input 2. That is, the ordered pairs $(-2, 4)$ and $(2, 4)$ are both in the function defined by $f(x) = x^2$. This situation is permissible in a function. It's okay that the outputs of distinct ordered pairs are the same, as long as their inputs are different.

Note: Although, by definition, a function f is a set of ordered pairs, it is commonplace to refer to the equation that defines a function as the function; that is, to speak of "the function $y = 2x + 1$" or "the function $f(x) = x^2$."

Evaluating a function means finding the corresponding output for a given input.

Here are two practice problems.

Problem: If $f(x) = 8x - 13$, find $f\left(\dfrac{3}{4}\right)$.

Solution: $f\left(\dfrac{3}{4}\right) = 8\left(\dfrac{3}{4}\right) - 13 = 6 - 13 = -7$

Problem: If $g(x) = \dfrac{2x+3}{x-1}$, $x \neq 1$, determine $g(5a+1)$.

Solution: $g(5a+1) = \dfrac{2(5a+1)+3}{(5a+1)-1} = \dfrac{10a+2+3}{5a+1-1} = \dfrac{10a+5}{5a} = \dfrac{2a+1}{a}$, $a \neq 0$

Domain and Range of Functions

The set of possible x values for a function f is the **domain** of f, denoted D_f, and the set of possible y values is the **range** of f, denoted R_f. In a real-valued function, the range consists of real numbers.

Note: The functions on the TExES Math exams are real-valued functions. Hereafter in this book, all functions are real-valued functions.

When a function f is defined by an equation $y = f(x)$ and no domain is specified, the domain of f is the largest possible subset of the real numbers for which each x value gives a corresponding y value that is a *real* number. To determine the domain, start with the set of real numbers and exclude all values for x, if any, that would make the equation undefined over the real numbers. If $y = f(x)$ contains a rational expression, to avoid division by zero, exclude values for x, if any, that would make a denominator zero. If $y = f(x)$ contains a radical with an *even* index, to avoid even roots of negative numbers, exclude all values for x, if any, that would cause the expression under the radical to be negative.

Tip: Division by zero and even roots of negative numbers are the two types of domain problems that you are most likely to encounter on the TExES Math exams.

You can determine the range of f in a manner similar to that used to find the domain of f if you can first solve the equation $y = f(x)$ explicitly for x. Otherwise, analyze $y = f(x)$ for insight into the possible values of y.

Here are two practice problems.

Problem: Determine the domain, D_f, and the range, R_f, for the function f defined by $y = \dfrac{1}{x-3}$.

Solution: When $x = 3$, the rational expression $\dfrac{1}{x-3}$ is $\dfrac{1}{0}$, which is undefined. Therefore, the number 3 is excluded from D_f. For every real number x, except 3, the quantity $\dfrac{1}{x-3}$ is a real number. Thus, the domain of f consists of all real numbers except 3, written $D_f = \{x \mid x \neq 3\}$.

To determine the range of f, solve $y = \dfrac{1}{x-3}$ explicitly for x to obtain $x = \dfrac{1+3y}{y}$. For every real number y, except 0, the quantity $\dfrac{1+3y}{y}$ is a real number. So, the range of f consists of all real numbers except 0, written $R_f = \{y \mid y \neq 0\}$.

Problem: Determine the domain and range of the function g defined by $g(x) = \sqrt{x-5} + 2$.

Solution: When $x - 5 < 0$, the expression $\sqrt{x-5}$ is the square root of a negative number, so it is not defined over the real numbers. However, for every real number x for which $x - 5 \geq 0$, the quantity $\sqrt{x-5}$ is a real number. Therefore, the domain of g is all real numbers such that $x - 5 \geq 0$; therefore, $D_g = \{x \mid x \geq 5\}$. For all real numbers x, the quantity $\sqrt{x-5}$ is nonnegative. So, $y = g(x) = \sqrt{x-5} + 2 \geq 2$. Therefore, $R_g = \{y \mid y \geq 2\}$.

Graphs of Functions

Because a function is a set of ordered pairs, its graph can be plotted in a coordinate plane. Each ordered pair is represented by a point in the plane. The **graph** of a function f is the set of all ordered pairs (x, y) for which x is in the domain of f and $y = f(x)$. The graph of a function is a visual representation of its solutions, the set of ordered pairs that make the statement $y = f(x)$ true.

Vertical Line Test

Vertical line test: A relation is a function if any vertical line in the plane intersects the graph of the relation in no more than one point. By definition, each element in the domain of a function is paired with exactly one element in the range. Thus, if a vertical line can be drawn so that it cuts the graph of a relation at more than one point, the relation is not a function. Here is an illustration of a relation that does *not* pass the vertical line test, so it is *not* a function. There are two points on the graph that correspond to $x = 2$, namely $(2, 1.7)$ and $(2, -1.7)$.

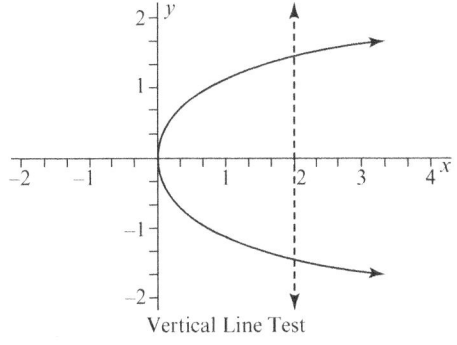

Vertical Line Test

Chapter 2: Patterns and Algebra

One-to-One Function and Horizontal Line Test

A function f is **one-to-one** if and only if $f(a) = f(b)$ implies that $a = b$; that is, if (a, c) and (b, c) are elements of f, then $a = b$. In a one-to-one function, each first component is paired with *exactly one* second component *and* each second component is paired with *exactly one* first component. Therefore, you have the **horizontal line test:** A function is one-to-one if any horizontal line in the plane intersects the graph of the function in no more than one point. Here is an illustration of a function that does *not* pass the horizontal line test, so it is *not* a one-to-one function.

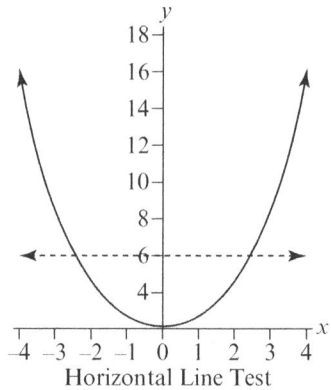
Horizontal Line Test

Increasing-Decreasing-Constant Behavior

Suppose a function f is defined over an interval. Then the following are true:

- f is **increasing** in the interval if, for every pair of numbers x_1 and x_2 in the interval, $f(x_1) < f(x_2)$ whenever $x_1 < x_2$.
- f is **decreasing** in the interval if, for every pair of numbers x_1 and x_2 in the interval, $f(x_1) > f(x_2)$ whenever $x_1 < x_2$.
- f is **constant** in the interval if $f(x_1) = f(x_2)$ for every pair of numbers x_1 and x_2 in the interval.

Thus, a function is increasing in an interval if its graph moves upward from left to right as the independent variable assumes values from left to right in the interval. A function is decreasing in an interval if its graph moves downward from left to right as the independent variable assumes values from left to right in the interval. A function is constant in an interval if the function value stays the same as the independent variable assumes values from left to right in the interval.

Here is a practice problem.

> Problem: For the graph of the function shown, list the intervals where the function is decreasing, increasing, or constant.

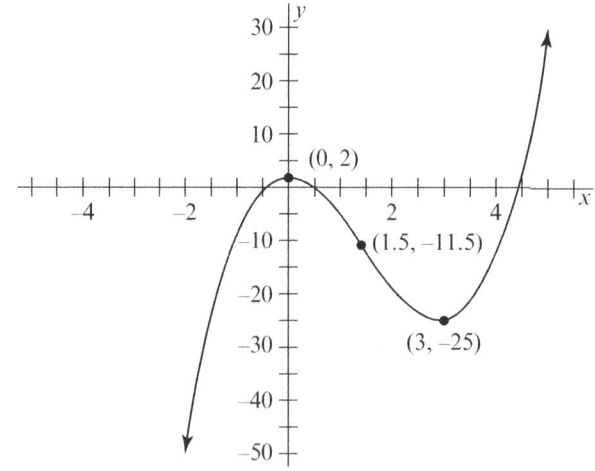

Solution: The function shown is decreasing in the interval $(-\infty, -2.5)$ and increasing in the interval $(-2.5, \infty)$. The function shows no constant behavior.

Tip: When you are determining intervals to describe increasing and decreasing behavior, give x-intervals, not y-intervals.

Monotonic Function

A function is **monotonic** if, on its entire domain, the function is either only increasing or only decreasing. A monotonic increasing or decreasing function is **one-to-one.** Here is an example.

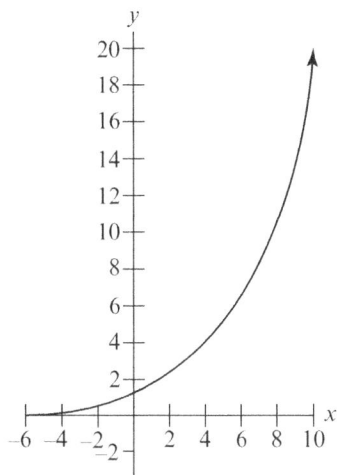

Monotonic Increasing Function

Extrema

Let c be in the domain of a function f. The number $f(c)$ is an **absolute minimum** of f if $f(c) \leq f(x)$ for all x in the domain of f. Similarly, $f(c)$ is an **absolute maximum** of f if $f(c) \geq f(x)$ for all x in the domain of f. The minimum and maximum values of a function are the **extreme values,** or **extrema** (plural of *extremum*), of the function.

Here is a practice problem.

Problem: Use the graph shown to identify absolute extrema.

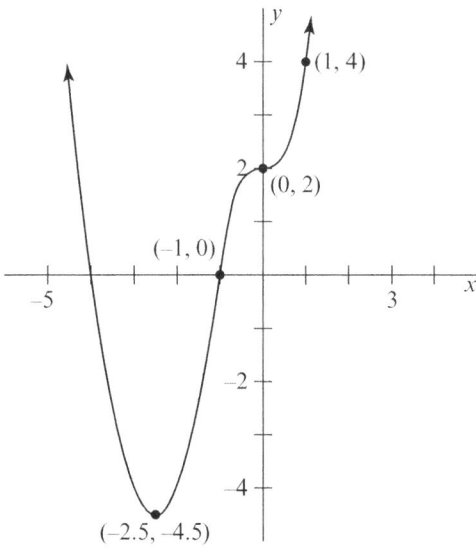

Solution: The point (−2.5, −4.5) is the lowest point on the graph. Thus, the graph has an absolute minimum of −4.5.

The number $f(c)$ is a **relative minimum** of a function f if there exists an open interval containing c in which $f(c)$ is a minimum; similarly, the number $f(c)$ is a **relative maximum** of a function f if there exists an open interval containing c in which $f(c)$ is a maximum. If $f(c)$ is a relative minimum or maximum of f, it is a **relative extremum** of f. Basically, a relative maximum occurs at a point where the function's graph changes direction from increasing to decreasing. Similarly, a relative minimum occurs at a point where the function's graph changes direction from decreasing to increasing.

Here is a practice problem.

Problem: Use the graph shown to identify relative extrema.

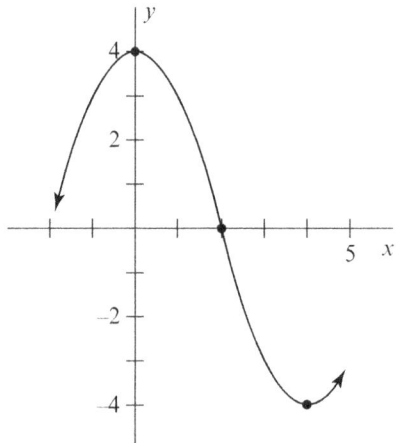

Solution: The function's graph changes direction from increasing to decreasing at (0, 4), so it has a relative maximum of 4. The function's graph changes direction from decreasing to increasing at (4, −4), so it has a relative minimum of −4.

Vertical and Horizontal Asymptotes

An **asymptote** of the graph of a function f is a line to which the graph gets closer and closer in at least one direction along the line. The vertical line $x = a$ is a **vertical asymptote** of the graph of a function f if, as x draws close to a from the left or right, the graph goes toward either $-\infty$ or ∞. A horizontal line $y = b$ is a **horizontal asymptote** of the graph of f if $f(x)$ approaches b as x approaches either $-\infty$ or ∞. See the following figure.

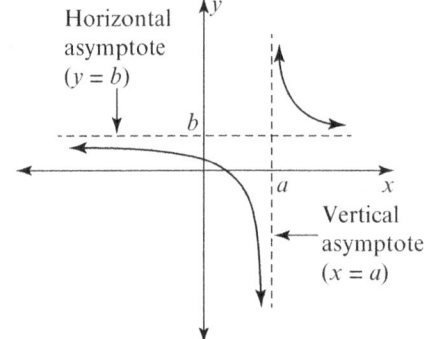

Vertical and Horizontal Asymptotes

Commonly, asymptotes are associated with rational functions (see "Rational Functions" later in this chapter for a more detailed discussion of rational functions). For a rational function f, defined by $f(x) = \dfrac{P(x)}{Q(x)}$, where $Q(x) \neq 0$, you find a vertical asymptote by setting the denominator $Q(x)$ equal to 0 and solving for x (provided the rational function is in simplified form and the degree of $Q(x)$ is at least 1). You find a horizontal asymptote by determining a value that $y = f(x)$ approaches as x approaches positive or negative infinity (again, provided the rational function is in simplified form).

Here is a practice problem.

Problem: Describe the asymptotes for the function defined by the equation $y = \dfrac{1}{x-2} + 4$.

Solution: The denominator $x - 2$ equals zero when $x = 2$. Thus, the vertical asymptote is $x = 2$. As x approaches ∞ or $-\infty$, $\dfrac{1}{x-2}$ approaches 0. Thus, as x approaches ∞ or $-\infty$, $\dfrac{1}{x-2} + 4$ approaches $0 + 4 = 4$, so $y = 4$ is a horizontal asymptote.

Note: A discussion of oblique asymptotes is presented in "More about Asymptotes" in Part 2 for candidates who plan to take the TExES Math 7–12.

Positive and Negative Behavior

A function f is positive in an interval if its graph lies above the x-axis for all x values in the interval; similarly, a function f is negative in an interval if its graph lies below the x-axis for all x values in the interval.

Here is a practice problem.

Problem: Describe the positive and negative behavior of the function f shown that crosses the x-axis at $(-1, 0), (0, 0), (2, 0),$ and $(3, 0)$.

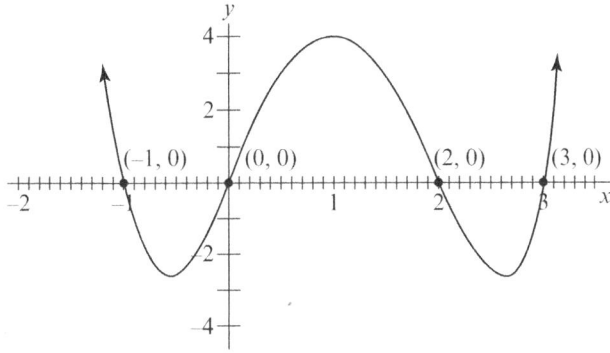

Solution: The function f is positive in the intervals $(-\infty, -1), (0, 2),$ and $(3, \infty)$, and negative in the intervals $(-1, 0)$ and $(2, 3)$.

Tip: Do not misread open interval notation as representing ordered pairs. The context of the notation should serve to remove the ambiguity. See "Intervals and Interval Notation" in Chapter 1 for a review of this topic.

Average and Instantaneous Rate of Change

If (x_1, y_1) and (x_2, y_2) are two distinct points on the graph of a function f, the **average rate of change** of f as x goes from x_1 to x_2 is given by

$$\frac{\Delta y}{\Delta x} = \frac{y_2 - y_1}{x_2 - x_1} = \frac{f(x_2) - f(x_1)}{x_2 - x_1}$$

where Δy is the change in y values and Δx is the change in x values. The average rate of change measures the "speed," *on average,* at which a function is changing over an interval of its domain. The line passing through points (x_1, y_1) and (x_2, y_2) is a **secant line.** The slope of the secant line is the average rate of change of the function over the interval.

Here are two practice problems.

Problem: Find the average rate of change of $f(x) = 2x$ **(a)** over the interval $[-4, -1]$ and **(b)** over the interval $[1, 4]$.

Solution:

(a) $\dfrac{\Delta y}{\Delta x} = \dfrac{f(x_2) - f(x_1)}{x_2 - x_1} = \dfrac{f(-1) - f(-4)}{(-1) - (-4)} = \dfrac{(2)(-1) - (2)(-4)}{-1 + 4} = \dfrac{-2 + 8}{3} = \dfrac{6}{3} = 2$

(b) $\dfrac{\Delta y}{\Delta x} = \dfrac{f(x_2) - f(x_1)}{x_2 - x_1} = \dfrac{f(4) - f(1)}{4 - 1} = \dfrac{2 \cdot 4 - 2 \cdot 1}{3} = \dfrac{6}{3} = 2$

Problem: Find the average rate of change of $g(x) = x^2$ **(a)** over the interval $[-4, -1]$ and **(b)** over the interval $[1, 4]$.

Solution:

(a) $\dfrac{\Delta y}{\Delta x} = \dfrac{g(x_2) - g(x_1)}{x_2 - x_1} = \dfrac{g(-1) - g(-4)}{(-1) - (-4)} = \dfrac{(-1)^2 - (-4)^2}{-1 + 4} = \dfrac{1 - 16}{3} = \dfrac{-15}{3} = -5$

(b) $\dfrac{\Delta y}{\Delta x} = \dfrac{g(x_2) - g(x_1)}{x_2 - x_1} = \dfrac{g(4) - g(1)}{4 - 1} = \dfrac{4^2 - 1^2}{3} = \dfrac{15}{3} = 5$

The **instantaneous rate of change** of a function $f(x)$ at $x = x_1$ is given by the slope of the tangent line to the function's graph at $(x_1, f(x_1))$. A **tangent line** is a line that touches a nonlinear function at only one point, as shown in the figure below.

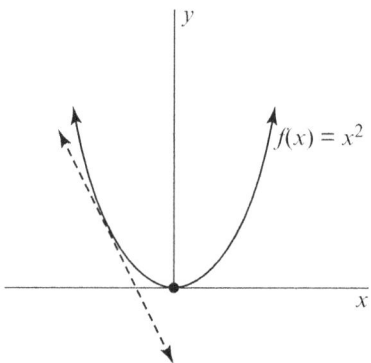

The slopes of tangent lines to nonlinear functions change; in fact, the slope could be different at every point along the curve. The slope provides information about the nature of change in y as a result of a change in x. This nature of change is expressed in the sign of the slope, which may be positive, negative, or zero.

Here is a practice problem.

Problem: In the graph below, describe the slopes of the tangent lines to $f(x) = x^2$ at points A, B, and C as positive, negative, or zero.

Chapter 2: Patterns and Algebra

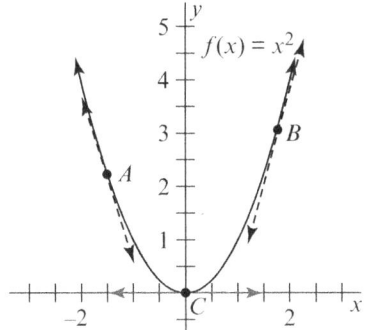

Solution: The slope of the tangent line at A is negative, the slope of the tangent line at B is positive, and the slope of the tangent line at C is zero.

Even and Odd Functions

A function is even if for every x in D_f, $-x$ is in D_f and $f(-x) = f(x)$. A function is odd if for every x in D_f, $-x$ is in D_f and $f(-x) = -f(x)$. The graphs of even functions are symmetric about the y-axis. The graphs of odd functions are symmetric about the origin. Here are illustrations.

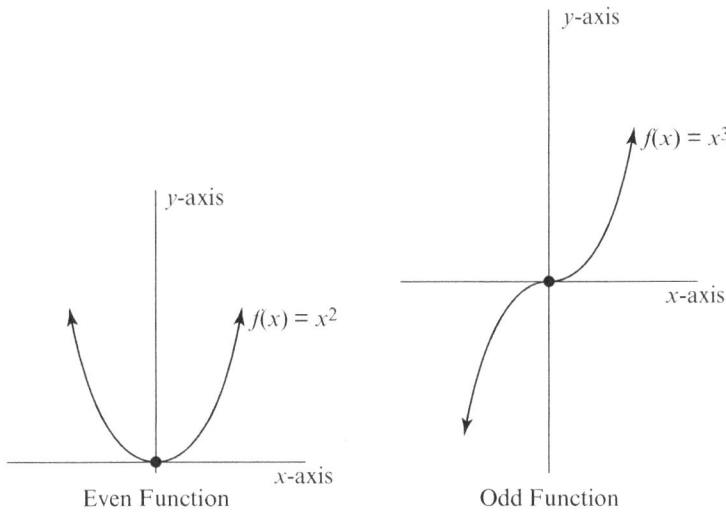

Even Function   Odd Function

Note: Many functions are neither even nor odd. Their graphs show no symmetry with respect to either the y-axis or the origin.

Zeros and Intercepts

A **zero** of a function f is a solution to the equation $f(x) = 0$. It is an input value that produces a zero output value. The zeros are determined by finding all values x for which $f(x) = 0$. For example, 2 and -2 are zeros of the function f defined by $f(x) = x^2 - 4$ because $f(2) = (2)^2 - 4 = 4 - 4 = 0$ and $f(-2) = (-2)^2 - 4 = 4 - 4 = 0$.

An **x-intercept** of the graph of a function is the x-coordinate of a point at which the graph intersects the x-axis, and the **y-intercept** is the y-coordinate of the point at which the graph intersects the y-axis. See the following figure.

Chapter 2: Patterns and Algebra

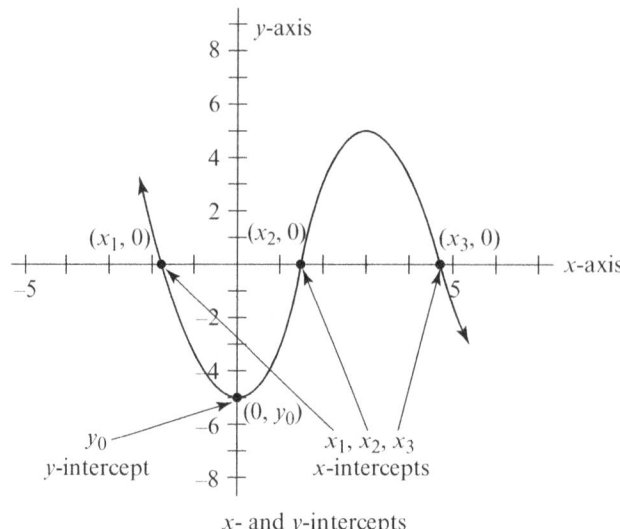

x- and y-intercepts

The graph of a function has at most *one* y-intercept. A function f cannot have more than one y-intercept because, by definition, each x value in the domain of f is paired with *exactly one* y value in the range. If 0 is in the domain of f, then f (0) is the y-intercept of the graph of f. To determine the y-intercept, if any, of a function f, let x = 0, provided that 0 is in the domain of f, and then solve f (0) = y for y.

A graph can have many x-intercepts, or it might not have any. To determine the x-intercept(s), if any, for a function f, set f(x) = 0 and then solve for x. The x-intercepts, if any, are the real zeros of f. You can describe a **real zero** of a function as one of the following: an x-intercept for the graph of y = f(x), a real number x for which f(x) = 0, or a real root of the equation f(x) = 0. See "Polynomial Functions" later in this chapter for an illustration of the zeros of a function.

Tip: It is important that you understand the distinction between x-intercepts and zeros. To clarify the relationship in general: For any function f, x-intercepts (if any) of the graph of f are *always* zeros of f; however, only *real* zeros (if any) of f are x-intercepts of its graph. Some functions have zeros that are not real numbers, so these zeros do not correspond to x-intercepts because these values do not lie on the x-axis.

Composition and Inverses of Functions

For this topic, you must be able to determine the composition of two functions, find the inverse of a one-to-one function in simple cases, and understand that only one-to-one functions have inverses.

Composition of Functions

The **composition**, denoted $f \circ g$ (read "f of g"), of two functions f and g is the function defined by $(f \circ g)(x) = f(g(x))$. The domain of $f \circ g$ is all x in the domain of g such that g(x) is defined and g(x) is in the domain of f. Hence, the range of g, R_g, is a subset of the domain of f, D_f.

Here are three practice problems.

>Problem: If f = {(–3, –5), (–2, –4), (0, –5), (1, 3), (2, 0), (4, 7)} and g = {(–4, 8), (–3, –8), (–2, –3), (0, 1), (1, 4)}, find **(a)** $f \circ g$ and **(b)** $g \circ f$.

Solution:

(a) Systematically determine the ordered pairs that are elements of $f \circ g$ as follows:
$(f \circ g)(-4) = f(g(-4)) = f(8)$ is undefined because 8 is not in the domain of f, $(f \circ g)(-3) = f(g(-3)) = f(-8)$ is undefined because -8 is not in the domain of f, $(f \circ g)(-2) = f(g(-2)) = f(-3) = -5$, $(f \circ g)(0) = f(g(0)) = f(1) = 3$, and $(f \circ g)(1) = f(g(1)) = f(4) = 7$. Thus, $f \circ g = \{(-2, -5), (0, 3), (1, 7)\}$.

(b) Systematically determine the ordered pairs that are elements of $g \circ f$ as follows:
$(g \circ f)(-3) = g(f(-3)) = g(-5)$ is undefined because -5 is not in the domain of g, $(g \circ f)(-2) = g(f(-2)) = g(-4) = 8$, $(g \circ f)(0) = g(f(0)) = g(-5)$ is undefined because -5 is not in the domain of g, $(g \circ f)(1) = g(f(1)) = g(3)$ is undefined because 3 is not in the domain of g, and $(g \circ f)(2) = g(f(2)) = g(0) = 1$. Thus, $g \circ f = \{(-2, 8), (2, 1)\}$.

Problem: Given $f(x) = 3x$ and $g(x) = x^2$, find **(a)** $f \circ g(x)$ and **(b)** $g \circ f(x)$.

Solution:

(a) $(f \circ g)(x) = f(g(x)) = 3(g(x)) = 3x^2$

(b) $(g \circ f)(x) = g(f(x)) = (f(x))^2 = (3x)^2 = 9x^2$

Problem: Let $f(x) = x^2$ and $g(x) = \sqrt{x+3}$. **(a)** Determine the domain of $f \circ g$, **(b)** write a simplified expression for $(f \circ g)(x)$, and, if possible, evaluate **(c)** $(f \circ g)(6)$, $(f \circ g)(-1)$, and $(f \circ g)(-6)$.

Solution:

(a) The domain of $f \circ g$ is all x in the domain of g such that $g(x)$ is defined and $g(x)$ is in the domain of f. The function g defined by $g(x) = \sqrt{x+3}$ has the domain $D_g = \{x \mid x \geq -3\}$. In the composition, $g(x)$ must be in the domain of f. The domain of f is all real numbers, so $g(x)$ is definitely in the domain of f. Therefore, the domain of $f \circ g$ is the same as the domain of g; that is, the domain of $f \circ g = \{x \mid x \geq -3\}$.

(b) $(f \circ g)(x) = f(g(x)) = f(\sqrt{x+3}) = (\sqrt{x+3})^2 = x + 3,\ x \geq -3$

(c) $(f \circ g)(6) = f(g(6)) = f(\sqrt{6+3}) = f(\sqrt{9}) = f(3) = 3^2 = 9$; $(f \circ g)(-1) = f(g(-1)) = f(\sqrt{-1+3}) = f(\sqrt{2}) = (\sqrt{2})^2 = 2$; $(f \circ g)(-6)$ is undefined because -6 is not in the domain of $f \circ g$.

Tip: Composition of functions is not commutative; that is, in general, $f \circ g(x) \neq g \circ f(x)$.

Inverses of Functions

If the function f is a one-to-one function, its **inverse,** denoted f^{-1} (read "f inverse"), is the function such that $(f^{-1} \circ f)(x) = x$ for all x in the domain of f and $(f \circ f^{-1})(x) = x$ for all x in the domain of f^{-1}, and $R_{f^{-1}} = D_f$ and $R_f = D_{f^{-1}}$. Graphically, f^{-1} is a reflection of f over the line $y = x$.

Tip: Do not interpret f^{-1} to mean $\dfrac{1}{f}$. The $^{-1}$ that is attached to f is *not* an exponent; it is a notation that is used to denote the inverse of a function.

If a function f defined by a set of ordered pairs is one-to-one, then f^{-1} may be found by interchanging x and y in each of the ordered pairs of f. For example, if $f = \{(-1, 2), (3, 5), (6, -1)\}$, then $f^{-1} = \{(2, -1), (5, 3), (-1, 6)\}$.

When a one-to-one function f is defined by an equation, you can find the equation of f^{-1} as follows:

First, in $y = f(x)$, replace x with y and y with x, and then solve $x = f(y)$ for y.

Here is a practice problem.

> Problem: Given $y = f(x) = 3x$, find $f^{-1}(x)$.
> Solution: First, interchanging x and y gives $x = 3y$. Next, solving for y gives $\frac{x}{3} = y$ or $y = \frac{x}{3}$.

Only one-to-one functions have inverses that are functions. However, when a function f is not one-to-one, it might be possible to restrict its domain so that f is one-to-one in the **restricted domain**. Then, f will have an inverse function in the restricted domain.

Features of Common Functions

This section presents features of common functions including their defining equations, domains and ranges, zeros, and intercepts.

Linear Functions

Linear functions are defined by equations of the form $y = mx + b$. The domain for all linear functions is R, the set of real numbers. When $m \neq 0$, the range is R. When $m = 0$, the range is the set $\{b\}$, containing the single value b.

The graph of a linear function f defined by $y = mx + b$ is always a nonvertical line with slope m and y-intercept b.

When $m \neq 0$, the graph has exactly one y-intercept, which is b, and exactly one x-intercept, which is $-\frac{b}{m}$.

Thus, the points $(0, b)$ and $\left(-\frac{b}{m}, 0\right)$ are contained in the graph. The only zero is the real number $-\frac{b}{m}$; thus, the graph crosses the x-axis at the point $\left(-\frac{b}{m}, 0\right)$. If $m > 0$, f is increasing; if $m < 0$, f is decreasing. The following figure shows the graph of the linear function $y = -\frac{1}{2}x + 6$ that has slope of $-\frac{1}{2}$, y-intercept of 6, and x-intercept of 12.

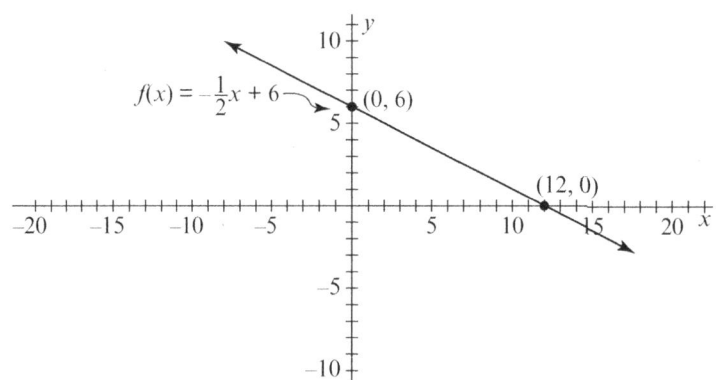

Note: The equation $y = mx + b$ is the **slope-intercept form** of the equation of a line. Every linear equation $Ax + By = C$ ($B \neq 0$) determines a linear function. (See "The Equation of a Line" earlier in this chapter for an additional discussion of linear equations.)

The **identity function** is the linear function defined by the equation $y = x$. It is called the identity function because it matches each x value with an identical y value. The domain and range are both R, the set of real numbers. The graph has slope of 1. The graph passes through the origin, so both the x- and y-intercepts are zero. The only zero is $x = 0$.

Constant functions are linear functions defined by equations of the form $y = b$, where $b \in R$. The domain is the set R of real numbers, and the range is the set $\{b\}$ containing the single element b. The slope is zero. Constant functions either have no zeros or infinitely many zeros according to the following guideline: If $b \neq 0$, they have no zeros; if $b = 0$, every real number x is a zero. The graph of a constant function is a horizontal line that is $|b|$ units above or below the x-axis when $b \neq 0$ and coincident with the real axis when $b = 0$.

Directly proportional functions are linear functions defined by equations of the form $y = kx$, where k is the non-zero **constant of proportionality.** A function is a directly proportional function when the output equals the input multiplied by a constant. The domain and range are both R, the set of real numbers. The graph has slope k. The graph passes through the origin, so both the x- and y-intercepts are zero. The only zero is $x = 0$. *Note:* Technically, the identity function is a directly proportional function in which the constant of proportionality k equals 1.

Here are examples of linear functions.

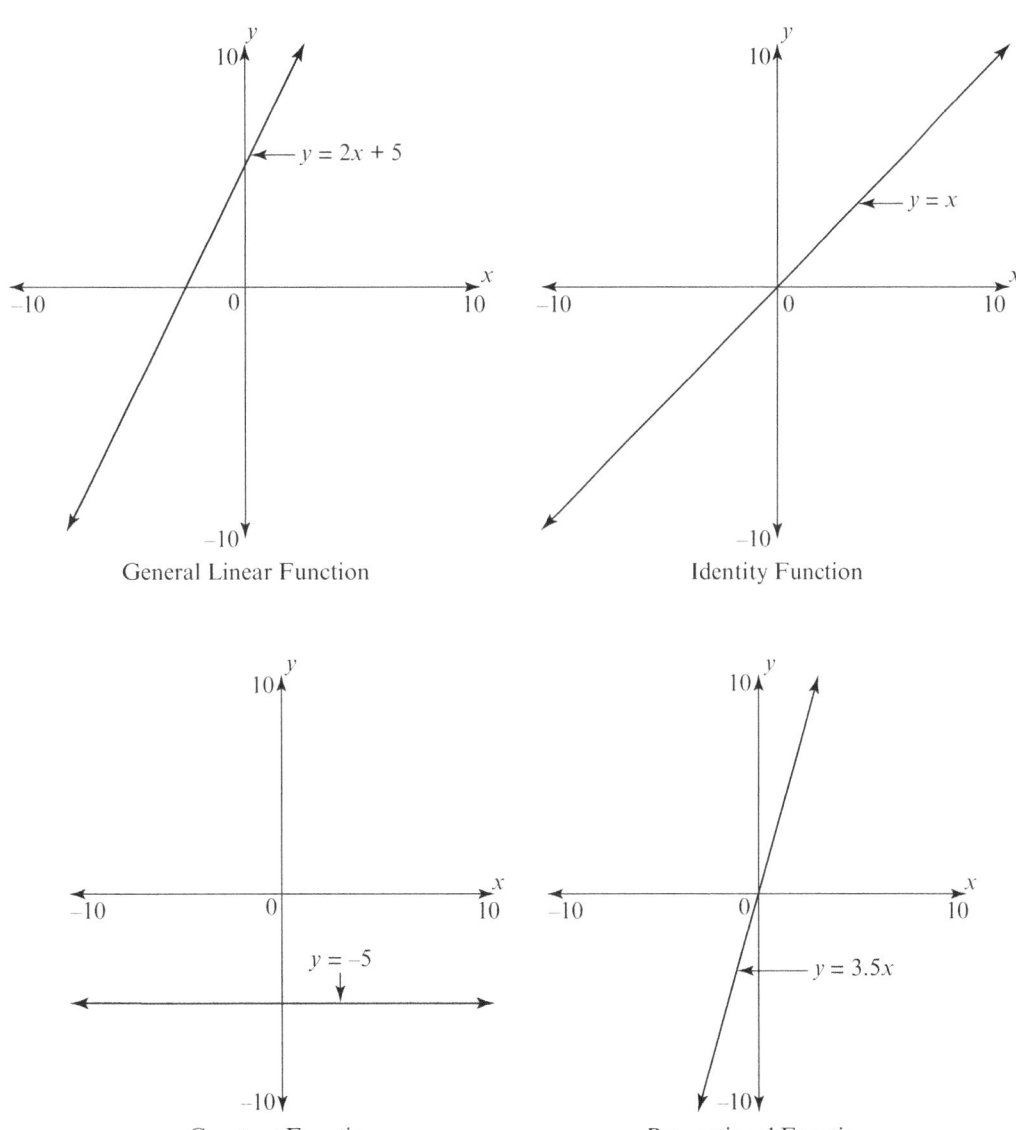

General Linear Function

Identity Function

Constant Function

Proportional Function

101

Rate of Change of a Linear Function

The slope m of a linear function's graph is the function's **rate of change.** Because the slope of a line is constant, a linear function's rate of change is constant over the entire graph. The rate of change describes how the output changes in relation to the input. For every 1-unit change in the input, there are m units of change in the output. If the input changes by k units, the output changes by km units.

Here is a practice problem.

> Problem: Given the function $y = 2x + 5$, for every 1-unit change in x, what is the change in y?
> Solution: For the function $y = 2x + 5$, for every 1-unit change in x, there is a 2-unit change in y.

In general, if (x_1, y_1) and (x_2, y_2) are any two distinct ordered pairs in a linear function's graph, the function's rate of change is $m = \dfrac{\text{change in } y}{\text{change in } x} = \dfrac{y_2 - y_1}{x_2 - x_1}$. Rates of change can be positive, negative, or zero.

A **positive rate of change** corresponds to an increase in the output when the input increases. When you trace the input, x, as it increases from left to right, you will observe that the output, y, increases from lower to higher values. The result is that the graph slants upward from left to right.

A **negative rate of change** corresponds to a decrease in the output when the input increases. When you trace the input, x, as it increases from left to right, you will observe that the output, y, decreases from higher to lower values. The result is that the graph slants downward from left to right.

A **zero rate of change** occurs when the output does not change as the input increases. When you trace the input, x, as it increases from left to right, you will observe that the value of the output, y, does not change. That is, the output's value remains constant. The result is that the graph is a horizontal line. Here are graphical illustrations.

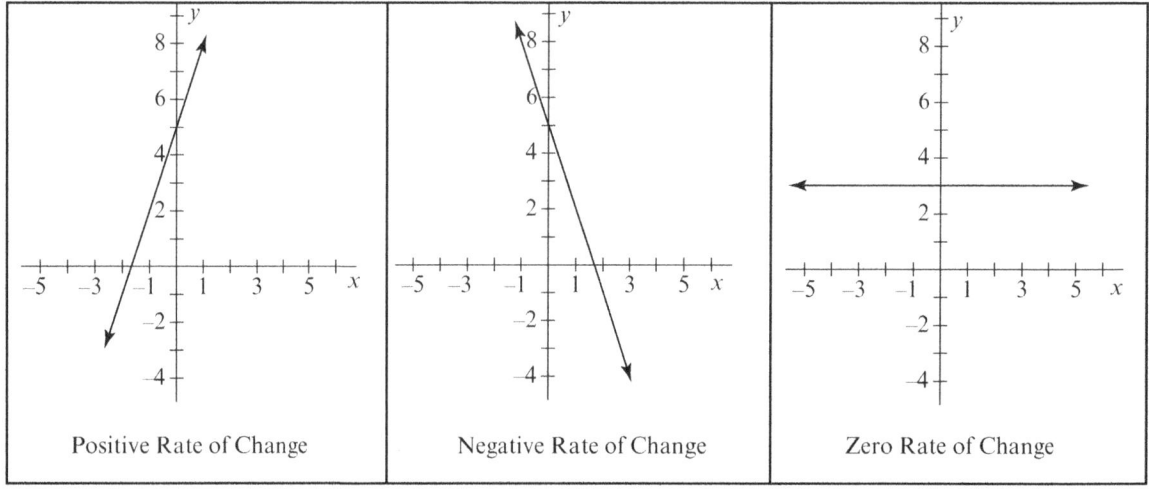

Positive Rate of Change   Negative Rate of Change   Zero Rate of Change

Therefore, linear functions are either increasing, decreasing, or remaining constant, from left to right, at a steady rate. Their graphs do not change direction.

Quadratic Functions

Quadratic functions are defined by equations of the form $y = ax^2 + bx + c$ ($a \neq 0$). The domain is the set R of real numbers, and the range is a subset of R. The zeros are the roots of the quadratic equation $ax^2 + bx + c = 0$. The quantity $b^2 - 4ac$ is the **discriminant** of the quadratic equation. It determines three cases for the zeros of the quadratic function:

- If $b^2 - 4ac > 0$, the quadratic function has two real *unequal* zeros.
- If $b^2 - 4ac = 0$, the quadratic function has one real zero (double root).
- If $b^2 - 4ac < 0$, the quadratic function has no real zeros.

The graph of $f(x) = ax^2 + bx + c$ is a parabola. The vertex is $\left(-\dfrac{b}{2a}, f\left(-\dfrac{b}{2a}\right)\right)$. When $a > 0$, the parabola opens upward and the *y*-coordinate of the vertex is an absolute minimum of f. When $a < 0$, the parabola opens downward and the *y*-coordinate of the vertex is an absolute maximum of f. The parabola is symmetric about its axis of symmetry, a vertical line, with the equation $x = -\dfrac{b}{2a}$ that passes through its vertex.

Depending on the solution set of $ax^2 + bx + c = 0$, the graph of a quadratic function might or might not intersect the *x*-axis. Three cases occur:

- If there are *two* real *unequal* roots, the parabola will intersect the *x*-axis at those *two* points.
- If there is exactly *one* real root, the parabola will intersect the *x*-axis at only that *one* point.
- If there are no real roots, the parabola will *not* intersect the *x*-axis.

Here are examples of quadratic functions defined by $y = ax^2 + bx + c$ with $a > 0$.

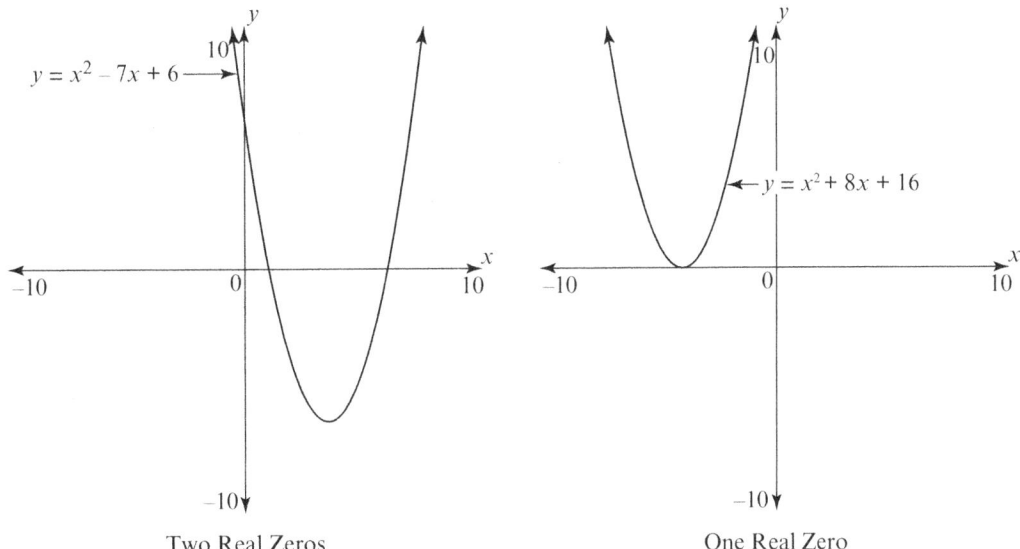

Two Real Zeros   One Real Zero

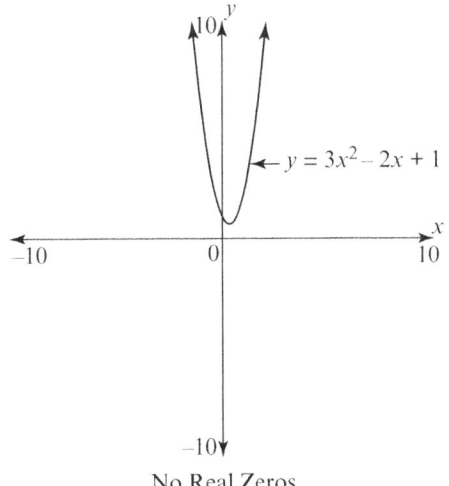

No Real Zeros

The **standard form** for the equation of a parabola that opens upward or downward is $y = a(x - h)^2 + k$ ($a \neq 0$) with vertex (h, k). Any quadratic function can be put in standard form by using the process of **completing the square**. (See "Solving Quadratic Equations by Completing the Square" earlier in this chapter for a discussion of completing the square.)

Polynomial Functions

Polynomial functions are defined by equations of the form $P(x) = a_n x^n + a_{n-1} x^{n-1} + \ldots + a_2 x^2 + a_1 x + a_0$, with **leading coefficient** $a_n \neq 0$. The **degree** of the polynomial function is n, a nonnegative integer. Linear and quadratic functions are polynomial functions of degree one and two, respectively. A constant polynomial function, defined by $P(x) = c$ (a nonzero constant), has degree zero. The degree of the zero polynomial function, defined as $P(x) = 0$, is undefined. The domain of any polynomial function is R. When n is odd, the range is R. When n is even, the range is a subset of R. The zeros are the roots of the equation $P(x) = 0$.

A number r is a zero of a polynomial function P that is defined by $y = P(x)$ if and only if $P(r) = 0$. If $r \in R$, the graph of $y = P(x)$ crosses the x-axis at the point $(r, 0)$ and has an x-intercept at r. The graph of a polynomial function P is a continuous smooth curve (or line) with no breaks of any kind; moreover, it has no **cusps** (meaning sharp corners). The y-intercept of the graph is $P(0)$. The x-intercepts correspond to the real zeros (if any) of P. As the degree of polynomial functions increases, their graphs become more complex. The graph below shows a polynomial function that has zeros (and x-intercepts) -1, 0, 2, and 3, and y-intercept 0.

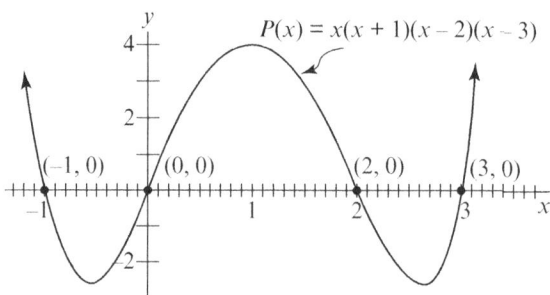

The graph of a polynomial function might have turning points. A **turning point** (x, y) occurs whenever the graph changes from increasing to decreasing or from decreasing to increasing. An nth degree polynomial function has at most $(n - 1)$ turning points. The y value of a turning point is either a relative maximum or relative minimum value for the function.

Tip: Do not confuse maximum or minimum values with turning points. A turning point, identified by an ordered pair (x, y), is a point on the graph where the graph changes from increasing to decreasing (or from decreasing to increasing). A maximum or minimum value is not a point on the graph. It is a value of the function.

Note: A further discussion of polynomial functions is presented in "More about Polynomial Functions" in Part 2 for candidates who plan to take the TExES Math 7–12.

Rational Functions

Rational functions are defined by equations of the form $f(x) = \dfrac{P(x)}{Q(x)} = \dfrac{a_n x^n + a_{n-1} x^{n-1} + \cdots + a_1 x + a_0}{b_m x^m + b_{m-1} x^{m-1} + \cdots + b_1 x + b_0}$, where $P(x)$

and $Q(x)$ are polynomials and $Q(x) \neq 0$. The domain is $\{x \in R \mid Q(x) \neq 0\}$. The range is a subset of R. When $f(x)$ is in simplified form (that is, when the numerator and denominator polynomials have no common factors), the zeros of f, if any, occur at x values for which $P(x) = 0$. If 0 is in the domain of f, the y-intercept is $f(0)$. When $f(x) = \dfrac{P(x)}{Q(x)}$ is in simplified form, the x-intercepts occur at real values for which $P(x) = 0$.

To graph $f(x) = \dfrac{P(x)}{Q(x)}$, first factor $P(x)$ and $Q(x)$ to identify possible "holes" in the graph of f. Intuitively, a **hole** is a missing point in the graph. If $P(x)$ and $Q(x)$ have a common factor, $(x - h)$, that will divide out completely from the denominator when $f(x)$ is simplified, then the graph will have a hole at $(h, f(h))$, where $f(h)$ is calculated after $f(x)$ is simplified.

Here is a practice problem.

Problem: Graph the rational function $f(x) = \dfrac{x+2}{x^2-4}$.

Solution: $f(x) = \dfrac{x+2}{x^2-4} = \dfrac{x+2}{(x+2)(x-2)}$. The common factor, $(x + 2)$, will divide out completely from the denominator. Thus, $f(x) = \dfrac{1}{x-2}$, when simplified. When $x = -2$, $f(-2) = \dfrac{1}{-2-2} = -\dfrac{1}{4}$. Therefore, the graph of f has a hole at $\left(-2, -\dfrac{1}{4}\right)$, given that the original function $f(x) = \dfrac{x+2}{x^2-4}$ is undefined when $x = -2$.

After identifying possible holes, next use the simplified form of $f(x)$ to determine asymptotes of the graph (see "Vertical and Horizontal Asymptotes" earlier in this chapter for a discussion of this topic). Because $f(x) = \dfrac{1}{x-2}$ is undefined when x is 2, the graph has a vertical asymptote at $x = 2$. The degree of the numerator of $f(x) = \dfrac{1}{x-2}$ is less than the degree of its denominator, so the x-axis is a horizontal asymptote of the graph. The graph of $f(x) = \dfrac{x+2}{x^2-4}$ is shown below.

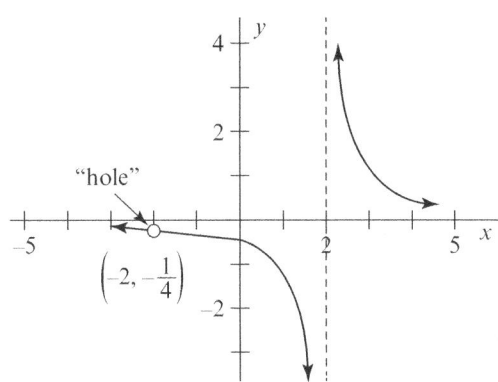

To determine the behavior of the rational function f defined by $f(x) = \dfrac{P(x)}{Q(x)} = \dfrac{a_n x^n + a_{n-1} x^{n-1} + \cdots + a_1 x + a_0}{b_m x^m + b_{m-1} x^{m-1} + \cdots + b_1 x + b_0}$, as x approaches ∞ or $-\infty$, separately factor out $a_n x^n$, the term with highest degree in the numerator, and $b_m x^m$, the term with highest degree in the denominator. Then as x approaches ∞ or $-\infty$, $f(x) = \dfrac{P(x)}{Q(x)}$ behaves as $\dfrac{a_n x^n}{b_m x^m}$ does.

Square Root Functions

Square root functions are defined by equations of the form $f(x) = \sqrt{ax+b}$. The domain is $\{x \in R \mid ax + b \geq 0\}$. The range is $\{y \in R \mid y \geq 0\}$. The graph is nonnegative with the only zero at $x = -\dfrac{b}{a}$. The following figure shows the square root function $f(x) = \sqrt{x}$.

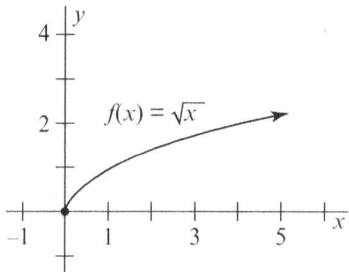

Power Functions

Power functions are defined by equations of the form $f(x) = x^a$, where a is a real number (provided that 0^0 does not occur). If a is a rational number $\frac{p}{q}$ [with p and q integers ($q \neq 0$) and $\frac{p}{q}$ simplified], then the domain is $[0, \infty)$ when q is even and is $(-\infty, \infty)$ when q is odd. If a is an irrational number, the domain is $[0, \infty)$. The range will vary depending on the value of a, and so will the zeros.

Piecewise Functions

A **piecewise function** is a function that is defined by two or more equations over a piecewise domain. Each of the equations in the definition applies to a different portion of the domain. The components of a piecewise function can have any functional form (linear, quadratic, cubic, exponential, and so on). A piecewise function can be continuous with no gaps or breaks in the graph or it can be discontinuous with gaps, breaks, and excluded points.

Here is a practice problem.

Problem: The figure below shows the graph of $f(x) = \begin{cases} \frac{1}{2}x^2 + 1, & x < 0 \\ x - 1, & x \geq 0 \end{cases}$. Evaluate the function when **(a)** $x = -2$, **(b)** $x = 0$, and **(c)** $x = 2$.

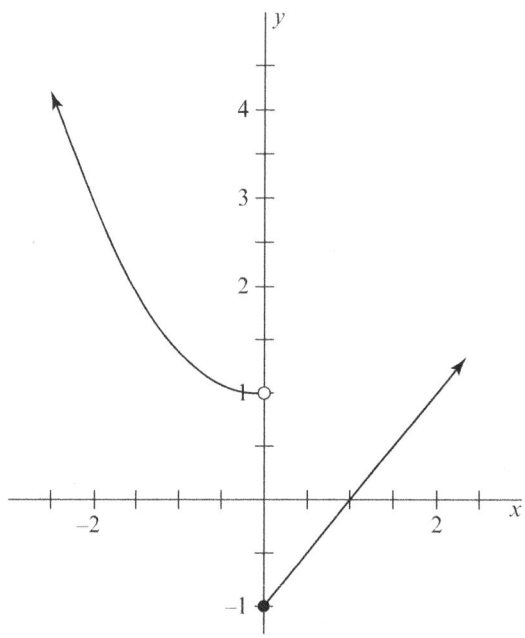

Solution:

(a) For $x = -2$, use $\frac{1}{2}x^2 + 1$ to obtain $f(-2) = \frac{1}{2}(-2)^2 + 1 = 3$.

(b) For $x = 0$, use $x - 1$ to obtain $f(0) = (0) - 1 = -1$.

(c) For $x = 2$, use $x - 1$ to obtain $f(2) = (2) - 1 = 1$.

Absolute Value Functions

Absolute value functions are defined by equations of the form $f(x) = |ax + b|$. The domain is R, and the range is $\{y \in R | y \geq 0\}$. The only zero occurs at $x = -\frac{b}{a}$, and the y-intercept is located at $|b|$. The absolute value function $f(x) = |ax + b|$ is a piecewise function because you can write it as $f(x) = \begin{cases} ax + b & \text{if } x \geq -\frac{b}{a} \\ -(ax + b) & \text{if } x < -\frac{b}{a} \end{cases}$. The following figure shows the absolute value function $f(x) = |x|$.

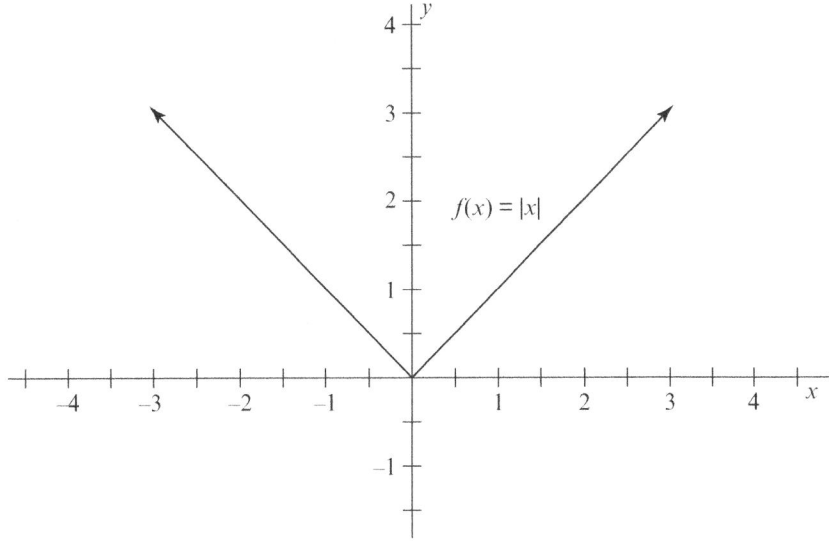

(See "Absolute Value" in Chapter 1 for the properties of absolute value.)

Greatest Integer Functions

The **greatest integer function** is a piecewise function defined by $y = f(x) = [\![x]\!]$, where the brackets denote to find the greatest integer less than or equal to x. The domain is the set R of real numbers, and the range is the set of integers. The zeros lie in the interval $[0, 1)$.

Here is an example.

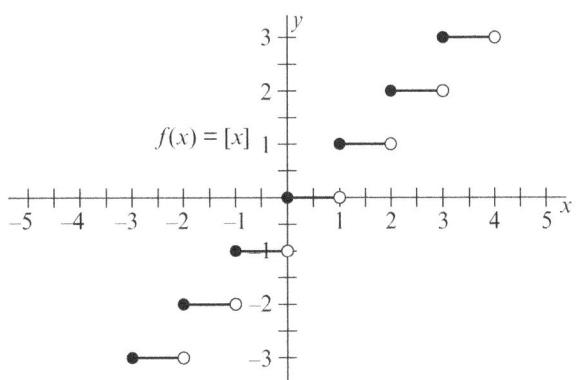

Exponential Functions

Exponential functions are defined by equations of the form $f(x) = b^x$ ($b > 0$, $b \neq 1$), where b, a constant, is the base of the exponential function. The domain is R, and the range is $(0, \infty)$, which is to say that $b^x > 0$ for every real number x. Because $f(x) = b^x = 0$ has no solution, there are no zeros.

The graph of $f(x) = b^x$ ($b > 0$, $b \neq 1$) is a smooth, continuous curve. The graph passes through the points $(0, 1)$ and $(1, b)$ and is located in the first and second quadrants only. The y-intercept is 1. The graph of the function does not cross the x-axis, so it has no x-intercepts. The x-axis is a horizontal asymptote.

If $b > 1$, the function is increasing: As x approaches ∞, $f(x) = b^x$ approaches ∞; and as x approaches $-\infty$, $f(x) = b^x$ approaches 0 (but never reaches 0). If $0 < b < 1$, the function is decreasing: As x approaches ∞, $f(x) = b^x$ approaches 0 (but never reaches 0); and as x approaches $-\infty$, $f(x) = b^x$ approaches ∞.

The following figure shows the graph of the exponential function $f(x) = 2^x$.

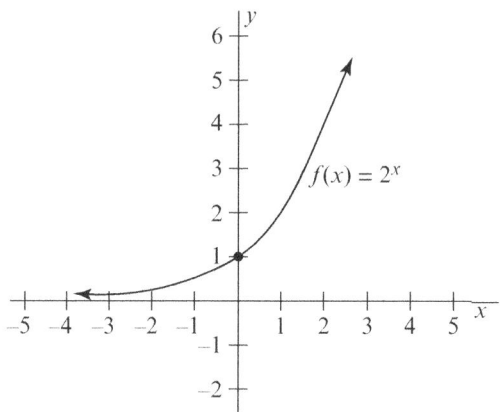

The **natural exponential function** is defined by $f(x) = e^x$, where the base e is the irrational number whose rational decimal approximation is 2.718281828 (to nine digits).

The **base-10 exponential function** is defined by $f(x) = 10^x$.

(See "Exponents" in Chapter 1 for a review of exponents.)

Tip: Do not confuse exponential functions with power functions. The exponents in exponential functions are variables, whereas the exponents in power functions are constants. For example, f(x) = 3^x defines an exponential function and g(x) = x³ defines a power function.

Logarithmic Functions

Logarithmic functions are defined by equations of the form $f(x) = \log_b x$, where $y = \log_b x$ if and only if $b^y = x$ ($b > 0$, $b \neq 1$). The constant b is the base of the logarithmic function. The domain is $(0, \infty)$ and the range is R. The function has one zero at $x = 1$.

The graph of $f(x) = \log_b x$ ($b > 0$, $b \neq 1$) is a smooth, continuous curve. The graph passes through $(1, 0)$ and $(b, 1)$ and is located in the first and fourth quadrants only. The graph of the function does not cross the y-axis, so it does not have a y-intercept. The y-axis is a vertical asymptote.

If $b > 1$, the function is increasing: As x approaches ∞, $f(x) = \log_b x$ approaches ∞; and as x approaches 0, $f(x) = \log_b x$ approaches $-\infty$. If $0 < b < 1$, the function is decreasing: As x approaches ∞, $f(x) = \log_b x$ approaches $-\infty$; and as x approaches 0, $f(x) = \log_b x$ approaches ∞.

The **natural logarithmic function** is defined by $g(x) = \log_e x$, denoted $\ln x$. The **common logarithmic function** is defined by $g(x) = \log_{10} x$, denoted $\log x$.

For a given base, the logarithmic function is the inverse of the corresponding exponential function, and the reverse is true. The logarithm function $g(x) = \log_{10} x$ (common logarithmic function) is the inverse of the exponential function $f(x) = 10^x$. The logarithm function $g(x) = \ln x$ (natural logarithmic function) is the inverse of the exponential function $f(x) = e^x$. (See "Inverses of Functions" earlier in this chapter for an explanation of inverses.)

The following figure shows the graphs of the logarithmic function defined by $g(x) = \ln x$ and its mutually inverse exponential function defined by $f(x) = e^x$.

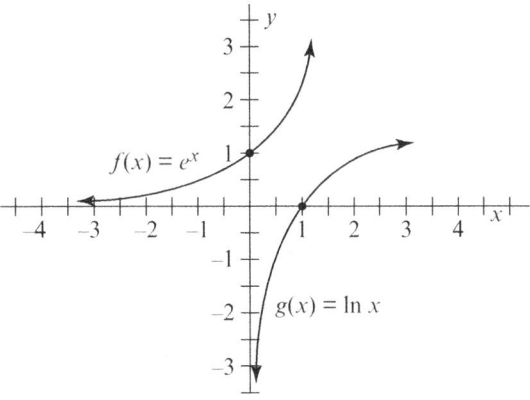

Transformations

Adding or subtracting a positive constant k to $f(x)$ is a **vertical shift**. Adding or subtracting a positive constant h to x is a **horizontal shift**. Vertical and horizontal shifts are summarized in the following table.

Vertical and Horizontal Shifts

Type of Change	Effect on $y = f(x)$
(h, k both positive)	
$y = f(x) + k$	Vertical shift: k units up
$y = f(x) - k$	Vertical shift: k units down
$y = f(x + h)$	Horizontal shift: h units to left
$y = f(x - h)$	Horizontal shift: h units to right

Multiplying $f(x)$ by $k > 1$ **stretches** the graph of f vertically. Multiplying $f(x)$ by $0 < k < 1$ compresses the graph of f vertically. The graph of $y = -f(x)$ is a **reflection** of $y = f(x)$ over the x-axis. Here are illustrations using the quadratic function $y = x^2$.

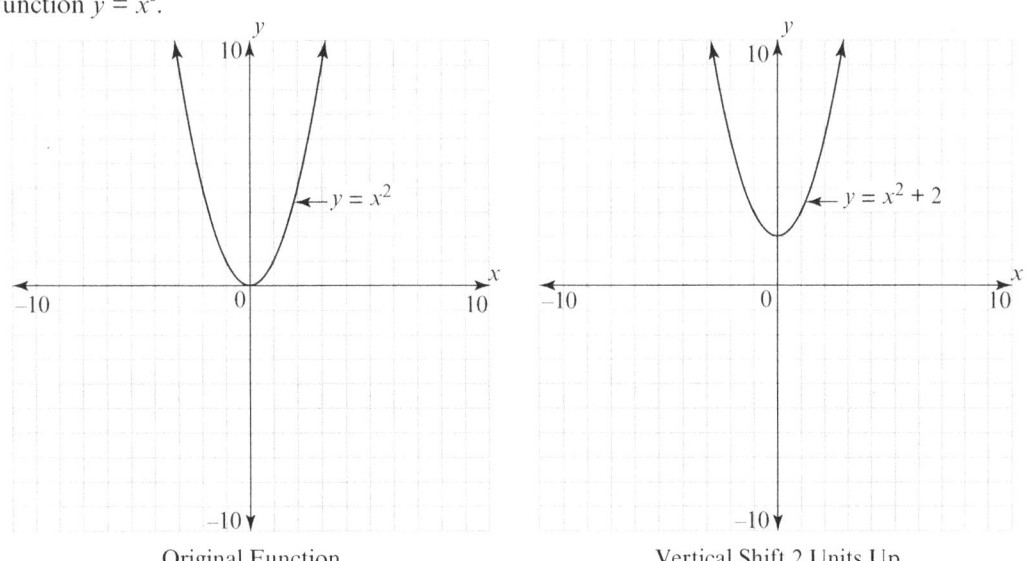

Original Function   Vertical Shift 2 Units Up

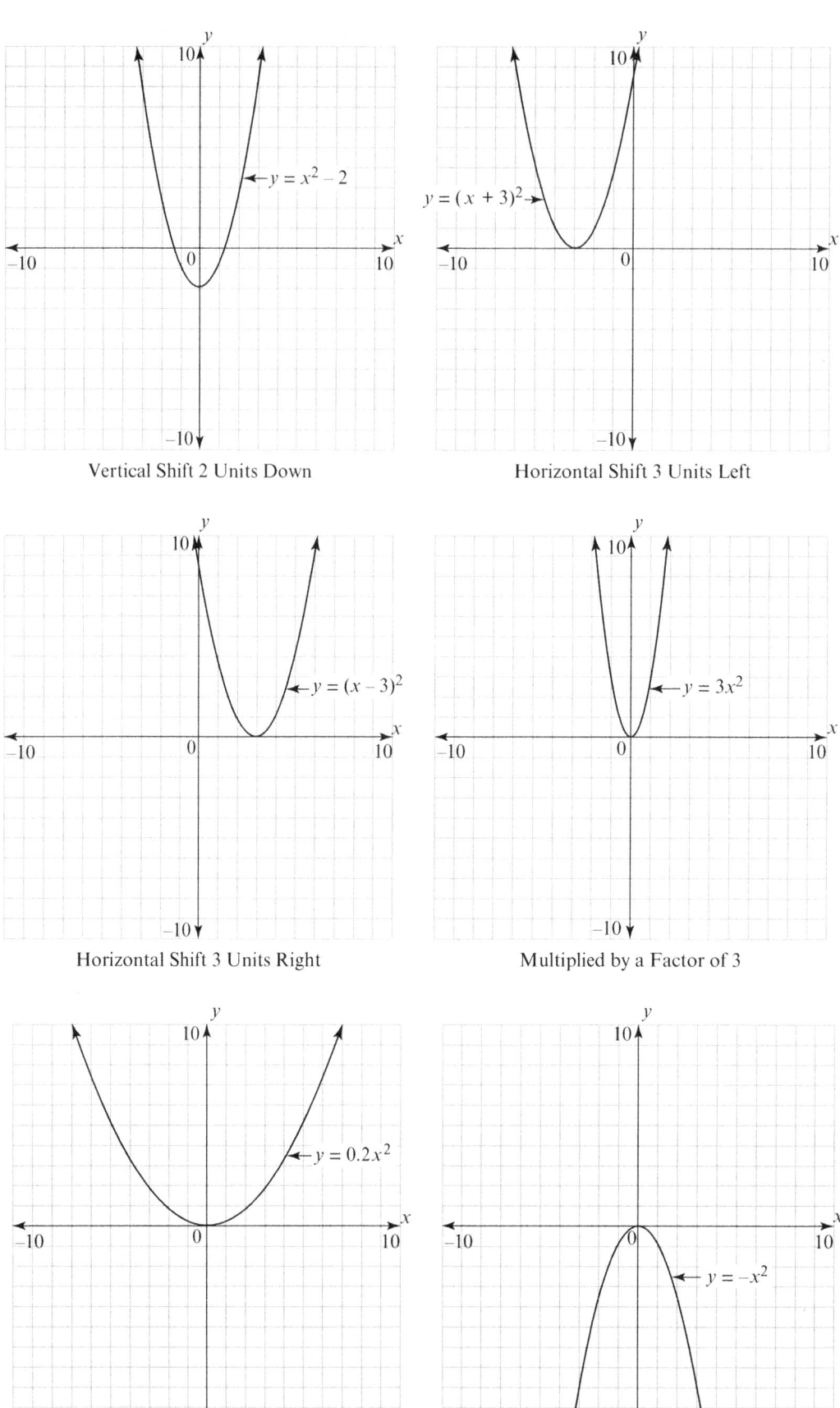

Note: For a general discussion of geometric transformations, see "Geometric Transformations" in Chapter 3.

Modeling with Functions

Families of functions (the families of linear functions, quadratic functions, step functions, exponential functions, and so on) are used to model phenomena in the real world.

Linear functions model processes in which the rate of change is constant. For example, in science a linear function can be used to model the distance a moving object travels at a constant rate of speed as a function of time or to model the volume occupied by a sample of gas at a constant pressure as a function of its absolute temperature.

Quadratic functions model processes that involve a maximum or a minimum value. For example, in business a quadratic function can be used to model the profit or revenue of a company as a function of the number of units sold.

Step functions model processes that increase or decrease in increments but remain constant over fixed intervals. For example, a step function can be used to model the cost of postage for a letter or package as a function of the weight of the letter or package.

Exponential functions model processes that grow or decline rapidly. For example, they are used to model physical phenomena such as population growth and population decay as a function of time. This family of functions is also used in business for determining the growth of money as a function of time when interest is compounded at a fixed rate.

Here are two practice problems.

Problem: A water tank that holds 1,000 gallons of water is one-fourth full. Suppose water is added to the tank at a constant rate of 150 gallons per hour. Let $f(t)$ be the amount of water (in gallons) in the tank after t hours.

(a) What is the rate of change of the function f?

(b) What is the amount of water in the tank at time $t = 0$?

(c) Write a formula for $f(t)$.

(d) At what time, t, will the water tank be filled to capacity?

Solution:

(a) The amount of water in the tank changes at a constant rate of 150 gallons per hour. Thus, the rate of change of f is 150 gallons per 1 hour of time.

(b) At time $t = 0$, the initial amount of water in the tank is $\frac{1}{4}(1{,}000 \text{ gallons}) = 250$ gallons.

(c) The amount of water in the tank after t hours is $\left(150\,\frac{\text{gallons}}{\text{hour}}\right)t + 250$ gallons. Thus, omitting units, $f(t) = 150t + 250$, a linear function.

(d) Find t when $f(t) = 1{,}000$.

$$1{,}000 = 150t + 250$$
$$750 = 150t$$
$$5 = t$$

The water tank is filled to capacity at time $t = 5$ hours.

Problem: A homeowner has 100 feet of fencing to enclose a rectangular region for a small garden. The homeowner will use a portion of the side of a large shed as one side of the rectangular region, as shown in the following figure.

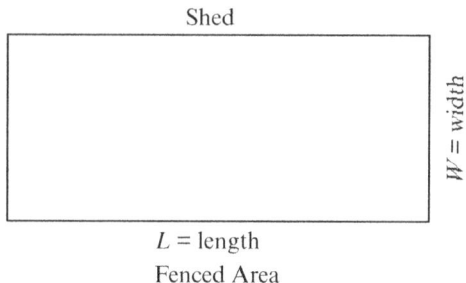

Let $f(W)$ be the area of the rectangular region expressed in terms of its width, W.
(a) Write a formula for $f(W)$.
(b) Find the dimensions of the rectangular region that give the maximum area for the garden.

Solution:

(a) Let W = the width (in feet) and L = the length (in feet) of the rectangular region. The fence does not go along the shed, so (omitting units) $100 = 2W + L$, which implies that $L = 100 - 2W$. The area of the rectangular region equals length times width. Thus, $f(W) = (100 - 2W)W = 100W - 2W^2 = -2W^2 + 100W$, a quadratic function.

(b) The graph of $f(W)$ is a parabola opening downward. The vertex formula is $\left(-\frac{b}{2a}, f\left(-\frac{b}{2a}\right)\right)$, so the maximum value for $f(W)$ occurs when $W = -\frac{b}{2a} = -\frac{100}{2(-2)} = 25$. The corresponding value of $L = 100 - 2W = 100 - 2 \cdot 25 = 100 - 50 = 50$. The dimensions that maximize the area are 50 feet by 25 feet.

Sequences

A **sequence** is a function whose domain is a subset of the integers, usually the natural numbers $N = \{1, 2, 3, ...\}$ or the whole numbers $W = \{0, 1, 2, ...\}$. (For this section, sequences are restricted, without loss of generality, to domains equal to N.) The notation a_n denotes the image of the integer n; that is, a_n is the **nth term** (or **element**) of the sequence. The **initial term** (or first term) of the sequence is denoted a_1. When a_n can be expressed as a formula that you can use to generate any term of the sequence, it is conventional to call a_n the **general term** of the sequence. Even though a sequence is a function (a set of ordered pairs), it is customary to describe a sequence by listing the terms in the order in which they correspond to the natural numbers. For example, the list of terms of the sequence with initial term a_1 is $a_1, a_2, a_3, a_4, ..., a_n, ...$.

Note: The three dots (...) indicate that the sequence continues in the same manner.

Tip: Sequences are discrete functions, so the points on their graphs are not connected.

Arithmetic Sequences

In an **arithmetic sequence,** the same number, called the **common difference,** is added (algebraically) to each term to obtain the subsequent term in the sequence. An arithmetic sequence (also called arithmetic progression) has the form $a_1, a_1 + d, a_1 + 2d, ..., a_1 + (n-1)d, ...$, where a_1 is the initial term, d is the common difference between terms, and $a_n = a_1 + (n-1)d$ is the general term.

Here is a practice problem.

Problem: What is the 50th term in the arithmetic sequence $-2, 2, 6, 10, 14, ...$?

Solution: The first term a_1 is -2. The common difference is 4. The general term is $a_n = a_1 + (n-1)d = -2 + (n-1)(4)$. Thus, the 50th term is $a_{50} = -2 + (50-1)(4) = -2 + (49)(4) = -2 + 196 = 194$.

Geometric Sequences

In a **geometric sequence,** each term is multiplied by the same number, called the **common ratio,** to obtain the subsequent term in the sequence. A geometric sequence (also called geometric progression) has the form $a_1, a_1 r, a_1 r^2, ..., a_1 r^{n-1}, ...$, where a_1 is the initial term, r is the common ratio between terms, and $a_n = a_1 r^{n-1}$ is the general term.

Here is a practice problem.

> Problem: What is the 9th term in the geometric sequence $-1, -2, -4, -8, -16, ...$?
>
> Solution: The first term a_1 is -1. The common ratio is 2. The general term is $a_n = a_1 r^{n-1} = (-1)2^{n-1}$. Thus, the 9th term is $a_9 = (-1)2^{9-1} = (-1)2^8 = (-1)(256) = -256$.
>
> Of course, you could have worked this problem by continuing to multiply by 2 until you reached the 9th term, as shown here.
>
> $$-1, -2, -4, -8, -16, -32, -64, -128, -256$$
> 1st 2nd 3rd 4th 5th 6th 7th 8th 9th

Tip: If you use this latter approach, count the terms to be sure you have the correct term.

Figurate-Number Sequences

Some sequences consist of numbers called **figurate numbers,** so called because they can be displayed as geometric shapes. Here is an example of a sequence of **triangular numbers** with their corresponding geometric shapes. The nth term is $\frac{n(n+1)}{2}$.

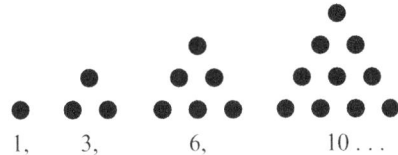

1, 3, 6, 10 . . .

Here is an example of a sequence of **square numbers** with their corresponding geometric shapes. The nth term is n^2.

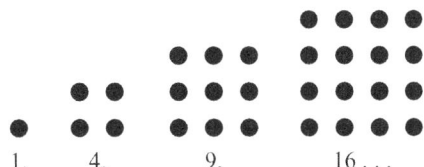

1, 4, 9, 16 . . .

Recursive Sequences

A **recursive sequence** is one whose terms are obtained by means of a recursive definition. A **recursive definition** for a sequence is a definition that includes the value of one or more initial terms of the sequence and a formula that tells you how to find each term from previous terms.

Here is a practice problem.

> Problem: List the first four terms of the sequence defined as follows: $f(1) = 1, f(n) = 3f(n-1) + 1$ for $n \geq 2$.

Solution: For the recursive formula given in the problem, you will need to find the previous term before you can find the next term. Proceed as shown here.

$f(1) = 1$

$f(2) = 3f(1) + 1 = 3(1) + 1 = 3 + 1 = 4$

$f(3) = 3f(2) + 1 = 3(4) + 1 = 12 + 1 = 13$

$f(4) = 3f(3) + 1 = 3(13) + 1 = 39 + 1 = 40$

Thus, the first four terms are 1, 4, 13, and 40.

A **Fibonacci sequence** is defined by the recursive definition: $a_1 = 1$, $a_2 = 1$, and $a_n = a_{n-1} + a_{n-2}$, $n \geq 3$. A list showing the first seven terms is 1, 1, 2, 3, 5, 8, 13, ...

Identifying Patterns for Sequences

For your TExES Math exam, you might be asked to determine the general term or the next term of a sequence when a few terms of the sequence are given.

Look for an identifiable model such as one of the following:

Polynomial: Use the method of **finite differences** to determine whether the terms of the sequence fit a polynomial model. Take differences of consecutive terms. Continue to take differences of the resulting differences, as needed. Only if the process eventually results in nonzero equal differences do the terms of the sequence fit a polynomial model, and the number of differences indicates the degree of the polynomial. If the first differences are equal, the polynomial model is linear; if the second differences are equal, the polynomial model is quadratic; if the third differences are equal, the polynomial model is cubic; and so on.

Here is a practice problem.

> Problem: Write a formula for the nth term of the sequence 1, 3, 6, 10, 15, 21, ...
>
> Solution: Using the method of finite differences yields

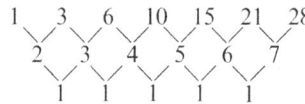

The second differences are equal, so the general term is quadratic. Let $f(n) = an^2 + bn + c$ be the polynomial model. Then using 1, 3, and 6, the first three terms of the sequence, as the outputs of $f(n)$ for $n = 1, 2$, and 3, respectively, you obtain the following system of three linear equations in three variables:

$a(1)^2 + b(1) + c = a + b + c = 1$; $a(2)^2 + b(2) + c = 4a + 2b + c = 3$; and $a(3)^2 + b(3) + c = 9a + 3b + c = 6$

Solving this system yields $a = \frac{1}{2}$, $b = \frac{1}{2}$, and $c = 0$. Thus, $f(n) = \frac{1}{2}n^2 + \frac{1}{2}n = \frac{1}{2}(n^2 + n)$. Therefore, the formula for the nth term is $\frac{1}{2}(n^2 + n) = \frac{n(n+1)}{2}$.

The method of finite differences applies only for polynomial models. Here are suggestions for identifying other models.

> **Geometric or Exponential:** Starting with the second term, divide each term by the previous term to check for a common ratio.
>
> **Factorial:** $n!$ Check whether each term is obtained by finding the product of all the previous terms.
>
> **Recursive:** $a_n = a_{n-1} \pm a_{n-2}$ Check whether the terms are obtained by adding or subtracting previous terms in some way.

Arithmetic and Geometric Series

Given a finite number of terms of a sequence, $a_1, a_2, a_3, a_4, \ldots, a_n$, the sum of the terms $s_n = a_1 + a_2 + a_3 + a_4 + \ldots + a_n$ is a **finite series**. You can write this sum using the **sigma (summation) notation** as $s_n = \sum_{k=1}^{n} a_k$, where k is the **summing index**. Some useful properties of sigma notation are the following:

$$\sum_{k=1}^{n} c = nc$$

$$\sum_{k=1}^{n} (a_k \pm b_k) = \sum_{k=1}^{n} a_k \pm \sum_{k=1}^{n} b_k$$

$$\sum_{k=1}^{n} ca_k = c \sum_{k=1}^{n} a_k$$

$$\sum_{k=1}^{n} a_k = \sum_{k=1}^{m} a_k + \sum_{k=m+1}^{n} a_k, \text{ where } 1 \le m \le n$$

$$\sum_{k=1}^{n} a_k = a_1 + a_2 + \sum_{k=3}^{n-1} a_k + a_n$$

Here is a practice problem.

    Problem: Expand and then sum: $\sum_{k=1}^{4} (5k - 3)$.

    Solution: $\sum_{k=1}^{4} (5k - 3) = (5 \cdot 1 - 3) + (5 \cdot 2 - 3) + (5 \cdot 3 - 3) + (5 \cdot 4 - 3) = 2 + 7 + 12 + 17 = 38$

The sum of a finite arithmetic series is given by $s_n = a_1 + a_2 + \ldots + a_n = \sum_{k=1}^{n} a_k = \dfrac{n(a_1 + a_n)}{2}$.

The sum of a finite geometric series is given by $s_n = a_1 + a_1 r + \ldots + a_1 r^{n-1} = \sum_{k=1}^{n} a_1 r^{k-1} = \dfrac{a_1 - a_1 r^n}{1 - r} = \dfrac{a_1(1 - r^n)}{1 - r}$, provided $r \ne 1$. If $r = 1$, then $s_n = na_1$.

Here is a practice problem.

    Problem: Find the sum of the first 60 positive odd numbers.

    Solution: The odd numbers are an arithmetic sequence with general term $a_n = 2n - 1$. Therefore, $s_{60} = 1 + 3 + 5 + \ldots + 119 = \dfrac{n(a_1 + a_n)}{2} = \dfrac{60(a_1 + a_{60})}{2} = \dfrac{60(1 + 119)}{2} = 3,600$.

If $|r| < 1$, then the sum of the infinite geometric series $a_1 + a_1 r + \ldots + a_1 r^{n-1} + \ldots$ is given by $S = \dfrac{a_1}{1 - r}$.

Here is a practice problem.

    Problem: Find the sum of the infinite geometric series $4 + 2 + 1 + \dfrac{1}{2} + \cdots$, if possible.

    Solution: The first term $a_1 = 4$ and the common ratio $r = \dfrac{1}{2}$. Because $|r| < 1$, $4 + 2 + 1 + \dfrac{1}{2} + \cdots = S = \dfrac{a_1}{1 - r} = \dfrac{4}{1 - \dfrac{1}{2}} = \dfrac{4}{\dfrac{1}{2}} = 8$.

If $|r| \ge 1$, then the infinite geometric series $a_1 + a_1 r + \ldots + a_1 r^{n-1} + \ldots$ does not have a sum.

Introductory Right Triangle Trigonometric Concepts

For this topic, you must be able to define and use the six basic trigonometric ratios using the degree measure of angles and to know the trigonometric ratios of two special acute triangles. *Note:* A general discussion of trigonometric concepts is presented in "Trigonometry" in Part 2 for candidates who plan to take the TExES Math 7–12.

Right Triangle Ratios

To define the six **basic trigonometric ratios,** begin with a right triangle ABC and label its six parts as follows:

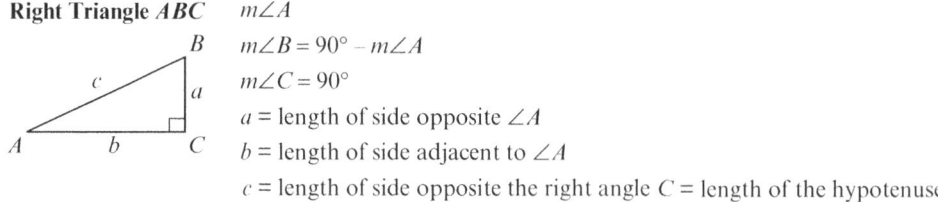

Right Triangle ABC

$m\angle A$
$m\angle B = 90° - m\angle A$
$m\angle C = 90°$
a = length of side opposite $\angle A$
b = length of side adjacent to $\angle A$
c = length of side opposite the right angle C = length of the hypotenuse

Note: In the above figure, $m\angle X$ denotes "the measure of angle X."

The ratios relative to angle A in the right triangle ABC are as follows:

sine of $\angle A = \sin A = \dfrac{\text{side opposite}}{\text{hypotenuse}} = \dfrac{a}{c}$ 　　　**cosecant** of $\angle A = \csc A = \dfrac{\text{hypotenuse}}{\text{side opposite}} = \dfrac{c}{a}$

cosine of $\angle A = \cos A = \dfrac{\text{side adjacent}}{\text{hypotenuse}} = \dfrac{b}{c}$ 　　　**secant** of $\angle A = \sec A = \dfrac{\text{hypotenuse}}{\text{side adjacent}} = \dfrac{c}{b}$

tangent of $\angle A = \tan A = \dfrac{\text{side opposite}}{\text{side adjacent}} = \dfrac{a}{b}$ 　　　**cotangent** of $\angle A = \cot A = \dfrac{\text{side adjacent}}{\text{side opposite}} = \dfrac{b}{a}$

Note: The designations "side opposite," "side adjacent," and "hypotenuse" refer to the length of the side opposite an angle, the length of the side adjacent to an angle, and the length of the hypotenuse, respectively.

Tip: The mnemonic SOH-CAH-TOA (soh-kuh-toh-uh) can help you remember that S (sine) is O (opposite) over H (hypotenuse), that C (cosine) is A (adjacent) over H (hypotenuse), and T (tangent) is O (opposite) over A (adjacent).

It is customary to use the abbreviated names of the ratios. Also, instead of using the angle notation $\angle A$ to denote an angle, you can just use a capital letter by itself (e.g., A, B, or C), a lowercase variable name (e.g., x, y, or t), or a letter from the Greek alphabet [e.g., α (alpha), β (beta), γ (gamma), θ (theta), or φ (phi)] to represent angles. In the same vein, it is convenient to write, for example, $A = 60°$ instead of $m\angle A = 60°$ when no confusion can occur.

Here is a practice problem.

Problem: Find the six trigonometric ratios for angle A in the right triangle ABC shown below.

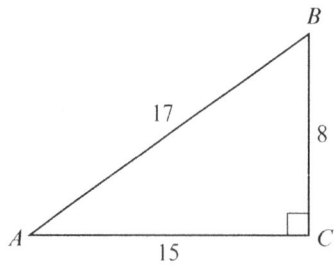

Solution:

$$\sin A = \frac{\text{opposite}}{\text{hypotenuse}} = \frac{8}{17} \qquad \cos A = \frac{\text{adjacent}}{\text{hypotenuse}} = \frac{15}{17} \qquad \tan A = \frac{\text{opposite}}{\text{adjacent}} = \frac{8}{15}$$

$$\csc A = \frac{\text{hypotenuse}}{\text{opposite}} = \frac{17}{8} \qquad \sec A = \frac{\text{hypotenuse}}{\text{adjacent}} = \frac{17}{15} \qquad \cot A = \frac{\text{adjacent}}{\text{opposite}} = \frac{15}{8}$$

Tip: The values of the trigonometric ratios have no units, so they are pure numbers.

From the definitions of the trigonometric ratios, you can see that sine and cosecant are reciprocals of each other, that cosine and secant are reciprocals of each other, and that tangent and cotangent are reciprocals of each other. Therefore, it is necessary to remember only the sine, cosine, and tangent ratios because the other ratios can be determined by using the reciprocal relationships. *Note:* Because of the reciprocal relationships of trigonometric ratios, for practical reasons most real-world applications employ the more frequently used sine, cosine, and tangent ratios.

Trigonometric Ratios of Special Acute Angles

Two special right triangles of trigonometry that are useful to know are the **30°-60°-90° right triangle** and the **45°-45°-90° right triangle** shown here.

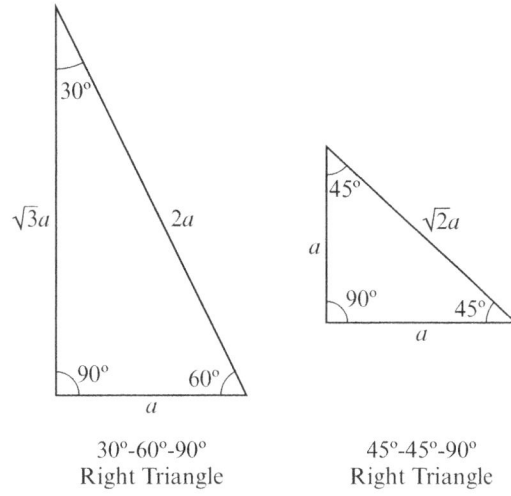

30°-60°-90° Right Triangle   45°-45°-90° Right Triangle

Note: a is a nonzero factor.

The trigonometric ratios associated with these triangles are given in the following table.

Special Trigonometric Ratios

Angle	Sine	Cosine	Tangent
30°	$\frac{1}{2}$	$\frac{\sqrt{3}}{2}$	$\frac{1}{\sqrt{3}} = \frac{\sqrt{3}}{3}$
45°	$\frac{1}{\sqrt{2}} = \frac{\sqrt{2}}{2}$	$\frac{1}{\sqrt{2}} = \frac{\sqrt{2}}{2}$	1
60°	$\frac{\sqrt{3}}{2}$	$\frac{1}{2}$	$\sqrt{3}$

Rather than trying to memorize this table, it is better to remember the triangles and how the ratios are defined. All triangles similar to these two have the same ratio values.

Here is a practice problem.

Problem: Given $C = 90°$, $A = 60°$, and $b = 5$, find a and c for the triangle shown.

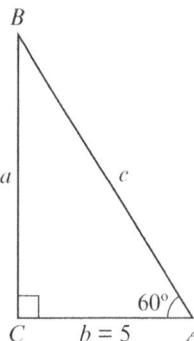

Solution: Given $A = 60°$, then $B = 90° - 60° = 30°$. Hence, the triangle is a 30°-60°-90° right triangle. Therefore, $\cos A = \dfrac{5}{c} = \dfrac{1}{2}$, which yields $c = 10$. Also, $\sin A = \dfrac{a}{c} = \dfrac{a}{10} = \dfrac{\sqrt{3}}{2}$, which yields $a = 5\sqrt{3}$.

Tip: Angle measurements can also be expressed in **radians.** In the radian system of angular measurement, $360° = 2\pi$ radians. Thus, $1° = \dfrac{\pi}{180}$ radians and 1 radian $= \dfrac{180}{\pi}°$.

Three Central Calculus Concepts

For this topic, you must demonstrate an understanding of the three central calculus concepts of limit, derivative, and integral. *Note:* A fuller discussion of calculus concepts is presented in "Calculus" in Part 2 for candidates who plan to take the TExES Math 7–12.

Limits

Limits are a fundamental part of calculus. Intuitively, finding the limit of a function *f* means determining what value $f(x)$ approaches as x gets closer and closer to a certain value. For example, finding the limit of the function $f(x) = 5x + 2$ as x gets near to 0 means finding the number, if any, that $f(x) = 5x + 2$ approaches as x gets closer and closer to 0. The limit process lets you zoom in on the number if it exists. In the case of $f(x) = 5x + 2$, you might reasonably predict that as x get closer and closer to 0, then $5x$ also gets closer and closer to 0, so $5x + 2$ gets closer and closer to 2.

The concept of limit is necessary in calculus, both as a stand-alone idea and as the basis for defining the two other central calculus concepts of derivative and integral.

Derivatives

Derivatives allow you to find the instantaneous rate of change of linear and nonlinear functions. For a linear function, the slope of its graph tells you the rate of change, which is constant over the function's domain. Derivatives provide a means for finding the instantaneous rate of change at a point on a nonlinear function's graph. In other words, you can use the concept of derivative to find the slope of a tangent line at a point on a nonlinear function's graph. Thus, you can track the function's rate of change as you move along its graph.

Integrals

The simplest way to describe an integral is to say that it is used to compute the area under a curve or between two curves. It can also be used to compute the volume of three-dimensional figures, accrued production, accumulated distance, the total of a continuous progression, and the results of other limiting sum processes.

Another useful feature of integrals is that you can undo a derivative with integration (and vice versa). They are reverse processes of each other.

Part 2

Part 2 of this chapter is for candidates who plan to take the TExES Math 7–12. This review material goes beyond the standards for the TExES Math 4–8.

Solving General Exponential Equations

An **exponential equation** is one in which the variable appears in an exponent. For example, $5^{2x-1} = 125$ and $2^x = 20$ are exponential equations. In some cases, you can solve simple exponential equations such as $5^{2x-1} = 125$ by equating exponents of like bases, as shown in "Solving Simple Exponential Equations" in Part 1 of this chapter. However, solving $2^x = 20$ requires the use of logarithms because 2 and 20 are not integral powers of the same base.

In general, to solve an exponential equation, use the following procedure:

1. Isolate the exponential term.
2. Take the natural log (base e) or the common log (base 10) of both sides of the equation.
3. Use $\ln b^x = x \ln b$ (or $\log b^x = x \log b$) to simplify the logarithmic term.
4. Solve the resulting equation for the variable, using the ln key (or the log key) on your calculator to approximate the solution.

Tip: The solution is the same whether you use the natural log or the common log to transform the equation to logarithmic form.

Here is a practice problem.

Problem: Solve $2^x = 20$ (round to the nearest tenth).
Solution:
$$2^x = 20$$
$$\ln(2^x) = \ln(20)$$
$$x \ln 2 = \ln 20$$
$$x = \frac{\ln 20}{\ln 2}$$
$$x \approx 4.3$$

Note: See "Exponents" in Chapter 1 for a review of exponents.

Solving General Logarithmic Equations

A **logarithmic equation** is one in which the variable appears in a logarithm. For example, $\log_{10}(x) = -2$ and $\log_5(x) + \log_5(10) = 4$ are logarithmic equations. In some cases, you can solve simple logarithmic equations such as $\log_{10}(x) = -2$ by writing the logarithmic equation in exponential form and evaluating to determine the value of the variable, as shown in "Solving Simple Logarithmic Equations" in Part 1 of this chapter. However, solving $\log_5(x) + \log_5(10) = 4$ is more complicated.

In general, to solve a logarithmic equation, use the following procedure:

1. If needed, use the rules for logarithms (shown below) to create one logarithmic term.
2. Isolate the logarithmic term.
3. Write the logarithmic equation in exponential form.
4. Solve the resulting equation for the variable.

Here is a practice problem.

Problem: Solve $\log_5(x) + \log_5(10) = 4$.
Solution:

$$\log_5(x) + \log_5(10) = 4$$
$$\log_5(10x) = 4, \text{ which implies}$$
$$10x = 5^4$$
$$10x = 625$$
$$x = 62.5$$

The following rules for logarithms are based on the rules for exponents.

Rules for Logarithms

Rule	Example
$\log_b 1 = 0$	$\log_2(1) = 0$
$\log_b b = 1$	$\log_5(5) = 1$
$\log_b b^x = x$	$\log_2 2^5 = 5$
$\log_b\left(\dfrac{1}{x}\right) = -\log_b x$ (reciprocal rule)	$\log_2\left(\dfrac{1}{8}\right) = -\log_2(8) = -3$
$\log_b(uv) = \log_b u + \log_b v$ (product rule)	$\log_2(8 \cdot 16) = \log_2(8) + \log_2(16) = 3 + 4 = 7$
$\log_b\left(\dfrac{u}{v}\right) = \log_b u - \log_b v$ (quotient rule)	$\log_3\left(\dfrac{243}{27}\right) = \log_3(243) - \log_3(27) = 5 - 3 = 2$
$\log_b(x^p) = p\log_b x$ (power rule)	$\log_2(8^{12}) = 12\log_2(8) = 12 \cdot 3 = 36$
Change-of-base formula: $\log_b x = \dfrac{\log_a x}{\log_a b} = \dfrac{\ln x}{\ln b} = \dfrac{\log_{10} x}{\log_{10} b}$ $(a > 0, a \neq 1)$	$\log_5 600 = \dfrac{\ln 600}{\ln 5} \approx 3.97;\ \log_2 100 = \dfrac{\log_{10} 100}{\log_{10} 2} \approx 6.64$
If $\log_b x = \log_b k$, then $x = k$ (one-to-one property)	$\ln x = \ln 7$ implies $x = 7$

Matrix Solutions of Systems of Linear Equations

For this topic, you use matrix techniques to solve systems of linear equations.

A **system** of three linear equations with three variables, x, y, and z, is given by $\begin{array}{l} a_{11}x + a_{12}y + a_{13}z = c_1 \\ a_{21}x + a_{22}y + a_{23}z = c_2 \\ a_{31}x + a_{32}y + a_{33}z = c_3 \end{array}$, where the coefficients a_{ij} and c_i are constants.

This system can be solved using the algebraic methods of substitution and elimination (which are presented in "Systems of Equations and Inequalities" in Part 1 of this chapter), or the system can be solved using a technique called **transformation of the augmented matrix,** which will be presented in this section. The system is said to be **consistent** if it has a solution; otherwise, the system is **inconsistent.**

The augmented matrix for the system is the matrix $\begin{bmatrix} a_{11} & a_{12} & a_{13} & c_1 \\ a_{21} & a_{22} & a_{23} & c_2 \\ a_{31} & a_{32} & a_{33} & c_3 \end{bmatrix}$.

To solve the system, employ, as needed, the following **elementary row operations** to transform the submatrix of coefficients a_{ij} as close as possible into the identity matrix:

Interchange two rows (for example, interchange row 1 and row 2, abbreviated R1 ↔ R2).

Multiply a row by a nonzero scalar (for example, multiply row 2 by $\frac{1}{5}$, abbreviated R2 → $\frac{1}{5}$R2).

Multiply a row by a nonzero scalar, and add the result to another row (for example, multiply row 1 by –2 and add the result to row 3, abbreviated R3 → –2R1 + R3).

When the system is consistent, the results will be one of the following reduced row-echelon forms:

$\begin{bmatrix} 1 & 0 & 0 & x_0 \\ 0 & 1 & 0 & y_0 \\ 0 & 0 & 1 & z_0 \end{bmatrix}$, which yields the unique solution $x = x_0$, $y = y_0$, $z = z_0$;

$\begin{bmatrix} 1 & 0 & k_1 & x_0 \\ 0 & 1 & k_2 & y_0 \\ 0 & 0 & 0 & 0 \end{bmatrix}$, which yields the nonunique solution $x = x_0 - k_1 t$, $y = y_0 - k_2 t$, $z = t$, where t is an arbitrarily chosen value for the "free" variable z; or

$\begin{bmatrix} 1 & j_1 & k_1 & x_0 \\ 0 & 0 & 0 & 0 \\ 0 & 0 & 0 & 0 \end{bmatrix}$, which yields the nonunique solution $x = x_0 - j_1 s - k_1 t$, $y = s$, $z = t$, where s and t are arbitrarily chosen values for the free variables y and z.

Here is a practice problem.

Problem: Solve the system: $\begin{aligned} x - 2y + 3z &= 1 \\ x + 3y - z &= 4 \\ 2x + y - 2z &= 13 \end{aligned}$.

Solution: The augmented matrix for the system is the matrix $\begin{bmatrix} 1 & -2 & 3 & 1 \\ 1 & 3 & -1 & 4 \\ 2 & 1 & -2 & 13 \end{bmatrix}$. Proceed with elementary row operations.

$\begin{bmatrix} 1 & -2 & 3 & 1 \\ 1 & 3 & -1 & 4 \\ 2 & 1 & -2 & 13 \end{bmatrix} \xrightarrow{R2 \to -1R1 + R2} \begin{bmatrix} 1 & -2 & 3 & 1 \\ 0 & 5 & -4 & 3 \\ 2 & 1 & -2 & 13 \end{bmatrix} \xrightarrow{R3 \to -2R1 + R3} \begin{bmatrix} 1 & -2 & 3 & 1 \\ 0 & 5 & -4 & 3 \\ 0 & 5 & -8 & 11 \end{bmatrix}$

$\xrightarrow{R2 \to \frac{1}{5}R2} \begin{bmatrix} 1 & -2 & 3 & 1 \\ 0 & 1 & -0.8 & 0.6 \\ 0 & 5 & -8 & 11 \end{bmatrix} \xrightarrow{R1 \to 2R2 + R1} \begin{bmatrix} 1 & 0 & 1.4 & 2.2 \\ 0 & 1 & -0.8 & 0.6 \\ 0 & 5 & -8 & 11 \end{bmatrix} \xrightarrow{R3 \to -5R2 + R3} \begin{bmatrix} 1 & 0 & 1.4 & 2.2 \\ 0 & 1 & -0.8 & 0.6 \\ 0 & 0 & -4 & 8 \end{bmatrix}$

$\xrightarrow{R3 \to -\frac{1}{4}R3} \begin{bmatrix} 1 & 0 & 1.4 & 2.2 \\ 0 & 1 & -0.8 & 0.6 \\ 0 & 0 & 1 & -2 \end{bmatrix} \xrightarrow{R1 \to -1.4R3 + R1} \begin{bmatrix} 1 & 0 & 0 & 5 \\ 0 & 1 & -0.8 & 0.6 \\ 0 & 0 & 1 & -2 \end{bmatrix} \xrightarrow{R2 \to 0.8R3 + R2} \begin{bmatrix} 1 & 0 & 0 & 5 \\ 0 & 1 & 0 & -1 \\ 0 & 0 & 1 & -2 \end{bmatrix}$

Thus, the solution is $x = 5$, $y = -1$, $z = -2$.

The technique of solving a system of linear equations by transformation of the augmented matrix can be applied to a system of n equations with n variables such as

$$\begin{aligned} a_{11}x_1 + a_{12}x_2 + \cdots + a_{1n}x_n &= c_1 \\ a_{21}x_1 + a_{22}x_2 + \cdots + a_{2n}x_n &= c_2 \\ \cdots \quad \cdots \quad \cdots \quad \cdots \quad \cdots & \\ a_{n1}x_1 + a_{n2}x_2 + \cdots + a_{nn}x_n &= c_n \end{aligned}.$$

You would proceed in the same manner as shown for systems with three equations and three variables.

Tip: Your TI calculator has matrix features that you can use to solve systems of linear equations. Refer to the calculator guidebook for instructions or search for relevant online videos.

More about Asymptotes

Recall from "Vertical and Horizontal Asymptotes" earlier in this chapter that an **asymptote** of the graph of a function f is a line to which the graph gets closer and closer in at least one direction along the line. The vertical line $x = a$ is a **vertical asymptote** of the graph of a function f if, as x draws close to a from the left or right, the graph goes toward either $-\infty$ or ∞. A horizontal line $y = b$ is a **horizontal asymptote** of the graph of f if $f(x)$ approaches b as x approaches either $-\infty$ or ∞.

A line $y = g(x)$ is an **oblique asymptote** (or slant asymptote) of a function f if the graph of the function approaches $y = g(x)$ as x approaches either ∞ or $-\infty$. See the following figure that shows an oblique asymptote (along with a vertical asymptote).

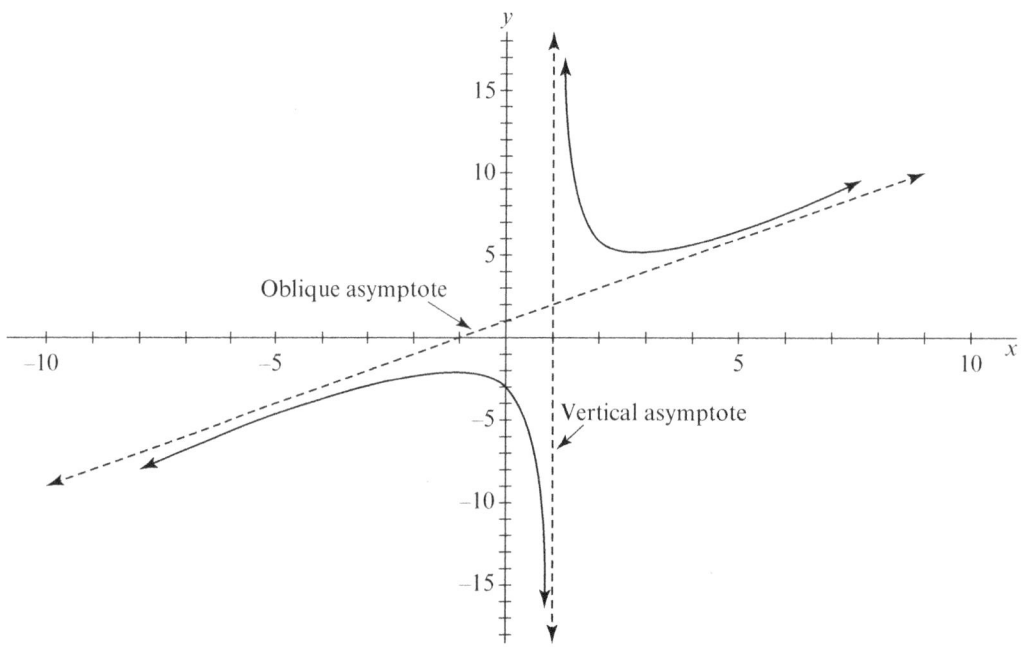

Oblique and Vertical Asymptotes

You find horizontal asymptotes by determining the value that $y = f(x)$ approaches as x approaches either ∞ or $-\infty$ (again, provided the rational function is in simplified form and the degree of $q(x)$ is at least 1).

A rational function will have at most one horizontal asymptote. The following guidelines will help you identify a horizontal asymptote of a rational function defined by $f(x) = \dfrac{P(x)}{Q(x)}$, where $f(x)$ is in simplified form and the degree of $Q(x)$ is at least 1:

- If the degree of $P(x)$ is less than the degree of $Q(x)$, then the x-axis ($y = 0$) is a horizontal asymptote.

Here is a practice problem.
Problem: Describe the horizontal asymptote, if any, of $f(x) = \dfrac{1}{x-3}$.

Solution: For $f(x) = \dfrac{1}{x-3}$, which is in simplified form, the degree of the numerator polynomial is less than the degree of the denominator polynomial, so the x-axis is a horizontal asymptote.

- If the degree of $P(x)$ equals the degree of $Q(x)$, then the graph will have a horizontal asymptote at $y = \dfrac{a_n}{b_m}$, where a_n is the leading coefficient of $P(x)$ and b_m is the leading coefficient of $Q(x)$.

Here is a practice problem.
Problem: Describe the horizontal asymptote, if any, of $g(x) = \dfrac{3x^2 - 4}{4x^2 + 1}$, and then graph the function.

Solution: For $g(x) = \dfrac{3x^2 - 4}{4x^2 + 1}$, which is in simplified form, the degree of the numerator polynomial equals the degree of the denominator polynomial, so $y = \dfrac{3}{4}$ is a horizontal asymptote. The graph is shown below with a dashed horizontal line at $y = \dfrac{3}{4}$, the horizontal asymptote.

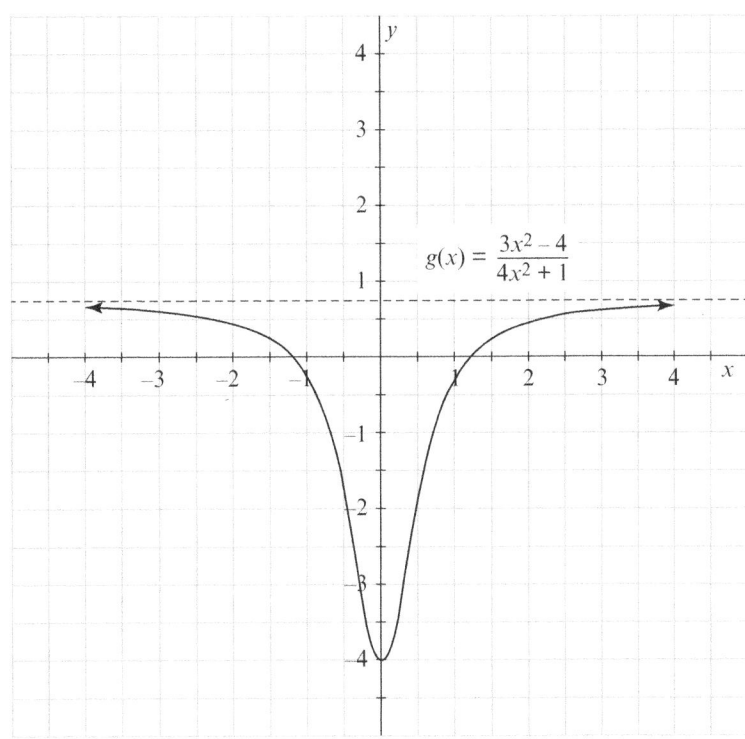

- If the degree of $P(x)$ exceeds the degree of $Q(x)$ by more than 1, the graph will *not* have a horizontal asymptote.

Here is a practice problem.
Problem: Describe the horizontal asymptote, if any, of $h(x) = \dfrac{x^6 - 1}{x^2 + 2}$.

Solution: For $h(x) = \dfrac{x^6 - 1}{x^2 + 2}$, which is in simplified form, the degree of the numerator polynomial exceeds the degree of the denominator polynomial by more than 1 degree, so $h(x) = \dfrac{x^6 - 1}{x^2 + 2}$ has no horizontal asymptote.

A rational function, defined by $f(x) = \dfrac{P(x)}{Q(x)}$, where $f(x)$ is in simplified form and the degree of $Q(x)$ is at least 1, will have at most one oblique asymptote. If the degree of $P(x)$ exceeds the degree of $Q(x)$ by *exactly* 1, the graph will have an oblique asymptote. To find the equation of the oblique asymptote, use long division to rewrite

Chapter 2: Patterns and Algebra

$f(x) = \dfrac{P(x)}{Q(x)}$ as quotient plus $\dfrac{\text{remainder}}{Q(x)}$ (see Appendix B for a review of long division of polynomials). The line with equation y = quotient is an oblique asymptote.

Here is a practice problem.

Problem: Describe the asymptotes of $f(x) = \dfrac{x^2+3}{x-1}$ and then graph the function.

Solution: Using division of polynomials, $f(x) = \dfrac{x^2+3}{x-1} = (x+1) + \dfrac{4}{x-1}$. Thus, $y = x + 1$ is an oblique asymptote of the graph of f. The rational function $f(x) = \dfrac{x^2+3}{x-1}$ is in simplified form, so because its denominator $x - 1$ equals 0 when $x = 1$, the graph has a vertical asymptote at $x = 1$. The graph is shown below with a dashed vertical line at $x = 1$ and a dashed oblique line representing $y = x + 1$.

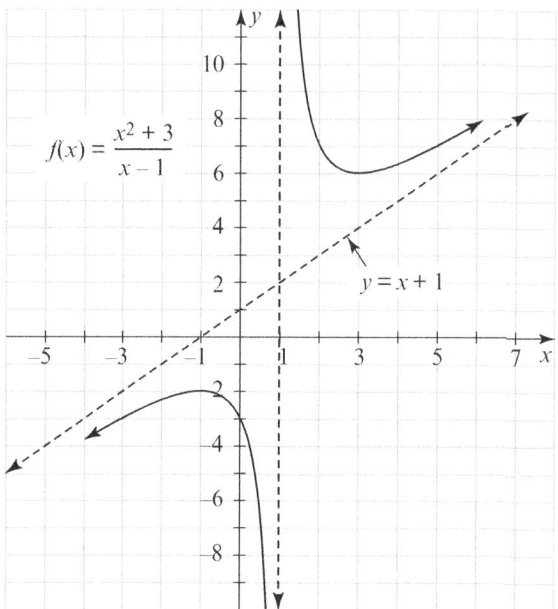

The graph of a function can *never* intersect a vertical asymptote of the function. However, the graph of a function may cross a line that is a horizontal or oblique asymptote as long as the graph eventually draws asymptotically close to the line.

In an informal sense, a function has **discontinuities** if the graph of the function has vertical asymptotes, holes, or jumps that make it impossible to sketch the graph of the function without lifting the pencil. See "Calculus" later in this chapter for a mathematically rigorous discussion of continuity and discontinuity.

More about Polynomial Functions

Useful theorems to know about polynomial functions are the following:

- **Intermediate Value Theorem for Polynomials:** If $a, b \in R$ such that $P(a)$ and $P(b)$ have opposite signs, then P has at least one zero between a and b.
- **Factor Theorem:** $P(r) = 0$ if and only if $x - r$ is a factor of $P(x) = a_n x^n + a_{n-1} x^{n-1} + \ldots + a_2 x^2 + a_1 x + a_0$. Thus, you can factor $P(x)$ by determining the zeros of P; and, conversely, you can determine the zeros of P by factoring $P(x)$.
- **Remainder Theorem:** If $P(x) = a_n x^n + a_{n-1} x^{n-1} + \ldots + a_2 x^2 + a_1 x + a_0$ is divided by $x - r$, the remainder is $P(r)$.

- **Rational Root Theorem:** If $P(x) = a_n x^n + a_{n-1} x^{n-1} + \ldots + a_2 x^2 + a_1 x + a_0$ with integer coefficients a_i (and both a_n and a_0 are not zero) and $\frac{p}{q}$ is a rational root of $P(x) = 0$ in simplified form, then p is a factor of a_0 and q is a factor of a_n.
- **Descartes' Rule of Signs:** If $P(x)$ has real coefficients and is written in descending (or ascending) powers of x, then the number of positive real roots of $P(x) = 0$ is either the number of sign changes, from left to right, occurring in the coefficients of $P(x)$, or it is less than this number by an even number. Similarly, the number of negative real roots of $P(x) = 0$ is either the number of sign changes, from left to right, occurring in the coefficients of $P(-x)$, or it is less than this number by an even number. *Note:* When using this rule, ignore missing powers of x.
- **Fundamental Theorem of Algebra:** Over the complex numbers, every polynomial function P of degree $n \geq 1$ has at least one zero. It follows that if you allow complex zeros and count a zero again each time it occurs more than once, a polynomial function of degree n has exactly n zeros. This theorem guarantees that for every polynomial function P of degree $n \geq 1$ there exist complex zeros $r_1, r_2, \ldots,$ and r_n, so that you can factor $P(x)$ completely as $P(x) = a_n(x - r_1)(x - r_2) \ldots (x - r_n)$, where a_n is the leading coefficient of $P(x)$. In general, a zero r of a polynomial function P has **multiplicity k,** meaning it occurs as a zero exactly k times, if $(x - r)^k$ is a factor of $P(x)$ and $(x - r)^{k+1}$ is not a factor of $P(x)$. Hence, the n zeros of a polynomial function P are not necessarily all different from each other. For example, 3 is a zero of multiplicity 2 for the second degree polynomial function P defined by $P(x) = x^2 - 6x + 9 = (x - 3)(x - 3)$.
- **Complex Conjugate Rule:** If $P(x)$ has real coefficients and $a + bi$, $(b \neq 0)$, is a complex root of $P(x) = 0$, then its complex conjugate $a - bi$ is also a root of $P(x) = 0$.

Here are two practice problems.

Problem: Find the zeros of the polynomial function P defined by $P(x) = 2x^3 - 3x^2 - 11x + 6$.

Solution: Using Descartes' rule of signs, the number of sign changes in $P(x) = 2x^3 - 3x^2 - 11x + 6$ is two. So, there are two or zero positive real roots. The number of sign changes in $P(-x) = -2x^3 - 3x^2 + 11x + 6$ is one. So, there is at most one negative real root. If $\frac{p}{q}$ is a rational root of $P(x) = 0$, then possible values for p are factors of 6 and possible values for q are factors of 2. Thus, p could be $\pm 1, \pm 2, \pm 3,$ or ± 6, and q could be ± 1 or ± 2. Hence, $\frac{p}{q}$ is possibly $\pm 1, \pm 2, \pm 3, \pm 6, \pm \frac{1}{2},$ or $\pm \frac{3}{2}$. Substituting into $P(x)$, $P(1) = -6$, $P(-1) = 12$, $P(2) = -12$, and $P(-2) = 0$. Thus, -2 is a zero, and $(x + 2)$ is a factor of $P(x)$ by the factor theorem. There are no other negative zeros, so eliminate $-3, -6, -\frac{1}{2},$ and $-\frac{3}{2}$ as possible zeros. Testing $x = 3$ yields $P(3) = 0$, so $(x - 3)$ is a factor of $P(x)$ by the factor theorem. The second positive zero can be found by dividing $P(x)$ by the product $(x + 2)(x - 3)$, which is $x^2 - x - 6$. The result is a quotient of $(2x - 1)$ with remainder zero. Therefore, $P(x) = 2x^3 - 3x^2 - 11x + 6 = (x - 3)(x + 2)(2x - 1)$. Hence, the zeros of the polynomial function P are $-2, \frac{1}{2},$ and 3. There are no complex zeros.

Tip: This solution is one way to determine the zeros, but other approaches also could be used to yield the same result.

Problem: Find the zeros of the polynomial function P defined by $P(x) = x^3 - 1$.

Solution: The zeros of P are the roots of $x^3 - 1 = 0$. Since $P(x)$ has degree 3, the equation $x^3 - 1 = 0$ has exactly three roots. Solve by factoring the difference of two cubes and then using the quadratic formula to determine the roots of the trinomial factor.

$$x^3 - 1 = 0$$
$$(x - 1)(x^2 + x + 1) = 0$$
$$(x - 1) = 0 \text{ or } (x^2 + x + 1) = 0$$
$$x = 1 \text{ or } x = \frac{-1 \pm \sqrt{1^2 - 4(1)(1)}}{2(1)} = \frac{-1 \pm \sqrt{-3}}{2} = -\frac{1}{2} \pm \frac{\sqrt{3}}{2} i$$

Thus, $1, -\frac{1}{2} + \frac{\sqrt{3}}{2} i,$ and $-\frac{1}{2} - \frac{\sqrt{3}}{2} i$ are the zeros of P.

Tip: When a polynomial function P has only real coefficients, the complex zeros of P occur in conjugate pairs (as shown in the second problem above). Also, even though P has three zeros, it has only one real zero, namely 1, so its graph will intersect the x-axis only once—at x = 1, as shown in the following figure.

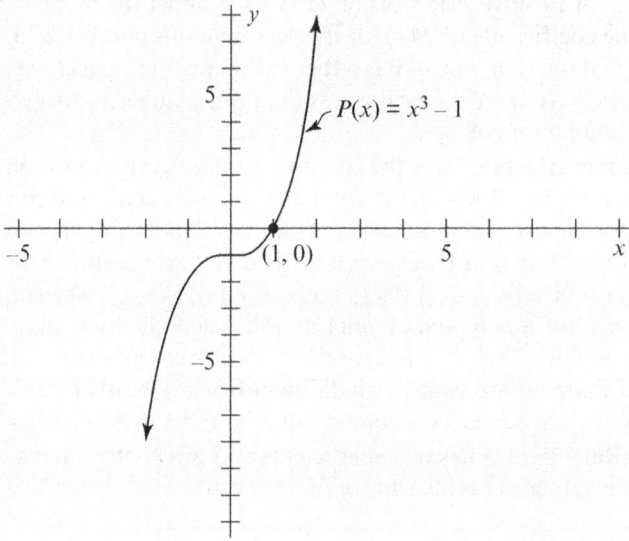

End Behavior: The **end behavior** of a polynomial function is the behavior of its graph as x approaches positive infinity or negative infinity. To determine the end behavior of a polynomial function defined by $P(x) = a_n x^n + a_{n-1} x^{n-1} + \ldots + a_2 x^2 + a_1 x + a_0$ as x approaches ∞ or $-\infty$, factor out $a_n x^n$, the term with highest degree. Then as x approaches ∞ or $-\infty$, $P(x)$ behaves as $a_n x^n$ does.

Here is a practice problem.

Problem: Describe the end behavior of the polynomial function defined by $P(x) = 3x^4 - 500{,}000x^3 + 40x^2 + 100x - 80$.

Solution: Factoring out $3x^4$ yields $P(x) = 3x^4 - 500{,}000x^3 + 40x^2 + 100x - 80 = 3x^4 \left(1 - \dfrac{500{,}000}{3x} + \dfrac{40}{3x^2} + \dfrac{100}{3x^3} - \dfrac{80}{3x^4}\right)$. As x approaches ∞ or $-\infty$, the quantity in parentheses approaches 1, so $P(x)$ will behave as $3x^4$ does. Given that $3x^4$ is always positive, then as x approaches ∞, $P(x)$ will become increasingly positive, and as x approaches $-\infty$, again $P(x)$ will become increasingly positive.

Arithmetic of Functions

Suppose that both $f(x)$ and $g(x)$ exist. For all real numbers x such that $x \in D_f \cap D_g$, the following definitions for the arithmetic of functions hold:

the **sum of f and g** is the function $f + g$, defined by $(f + g)(x) = f(x) + g(x)$;
the **difference of f and g** is the function $f - g$, defined by $(f - g)(x) = f(x) - g(x)$;
the **product of f and g** is the function fg, defined by $(fg)(x) = f(x) \cdot g(x)$; and
the **quotient of f and g** is the function $\dfrac{f}{g}$, defined by $\left(\dfrac{f}{g}\right)(x) = \dfrac{f(x)}{g(x)}$, where $g(x) \ne 0$.

Here is a practice problem.

Problem: Let $f(x) = x^2 + 1$ and $g(x) = \sqrt{x} - 3$. **(a)** Find the domain of $\dfrac{f}{g}$, and **(b)** write a simplified expression for $\left(\dfrac{f}{g}\right)(x)$.

Solution:

(a) The domain of $\frac{f}{g}$ must exclude negative values of x and also values of x for which $g(x) = \sqrt{x} - 3 = 0$. Solving $\sqrt{x} - 3 = 0$ yields $x = 9$, so the domain of $\frac{f}{g}$ is $\{x \mid x \geq 0, x \neq 9\}$.

(b) $\left(\frac{f}{g}\right)(x) = \frac{f(x)}{g(x)} = \frac{x^2 + 1}{\sqrt{x} - 3}$

The product function fg is fundamentally different from the composition function $f \circ g$ (see "Composition and Inverses of Functions" in Part 1 for a discussion of composition of functions).

Here is a practice problem.

Problem: Given $f(x) = 3x$ and $g(x) = x^2$, write simplified expressions for (a) $fg(x)$ and (b) $(f \circ g)(x)$.

Solution:

(a) $fg(x) = f(x) \cdot g(x) = (3x) \cdot (x^2) = 3x^3$

(b) $(f \circ g)(x) = f(g(x)) = f(x^2) = 3(x^2) = 3x^2$

Trigonometry

For this topic, you must be able to use trigonometric relationships to solve oblique triangles, understand trigonometric and circular functions and analyze their graphs, and solve trigonometric equations.

The Law of Sines and the Law of Cosines

The **law of sines** and the **law of cosines** are given below for the triangle ABC labeled as shown here.

Law of Sines: $\dfrac{\sin A}{a} = \dfrac{\sin B}{b} = \dfrac{\sin C}{c}$

Law of Cosines: $c^2 = a^2 + b^2 - 2ab \cos C$

$a^2 = b^2 + c^2 - 2bc \cos A$

$b^2 = a^2 + c^2 - 2ac \cos B$

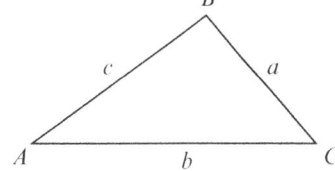

Note: The formulas for the law of sines and the law of cosines will be available to you as reference material during your TExES Math exam.

Every triangle has six parts: three sides and three angles. To **solve a triangle** means to determine all missing measures of the six parts. The law of sines and the law of cosines are used to find missing measures of parts of **oblique triangles** (triangles that are not right triangles). Three possibilities can result: one solution, two solutions (called the ambiguous case), or no solution. The following table summarizes when to use the two laws.

Situation in the Problem	Use	Number of Solutions
You are given the measures of three sides (SSS), and the sum of the lengths of the two smaller sides is greater than the length of the larger side.	law of cosines	one
You are given the measures of three sides (SSS), and the sum of the lengths of the two smaller sides is less than or equal to the length of the larger side.	neither	no solution
You are given the measures of two sides and the included angle (SAS).	law of cosines	one solution
You are given the measures of two angles and the included side (ASA), and the sum of the given angles is less than 180°.	law of sines	one solution

continued

Situation in the Problem	Use	Number of Solutions
You are given the measures of two angles and a nonincluded side (AAS), and the sum of the given angles is less than 180°.	law of sines	one solution
You are given the measures of two angles and either the included side (ASA) or a nonincluded side (AAS), and the sum of the given angles is greater than or equal to 180°.	neither	no solution
You are given the measures of two sides and a nonincluded obtuse angle (SSA), and the length of the side opposite the given angle is greater than the length of the side adjacent to the given angle.	law of sines	one solution
You are given the measures of two sides and a nonincluded obtuse angle, and the length of the side opposite the given angle is less than or equal to the length of the side adjacent to the given angle.	neither	no solution
You are given the measures of two sides and a nonincluded acute angle (SSA), and the length of the side opposite the given angle is greater than or equal to the length of the side adjacent to the given angle.	law of sines	one solution
You are given the measures of two sides and a nonincluded acute angle (SSA), and the length of one side falls between the length of the altitude from the vertex where the two given sides meet and the length of the other side.	law of sines	two solutions
You are given the measures of two sides and a nonincluded acute angle (SSA), and the length of the altitude from the vertex where the two given sides meet falls between the lengths of the two given sides.	neither	no solution
You are given the measures of three angles (AAA).	neither	no unique solution

Here are two practice problems.

Problem: Solve triangle ABC, given $A = 40°$, $a = 50$, and $b = 30$.

Solution: Sketch a figure.

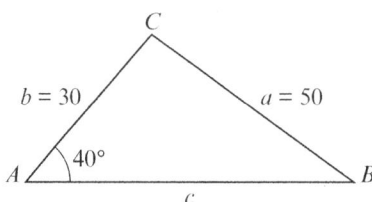

You are given the measures of two sides and a nonincluded acute angle (SSA), and the length of the side opposite the given angle is greater than the length of the side adjacent to the given angle, so there is one solution.

Using the law of sines, $\dfrac{\sin B}{30} = \dfrac{\sin 40°}{50}$. Thus, $\sin B = \dfrac{30 \sin 40°}{50} \approx 0.3857$. The sine of an angle is positive in quadrants I and II, so there are two values of B to consider (see "The Unit Circle and Trigonometric Functions" that follows for a discussion of the signs of trigonometric functions). Using the $\sin^{-1}$ key (which is the second function above the sin key) on your calculator yields $\sin^{-1}(0.3857) \approx 22.7°$. Thus, either $B \approx 22.7°$ or $B \approx 180° - 22.7° = 157.3°$. The latter value will not work because $40° + 157.3° > 180°$, so $B \approx 22.7°$. It follows that $C \approx 180° - 40° - 22.7° = 117.3°$. Using this result and again applying the law of sines,

$$\frac{\sin 40°}{50} = \frac{\sin 117.3°}{c}; \text{ so } c = \frac{50 \sin 117.3°}{\sin 40°} \approx 69.1.$$ Therefore, the triangle is solved because all missing measures have been determined.

Problem: Solve triangle ABC, given $a = 15$, $b = 25$, and $c = 28$.

Solution: Sketch a figure.

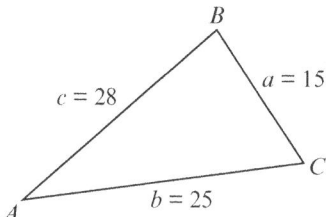

You are given the measures of three sides (SSS), and the sum of the lengths of the two smaller sides is greater than the length of the larger side, so there is one solution. Applying the law of cosines, solve for A.

$$15^2 = 25^2 + 28^2 - 2(25)(28)\cos A$$
$$225 = 625 + 784 - 1400 \cos A$$
$$225 = 1409 - 1400 \cos A$$
$$-1184 = -1400 \cos A$$
$$\cos A \approx 0.8457$$

The cosine of an angle is positive in quadrants I and IV (see "The Unit Circle and Trigonometric Functions" that follows for a discussion of the signs of trigonometric functions). Angles in quadrant IV could not be angles of a triangle, so there is only one value of A to consider. Using the $\cos^{-1}$ key (which is the second function above the cos key) on your calculator yields $A = \cos^{-1}(0.8457) \approx 32.3°$.

Applying the law of cosines a second time, solve for B.

$$25^2 = 15^2 + 28^2 - 2(15)(28)\cos B$$
$$625 = 225 + 784 - 840 \cos B$$
$$625 = 1009 - 840 \cos B$$
$$-384 = -840 \cos B$$
$$\cos B \approx 0.4571$$
$$B \approx \cos^{-1}(0.4571) \approx 62.8°$$

Then $C \approx 180° - 32.3° - 62.8° \approx 84.9°$.

Therefore, the triangle is solved because all missing measures have been determined.

Tip: When solving an oblique triangle, be sure to set your calculator to DEGREE mode if the angle measurements are in degrees and to RADIAN mode if the angle measurements are given in radians.

The Unit Circle and Trigonometric Functions

The **unit circle** is a circle centered at (0, 0) with radius equal to 1. If the unit circle is plotted in the Cartesian coordinate plane, then the sine and cosine trigonometric functions are associated with the circle in the manner shown.

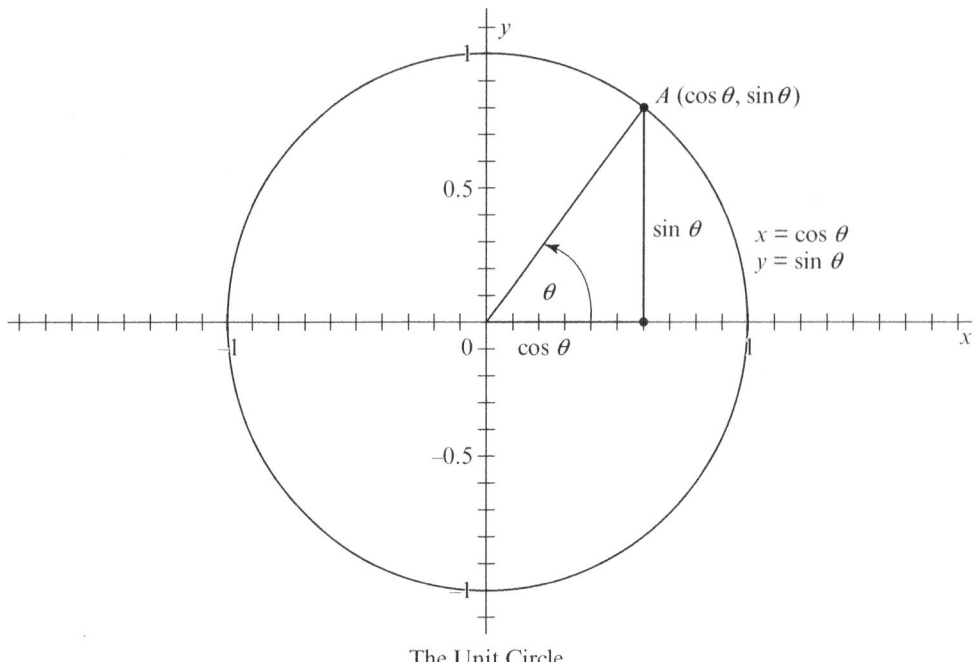

The Unit Circle

Because the radius is 1, $\cos \theta$ is the x-coordinate and $\sin \theta$ is the y-coordinate of the point on the circle intercepted by the ray determined by the central angle θ.

If the point on the circle is rotated counterclockwise to the y-axis, then $\sin \theta = 1$ and $\cos \theta = 0$. Thus, $\sin 90° = 1$ and $\cos 90° = 0$. By the same token, $\sin 0° = 0$ and $\cos 0° = 1$, $\sin 180° = 0$ and $\cos 180° = -1$, and $\sin 270° = -1$ and $\cos 270° = 0$.

If an angle θ is placed in the Cartesian coordinate plane such that the vertex is at the origin and one side is along the x-axis, then θ is said to be in **standard position.** The side along the x-axis is the **initial side,** and the other side is the terminal side. An angle can be thought of as being formed by a rotation of the **terminal side.** If the rotation is counterclockwise, the angle is positive; if the rotation is clockwise, the angle is negative.

As the terminal side of θ moves around the unit circle passing through the four quadrants of the coordinate plane, the values of the trigonometric functions $y = \sin \theta$, $y = \cos \theta$, $y = \tan \theta$, $y = \csc \theta$, $y = \sec \theta$, and $y = \cot \theta$ can be determined by using the appropriate reference angle. The **reference angle** for an angle in standard position is the positive acute angle formed by the x-axis and the terminal side of the angle (disregarding the direction of rotation). For example, the reference angle for 240° is 60°. *Tip:* All reference angles have measure between 0° and 90°.

The relationship of a positive angle A that is less than 360° and its reference angle A_r in each quadrant is given in the following table.

A's Quadrant	Relationship
I	$A_r = A$
II	$A_r = 180° - A$
III	$A_r = A - 180°$
IV	$A_r = 360° - A$

Referring to the unit circle, with $y = \sin \theta$ and $x = \cos \theta$, the **sign of a trigonometric function** may be positive or negative, depending in which quadrant the terminal side of θ is located. For your TExES Math exam, it is necessary to remember only in which quadrants the sine, cosine, and tangent are positive because they will be negative in the other quadrants. Moreover, their reciprocals will have the same signs as the functions themselves do.
The sine function is positive in quadrants I and II; the cosine function is positive in quadrants I and IV; and the tangent function is positive in quadrants I and III.

Tip: Use the mnemonic "**A**ll **S**tudents **T**ake **C**alculus" to help you remember the correct sign of a trigonometric function as you move in a counterclockwise direction from quadrant I to quadrant IV. The initial letters A-S-T-C in the mnemonic remind you that **A**ll the functions are positive in quadrant I; the **S**ine function is positive in quadrant II; the **T**angent function is positive in quadrant III; and the **C**osine function is positive in quadrant IV.

Here is a practice problem.

Problem: Use a reference angle to determine $\sin \theta$, $\cos \theta$, and $\tan \theta$ for $\theta = 315°$.
Solution: The angle $\theta = 315°$ is in quadrant IV. The reference angle is $360° - 315° = 45°$. Thus,
$\sin 315° = -\sin 45° = -\frac{\sqrt{2}}{2}$, $\cos 315° = \cos 45° = \frac{\sqrt{2}}{2}$, and $\tan 315° = -\tan 45° = -1$.

The trigonometric functions, of course, can be associated with any circle of radius r. The ratios then take on the following forms: $\sin \theta = \frac{y}{r}$, $\cos \theta = \frac{x}{r}$, $\tan \theta = \frac{y}{x}$. Note that $y = r \sin \theta$ and $x = r \cos \theta$.

Trigonometric Functions of Real Numbers

The argument θ of a trigonometric function can be expressed in degrees or radians. If $\theta = x$ radians, where x is a real number, the six basic trigonometric functions of x are $y = \sin x$, $y = \cos x$, $y = \tan x$, $y = \csc x$, $y = \sec x$, and $y = \cot x$.

Trigonometric Function	Domain	Range	Vertical Asymptote
	Let k be any integer		Let k be any integer
$y = \sin x$	all reals	$[-1, 1]$	none
$y = \cos x$	all reals	$[-1, 1]$	none
$y = \tan x$	$\{x \in \text{reals}, x \neq \frac{\pi}{2} + k\pi\}$	all reals	$x = \frac{\pi}{2} + k\pi$
$y = \csc x$	$\{x \in \text{reals}, x \neq k\pi\}$	$(-\infty, -1] \cup [1, \infty)$	$x = k\pi$
$y = \sec x$	$\{x \in \text{reals}, x \neq \frac{\pi}{2} + k\pi\}$	$(-\infty, -1] \cup [1, \infty)$	$x = \frac{\pi}{2} + k\pi$
$y = \cot x$	$\{x \in \text{reals}, x \neq k\pi\}$	all reals	$x = k\pi$

Tip: When evaluating a trigonometric function, switch to RADIAN mode when the argument is a real number.

The following table summarizes the values of the trigonometric functions for some **special angles**.

Angle (°)	Angle (radians)	Sine	Cosine	Tangent	Cotangent	Secant	Cosecant
0°	0	0	1	0	undefined	1	undefined
30°	$\frac{\pi}{6}$	$\frac{1}{2}$	$\frac{\sqrt{3}}{2}$	$\frac{1}{\sqrt{3}}$	$\sqrt{3}$	$\frac{2}{\sqrt{3}}$	2
45°	$\frac{\pi}{4}$	$\frac{1}{\sqrt{2}}$	$\frac{1}{\sqrt{2}}$	1	1	$\sqrt{2}$	$\sqrt{2}$
60°	$\frac{\pi}{3}$	$\frac{\sqrt{3}}{2}$	$\frac{1}{2}$	$\sqrt{3}$	$\frac{1}{\sqrt{3}}$	2	$\frac{2}{\sqrt{3}}$
90°	$\frac{\pi}{2}$	1	0	undefined	0	undefined	1

Here is a practice problem.

> Problem: Determine the exact value of $\sin\frac{\pi}{3}$.
> Solution: $\sin\frac{\pi}{3} = \frac{\sqrt{3}}{2}$

Graphs of the Trigonometric Functions

A function f is **periodic** if there is a positive number P such that $f(x + P) = f(x)$ for all x in the domain. The least number P for which this is true is the **period** of f. The sine, cosine, secant, and cosecant functions are periodic with period 2π. The tangent and cotangent functions are periodic with period π.

Note: In graphing the trigonometric functions, commonly the radian measure for angles is used.

The graphs of $y = \sin x$, $y = \cos x$, and $y = \tan x$—the three main trigonometric functions—are shown in the following figures.

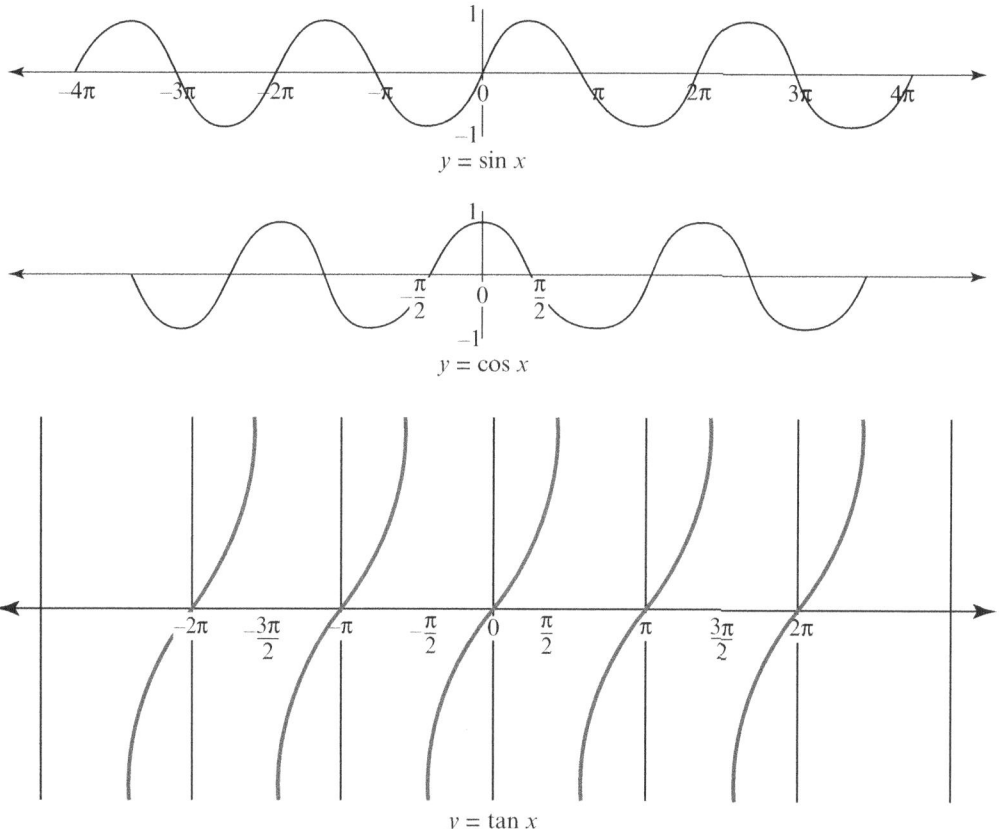

Notice that the graphs of the sine and cosine functions are smooth and continuous with a wavelike pattern. They have no vertical asymptotes, holes, gaps, jumps, or corners. These graphs provide models for oscillating, harmonic, or wave motion. The sine function is odd, meaning $\sin(-x) = -\sin(x)$, so its graph is symmetric about the origin. The cosine function is even, meaning $\cos(-x) = \cos(x)$, so its graph is symmetric about the origin.

The **amplitude** of a sine or cosine function is the height of the wave. It equals one-half the absolute difference between the function's maximum value (max) and minimum value (min); that is, amplitude $= \frac{1}{2}|\text{max} - \text{min}|$.

The graph of $y = \tan x$ has vertical asymptotes at multiples of $\frac{\pi}{2}$. The tangent is odd, meaning $\tan(-x) = -\tan(x)$, so its graph is symmetric about the origin.

Transformations of the Trigonometric Functions

If $b > 0$, the general forms for the sine and cosine functions, $y = a \sin(bx + c) + k$ and $y = a \cos(bx + c) + k$, have graphs with amplitude = $|a|$, period = $\frac{2\pi}{b}$, a horizontal or phase shift of $\frac{|c|}{b}$ units (to the left of the origin if $\frac{c}{b}$ is positive; to the right of the origin if $\frac{c}{b}$ is negative), and a vertical shift of $|k|$ units (up from the origin if k is positive; down from the origin if k is negative). The constant a is either a vertical stretch factor or a vertical compression factor. If $|a| > 1$, the graph is stretched vertically away from the x-axis by the multiple $|a|$, and if $|a| < 1$, the graph is compressed vertically toward the x-axis by the multiple $|a|$. The maximum height of the graph is $|a| + k$ and the minimum height is $-|a| + k$. If $a < 0$, the graph is reflected over $y = k$, and over the x-axis when $k = 0$.

If $b > 0$, the general form for the tangent function, $y = a \tan(bx + c) + k$, has a graph with period = $\frac{\pi}{b}$, a horizontal or phase shift of $\frac{|c|}{b}$ units (to the left of the origin if $\frac{c}{b}$ is positive; to the right of the origin if $\frac{c}{b}$ is negative), and a vertical shift of $|k|$ units (up from the origin if k is positive; down from the origin if k is negative). As with the sine and cosine functions, the coefficient a causes the function to be "stretched" *away* from the x-axis or "compressed" *toward* the x-axis in the vertical direction by the multiple $|a|$; however, unlike the sine and cosine functions, the tangent function has neither a maximum nor a minimum value. If $a < 0$, the graph is reflected over $y = k$, and over the x-axis when $k = 0$.

Here are two practice problems.

> Problem: Describe the major features of the graph of $y = \frac{1}{2}\sin\left(4x - \frac{\pi}{3}\right)$.
>
> Solution: The graph of $y = \frac{1}{2}\sin\left(4x - \frac{\pi}{3}\right)$ has an amplitude of $\frac{1}{2}$, a period of $\frac{\pi}{2}\left(=\frac{2\pi}{4}\right)$, a phase shift of $\frac{\pi}{12}\left(=\frac{\frac{\pi}{3}}{4}\right)$ to the right, and no vertical shift.
>
> Problem: Describe the major features of the graph of $y = -\cos(2x + \pi) + 3$.
> Solution: The graph of $y = -\cos(2x + \pi) + 3$ has an amplitude of 1, a period of $\pi\left(=\frac{2\pi}{2}\right)$, a phase shift of $\frac{\pi}{2}$ to the left, a vertical shift of 3 units up, and is reflected over $y = 3$.

If $b < 0$, rewrite the argument of the function as -1 times a factor, then use the function's even or odd property to write the function as an equivalent function with $b > 0$.

Here is a practice problem.

> Problem: Write $y = -2\cos(\pi - 3x)$ as an equivalent cosine function in which the coefficient of x is positive.
> Solution: Because cosine is an even function, $y = -2\cos(\pi - 3x) = -2\cos[(-1)(3x - \pi)] = -2\cos(3x - \pi)$.

Inverse Trigonometric Functions

For a function to have an inverse function, the original function must be one-to-one. Because the trigonometric functions are periodic on the real numbers, *none* of them are one-to-one functions on their domains. However, if you restrict the domain of a trigonometric function to a portion on which the function *is* one-to-one, then the trigonometric function has a unique inverse function on that restricted domain.

Chapter 2: Patterns and Algebra

The restricted domains of the sine, cosine, and tangent functions are given in the following table.

Trigonometric Function	Restricted Domain
$y = \sin x$	$-\frac{\pi}{2} \leq x \leq \frac{\pi}{2}$
$y = \cos x$	$0 \leq x \leq \pi$
$y = \tan x$	$-\frac{\pi}{2} < x < \frac{\pi}{2}$

Using the restricted domains from the preceding table, the inverse sine, cosine, and tangent functions (represented using the notations $\sin^{-1} x$, $\cos^{-1} x$, and $\tan^{-1} x$, respectively) are defined so that their domains and ranges are as given in the following table.

Domains and Ranges of the Inverse Sine, Cosine, and Tangent Functions

Function	Domain	Range
$y = \sin^{-1} x$	$-1 \leq x \leq 1$	$-\frac{\pi}{2} \leq y \leq \frac{\pi}{2}$
$y = \cos^{-1} x$	$-1 \leq x \leq 1$	$0 \leq y \leq \pi$
$y = \tan^{-1} x$	$-\infty < x < \infty$	$-\frac{\pi}{2} < y < \frac{\pi}{2}$

Notice that the outputs of the inverse trigonometric functions are limited to specific range values. These limitations are necessary so that each input value yields one and only one output value.

Note: You can read $\sin^{-1} x$ as "inverse sine of x" and do similarly with $\cos^{-1} x$ and $\tan^{-1} x$. Other notations for the inverse trigonometric functions use an arc- prefix (e.g., arcsin x, read "an angle whose sine is x").

Tip: The small raised "–1" on an inverse function is not an exponent. Instead, it simply is an inverse notation.

Here are three practice problems.

Problem: Determine $\sin^{-1}\left(\frac{1}{2}\right)$.

Solution: $\sin^{-1}\frac{1}{2} = \frac{\pi}{6}$ because $\frac{\pi}{6}$ is the one and only angle in the interval $\left[-\frac{\pi}{2}, \frac{\pi}{2}\right]$ whose sine is $\frac{1}{2}$.

Problem: Determine $\cos^{-1}\left(-\frac{\sqrt{2}}{2}\right)$.

Solution: $\cos^{-1}\left(-\frac{\sqrt{2}}{2}\right) = \frac{3\pi}{4}$ because $\frac{3\pi}{4}$ is the one and only angle in the interval $[0, \pi]$ whose cosine is $-\frac{\sqrt{2}}{2}$.

Problem: Determine $\tan^{-1}(-1)$.

Solution: $\tan^{-1}(-1) = -\frac{\pi}{4}$ because $-\frac{\pi}{4}$ is the one and only angle in the interval $\left(-\frac{\pi}{2}, \frac{\pi}{2}\right)$ whose sine is -1.

Special Angle Formulas and Identities

For your TExES Math exam, you need to know certain fundamental identities and formulas that can be used to simplify or change trigonometric expressions. The following is a list of important identities to commit to memory before the test.

Chapter 2: Patterns and Algebra

Reciprocal Identities	$\sec\theta = \dfrac{1}{\cos\theta}$, $\csc\theta = \dfrac{1}{\sin\theta}$, and $\cot\theta = \dfrac{1}{\tan\theta}$
Ratio Identities	$\tan\theta = \dfrac{\sin\theta}{\cos\theta}$ and $\cot\theta = \dfrac{\cos\theta}{\sin\theta}$
Pythagorean Identities	$\sin^2\theta + \cos^2\theta = 1$, $\tan^2\theta + 1 = \sec^2\theta$, and $1 + \cot^2\theta = \csc^2\theta$
Cofunction Identities	$\cos\theta = \sin(90° - \theta)$, $\csc\theta = \sec(90° - \theta)$, and $\cot\theta = \tan(90° - \theta)$
Even-Odd Identities	$\sin(-\theta) = -\sin\theta$, $\cos(-\theta) = \cos\theta$, and $\tan(-\theta) = -\tan\theta$

Tip: The notation $\sin^2\theta = (\sin\theta)^2$. Similarly, $\cos^2\theta = (\cos\theta)^2$, $\tan^2\theta = (\tan\theta)^2$, and so forth.

For your TExES Math exam, you might have to select which trigonometric expression is an identity for a given trigonometric expression. Here are some helpful strategies.

- Change all the trigonometric functions in the given expression to sines and cosines and simplify.
- Combine fractions and simplify.
- If the numerator or denominator of a fraction has the form $f(x) + 1$, multiply the numerator and denominator by $f(x) - 1$ to obtain the difference of two squares, and then look for a Pythagorean identity; for $f(x) - 1$ multiply by $f(x) + 1$.
- Evaluate the given trigonometric expression for a convenient value of the angle, and then evaluate each of the answer choices for the same value of the angle to find one that evaluates to be the same value you obtained for the given trigonometric expression.

Trigonometric Equations and Inequalities

Trigonometric equations and inequalities are solved in a manner similar to that used in solving algebraic equations and inequalities. The main difference is that because of the periodic nature of the trigonometric functions, there could be multiple solutions to the equation, depending on the specifications in the problem. For example, to solve $\cos x = \dfrac{1}{2}$, you must find all values of x that make the equation true. For simplicity, suppose you want to express the answer in radians. Because $\dfrac{1}{2}$ is the cosine of a special angle (see "Trigonometric Functions of Real Numbers" earlier in this section for a table that summarizes the values of the trigonometric functions for some special angles), you know that $\dfrac{\pi}{3}$ is a value for x that makes the equation true. However, the cosine function is also positive in quadrant IV. The angle in quadrant IV with reference angle $\dfrac{\pi}{3}$ is $\dfrac{5\pi}{3}$, which is also a value for x that makes the equation true. Because the cosine function is periodic with period 2π, you have many more values for x that satisfy $\cos x = \dfrac{1}{2}$. To list all of them, add multiples of 2π to each of the values $\dfrac{\pi}{3}$ and $\dfrac{5\pi}{3}$. Thus, the solutions are $x = \dfrac{\pi}{3} + k \cdot 2\pi$ and $\dfrac{5\pi}{3} + k \cdot 2\pi$ where k is any integer.

If a problem specifies that you are to find only values in a particular interval, then you omit any values outside the given interval. Otherwise, to determine all solutions of a trigonometric equation, write a **general solution** by adding multiples of the period to the solutions that occur in one cycle of the trigonometric function.

You can use your calculator to solve trigonometric equations by using the keys for the inverse trigonometric functions: $y = \sin^{-1} x$ (use the second function above the sin key), $y = \cos^{-1} x$ (use the second function above the cos key), and $y = \tan^{-1} x$ (use the second function above the tan key). The range for an inverse trigonometric function is restricted. When you use the keys for the inverse functions, the values returned will be in the restricted ranges.

You will have to use your knowledge of reference angles and the periodicity of the functions to determine other values in the solution set, if needed.

Tip: If the answer choices are given as radians expressed in terms of π, set your graphing calculator to DEGREE mode when obtaining the angle's value, and then convert the angle into radians using the relationship that $1° = \frac{\pi}{180}$ radians. If you set the calculator to RADIAN mode, the solution's value will be displayed as a real number. You will have to convert the answer choices to real numbers to decide which answer is the same as your solution.

Here is a practice problem.

Problem: Solve $2\sin\theta - \sqrt{2} = 0$ for all solutions in $[0, 3\pi]$.

Solution: First, solve for $\sin\theta$, then determine θ.

$$2\sin\theta - \sqrt{2} = 0$$

$$\sin\theta = \frac{\sqrt{2}}{2}$$

$$\sin^{-1}(\sin\theta) = \sin^{-1}\left(\frac{\sqrt{2}}{2}\right)$$

$$\theta = \frac{\pi}{4}$$

All solutions in $[0, 3\pi]$ are $\frac{\pi}{4}, \frac{3\pi}{4}, \frac{9\pi}{4}$, and $\frac{11\pi}{4}$.

Tip: You will find that visualizing the unit circle and the algebraic sign of the given function in the various quadrants is helpful when you are determining all solutions for trigonometric equations.

Trigonometric Form of a Complex Number

The trigonometric form of a complex number $z = x + yi$ (standard form) is $r\cos\theta + ir\sin\theta$, where $r = \sqrt{x^2 + y^2}$ and $\tan\theta = \frac{y}{x}$, provided $x \neq 0$.

De Moivre's theorem says that $(r\cos\theta + ir\sin\theta)^k = r^k[\cos(k\theta) + i\sin(k\theta)]$. This theorem is useful for finding powers and roots of complex numbers.

Here is a practice problem.

Problem: Use De Moivre's theorem to find $\left(-3 - i3\sqrt{3}\right)^3$. Express the result as a complex number in standard form.

Solution: First, write $-3 - i3\sqrt{3}$ in trigonometric form. Next, apply De Moivre's theorem. Finally, convert the result to standard form.

Given the complex number $-3 - i3\sqrt{3}$, $r = \sqrt{x^2 + y^2} = \sqrt{3^2 + \left(3\sqrt{3}\right)^2} = \sqrt{9 + 27} = \sqrt{36} = 6$ and

$\tan\theta = \frac{y}{x} = \frac{-3\sqrt{3}}{-3} = \sqrt{3}$, which implies that $\theta = 240°$ (because $-3 - i3\sqrt{3}$ is in quadrant III). Applying De Moivre's theorem yields the following:

$$\left(-3 - i3\sqrt{3}\right)^3 = (6\cos 240° + i6\sin 240°)^3$$

$$= 6^3[\cos(3 \cdot 240°) + i\sin(3 \cdot 240°)] = 216(\cos 720° + i\sin 720°) = 216(1 + 0) = 216$$

Calculus

For this topic, you must understand and be able to apply the concepts of limit, derivatives, and integrals.

Limits

The study of calculus begins with the study of limits. For your TExES Math exam, the following definitions and properties of limit are essential to know.

Definition of Limit

Let f be a function defined on an open interval containing the number a, except possibly at a, then the $\lim_{x \to a} f(x) = L$ (read "the limit of $f(x)$ as x approaches a equals L") if for every number $\varepsilon > 0$, there exists a number $\delta > 0$ such that if $0 < |x - a| < \delta$, then $|f(x) - L| < \varepsilon$ for every x in the domain of f. That is, a function f has a limit L as x gets closer and closer to the number a, written $\lim_{x \to a} f(x) = L$, provided the error between $f(x)$ and L, written $|f(x) - L|$, can be made less than any preassigned positive number ε by making x sufficiently close to, but not equal to, the number a. *Note: ε and δ are the lowercase Greek letters epsilon and delta, respectively.*

The $\lim_{x \to a^-} f(x) = M$ is the **left-hand limit** of $f(x)$ provided $f(x)$ approaches M as x gets closer and closer to the number a from the left, and $\lim_{x \to a^+} f(x) = N$ is the **right-hand limit** of $f(x)$ provided $f(x)$ approaches N as x gets closer and closer to the number a from the right.

The limit $\lim_{x \to a} f(x) = L$ *exists* only if the following conditions are satisfied:

1. the limit L is a single finite real number; and
2. the left-hand and right-hand limits of $f(x)$ as x approaches the number a both exist; and
3. $\lim_{x \to a^-} f(x) = \lim_{x \to a^+} f(x) = L$.

If no such L exists, then the $\lim_{x \to a} f(x)$ *does not exist*. Common situations that occur when the limit of a function f as x approaches the number a does *not* exist are the following:

- $\lim_{x \to a^+} f(x) \neq \lim_{x \to a^-} f(x)$,
- $f(x)$ increases or decreases without bound as x gets closer and closer to a, or
- $f(x)$ oscillates between two fixed values as x gets closer and closer to a.

Here is a practice problem.

Problem: Determine $\lim_{x \to 5} \dfrac{10}{x-5}$.

Solution: From the limit definition, $\lim_{x \to 5} \dfrac{10}{x-5}$ exists only if $\dfrac{10}{x-5}$ approaches a single finite value as x approaches 5 from both the left and right. As x gets closer and closer to 5 from the left, the number $\dfrac{10}{x-5}$ is decreasing without bound; symbolically, you indicate this behavior as $\lim_{x \to 5^-} \dfrac{10}{x-5} = -\infty$. As x gets closer and closer to 5 from the right, the number $\dfrac{10}{x-5}$ is increasing without bound, indicated as $\lim_{x \to 5^+} \dfrac{10}{x-5} = \infty$. Since $\dfrac{10}{x-5}$ does not approach a single finite value as x approaches 5 from both the left and right of 5, $\lim_{x \to 5} \dfrac{10}{x-5}$ does not exist.

Intuitively, the "ε-δ" definition of limit means that if the values of f(x) get arbitrarily close to a single value L as x approaches the number a from both sides, then $\lim_{x \to a} f(x) = L$. When $\lim_{x \to a} f(x)$ exists, the limit is unique. Furthermore, its value is independent of the value of f at the number a.

Here is a practice problem.

> Problem: Determine $\lim_{x \to 5}(x^2 + 3)$ using an intuitive approach.
>
> Solution: If x gets very close to but unequal to 5 in value, either from the left or right, $(x^2 + 3)$ is very close to 28 in value (for example, when $x = 4.99$, $x^2 + 3 = 27.9001$; and when $x = 5.01$, $x^2 + 3 = 28.1001$). Thus, $(x^2 + 3)$ approaches a single finite value, namely 28, as x approaches 5 from either the left or right.
>
> Therefore, $\lim_{x \to 5}(x^2 + 3) = 28$.

When $\lim_{x \to a} f(x)$ exists, three situations that might occur at the number a are the following:

$f(a) = \lim_{x \to a} f(x)$; $f(a)$ is undefined; or $f(a)$ is defined, but $f(a) \neq \lim_{x \to a} f(x)$.

Limits of Continuous Functions

Notice that in the limit concept, you do not consider what happens at $x = a$, only what happens when x is close to the value of a. Therefore, you must be cautious about assuming that $\lim_{x \to a} f(x) = f(a)$; that is, that you determine the limit by substituting $x = a$ into the expression that defines $f(x)$ and then evaluating. However, when a function is continuous at a number a, you have the situation whereby the limit *can* be calculated by actually evaluating the function at the number a. Thus, when a function f is *continuous* at $x = a$, then $\lim_{x \to a} f(x) = f(a)$, so you can find the limit by direct substitution (see "Continuity" later in this chapter for a discussion of the term *continuous*). Here are some common limits that can be evaluated using direct substitution.

$\lim_{x \to a} b = b$

$\lim_{x \to a} x = a$

$\lim_{x \to a} \dfrac{1}{x} = \dfrac{1}{a}$, $a \neq 0$

$\lim_{x \to a} x^2 = a^2$

$\lim_{x \to a} x^n = a^n$, for n a positive integer

$\lim_{x \to a} \sqrt{x} = \sqrt{a}$, $a \geq 0$

$\lim_{x \to a} \sqrt[n]{x} = \sqrt[n]{a}$, for n a positive integer with the restriction that if n is even, $a \geq 0$

$\lim_{x \to a} |x| = |a|$

$\lim_{x \to a} e^x = e^a$ and $\lim_{x \to a} b^x = b^a$, $b > 0$, $b \neq 1$

$\lim_{x \to a} \ln x = \ln a$, $a > 0$ and $\lim_{x \to a} \log_b x = \log_b a$, $a > 0$, $b > 0$, $b \neq 1$

If f is a polynomial function given by $f(x) = c_n x^n + c_{n-1} x^{n-1} + c_{n-2} x^{n-2} + \ldots + c_2 x^2 + c_1 x + c_0$, then

$\lim_{x \to a} f(x) = c_n a^n + c_{n-1} a^{n-1} + c_{n-2} a^{n-2} + \cdots + c_2 a^2 + c_1 a + c_0$.

If f is a rational function given by $f(x) = \dfrac{P(x)}{Q(x)}$, then $\lim_{x \to a} f(x) = \dfrac{P(a)}{Q(a)}$, provided $Q(a) \neq 0$.

For a in the domain of the function,

$$\lim_{x \to a} \sin x = \sin a, \ \lim_{x \to a} \cos x = \cos a, \ \lim_{x \to a} \tan x = \tan a, \ \lim_{x \to a} \csc x = \csc a, \ \lim_{x \to a} \sec x = \sec a, \text{ and } \lim_{x \to a} \cot x = \cot a$$

Here is a practice problem:

Problem: Evaluate the following limits:

(a) $\lim_{x \to 5} \dfrac{1}{x}$, **(b)** $\lim_{x \to 3} x^4$, **(c)** $\lim_{x \to 36} \sqrt{x}$, **(d)** $\lim_{x \to 32} \log_2 x$, **(e)** $\lim_{x \to 3} 4^x$, **(f)** $\lim_{x \to \frac{\pi}{6}} \sin x$

Solution:

(a) $\lim_{x \to 5} \dfrac{1}{x} = \dfrac{1}{5}$, **(b)** $\lim_{x \to 3} x^4 = 3^4 = 81$, **(c)** $\lim_{x \to 36} \sqrt{x} = \sqrt{36} = 6$, **(d)** $\lim_{x \to 32} \log_2 x = \log_2 32 = 5$, **(e)** $\lim_{x \to 3} 4^x = 4^3 = 64$,

(f) $\lim_{x \to \frac{\pi}{6}} \sin x = \sin\left(\dfrac{\pi}{6}\right) = \dfrac{1}{2}$

Limit of a composite function: If f and g are functions such that g is continuous at a and f is continuous at $g(a)$,

then $\lim_{x \to a} f \circ g(x) = \lim_{x \to a} f(g(x)) = f\left(\lim_{x \to a} g(x)\right) = f(g(a))$.

Here is a practice problem.

Problem: Let $f(x) = |x|$ and $g(x) = \tan x$. Evaluate $\lim_{x \to \frac{7\pi}{4}} f \circ g(x)$.

Solution: $\lim_{x \to \frac{7\pi}{4}} |\tan x| = \left|\lim_{x \to \frac{7\pi}{4}} \tan x\right| = \left|\tan \dfrac{7\pi}{4}\right| = |-1| = 1$

L'Hôpital's Rule

If $\lim_{x \to a} p(x) = 0$ and $\lim_{x \to a} q(x) = 0$, then direct substitution into $\lim_{x \to a} \dfrac{p(x)}{q(x)}$ yields $\dfrac{0}{0}$, which is an **indeterminate form.**
When this problem occurs, maybe you can factor $(x - a)$ from $p(x)$ and $q(x)$, thereby reducing the algebraic fraction $\dfrac{p(x)}{q(x)}$, and then find the limit of the resulting expression, if it exists.

Here is a practice problem.

Problem: Find $\lim_{x \to 4} \dfrac{x^2 - 16}{x - 4}$.

Solution: Direct substitution into $\lim_{x \to 4} \dfrac{x^2 - 16}{x - 4}$ yields $\dfrac{0}{0}$. Reducing $\dfrac{x^2 - 16}{x - 4}$ first and then finding the limit

results in the following: $\lim_{x \to 4} \dfrac{x^2 - 16}{x - 4} = \lim_{x \to 4} \dfrac{(x+4)\cancel{(x-4)}}{\cancel{(x-4)}} = \lim_{x \to 4} (x + 4) = 8$.

Another way to approach problems that result in an indeterminate form is to apply **L'Hôpital's rule** using derivatives (see "Derivatives" later in this chapter for an explanation of derivatives and related terminology). A function is **differentiable** if its derivative exists. By L'Hôpital's rule, if p and q are differentiable at every number x in an open interval, I, except possibly at a, and $\lim_{x \to a} p(x) = 0$ and $\lim_{x \to a} q(x) = 0$, then $\lim_{x \to a} \dfrac{p(x)}{q(x)} = \lim_{x \to a} \dfrac{p'(x)}{q'(x)}$, provided $q'(x) \neq 0$ for all $x \neq a$ in I and $\lim_{x \to a} \dfrac{p'(x)}{q'(x)}$ exists. (*Note:* $p'(x)$ and $q'(x)$ are the derivatives of p and q, respectively.) L'Hôpital's rule also applies when $\lim_{x \to a} p(x) = \pm\infty$ and $\lim_{x \to a} q(x) = \pm\infty$.

Here are examples (refer to "Differentiation Formulas" on the next page).

$$\lim_{x \to 4} \frac{x^2 - 16}{x - 4} = \lim_{x \to 4} \frac{D_x(x^2 - 16)}{D_x(x - 4)} = \lim_{x \to 4} \frac{2x}{1} = 8$$

$$\lim_{x \to 0} \frac{\sin x}{6x} = \lim_{x \to 0} \frac{D_x(\sin x)}{D_x(6x)} = \lim_{x \to 0} \frac{\cos x}{6} = \frac{1}{6}$$

Note: $D_x f(x) = f'(x)$

Properties of Limits

Assuming that the functions f and g have limits that exist as x approaches the number a, the following fundamental properties of limits hold.

Sum or Difference	$\lim_{x \to a}[f(x) \pm g(x)] = \lim_{x \to a} f(x) \pm \lim_{x \to a} g(x)$
Product	$\lim_{x \to a}[f(x) \cdot g(x)] = \lim_{x \to a} f(x) \cdot \lim_{x \to a} g(x)$
Quotient	$\lim_{x \to a} \frac{f(x)}{g(x)} = \frac{\lim_{x \to a} f(x)}{\lim_{x \to a} g(x)}$, provided $g(x) \neq 0$ and $\lim_{x \to a} g(x) \neq 0$
Power	$\lim_{x \to a}[f(x)]^n = [\lim_{x \to a} f(x)]^n$
Root	$\lim_{x \to a} \sqrt[n]{f(x)} = \sqrt[n]{\lim_{x \to a} f(x)}$ for n a positive integer, provided both $f(x) \geq 0$ and $\lim_{x \to a} f(x) \geq 0$ when n is even
Scalar Multiplication	$\lim_{x \to a} k f(x) = k \lim_{x \to a} f(x)$, for any real number k

Here are two practice problems.

Problem: Evaluate $\lim_{x \to 2} \frac{3x - 5}{5x + 2}$.

Solution: $\lim_{x \to 2} \frac{3x - 5}{5x + 2} = \frac{\lim_{x \to 2}(3x - 5)}{\lim_{x \to 2}(5x + 2)} = \frac{\lim_{x \to 2} 3x - \lim_{x \to 2} 5}{\lim_{x \to 2} 5x + \lim_{x \to 2} 2} = \frac{3 \lim_{x \to 2} x - \lim_{x \to 2} 5}{5 \lim_{x \to 2} x + \lim_{x \to 2} 2} = \frac{3(2) - 5}{5(2) + 2} = \frac{1}{12}$

Problem: Evaluate $\lim_{x \to 4}(3x + \sqrt{16x})$.

Solution:

$\lim_{x \to 4}(3x + \sqrt{16x}) = \lim_{x \to 4} 3x + \lim_{x \to 4} \sqrt{16x} = 3\lim_{x \to 4} x + \sqrt{\lim_{x \to 4} 16x} = 3\lim_{x \to 4} x + \sqrt{16 \lim_{x \to 4} x} = 3(4) + \sqrt{16(4)} = 12 + \sqrt{64}$
$= 12 + 8 = 20$

Derivatives

For this topic, you must demonstrate an understanding of the derivative of a function as a limit, as the slope of a curve, and as a rate of change.

Definition of Derivative

The derivative f' (read "f prime") of the function f at the number x is defined as $f'(x) = \lim_{h \to 0} \frac{f(x+h) - f(x)}{h}$, provided this limit exists. If this limit does not exist, then f does not have a derivative at x.

Here is a practice problem.

Problem: Given the function f defined by $f(x) = -2x + 3$, use the definition of the derivative to find $f'(x)$.
Solution:

$$f'(x) = \lim_{h \to 0} \frac{f(x+h) - f(x)}{h} = \lim_{h \to 0} \frac{(-2(x+h) + 3) - (-2x + 3)}{h} = \lim_{h \to 0} \frac{(-2x - 2h + 3) + 2x - 3}{h}$$

$$= \lim_{h \to 0} \frac{-2x - 2h + 3 + 2x - 3}{h} = \lim_{h \to 0} \frac{-2h}{h} = \lim_{h \to 0} (-2) = -2$$

A **differentiable function** is a function that has a derivative. If $f'(c)$ exists, then f is differentiable at c; otherwise, f does not have a derivative at c. Various symbols are used to represent the derivative of a function f. For the notation $y = f(x)$, you can symbolize the derivative of f by $f'(x)$, $\frac{dy}{dx}$, $D_x f(x)$, y', $D_x y$, or $\frac{d}{dx} f(x)$.

The derivative $f'(x)$ is the **first derivative** of f. The derivative of $f'(x)$ is the **second derivative** of f and is denoted $f''(x)$. Similarly, the derivative of $f''(x)$ is the **third derivative** of f and is denoted $f'''(x)$. In general, the **nth derivative** of f is denoted $f^{(n)}(x)$.

Differentiation Formulas

The process of finding the derivative of a function is called *differentiation*. You should know the following differentiation formulas for your TExES Math exam.

$D_x k = 0$, for k a real number $D_x x = 1$ $D_x (mx) = m$

$D_x x^n = nx^{n-1}$, for n a rational number $D_x \ln x = \frac{1}{x}$, $x > 0$ $D_x e^x = e^x$

$D_x \sin x = \cos x$ $D_x \cos x = -\sin x$ $D_x \tan x = \sec^2 x$

$D_x \sec x = \sec x \tan x$ $D_x \csc x = -\csc x \cot x$ $D_x \cot x = -\csc^2 x$

If f and g are differentiable at x, then the following derivative formulas are true.

Scalar Multiplication	$D_x(kf(x)) = k \cdot f'(x)$ for k a real number
Sum and Difference	$D_x(f(x) \pm g(x)) = f'(x) \pm g'(x)$
Product	$D_x(f(x)g(x)) = f(x) \cdot g'(x) + g(x) \cdot f'(x)$
Quotient	$D_x\left(\frac{f(x)}{g(x)}\right) = \frac{g(x) \cdot f'(x) - f(x) \cdot g'(x)}{(g(x))^2}$, $g(x) \neq 0$
Chain Rule	$D_x[f(g(x))] = f'(g(x)) \cdot g'(x)$

Here is a practice problem.

Problem: Use the appropriate formula to find the indicated derivative.
(a) $D_x(-2x + 3)$ (b) $D_x(2x^3 - 9x^2 + 2)$ (c) $D_x \ln x$, $x > 0$

(d) $\frac{d}{dx}(x^2 \sin x)$ (e) $D_x\left(\frac{3x+5}{2-x}\right)$ (f) $\frac{d}{dx}\left(\frac{1}{\sqrt{x}}\right)$ (g) $D_x(x^2 - 1)^3$

Solution:

(a) $D_x(-2x + 3) = -2 + 0 = -2$

(b) $D_x(2x^3 - 9x^2 + 2) = 6x^2 - 18x + 0 = 6x^2 - 18x$

(c) $D_x \ln x = \dfrac{1}{x}, \ x > 0$

(d) $\dfrac{d}{dx}(x^2 \sin x) = x^2 \cdot \cos x + \sin x \cdot 2x = x^2 \cos x + 2x \sin x$

(e) $D_x\left(\dfrac{3x+5}{2-x}\right) = \dfrac{(2-x)(3)-(3x+5)(-1)}{(2-x)^2} = \dfrac{6-3x+3x+5}{(2-x)^2} = \dfrac{11}{(2-x)^2}$

(f) $\dfrac{d}{dx}\left(\dfrac{1}{\sqrt{x}}\right) = \dfrac{d}{dx}\left(x^{-\frac{1}{2}}\right) = -\dfrac{1}{2}x^{-\frac{3}{2}} = -\dfrac{1}{2x^{\frac{3}{2}}}$

(g) $D_x(x^2 - 1)^3 = 3(x^2 - 1)^2 \cdot 2x = 6x(x^2 - 1)^2$

Slope of Tangent Line

If $f'(a)$ exists, then the tangent line to the graph of the function f at the point $P(a, f(a))$ is the line through P that has slope $m = f'(a)$.

Here is a practice problem (refer to "Differentiation Formulas," above).

> Problem: Find the slope of the tangent line to the parabola $y = f(x) = x^2 + 1$ at the point (2, 5) and graph the result.
>
> Solution: Given that $f(x) = x^2 + 1$, then $f'(x) = 2x$. Therefore, the slope at point (2, 5) $= m = f'(2) = 4$. The graph is shown below.

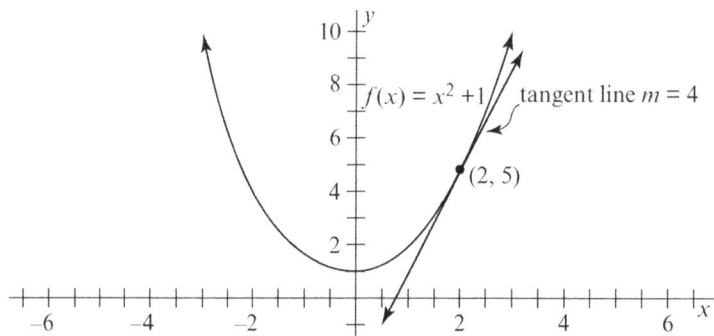

Instantaneous Rate of Change

If $f'(t)$ exists, then the **instantaneous rate of change** of f at t is $f'(t)$. For example, if $s(t)$ is the **position function** of a moving object, then the **velocity** (the instantaneous rate of change) of the object at time t is $s'(t)$. Additionally, the **acceleration** of the object at time t is $s''(t)$.

Here is a practice problem (refer to "Differentiation Formulas," above).

> Problem: Suppose $s(t) = 100t^2 + 100t$ describes the position (in feet) of a moving object as a function of time t (in seconds). Find the velocity (in feet per second) and acceleration (in feet per second^2) of the object at time $t = 2$ seconds.
>
> Solution: Velocity $= s'(t) = 200t + 100$, so at time $t = 2$ seconds, velocity $= s'(2) = 200(2) + 100 = 500$ feet per second.
>
> Acceleration $= s''(t) = 200$, so at time $t = 2$ seconds, acceleration $= 200$ feet per second^2.

Chapter 2: Patterns and Algebra

Continuity

For this topic, you must be able to show that a particular function is continuous and demonstrate an understanding of the relationship between continuity and differentiability.

Definition of Continuous Function

The function f is **continuous at the number** $x = a$ in the domain of f if *all three* of the following conditions are met:

$f(a)$ is defined; $\lim_{x \to a} f(x)$ exists; and $\lim_{x \to a} f(x) = f(a)$.

A function that does not satisfy the above conditions is **discontinuous at** a.

Here are two practice problems.

Problem: Given $f(x) = \sqrt{2x+17}$, is f continuous at $x = 4$?

Solution: $\lim_{x \to 4} \sqrt{2x+17} = \sqrt{\lim_{x \to 4}(2x+17)} = \sqrt{25} = 5$ exists and is equal to $f(4) = \sqrt{2(4)+17} = \sqrt{25} = 5$; therefore, f is continuous at 4.

Problem: Given $g(x) = \dfrac{15}{x-2}$, is g continuous at $x = 2$?

Solution: $\lim_{x \to 2} \dfrac{15}{x-2}$ does not exist; therefore, g is discontinuous at 2.

A function f is **continuous** if for every value a in its domain, $f(a)$ exists and $\lim_{x \to a} f(x) = f(a)$. Otherwise, f is **discontinuous**.

A function f is **continuous in an open interval** if it is continuous at each point in the interval. If a function is continuous on the entire real line, the function is **continuous everywhere**; that is to say, its graph is a single, unbroken curve that has no holes, jumps, or gaps in it.

Common Continuous Functions

A function is a **continuous function** if it is continuous on its domain. The following types of functions are continuous at every point in their domains.

Constant Functions	$f(x) = k$, where k is a constant
Identity Functions	$f(x) = x$
Reciprocal Functions	$f(x) = \dfrac{1}{x}$, $x \neq 0$
Power Functions	$f(x) = x^n$, where n is a real number
Quadratic Functions	$f(x) = x^2$
Square Root Functions	$f(x) = \sqrt{x}$, $x \geq 0$
Radical Functions	$f(x) = \sqrt[n]{x}$, for n a positive integer, provided that if n is even, $x \geq 0$
Absolute Value Functions	$f(x) = |x|$
Polynomial Functions	$f(x) = c_n x^n + c_{n-1} x^{n-1} + c_{n-2} x^{n-2} + \ldots + c_2 x^2 + c_1 x + c_0$
Rational Functions	$f(x) = \dfrac{P(x)}{Q(x)}$, $Q(x) \neq 0$

continued

Exponential Functions	$f(x) = b^x$, $b > 0$, $b \neq 1$
Logarithmic Functions	$f(x) = \log_b x$, $b > 0$, $b \neq 1$, $x > 0$
Trigonometric Functions	$f(x) = \sin x$; $f(x) = \cos x$; $f(x) = \tan x$, $x \neq \frac{\pi}{2} + \pi$; $f(x) = \csc x$, $x \neq k\pi$; $f(x) = \cot x$, $x \neq k\pi$; and $f(x) = \sec x$, $x \neq \frac{\pi}{2} + \pi$

Properties of Continuity

If f and g are continuous at $x = a$, then the following functions are also continuous at $x = a$.

Sum and Difference	$f \pm g$
Product	fg
Scalar Multiple	kf, for k a real number
Quotient	$\dfrac{f}{g}$, $g(a) \neq 0$
Composition	If g is continuous at a and f is continuous at $g(a)$, then $f \circ g$ is continuous at a, where $(f \circ g)(x) = f(g(x))$.

If a function f is differentiable at $x = a$, then f is continuous at $x = a$; in other words, *differentiability implies continuity*. Therefore, if f is *not* continuous at $x = a$, then f is also *not* differentiable at $x = a$. **Caution:** Continuity does *not* imply differentiability. A function can be continuous at $x = a$ even though $f'(x)$ does not exist at $x = a$. This circumstance occurs when there is a cusp (a sharp corner) or a vertical tangent line at a. For example, the absolute value function (shown below) is continuous at $x = 0$; however, $f'(x)$ does not exist at $x = 0$.

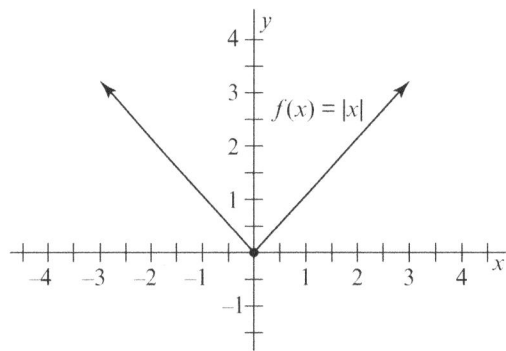

Analyzing the Behavior of a Function

For this topic, you must be able to analyze the behavior of a function (for example: find relative extrema, concavity), solve problems involving related rates, and solve applied extrema problems.

Increasing and Decreasing Behavior

If f is continuous on a closed interval $[a, b]$ and differentiable on the open interval (a, b), then

- f is **increasing** in $[a, b]$ if $f'(x) > 0$ in (a, b); and
- f is **decreasing** in $[a, b]$ if $f'(x) < 0$ in (a, b).

Tip: The sign of $f'(x)$ determines the increasing or decreasing behavior of f.

You can find the intervals in which a function is increasing or decreasing by solving the inequalities $f'(x) > 0$ and $f'(x) < 0$.

Here is a practice problem (refer to "Differentiation Formulas" earlier in this section).

> Problem: For the function f defined by $f(x) = x^2 + 2x + 1$, determine where f is increasing and where f is decreasing.
>
> Solution: $f'(x) = 2x + 2$, so solving the inequalities $2x + 2 < 0$ and $2x + 2 > 0$ yields $x < -1$ and $x > -1$, respectively. Therefore, $f'(x) < 0$ if $x < -1$ and $f'(x) > 0$ when $x > -1$. Hence, f is decreasing in the interval $(-\infty, -1]$ and f is increasing in the interval $(-\infty, -1]$.

Extrema and the Extreme Value Theorem

Let f be defined on an interval containing c. The value $f(c)$ is a **minimum** (also called the absolute minimum) of f in the interval if $f(c) \leq f(x)$ for every number x in the interval; similarly, $f(c)$ is a **maximum** (also called the absolute maximum) of f in the interval if $f(c) \geq f(x)$ for every number x in the interval. The minimum and maximum values of a function in an interval are the **extreme values,** or **extrema,** of the function in the interval.

Extreme Value Theorem: If f is continuous on a closed interval $[a, b]$, then f has both a minimum and a maximum value in $[a, b]$.

Here is a practice problem.

> Problem: Describe the extrema for the function f defined by $f(x) = x^3$ on the interval $[-2, 2]$ and graph the result.
>
> Solution: The function f defined by $f(x) = x^3$ is continuous everywhere, so it is continuous in the interval $[-2, 2]$. By the extreme value theorem, f has a minimum and a maximum value in $[-2, 2]$. The minimum value is $f(-2) = (-2)^3 = -8$, and the maximum value is $f(2) = (2)^3 = 8$. The graph is shown below.

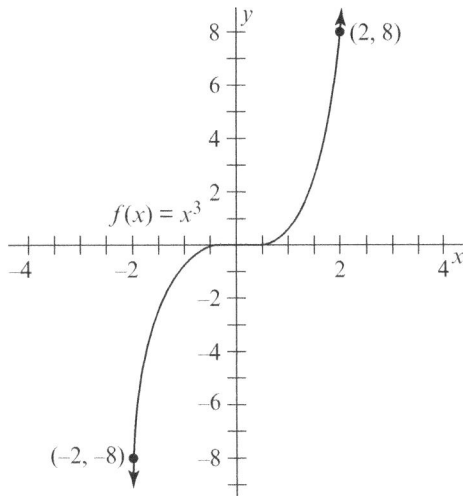

Tip: The extreme value theorem tells you when the minimum and maximum of a function exist, but not how to find these values. You can use features of your graphing calculator to find the extreme values of a function. Refer to the calculator guidebook for instructions or search for relevant tutorials online.

The number $f(c)$ is a **relative minimum** of a function f if there exists an open interval containing c in which $f(c)$ is a minimum; similarly, the number $f(c)$ is a **relative maximum** of a function f if there exists an open interval containing c in which $f(c)$ is a maximum. If $f(c)$ is a relative minimum or maximum of f, it is called a **relative extremum** of f. If f has a relative extremum at c, then either $f'(c) = 0$ or $f'(c)$ does not exist.

First and Second Derivative Tests

Given c is in the domain of f, then c is a **critical number** of f if either $f'(c) = 0$ or $f'(c)$ does not exist. The critical numbers determine points at which $f'(x)$ can change signs; that is, these are the only numbers for which the graph of f can have turning points, cusps, or discontinuities. If c is a critical number for f, then $f(c)$ is a **critical value** of f and the point $(c, f(c))$ is a **critical point** of the graph.

A **sign diagram** for $f'(x)$ is a diagram along the real line showing the signs for $f'(x)$ between critical numbers for f. You can use a sign diagram to predict the shape of the graph of f. (See the next section, "Concavity," for an example of a sign diagram.)

First Derivative Test: Given c is a critical number of a function f that is continuous on an open interval I containing c, then

- if $f'(x)$ changes sign at c from negative (for x values in I less than c) to positive (for x values in I greater than c), then $f(c)$ is a relative minimum of f; and
- if $f'(x)$ changes sign at c from positive (for x values in I less than c) to negative (for x values in I greater than c), then $f(c)$ is a relative maximum of f.

(See the next section, "Concavity," for an example of an application of the first derivative test.)

Second Derivative Test: Given c is a critical number of f and $f''(c)$ exists on an open interval containing c, then

- $f(c)$ is a relative minimum of f if $f''(c) > 0$; and
- $f(c)$ is a relative maximum of f if $f''(c) < 0$.
- If $f''(c) = 0$, the test is inconclusive.

(See the next section, "Concavity," for an example of an application of the second derivative test.)

Concavity

Given f is a function whose first and second derivatives exist on some open interval containing the number c, then

- the graph of f is **concave upward** at $(c, f(c))$ if $f''(c) > 0$; and
- the graph of f is **concave downward** at $(c, f(c))$ if $f''(c) < 0$.

The point $(c, f(c))$ is a point of **inflection** if the concavity of the graph of f changes at $(c, f(c))$. If a graph has an inflection point at $x = c$, then either $f''(c)$ is 0 or does not exist.

Tip: When a curve is concave up, it looks like it could hold water; when a curve is concave down, it looks like it would spill water.

A methodical way to analyze the behavior of a function is to proceed as follows:

1. First, find the critical number(s) of f by using $f'(c)$.
2. Next, use the first derivative test, a sign diagram, and, if applicable, the second derivative test to find relative extrema.
3. Finally, use $f''(c)$, if it exists, to investigate concavity and identify points of inflection.

Here is a practice problem (refer to "Differentiation Formulas" earlier in this section).

Problem: Given $f(x) = 2x^3 - 9x^2 + 2$, discuss critical points, the sign diagram, turning points, extrema, concavity, and points of inflection with regard to f. Then, graph the function.

Solution: Given $f(x) = 2x^3 - 9x^2 + 2$, then $f'(x) = 6x^2 - 18x$. Set $f'(x)$ equal to zero. If $f'(x) = 6x^2 - 18x = 6x(x-3) = 0$, then $x = 0$ and $x = 3$ are critical numbers. Create a sign diagram for $f'(x)$ as shown here.

	$x < 0$	$x = 0$	$0 < x < 3$	$x = 3$	$x > 3$
$f'(x)$	+	0	–	0	+
$f(x)$	increasing	2	decreasing	–25	increasing

Next, evaluate the second derivative $f''(x) = 12x - 18$ at the critical numbers, 0 and 3, to obtain $f''(0) = 12(0) - 18 = -18$ and $f''(3) = 12(3) - 18 = 18$. Thus, by the second derivative test, $f(0) = 2(0)^3 - 9(0)^2 + 2 = 2$ is a relative maximum because $f''(0) = -18 < 0$, and $f(3) = 2(3)^3 - 9(3)^2 + 2 = -25$ is a relative minimum because $f''(3) = 18 > 0$. For $x < 0$, $f''(x) = 12x - 18 < 0$, so the graph of f is concave downward in that interval. For $x > 3$, $f''(x) = 12x - 18 > 0$, so the graph of f is concave upward in that interval. Solving $f''(x) = 12x - 18 = 0$ yields $x = 1.5$ as a possible point of inflection. For $0 < x < 1.5$, $f''(x) = 12x - 18 < 0$, so the graph of f is concave downward from 0 to 1.5. From $1.5 < x < 3$, $f''(x) = 12x - 18 > 0$, so the graph of f is concave upward from 1.5 to 3. The concavity of the graph of f changes at $(1.5, -11.5)$, so $(1.5, -11.5)$ is a point of inflection. See the graph below.

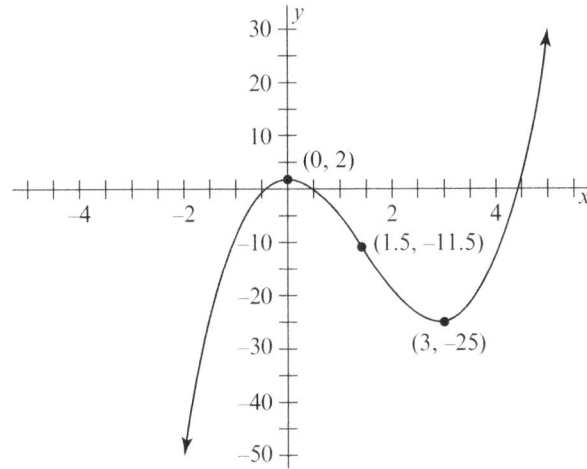

The Mean Value Theorem for Derivatives

Mean Value Theorem for Derivatives: If the function f is continuous on the closed interval $[a, b]$ and $f'(x)$ exists on the open interval (a, b), then there exists a number c in (a, b) such that $f'(c) = \dfrac{f(b) - f(a)}{b - a}$.

This theorem tells you that if f is continuous on $[a, b]$ and differentiable on (a, b), there exists some value c in (a, b) where the slope of the tangent line at $(c, f(c))$ is equal to the slope of the secant line between $(a, f(a))$ and $(b, f(b))$.

Here is a practice problem.

> Problem: Find the value of c, if any, in the interval $(1, 3)$ that satisfies the mean value theorem for derivatives for the function f defined by $f(x) = x^2$.
>
> Solution: The function f is quadratic and, therefore, is continuous on $[1, 3]$ and differentiable on $(1, 3)$. Find c such that $f'(c) = \dfrac{f(3) - f(1)}{3 - 1} = \dfrac{9 - 1}{3 - 1} = 4$. Because $f'(x) = 2x$, you have $2c = 4$, which yields $c = 2$.

Integrals

For this topic, you must understand and apply the fundamental theorems of calculus and solve problems involving integrals.

Fundamental Theorems of Calculus

The function F is called an **antiderivative** (or **indefinite integral**) of the function f if $F'(x) = f(x)$.

Chapter 2: Patterns and Algebra

First Fundamental Theorem of Calculus: If f is continuous on the closed interval $[a, b]$ and F is an antiderivative of f on $[a, b]$, then the evaluation of the **definite integral** $\int_a^b f(x)dx$ is given by $\int_a^b f(x)dx = F(b) - F(a)$. (See "Properties of the Definite Integral" later in this section for a further discussion of definite integrals.)

The following notations are used when applying the first fundamental theorem of calculus:

$$\int_a^b f(x)dx = F(b) - F(a) = F(x)\Big|_a^b = F(x)\Big|_a^b = [F(x)]_a^b = [F(x)]_{x=a}^{x=b}$$

Thus, to find the numerical value of the integral $\int_a^b f(x)dx$, you first find an antiderivative, say $F(x)$, for $f(x)$, evaluate that antiderivative at a and b, and then find the difference, $F(b) - F(a)$.

Here are two practice problems (refer to "Integration Formulas and Techniques" later in this section).

Problem: Evaluate the integral $\int_1^4 15x^2\, dx$.

Solution: $\int_1^4 15x^2\, dx = 5x^3\Big|_1^4 = 5(4)^3 - 5(1)^3 = 320 - 5 = 315$

Problem: Evaluate the integral $\int_3^6 \frac{1}{x} dx$.

Solution: $\int_3^6 \frac{1}{x} dx = \ln|x|\Big|_3^6 = \ln|6| - \ln|3| = \ln 6 - \ln 3 = \ln\left(\frac{6}{3}\right) = \ln 2$

The following statements about the definite integral are useful to know:

If a function f is continuous on a closed interval $[a, b]$, then the definite integral $\int_a^b f(x)dx$ is a value that always exists.

If the function f is continuous on the closed interval $[a, b]$, then the average value of f on $[a, b]$ is

$$\frac{1}{b-a}\int_a^b f(x)dx.$$

Second Fundamental Theorem of Calculus: If f is continuous on an open interval containing c, then for every x in the interval, $D_x\left[\int_c^x f(t)dt\right] = f(x)$.

Here is a practice problem.

Problem: Differentiate as indicated.

(a) $D_x \int_3^x (3t^2 - 7)dt$

(b) $D_x \int_0^x \sin t\, dt$

Solution:

(a) $D_x \int_3^x (3t^2 - 7)dt = 3x^2 - 7$

(b) $D_x \int_0^x \sin t\, dt = \sin x$

Try this practice problem.

Problem: Suppose f is a continuous function in the closed interval $[0, 3]$ and $F(x) = \int_0^x f(t)dt$, where $0 \le x \le 3$; then $F'(x) = D_x \int_0^x f(t)dt = f(x)$. If f has the graph shown, at which of the labeled points is F increasing?

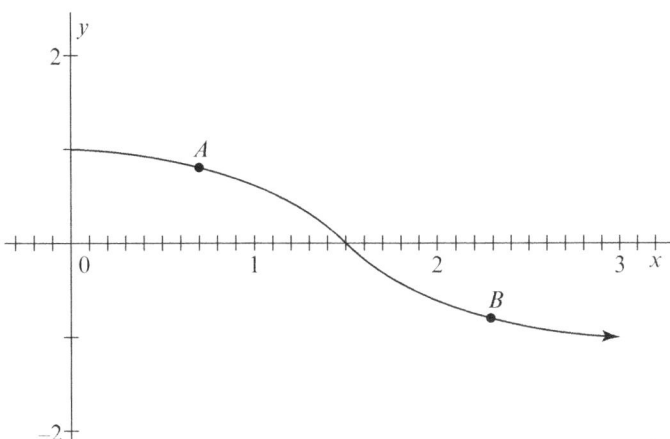

Solution: Given f is the first derivative of F, its graph tracks the slope of the tangent line to F at any point $x \in [0, 3]$. Thus, F is increasing when the graph of f is positive and decreasing when the graph of f is negative. Therefore, F is increasing at the point A.

Note: The expression $\int_c^x f(t)dt$ is an integral with a variable upper limit. The t appearing in this expression is called a "dummy variable" and can be replaced with any other letter not already being used.

The Mean Value Theorem for Integrals

Mean Value Theorem for Integrals: If the function f is continuous on a closed interval $[a, b]$, then there exists a number c in (a, b) such that $\int_a^b f(x)dx = f(c)(b-a)$.

This theorem tells you that if f is continuous on a closed interval $[a, b]$, there exists a number c in (a, b) such that the area of the region bounded by the graph of f, the x-axis, and the vertical lines $x = a$ and $x = b$ is the same as the area of a rectangle of height $f(c)$ and width $(b - a)$.

Here is a practice problem.

Problem: Find the value of c, if any, in the interval $(1, 3)$ that satisfies the mean value theorem for integrals for the function f defined by $f(x) = x^2$.

Solution: The function f is quadratic and, therefore, is continuous on $[1, 3]$. Find c such that

$$\int_1^3 x^2 dx = f(c)(3-1). \text{ Solving for } f(c) \text{ yields } f(c) = \frac{1}{2}\int_1^3 x^2 dx = \frac{1}{2}\left(\frac{x^3}{3}\right)\bigg|_1^3 = \frac{1}{2}\left(\frac{3^3}{3}\right) - \frac{1}{2}\left(\frac{1^3}{3}\right) = \frac{27}{6} - \frac{1}{6} = \frac{26}{6} = \frac{13}{3}.$$

Because $f(x) = x^2$, you have $c^2 = \frac{13}{3}$, which implies $c = \pm\sqrt{\frac{13}{3}}$. However, because c must lie in $(1, 3)$ and is therefore positive, $c = \sqrt{\frac{13}{3}}$.

Properties of the Definite Integral

- If f is defined at $x = a$, then $\int_a^a f(x)\,dx = 0$.
- If f is integrable on $[a, b]$, then $\int_a^b f(x)\,dx = -\int_b^a f(x)\,dx$.
- If f is integrable on $[a, b]$ and k is a constant, then the function kf is integrable on $[a, b]$ and $\int_a^b kf(x)\,dx = k\int_a^b f(x)\,dx$.
- If f and g are integrable on $[a, b]$, then the functions $f \pm g$ are integrable on $[a, b]$ and $\int_a^b (f(x) \pm g(x))\,dx = \int_a^b f(x)\,dx \pm \int_a^b g(x)\,dx$.
- If f is integrable on $[a, b]$, $[a, c]$, and $[c, b]$, then $\int_a^b f(x)\,dx = \int_a^c f(x)\,dx + \int_c^b f(x)\,dx$.
- If f is integrable and nonnegative on $[a, b]$, then $\int_a^b f(x)\,dx \geq 0$.
- If f and g are integrable on $[a, b]$, and $f(x) \leq g(x)$ for $a \leq x \leq b$, then $\int_a^b f(x)\,dx \leq \int_a^b g(x)\,dx$.
- If f is integrable on $[-a, a]$ and f is even, then $\int_{-a}^a f(x)\,dx = 2\int_0^a f(x)\,dx$.
- If f is integrable on $[-a, a]$ and f is odd, then $\int_{-a}^a f(x)\,dx = 0$.
- If k is a constant, then $\int_a^b k\,dx = k(b-a)$.

Integration Formulas and Techniques

The process of integrating a function is called **integration**. You should know the following integration formulas for your TExES Math exam. The constant C in the formulas is the **constant of integration,** and the result is an **indefinite integral.**

$$\int dx = x + C \qquad \int k\,dx = kx + C \qquad \int x^n\,dx = \frac{x^{n+1}}{n+1} + C,\ n \neq -1$$

$$\int \frac{1}{x}\,dx = \ln x + C,\ x > 0 \qquad \int e^x\,dx = e^x + C$$

$$\int \cos x\,dx = \sin x + C \qquad \int \sin x\,dx = -\cos x + C \qquad \int \sec^2 x\,dx = \tan x + C$$

$$\int \sec x \tan x\,dx = \sec x + C \qquad \int \csc x \cot x\,dx = -\csc x + C \qquad \int \csc^2 x\,dx = -\cot x + C$$

Change of Variable: $\int_a^b f(g(x))g'(x)\,dx = \int_{g(a)}^{g(b)} f(u)\,du$, where $u = g(x)$ and $du = g'(x)dx$

Integration by Parts: $\int u\,dv = u \cdot v - \int v\,du$

Here is a practice problem.

Problem: Use an appropriate formula or technique to find the indefinite integral.

(a) $\int (x^e + e^x)\,dx$

(b) $\int (x^2 + 1)\sqrt{x}\,dx$

Solution:

(a) $\int (x^e + e^x)\,dx = \int x^e\,dx + \int e^x\,dx = \dfrac{x^{e+1}}{e+1} + e^x + C$

(b) $\int (x^2+1)\sqrt{x}\,dx = \int (x^2+1)x^{\frac{1}{2}}\,dx = \int \left(x^{\frac{5}{2}} + x^{\frac{1}{2}}\right)dx = \int x^{\frac{5}{2}}\,dx + \int x^{\frac{1}{2}}\,dx = \dfrac{x^{\frac{7}{2}}}{\frac{7}{2}} + \dfrac{x^{\frac{3}{2}}}{\frac{3}{2}} + C = \dfrac{2}{7}x^{\frac{7}{2}} + \dfrac{2}{3}x^{\frac{3}{2}} + C$

Now try this practice problem.

Problem: Find $\int x\sin(3x)\,dx$.

Solution: Using the integration by parts formula, let $u = x$ and $dv = \sin 3x\,dx$. Then $du = dx$ and $v = \int \sin(3x)\,dx = -\dfrac{1}{3}\cos(3x)$. *Note:* The constant of integration is added at the end of the process.

Therefore, by $\int u\,dv = u \cdot v - \int v\,du$,

$\int x\sin(3x)\,dx = (x)\left(-\dfrac{1}{3}\cos(3x)\right) - \int \left(-\dfrac{1}{3}\cos(3x)\right)\cdot dx = -\dfrac{1}{3}x\cos(3x) + \dfrac{1}{3}\int \cos(3x)\,dx$

$= -\dfrac{1}{3}x\cos(3x) + \dfrac{1}{3}\cdot\dfrac{1}{3}\sin(3x) = -\dfrac{1}{3}x\cos(3x) + \dfrac{1}{9}\sin(3x) + C$

Applications of Definite Integrals

If f is a nonnegative, continuous function on the closed interval $[a, b]$, then the **area of the region** bounded by the graph of f, the x-axis, and the vertical lines $x = a$ and $x = b$ is $\int_a^b f(x)\,dx$.

Here is a practice problem.

Problem: Find the area, in square units, of the region under the continuous curve $y = x^2 + 2x$ bounded by the x-axis and the vertical lines $x = 4$ and $x = 6$.

Solution: The area, in square units, of the specified region equals

$\int_4^6 (x^2 + 2x)\,dx = \left[\dfrac{x^3}{3} + \dfrac{2x^2}{2}\right]_4^6 = \left(\dfrac{6^3}{3} + 6^2\right) - \left(\dfrac{4^3}{3} + 4^2\right) = 70\dfrac{2}{3}$

If f and g are continuous functions on the closed interval $[a, b]$ and $f(x) \geq g(x)$ on $[a, b]$, then the area of the region bounded by $y = f(x)$, $y = g(x)$, and the vertical lines $x = a$ and $x = b$ is $\int_a^b (f(x) - g(x))\,dx$.

Here is a practice problem.

Problem: Find the area, in square units, in the first quadrant enclosed by the continuous curves $y = x^2$ and $y = x^3$.

Solution: The graphs of $y = x^2$ and $y = x^3$ intersect when $x^3 = x^2$. Sketch a figure.

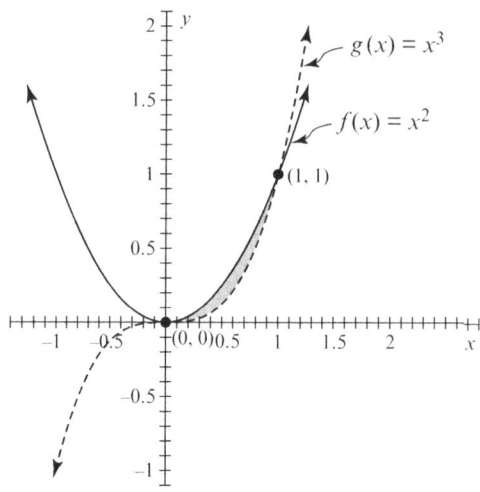

Solving this equation yields

$$x^3 = x^2$$
$$x^3 - x^2 = 0$$
$$x^2(x-1) = 0$$
$$x = 0 \text{ or } x = 1$$

Because $x^2 \geq x^3$ on the interval from $x = 0$ to $x = 1$, the shaded area enclosed by the two curves is

$$\int_0^1 (x^2 - x^3)\,dx = \left(\frac{x^3}{3} - \frac{x^4}{4}\right)\Big|_0^1 = \frac{1}{3} - \frac{1}{4} = \frac{1}{12}.$$

Tip: For your TExES Math exam, if asked to find the area enclosed by two curves, first, you might need to find the points of intersection of the two curves to determine *a* and *b*. You can use your graphing calculator to find where the curves intersect, or you might elect to find the points of intersection algebraically. After determining *a* and *b*, you can numerically evaluate the integral.

The definite integral can be used to compute the area under a curve or between two curves, as shown in this section. It can also be used to compute the volume of three-dimensional figures, accumulated distance, accumulated production, the total of a continuous income stream, and the results of other limiting sum processes.

Chapter 3

Geometry and Measurement

This chapter provides a review of key ideas of geometry and measurement concepts and principles.

Part 1

Part 1 of this chapter is for all candidates who plan to take a TExES Math exam. Carefully study the review material, being sure to concentrate as you go through it. Work through the examples and the practice problems and make sure you understand them thoroughly. When working a practice problem, you should cover up the solution. Then check your answer when you've finished.

Geometry

For this topic, you must understand geometric relationships, know concepts and properties of two- and three-dimensional figures, and understand and apply transformational geometry.

Congruence, Similarity, and Symmetry

Congruent (symbolized by ≅) geometric figures have exactly the same size and same shape. They are superimposable, meaning they will fit exactly on top of each other. Corresponding parts of congruent figures are congruent, and thereby, have the same measure. That is, corresponding lengths are equal and corresponding angles have the same measure.

You can use hash marks (as in the pair of congruent triangles shown below) to draw attention to corresponding congruent parts. *Tip:* Corresponding parts are marked with the same number of strokes.

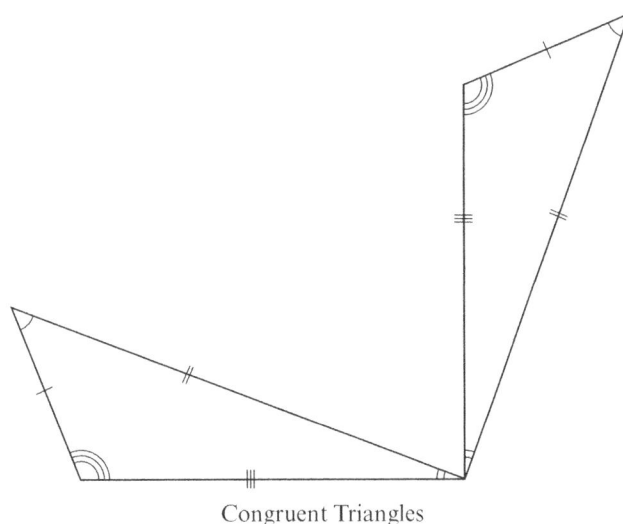
Congruent Triangles

Similar (symbolized by ~) geometric figures have the same shape but not necessarily the same size. Corresponding angles of similar shapes are congruent, and corresponding lengths of similar shapes are proportional.

Here are examples of similar figures. Notice that congruent figures are also similar figures.

153

Chapter 3: Geometry and Measurement

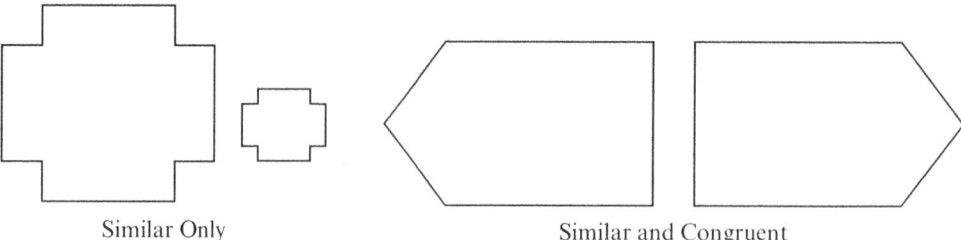

Similar Only   Similar and Congruent

Symmetry describes a characteristic of the shape of a figure or object. A figure has **reflective** (or **bilateral**) **symmetry** if it can be folded exactly in half and the resulting two parts are congruent. The line along the fold is the **line of symmetry**. A figure has **rotational symmetry** if it can be rotated onto an exact copy of itself before it comes back to its original position. The center of rotation is the **center of symmetry.** Here are illustrations.

Reflective Symmetry Only   Both Reflective and Rotational Symmetry

Note: See "Geometric Transformations" later in this chapter for additional discussions of congruence, similarity, and rotation of geometric figures.

Angles and Lines

In geometry, the terms *point, line,* and *plane* are undefined. Think of a **point** as a location in space. Think of a **line** as a set of points that extends infinitely in both directions. Think of a **plane** as a set of points that forms a flat infinite surface. *Note:* For discussions in this chapter, unless specifically stated otherwise, all plane figures and objects are considered to lie in the same plane.

Angles

A **ray** is a portion of a line extending infinitely from a point in one direction. $\overrightarrow{AB}$ is the ray that starts at A, goes through B, and continues on.

When two rays meet at a common point, they form an **angle.** The point where the rays meet is the angle's **vertex** (the plural is vertices), and the rays are its **sides.** The symbol for angle is ∠.

You measure an angle with reference to a circle with its center as the vertex of the angle. The amount of rotation required to form the angle can be expressed as a number of **degrees.** The symbol for degrees is °. A full rotation around the circle is 360°. An angle that turns $\frac{1}{360}$ of a complete rotation around the circle measures 1°.

A counterclockwise rotation results in a positive measure. A clockwise rotation results in a negative measure.

The number of degrees in an angle is its measure. If there are k degrees in angle A, then you write $m\angle A = k°$. Angles are congruent if they have the same measure. *Note:* Informally, you might write "$\angle A = k°$" or even "$A = k°$" as long as there is a clear understanding that the meaning is "$m\angle A = k°$."

An **acute angle** measures between 0° and 90°; that is, if angle A is acute, $0° < m\angle A < 90°$. An **obtuse angle** measures between 90° and 180°; that is, if angle B is obtuse, $90° < m\angle B < 180°$. A **right angle** measures exactly

90°; that is, if angle C is a right angle, $m\angle C = 90°$. A **straight angle** measures exactly 180°; that is, if angle D is a straight angle, $m\angle D = 180°$. Here are illustrations.

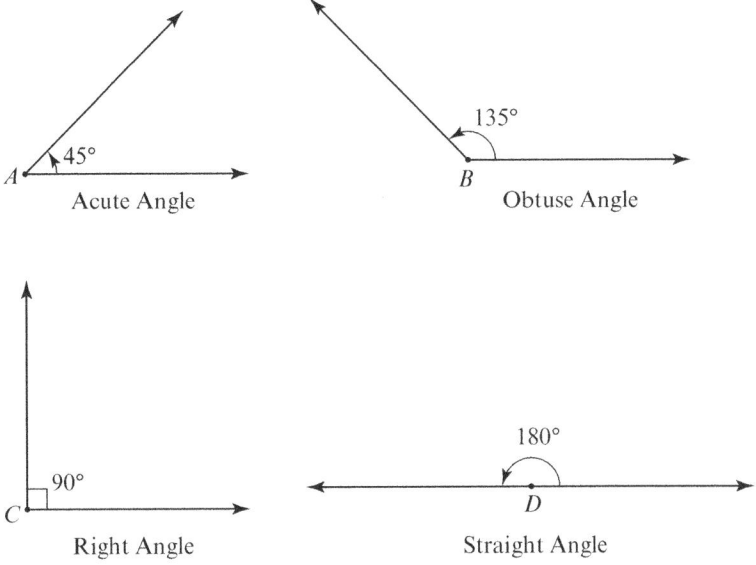

Tip: The box in the corner of ∠C denotes a right angle.

Two angles whose measures sum to 90° are **complementary angles.** Each angle is the other angle's **complement.** Two angles whose measures sum to 180° are **supplementary angles.** Each angle is the other angle's **supplement.**

Here is a practice problem.

Problem: What is the complement of an angle that measures 30°?
Solution: The complement is 90° − 30° = 60°.

Adjacent angles are angles that have a common vertex and a common side with no overlap. Here is an illustration.

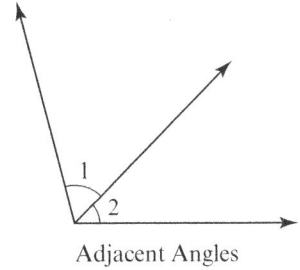
Adjacent Angles

A **bisector of an angle** is a line or ray that passes through the vertex of the angle and divides it into two congruent angles. Here is an illustration.

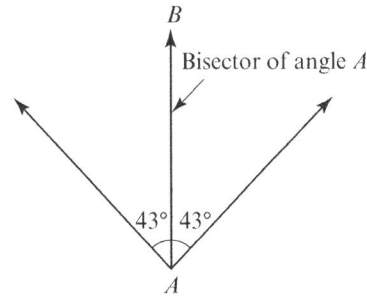

155

The following are theorems about angles that are useful to know.

- Two angles that are complementary are both acute.
- Two angles that are both congruent and supplementary are both right angles.
- Supplements of congruent angles are congruent.
- Complements of congruent angles are congruent.
- If one angle of two intersecting lines is a right angle, then all four of the angles formed by the two lines are right angles.

Lines

The notation $\overleftrightarrow{PQ}$ denotes the line containing the points P and Q and extending infinitely in both directions.

A **line segment** $\overline{PQ}$ is a part of a line that connects the points P and Q and includes P and Q. The points P and Q are the segment's **endpoints.** Its length is denoted PQ. Congruent segments have equal lengths.

Two lines in a plane can be *coincident lines, parallel lines,* or *intersecting lines*. Two lines are **coincident** if they have all points in common. **Parallel** lines have no points in common. **Intersecting** lines cross at exactly one point in the plane. Here are illustrations.

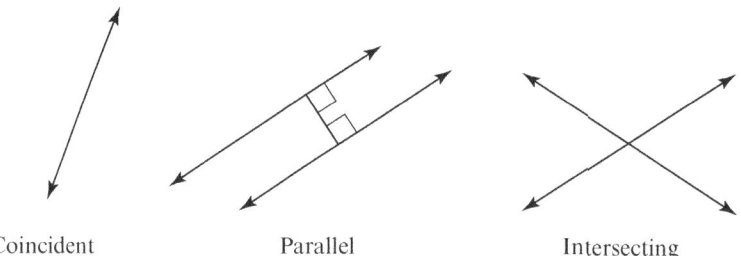

Coincident   Parallel   Intersecting

Two intersecting lines form four angles. **Vertical angles** are two *nonadjacent* angles formed by the two intersecting lines with a common vertex at the intersection of the two lines. Vertical angles formed by two intersecting lines are congruent. In the following figure, ∠1 and ∠3 are congruent vertical angles, and ∠2 and ∠4 are congruent vertical angles.

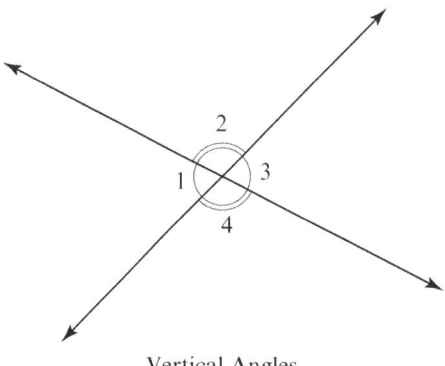

Vertical Angles

Parallel lines (in a plane) never meet. The distance between them is always the same. To indicate that line *l* is parallel to line *m*, write *l* ∥ *m*. A **transversal** is a straight line that intersects two or more given lines. When two parallel lines are cut by a transversal, eight angles are formed. In the following figure, parallel lines *l* and *m* are cut by a transversal *n*.

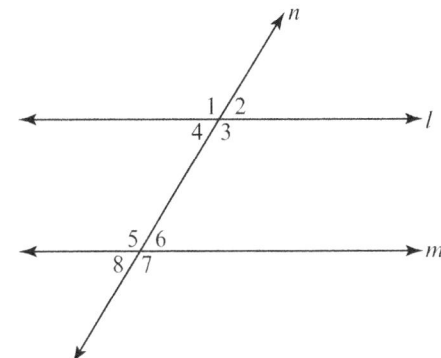

The interior angles are ∠3, ∠4, ∠5, and ∠6. The exterior angles are ∠1, ∠2, ∠7, and ∠8. The corresponding angles are the pair of angles ∠1 and ∠5, the pair of angles ∠2 and ∠6, the pair of angles ∠4 and ∠8, and the pair of angles ∠3 and ∠7. The alternate exterior angles are the pair of angles ∠1 and ∠7 and the pair of angles ∠2 and ∠8. The alternate interior angles are the pair of angles ∠4 and ∠6 and the pair of angles ∠3 and ∠5.

Perpendicular lines intersect at right angles. To indicate that line *l* is perpendicular to line *m*, write *l* ⊥ *m*. The **perpendicular bisector** of a line segment is the set of all points in the plane of the line segment that are equidistant from the endpoints of the line segment. In the following figure, line *m* is the perpendicular bisector of line segment $\overline{AB}$.

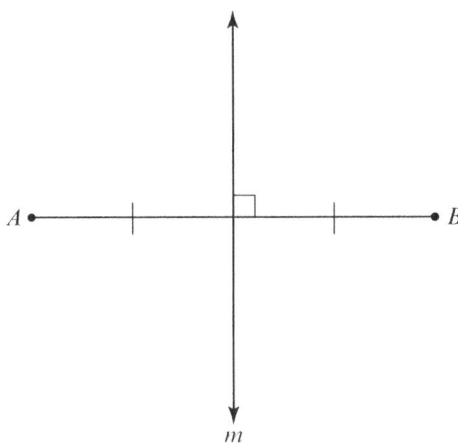

Two or more lines in a plane are **concurrent** if there is a single point, called the **point of concurrency**, that lies on all of them. Here is an illustration.

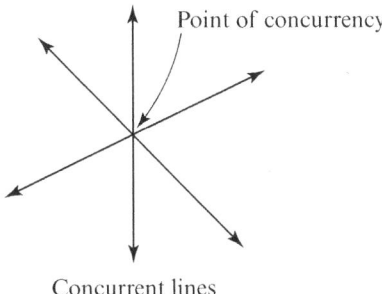

Concurrent lines

The following theorems about lines are useful to know.

- **Euclid's Parallel Postulate:** Given a line and a point in the same plane but not on the line, there is one and only one line through the given point that is parallel to the given line.
- If two intersecting lines form one right angle, then they form four right angles.

- Two distinct lines (in a plane) that are perpendicular to the same line are parallel.
- A line in a plane that is perpendicular to one of two parallel lines is perpendicular to the other parallel line.
- A line in a plane that intersects one of two parallel lines in exactly one point intersects the other parallel line.
- If two parallel lines are cut by a transversal, then any pair of corresponding angles, alternate exterior angles, or alternate interior angles are congruent.
- Two lines that are cut by a transversal are parallel if any pair of corresponding angles, alternate exterior angles, or alternate interior angles are congruent.
- Two lines that are cut by a transversal are parallel if a pair of interior angles on the same side of the transversal are supplementary.
- The shortest distance from a point to a line is the length of the perpendicular line segment from the point to the line.

Polygons

A **polygon** is a simple, closed-plane figure composed of line segments, fitted end to end. The segments meet only at their endpoints, and no two segments with a common endpoint are collinear. The segments are the polygon's **sides.** The point at which two sides of a polygon intersect is a **vertex.**

Polygons are classified by the number of sides they have. A **triangle** is a three-sided polygon. A **quadrilateral** is a four-sided polygon. A **pentagon** is a five-sided polygon. A **hexagon** is a six-sided polygon. A **heptagon** is a seven-sided polygon. An **octagon** is an eight-sided polygon. A **nonagon** is a nine-sided polygon. A **decagon** is a ten-sided polygon. In general, an ***n*-gon** is an *n*-sided polygon. A **regular polygon** is a polygon for which all sides and angles are congruent.

An *n*-sided polygon has *n* interior angles and *n* exterior angles. An **interior angle** of a polygon is formed at a vertex by two adjacent sides and lies within the polygon. The sum of the measures of an *n*-sided polygon's interior angles equals $(n-2)180°$. An **exterior angle** of a polygon is formed at a vertex by one side of the polygon and the extension of the adjacent side. The sum of the measures of a polygon's exterior angles equals 360°, no matter how many sides the polygon has. An interior and an exterior angle at a vertex of a polygon are supplementary. *Note:* It is possible to draw two congruent exterior angles at each vertex of a polygon, but only one is considered when speaking of the exterior angle at a particular vertex. The following figure shows an interior and exterior angle of a pentagon.

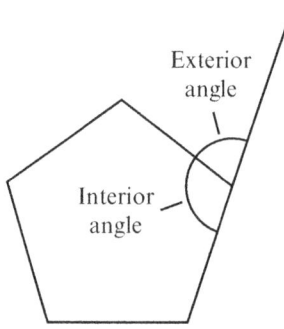

Here are two practice problems.

Problem: What is the measure of an interior angle of a regular pentagon?
Solution: The sum of the five interior angles of a regular pentagon is $(5-2)180° = 540°$. Thus, each interior angle has a measure of $\frac{540°}{5} = 108°$.

Problem: What is the measure of an exterior angle of a regular decagon?

Solution: The sum of the 10 exterior angles of a regular decagon is 360°. Thus, each exterior angle has a measure of $\frac{360°}{10} = 36°$.

A line segment that connects two nonconsecutive vertices of a polygon is a **diagonal.** The number of diagonals of an *n*-sided polygon is $\frac{n(n-3)}{2}$. Here are illustrations of regular polygons with the number of diagonals indicated below the figure.

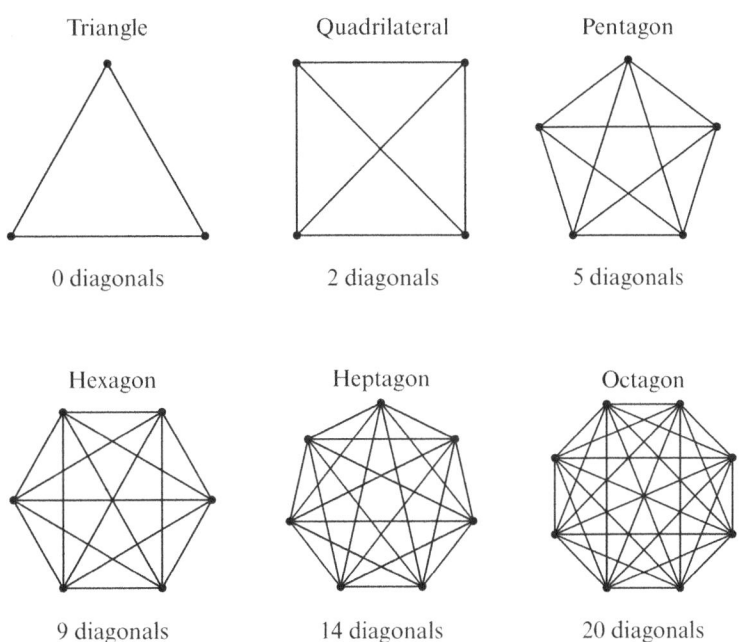

Here is a practice problem.

Problem: A decagon has how many diagonals?

Solution: The number of diagonals of a decagon is $\frac{10(10-3)}{2} = 35$.

A polygon in which each interior angle is less than 180° is **convex.** All the diagonals of a convex polygon lie within the polygon's interior. A polygon in which at least one interior angle is greater than 180° is **concave.** Not all the diagonals of a concave polygon lie within the polygon's interior. Here are illustrations.

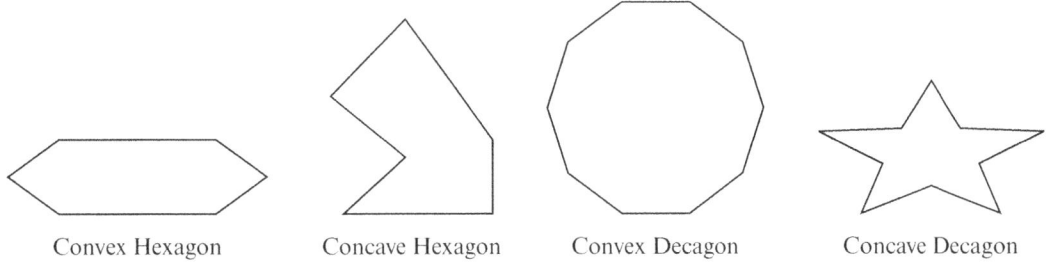

Triangles

A **triangle** is a three-sided polygon. For this topic, you must demonstrate an understanding of the properties of triangles.

Classifying Triangles

You can classify triangles according to their sides. A **scalene triangle** has no two sides congruent. An **isosceles triangle** has at least two congruent sides (and the angles opposite the congruent sides are congruent **base angles**). An **equilateral triangle** has three congruent sides (and three congruent angles). Here are examples.

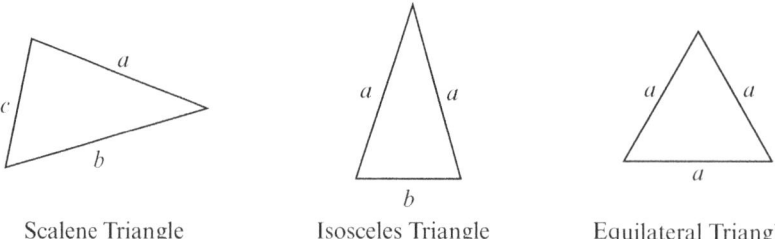

Scalene Triangle   Isosceles Triangle   Equilateral Triangle

You can classify triangles according to the measures of their interior angles. The sum of the measures of a triangle's interior angles is 180°. An **acute triangle** has three acute interior angles. A **right triangle** has one right interior angle. An **obtuse triangle** has one obtuse interior angle.

Here is a practice problem.

> Problem: Describe each triangle shown as an acute triangle, a right triangle, or an obtuse triangle.

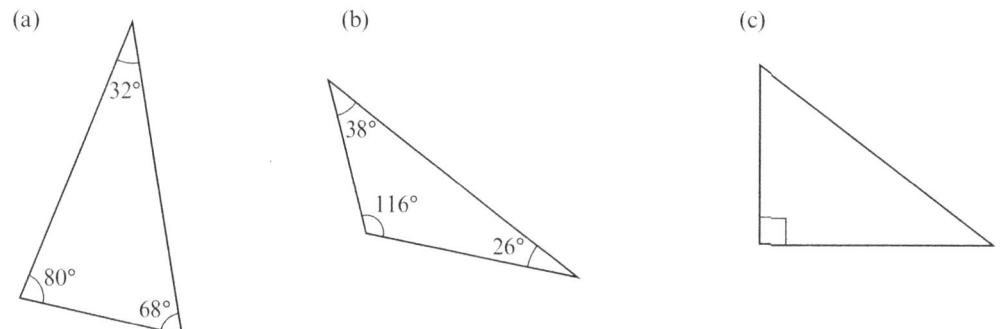

> Solution: **(a)** acute triangle; **(b)** obtuse triangle; **(c)** right triangle

The Triangle Inequality Theorem

The **triangle inequality theorem** asserts that the sum of the lengths of any two sides of a triangle is greater than the length of the third side. In simple terms, the triangle inequality theorem means that any side of a triangle must be shorter than the sum of the other two sides; otherwise, the three sides will not make a triangle.

Here are two practice problems.

> Problem: Can the lengths 4, 9, and 11 be the lengths of the sides of a triangle? Yes or No? Justify your answer.
> Solution: The longest side is 11. Compare 4 + 9 and 11. Because 4 + 9 = 13, which is greater than 11, the answer is yes.
> Problem: Can the lengths 2, 6, and 9 be the lengths of the sides of a triangle? Yes or No?
> Solution: The longest side is 9. Compare 2 + 6 and 9. Because 2 + 6 = 8, which is less than 9, the answer is no.

Points of Concurrency Associated with Triangles

A triangle's **altitude** is a perpendicular line segment from a vertex to a line containing the opposite side, called the **base**. The **height** of a triangle is the length of the altitude. *Note:* The term *altitude* is sometimes used to mean the *height* of the triangle, rather than the line segment that determines the height. On your TExES Math exam, you will be able to tell from the context of the problem what meaning is intended for the term *altitude*.

Every triangle has three altitudes, one from each vertex. The lines containing a triangle's altitudes are **concurrent,** meaning they intersect in a point. This point of concurrency of a triangle's altitudes is the triangle's **orthocenter.** See the following figure.

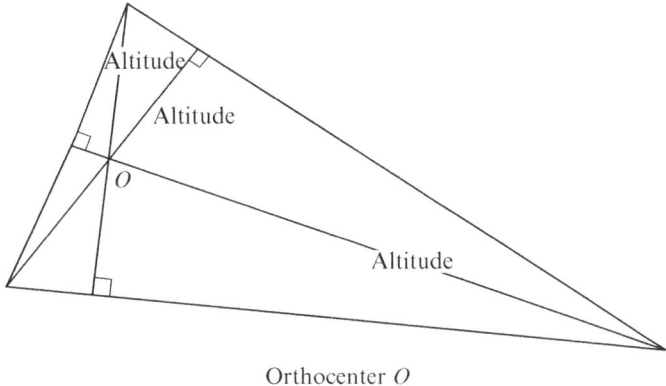

Orthocenter O

A **median** in a triangle is a line segment connecting a vertex of the triangle to the midpoint of the side opposite that vertex. The lines containing the triangle's medians are concurrent and the **centroid,** their point of concurrency, is two-thirds of the way along each median, from the vertex to the opposite side. See the following figure.

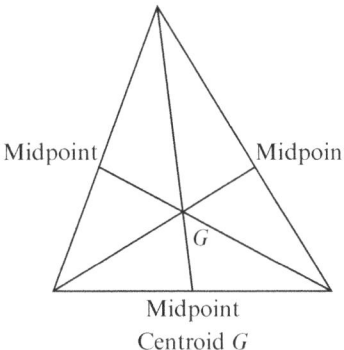

Centroid G

A **perpendicular bisector** of a triangle's side is a line perpendicular to that side at its midpoint. The perpendicular bisectors of a triangle's sides are concurrent, and the **circumcenter,** their point of concurrency, is equidistant from the triangle's vertices. Thus, if a circle is circumscribed about triangle XYZ, the circumcenter is the center of the circumscribed circle. A circle that is **circumscribed** about a triangle passes through the triangle's three vertices and contains the entire triangle in its interior. See the following figure.

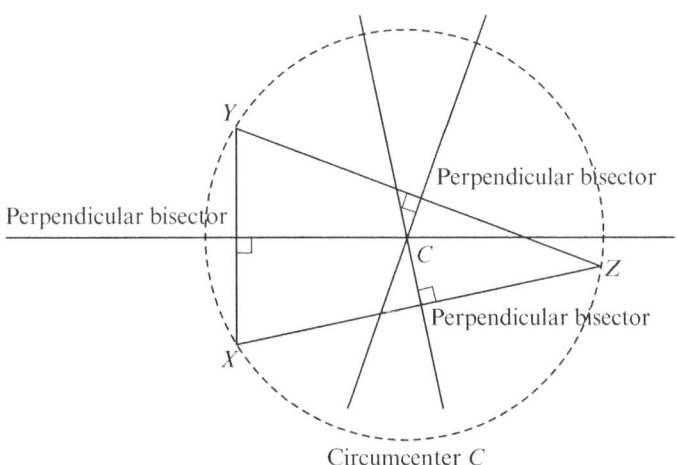

Circumcenter C

161

The **angle bisectors** of a triangle's interior angles are concurrent and the **incenter,** their point of concurrency, is equidistant from the three sides. Therefore, if a circle is inscribed in a triangle, the incenter is the center of the inscribed circle. A circle that is **inscribed** in a triangle touches each side of the triangle in only one point and is the largest circle contained entirely within the triangle's interior. See the following figure.

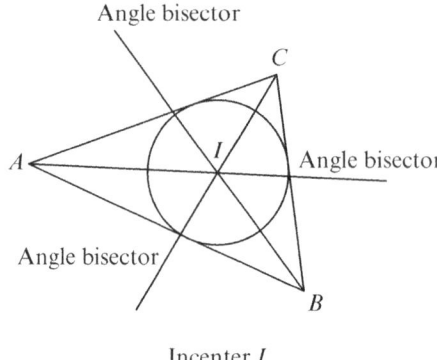

Incenter *I*

Congruent and Similar Triangles

Congruent triangles are triangles for which corresponding sides and corresponding angles are congruent. You can use the following theorems to prove two triangles are congruent. ***Remember:*** To make sure a triangle exists, the sum of the lengths of any two sides must be greater than the length of the third side.

- If three sides of one triangle are congruent, correspondingly, to three sides of another triangle, then the two triangles are congruent (SSS).
- If two sides and the included angle of one triangle are congruent, correspondingly, to two sides and the included angle of another triangle, then the two triangles are congruent (SAS).
- If two angles and the included side of one triangle are congruent, correspondingly, to two angles and the included side of another triangle, then the two triangles are congruent (ASA).
- If two angles and the nonincluded side of one triangle are congruent, correspondingly, to two angles and the nonincluded side of another triangle, then the two triangles are congruent (AAS).

Tip: Two methods that are not guaranteed to improve congruence are AAA (three corresponding angles congruent) and SSA (two corresponding sides and the nonincluded angle congruent).

Similar triangles are triangles for which corresponding sides are proportional and corresponding angles are congruent. You can use the following theorems to prove two triangles are similar.

- If corresponding angles of two triangles are congruent, the two triangles are similar.
- If corresponding sides of two triangles are proportional, the two triangles are similar.
- If two angles of one triangle are congruent to two corresponding angles of another triangle, then the two triangles are similar.
- If two sides of one triangle are proportional to two corresponding sides of another triangle, and the included angles are congruent, then the two triangles are similar.

(See "Geometric Transformations" later in this chapter for an additional discussion of *congruence* and *similarity*.)

Here are other theorems about triangles that are useful to know.

- The measure of an exterior angle of a triangle equals the sum of the measures of the nonadjacent (remote) interior angles.
- The segment drawn between the midpoints of two sides of a triangle is parallel to the third side and half as long.

- A line that is parallel to one side of a triangle and cuts the other two sides in distinct points cuts off segments that are proportional to these two sides; for instance, the ratio of the length of one side to the length of its top segment equals the ratio of the length of the other side to the length of its top segment.
- A line that intersects two sides of a triangle and cuts off segments proportional to these two sides is parallel to the third side.
- The bisector of an interior angle of a triangle divides the opposite side in the ratio of the sides that form the angle bisected.
- If two sides of a triangle are congruent, then the angles opposite those sides are congruent, and the reverse is true.
- The ratio of the perimeters of two similar triangles is the same as the ratio of any two corresponding sides.
- The ratio of the areas of two similar triangles is the square of the ratio of any two corresponding sides.

The Pythagorean Theorem

In a right triangle, the side opposite the right angle is the **hypotenuse** of the right triangle. The hypotenuse is *always* the longest side of the right triangle. The other two sides are the right triangle's **legs**. See the following figure.

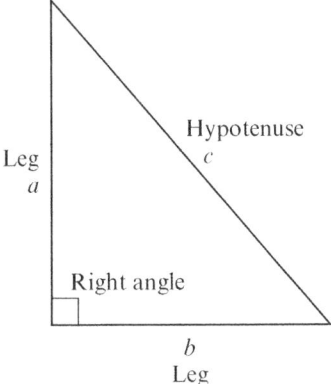

The **Pythagorean theorem** states that, in a right triangle, $c^2 = a^2 + b^2$, where c is the length of the hypotenuse and a and b are the lengths of the legs of the right triangle. This relationship applies only to right triangles. If you know any two sides of a right triangle, you can find the third side by using the formula $c^2 = a^2 + b^2$.

Here are two practice problems.

Problem: Find the length of the hypotenuse of a right triangle that has legs of 9 centimeters and 12 centimeters.

Solution: Use the Pythagorean theorem, omitting the units for convenience, to solve for c.

$$c^2 = 9^2 + 12^2 = 81 + 144 = 225$$

Hence, $c = \sqrt{225} = 15$. The length of the hypotenuse is 15 centimeters.

Tip: The number 225 has two square roots, 15 and –15. The negative value is rejected because the length of the hypotenuse (or any side of a triangle) cannot be negative.

Problem: Find b in the right triangle shown.

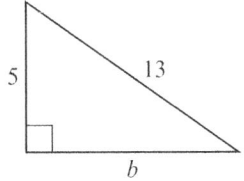

Solution: Use the Pythagorean theorem to solve for b.
$$b^2 = 13^2 - 5^2 = 169 - 25 = 144$$
Hence, $b = \sqrt{144} = 12$.

The converse of the Pythagorean theorem also is true. To be precise: If the square of the length of the longest side of a triangle equals the sum of the squares of the lengths of the other two sides, the triangle is a right triangle, with its right angle opposite the longest side.

Here is a practice problem.

>   Problem: Is the triangle with sides of lengths 3, 4, and 5 a right triangle? Yes or No? Justify your answer.
>   Solution: Yes, a triangle with sides of lengths 3, 4, and 5 is a right triangle because $3^2 + 4^2 = 9 + 16 = 25 = 5^2$.

The numbers (3, 4, 5) are a **Pythagorean triple**, so called because they are natural numbers that satisfy the relation $a^2 + b^2 = c^2$. Other well-known Pythagorean triples are (5, 12, 13), (8, 15, 17), and (7, 24, 25). After you identify a Pythagorean triple, any multiple of the three numbers is also a Pythagorean triple. That is, if each number of a Pythagorean triple is multiplied by a positive number k, the resulting triple also satisfies $a^2 + b^2 = c^2$.

Here is a practice problem.

>   Problem: Is the triangle with sides of lengths 30, 40, and 50 a right triangle? Yes or No? Justify your answer.
>   Solution: Yes, because (30, 40, 50) is a Pythagorean triple derived from (3, 4, 5).

Here are additional theorems about right triangles that are useful to know.

- The length of the median to the hypotenuse of a right triangle is one-half the length of the hypotenuse.
- The altitude to a right triangle's hypotenuse divides the triangle into two right triangles that are similar to each other and to the original right triangle. Furthermore, the altitude's length is the geometric mean of the lengths of the two segments into which it separates the hypotenuse. In the figure shown below, $\triangle ACB \sim \triangle AHC \sim \triangle CHB$; and $\dfrac{AH}{h} = \dfrac{h}{HB}$.

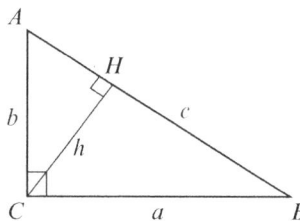

- The lengths of the sides of a 45°-45°-90° right triangle are in the ratio $\dfrac{1}{\sqrt{2}} : \dfrac{1}{\sqrt{2}} : 1$ or, equivalently, $1 : 1 : \sqrt{2}$.
- The lengths of the sides of a 30°-60°-90° right triangle are in the ratio $\dfrac{1}{2} : \dfrac{\sqrt{3}}{2} : 1$, or equivalently, $1 : \sqrt{3} : 2$, where the shortest side is opposite the 30° angle.
- If the length of one leg of a right triangle is one-half the length of the hypotenuse, the triangle is a 30°-60°-90° right triangle.
- If the base of an isosceles triangle is $\sqrt{2}$ times as long as each of the two congruent sides, then the angle opposite the base is a right triangle.
- Given two right triangles, if the hypotenuse and one leg of one triangle are congruent to the hypotenuse and the corresponding leg of the other triangle, then the two right triangles are congruent.

Quadrilaterals

A **quadrilateral** is a four-sided polygon. Special quadrilaterals are trapezoids, kites, and parallelograms.

Trapezoids

A **trapezoid** is a quadrilateral that has *exactly* one pair of parallel sides. (*Note:* This definition excludes parallelograms as a special case.) The parallel sides are its **bases.** Its nonparallel sides are its **legs.** Its **altitude** is a perpendicular line segment from any point on a line containing one of its bases to the line containing the opposite base. The segment joining the midpoints of the legs is its **median.** Shown below is isosceles trapezoid $ABCD$, in which $AD \parallel BC$ and $AB = DC$.

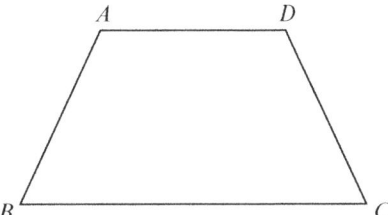

Some useful properties of a trapezoid are the following:

- It has exactly one pair of parallel sides.
- The median is parallel to each base, and its length equals one-half the sum of the lengths of the two bases.
- Lower base angles and upper base angles on the same leg are supplementary.
- The legs of an isosceles trapezoid are congruent.
- The lower base angles of an isosceles trapezoid are congruent.
- The upper base angles of an isosceles trapezoid are congruent.
- The diagonals of an isosceles trapezoid are congruent.

Kites

A **kite** is a quadrilateral in which exactly one diagonal is the perpendicular bisector of the other diagonal. Shown below is kite $EFGH$, in which $HE = HG$, $EF = GF$, and $\angle HEF \cong \angle HGF$.

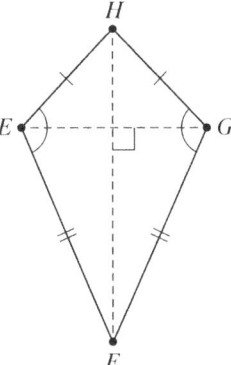

Here are properties of kites.

- A kite has no parallel sides.
- A kite has two distinct pairs of adjacent congruent sides.
- Exactly one pair of diagonally opposite angles are congruent.
- The opposite sides of a kite are not congruent.

Parallelograms

A **parallelogram** is a quadrilateral in which both pairs of opposite sides are parallel. Shown below is parallelogram *PQRS*.

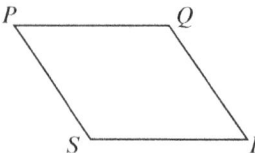

Some useful properties of a parallelogram are the following:

- Opposite sides are congruent.
- The sum of the four interior angles is 360°.
- Opposite interior angles are congruent.
- Consecutive interior angles are supplementary.
- If one interior angle is a right angle, then all the angles are right angles.
- The diagonals bisect each other.
- Each diagonal divides the parallelogram into two congruent triangles.

Some parallelograms have special names because of their special properties. A **rhombus** is a parallelogram that has four congruent sides. A **rectangle** is a parallelogram that has four right angles. A **square** is a parallelogram that has four right angles and four congruent sides. These three figures have all the general properties of parallelograms. In addition, in rectangles and squares, the diagonals are congruent. In rhombuses and squares, the diagonals intersect at right angles. Here are illustrations.

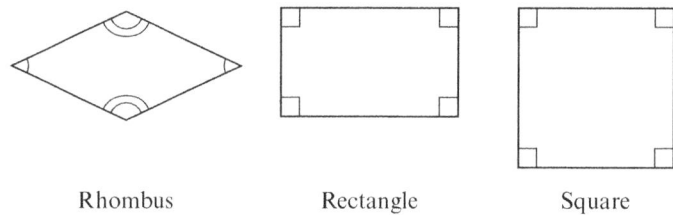

Rhombus   Rectangle   Square

Theorems about Quadrilaterals

The following are theorems about quadrilaterals that are useful to know.

- The sum of the interior angles of a quadrilateral is 360°.
- If the diagonals of a quadrilateral bisect each other, the quadrilateral is a parallelogram.
- If both pairs of opposite sides of a quadrilateral are congruent, the quadrilateral is a parallelogram.
- If two sides of a quadrilateral are parallel and congruent, the quadrilateral is a parallelogram.
- If the diagonals of a quadrilateral are perpendicular bisectors of each other, the quadrilateral is a rhombus.
- If a parallelogram has one right angle, it has four right angles and is a rectangle.
- If a rhombus has one right angle, it has four right angles and is a square.

Circles

A **circle** is a closed-plane figure for which all points are the same distance from a point within, called the **center**. A circle's **radius** is a line segment joining the circle's center to any point on the circle. *Note:* The plural of radius is **radii**. A **tangent** is a line that intersects the circle in exactly one point. A **secant** is a line that intersects the circle in two points. An **arc** is a portion of the circle. A **chord** is a line segment with both endpoints on the circle. A **diameter** is a chord that passes through the circle's center. A circle's diameter is twice the radius. Conversely, a circle's radius is half the diameter. See the following illustration.

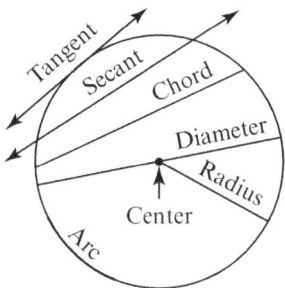

In a circle, a radius perpendicular to a chord bisects the chord. Consequently, a chord's perpendicular bisector passes through the circle's center as shown below.

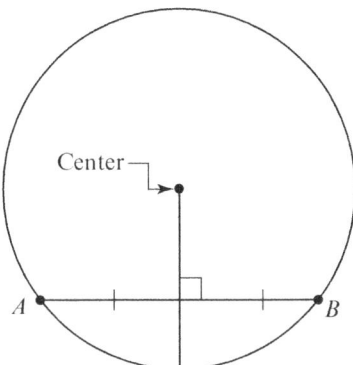

An **arc** is a portion of a circle; it is the set of points between and including two points on the circle. The two points determine two arcs on the circle. Arcs are measured in degrees. If the two arcs are of unequal measure, the arc with the smaller measure is the **minor arc,** and the arc with the greater measure is the **major arc.** A **semicircle** is an arc whose endpoints are the endpoints of the circle's diameter. The degree measure of a semicircle is 180°.

A **central angle** of a circle is an angle that has its vertex at the circle's center. A central angle and its **intercepted arc** have the same degree measure.

Here is a practice problem.

    Problem: In the circle shown, what is the measure of minor arc $\overparen{AB}$?

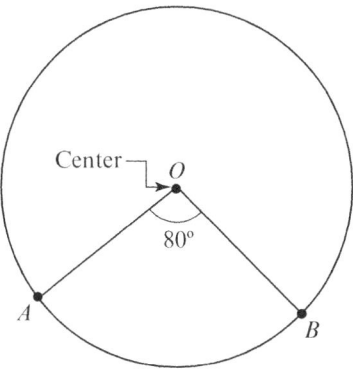

    Solution: $m\overparen{AB} = m\angle AOB = 80°$

An **inscribed angle** is an angle whose vertex is on a circle and whose sides are chords of the circle. The arc of the circle that is in the inscribed angle's interior and whose endpoints are on the angle's sides is its intercepted arc. The measure of an inscribed angle is half the measure of its intercepted arc. An angle inscribed in a semicircle is a right angle.

167

Here is a practice problem.

Problem: In the circle shown, what is the measure of $\angle ADB$?

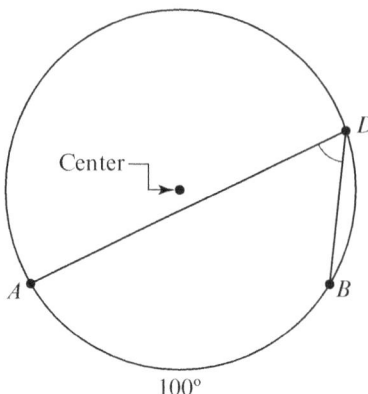

Solution: $m\angle ADB = \frac{1}{2}(100°) = 50°$

If two chords intersect within a circle, each of the angles formed equals one-half the sum of its intercepted arcs. Furthermore, the product of the lengths of the segments formed for one chord equals the product of the lengths of the segments formed for the other chord. In the circle shown below,

$m\angle RVU = m\angle SVT = \frac{1}{2}(50° + 70°) = \frac{1}{2}(120°) = 60°$; and $(RV)(VS) = (UV)(VT)$.

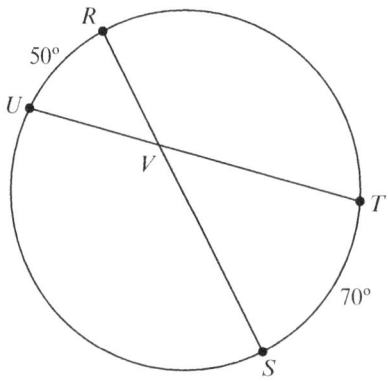

The point of contact of a tangent to a circle is the **point of tangency.** If a line is tangent to a circle, then the radius drawn to the point of tangency will be perpendicular to the tangent. See the following figure.

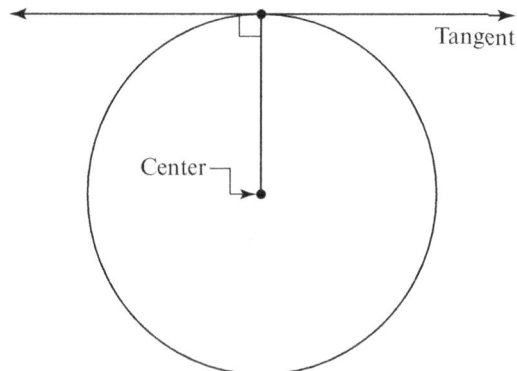

The length, L, of an arc that has measure $a°$ is $L = \dfrac{a°}{360°} \cdot 2\pi r = \dfrac{a}{180} \cdot \pi r$.

Here is a practice problem.

Problem: In a circle that has radius 18 cm, what is the length, L, of an arc of 60°?

Solution: $L = \dfrac{60}{180} \cdot \pi (18 \text{ cm}) = 6\pi$ cm

A **sector** of a circle is a region bounded by two radii and an arc of the circle. The **area**, A, of a sector with radius r and arc measure of $a°$ is $A = \dfrac{a}{360} \cdot \pi r^2$.

Here is a practice problem.

Problem: In a circle that has radius 18 cm, what is the area of a sector whose arc has measure of 60°?

Solution: area of sector $= \dfrac{60}{360} \cdot \pi (18 \text{ cm})^2 = \dfrac{1}{6} \cdot \pi \left(324 \text{ cm}^2\right) = 54\pi$ cm^2

The following are additional properties of circles that are useful to know.

- The measure of an angle formed outside a circle by the intersection of two secants, two tangents, or a tangent and a secant equals one-half the difference of the measures of the intercepted arcs.
- The measure of an angle with its vertex on a circle formed by a secant and a tangent equals one-half the measure of the intercepted arc.
- The ratio of the length of the arc intercepted by a central angle to the circumference of the circle equals the ratio of the degree measure of the central angle to 360°.
- Two tangent segments to a circle from an exterior point are congruent. *Note:* If a line through a point E that is exterior to a circle is tangent to the circle at point T, then $\overline{ET}$ is a **tangent segment** from E to the circle.
- If two arcs have congruent radii, then the lengths of the arcs are proportional to their measures.
- Concentric circles are circles that have the same center.
- A polygon is inscribed in a circle if each of its vertices lies on the circle.
- A polygon is circumscribed about a circle if each of its sides is tangent to the circle.
- Opposite pairs of interior angles of a quadrilateral inscribed in a circle are supplementary.

Geometric Transformations

A **geometric transformation** is a one-to-one mapping between the points of the plane and themselves. A transformation maps a **preimage** point, P, onto a unique **image** point, P'. Each point is associated with itself or with some other point in the plane. In symbols, this mapping is represented as $P \rightarrow P'$ and is read as "the image of P is P prime." In this section, you will learn about four common transformations in the plane: reflections, translations, rotations, and dilations.

Reflections

A **reflection over a line** is a geometric transformation in which every point P is mapped to a new point P' that is the same distance from a fixed line, but on the opposite side of the line. The fixed line is the **line of reflection**. This line is the perpendicular bisector of the segment joining any point to its image. *Note:* Any line in the plane can serve as a line of reflection.

A **reflection over the x-axis** is a transformation in which $P(x, y) \rightarrow P'(x, -y)$. Corresponding points are equidistant from the x-axis as shown below.

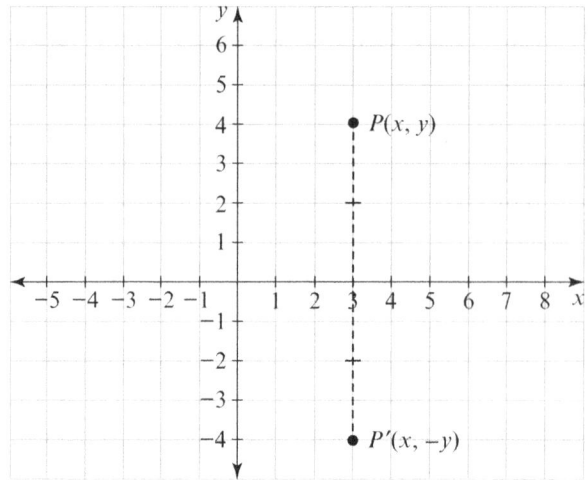

Tip: Under a reflection over the x-axis, every x-coordinate stays the same and every y-coordinate is changed to its opposite.

A **reflection over the y-axis** is a transformation in which $P(x, y) \to P'(-x, y)$. Corresponding points are equidistant from the y-axis as shown below.

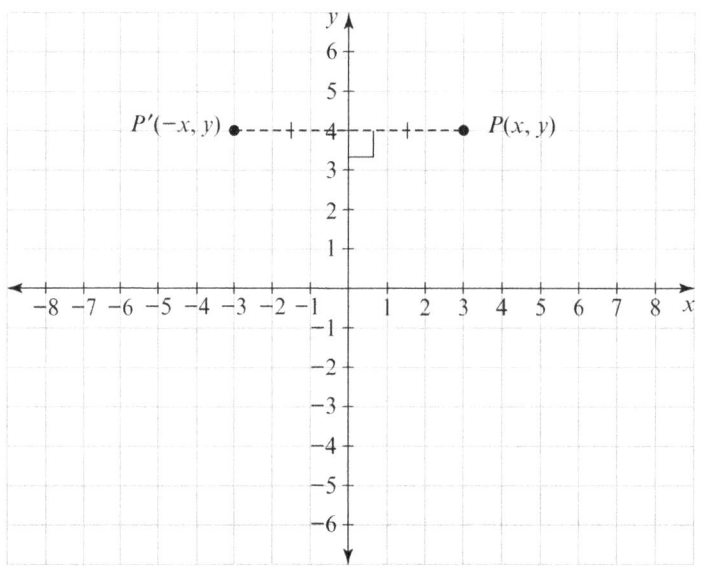

Tip: Under a reflection over the y-axis, every y-coordinate stays the same and every x-coordinate is changed to its opposite.

Here is a practice problem.

> Problem: Given triangle ABC with vertices $A(-4, 3)$, $B(-4, 1)$, and $C(2, 1)$, determine the corresponding coordinates of the vertices of triangle $A'B'C'$, the image of triangle ABC under a reflection over the x-axis. Sketch your results.
>
> Solution: Under a reflection over the x-axis, $P(x, y) \to P'(x, -y)$. Thus, as shown below, $A(-4, 3) \to A'(-4, -3)$, $B(-4, 1) \to B'(-4, -1)$, and $C(2, 1) \to C'(2, -1)$.

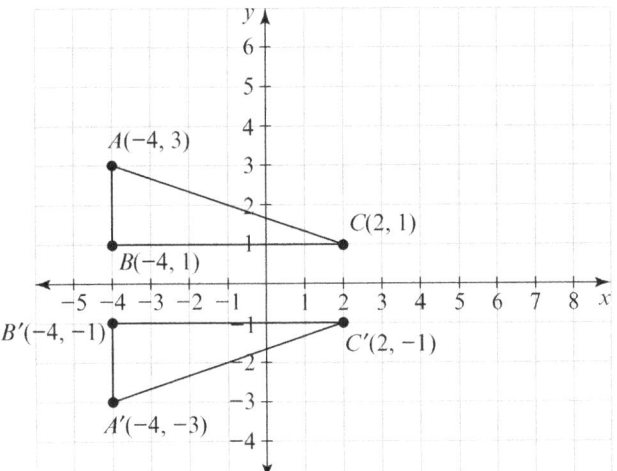

A **reflection in a point** is a geometric transformation about a fixed **point of reflection** for which every point P is mapped to a new point P' directly opposite it on the other side of the point of reflection, so that the point of reflection is the midpoint of the segment joining the original point with its image. *Note:* Any point in the plane can serve as a point of reflection.

A **reflection in the origin** is a transformation in which $P(x, y) \rightarrow P'(-x, -y)$. The origin is the midpoint of segment $\overline{PP'}$ joining corresponding points as shown below.

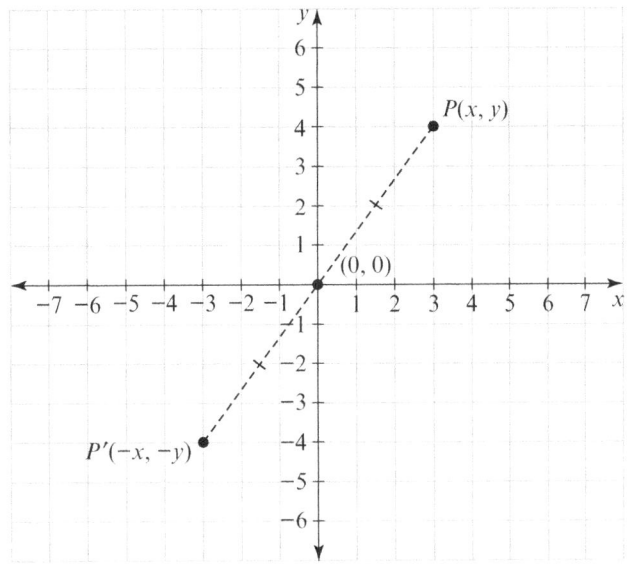

Tip: Under a reflection in the origin, every x-coordinate and every y-coordinate is changed to its opposite.

Here is a practice problem.

Problem: Given rectangle $ABCD$ with vertices $A(2, -3)$, $B(2, -5)$, $C(5, -5)$, and $D(5, -3)$, determine the corresponding coordinates of the vertices of rectangle $A'B'C'D'$, the image of rectangle $ABCD$ under a reflection in the origin. Sketch your results.

Solution: Under a reflection in the origin, $P(x, y) \rightarrow P'(-x, -y)$. Thus, as shown below, $A(2, -3) \rightarrow A'(-2, 3)$, $B(2, -5) \rightarrow B'(-2, 5)$, $C(5, -5) \rightarrow C'(-5, 5)$, and $D(5, -3) \rightarrow D'(-5, 3)$.

Chapter 3: Geometry and Measurement

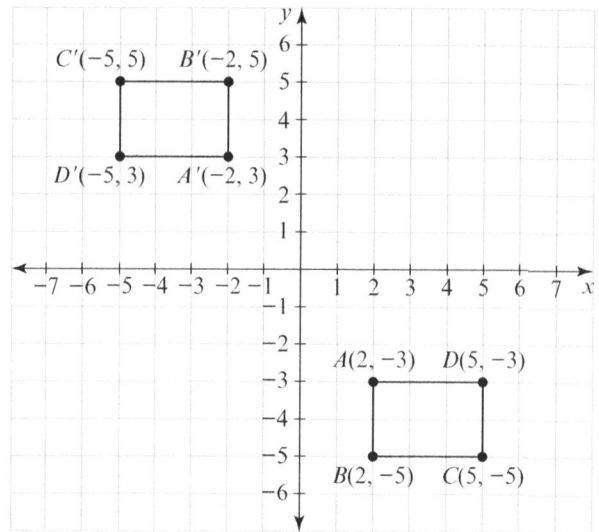

Tip: Think of reflections as "flips." The image is the result of flipping the preimage over the line (or point) of reflection so that the new figure is a mirror image of the original.

Translations

A **translation** is a geometric transformation in which every point P is mapped a fixed distance in the same direction along a straight line to a new point P'. A **translation of h units in the horizontal direction and k units in the vertical direction** is a transformation in which $P(x, y) \rightarrow P'(x + h, y + k)$. A translation moves every point h units horizontally and k units vertically.

Tip: In a translation, you merely add h to each x-coordinate and k to each y-coordinate.

Here is a practice problem.

> **Problem:** Given segment $\overline{AB}$ with endpoints $A(2, 4)$ and $B(3, 1)$, determine the corresponding coordinates of the endpoints of $\overline{A'B'}$, the image of $\overline{AB}$ under a translation of 3 units horizontally and –2 units vertically. Sketch your results.
>
> **Solution:** Under a translation, $P(x, y) \rightarrow P'(x + h, y + k)$. Thus, as shown below, $A(2, 4) \rightarrow A'(5, 2)$ and $B(3, 1) \rightarrow B'(6, -1)$.

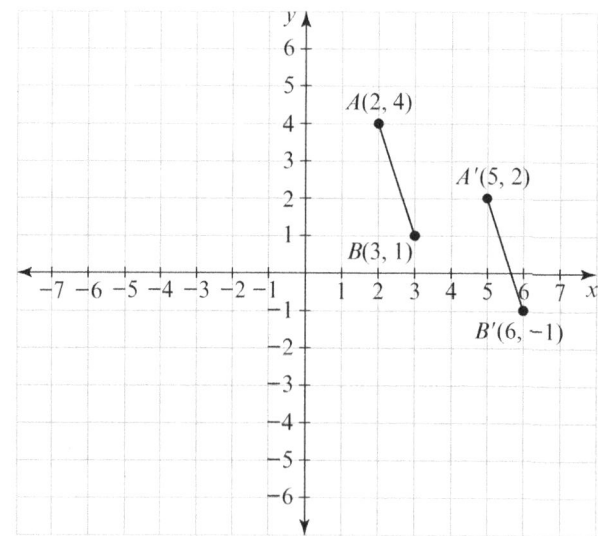

Tip: Think of translations as "slides." You slide the preimage right or left or up or down, or a combination of these moves. The result is the image.

Rotations

A **rotation** is a geometric transformation in which every point P is "rotated" through an angle around a fixed point, called the **center of rotation**. A figure has **rotational symmetry** if there is a rotation of less than 360° in which the image and its preimage coincide under the rotation.

The following discussion presents coordinate rules for three types of rotations about the origin O: a counterclockwise rotation of 90° about O, a counterclockwise rotation of 180° about O, and a counterclockwise rotation of 270° about O.

Tip: Think of rotations as "turns" around a point.

A **counterclockwise rotation of 90° about the origin O** is a transformation in which $P(x, y) \rightarrow P'(-y, x)$. The angle POP' is a right angle as shown below.

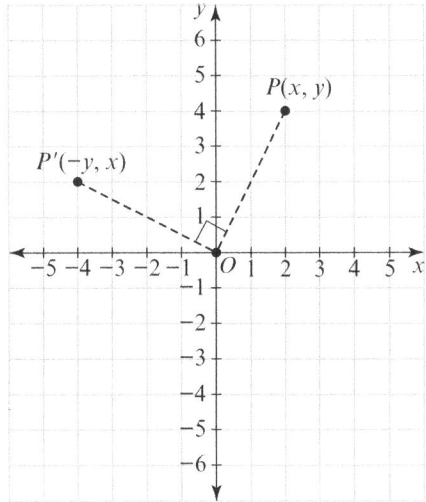

A **counterclockwise rotation of 180° about the origin O** is a transformation in which $P(x, y) \rightarrow P'(-x, -y)$. The measure of angle POP' is 180° as shown below.

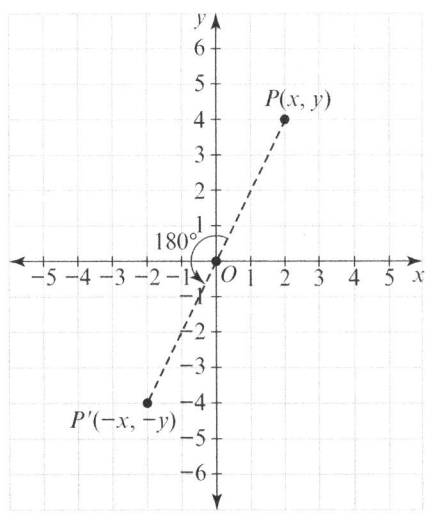

Tip: A counterclockwise rotation of 180° about the origin O is equivalent to a reflection in the origin.

A **counterclockwise rotation of 270°** about the origin O is a transformation in which $P(x, y) \to P'(y, -x)$. The measure of angle POP' is 270° as shown below. The angle is measured *counterclockwise* from $\overline{OP}$ to $\overline{OP'}$.

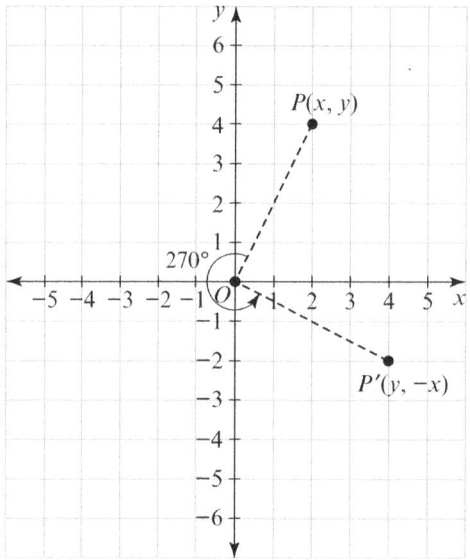

Here is a practice problem.

Problem: Given rectangle $ABCD$ with vertices $A(2, -3)$, $B(2, -5)$, $C(5, -5)$, and $D(5, -3)$, determine the corresponding coordinates of the vertices of rectangle $A'B'C'D'$, the image of rectangle $ABCD$ under a counterclockwise rotation of 90° about the origin. Sketch your results.

Solution: Under a counterclockwise rotation of 90° about the origin, $P(x, y) \to P'(-y, x)$. Thus, as shown below, $A(2, -3) \to A'(3, 2)$, $B(2, -5) \to B'(5, 2)$, $C(5, -5) \to C'(5, 5)$, and $D(5, -3) \to D'(3, 5)$.

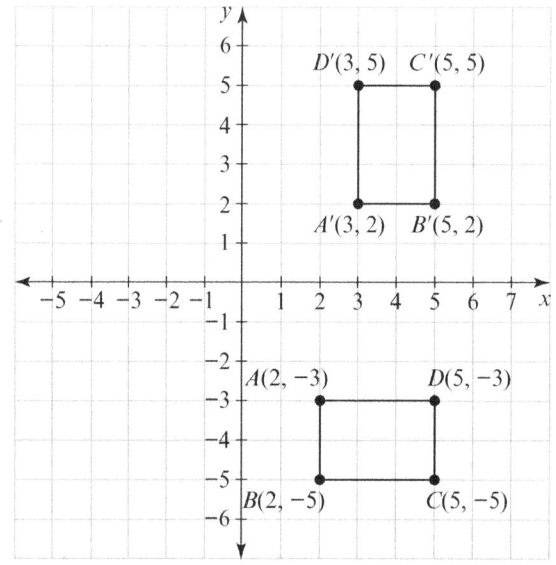

Dilations

A **dilation** is a geometric transformation in which every point P is mapped to a new point P', where the point P' lies on a ray through a fixed point O and the point P, so that $OP' = |r|OP$, where r is a nonzero real number, called the **scale factor**. Informally, a dilation is an expanding ($|r| > 1$) or contracting ($|r| < 1$) of a geometric shape using a scale factor, while its shape, location, and orientation remain the same. In the case that $|r| = 1$, the dilated image is congruent to the original geometric shape, and the dilation is a rigid motion.

A **dilation of scale factor r where the center of dilation is the origin O** is a transformation in which $P(x, y) \rightarrow P'(rx, ry)$, where $r > 0$. Under a dilation, the ratio of OP' to OP equals the dilation's scale factor r. That is, $\dfrac{OP'}{OP} = r$.

Note: Any point can be chosen as the center of dilation. Also, scale factors can be negative. In this book, dilations are limited to those where the origin is the center of dilation and scale factors are positive.

Under a dilation, if the scale factor r is greater than 1, the image is an **enlargement** of the preimage and has the same shape. If the scale factor is between 0 and 1, the image is a **reduction** of the preimage and has the same shape. If the scale factor equals 1, the preimage and image are the same size and shape.

Here is a practice problem.

> Problem: Given rectangle $ABCD$ with vertices $A(-4, 5)$, $B(-4, -5)$, $C(4, -5)$, and $D(4, 5)$, determine the corresponding coordinates of the vertices of rectangle $A'B'C'D'$, the image of rectangle $ABCD$ under a dilation of $\dfrac{1}{2}$ with the origin as the center of dilation. Sketch your results.
>
> Solution: Under a dilation of scale factor $\dfrac{1}{2}$ with the origin as the center of dilation $P(x, y) \rightarrow P'\left(\dfrac{1}{2}x, \dfrac{1}{2}y\right)$. Thus, as shown below, $A(-4, 5) \rightarrow A'(-2, 2.5)$, $B(-4, -5) \rightarrow B'(-2, -2.5)$, $C(4, -5) \rightarrow C'(2, -2.5)$, and $D(4, 5) \rightarrow D'(2, 2.5)$.

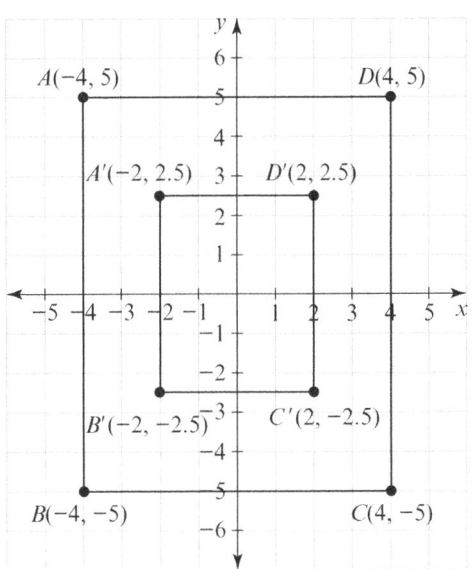

Summary of Coordinate Rules for Geometric Transformations

The following is a summary of the coordinate rules for the common transformation types presented in this chapter.

Transformation	Coordinate Rule
Reflection over the x-axis	$P(x, y) \to P'(x, -y)$
Reflection over the y-axis	$P(x, y) \to P'(-x, y)$
Reflection in the origin	$P(x, y) \to P'(-x, -y)$
Counterclockwise rotation of 90° about the origin	$P(x, y) \to P'(-y, x)$
Counterclockwise rotation of 180° about the origin	$P(x, y) \to P'(-x, -y)$
Counterclockwise rotation of 270° about the origin	$P(x, y) \to P'(y, -x)$
Translation of h units in the horizontal direction and k units in the vertical direction	$P(x, y) \to P'(x + h, y + k)$
Dilation of scale factor r where the center of dilation is the origin	$P(x, y) \to P'(rx, ry), r > 0$

Here is a practice problem.

> Problem: In a coordinate plane, triangle ABC has vertices $A(2, 1)$, $B(2, 5)$, and $C(5, 2)$. Triangle $A'B'C'$ is the image of triangle ABC after a reflection over the y-axis followed by a translation of 4 units to the right and 2 units down. What are the coordinates of B'?
>
> Solution: Under a reflection over the y-axis, $(2, 5) \to (-2, 5)$. Under a translation of 4 units right and 2 units down, $(-2, 5) \to (-2 + 4, 5 - 2) = (2, 3)$. The coordinates of B' are $(2, 3)$.

Properties Preserved Under Geometric Transformations

The following five properties are preserved under reflections, translations, and rotations:

- Distance—Lengths in the image equal their corresponding lengths in the preimage.
- Angle measure—Angles in the image have the same measure as their corresponding angles in the preimage.
- Parallelism—The images of two parallel lines are also parallel lines.
- Collinearity—The images of three or more points that lie on a straight line (that is, the points are collinear) will also lie on a straight line in the same order.
- Midpoint—The image of the midpoint of a line segment is the midpoint of the line segment's image.

The properties preserved under *dilations* include only four of the five properties preserved under reflections, translations, and rotations. These properties are angle measure, parallelism, collinearity, and midpoint. Dilations do not preserve distance (except when the scale factor is 1). Lengths in the image figure are equal to their corresponding lengths in the preimage figure multiplied by the scale factor r.

Congruence and Similarity in the Context of Geometric Transformations

Reflections, translations, and rotations are **rigid motions**. These transformations are rigid motions because they move a figure to a different location in the plane without altering its shape or size. They take lines to lines. They take line segments to line segments of the same length. They take angles to angles of the same measure. They take parallel lines to parallel lines. And they take points to their same relative locations.

Under reflections, translations, and rotations, figures (preimages) and their corresponding images are congruent. Therefore, **congruence** of two plane geometric figures is defined as follows: A two-dimensional figure is congruent to another if the first can be transformed into the second by a sequence of rotations, reflections, and translations.

Tip: The sequence of transformations that results in two congruent figures is not necessarily unique.

In the diagram, trapezoids I and II are congruent. One possible sequence of transformations whereby Trapezoid I can be transformed into Trapezoid II is a reflection across the y-axis, followed by a translation of 1 unit right and 8 units down. Specifically, $(-5, 5) \to (5, 5) \to (6, -3)$; $(-5, 3) \to (5, 3) \to (6, -5)$; $(-2, 3) \to (2, 3) \to (3, -5)$; $(-3, 5) \to (3, 5) \to (4, -3)$.

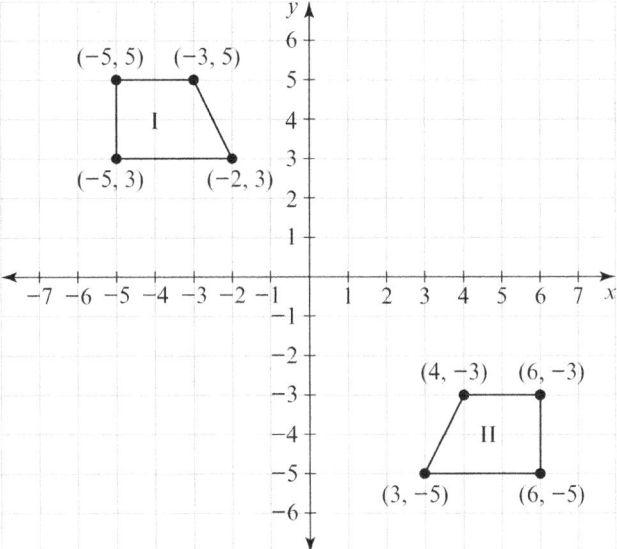

Dilations are *not* rigid motions. However, dilations *do* take angles to angles of the same measure. They take parallel lines to parallel lines. And they take points to their same relative locations. Under dilations, figures (preimages) and their images are similar. Therefore, **similarity** of two plane geometric figures is defined as follows: A two-dimensional figure is similar to another if the first can be transformed into the second by a sequence of rotations, reflections, translations, and dilations.

Tip: The sequence of transformations that results in two similar figures is not necessarily unique.

In the diagram, triangles I and II are similar. A possible sequence of transformations that transforms Triangle I into Triangle II is a counterclockwise rotation of 90°, followed by a dilation of 1.5. Specifically, (2, 5) → (−5, 2) → (−7.5, 3); (3, 2) → (−2, 3) → (−3, 4.5); (6, 4) → (−4, 6) → (−6, 9).

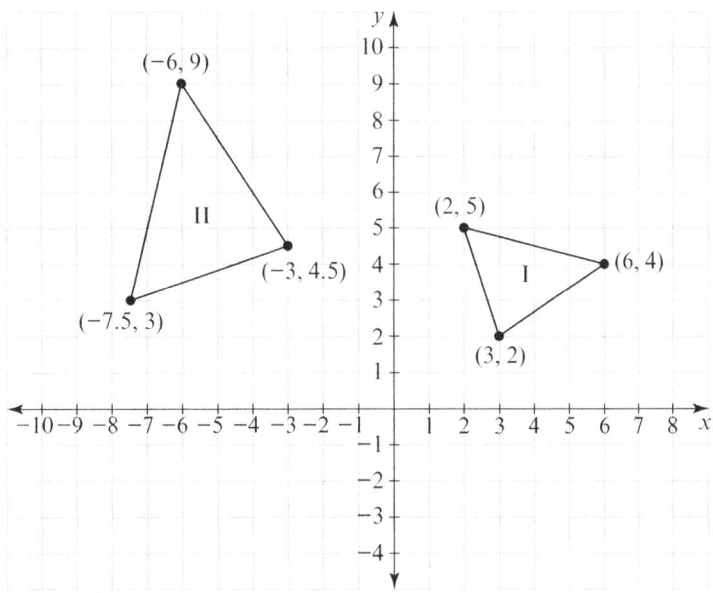

Note: See "Congruence, Similarity, and Symmetry" and "Triangles" earlier in this chapter for additional discussions of congruence and similarity.

177

Measurement

For this topic, you must understand and apply dimensional analysis and use and understand the development of formulas to find lengths, perimeters, areas, and volumes of basic geometric figures.

Dimensional Analysis

On your TExES Math exam, you have to demonstrate your knowledge of measurement using the U.S. customary system and the metric system. See Appendix C, "Measurement Units and Conversions," for some common conversion facts you should know.

Convert from one measurement unit to another by using an appropriate "conversion fraction." You make conversion fractions by using a conversion fact, such as 1 gallon = 4 quarts. For each conversion fact, you can write *two* conversion fractions. For example, for the conversion fact given, you have $\frac{1 \text{ gal}}{4 \text{ qt}}$ and $\frac{4 \text{ qt}}{1 \text{ gal}}$ as your two conversion fractions.

Every conversion fraction is equivalent to the number 1 because the numerator and denominator are different names for measures of the same quantity. Therefore, if you multiply a quantity by a conversion fraction, you will not change the value of the quantity.

To change one measurement unit to another unit, multiply by the conversion fraction whose *denominator has the same units as those of the quantity to be converted*. This strategy falls under **dimensional analysis,** a powerful tool used by scientists (including mathematicians) and engineers to analyze units and to guide or check equations and calculations. When you do the multiplication, the units you started out with will "cancel" (divide) out, and you will be left with the desired new units. If this doesn't happen, then you used the wrong conversion fraction. Do it over again with the other conversion fraction.

Additionally, for some conversions you might need to make a "chain" of conversion fractions to obtain your desired units.

Here is a practice problem.

> Problem: Convert 3 gallons to cups.
>
> Solution: Relevant conversion facts are the following: 1 pint = 2 cups, 1 quart = 2 pints, and 1 gallon = 4 quarts. These facts yield six conversion fractions, respectively:
>
> $$\frac{1 \text{ pt}}{2 \text{ c}} \text{ and } \frac{2 \text{ c}}{1 \text{ pt}}, \quad \frac{1 \text{ qt}}{2 \text{ pt}} \text{ and } \frac{2 \text{ pt}}{1 \text{ qt}}, \quad \frac{1 \text{ gal}}{4 \text{ qt}} \text{ and } \frac{4 \text{ qt}}{1 \text{ gal}}$$
>
> Start with the quantity to be converted and keep multiplying by conversion fractions until, after canceling like units, you obtain the desired units.
>
> $$\frac{3 \text{ gal}}{1} \cdot \frac{4 \text{ qt}}{1 \text{ gal}} \cdot \frac{2 \text{ pt}}{1 \text{ qt}} \cdot \frac{2 \text{ c}}{1 \text{ pt}} = \frac{3 \text{ g\!\!\!/al}}{1} \cdot \frac{4 \text{ q\!\!\!/t}}{1 \text{ g\!\!\!/al}} \cdot \frac{2 \text{ p\!\!\!/t}}{1 \text{ q\!\!\!/t}} \cdot \frac{2 \text{ c}}{1 \text{ p\!\!\!/t}} = 48 \text{ c}$$
>
> Thus, 3 gallons equals 48 cups.

It is a good idea to assess your final answer to see if it makes sense. When you convert from a larger unit to a smaller unit, you should expect that it will take more of the smaller units to equal the same amount. When you convert from a smaller unit to a larger unit, you should expect that it will take fewer of the larger units to equal the same amount.

Here is a practice problem that involves converting from a larger unit to a smaller unit.

> Problem: Convert 5 yards to feet.
>
> Solution: 5 yards = $\frac{5 \text{ yd}}{1} \times \frac{3 \text{ ft}}{1 \text{ yd}} = \frac{5 \text{ y\!\!\!/d}}{1} \times \frac{3 \text{ ft}}{1 \text{ y\!\!\!/d}} = 15$ feet

Tip: Feet are smaller than yards, so it should take more of them to equal the same length as 5 yards.

Here is a practice problem that involves converting from a smaller unit to a larger unit.

Problem: Convert 250 centimeters to meters.

Solution: 250 centimeters = $\dfrac{250 \text{ cm}}{1} \times \dfrac{1 \text{ m}}{100 \text{ cm}} = \dfrac{250 \text{ cm}}{1} \times \dfrac{1 \text{ m}}{100 \text{ cm}} = \dfrac{250 \text{ m}}{100} = 2.5$ meters

Tip: Meters are larger than centimeters, so it should take fewer of them to equal the same length as 250 centimeters.

As seen in conversion of units, in calculations involving measured quantities that have units, the units are part of the completed defined measure and must undergo the same mathematical operations. You can add or subtract like units, but not unlike units. You can multiply or divide whether you have like or unlike units, provided the product or quotient has meaning.

Perimeter, Area, and Volume

For your TExES Math exam, you are expected to know how to compute perimeter and area of triangles, quadrilaterals, circles, and regions that are combinations of these figures; and how to compute the surface area and volume of right prisms, cones, cylinders, spheres, and solids that are combinations of these figures. For particular questions on the test, applicable formulas might be provided in the on-screen "Definitions and Formulas" reference material. To be on the safe side, you should memorize formulas that are commonly used. Here are important formulas for perimeter, area, surface area, and volume that you should know for your TExES Math exam.

Triangle: height h, base b

area = $\dfrac{1}{2}bh$

sides a, b, and c

perimeter = $a + b + c$

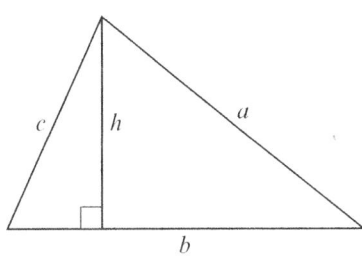

Rectangle: length l, width w

area = lw

perimeter = $2l + 2w = 2(l + w)$

Square: side s

area = s^2

perimeter = $4s$

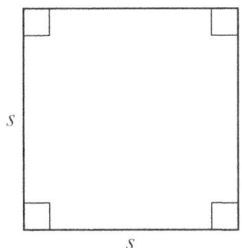

Parallelogram: height h, base b, width a

area = bh

perimeter = $2a + 2b = 2(a + b)$

Circle: radius r, diameter d

area $= \pi r^2$

circumference $= 2\pi r = \pi d$

diameter $d = 2r$

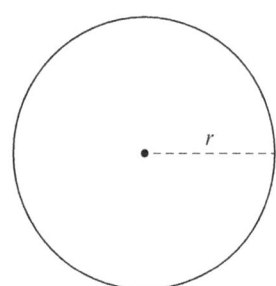

Trapezoid: height h, bases a, b

area $= \frac{1}{2}h(a+b)$

perimeter $= a + b + c + d$

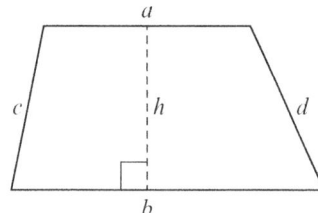

Sphere: radius r

volume $= \frac{4}{3}\pi r^3$

lateral surface area $= 4\pi r^2$

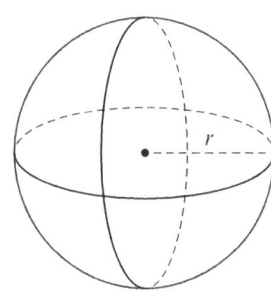

Right prism: height h, area of base B

volume $= Bh$

total surface area $= 2B +$ sum of areas of rectangular sides

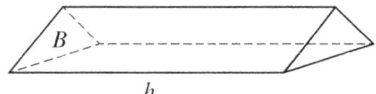

Rectangular prism: length l, width w, height h

volume $= lwh$

total surface area $= 2hl + 2hw + 2lw$

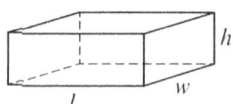

Cube: edge e

volume $= e^3$

total surface area $= 6e^2$

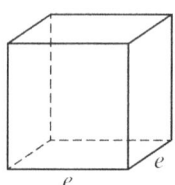

Right circular cylinder: height h, radius of base r

volume $= \pi r^2 h$

lateral surface area $= 2\pi r h$

total surface area $= (2\pi r)h + 2(\pi r^2)$

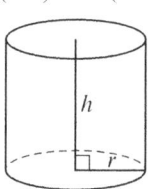

Right pyramid: height h, area of base B

volume $= \frac{1}{3}Bh$

total surface area $= B +$ sum of areas of triangular lateral faces

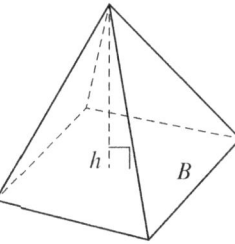

Right circular cone: height h, radius of base r

volume $= \frac{1}{3}\pi r^2 h$

lateral surface area $= \pi r\sqrt{r^2 + h^2} = \pi r s$, where s is the slant height $= \sqrt{r^2 + h^2}$

total surface area $= \pi r\sqrt{r^2 + h^2} + \pi r^2 = \pi r s + \pi r^2$

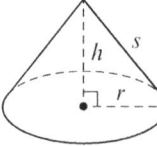

Perimeter and Circumference

The **perimeter** of a figure is the distance around it. You measure perimeter in units of length, such as inches (in), feet (ft), yards (yd), miles (mi), kilometers (km), meters (m), centimeters (cm), and millimeters (mm). To find the perimeter of a closed figure that is made up of line segments, add up the lengths of the line segments.

Here is a practice problem.

Problem: Find the perimeter, in centimeters, of the figure shown.

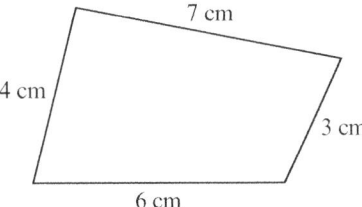

Solution: Perimeter = 6 cm + 3 cm + 7 cm + 4 cm = 20 cm

The perimeter of a circle is called its **circumference.** The formula for the circumference of a circle is $C = \pi d = 2\pi r$, where d and r are the diameter and radius of the circle, respectively.

Here is a practice problem to find the circumference of a circle.

Problem: Find the circumference, in inches, of the circle in the figure shown. Round your answer to the nearest inch.

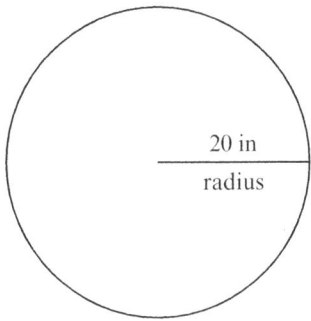

Solution: From the figure, the radius is 20 in. Substitute into the formula: $C = 2\pi r = 2\pi(20 \text{ in}) \approx 126$ inches.

Tip: Use your TI calculator's π key when doing calculations involving π unless you have instructions to use an approximation for π.

Here is a practice problem to find the perimeter of a figure that is a combination of figures.

Problem: The figure shown consists of a semicircle of radius r and a rectangle whose longer side is $2r$ and whose shorter side is r. What is the perimeter of the figure in terms of r?

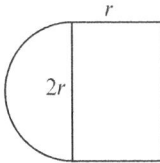

Solution: Perimeter = the circumference of the semicircle + 2 times the length of the shorter side of the rectangle + the length of the longer side of the rectangle = $\frac{1}{2}(2\pi r) + 2 \cdot r + 2r = \pi r + 4r$.

181

Area

The **area** of a plane figure is the amount of surface enclosed by the boundary of the figure. You measure area in square units, such as square inches (in^2), square feet (ft^2), square miles (mi^2), square meters (m^2), square kilometers (km^2), square centimeters (cm^2), and square millimeters (mm^2). The area is always described in terms of square units, regardless of the shape of the figure.

Plane figures are two-dimensional (for example, a rectangle has length and width). The measurement units for the dimensions are linear units (for example, inches, feet, miles, and meters). You obtain the square units needed to describe area when you multiply a unit by itself. For example, 1 in × 1 in = 1 in^2 = 1 square inch.

Here is a practice problem to find the area of a rectangle.

   Problem: What is the area, in cm^2, of a rectangle that is 8.5 cm by 6 cm?
   Solution: Sketch a diagram and label it.

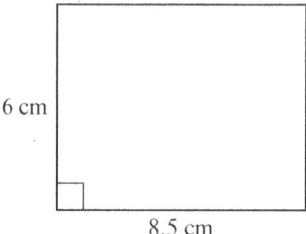

   The formula for the area of a rectangle is $A = lw$, where l is the length and w is the width. Substitute into the formula.
   $A = lw = (8.5 \text{ cm})(6 \text{ cm}) = 51 \text{ cm}^2$. Thus, the rectangle has an area of 51 cm^2.

Tip: When you work problems involving geometric figures, it is helpful to sketch a diagram if no diagram is given.

Here is a practice problem to find the area of a triangle.

   Problem: Find the area, in cm^2, of the triangle shown.

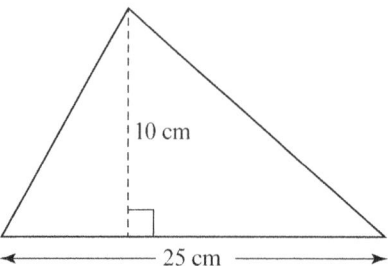

   Solution: The formula for the area of a triangle is $A = \frac{1}{2}bh$, where b is the length of a base of the triangle and h is the height for that base. When you are finding the area of a triangle, you can pick any convenient side of the triangle to serve as the base in the formula.

   From the figure, you can see that $b = 25$ cm and $h = 10$ cm. Substitute into the formula.

$$A = \frac{1}{2}bh = A = \frac{1}{2}(25 \text{ cm})(10 \text{ cm}) = \frac{(25 \text{ cm})(10 \text{ cm})}{2} = 125 \text{ cm}^2$$

The triangle has an area of 125 cm^2.

Here is a practice problem to find the area of a circle.

Problem: Find the area, in in², of the circle in the figure. Round your answer to the nearest in².

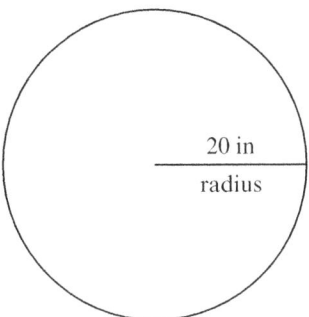

Solution: The formula for the area of a circle is $A = \pi r^2$, where r is the radius of the circle. From the figure, the radius is 20 in. Substitute into the formula.

$$A = \pi r^2 = \pi(20 \text{ in})^2 = \pi(400 \text{ in}^2) \approx 1{,}257 \text{ in}^2$$

The circle's area is approximately 1,257 in².

Here is a practice problem to find the area of a triangle in the coordinate plane.

Problem: The vertices of the triangle shown are $A(-3, 3)$, $B(1, 5)$, and $C(4, 2)$. Determine the area of $\triangle ABC$.

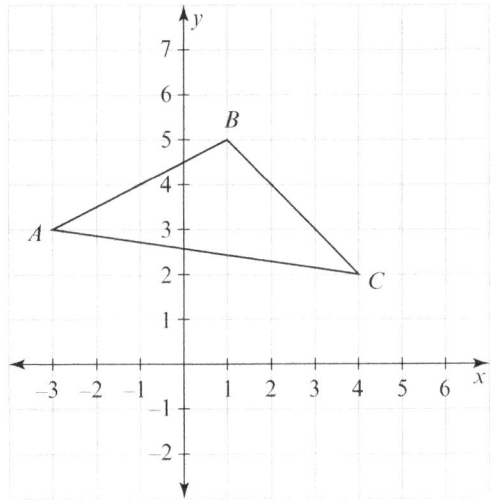

Solution: The figure has no horizontal or vertical sides, so you cannot easily find the lengths of the sides or altitudes. To determine the area, enclose the triangle in a rectangle as shown below. Make the rectangle's top side parallel to the x-axis and passing through vertex B of the triangle. Make the rectangle's bottom side parallel to the x-axis and passing through vertex C of the triangle. Make the left side of the rectangle perpendicular to its top and bottom sides and passing through vertex A. Make the right side of the rectangle perpendicular to its top and bottom sides and passing through vertex C. To help keep track of your work, label the coordinates of the vertices in the figure.

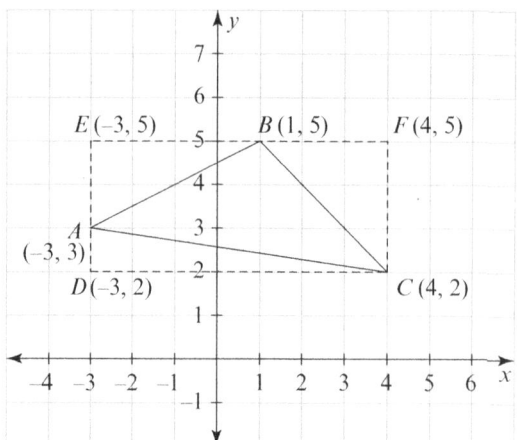

The area, A, of $\triangle ABC$ equals the area of rectangle $EDCF$ minus the sum of the areas of right triangles ADC, CFB, and BEA. In this figure, you can find the lengths of the sides of the figures by counting.

Rectangle $EDCF$ has dimensions 7 units by 3 units. Triangle ADC has base 7 units and height 1 unit. Triangle CFB has base 3 units and height 3 units. And triangle BEA has base 4 units and height 2 units.

$$A = (7 \text{ units})(3 \text{ units}) - \frac{1}{2}(7 \text{ units})(1 \text{ unit}) - \frac{1}{2}(3 \text{ units})(3 \text{ units}) - \frac{1}{2}(4 \text{ units})(2 \text{ units})$$
$$= 21 \text{ units}^2 - 3.5 \text{ units}^2 - 4.5 \text{ units}^2 - 4 \text{ units}^2$$
$$= 9 \text{ units}^2$$

$\triangle ABC$ has area of 9 units^2.

Surface Area

When you have a solid figure such as a rectangular prism (a box), a cylinder, or a pyramid, you can find the area of every face (surface) and add the areas together. The sum is the **surface area** ($S.A.$) of the solid figure.

Here is a practice problem to find the surface area of a rectangular box.

Problem: What is the surface area, in in^2, of the box shown?

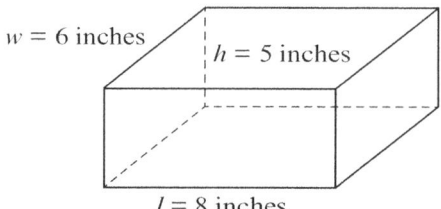

Solution: The box is composed of six **faces,** all of which are rectangles. Use the length and height to find the areas of the front and back faces. Use the length and width to find the areas of the top and bottom faces. Use the width and height to find the areas of the two side faces.

$$S.A. = 2(8 \text{ in})(5 \text{ in}) + 2(8 \text{ in})(6 \text{ in}) + 2(6 \text{ in})(5 \text{ in}) = 80 \text{ in}^2 + 96 \text{ in}^2 + 60 \text{ in}^2 = 236 \text{ in}^2$$

The box has surface area of 236 in^2.

Nets are helpful when you want to find the surface area of a solid figure. A **net** is a two-dimensional shape that can be folded to make a three-dimensional solid figure in which each face is a flat surface. Here are six three-dimensional solids and a corresponding net for each. *Tip:* Nets are not unique. A solid can have more than one net configuration.

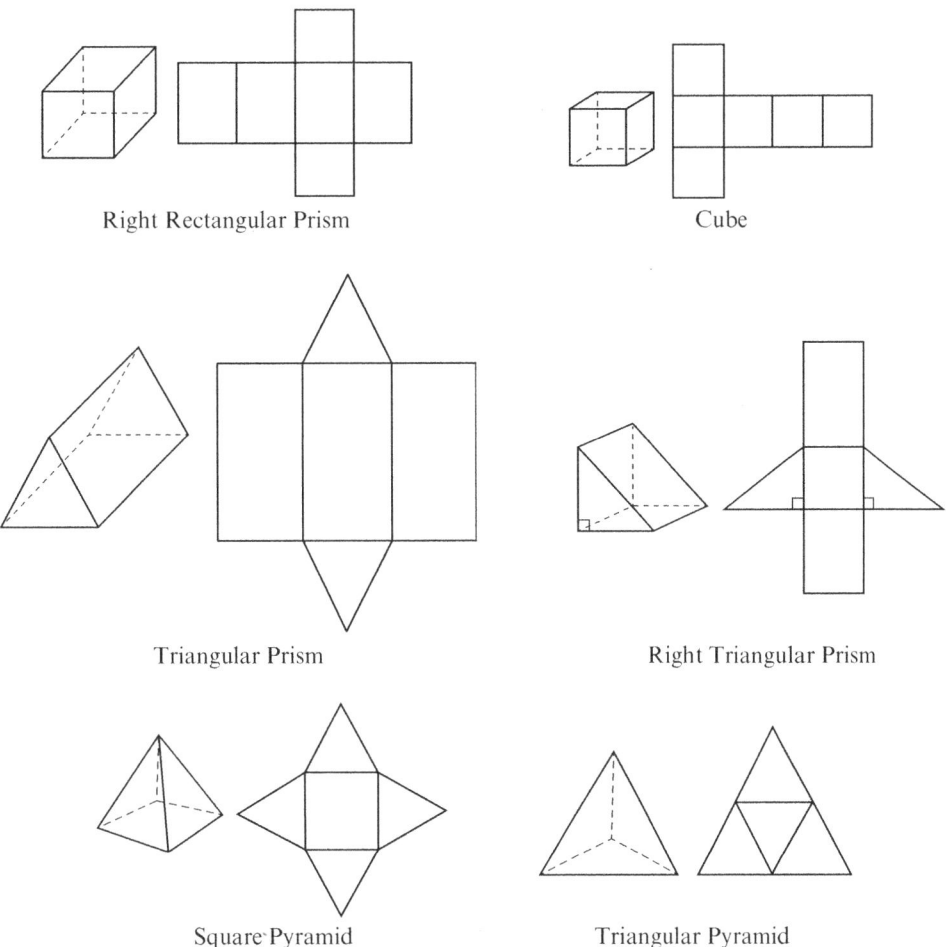

Here is a practice problem.

Problem: The grid shows the net for a square pyramid. Find the surface area, in in², of the pyramid. Assume each grid box represents a 1-inch by 1-inch square.

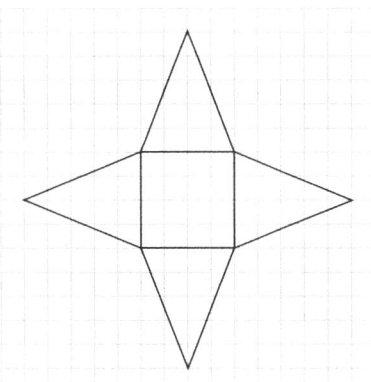

Solution: The surface area of the pyramid is the sum of the area of its square base and the areas of its four triangular faces. The square base measures 4 inches by 4 inches. Each triangle has base 4 inches and height 5 inches.

$$S.A. = (4\text{ in})(4\text{ in}) + 4\left(\frac{1}{2}\right)(4\text{ in})(5\text{ in}) = 16\text{ in}^2 + 40\text{ in}^2 = 56\text{ in}^2$$

The pyramid has surface area of 56 in².

Volume

The **volume** of a solid figure is the amount of space inside the solid. Solid figures have three dimensions (for example, length, width, and height of a box). When you use the dimensions of a solid to find its volume, the units for the volume are cubic units, such as cubic inches (in^3), cubic feet (ft^3), cubic miles (mi^3), cubic meters (m^3), cubic kilometers (km^3), cubic centimeters (cm^3), and cubic millimeters (mm^3).

Here is a practice problem to find the volume of a rectangular prism.

Problem: What is the volume, in in^3, of the box shown?

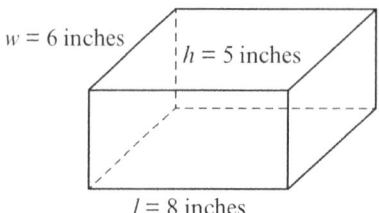

Solution: The box is in the shape of a right prism. A **right prism** is a prism whose bases are perpendicular to its sides. The formula for the volume of a right prism is $V = Bh$, where B = the area of the base of the prism. For a rectangular prism, $B = lw$. Thus, the formula for the volume of a rectangular prism is $V = lwh$, where l is the length, w is the width, and h is the height.

Determine the dimensions from the figure and substitute into the formula.

$$V = Bh = lwh = (8 \text{ in})(6 \text{ in})(5 \text{ in}) = 240 \text{ in}^3$$

The box has volume of 240 in^3.

Tip: Notice that the units for the volume of the box are in^3 = cubic inches. Cubic units are obtained when a unit is used as a factor in a product three times, as in the following: (in)(in)(in) = in^3.

Precision, Accuracy, and Approximate Error

In the physical world, measurement of continuous quantities is always approximate. The precision and accuracy of the measurement relate to the worthiness of the approximation.

Precision refers to the degree to which a measurement is repeatable and reliable; that is, consistently getting the same data each time the measurement is taken. The precision of a measurement depends on the magnitude of the smallest measuring unit used to obtain the measurement (for example, to the nearest meter, to the nearest centimeter, or to the nearest millimeter). In theory, the smaller the measurement unit used, the more precise the measurement.

Accuracy refers to the degree to which a measurement is true or correct. A measurement can be precise without being accurate. This can occur, for example, when a measuring instrument needs adjustment, so that the measurements obtained, no matter how precisely measured, are inaccurate.

The amount of error involved in a physical measurement is the **approximate error** of the measurement. The **maximum possible error** of a measurement is half the magnitude of the smallest measurement unit used to obtain the measurement. For example, if the smallest measurement unit is 1 inch, the maximum possible error is 0.5 inch. The most accurate way of expressing a measurement is as a **tolerance interval**. For example, a measurement of 10 inches, to the nearest inch, should be reported as 10 inches ± 0.5 inches. In other words, the true measurement lies between 9.5 inches and 10.5 inches. Closer approximations can be obtained by refining the measurement to a higher degree of precision (for example, by measuring to the nearest half-inch).

Two ways of conveying the magnitude of error in a measurement are absolute error and relative error (which can be expressed as a decimal or a percent). The **absolute error** of the measurement is the amount of physical error in the measurement, and the **relative error** of the measurement is the ratio of the absolute error to the correct value, or, if the correct value is unknown, to the measurement taken. The formula for relative error is given by $\frac{\text{absolute error}}{\text{correct value}}$ or $\frac{\text{absolute error}}{\text{measured value}}$ (if the correct value is unknown). When relative error is expressed as a percent, it is called **percent error.**

Here is a practice problem.

> Problem: If a protractor is used to measure the sum of the measures of the interior angles of a triangle yielding a measurement of 178.2°, what are the absolute error, relative error, and percent error of the measurement?
>
> Solution: The absolute error is the difference between the correct value 180° and the measured value 178.2°. That is, the absolute error = 180° − 178.2° = 1.8°. The relative error is $\frac{1.8°}{180°} = 0.01$, and the percent error is 1%.

Tip: Notice that the absolute error has the same units as the units of the measurement, while the relative error and percent error have no units.

Results of calculations with approximate measurements should not be reported with a degree of precision that would be misleading; that is, suggesting a degree of accuracy greater than the actual accuracy that could be obtained using the approximate measurements. Generally, such calculations should be rounded, *after* all calculations have been made, to have the same precision as the measurement with least precision in the calculation. *Caution:* Rounding before final calculations can compound and inflate error.

Part 2

Part 2 of this chapter is for candidates who plan to take the TExES Math 7–12. This review material goes beyond the standards for the TExES Math 4–8.

Geometry (Continued)

Two additional geometry topics for TExES Math 7–12 candidates are matrix representation of geometric transformations and algebraic representation of conic sections.

Matrix Representation of Geometric Transformations

Four geometric transformations are translations, reflections, rotations, and dilations. You can think of geometric transformations as ways to change geometric figures without changing their basic properties. (See "Geometric Transformations" earlier in Part 1 of this chapter for an introductory discussion of geometric transformations.)

A convenient way to represent geometric transformations is by using matrices. (See "Matrices" in Chapter 1 for a full discussion of matrices.) A geometric figure in the plane can be represented by a $2 \times n$ **vertex matrix** whose columns' elements are the n vertices of the figure. For example, the triangle T with vertices (x_1, y_1), (x_2, y_2), and (x_3, y_3) shown in the following figure can be represented as $T = \begin{bmatrix} x_1 & x_2 & x_3 \\ y_1 & y_2 & y_3 \end{bmatrix}$.

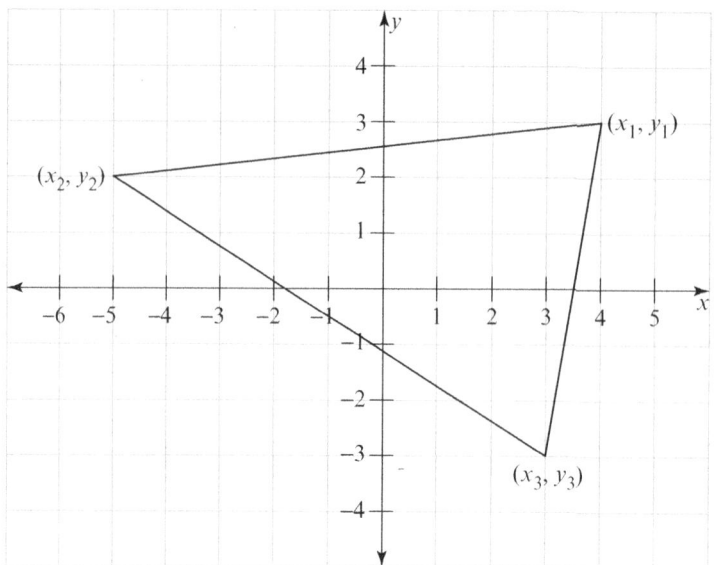

A translation h units horizontally and k units vertically is accomplished by adding the 2×3 translation matrix $\begin{bmatrix} h & h & h \\ k & k & k \end{bmatrix}$ to T as shown below.

$$\begin{bmatrix} x_1 & x_2 & x_3 \\ y_1 & y_2 & y_3 \end{bmatrix} + \begin{bmatrix} h & h & h \\ k & k & k \end{bmatrix} = \begin{bmatrix} x_1+h & x_2+h & x_3+h \\ y_1+k & y_2+k & y_3+k \end{bmatrix}$$

A reflection over the x-axis is accomplished by premultiplying T by the 2×2 matrix $\begin{bmatrix} 1 & 0 \\ 0 & -1 \end{bmatrix}$ as shown below.

$$\begin{bmatrix} 1 & 0 \\ 0 & -1 \end{bmatrix} \begin{bmatrix} x_1 & x_2 & x_3 \\ y_1 & y_2 & y_3 \end{bmatrix} = \begin{bmatrix} x_1 & x_2 & x_3 \\ -y_1 & -y_2 & -y_3 \end{bmatrix}$$

A reflection over the y-axis is accomplished by premultiplying T by the 2×2 matrix $\begin{bmatrix} -1 & 0 \\ 0 & 1 \end{bmatrix}$ as shown below.

$$\begin{bmatrix} -1 & 0 \\ 0 & 1 \end{bmatrix} \begin{bmatrix} x_1 & x_2 & x_3 \\ y_1 & y_2 & y_3 \end{bmatrix} = \begin{bmatrix} -x_1 & -x_2 & -x_3 \\ y_1 & y_2 & y_3 \end{bmatrix}$$

A reflection in the origin is accomplished by premultiplying T by the 2×2 matrix $\begin{bmatrix} -1 & 0 \\ 0 & -1 \end{bmatrix}$ as shown below.

$$\begin{bmatrix} -1 & 0 \\ 0 & -1 \end{bmatrix} \begin{bmatrix} x_1 & x_2 & x_3 \\ y_1 & y_2 & y_3 \end{bmatrix} = \begin{bmatrix} -x_1 & -x_2 & -x_3 \\ -y_1 & -y_2 & -y_3 \end{bmatrix}$$

A reflection over the line $y = x$ is accomplished by premultiplying T by the 2×2 matrix $\begin{bmatrix} 0 & 1 \\ 1 & 0 \end{bmatrix}$ as shown below.

$$\begin{bmatrix} 0 & 1 \\ 1 & 0 \end{bmatrix} \begin{bmatrix} x_1 & x_2 & x_3 \\ y_1 & y_2 & y_3 \end{bmatrix} = \begin{bmatrix} y_1 & y_2 & y_3 \\ x_1 & x_2 & x_3 \end{bmatrix}$$

A counterclockwise rotation of θ degrees about the origin is accomplished by premultiplying T by the 2 × 2 matrix $\begin{bmatrix} \cos\theta & -\sin\theta \\ \sin\theta & \cos\theta \end{bmatrix}$. Here are three examples.

For a counterclockwise rotation of 90° about the origin, premultiply T by the 2 × 2 matrix

$$\begin{bmatrix} \cos 90° & -\sin 90° \\ \sin 90° & \cos 90° \end{bmatrix} = \begin{bmatrix} 0 & -1 \\ 1 & 0 \end{bmatrix}$$ as shown below.

$$\begin{bmatrix} 0 & -1 \\ 1 & 0 \end{bmatrix} \begin{bmatrix} x_1 & x_2 & x_3 \\ y_1 & y_2 & y_3 \end{bmatrix} = \begin{bmatrix} -y_1 & -y_2 & -y_3 \\ x_1 & x_2 & x_3 \end{bmatrix}$$

For a counterclockwise rotation of 180° about the origin, premultiply T by the 2 × 2 matrix

$$\begin{bmatrix} \cos 180° & -\sin 180° \\ \sin 180° & \cos 180° \end{bmatrix} = \begin{bmatrix} -1 & 0 \\ 0 & -1 \end{bmatrix}$$ as shown below.

$$\begin{bmatrix} -1 & 0 \\ 0 & -1 \end{bmatrix} \begin{bmatrix} x_1 & x_2 & x_3 \\ y_1 & y_2 & y_3 \end{bmatrix} = \begin{bmatrix} -x_1 & -x_2 & -x_3 \\ -y_1 & -y_2 & -y_3 \end{bmatrix}$$

For a counterclockwise rotation of 270° about the origin, premultiply T by the 2 × 2 matrix

$$\begin{bmatrix} \cos 270° & -\sin 270° \\ \sin 270° & \cos 270° \end{bmatrix} = \begin{bmatrix} 0 & 1 \\ -1 & 0 \end{bmatrix}$$ as shown below.

$$\begin{bmatrix} 0 & 1 \\ -1 & 0 \end{bmatrix} \begin{bmatrix} x_1 & x_2 & x_3 \\ y_1 & y_2 & y_3 \end{bmatrix} = \begin{bmatrix} y_1 & y_2 & y_3 \\ -x_1 & -x_2 & -x_3 \end{bmatrix}$$

A dilation by a nonzero scale factor r is accomplished by premultiplying T by the 2 × 2 matrix $\begin{bmatrix} r & 0 \\ 0 & r \end{bmatrix}$ as shown below.

$$\begin{bmatrix} r & 0 \\ 0 & r \end{bmatrix} \begin{bmatrix} x_1 & x_2 & x_3 \\ y_1 & y_2 & y_3 \end{bmatrix} = \begin{bmatrix} rx_1 & rx_2 & rx_3 \\ ry_1 & ry_2 & ry_3 \end{bmatrix}$$

Here is a practice problem.

Problem: Use matrix multiplication to determine the coordinates of the endpoints of the image, $\overline{A'B'}$, of the segment $\overline{AB}$, with endpoints $A(2, 4)$ and $B(5, 1)$, after it is rotated 90° counterclockwise about the origin. Sketch your results.

Solution: The vertex matrix for $\overline{AB}$ is $\begin{bmatrix} 2 & 5 \\ 4 & 1 \end{bmatrix}$. Premultiplying by $\begin{bmatrix} 0 & -1 \\ 1 & 0 \end{bmatrix}$ yields

$\begin{bmatrix} 0 & -1 \\ 1 & 0 \end{bmatrix} \begin{bmatrix} 2 & 5 \\ 4 & 1 \end{bmatrix} = \begin{bmatrix} -4 & -1 \\ 2 & 5 \end{bmatrix}$. Therefore, as shown below, $\overline{A'B'}$ has coordinates $A'(-4, 2)$ and $B'(-1, 5)$.

Chapter 3: Geometry and Measurement

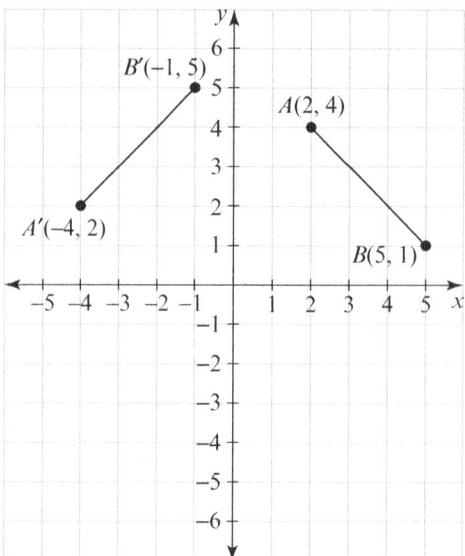

To accomplish translations in combination with rotations, reflections, or dilations using one transformation matrix, write the vertex matrix as a $3 \times n$ matrix with ones as the elements in the third row. Then, for example, to reflect over the line $y = x$, and then translate h units horizontally and k units vertically, premultiply by the 3×3 matrix $\begin{bmatrix} 0 & 1 & h \\ 1 & 0 & k \\ 0 & 0 & 1 \end{bmatrix}$ as shown below.

$$\begin{bmatrix} 0 & 1 & h \\ 1 & 0 & k \\ 0 & 0 & 1 \end{bmatrix} \begin{bmatrix} x_1 & x_2 & x_3 \\ y_1 & y_2 & y_3 \\ 1 & 1 & 1 \end{bmatrix} = \begin{bmatrix} y_1+h & y_2+h & y_3+h \\ x_1+k & x_2+k & x_3+k \\ 1 & 1 & 1 \end{bmatrix}$$

The technique of premultiplying the vertex matrix by either a 2×2 or a 3×3 **transformation matrix** can be applied when the number of vertices is extended to $n > 3$. You would proceed in the same manner as shown for a figure with three vertices.

Tip: When you are working problems involving geometric transformations, sketch a figure to help you visualize the situation.

Algebraic Representation of Conic Sections

The four basic kinds of conics are the circle, parabola, ellipse, and hyperbola. Geometrically, these conic sections are two-dimensional figures realized as the result of cutting a double-napped right-circular cone with a plane. They are formed by altering the angle of the cutting plane as shown here.

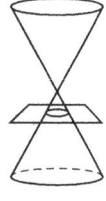
Circle

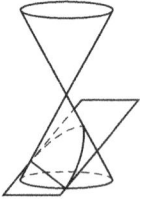
Parabola

Ellipse

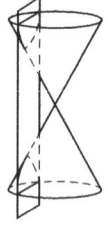
Hyperbola

The **equation of a conic** with axis (or axes) on or parallel to a coordinate axis (or axes) can be written as $Ax^2 + By^2 + Cx + Dy + E = 0$, where A, B, C, D, and E are constants and A and B are not both 0.

This equation defines a relation that has different graphs depending on the values of the coefficients A and B according to the following:

- If $A = B$, the equation is a circle. A **circle** is a set of points in the plane such that each point is equidistant from a fixed point in the circle's center. It has standard form: $(x - h)^2 + (y - k)^2 = r^2$, where (h, k) is the circle's **center** and the **radius** is $|r|$ units. Here is the graph of the circle, $x^2 + y^2 = 25$, with center at $(0, 0)$ and radius 5.

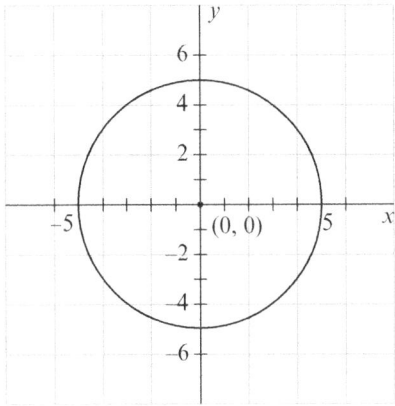

- If either A or B is 0, the equation is a parabola. A **parabola** is a set of points in the plane such that each point is equidistant from a line, called the **directrix**, and a fixed point, called the **focus**. It has the following standard forms, where $p\ (> 0)$ is the distance from the vertex of the parabola to the focus or directrix:
  - $(x - h)^2 = 4p(y - k)$. This parabola opens upward with vertex (h, k), focus $(h, k + p)$, and directrix $y = k - p$. It is symmetric about a vertical line through its vertex at $x = h$.
  - $(x - h)^2 = -4p(y - k)$. This parabola opens downward with vertex (h, k), focus $(h, k - p)$, and directrix $y = k + p$. It is symmetric about a vertical line through its vertex at $x = h$.
  - $(y - k)^2 = 4p(x - h)$, with vertex (h, k). This parabola opens right with vertex (h, k), focus $(h + p, k)$, and directrix $x = h - p$. The parabola is symmetric about a horizontal line through its vertex at $y = k$.
  - $(y - k)^2 = -4p(x - h)$, with vertex (h, k). This parabola opens left with vertex (h, k), focus $(h - p, k)$, and directrix $x = h + p$. The parabola is symmetric about a horizontal line through its vertex at $y = k$.

Here is the graph of the parabola, $x^2 = 8y$, with vertex at $(0, 0)$, focus $(0, 2)$, and directrix $y = -2$.

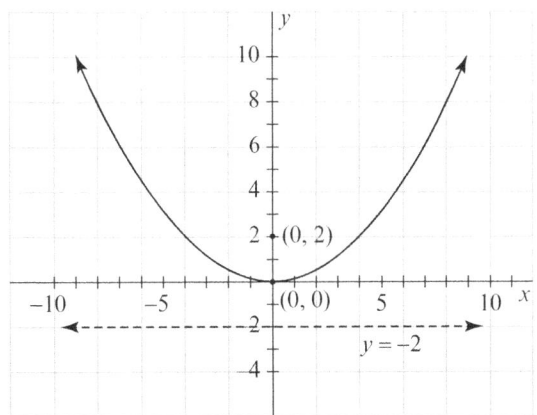

- If $AB > 0$, the equation is an ellipse. An **ellipse** is a set of points, the sum of whose distances from two fixed points, called the **foci**, is a constant. It has the following standard forms:

  - $\dfrac{(x-h)^2}{a^2} + \dfrac{(y-k)^2}{b^2} = 1$, $a > b > 0$ with a horizontal axis, center at (h, k), vertices at $(h \pm a, k)$, co-vertices at $(h, k \pm b)$, and foci at $(h \pm c, k)$, where $c = \sqrt{a^2 - b^2}$, which is the horizontal distance from the center to each foci. The line segment joining the vertices $(h - a, k)$ and $(h + a, k)$ is the major axis, is a horizontal axis of symmetry, and has length $2a$. The line segment joining the co-vertices $(h, k - b)$ and $(h, k + b)$ is the minor axis, is a vertical axis of symmetry, and has length $2b$.

  - $\dfrac{(x-h)^2}{b^2} + \dfrac{(y-k)^2}{a^2} = 1$, $a > b > 0$ with a vertical axis, center at (h, k), vertices at $(h, k \pm a)$, co-vertices at $(h \pm b, k)$, and foci at $(h, k \pm c)$, where $c = \sqrt{a^2 - b^2}$, which is the vertical distance from the center to each foci. The line segment joining the vertices $(h, k - a)$ and $(h, k + a)$ is the major axis, is a vertical axis of symmetry, and has length $2a$. The line segment joining the co-vertices $(h - b, k)$ and $(h + b, k)$ is the minor axis, is a horizontal axis of symmetry, and has length $2b$.

  Here is the graph of the ellipse, $\dfrac{x^2}{25} + \dfrac{y^2}{9} = 1$, with a horizontal axis, center at $(0, 0)$, vertices at $(\pm 5, 0)$, co-vertices at $(0, \pm 3)$, and foci at $(\pm 4, 0)$.

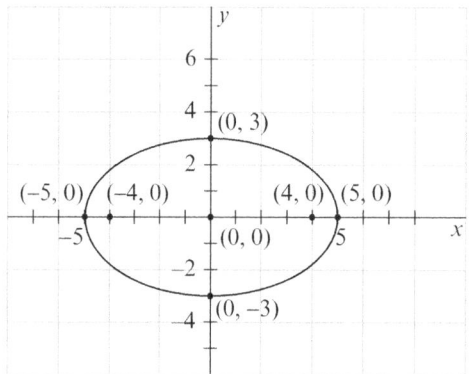

- If $AB < 0$, the equation is a hyperbola. A **hyperbola** is a set of points, the difference of whose distances from two fixed points, called the **foci**, is a constant. It has the following standard forms:

  - $\dfrac{(x-h)^2}{a^2} - \dfrac{(y-k)^2}{b^2} = 1$, $a > 0$, $b > 0$ with a horizontal axis, center at (h, k), vertices at $(h \pm a, k)$, and foci at $(h \pm c, k)$, where $c = \sqrt{a^2 + b^2}$, which is the horizontal distance from the center to each foci. The line segment joining the vertices $(h - a, k)$ and $(h + a, k)$ is the major axis, is a horizontal axis of symmetry, and has length $2a$. The hyperbola opens left and right along the line $y = k$, and it passes through the vertices $(h - a, k)$ and $(h + a, k)$. It has two intersecting lines $y = k + \dfrac{b}{a}(x - h)$ and $y = k - \dfrac{b}{a}(x - h)$ as (slanting) asymptotes. The asymptotes are the diagonals of a rectangle with dimensions $2a$ by $2b$ centered at (h, k).

  - $\dfrac{(y-k)^2}{a^2} - \dfrac{(x-h)^2}{b^2} = 1$, $a > 0$, $b > 0$ with a vertical axis, center at (h, k), vertices at $(h, k \pm a)$, and foci at $(h, k \pm c)$, where $c = \sqrt{a^2 + b^2}$, which is the vertical distance from the center to each foci. It opens up and down along the line $x = h$, and it passes through the vertices $(h, k - a)$ and $(h, k + a)$. It has two intersecting lines $y = k + \dfrac{a}{b}(x - h)$ and $y = k - \dfrac{a}{b}(x - h)$ as (slanting) asymptotes. The asymptotes are the diagonals of a rectangle with dimensions $2a$ by $2b$ centered at (h, k).

Here is the graph of the hyperbola, $\dfrac{x^2}{16} - \dfrac{y^2}{9} = 1$, with a horizontal axis, center at (0, 0), vertices at (±4, 0), foci at (±5, 0), and asymptotes $y = \pm\dfrac{3}{4}x$.

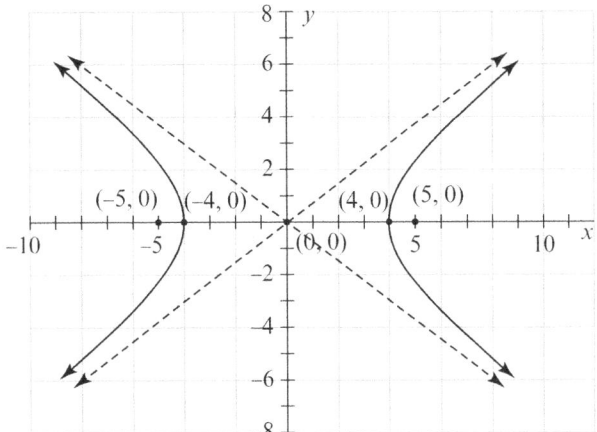

The **eccentricity**, $e = \dfrac{c}{a}$, of a conic section is a measure of the degree to which the shape varies from circular.

The eccentricity of a circle is 0, of a parabola is 1, of an ellipse is between 0 and 1, and of a hyperbola is greater than 1.

If the equation of a conic section is not in standard form, it can be put in standard form by completing the squares on the x and y terms.

Algebraic Representation of Spheres

A **sphere** is a three-dimensional figure, all of whose points are equidistant from its **center,** a fixed point within the sphere. The general equation for a sphere in a three-dimensional coordinate system is $(x - x_0)^2 + (y - y_0)^2 + (z - z_0)^2 = r^2$, with **center** (x_0, y_0, z_0) and **radius** $|r|$. Here is an illustration.

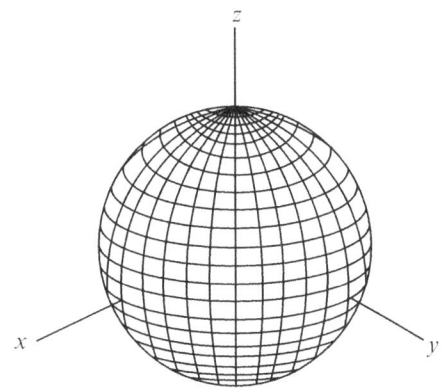

Chapter 4

Probability and Statistics

This chapter provides a review of concepts related to the study of probability and statistics, including counting techniques, probability theory, and statistical analysis.

Part 1

Part 1 of this chapter is for all candidates who plan to take a TExES Math exam. Carefully study the review material, being sure to concentrate as you go through it. Work through the examples and the practice problems and make sure you understand them thoroughly. When working a practice problem, you should cover up the solution. Then check your answer when you've finished.

Preliminaries: Counting Techniques

To be adequately prepared for probability, you must be able to solve basic problems that involve counting techniques, including the fundamental counting principle and permutations and combinations (for example, the number of arrangements of a set of objects or the number of ways to choose a committee from a club's membership).

Fundamental Counting Principle

Fundamental Counting Principle (FCP): If one of two tasks can be done in any one of m different ways, and, for each of these ways, a subsequent second task can be done in any one of n different ways, then the first task *and* the second task can both be done, in the order given, in $m \cdot n$ ways.

You can extend the FCP to any number of tasks. Thus, in general, for a sequence of k tasks, if a first task can be done in any one of n_1 different ways, and, for each of these ways, a subsequent second task can be done in any one of n_2 different ways, and, for each of these ways, a subsequent third task can be done in any one of n_3 different ways, and so on to the kth task, which can be done in any one of n_k different ways, then the total number of different ways the sequence of k tasks can be done, in the order given, is $n_1 \cdot n_2 \cdot n_3 \cdots n_k$. **Note:** This counting technique produces results in which *order determines different outcomes*.

Here are two practice problems.

> Problem: How many different 10-digit telephone numbers can begin with area code 210 and prefix 569?
>
> Solution: Four additional digits are needed to complete telephone numbers that begin (210) 569-. Therefore, in this problem, there are four tasks to do: Namely, determine each of the additional four digits. Think of each of the positions of the four digits as a slot to fill. In this example, you make your selection for each slot from the same set: the 10 digits 0 to 9. Since digits in a telephone number can repeat, you say that "repetitions are allowed." There are 10 ways to fill the first slot, and for each of these ways, 10 ways to fill the second slot, and for each of these, 10 ways to fill the third slot, and for each of these, 10 ways to fill the fourth slot. Thus, the total number of different telephone numbers that can begin (210) 569- is $10 \cdot 10 \cdot 10 \cdot 10 = 10,000$.
>
> Problem: In how many possible ways can a president, vice-president, secretary, and membership chairperson be selected from 25 members of a club if all members are eligible for each position and no member can hold more than one office?
>
> Solution: In this problem, there are four tasks: Namely, to select each of the four officers. Think of each of the officer positions as a slot to fill. Because the officers must all be different people, repetitions are not allowed in the selection process. There are 25 ways to fill the president's slot; after that, there are 24 ways remaining to fill the vice-president's slot; after that, there are 23 ways remaining to fill the secretary's

slot; and, finally, there are 22 ways remaining to fill the membership chairperson's slot. Thus, there are 25 · 24 · 23 · 22 = 303,600 possible ways to select a president, vice-president, secretary, and membership chairperson from the 25 members of the club.

Addition Principle

Addition Principle: If one task can be done in any one of m ways and a second task can be done in any one of n ways and if the two tasks *cannot* be done at the same time, then the number of different ways to do the first *or* the second task is $m + n$ ways. This principle can be extended to more than one task.

Here is a sample problem.

Problem: A student must select 1 elective from a list of 3 art classes, 10 kinesiology classes, and 2 music classes. How many possible classes are there from which to choose?

Solution: The student can choose an elective from the art classes in 3 ways, from the kinesiology classes in 10 ways, and from the music classes in 2 ways. The student can choose only one elective. Therefore, there are $3 + 10 + 2 = 15$ classes from which to choose.

You can modify the addition principle for situations in which two tasks overlap; that is, when the two tasks can be done at the same time. If one task can be done in any one of m ways and a second task can be done in any one of n ways and if the two tasks *can* be done at the same time in k different ways, then the number of ways to do the first or the second task is $m + n - k$.

Here is a practice problem.

Problem: In drawing one card at random (that is, without looking or making a special selection) from a well-shuffled deck of standard playing cards, how many different ways can a king or a diamond be selected?

Solution: In a random drawing of a card from a well-shuffled deck of standard playing cards, there are 52 possible outcomes: ace, 2, 3, 4, 5, 6, 7, 8, 9, 10, jack, queen, and king of clubs (♣); ace, 2, 3, 4, 5, 6, 7, 8, 9, 10, jack, queen, and king of spades (♠); ace, 2, 3, 4, 5, 6, 7, 8, 9, 10, jack, queen, and king of hearts (♥); and ace, 2, 3, 4, 5, 6, 7, 8, 9, 10, jack, queen, and king of diamonds (♦). Clubs and spades have black coloration, and hearts and diamonds have red coloration. Jacks, queens, and kings are face cards. Here is a black-and-white illustration of a standard deck of 52 playing cards.

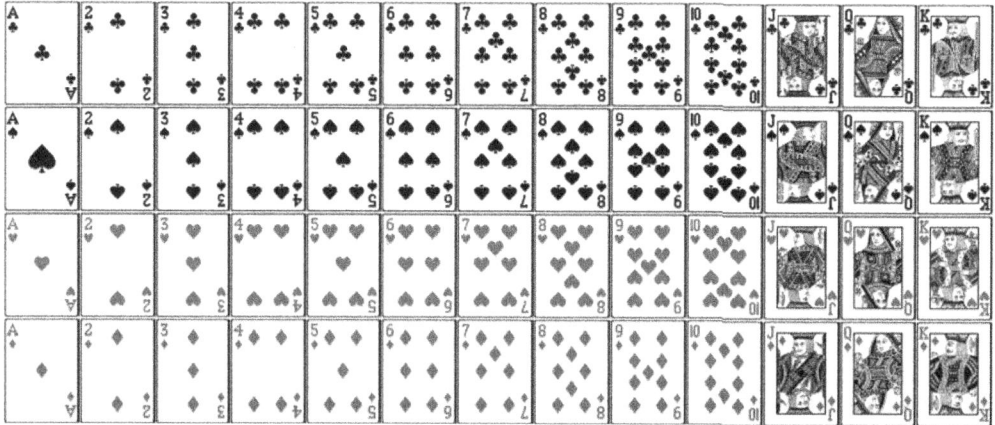

Source: *www.jfitz.com/cards/*

There are 4 ways to select a king, 13 ways to select a diamond, and 1 way to select a king and a diamond at the same time (the king of diamonds). Therefore, there are $4 + 13 - 1 = 16$ ways to select a king or a diamond.

Permutations

A **permutation** is an ordered arrangement of a set of distinctly different objects. For permutations, different orderings of the same objects are counted as different permutations. For example, two different permutations of the numbers 1 through 4 are 1234 and 4213. Thus, when the order of the objects in an arrangement is a differentiating factor in a problem, you are working with permutations.

Through a direct application of the FCP, the number of permutations of n distinct objects is $n! = n(n-1)(n-2)\ldots(2)(1)$.

Note: The notation $n!$ is read "n factorial." A factorial is the product of all positive integers less than or equal to a given positive integer. By definition, $0! = 1$.

Here is a practice problem.

> Problem: In how many different ways can five people be seated in a row of five identical seats?
>
> Solution: You can work this problem using the FCP, or you can recognize that the seating arrangement is the permutation of five distinct objects (persons). Thus, there are $5! = 5 \cdot 4 \cdot 3 \cdot 2 \cdot 1 = 120$ different ways for the five people to be seated.

Tip: On your TI calculator, you will find ! (factorial) under the PRB menu (for example, 5! returns 120).

The number of permutations of r objects selected from n distinct objects is $_nP_r = \dfrac{n!}{(n-r)!}$. When you apply this formula, it is important that you make sure the following conditions are met: The n objects must be n *distinct* objects, the r objects must be selected *without repetition* from the same set, and you must count different orderings of the same objects as *different* outcomes.

Here is a practice problem.

> Problem: In how many possible ways can a president, vice-president, secretary, and membership chairperson be selected from 25 members of a club if all members are eligible for each position and no member can hold more than one office?
>
> Solution: This problem was previously worked using the FCP, but now you can recognize that this problem satisfies the conditions for a permutation; that is, the 25 members of the club are distinct individuals, the 4 officers are selected without repetition from the same set of 25 members (no member can hold more than one office), and different orderings of the same people are counted as a different slate of officers. Thus, the number of permutations of 4 people selected from 25 people is
>
> $$_{25}P_4 = \dfrac{25!}{(25-4)!} = \dfrac{25!}{(21)!} = \dfrac{25 \cdot 24 \cdot 23 \cdot 22 \cdot 21!}{21!} = 25 \cdot 24 \cdot 23 \cdot 22 = 303{,}600.$$
>
> There are 303,600 possible ways to select a president, vice-president, secretary, and membership chairperson from the 25 members of the club.

Tip: On your TI calculator, the function $_nP_r$ is under the PRB menu. It returns the number of permutations of n distinct objects taken r at a time (for example, 25 $_nP_r$ 4 returns 303600).

The number of permutations of n objects of which n_1 are identical objects of a first kind, n_2 are identical objects of a second kind, …, n_k are identical objects of a kth kind is $\dfrac{n!}{n_1!n_2!\cdots n_k!}$.

Here is a practice problem.

> Problem: How many different "words" can you make using the 11 letters in the word *MISSISSIPPI* if you use all 11 letters each time?
>
> Solution: Because the order in which different letters appear results in different so-called "words," this is a permutation problem. The word *MISSISSIPPI* consists of 11 letters: one *M*, four *I*'s, four *S*'s, and two *P*'s. Since the 11 objects (that is, the letters) to be arranged are not all mutually different objects, the number of different words is $\dfrac{n!}{n_1! n_2! \cdots n_k!} = \dfrac{11!}{4!4!2!} = 34{,}650$.

Combinations

A **combination** is an arrangement of a set of distinct objects in which different orderings of the same objects are considered to be identical arrangements. For example, the set of three coins quarter, dime, and nickel is the same as the set nickel, dime, and quarter. That is, in a combination problem, different orderings of the same objects are *not* counted as separate results. When the order in which objects are arranged does *not* determine different outcomes, you are working with combinations.

The number of combinations of *r* objects selected from *n* distinct objects is $_nC_r = \dfrac{n!}{r!(n-r)!}$.

Note: The notation $_nC_r$ is also written as $\binom{n}{r}$.

When you apply this formula, it is important that you make sure the following conditions are met: The *n* objects must be *n distinct* objects, the *r* objects must be selected *without repetition* from the same set, and you must consider different orderings of the same objects to be *indistinguishable*.

Here is a practice problem.

> Problem: How many ways can a 4-member committee be formed from the 25 members of a club?
>
> Solution: Since the order in which committee members are arranged does not change the makeup of the committee, you would *not* try to work this problem using the FCP because it produces results in which order determines different outcomes. This example satisfies the conditions for a combination. That is, the 25 members of the club are distinct individuals, the 4 committee members are selected without repetition from the same set of 25 members, and different orderings of the same people are counted as the same committee. The number of combinations of 4 people selected from 25 people is
>
> $_{25}C_4 = \dfrac{25!}{4!(25-4)!} = \dfrac{25!}{4!(21)!} = \dfrac{25 \cdot 24 \cdot 23 \cdot 22 \cdot 21!}{4!21!} = \dfrac{25 \cdot 24 \cdot 23 \cdot 22}{4 \cdot 3 \cdot 2 \cdot 1} = 12{,}650$. There are 12,650 possible ways to form a 4-member committee from the 25 members of the club.

Tip: On your TI calculator, the function $_nC_r$ is under the PRB menu. It returns the number of combinations of *n* distinct objects taken *r* at a time (for example, 25 $_nC_r$ 4 returns 12650).

Situations Indicating Permutations or Combinations

One important way that combinations and permutations differ is that different orderings of the same objects are counted as separate results for permutation problems, but not for combination problems. The following table categorizes some situations as (most likely) indicating either a permutation or combination problem.

Permutations	Combinations
• creating passwords, license plates, words, or codes • assigning roles • filling positions • making ordered arrangements of things (people, books, colors, and so on) • selecting first, second, third place, and such • distributing objects among several people or things	• forming a committee • making a collection of things (coins, books, and so on) • counting subsets of a set • dealing hands from a deck of cards • listing the combinations from a set of objects • selecting pizza toppings • selecting questions from a test • selecting students for groups

For your TExES Math exam, you should be able to work most, if not all, of the permutation problems you might encounter by using the FCP rather than the formula $_nP_r$. For the situations similar to those given for combinations in the table, you should use $_nC_r$ (unless you can easily list the possibilities).

You can use the combination formula in conjunction with the FCP to determine the number of possible outcomes in certain situations.

Here is a practice problem.

> Problem: A party planner chooses 3 toy trucks, 7 toy cars, and 10 action figures from collections of 8 different toy trucks, 10 different toy cars, and 12 different action figures. How many possible ways can the party planner make the combined selections?
>
> Solution: Thinking in terms of the FCP, the party planner has three tasks to do: Select 3 of the 8 toy trucks, select 7 of the 10 toy cars, and select 10 of the 12 action figures. Since the arrangement of the toy items in the individual selections of trucks, cars, and action figures is not a differentiating factor in the problem, you can determine the number of ways to select each of the toy items using the combination formula. Then, following those calculations, you can use the FCP to determine the total number of possible ways the party planner can make the combined selections. Thus, the number of possible ways the party planner can make the combined selections is
>
> (number of ways to select 3 of 8 toy trucks) × (number of ways to select 7 of 10 toy cars) × (number of ways to select 10 of 12 action figures) =
>
> $$_8C_3 \cdot {}_{10}C_7 \cdot {}_{12}C_{10} = \frac{8!}{3!(8-3)!} \cdot \frac{10!}{7!(10-7)!} \cdot \frac{12!}{10!(12-10)!} = \frac{8!}{3!5!} \cdot \frac{10!}{7!3!} \cdot \frac{12!}{10!2!} = 56 \cdot 120 \cdot 66 = 443,520$$

Tip: Your TI calculator can numerically evaluate both $_nP_r$ and $_nC_r$. Make a point to practice using this time-saving feature under the PRB menu before you take your TExES Math exam.

The Binomial Theorem and Pascal's Triangle

This section presents the binomial theorem and Pascal's triangle.

The Binomial Theorem

The binomial theorem is used to expand a binomial to a power using the following formula:

$$(x+y)^n = \sum_{k=0}^{n} \binom{n}{k} x^{n-k} y^k$$

The values $\binom{n}{k}$ are the **binomial coefficients**.

Tip: In each term, the sum of the exponents on x and y is n, and the exponent on x decreases from n to 0, while the exponent on y increases from 0 to n.

Here is a practice problem.

Problem: Expand $(x + y)^3$.
Solution:

$$(x+y)^3 = \sum_{k=0}^{3}\binom{3}{k}x^{3-k}y^k = \binom{3}{0}x^3y^0 + \binom{3}{1}x^2y^1 + \binom{3}{2}x^1y^2 + \binom{3}{3}x^0y^3 = x^3 + 3x^2y + 3xy^2 + y^3$$

Tip: Notice that $\binom{3}{0} = \binom{3}{3}$ and $\binom{3}{1} = \binom{3}{2}$. In general, $\binom{n}{r} = \binom{n}{n-r}$.

You can use the binomial theorem to show that, counting the empty set, the number of subsets of a set consisting of n elements is 2^n.

Here is a practice problem:

Problem: Use the binomial theorem to show that the number of subsets of a set consisting of 3 elements is $2^3 = 8$.
Solution: The number of subsets of size 0 is $\binom{3}{0}$, of size 1 is $\binom{3}{1}$, of size 2 is $\binom{3}{2}$, and of size 3 is $\binom{3}{3}$ for a total of $= \binom{3}{0} + \binom{3}{1} + \binom{3}{2} + \binom{3}{3} = \sum_{k=0}^{3}\binom{3}{k}1^{3-k}1^k = (1+1)^3 = 2^3$ (which is 8).

Pascal's Triangle

Pascal's triangle is a triangular array of numbers that can be derived from the formula $\binom{n}{r}$. Row 0, the top row, of the triangle has one element; Row 1, the next row, has two elements; Row 2 has three elements; Row 3 has four elements; and so on. Each row begins and ends with a 1 and is symmetric from left to right, including Row 0, whose one element is 1. An element, other than a 1, in a row is the sum of the two elements most directly above it. Here is an example of Pascal's triangle showing Row 0 through Row 8.

```
0:                         1
1:                       1   1
2:                     1   2   1
3:                   1   3   3   1
4:                 1   4   6   4   1
5:               1   5  10  10   5   1
6:             1   6  15  20  15   6   1
7:           1   7  21  35  35  21   7   1
8:         1   8  28  56  70  56  28   8   1
           ⋮   ⋮   ⋮   ⋮   ⋮   ⋮   ⋮   ⋮
```

For any row n in Pascal's triangle, the elements are the numbers $\binom{n}{r}$ for $r = 0, \ldots, n$, in this order.

These numbers also are the **binomial coefficients** in the expansion of $(x + y)^n$. For example, the elements in Row 3 of Pascal's triangle are $\binom{3}{0} = 1$, $\binom{3}{1} = 3$, $\binom{3}{2} = 3$, and $\binom{3}{3} = 1$. When you expand $(x + y)^3$, you obtain $x^3 + 3x^2y + 3xy^2 + y^3$, which has coefficients 1, 3, 3, 1, the same numbers that are in Row 3 of Pascal's triangle.

If you find it convenient, you can use Pascal's triangle to find values of $\binom{n}{r}$, rather than working out the formula $_nC_r$ or using your calculator. For example, to determine $\binom{6}{2}$, locate the third term in Row 6 of Pascal's triangle, which is 15.

Tip: Keep in mind that for each row in Pascal's triangle, $\binom{n}{r}$ starts at $r = 0$, not 1.

Probability

For this topic, you must demonstrate an understanding of probability theory including random experiments, sample spaces, and probability measures and be able to use probability models to solve problems.

Random Experiments and Sample Spaces

A **chance process** gives results that cannot be determined beforehand. A **random experiment** is a chance process such that, on any single repetition of the experiment, exactly one outcome occurs. It is assumed that all the possible outcomes are known before the random experiment is performed, but which of the possibilities will in fact occur is uncertain. Here are examples. (*Note:* To facilitate the discussion that follows, the experiments are numbered; when no confusion might occur, experiment means "random experiment.")

> **Experiment 1:** Flip a U.S. coin one time and observe the coin's up face.
>
> **Experiment 2:** Perform one toss of a number cube, whose six faces are numbered 1 through 6, and observe the up face.
>
> **Experiment 3:** Draw one card (without looking) from a well-shuffled standard deck of 52 playing cards and observe which card was drawn. (*Note:* When you draw without looking you are making a random selection.)
>
> **Experiment 4:** Draw one tile (without looking) from a box containing five wooden, 1-inch square tiles numbered 1 through 5, and observe the up face.
>
> **Experiment 5:** Spin the pointer of a circular spinner one time. In one spin, the pointer will turn a random number of times and stop. The spinner has three sectors. The color of each sector and the percentage of the spinner that color occupies are blue (25%), green (25%), and red (50%).

For each of these random experiments you get a single **outcome** that occurs by chance. You cannot determine with certainty the outcome beforehand. That is, you cannot say for certain what the exact outcome will be. However, for each experiment you can produce its set of *possible* outcomes. The set, S, of possible outcomes of a random experiment is its **sample space**. Each element of S is an outcome (or **simple event, sample point,** or **elementary outcome**). Here are the sample spaces of the five experiments listed above.

Experiment 1: $S = \{H, T\}$, where "H" represents the outcome "Heads appears on the up face" and "T" represents the outcome "Tails appears on the up face." *Note:* U.S. coins have an image of a historical figure (person) on one side, which is referred to as "Heads." The image on the opposite side is referred to as "Tails."

Experiment 2: $S = \{1, 2, 3, 4, 5, 6\}$, where "1" represents "1 appears on the up face," "2" represents "2 appears on the up face," and so on to "6" represents "6 appears on the up face."

Experiment 3: $S = \{♣A, ♣2, ♣3, ♣4, ♣5, ♣6, ♣7, ♣8, ♣9, ♣10, ♣J, ♣Q, ♣K, ♠A, ♠2, ♠3, ♠4, ♠5, ♠6, ♠7, ♠8, ♠9, ♠10, ♠J, ♠Q, ♠K, ♥A, ♥2, ♥3, ♥4, ♥5, ♥6, ♥7, ♥8, ♥9, ♥10, ♥J, ♥Q, ♥K, ♦A, ♦2, ♦3, ♦4, ♦5, ♦6, ♦7, ♦8, ♦9, ♦10, ♦J, ♦Q, ♦K\}$, where ♣A represents the ace of clubs, ♣2 represents the 2 of clubs, . . ., ♣J represents the jack of clubs, ♣Q represents the queen of clubs, ♣K represents the king of clubs, and so on to ♦A represents the ace of diamonds,

♦2 represents the 2 of diamonds, . . ., ♦J represents the jack of diamonds, ♦Q represents the queen of diamonds, and ♦K represents the king of diamonds. *Note:* A standard deck of 52 playing cards consists of four suits: clubs (♣), spades (♠), hearts (♥), and diamonds (♦). Clubs and spades are black-colored suits; hearts and diamonds are red-colored suits. Each suit has 13 cards consisting of three face cards (king, queen, and jack) and number cards from 1 (ace) to 10, as shown in the following black and white illustration.

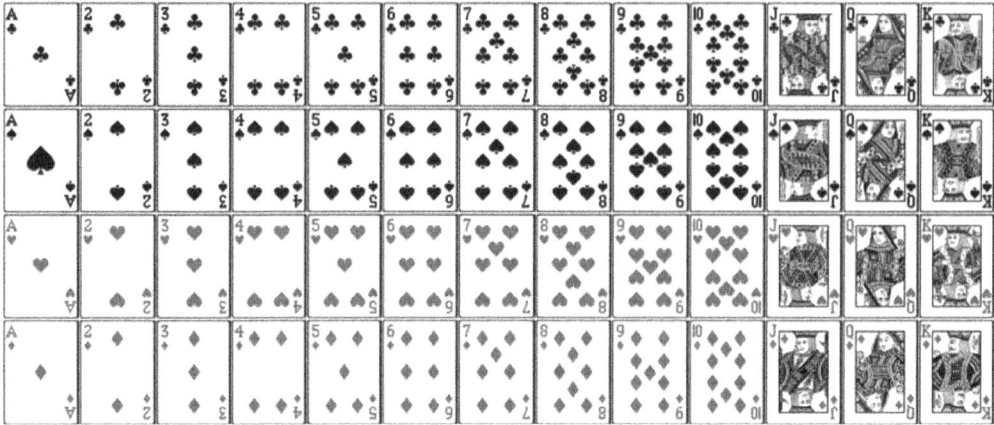

Source: *www.jfitz.com/cards/*

Experiment 4: $S = \{1, 2, 3, 4, 5\}$, where "1" represents the outcome "the tile drawn shows a 1," "2" represents the outcome "the tile drawn shows a 2," and so on to "5" represents the outcome "the tile drawn shows a 5."

Experiment 5: $S = \{B, G, R\}$, where "B" represents the outcome "the pointer stops on blue," "G" represents the outcome "the pointer stops on green," and "R" represents the outcome "the pointer stops on red."

Note: A sample space can be finite or infinite. In this book, only finite sample spaces are considered.

Sometimes random experiments have several stages. For example, consider the experiment of flipping two coins and observing the up faces. Think of the experiment as having two stages. First, flip the first coin and observe the up face. Next, flip the second coin and observe the up face. Three common methods for generating the possible outcomes for such an experiment are organized lists, tables, and tree diagrams.

Here is a practice problem.

Problem: Write the sample space for the experiment of flipping two coins and observing the up faces.
Solution:
Method 1: Use an **organized list** to generate the possible outcomes.
Proceed systematically. First, list H twice on the first coin with each of the possibilities (H, T) for the second coin. Next, list T twice on the first coin with each of the possibilities (H, T) for the second coin.

First Coin	Second Coin
H	H
H	T
T	H
T	T

Tip: When you use an organized list to count possibilities, be careful to proceed in a systematic manner, as shown in the problem above. Otherwise, you might overlook a possibility or count one more than once.

Method 2: Use a **table** to generate the possible outcomes.

Proceed systematically. Use H and T for the row headings and H and T for the column headings. Fill in the table cells according to the row and column headings.

	Second Coin	
First Coin	H	T
H	HH	HT
T	TH	TT

Method 3: Use a **tree diagram** to generate the possible outcomes.

First, draw a branch for each possibility for the first stage (in this case, the first coin). Next, attach branches for each possibility for the second stage (in this case, the second coin) to each of the possibilities for the first stage. Then, list the possible outcomes by tracing along the branches.

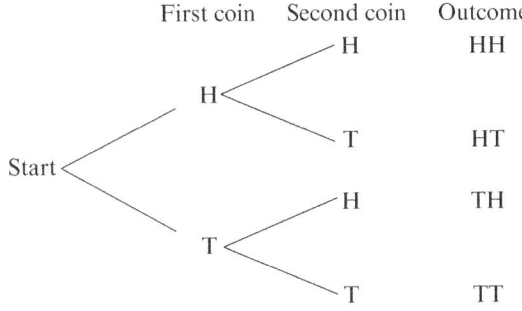

Each of the three methods results in the same four outcomes. The possible outcomes when two coins are flipped are HH (representing heads on the first coin and heads on the second coin), HT (representing heads on the first coin and tails on the second coin), TH (representing tails on the first coin and heads on the second coin), and TT (representing tails on the first coin and tails on the second coin). Therefore, $S = \{HH, HT, TH, TT\}$ is the sample space for flipping two coins.

Tip: Notice that HT and TH are *not* the same outcome. HT is the outcome of heads on the first coin and tails on the second coin, but TH is the outcome of tails on the first coin and heads on the second coin.

You can extend organized lists and tree diagrams to three or more stages.

Here is a practice problem.

Problem: Use a tree diagram to determine the sample space for the experiment of flipping three coins and observing the up faces.

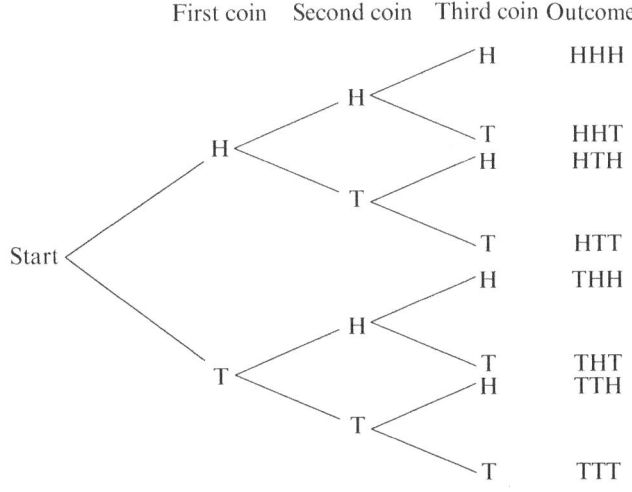

Solution: $S = \{HHH, HHT, HTH, HTT, THH, THT, TTH, TTT\}$ is the sample space for flipping three coins. The number of possible outcomes is 8.

Determining the outcomes in a sample space is a critical step in solving a probability problem. For simple experiments, organized lists, tables, and tree diagrams are useful ways to generate a list of the outcomes. More sophisticated counting techniques, which include the fundamental counting principle, permutations, and combinations, are needed for problems that are less straightforward. See "Preliminaries: Counting Techniques" earlier in this chapter for a discussion of these methods.

Probability Measures

A **probability measure** on a sample space, S, is a function that assigns to each outcome in S a real number between 0 and 1, inclusive, so that the values assigned to the outcomes in S sum to 1. (For a general discussion of functions, see Chapter 2.) The value assigned to an outcome in S is the **probability value** of that outcome.

Consider the sample space $S = \{1, 2, 3, 4, 5\}$ from Experiment 4 of drawing one tile (without looking) from a box containing five wooden, 1-inch square tiles numbered 1 through 5. Given that the tiles are physically identical and the drawing is performed without looking (that is, randomly), each tile has a 1 in 5 chance of being drawn. Thus, a logical probability value for each of the five outcomes in S is $\frac{1}{5}$. The sum of the probability values of the five outcomes in S is $\frac{1}{5} + \frac{1}{5} + \frac{1}{5} + \frac{1}{5} + \frac{1}{5} = \frac{5}{5} = 1$.

Consider the sample space $S = \{B, G, R\}$ from Experiment 5 of spinning the pointer of a circular spinner one time, where the spinner has three sectors that are colored blue (25%), green (25%), and red (50%). A logical probability value for the outcome B is $\frac{1}{4}$, for the outcome G is $\frac{1}{4}$, and for the outcome R is $\frac{1}{2}$. The sum of the probability values of the three outcomes in S is $\frac{1}{4} + \frac{1}{4} + \frac{1}{2} = \frac{4}{4} = 1$.

Consider the sample space $S = \{HHH, HHT, HTH, HTT, THH, THT, TTH, TTT\}$ from the experiment of flipping three coins and observing the up faces. A logical probability value for each of the eight outcomes in S is $\frac{1}{8}$. The sum of the probability values of the eight outcomes in S is $\frac{1}{8} + \frac{1}{8} + \frac{1}{8} + \frac{1}{8} + \frac{1}{8} + \frac{1}{8} + \frac{1}{8} + \frac{1}{8} = \frac{8}{8} = 1$.

Tip: For a sample space resulting from a real-world chance experiment, usually there is only one probability measure that is considered appropriate. In particular, objects such as coins and number cubes are considered to be fair; that is, such objects do not favor one outcome over another.

According to the frequency theory of probability, the probability values assigned to the outcomes of a sample space are the limiting values of the proportions of times over many repetitions that the experiment will result in the different possible outcomes. (See "Frequency Theory of Probability" later in this chapter for a discussion of this topic.)

Random Variables, Probability Distributions, and Expected Value

This topic presents the concept of random variables and their related probability distributions. You will calculate the expected value of a random variable and interpret the result as the mean of the probability distribution.

Random Variables and Probability Distributions

A **random variable** is a function X that assigns a real number x, determined by chance, to each and every outcome in a sample space S. The number x is the **value** of the random variable. It is determined by the outcome of a random experiment.

Note: Random variables are usually denoted by uppercase letters, often X, Y, or Z.

Like probability measures, a random variable is a function over a sample space; however (unlike probability measures), there are no restrictions on the values assigned to the outcomes of S, nor to their sum.

Note: Random variables can be discrete or continuous. This discussion deals only with discrete random variables. A discrete random variable is one in which its values can be counted or listed.

The **probability distribution** of a discrete random variable gives the probability for each of the random variable's values in a graph, chart, or table, or by means of a formula.

Consider the sample space $S = \{1, 2, 3, 4, 5\}$ from Experiment 4 (given previously) of drawing one tile (without looking) from a box containing five wooden, 1-inch square tiles numbered 1 through 5. Define the random variable X as the function that assigns the value 1 to the outcomes that show an even number on the drawn tile and the value 6 to the outcomes that show an odd number on the drawn tile. The possible values for the random variable X are 1 and 6. Specifically, $X(1) = 6$, $X(2) = 1$, $X(3) = 6$, $X(4) = 1$, and $X(5) = 6$. Notice that a random variable can assign the same value to more than one outcome in the sample space. The following table represents the probability distribution for X.

x	$P(X = x)$
1	$\frac{2}{5}$
6	$\frac{3}{5}$

The entries in the $P(X = x)$ column sum to 1 (that is, $\frac{2}{5} + \frac{3}{5} = \frac{5}{5} = 1$) because X assigns every outcome in S one and only one of the values 1 or 6.

Here is a practice problem.

> Problem: Consider the sample space $S = \{$HHH, HHT, HTH, HTT, THH, THT, TTH, TTT$\}$ from the experiment (given previously) of flipping three coins. Define the random variable Y as the number of heads observed in an outcome. Graph the probability distribution for Y.
>
> Solution: The possible values for the random variable Y are 0, 1, 2, and 3. Specifically, $Y(HHH) = 3$, $Y(HHT) = 2$, $Y(HTH) = 2$, $Y(HTT) = 1$, $Y(THH) = 2$, $Y(THT) = 1$, $Y(TTH) = 1$, and $Y(TTT) = 0$. The following graph represents the probability distribution for Y.

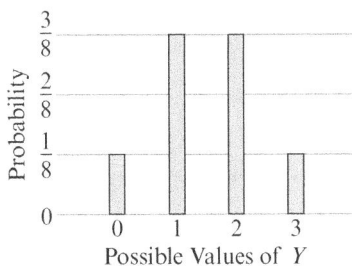

Note: The probabilities for the possible values of Y sum to 1 (that is, $\frac{1}{8} + \frac{3}{8} + \frac{3}{8} + \frac{1}{8} = \frac{8}{8} = 1$) because Y assigns every outcome in S one and only one of the values 0, 1, 2, or 3.

Expected Value

If X is a discrete random variable that takes on values $x_1, x_2, \ldots, x_n$, with respective probabilities $P(x_1), P(x_2), \ldots, P(x_n)$, the **expected value,** denoted $E(X)$, is the **theoretical mean** μ of X and is given by

$$\mu = E(X) = x_1 P(x_1) + x_2 P(x_2) + \ldots + x_n P(x_n)$$

Suppose X is the random variable that has the probability distribution shown.

x	$P(X = x)$
1	$\frac{2}{5}$
6	$\frac{3}{5}$

The expected value of X is given by

$$\mu = E(x) = x_1 P(x_1) + x_2 P(x_2) = 1\left(\frac{2}{5}\right) + 6\left(\frac{3}{5}\right) = \frac{20}{5} = 4$$

You can use your understanding of probability distributions and expected value to decide whether a game is fair. *Note:* A game is **fair** if there is an equal chance of winning or losing.

Here is a practice problem.

> Problem: Consider the experiment of drawing one tile (without looking) from a box containing five wooden, 1-inch square tiles numbered 1 through 5, and observing the up face. You pay 5 chips to play a game with the numbered tiles. You receive 6 chips if the tile drawn shows an odd number and 1 chip if the tile drawn shows an even number. Is the game fair?
>
> Solution: Your expected value for the game is $(1 \text{ chip})\left(\frac{2}{5}\right) + (6 \text{ chips})\left(\frac{3}{5}\right) = 4$ chips. Because you are paying a 5-chip fee to play the game, on average, you lose 1 chip per play. The game is not fair, since you, the player, can expect to lose.

Determining Probabilities of Events Using Binomial Probability Distributions

Consider n independent trials of an experiment where at each trial there are exactly two possible outcomes: success with probability p that is constant from trial to trial and failure with probability $1 - p$. Let X equal the number of successes out of the n repeated trials. The random variable X is called a **binomial random variable** and its probability distribution is called a **binomial distribution.** To summarize, a binomial distribution results from a process that has the following characteristics:

1. There are a fixed number n of identical trials.
2. Each trial results in exactly one of only two outcomes, which, by convention, are labeled "success" and "failure."
3. The probability of success, denoted p, on a single trial remains the same from trial to trial.
4. The trials are independent.
5. The binomial random variable X is the number of successes out of the n repeated trials.

Let the random variable X denote the number of successes in n trials of a binomial experiment. Then X has a binomial distribution and the **formula for the probability of observing exactly x successes in n trials** is given by

$$P(X = x) = \binom{n}{x} p^x q^{n-x} \text{ for } x = 0, 1, 2, \ldots, n$$

where n = number of trials

x = number of successes among n trials

p = probability of success in a single trial

$q = 1 - p$

Tip: Recall from "The Binomial Theorem," earlier in this chapter, that $\binom{n}{x} = {}_nC_x = \dfrac{n!}{x!(n-x)!}$.

Note: The word *success* as used in describing a binomial distribution is not meant to convey the message that the targeted success outcome is something you would ordinarily consider successful, good, or even desirable. The word *success* is simply used to designate whichever outcome is being counted in the n trials of the binomial experiment. Either outcome may be named the "success" outcome. However, once the success outcome is identified, then its probability of occurrence is designated as p.

Here are two practice problems.

> Problem: If you toss a six-sided die five times and record the number of dots on the up face of the die, what is the probability that four dots on the up face occurs exactly three times?
>
> Solution:
>
> $n = 5$
> $x = 3$
> p = probability four dots appears on the up face of the die in one toss = $\dfrac{1}{6}$
> $q = 1 - \dfrac{1}{6} = \dfrac{5}{6}$
>
> $$P(X = 3) = \binom{5}{3}\left(\dfrac{1}{6}\right)^3\left(\dfrac{5}{6}\right)^2 = (10)\left(\dfrac{1}{216}\right)\left(\dfrac{25}{36}\right) \approx 0.03215$$

> Problem: If you flip a coin six times and record the up face of the coin, what is the probability that heads shows on the up face fewer than three times?
>
> Solution:
>
> $$P(X < 3) = P(X = 0) + P(X = 1) + P(X = 2)$$
> $$= \binom{6}{0}\left(\dfrac{1}{2}\right)^0\left(\dfrac{1}{2}\right)^6 + \binom{6}{1}\left(\dfrac{1}{2}\right)^1\left(\dfrac{1}{2}\right)^5 + \binom{6}{2}\left(\dfrac{1}{2}\right)^2\left(\dfrac{1}{2}\right)^4$$
> $$= 0.015625 + 0.09375 + 0.234375 = 0.34375$$

Events

An **event**, E, is a collection of outcomes from a sample space S; that is, an event E is a subset of S. (See "Basic Set Theory" in Chapter 5 for a discussion of sets and subsets.) E can consist of no outcomes (the null set) or from a single outcome up to all the outcomes in S. *Note:* By convention, capital letters are used to designate events, with the word *event* being omitted in cases where the meaning is clear.

An event E is said to **occur** if a member of E occurs when the experiment is performed. The **probability of E**, denoted $P(E)$, is the sum of the probability values assigned to the outcomes in E. It is a numerical value between 0 and 1, inclusive, that quantifies the chance or likelihood that E will occur.

Chapter 4: Probability and Statistics

An **impossible event** is one that cannot occur. The probability of an impossible event is 0. A **certain event** is one that is guaranteed to occur. The probability of a certain event is 1. A probability near zero indicates an unlikely event; a probability around $\frac{1}{2}$ is neither likely nor unlikely; and a probability near 1 indicates a likely event. Thus, the lowest probability you can have is 0, and the highest probability you can have is 1. All other probabilities fall between 0 and 1. Symbolically, $0 \le P(E) \le 1$, for any event E.

Tip: If you determine a probability and your answer is greater than 1 or your answer is negative, you've made a mistake! Go back and check your work.

Here is a practice problem.

> Problem: Determine the probability of the given event from the sample space $S = \{1, 2, 3, 4, 5\}$, the set of outcomes from Experiment 4, the tile-drawing experiment.
> **(a)** $E_1 = \{1\}$, **(b)** $E_2 = \{1, 3, 5\}$, **(c)** $E_3 = \{4, 5\}$, **(d)** E_4 is the event that the tile drawn shows a number greater than 5, and **(e)** E_5 is the event that the tile drawn shows a whole number.
> Solution:
> **(a)** $P(E_1) = P(\{1\}) = \frac{1}{5}$. *Note:* Hereafter, probability of single outcomes, such as $P(\{1\})$, will be written as $P(1)$.
> **(b)** $P(E_2) = P(1) + P(3) + P(5) = \frac{1}{5} + \frac{1}{5} + \frac{1}{5} = \frac{3}{5}$
> **(c)** $P(E_3) = P(4) + P(5) = \frac{1}{5} + \frac{1}{5} = \frac{2}{5}$
> **(d)** E_4 is an impossible event; thus, $P(E_4) = 0$.
> **(e)** E_5 is a certain event; thus, $P(E_5) = 1$.

Determining Probabilities of Events Using Uniform Probability Distributions

When each of the possible outcomes in a sample space has an equal chance of occurring, the sample space has **equally likely outcomes**. The probability distribution for a sample space with equally likely outcomes is a **uniform probability distribution**. The probability of each outcome is $\frac{1}{n}$, where n is the number of possible outcomes. You write $P(\text{outcome}) = \frac{1}{n}$ to mean "the probability of an outcome is $\frac{1}{n}$."

If all outcomes in the sample space are equally likely, the **classical method** for computing the **probability of an event E** is given by $P(E) = \dfrac{\text{Number of outcomes in } E}{\text{Total number of outcomes in the sample space}}$.

Here is a practice problem.

> Problem: The sample space is $S = \{1, 2, 3, 4, 5\}$, containing the set of outcomes from the tile-drawing experiment. Let E be the event the tile drawn shows an odd number. Find $P(E)$.
>
> Solution: $E = \{1, 3, 5\}$. Thus, $P(E) = \dfrac{\text{Number of outcomes in } E}{\text{Total number of outcomes in the sample space}} = \dfrac{3}{5}$.

Tip: In a probability problem involving equally likely outcomes, the number of total outcomes possible will always be greater than or equal to the number of outcomes in the event, so check to make sure that the denominator is *larger than or equal to* the numerator when you plug into the formula.

Probabilities can be expressed as fractions, decimals, or percents. In the example given, the probability of drawing an odd-numbered tile can be expressed as $\frac{3}{5}$, 0.6, or 60 percent.

Keep in mind that the rule for the classical method of computing probability will *not* apply to sample spaces in which the events are not equally likely. For example, the sample space for spinning the pointer of the spinner shown below is $S = \{\text{green, red, yellow}\}$.

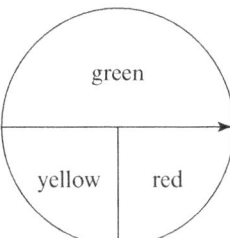

The probabilities for the different outcomes are the following: $P(\text{red}) = \frac{1}{4}$, $P(\text{yellow}) = \frac{1}{4}$, and $P(\text{green}) = \frac{1}{2}$. The three outcomes are not equally likely because the green section is larger than the other two sections.

Tip: Always remember to check whether the outcomes are equally likely before using the rule for the classical method of computing probability.

Combinations of Events

For this topic, you must demonstrate an understanding of complements, unions, and intersections of events.

Complement of an Event

The **complement of an event** E, denoted E', is the event that E does not occur. The probability of the complement of an event E is $P(E') = 1 - P(E)$. For example, if $P(E) = 0.06$, then $P(E') = 1 - P(E) = 1 - 0.06 = 0.94$.

Conversely, $P(E) = 1 - P(E')$.

Here is a practice problem.

> Problem: If the probability of not guessing correctly on a multiple-choice test question is $\frac{3}{4}$, what is the probability of guessing correctly on that question?
> Solution: The probability of guessing correctly on that question is $1 - \frac{3}{4} = \frac{1}{4}$.

Compound Events

Suppose A and B are two events defined over the same sample space S.

The event $A \cup B$ (read "A union B") is the event consisting of all outcomes in S that are in at least one of the events A or B. That is, the event $A \cup B$ includes all the outcomes that are in only one or the other of the two events as well as those that are common to both events.

Then, $P(A \cup B)$ is the probability that event A occurs or event B occurs or that both events occur simultaneously.

Tip: You will find it helpful to know that $P(A \cup B)$ is the probability that at least one of the events A or B occurs.

Chapter 4: Probability and Statistics

To find $P(A \cup B)$, sum the number of ways that A can occur and the number of ways that B can occur, being sure to add in such a way that *no outcome is counted twice,* and then divide by the number of outcomes in the sample space.

Here is a practice problem.

Problem: In one spin of the spinner shown below, the pointer will turn a random number of times and stop. What is the probability the pointer will stop on a number divisible by 4 or a number greater than 30?

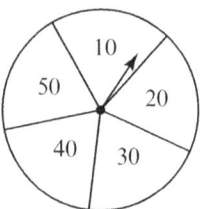

Solution: The sample space $S = \{10, 20, 30, 40, 50\}$. The number of outcomes in the sample space is 5. Let event A be the number is divisible by 4. Let event B be the number is greater than 30. Then $A = \{20, 40\}$ and $B = \{40, 50\}$. Looking at A and B, you can see that 40 is an outcome in both events. You do not want to count 40 twice, so $(A \cup B) = \{20, 40, 50\}$. Thus, there are three outcomes in $(A \cup B)$, leading to the following result: $P(\text{number divisible by 4 or number greater than 30}) = P(A \cup B) = \frac{3}{5}$.

From this example, you can see you must be careful when events overlap. But, if there is no overlap, you simply sum the outcomes in the two events.

Here is a practice problem.

Problem: A bag contains 5 black marbles numbered 1 to 5, 3 green marbles numbered 1 to 3, and 2 red marbles numbered 1 and 2, all identical in size and shape. If one marble is randomly drawn from the bag, what is the probability that the marble is green or red?

Solution: There are 10 outcomes in the sample space.

Let event A be the marble is green. Let event B be the marble is red. These two events have no overlap. The number of outcomes in $(A \cup B)$ is $3 + 2 = 5$, leading to the following result.

$$P(\text{green or red}) = P(A \cup B) = \frac{5}{10} = \frac{1}{2}$$

The event $A \cap B$ (read "*A* **intersection** *B*") is the event consisting of all outcomes in S that are in both events A and B. That is, the event $A \cap B$ includes all the outcomes that are common to both events. Then, $P(A \cap B)$ is the probability that events A and B occur simultaneously.

To find $P(A \cap B)$, count the number of ways that both A and B can occur at the same time, and then divide by the number of outcomes in the sample space.

Here is a practice problem.

Problem: In one spin of the spinner shown below, the pointer will turn a random number of times and stop. What is the probability the pointer will stop on a number divisible by 4 and a number greater than 30?

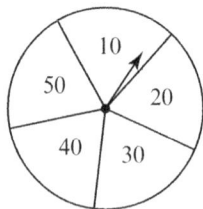

Solution: The sample space $S = \{10, 20, 30, 40, 50\}$. The number of outcomes in the sample space is 5. Let event A be the number is divisible by 4. Let event B be the number is greater than 30. Then $A = \{20, 40\}$ and $B = \{40, 50\}$. Looking at A and B, you can see that 40 is the only outcome common to both events, so $(A \cap B) = \{40\}$. Thus, there is 1 outcome in $(A \cap B)$, leading to the following result:

$$P(\text{number divisible by 4 and number greater than 30}) = P(A \cap B) = \frac{1}{5}$$

Mutually Exclusive Events

Events A and B defined over the same sample space S are **mutually exclusive** if they have no outcomes in common; that is, if $(A \cap B) = \emptyset$, where $\emptyset$ is the empty set. Mutually exclusive events cannot occur at the same time. Therefore, events A and B are mutually exclusive if and only if $P(A \cap B) = 0$.

Here is a practice problem.

Problem: A bag contains 5 black marbles numbered 1 to 5, 3 green marbles numbered 1 to 3, and 2 red marbles numbered 1 and 2, all identical in size and shape. If one marble is randomly drawn from the bag, what is the probability that the marble is green and red?

Solution: There are 10 outcomes in the sample space. Let event A be the marble is green. Let event B be the marble is red. These two events have no overlap. Therefore, $(A \cap B) = \emptyset$, so A and B are mutually exclusive.

The Addition Rule

Addition Rule: Given events A and B, $P(A \cup B) = P(A) + P(B) - P(A \cap B)$. For the addition rule, the events under consideration are associated with one task (getting a job offer, drawing one card, selecting one number, and so on).

Here is a practice problem.

Problem: Jaiden, a recent college graduate, applies for jobs at two different companies, Company X and Company Y. Let $P(X)$ be the probability that Jaiden gets a job offer from Company X, $P(Y)$ be the probability Jaiden gets a job offer from Company Y, and $P(X \cap Y)$ be the probability Jaiden gets job offers from both companies. Suppose $P(X) = 0.8$, $P(Y) = 0.6$, and $P(X \cap Y) = 0.5$. What is the probability that Jaiden will get a job offer from at least one of the companies?

Solution: The probability that Jaiden will get a job offer from at least one of the companies is $P(X \cup Y) = P(X) + P(Y) - P(X \cap Y) = 0.8 + 0.6 - 0.5 = 0.9$.

In many situations, you must calculate the probabilities used in the addition rule.

Here is a practice problem.

Problem: Suppose a card is drawn at random from a well-shuffled standard deck of 52 playing cards. What is the probability that the card drawn is a face card or a diamond? (See "Random Experiments and Sample Spaces" earlier in this chapter for an illustration of a standard deck of 52 playing cards.)

Solution: There are 12 face cards, so $P(\text{face card}) = \frac{12}{52}$. There are 13 diamonds, so $P(\text{diamond}) = \frac{13}{52}$. There are 3 diamond face cards, so $P(\text{face card} \cap \text{diamond}) = \frac{3}{52}$; thus, $P(\text{face card or diamond}) =$
$P(\text{face card} \cup \text{diamond}) = P(\text{face card}) + P(\text{diamond}) - P(\text{face card} \cap \text{diamond}) = \frac{12}{52} + \frac{13}{52} - \frac{3}{52} = \frac{22}{52} = \frac{11}{26}$.

In applying the addition rule, you can reduce fractions as you go along or wait until your final computation to reduce fractions. Waiting until the final computation to reduce fractions (as shown in the above problem) can save time. Given that the number of elements in S is the same for $P(A)$, $P(B)$, and $P(A \cap B)$, the denominators for these probabilities in the computation will be the same number if you do not reduce fractions beforehand.

When you can determine the possible outcomes for the sample space, an efficient and straightforward way to find $P(A \cup B)$ is to sum the number of ways that event A can occur and the number of ways that event B can occur, being sure to add in such a way that *no outcome is counted twice,* and then to divide by the total number of outcomes in the sample space.

Employing this strategy for the practice problem given above, you have the following: There are 12 face cards. There are 10 diamonds that are *not* face cards. Thus, there are 12 + 10 = 22 distinct cards in the event "face card or diamond." Therefore, $P(\text{face card} \cup \text{diamond}) = \frac{12+10}{52} = \frac{22}{52} = \frac{11}{26}$.

When two events A and B are mutually exclusive, the addition rule is $P(A \cup B) = P(A) + P(B)$. Here is a practice problem.

> Problem: One card is randomly drawn from a well-shuffled standard deck of 52 playing cards. Find the probability that the card drawn is a king or an ace. (See "Random Experiments and Sample Spaces" earlier in this chapter for an illustration of a standard deck of 52 playing cards.)
>
> Solution: There are 4 kings in the deck, so $P(\text{king}) = \frac{4}{52}$. There are 4 aces in the deck, so $P(\text{ace}) = \frac{4}{52}$.
>
> The event of drawing a king and the event of drawing an ace are mutually exclusive (because you cannot draw both at the same time on one draw from the deck). Hence, $P(\text{king or ace}) = P(\text{king} \cup \text{ace}) = P(\text{king}) + P(\text{ace}) = \frac{4}{52} + \frac{4}{52} = \frac{1}{13} + \frac{1}{13} = \frac{2}{13}$.

Conditional Probability

The probability of an event E, given that an event A has occurred, is a **conditional probability,** denoted $P(E|A)$ (read as "the probability of E given A").

A direct approach to obtaining the conditional probability, $P(E|A)$, is to compute the probability of event E in a "reduced" sample space S', containing fewer outcomes, that you determine after taking into account that the event A has already occurred.

Here are two practice problems.

> Problem: Suppose you draw one card at random from a well-shuffled standard deck of 52 playing cards; find the probability that the card drawn is a 6, given that the card drawn is greater than 2 and less than 8. (See "Random Experiments and Sample Spaces" earlier in this chapter for an illustration of a standard deck of 52 playing cards.)
>
> Solution: Let E be the event "the card drawn is a 6" and A be the event "the card drawn is greater than 2 and less than 8." There are 20 cards between 2 and 8 (four 3s, four 4s, four 5s, four 6s, and four 7s). Of these 20 cards, four are 6s. Hence, $P(E|A) = \frac{4}{20} = \frac{1}{5}$.
>
> Problem: The table below shows the gender and type of residence of 2,000 senior students at a university. Use the information in the table to find **(a)** the probability that a senior selected at random lives in a dorm given that the senior is female, and **(b)** the probability that a senior selected at random is a female given that the senior lives in a dorm. Express your answers as decimals rounded to the nearest hundredth.

Chapter 4: Probability and Statistics

Gender and Type of Residence of Senior Students (n = 2,000)

	Female	Male	Row Total
Apartment	229	180	409
Dorm	203	118	321
House	258	272	530
With Parent(s)	200	201	401
Sorority/Fraternity House	241	98	339
Column Total	1,131	869	2,000

Solution:

(a) Let D be the event "the senior selected lives in the dorm" and F be the event "the senior selected is female." The total number of female seniors is 1,131. Of that total, 203 live in a dorm; thus,

$$P(D|F) = \frac{203}{1,131} \approx 0.18.$$

(b) Let F be the event "the senior selected is female" and D be the event "the senior selected lives in the dorm." The total number of seniors living in a dorm is 321. Of that total, 203 are female; thus,

$$P(F|D) = \frac{203}{321} \approx 0.63.$$

Note: Notice that in the above problems, the number of outcomes under consideration is "reduced" to a lower number than the number of outcomes in the original sample space.

Here is a formula for obtaining the conditional probability, $P(E|A)$, using the original sample space S:

$$P(E|A) = \frac{P(E \cap A)}{P(A)}, \text{ provided } P(A) > 0$$

Here is the formula applied to the previous two practice problems.

Problem: Suppose you draw one card at random from a well-shuffled standard deck of 52 playing cards; find the probability that the card drawn is a 6, given that the card drawn is greater than 2 and less than 8. (See "Random Experiments and Sample Spaces" earlier in this chapter for an illustration of a standard deck of 52 playing cards.)

Solution: Let E be the event "the card drawn is a 6" and A be the event "the card drawn is greater than 2 and less than 8." Then, $P(E \cap A) = \frac{4}{52}$ and $P(A) = \frac{20}{52}$. Hence, $P(E|A) = \frac{P(E \cap A)}{P(A)} = \frac{\frac{4}{52}}{\frac{20}{52}} = \frac{4}{20} = \frac{1}{5}.$

Problem: The table below shows the gender and type of residence of 2,000 senior students at a university. Use the information in the table to find **(a)** the probability that a senior selected at random lives in a dorm given that the senior is female, and **(b)** the probability that a senior selected at random is a female given that the senior lives in a dorm. Express your answers as decimals rounded to the nearest hundredth.

Gender and Type of Residence of Senior Students (n = 2,000)

	Female	Male	Row Total
Apartment	229	180	409
Dorm	203	118	321
House	258	272	530
With Parent(s)	200	201	401
Sorority/Fraternity House	241	98	339
Column Total	1,131	869	2,000

Solution:

(a) Let D be the event "the senior selected lives in the dorm" and F be the event "the senior selected is female." $P(D \cap F) = \dfrac{203}{2,000}$ and $P(F) = \dfrac{1,131}{2,000}$; thus $P(D|F) = \dfrac{P(D \cap F)}{P(F)} = \dfrac{\frac{203}{2,000}}{\frac{1,131}{2,000}} = \dfrac{203}{1,131} \approx 0.18$.

(b) Let F be the event "the senior selected is female" and D be the event "the senior selected lives in the dorm." $P(F \cap D) = \dfrac{203}{2,000}$ and $P(D) = \dfrac{321}{2,000}$; thus, $P(F|D) = \dfrac{P(F \cap D)}{P(D)} = \dfrac{\frac{203}{2,000}}{\frac{321}{2,000}} = \dfrac{203}{321} \approx 0.63$.

As you can see, for both practice problems, you get the same answers as previously obtained.

The Multiplication Rule and Independent and Dependent Events

For this topic, you must demonstrate an understanding of the multiplication rule and independent and dependent events.

Multiplication Rule

Multiplication Rule: Given events A and B, $P(A \cap B) = P(A)P(B|A)$. For the multiplication rule, the events under consideration are associated with two or more tasks (drawing two cards, flipping a coin followed by tossing a number cube, and so on).

Here is a practice problem.

> Problem: Two cards are drawn at random, one after the other, from a standard deck of 52 playing cards. Let J be the event "a jack is drawn on the first draw" and K be the event "a king is drawn on the second draw." (See "Random Experiments and Sample Spaces" earlier in this chapter for an illustration of a standard deck of 52 playing cards.)
>
> **(a)** What is the probability of drawing a jack on the first draw, without replacement, and a king on the second draw? *Note:* "Without replacement" means the first item selected is *not* put back before the second selection takes place.
>
> **(b)** What is the probability of drawing a jack on the first draw, with replacement, and a king on the second draw? *Note:* "With replacement" means the first card is put back before the second drawing takes place.
>
> Solution:
>
> **(a)** $P(J) = \dfrac{4}{52} = \dfrac{1}{13}$ (this is true because there are 4 jacks in the deck of 52 cards), and $P(K|J) = \dfrac{4}{51}$ (this is true because after the jack is drawn and not put back in the deck, there are 4 kings in the remaining deck of 51 cards). Therefore, $P(J \cap K) = \dfrac{1}{13} \cdot \dfrac{4}{51} = \dfrac{4}{663}$.
>
> **(b)** $P(J) = \dfrac{4}{52} = \dfrac{1}{13}$ (this is true because there are 4 jacks in the deck of 52 cards), and $P(K|J) = \dfrac{4}{52} = \dfrac{1}{13}$ (this is true because after the jack is drawn and put back in the deck, there are 4 kings in the remaining deck of 52 cards). Therefore, $P(J \cap K) = \dfrac{1}{13} \cdot \dfrac{1}{13} = \dfrac{1}{169}$.

Chapter 4: Probability and Statistics

Tip: For your TExES Math exam, remember that to obtain the probability that event A occurs followed by event B, you multiply the probability of event A times the *conditional* probability of event B. This means you must take into account that event A has already occurred when determining the second factor.

Independent and Dependent Events

Two events A and B are **independent** if $P(A \mid B) = P(A)$ and $P(B \mid A) = P(B)$. This definition means events A and B are independent if the occurrence of one does not affect the probability of the occurrence of the other. It follows that if events A and B are independent, then the multiplication rule is $P(A \cap B) = P(A)P(B)$.

Here is a practice problem.

Problem: Suppose you flip a coin, and then toss a number cube, whose faces are numbered 10, 20, 30, 40, 50, and 60. Find the probability that a head appears on the up face of the coin and the number 50 appears on the up face of the number cube.

Solution: Let H be the event "a head appears on the up face of the coin" and F be the event "the number 50 appears on the up face of the number cube." $P(H \mid F) = P(H) = \frac{1}{2}$ (this is true because what happens with the coin is not affected by what happens with the number cube) and $P(F \mid H) = P(F) = \frac{1}{6}$ (this is true because what happens with the number cube is not affected by what happens with the coin). Therefore, $P(H \cap F) = P(H)P(F) = \frac{1}{2} \cdot \frac{1}{6} = \frac{1}{12}$.

You can extend the multiplication rule for two independent events to any number of independent events.

Here are two practice problems.

Problem: If you flip a coin three times in a row, what is the probability of obtaining three heads?

Solution: Each flip of the coin is independent of the other flips. Thus, the probability of three heads in a row is $P(H) \cdot P(H) \cdot P(H) = \frac{1}{2} \cdot \frac{1}{2} \cdot \frac{1}{2} = \frac{1}{8}$.

Problem: If you draw 2 marbles at random, one after the other, from a box containing 6 red marbles and 4 blue marbles, what is the probability of drawing a red marble, with replacement, on the first draw and then drawing a blue marble on the second draw?

Solution: Let R be the event "the first marble drawn is red" and B be the event "the second marble drawn is blue." $P(R) = \frac{6}{10} = \frac{3}{5}$ (this is true because on the first draw, there are 6 red marbles in the box of 10 marbles), and $P(B \mid R) = P(B) = \frac{4}{10} = \frac{2}{5}$ (this is true because after the red marble is drawn and replaced, the probability of drawing a blue marble has not changed given there are still 4 blue marbles and 6 red marbles in the box). Therefore, $P(R \cap B) = P(R)P(B) = \frac{3}{5} \cdot \frac{2}{5} = \frac{6}{25}$.

If events A and B are not independent, they are said to be **dependent**.

Here is a practice problem.

Problem: Suppose you draw 2 marbles, one after the other, from a box containing 6 red marbles and 4 blue marbles. Find the probability of drawing a red marble, without replacement, on the first draw and then drawing a blue marble on the second draw.

215

Solution: Let R be the event "the first marble drawn is red" and B be the event "the second marble drawn is blue." $P(R) = \frac{6}{10} = \frac{3}{5}$ (this is true because on the first draw, there are 6 red marbles in the box of 10 marbles) and $P(B|R) = \frac{4}{9}$ (this is true because after the red marble is drawn without replacement, there are 4 blue marbles and 5 red marbles remaining in the box). Therefore, $P(R \cap B) = P(R)P(B|R) = \frac{3}{5} \cdot \frac{4}{9} = \frac{4}{15}$.

Notice that selecting "with replacement" results in independent events, while selecting "without replacement" results in dependent events.

The Complement Rule

For some problems, you might find it convenient to determine the probability that at least one of something of interest occurs by using the following **complement rule**: $P(\text{at least one}) = 1 - P(\text{none})$.

Here is a practice problem.

Problem: A coin is flipped three times. Find the probability that at least one tails occurs.
Solution: The sample space is {HHH, HHT, HTH, HTT, THH, THT, TTH, TTT}. Thus, P(at least one tails) $= 1 - P(\text{no tails}) = 1 - P(\text{HHH}) = 1 - \frac{1}{8} = \frac{7}{8}$. By looking at the sample space, you can see that this answer is correct because there are seven outcomes in which tails occurs. In fact, you could have worked the problem directly as follows: P(at least one tails) $= \frac{7}{8}$. With larger sample spaces, rather than working out the probability directly, it is often more convenient to determine the probability of "at least one" by using $1 - P(\text{none})$.

Odds

The **odds in favor of an event** E are given by $\frac{P(E)}{1 - P(E)}$, usually expressed in the form $p: q$ (or p to q), where p and q are integers with no common factors and $\frac{P(E)}{1 - P(E)} = \frac{p}{q}$. The **odds against an event** E are given by $\frac{1 - P(E)}{P(E)}$, usually expressed in the form $q: p$ (or q to p), where p and q are integers with no common factors and $\frac{1 - P(E)}{P(E)} = \frac{q}{p}$, where $P(E) \neq 1$ or 0.

Here is a practice problem.

Problem: If you perform one toss of a number cube, whose six faces are numbered 1 through 6, and observe the up face, what are the odds **(a)** in favor of observing a 2 on the up face and **(b)** against observing a 2 on the up face?
Solution: The probability of observing a 2 on the up face is $\frac{1}{6}$ (this is true because 2 has a 1 in 6 chance of showing on the up face). **(a)** Therefore, the odds in favor of observing a 2 on the up face are $\frac{\frac{1}{6}}{1 - \frac{1}{6}} = \frac{\frac{1}{6}}{\frac{5}{6}} = \frac{1}{5}$, which is 1 to 5. **(b)** The odds against observing a 2 on the up face are 5 to 1.

Chapter 4: Probability and Statistics

Frequency Theory of Probability

An empirical way to assign probability to a random experiment is to view probability as long-run relative frequency. The **frequency theory of probability** assumes that as the number of trials increases, the proportion of times that E occurs approaches E's true probability. For example, as a coin is flipped repeatedly, the proportion of heads obtained gets closer and closer to $\frac{1}{2}$ as the number of repetitions increases. The value of $\frac{1}{2}$ is the limiting value of this process and, as a result, is called the probability of heads.

In general, the **probability of an event** E is interpreted to mean the limiting value of the relative frequency of the occurrence of E if the experiment were conducted an indefinitely large number of times. It is the proportion of times the event would occur in a large number of repetitions (called trials) of the experiment.

In some situations, the only feasible way to assign a probability to an event is to make a relative frequency interpretation of probability. This way of assigning probability is the **relative frequency method.** The probability of an event E is estimated by conducting the experiment a large number of times and counting the number of times that event E actually occurred. Based on these results, the probability of E is estimated as

$P(E) \approx \frac{\text{Number of times } E \text{ occurred}}{\text{Total number of trials}}$. Here is a practice problem.

> Problem: Out of 100 light bulbs tested at Company X, two were defective. What is the estimated probability that a Company X light bulb is defective?
>
> Solution: $P(\text{Company X light bulb is defective}) \approx \frac{2}{100} = 0.02 = 2\%$

Geometric Probability

Geometric probability involves determining probabilities associated with geometric objects.

Here is a practice problem.

> Problem: The figure shown is a circle inscribed in a 10-inch square. A point is randomly selected within the square. What is the probability that the point will lie inside the circle?
>
>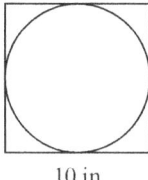
>
> 10 in
>
> Solution: To calculate the probability that the point will lie inside the circle, calculate the ratio of the area of the circle to the area of the square. (See "Perimeter, Area, and Volume" in Chapter 3 for formulas for the area of geometric shapes.)
>
> $P(\text{point lies inside circle}) = \frac{\text{area of circle}}{\text{area of square}} = \frac{\pi r^2}{s^2} = \frac{\pi (5 \text{ in})^2}{(10 \text{ in})^2} = \frac{25\pi}{100} \approx 0.785$

Statistics

For this topic, you must demonstrate an understanding of statistical concepts including categorical and quantitative data, graphical representation of data, measures of central tendency, and measures of variability, and be able to analyze and interpret one-variable and bivariate data.

217

Statistical Questions and Types of Data

When you have a statistical question, you need information, called **data,** to answer it. A **statistical question** is one that anticipates the data collected to answer it will vary. The question does not have a specific predetermined answer. For example, "What is the average salary of teachers in your state?" is a statistical question. You expect the salaries of teachers to vary from teacher to teacher. However, "What is the salary of the high school band director at a particular school in your state?" is *not* a statistical question. The band director has a specific salary. There is no variability in the answer at the time of the question. Accounting for the **variability** in data is the main purpose of statistical analysis.

The salary of a randomly selected teacher in your state is a variable. In statistics, a **variable** is a characteristic (or attribute) that describes an object, person, or thing. The variable's value varies from entity to entity. When you collect data related to a variable, the data are categorical data or quantitative data.

Categorical data (also called **qualitative data**) are nonnumerical data for which representation on a numerical scale is *not* naturally meaningful such as names, labels, codes, colors, race, educational level, and other qualities that result from sorting objects, things, or people into categories.

Quantitative data are numerical data for which representation on a numerical scale is naturally meaningful. Quantitative data can be either continuous data (which includes measurements of lengths, heights, weights, temperature, test scores, and other amounts) or discrete data (which includes counts of family size, number of pets, and so forth). Quantitative data that results from taking a measurement is also termed **measurement data.**

The **distribution** of a variable reveals the variability that occurs in a variable's data. For example, a frequency distribution shows what values the variable assumes and the frequency of those values. It models how the data vary about a central value.

Graphical Representations of Data

Graphical representations of data show the distributions of variables. For your TExES Math exam, you should be able to read and interpret information about variables from tables, pictographs, circle graphs, bar graphs, line graphs, dot plots, stem-and-leaf plots, and histograms.

Tables

A **table** organizes information as entries in rows and columns. Row and column labels explain the data recorded in the table. A **frequency table** is a tabular representation of data that shows the frequency of each value in the data set. A **relative frequency table** shows the frequency of each value as a proportion or percentage of the whole data set. The total of all relative frequencies should be 1.00 or 100 percent (but instead might be very close to 1.00 or 100 percent due to round-off error).

Here is a practice problem.

> Problem: According to the information shown in the table below, what percent of the students received a C or better on Test 1?

Grade Distribution of 25 Students for Test 1

Grade	Frequency	Relative Frequency
A	5	0.20
B	8	0.32
C	9	0.36
D	2	0.08
F	1	0.04
Total	25	1.00

Solution: According to the information in the table, 0.20 + 0.32 + 0.36 = 0.88 or 88% of the students received a C or better on Test 1.

Pictographs

A **pictograph** (or **picture graph**) uses symbols or pictures to represent data. Each symbol stands for a definite number of a specific item. This information should be stated on the graph. To read a pictograph, you count the number of symbols shown and then multiply by the number it represents. Fractional portions of symbols are approximated and used accordingly.

Here is a practice problem.

Problem: According to the pictograph shown below, how many of the 75 dog owners surveyed responded "yes" to the survey question?

Solution: According to the graph, 4 × 5 = 20 of the 75 dog owners surveyed responded "yes" to the survey question.

Circle Graphs

A **circle graph** (or **pie chart**) is a graph in the shape of a circle. A circle graph visually displays the relative contribution of each category of data within a set of data belonging to a whole, which is represented by the circle. A circle graph can only compare parts of a whole. Circle graphs are also called **pie charts** because each looks like a pie cut into wedges. The wedges are labeled to show the categories for the graph. Usually the portion of the graph that corresponds to each category is shown as a percent. The total amount of percentage on the graph is 100 percent. The graph is made by dividing the 360 degrees of the circle into portions that are proportional to the percentages for each category. You read a circle graph by reading the percentages displayed on the graph for the different categories.

Here is a practice problem.

Problem: According to the graph, what percent of the 25 students received a B or better on Test 1?

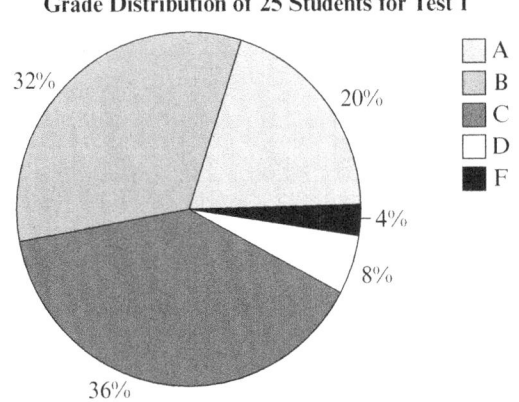

Solution: According to the graph, 32% + 20% = 52% of the 25 students received a B or better on Test 1.

Bar Graphs

A **bar graph** is a useful way to organize and represent categorical data. Bar graphs can display categories that are not parts of a whole as well as categories that are parts of a whole. A bar graph uses rectangular bars of the same width to show the frequency (or relative frequency) of the different categories in which the data are classified. Labels at the base of the bars specify the categories. The bars are equally spaced from each other and may be oriented vertically or horizontally. (*Note:* For ease of discussion, the following explanation is limited to bar graphs that are oriented vertically; the explanation for bar graphs that are oriented horizontally is similar.) The categories for the data are labeled on the horizontal axis. The horizontal axis is not a scale as such, meaning the ordering of the categories and their horizontal positions are not dictated by the data. A bar's length or height indicates the frequency (or relative frequency) for the category represented by that particular bar. A vertical scale, marked in whole numbers for determining the frequency counts (or marked as proportions/percentages for determining relative frequencies) corresponding to the bars' categories, is shown on the graph. To read a bar graph, examine the vertical scale to determine the count (or relative frequency) represented by each tick mark. Then determine where the bars' heights fall relative to the scale.

Here is a practice problem.

> Problem: According to the graph shown, how many of the 25 students received a grade of C or better on Test 1?
>
>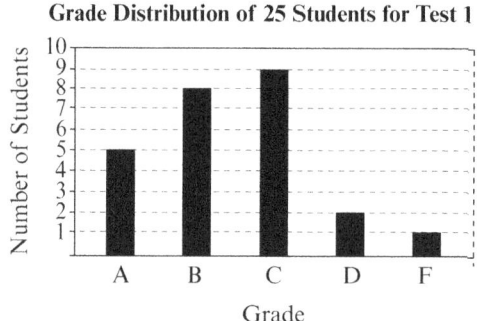
>
> Solution: The graph shows that 9 + 8 + 5 = 22 students received a grade of C or better on Test 1.

Two or more sets of data can be displayed on the same graph to facilitate comparison of the data sets to each other. Here is a practice problem.

> Problem: According to the graph shown, in general, which class performed better on Test 1: Class X or Class Y?
>
>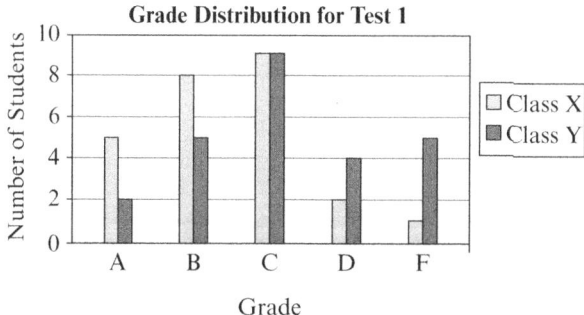
>
> Solution: The graph shows that Class X had more As and Bs and fewer Ds and Fs than did Class Y; so, in general, Class X performed better on Test 1 than did Class Y.

Line Graphs

A **line graph** displays measurement data that have been collected over equal consecutive time intervals. The data values are plotted as ordered pairs on a grid that has a horizontal time scale. The vertical scale corresponds to the measurement scale that was used to obtain the data. Consecutive points are connected by line segments to aid the eye in identifying changes over time. The slants of the line segments between points indicate which direction the data might be trending. Upward slants from left to right indicate increasing data values, downward slants from left to right indicate decreasing data values, and line segments with no slant (horizontal lines) indicate that the data values are remaining constant. **Trends** are patterns of (relatively) long-term upward or downward changes.

Here is a practice problem.

> Problem: The graph below shows the Fahrenheit temperature at 2-hour intervals from 8 a.m. to 8 p.m. on a given day. Describe any noticeable trends in the data.

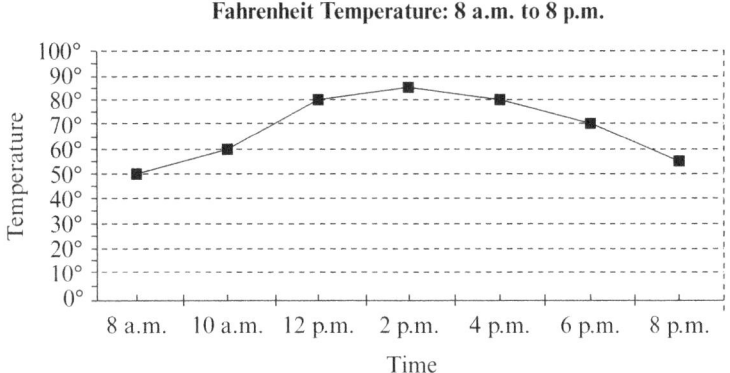

> Solution: The graph shows that the temperature steadily increased between 8 a.m. and 2 p.m. (upward trend), and then steadily decreased between 2 p.m. and 8 p.m. (downward trend).

You can plot two or more sets of data on the same graph, a display that facilitates comparisons between the data sets. Here is a practice problem.

> Problem: According to the graph shown below, in what month did the maximum difference between revenue sales and expenses occur?

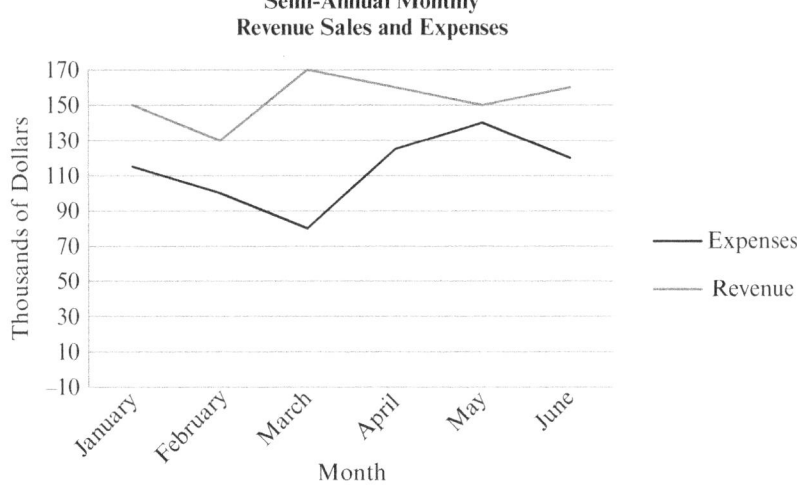

> Solution: The graph shows that the maximum difference between revenue sales and expenses occurred in March, and the minimum difference occurred in May.

221

Dot Plots

A **dot plot** (or **line plot**) is a graph in which the data's possible values are indicated along the horizontal axis, and dots (or other similar symbols) are placed above each value to indicate the number of times that particular value occurs in the data set. The horizontal axis corresponds to the measurement scale that was used to obtain the data. An important advantage of dot plots is that they show a symbol for every data value. You can easily determine the minimum (least) and the maximum (greatest) data values and the frequency of occurrence of values. Features of the data's distribution including clusters, gaps, and outliers are visually apparent. A **cluster** is a group of data that are close together. A **gap** is an interval where no data are plotted. An **outlier** is a data value that is extremely high or extremely low in comparison to most of the other data values.

Here is a practice problem.

> Problem: The dot plot below shows the social studies test scores of 20 sixth-grade students. Describe visually apparent features of the graph related to the shape, spread, and variability of the data distribution.

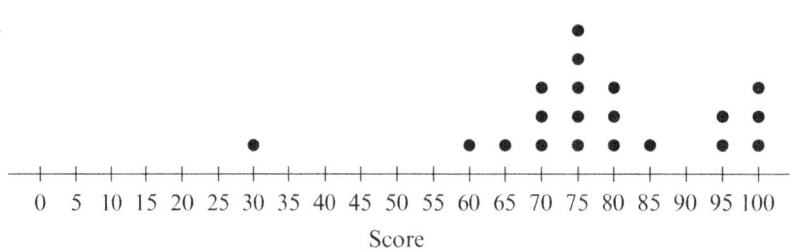

> Solution: The dot plot shows a cluster of scores between 60 and 85 and a smaller cluster between 95 and 100. There is a large gap between 30 and 60 and a smaller one between 85 and 95. Because the gap between 30 and 60 is very large (indicating 30 is extremely low in comparison to the other data values), 30 is an outlier in the data set. The score that occurs most frequently is 75. The least score is 30 and the greatest score is 100.

Tip: Dot plots are used mostly with small data sets (those with fewer than 50 data values).

Stem-and-Leaf Plots

A **stem-and-leaf plot** is a graphical display of data in which each data value is separated into two parts: a stem and a leaf. For a given data value, the leaf is the last digit, and the stem, the remaining digits. For example, for the data value 198, 19 is the stem and 8 is the leaf. A stem-and-leaf plot includes a legend that explains what the stem and leaf represent so the reader can interpret the information in the plot; for example, 19|8 = 198. Usually, the stems are listed vertically, from smallest to largest, in a column labeled "Stem." The leaves are listed horizontally, from smallest to largest, in the row of their corresponding stem in a column labeled "Leaf." Each leaf is listed to the right of its corresponding stem as many times as it occurs in the original data set. A feature of a stem-and-leaf plot is that the original data are retained and displayed in the plot. Reading information from a stem-and-leaf plot is a matter of interpreting the plot's stems and leaves.

Here is a practice problem.

> Problem: According to the stem-and-leaf plot below, of the 40 attendees, how many were in their 40s, how many were in their 50s, how many were in their 60s, how many were in their 70s, how many were in their 80s, and how many were in their 90s?

Ages of 40 Attendees at a Retirement Party

Stem	Leaf
4	0 3 3 5 6 9
5	3 4 4 5 6 6 7 7 7 7 7 8 8 8 9
6	0 0 0 1 1 1 2 3 3 3 7
7	1 4 7 8
8	1 3
9	0 1
Legend: 4|6 = 46	

Solution: According to the stem-and-leaf plot, of the 40 attendees, 6 were in their 40s, 15 were in their 50s, 11 were in their 60s, 4 were in their 70s, 2 were in their 80s, and 2 were in their 90s.

Histograms

A **histogram** summarizes measurement data that have been grouped by nonoverlapping **class intervals.** Histograms have two scales: a measurement scale, corresponding to the measurement scale used to obtain the data, and a frequency (or relative frequency) scale. The histogram displays the data's frequencies (or relative frequencies) within the successive class intervals that lie along the measurement scale. Class intervals are of equal width and cover from the lowest to the highest data value. The left and right endpoints for the class intervals are selected so that each data value clearly falls within one and only one class interval. The frequency or relative frequency of the data's occurrence within a class interval is represented by a rectangular bar, whose width is the same as the width of the class interval. The height of the bar is proportional to the data's frequency (or relative frequency) within that interval. *Tip:* There are no horizontal spaces between the bars of a histogram unless a bar's height is zero, meaning no data values fall in its class interval.

In a **frequency histogram,** the scale for measuring the bars' heights is marked with actual frequencies (or counts). The frequency of an interval is the number of data values that fall in that interval. (*Tip:* The sum of the frequencies is the same as the number of data values.) In a **relative frequency histogram,** the scale is marked with relative frequencies instead of actual frequencies. The relative frequency of an interval is the proportion of the data values that fall in that interval. The total of the relative frequencies corresponding to the class intervals should be 1.00 or 100 percent (but might instead be very close to 1.00 or 100 percent due to round-off error).

Tip: Relative frequency histograms are useful because proportions or percentages make it easier to consider portions of the data compared to the whole.

A histogram provides visual information about the shape and spread of the data distribution. However, because of the grouping of data into intervals, histograms do not provide the high level of specific information about data values that, for example, dot plots and stem-and-leaf plots provide. The exact data values are not displayed in a histogram. Therefore, outliers and maximum and minimum values cannot be identified. Neither can the frequency of occurrence of particular values. Nevertheless, histograms are useful for displaying large sets of data, and therefore are used frequently in statistics.

Here is a practice problem.

> Problem: According to the histogram below, how many of the 65 tenth-graders scored below 70 on the basic arithmetic skills assessment?

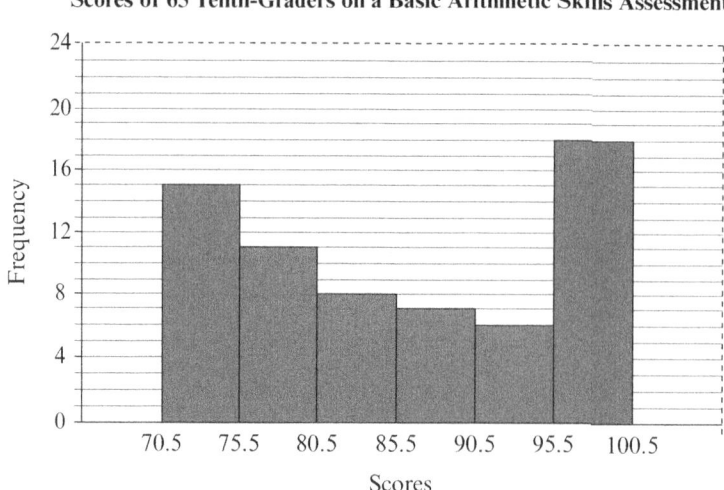

Solution: The histogram shows that the data are clustered between 70.5 and 100.5 with no student scoring below 70.

Misleading Graphs

Drawing valid conclusions from graphical representations of data requires that you have read the graph accurately and analyzed the graphical information correctly. Sometimes a graphical representation will distort the data in some way, leading you to draw an invalid conclusion.

At first glance, the data in the following graph look evenly distributed. However, upon closer examination, you can see that each of the first two intervals covers a 29-point spread, but the last interval covers only a 9-point spread, making it difficult to draw conclusions from the graph.

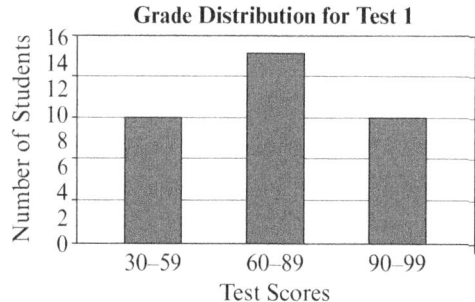

Guidelines for Interpreting Graphs

When you interpret graphical information on your TExES Math exam, follow these suggestions:

- Make sure you understand the graph's title.
- Read the labels on the graph's parts to understand what is being represented.
- Make sure you know what each symbol in a pictograph represents; check that the symbols are a uniform size.
- Examine carefully the horizontal and vertical scales; make sure the numbers are equally spaced.
- Look for trends such as rising values (upward-slanting line segments), falling values (downward-slanting line segments), and periods of inactivity (horizontal line segments) in line graphs.
- Look for clusters, gaps, and outliers and note the general shape of dot plots, stem-and-leaf plots, and histograms.

- Be ready to do simple arithmetic computations.
- Make sure the numbers add up correctly.
- Use only the information in the graph. Do not answer based on your personal knowledge or opinion.

Here is a practice problem of using graphical information to determine a probability (see "Probability" earlier in this chapter for a further discussion of this topic).

Problem: Given the frequency histogram of the scores of 65 tenth-graders (shown below), find the probability that a student randomly selected from the 65 tenth-graders scored 90.5 or higher on the basic arithmetic skills assessment.

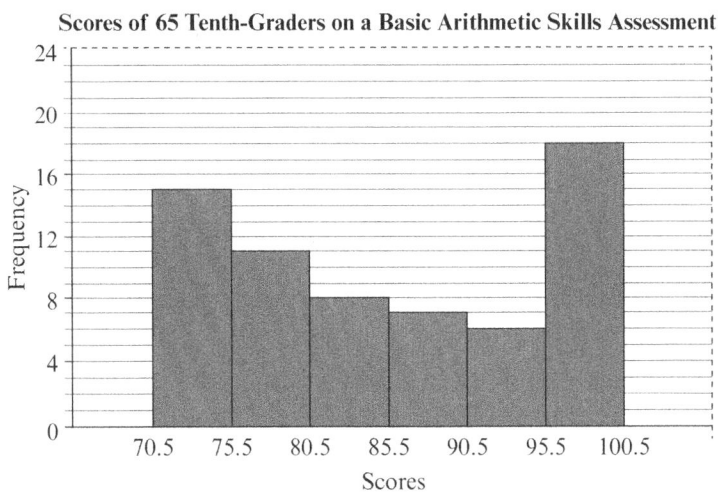

Solution: According to the graph, $6 + 18 = 24$ of the 65 students scored 90.5 or higher. Thus, since the student is randomly selected $P(\text{score is 90.5 or higher}) = \dfrac{\text{number of outcomes in the event}}{\text{total number of outcomes}} = \dfrac{24}{65}$.

Measures of Central Tendency

A measure of **central tendency** is a numerical value that describes a data set by attempting to provide a "central" or "typical" value of the data set. It is a single number that summarizes all the values in the data set. Three common measures of central tendency are the mean, median, and mode. Each of these measures represents a way to describe a set of data's central value.

Tip: Measures of central tendency should have the same units as those of the data values from which they are determined. If no units are specified for the data values, no units are specified for the measures of central tendency.

Tip: When determining a value for a central tendency measure, it's a good practice to list the values of a data set in order from least to greatest (or greatest to least). While reordering the values of a data set isn't necessary to find the mean, doing so is helpful in identifying the mode and *imperative* to finding the median.

Mean

A data set's **mean** is the data values' arithmetic average; thus, $\text{mean} = \dfrac{\text{sum of the data values}}{\text{number of data values}}$.

225

Here is a practice problem.

> Problem: Find the mean of the following data set: 21, 35, 34, 30, 32, 36, 24, 35, 28, 35.
>
> Solution: mean $= \dfrac{\text{sum of the data values}}{\text{number of data values}} = \dfrac{21+24+28+30+32+34+35+35+35+36}{10} = \dfrac{310}{10} = 31$

Tip: You can use the statistical features of your TI calculator to compute means of data sets. Check the calculator guidebook for instructions.

A *weighted mean* is a mean computed by assigning weights to the data values. To find a weighted mean, first multiply each data value by its assigned weight, and then sum the results. Next, divide the sum obtained by the sum of the weights. Thus, for data values $x_1, x_2, \ldots, x_n$ with respective assigned weights $w_1, w_2, \ldots, w_n$,

weighted mean $= \dfrac{\sum w_i x_i}{\sum w_i}$.

Here is a practice problem.

> Problem: A student scores 80, 60, and 50 on three exams. Find the weighted mean of the student's three scores, where the score of 80 counts 20 percent, the score of 60 counts 20 percent, and the score of 50 counts 60 percent.
>
> Solution: weighted mean $= \dfrac{\sum w_i x_i}{\sum w_i} = \dfrac{20\%(80)+20\%(60)+60\%(50)}{20\%+20\%+60\%} = \dfrac{16+12+30}{100\%} = \dfrac{58}{1} = 58$

Median

The **median** is the middle value or the average of the middle pair of values in an *ordered* set of data. For a small data set, you easily can determine a data set's median using a two-step process. First, put the data values in order from least to greatest (or greatest to least). Next, find the middle data value. If there is no single middle data value, find the average of the middle pair of data values. When the number of data values is *odd,* the median is the middle value. When the number of data values is *even,* the median is the average of the middle pair of values.

Here is a practice problem.

> Problem: Find the median of the data set consisting of the following 10 values: 21, 35, 34, 30, 32, 36, 24, 35, 28, 35.
>
> Solution:
>
> Step 1. Put the data values in order: 21, 24, 28, 30, 32, 34, 35, 35, 35, 36.
>
> Step 2. The number of data values is even, so find the average of the middle pair of values: $\dfrac{32+34}{2} = 33$.
> Therefore, the median is 33.

Tip: You can use the statistical features of your TI calculator to compute medians of data sets. Check the calculator guidebook for instructions.

Tip: When you are finding a median, don't make the common mistake of neglecting to put the numbers in order first.

In terms of position, the median is the $\dfrac{(n+1)}{2}$ data value in an ordered set of discrete values. You can find the median by counting up from the least data value to the $\dfrac{(n+1)}{2}$ position, which is the middle position of the ordered set of data. When *n* is odd, there is one number at the $\frac{(n+1)}{2}$ position. When *n* is even, the median is halfway between the two numbers on either side of the $\frac{(n+1)}{2}$ position.

Here is a practice problem.

Problem: Find the median of the data in the following stem-and-leaf plot.

Ages of 40 Attendees at a Retirement Party

Stem	Leaf
4	0 3 3 5 6 9
5	3 4 4 5 6 6 7 7 7 7 7 8 8 8 9
6	0 0 0 1 1 1 2 3 3 3 7
7	1 4 7 8
8	1 3
9	0 1
Legend: 4|6 = 46	

Solution: The median for the stem-and-leaf plot shown is in the $\frac{(40+1)}{2} = 20.5$th position. Thus, the median is halfway between the 20th data value, 58, and the 21st data value, 59. The median is 58.5.

Tip: $\frac{(n+1)}{2}$ does not give a median's value; it gives the median's position in an ordered data set.

Mode

The **mode** is the data value or values that occur with the highest frequency in a data set. A data set can have one mode, more than one mode, or no mode. If exactly two data values occur with the same frequency that is more often than that of any of the other data values, then the data set is bimodal. If three or more data values occur with the same frequency that is more often than that of any of the other data values, then the data set is multimodal. A data set in which each data value occurs the same number of times has no mode.

Here are two practice problems.

Problem: Find the mode of the following data set: 21, 35, 34, 30, 32, 36, 24, 35, 28, 35.

Solution: The value 35 occurs three times, which is the highest frequency of occurrence for any one value in the data set. Thus, the mode is 35.

Problem: What score is the mode for the data shown in the dot plot below?

Social Studies Test Scores of 20 Sixth-Grade Students

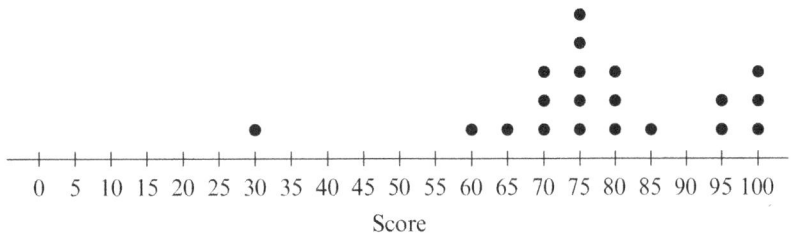

Solution: The data set displayed in the dot plot has one mode. The value 75 occurs five times, which is the greatest frequency. Therefore, 75 is the modal score of the 20 students.

Tip: The mode of a data set is the **modal** data value.

Selecting the Most Appropriate Measure of Central Tendency

The mean, median, and mode are ways to describe a data set's central value. To know which of these measures of central tendency you should use to describe a data set, consider the following information.

Mean

- The mean is preferred when the distribution of the data has a symmetric shape (or close to it).
  Tip: A distribution is **symmetric** if its lower half and upper half are mirror images of each other.
- The actual data values are used in the computation of the mean. If any one number is changed, the mean's value will change. For example, the mean of the data set consisting of 50, 50, 87, 78, and 95 is 72. If the 95 in this set is changed to 100, the new data set's mean is 73.
- Although the mean represents a data set's central or typical value, the mean does not necessarily have the same value as one of the numbers in the set. For example, the mean of 50, 50, 87, 78, and 95 is 72, yet none of the five numbers in this data set equals 72.
- A disadvantage of the mean is that it is influenced by outliers, especially in a small data set. It tends to be "pulled" toward an extreme value, much more so than does the median. (An **outlier** is a data value that is extremely high or extremely low in comparison to most of the other data values.)
  - If a data set contains extremely high values that are not balanced by corresponding low values, the mean is misleadingly high. The mean of the data set consisting of 15, 15, 20, 25, and 25 is 20. If the 20 in this set is changed to 100, the mean of the new data set is 36. The value 36 does not represent the data set consisting of 15, 15, 100, 25, and 25 very well, since four of the data values are less than 30.
  - If a data set contains extremely low values that are not balanced by corresponding high values, the mean is misleadingly low. The mean of the data set consisting of 100, 100, 130, and 150 is 120. If the 150 in this set is changed to 10, the mean of the new data set is 85. The value 85 does not represent the data set consisting of 100, 100, 130, and 10 very well, since three of the data values are greater than or equal to 100.

Median

- The median is the most useful alternative to the mean as a measure of central tendency. The median is preferred when the data distribution is "lopsided" with unbalanced extreme values or outliers on one side. Such distributions are **skewed**. **Right-skewed** distributions have unbalanced extreme values on the right side. **Left-skewed** distributions have unbalanced extreme values on the left side. (See "Skewness" later in this chapter for an additional discussion of this topic.)
- Like the mean, the median does not necessarily have the same value as one of the numbers in the set. If the data set contains an odd number of data values, the median will be the middle number; however, for an even number of data values, the median is the arithmetic average of the middle pair of numbers.
- The median is not strongly influenced by outliers. For example, the median of the data set consisting of 10, 15, 20, 25, and 30 is 20. If the 30 in this set is changed to 100, the new data set's median remains 20.
- A disadvantage of the median as an indicator of a central value is that it is based on relative size rather than on the actual numbers in the set. For example, a student who has test scores of 44, 47, and 98 shows improved performance that would not be reflected if the median of 47, rather than the mean of 63, was reported as the representative score.

Mode

- The mode is the simplest measure of central tendency to calculate.
- If a data set has a mode, the mode (or modes) is one of the data values.
- The mode is the only appropriate measure of central tendency for data that are strictly nonnumeric, like data on ice cream flavor preferences (vanilla, chocolate, strawberry, and so on). Although it makes no sense to determine a mean or median ice cream flavor for the data, the ice cream flavor that was named most frequently is the modal flavor.

- For numeric data, the mean and the median are preferred over the mode as measures of central tendency.
- A disadvantage of the mode as an indicator of a central value is that it is based on relative frequency, rather than on all the values in the set. For example, a student who has test scores of 45, 45, and 99 shows improved performance that would not be reflected if the mode of 45, rather than the mean of 63, was reported as the representative score.

When you are summarizing data, you might want to report more than one measure of central tendency, if appropriate. For numeric data, if you select only one measure, the mean is preferred for data sets in which outliers are not present. The median is the preferred measure when outliers are present. The mode is the preferred measure for nonnumeric categorical data.

Percentiles and Quartiles

Percentiles and quartiles are additional measures that are used to describe numerical data. The **Pth percentile** is a value at or below which P percent of the data fall. For example, the median is the 50th percentile because 50 percent of the data fall at or below the median. **Quartiles** are values that divide an ordered data set into four portions, each of which contains approximately one-fourth of the data. About 25 percent of the data values are at or below the first quartile (also called the 25th percentile). About 50 percent of the data values are at or below the second quartile (also called the 50th percentile), which is the same as the median. About 75 percent of the data values are at or below the third quartile (also called the 75th percentile).

The **first quartile,** denoted Q_1, is the median of the lower half of an ordered data set, and the **third quartile,** denoted Q_3, is the median of the upper half. When the number of data values is odd, exclude the median to create the two halves of the data set.

Here are two practice problems.

> Problem: Given the data set 21, 24, 28, 30, 32, 34, 35, 35, 35, 36, determine the median, and Q_1 and Q_3.
>
> Solution: The number of data values is even. The median is $\frac{32+34}{2} = 33$; Q_1 is 28, the median of 21, 24, 28, 30, 32; and Q_3 is 35, the median of 34, 35, 35, 35, 36.
>
> Problem: Given the data set 10, 12, 12, 13, 14, 15, 16, 17, 20, determine the median, and Q_1 and Q_3.
>
> Solution: The number of data values is odd. The median is 14; Q_1 is 12, the median of 10, 12, 12, 13; and Q_3 is 16.5, the median of 15, 16, 17, 20.

Note: Determining Q_1 and Q_3 by excluding the median to create the two halves when the number of data values is odd is not the only approach currently in use. You might encounter other methods for dividing the data set into two halves for the purposes of calculating Q_1 and Q_3 when the number of data values is odd.

Tip: Percentiles and quartiles are numbers along the horizontal axis. They are not percentages.

Tip: You can use the statistical features of your TI calculator to compute Q_1 and Q_3. Check the calculator guidebook for instructions.

Measures of Variability

A measure of **variability** is a single value that describes the spread of a data set about its central value. Measures of center are important for describing data sets. However, their interpretation is enhanced when the variability about the central value is known. For example, one set of scores may be extremely consistent, with scores like 60, 62, 65, 68, 70, 70, 72, 75, 78, and 80; while another set of scores may be very erratic, with scores like 40, 40, 50, 55, 60, 80, 85, 90, 100, and 100. The scores in the first set cluster more closely together than do the scores in the second set; the scores in the second set are more spread out.

For your TExES Math exam, measures of variability you should know are the range, standard deviation, variance, and interquartile range (IQR).

Range

The **range** of a data set is the difference between the maximum value (the greatest value) and the minimum value (least value) in the data set; that is, range = maximum value – minimum value. *Tip:* The range should have the same units as those of the data values from which it is computed. If no units are specified, then the range will not specify units.

Here are two practice problems.

Problem: Find the range of the following data set: 21, 35, 34, 30, 32, 36, 24, 35, 28, 35.
Solution: Range = maximum value – minimum value = 36 – 21 = 15.
Problem: Determine the range for the data shown in the stem-and-leaf plot below.

Ages of 40 Attendees at a Retirement Party

Stem	Leaf
4	0 3 3 5 6 9
5	3 4 4 5 6 6 7 7 7 7 7 8 8 8 9
6	0 0 0 1 1 1 2 3 3 3 7
7	1 4 7 8
8	1 3
9	0 1
Legend: 4|6 = 46	

Solution: Range = maximum value – minimum value = 91 – 40 = 51.

The range gives an indication of the spread of the values in a data set, but its value is determined by only two of the data values. The extent of spread of the other data values is not considered.

Standard Deviation and Variance

The **standard deviation** is a measure of the variability of a set of data values about the mean of the data set. If there is no variability in a data set, each data value equals the mean, giving a standard deviation of 0. The more the data values vary from the mean, the greater the standard deviation, meaning the data set has more spread. *Tip:* The standard deviation should have the same units as those of the data values from which it is computed. If no units are specified, then the standard deviation will not specify units. The **variance** is the square of the standard deviation.

Tip: The standard deviation and variance are used for data in which the mean is the appropriate measure of center.

The formula for the standard deviation σ of a population of size N with mean μ is $\sigma = \sqrt{\frac{\sum(x-\mu)^2}{N}}$, where the x in the formula represents the population's N data values. The formula for the standard deviation, s, of a sample of size n with mean $\bar{x}$ (read as "x-bar") is $s = \sqrt{\frac{\sum(x-\bar{x})^2}{n-1}}$, where x in the formula represents the sample's n data values. The variance of a population, σ^2, is the square of the standard deviation of the population. The variance of a sample, s^2, is the square of the standard deviation of the sample. (See "Statistical Inference" later in this chapter for definitions of the terms *population* and *sample*.)

Tip: For your TExES Math exam, if a problem requires that you calculate a standard deviation or variance, check whether the data are from a population or a sample to make sure you use the correct formula.

Tip: You can use the statistical features of your TI calculator to calculate standard deviations, either for populations or samples. Check the calculator guidebook for instructions.

When you are given two data sets, the standard deviation of the one whose data values are clustered closer to the mean of the data is less than the standard deviation of the other data set.

Here is a practice problem.

> Problem: The following two data sets both have a mean of 50. Which data set has the lesser standard deviation?
>
> Set 1: 30, 40, 50, 60, 70
> Set 2: 10, 10, 50, 90, 90
>
> Solution: It is not necessary to calculate the actual standard deviations for the two data sets because, by inspection, the data values in Set 1 cluster more closely around the mean of 50 than do the data values in Set 2. Therefore, the standard deviation of Set 1 is less than the standard deviation of Set 2. *Note:* Even though the two data sets have the same mean, the data in Set 2 have more spread than the data in Set 1.

Visually, in a manner of speaking, data sets whose distributions are "tall and thin" have standard deviations that are less than the standard deviations of data sets whose distributions are "short and wide."

Here is a practice problem.

> Problem: The dot plots below show the scores of 30 seventh-graders on the mathematics beginning-of-year (BOY) assessment and on the mathematics end-of-year (EOY) assessment. Which set of scores has the lesser standard deviation?

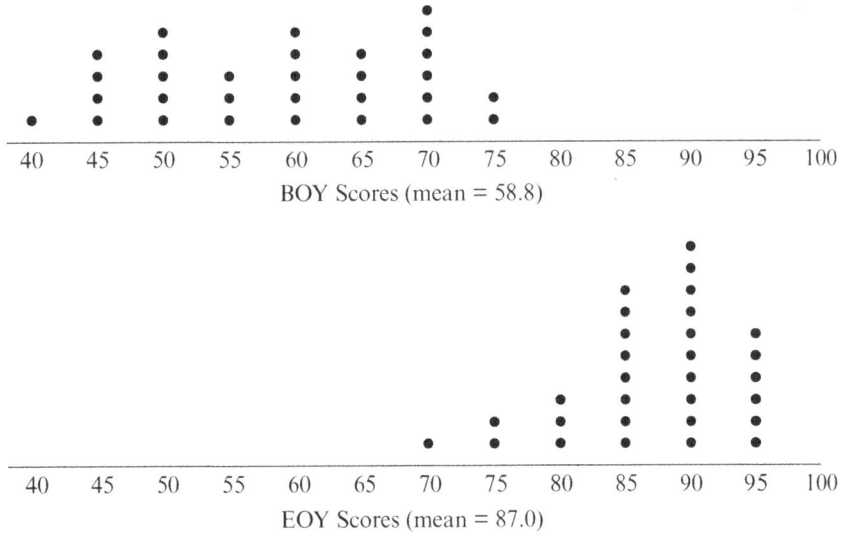

> Solution: The BOY scores show more variability than do the EOY scores. The BOY distribution looks shorter and wider than the EOY distribution. The EOY scores are clustered more closely around the EOY mean of 87.0 than are the BOY scores around the BOY mean of 58.8. Therefore, by visual inspection, the standard deviation of the EOY scores is less than the standard deviation of the BOY scores.

Interquartile Range

The **interquartile range (IQR)** is the difference between the upper and lower quartiles of a data set. That is, $IQR = Q_3 - Q_1$.

The IQR is the range of the middle 50 percent of the data. A small IQR indicates the middle half of the data clusters around the median. A large IQR indicates the middle half of the data is spread out away from the median.

Tip: The IQR is used for data in which the median is the appropriate measure of center.

To determine the IQR, you will need to do three steps. First, determine the data set's median. Next, determine the upper and lower quartiles. Then, compute the difference between the upper and lower quartiles. Here are examples using the data sets given in "Percentiles and Quartiles" earlier in this chapter.

Given the data set 21, 24, 28, 30, 32, 34, 35, 35, 35, 36, the median is 33, Q_1 is 28, and Q_3 is 35. Thus, the IQR = 35 − 28 = 7.

Given the data set 10, 12, 12, 13, 14, 15, 16, 17, 20, the median is 14, Q_1 is 12, and Q_3 is 16.5. Thus, the IQR = 16.5 − 12 = 4.5.

z-Scores

The **z-score** for a data value is its distance in standard deviations from the mean of the data values. To compute a z-score, use the following formula:

$$z\text{-score} = \frac{\text{data value} - \text{mean}}{\text{standard deviation}}$$

If a z-score is positive, the data value is greater than the mean; if a z-score is negative, the data value is less than the mean. The mean has a z-score of 0.

Here is a practice problem.

Problem: Suppose a student scored 80 on a chemistry test and 90 on a biology test. The mean and standard deviations of the scores from the entire class on the two tests are shown in the table below. On which test did the student perform better relative to the mean performance of the class on the test?

Course	Mean	Standard Deviation
Chemistry	70	5
Biology	84	6

Solution: The student's z-score for the chemistry test is $\frac{\text{score} - \text{mean}}{\text{standard deviation}} = \frac{80 - 70}{5} = 2$, indicating the student scored two standard deviations above the class mean on the chemistry test. The student's z-score for the biology test is $\frac{\text{score} - \text{mean}}{\text{standard deviation}} = \frac{90 - 84}{6} = 1$, indicating the student scored one standard deviation above the class mean on the biology test. Therefore, relative to the mean performance of the class, the student performed better on the chemistry test.

Five-Number Summary and Box Plots

For a set of data, the **five-number summary** consists of five measures: the minimum data value (Min), the first quartile (Q_1), the median, the third quartile (Q_3), and the maximum value (Max), written in order from smallest to largest. A **box plot** (shown below) is a graphical representation of the five-number summary for a data set. Box plots are also called **box-and-whisker plots**. Here is a practice problem. (*Note:* The dashed vertical lines are used for clarity but would not be included as part of the box plot.)

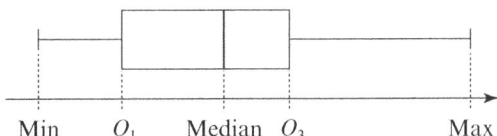

This box plot shows a rectangular box between Q_1 and Q_3, above the horizontal axis. The median is indicated with a vertical line in the interior of the box. The minimum value is at the end of the horizontal line extending from the left end of the box, and the maximum value is at the end of the horizontal line extending from the right end of the box. *Note:* Box plots also may be oriented vertically.

The box plot is a visual summary of the data. The five numbers of the five-number summary determine four groups from left to right, starting at the minimum value position in the box plot. Each group contains approximately 25% of the data values.

Tip: You can use the statistical features of your TI calculator to calculate the five numbers of the five-number summary for a box plot. Check the calculator guidebook for instructions.

Here is a practice problem.

> Problem: Create a box plot for the following five-number summary: MIN = 50, Q_1 = 70, MED = 75, Q_3 = 90, and MAX = 100.
> Solution: The box plot is shown below.

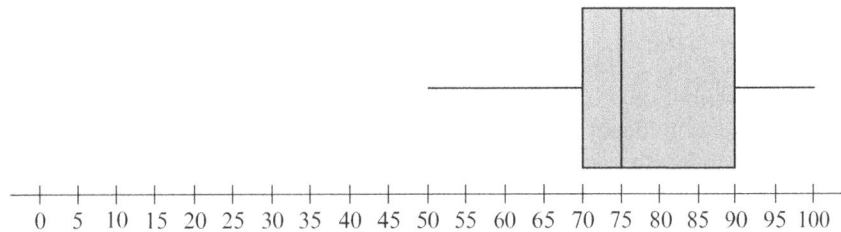

Skewness

Skewness describes the "lopsidedness" of a distribution. A distribution that is **symmetric,** meaning the lower half is a mirror image of the upper half, has no skew. A distribution is **skewed to the right** (or **positively skewed**) if it has a longer tail to the right, toward larger values. A distribution is **skewed to the left** (or **negatively skewed**) if it has a longer tail to the left. In a right-skewed distribution, the mean lies to the right of the median. In a left-skewed distribution, the mean lies to the left of the median. The mean and median coincide for a symmetric distribution (no skew). Here are examples.

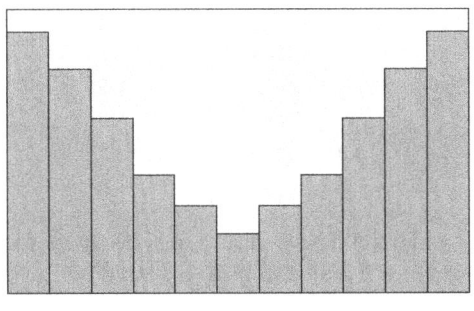

Symmetric

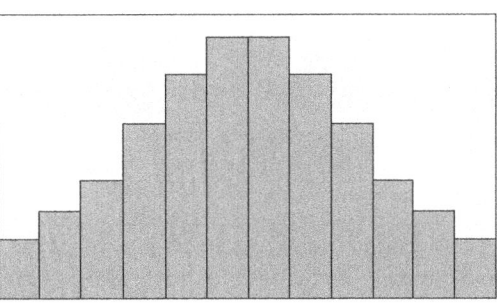

Symmetric

233

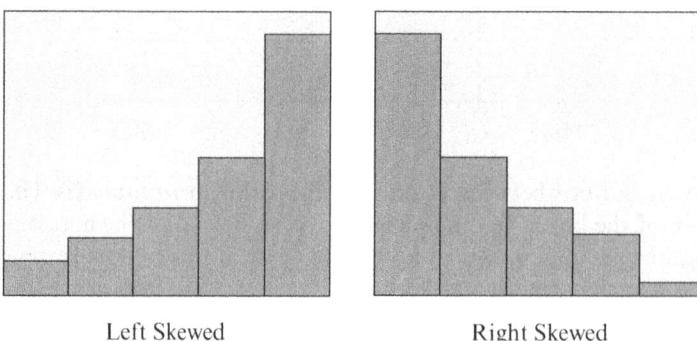

Left Skewed   Right Skewed

In box plots, skewness is detected by the position of the median. If the median is farther from the first quartile than it is from the third quartile, the distribution is skewed to the left. If the median is farther from the third quartile than it is from the first quartile, the distribution is skewed to the right. If the median is equidistant from the first and third quartiles, the distribution is symmetric. Here are examples.

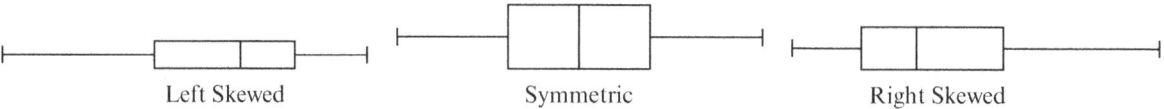

Left Skewed   Symmetric   Right Skewed

Normal Distributions

A **normal distribution** is a bell-shaped curve that is symmetric about its mean, μ. The standard deviation, σ, is the distance from μ to where the curvature of the bell-shaped graph changes on either side. The distribution is continuous, extending from $-\infty$ to ∞, and its mean, median, and mode coincide.

The mean, μ, of a normal distribution is a *location* parameter because it determines where the center of the distribution is located along the horizontal axis. For example, the figure below shows three normal distributions with identical standard deviations, but different means.

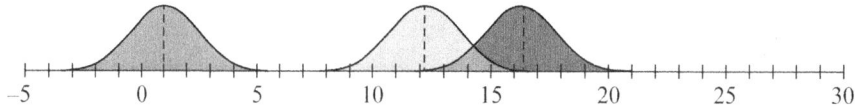

The standard deviation is a measure of the variability (or spread) of the distribution about its mean. Essentially, σ is a *shape* parameter because it determines whether the distribution is tall and thin (corresponding to small values of σ) or short and wide (corresponding to large values of σ). For example, the figure below shows three normal distributions with identical means, but different standard deviations.

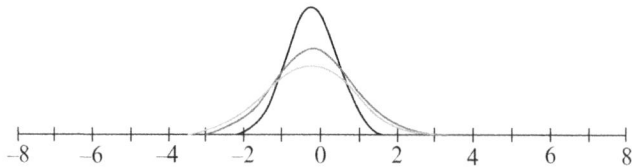

The normal distribution is completely defined by its mean, μ, and standard deviation, σ. The **standard normal distribution**, denoted Z, is the normal distribution that has mean $\mu = 0$ and standard deviation $\sigma = 1$. Due to its unique parameters, a point z along the horizontal axis of a standard normal distribution expresses the position of the value relative to the mean, with negative values lying to the left of the mean and positive values lying to the right of the mean. Furthermore, the z-value is in terms of standard deviations. For example, the value -1 is one standard deviation below the mean, and the value 1 is one standard deviation above the mean.

Because of the normal distribution's bell shape, most of the data fall in the middle of the distribution and taper off evenly in both directions as you move away from the center of the distribution. This characteristic of normal distributions is expressed by the **68-95-99.7 rule.** According to this rule, approximately 68 percent of the values of a normal distribution fall within one standard deviation of the mean, about 95 percent fall within two standard deviations of the mean, and about 99.7 percent fall within three standard deviations of the mean. Hence, about 68 percent of the values of a normal distribution fall between $\mu - 1\sigma$ and $\mu + 1\sigma$, 95 percent between $\mu - 2\sigma$ and $\mu + 2\sigma$, and 99.7 percent between $\mu - 3\sigma$ and $\mu + 3\sigma$.

A result of the 68-95-99.7 rule is that a normal distribution with mean μ and standard deviation σ can be subdivided as shown in the following figure.

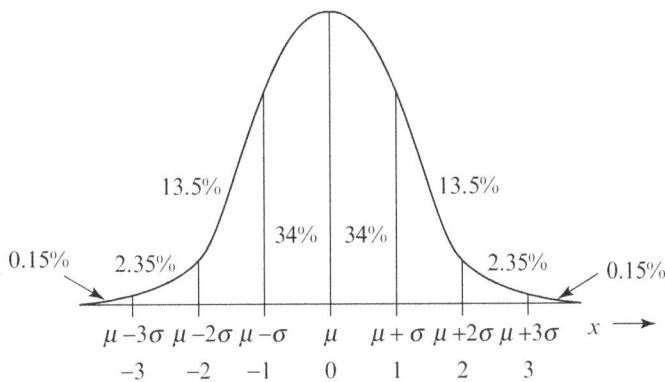

The numbers written horizontally along the bottom of the figure are measures of standard deviations from the mean, called z-scores.

Here is a practice problem.

> Problem: The Wechsler Adult Intelligence Scale (WAIS) is a test designed to measure intelligence in adults. A subject's overall score on the test is called the subject's intelligence quotient (IQ). The WAIS IQ scores have a normal distribution with mean, $\mu = 100$, and standard deviation, $\sigma = 15$. Based on the WAIS IQ test, approximately what percent of adults have IQs between 85 and 115, between 70 and 130, and between 55 and 145?
>
> Solution: According to the 68-95-99.7 rule, about 68 percent of WAIS IQ scores will fall between $100 - 1(15)$ and $100 + 1(15)$, 95 percent between $100 - 2(15)$ and $100 + 2(15)$, and 99.7 percent between $100 - 3(15)$ and $100 + 3(15)$. Thus, based on the WAIS IQ test, about 68 percent of adults have IQs between 85 and 115, about 95 percent have IQs between 70 and 130, and about 99.7 percent have IQs between 55 and 145.

In working problems involving normal distributions, you often will find it necessary to convert data values into z-scores using the formula $z\text{-score} = \dfrac{\text{data value} - \text{mean}}{\text{standard deviation}} = \dfrac{\text{data value} - \mu}{\sigma}$. The z-score expresses the position of the data value relative to the mean. (See "z-Scores" earlier in this chapter for an additional discussion of this topic.) Furthermore, z-scores are in terms of standard deviations. For example, a data value that has a z-score of –1 is one standard deviation below the mean, and a data value that has a z-score of 1 is one standard deviation above the mean.

Here is a practice problem.

> Problem: If scores on a national exam are normally distributed with mean, $\mu = 500$, and standard deviation, $\sigma = 100$, find the z-score for a score of 800. Interpret the z-score in terms of standard deviations relative to the mean.
>
> Solution: The z-score for $800 = \dfrac{\text{data value} - \mu}{\sigma} = \dfrac{800 - 500}{100} = 3$. Thus, 800 is three standard deviations above the mean.

Determining Probabilities Using Normal Distributions

Because the total area bounded by the normal curve and the horizontal axis is 1, the area over a particular interval along the horizontal axis equals the probability that the normal random variable will assume a value in that interval. Therefore, for the standard normal random variable Z, you have the following probabilities:

$P(-1 < Z < 1) \approx 0.68 = 68\%$

$P(-2 < Z < 2) \approx 0.95 = 95\%$

$P(-3 < Z < 3) \approx 0.997 = 99.7\%$

$P(Z < -1) = P(Z > 1) \approx 0.16 = 16\%$

$P(Z < -2) = P(Z > 2) \approx 0.025 = 2.5\%$

$P(Z < -3) = P(Z > 3) \approx 0.0015 = 0.15\%$

Considering that, geometrically, area is a region, the "area" above a point on the horizontal axis of a normal distribution is zero. Therefore, the probability that a normal random variable assumes any particular exact value is zero. Thus, in probability statements for the standard normal distribution, the probability is unchanged when the symbols "<" and "≤" are interchanged or the symbols ">" and "≥" are interchanged.

Here is a practice problem.

> Problem: If scores on a national exam are normally distributed with mean, $\mu = 500$, and standard deviation, $\sigma = 100$, find the probability that a randomly selected test-taker will score greater than 800.
>
> Solution: $P(X > 800) = P\left(Z > \dfrac{800 - 500}{100}\right) = P(Z > 3.00) = 0.0015 = 0.15\%$

Statistical Inference

This section presents basic terminology and concepts of statistical inference. In statistical inference, data are collected, summarized, and analyzed to answer questions or to inform decision making. The data provide information about the world around you.

Note: A further discussion of statistical inference is presented in "More about Inferential Statistics" in Part 2 for candidates who plan to take the TExES Math 7–12.

Populations and Samples

A **population** is the entire group of objects, persons, or things (subjects, experimental units) that you are interested in and want to know something about. *Note:* Although it is common to refer to populations as groups of entities, you can also view populations as the data collected from those entities. A **parameter** is a numerical measurement that describes a population. It is a fixed number. However, in investigations of the population, its value often is *unknown*. Customary symbols for the population mean, population standard deviation, and population proportion are μ, σ, and p, respectively.

A **sample** is a subset of the population. A **statistic** is a numerical measurement that describes a sample. Once you have data from a sample, the value of a statistic is *known* because you can compute it. However, its value varies from sample to sample. Customary symbols for the sample mean, sample standard deviation, and sample proportion are $\bar{x}$, s, and $\hat{p}$ (read as "p-hat"), respectively.

When you find it is impractical or impossible to obtain the value of parameters directly from an entire population, you collect the corresponding statistics from a sample of the population. In **inferential statistics**, information from samples is used to make estimates, predictions, decisions, generalizations, or comparisons about populations. Here is a diagram of the process.

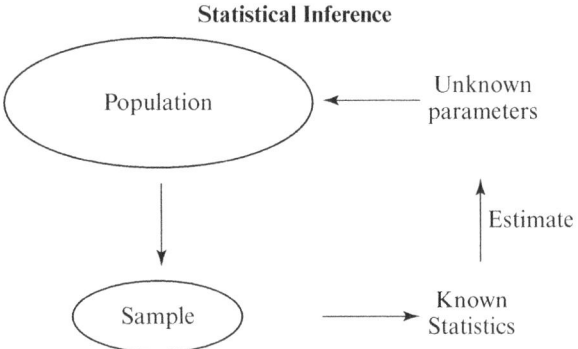

Statistical Inference

Tip: Conclusions of statistical inference are *always* about populations, *not* about samples.

Random Samples

Random sampling of a population means selecting entities from the population by choosing them at random. The result is a **random sample** from the population. In a **simple random sample (SRS)**, every possible sample of the same size has the same chance of being selected. Drawing without looking and without replacement from a bowl containing names written on slips of paper is a way to obtain an SRS. For many situations, however, this method is impractical. Computer-generated random digits or a table of random digits can be used to obtain a random sample. Hereafter, in this book, a random sample is assumed to be an SRS. An SRS results in a good representation of the population, meaning it has characteristics that mirror those of the population from which it was selected. Suppose your population is all teachers in your state. Your sample, for example, should have a similar age, race, and gender makeup as this population. An important advantage of random samples is that they guard against bias. **Bias** in a statistical study is a type of systematic error that favors particular results.

The **sample size** is the number of entities in the sample. Statistical formulas or guidelines are available for determining adequate sample size for various types of studies. In general, increasing the sample size leads to more precise results (because it reduces variability in the data), but with the caveat that a finite population correction factor should be used when the sample size is larger than 10% of the population size. It's important to note that larger populations do not require larger sample sizes. If a good sampling method is used, the population size has little impact on the precision of estimates. *Note:* Conclusions about populations should not be based on samples that are far too small (for example, an opinion survey that uses fewer than 10 subjects).

The powerful techniques of inferential statistics allow you to draw inferences about the entire population from information obtained from sample data as long as the sample is selected at random from the population and the sample size is not too small. Of course, you can't be positive your conclusions are correct because your data are not from the entire population. Fortunately, though, random sampling tends to produce representative samples. Representative samples provide meaningful results that will support valid inferences you make about populations. Making inferences about populations from information in samples is known as **generalizing to the population.**

Sampling Distributions

A **sampling distribution** is the probability distribution of the different values of a sample statistic obtained (theoretically) from all possible random samples of the same size. (See "Random Variables, Probability Distributions, and Expected Value" earlier in this chapter for an explanation of probability distributions.) The variation in the value of the sample statistic from sample to sample is **sampling variability.** The extent of sampling variability is related to the common sample size, with a small sample size yielding greater sample-to-sample variability than a large sample size.

Sampling distributions underlie all of statistical inference. You use probabilistic reasoning based on sampling distributions to make decisions about population parameters. Two important sampling distributions are the sampling distribution of the sample mean and the sampling distribution of the sample proportion.

Sampling Distribution of the Sample Mean

When you repeatedly calculate the sample mean $\bar{x}$ from random samples of size n from a population with mean μ, the value of the sample mean will vary from sample to sample. Therefore, the sample mean is a random variable and has a probability distribution. (See "Random Variables, Probability Distributions, and Expected Value" earlier in this chapter for an explanation of random variables.) The sample mean's probability distribution is known as the **sampling distribution of the sample mean** and has the following properties:

- Its mean is the same as the mean of the sampled population μ.
- Its standard deviation is $\frac{\sigma}{\sqrt{n}}$, the standard deviation σ of the sampled population divided by the square root of the sample size n.
- Its shape approaches a normal distribution as the sample size n increases (**Central Limit Theorem**). *Tip:* If the sample size is at least 30, then the sampling distribution of the sample mean is approximately normally distributed. (See "Normal Distributions" earlier in this chapter for a discussion of this topic.)

Sampling Distribution of the Sample Proportion

When you repeatedly calculate the sample proportion $\hat{p}$ from random samples of size n from a population with population proportion p, the value of the sample proportion will vary from sample to sample. Therefore, the sample proportion is a random variable and has a probability distribution. Its probability distribution is known as the **sampling distribution of the sample proportion** $\hat{p}$ and has the following properties:

- Its mean is the same as the population proportion p.
- Its standard deviation is $\sqrt{\frac{p(1-p)}{n}}$, where n is the sample size.
- It has approximately a normal distribution when the sample size is large. *Tip:* The sample size n is considered "large" if both np and $n(1-p)$ are both at least 5.

Estimating an Unknown Population Parameter

In practice, when you want to estimate an unknown population parameter, you select just *one* sample from the population. You calculate the sample statistic and use it as your best **point estimate** of the population parameter. If you use a random sample of adequate size, your point estimate should be close to the true value of the population parameter.

Statistical techniques allow to you to calculate a **margin of error,** a measure of sampling error based on the sampling distribution of the sample statistic. The margin of error lets you determine how far the point estimate is likely to be from the true value. The sample statistic plus or minus the margin of error produces an interval, called a **confidence interval,** that may or may not contain the true value. However, information from the sampling distribution allows you to make a statement of confidence that the true value is within the margin of error. For example, you might state that you are "95% confident" that the true value of the population parameter lies in the interval. Technically, "95% confident" means that the true value will lie within 95 percent of all possible intervals constructed in this manner.

Two-Way Frequency Tables of Categorical Data

When you collect data on two categorical variables from a sample of subjects, randomly selected from a population of interest to you, display the frequencies for the data in a two-way table. Then calculate row and column totals. Use relative frequencies (or proportions) to describe possible associations between the two variables.

Here is a practice problem.

> Problem: A random selection of 400 university students (200 freshmen students and 200 senior students) from a university of about 40,000 students was surveyed and asked whether they have a personal online social media account. One hundred fifty of the freshmen students and 112 of the senior students responded "yes" to the survey question. The following two-way table summarizes the information given. Do the data suggest that there is an association between classification as a freshman or senior and having a personal online social media account?

> **Responses of 400 Students to the Survey Question:**
> **Do you have a personal online social media account?**
>
> | Classification | Yes | No | Total |
> |---|---|---|---|
> | Freshmen | 150 | 50 | 200 |
> | Seniors | 112 | 88 | 200 |
> | Totals | 262 | 138 | 400 |

> Solution: The proportion of freshmen who have a personal online social media account is $\frac{150}{200} = 0.75$ or 75%. The proportion of seniors who have a social media online account is $\frac{112}{200} = 0.56$ or 56%. Using an informal inferential approach, note that the two proportions are based on an equal number of students and observe that 0.75 and 0.56 differ by 0.19 or 19%. This difference seems noteworthy. These findings suggest that, for students in that university, classification as a freshman or senior is associated with having a personal online social media account. It appears that freshmen are more likely than seniors to have a social media account.

Note: Statistical formulas are available to quantify and statistically evaluate information in two-way categorical tables.

Investigating Bivariate Data

For your TExES Math exam, you should have a basic understanding of how to detect relationships between two quantitative variables based on data that have been collected on both variables. These data are bivariate data. **Bivariate data** are paired values of data from two quantitative variables. The data are paired in a way that matches each value from one variable with a corresponding value from the other variable. Scatter plots, lines of best fit, simple linear regression, and correlation coefficients are used to investigate this type of data.

Scatter Plots

A **scatter plot** is a graph of the ordered pairs of a set of bivariate data plotted on a coordinate grid. The scale for one of the variables is along the horizontal axis and the scale for the other variable is along the vertical axis. Each plotted ordered pair represents a **data point** in the scatter plot. (*Note:* Do not connect the data points in a scatter plot.) Always plot the **predictor variable** (also called the **explanatory variable** or **independent variable**), if there is one, on the horizontal axis and the **response variable** (also called the **dependent variable**) on the vertical axis. The scatter plot's pattern provides visual cues as to whether there is a relationship between the two variables and, if there is, the nature of that relationship.

For your TExES Math exam, you should be able to examine scatter plots and distinguish between those that suggest linear relationships and those that suggest nonlinear relationships between two variables. The data points are often described as forming a "cloud." When the data points in a scatter plot appear to cluster around an imagined line passing through the points, the scatter plot suggests a **linear** relationship between the two variables.

Here is a practice problem.

> Problem: Which scatter plot below clearly shows a nonlinear relationship between variables X and Y?

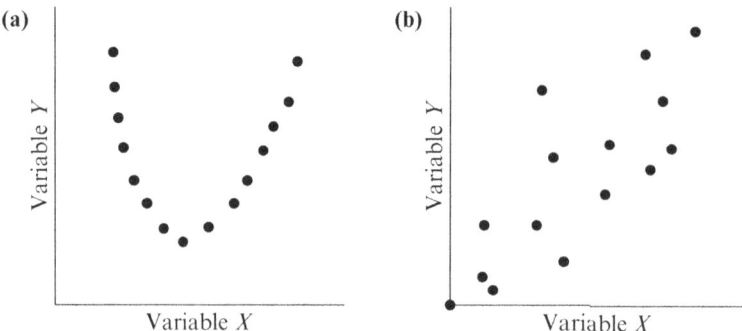

> Solution: The scatter plot in **(a)** shows a recognizable curved pattern. This pattern suggests a curved relationship between the variables X and Y. It is clearly nonlinear. The scatter plot in **(b)** shows a recognizable linear pattern. This pattern suggests a linear relationship between the variables X and Y.

A scatter plot that has no recognizable pattern points to no relationship between the two variables.

Here is a practice problem.

> Problem: Which scatter plot suggests that there is no relationship between the two variables?

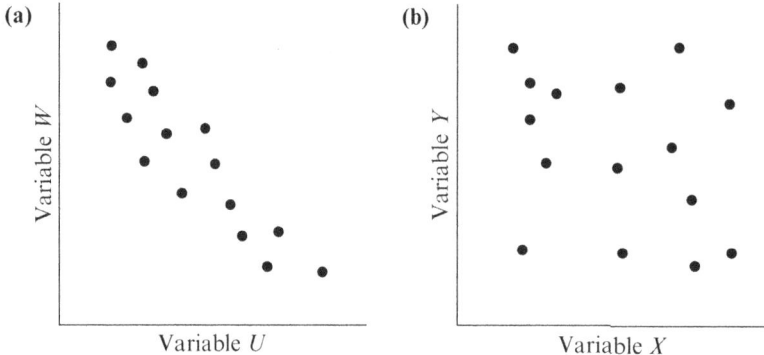

> Solution: The scatter plot in **(a)** shows a recognizable linear pattern that suggests a linear relationship between variables U and W. The scatter plot in **(b)** does not show a recognizable pattern to suggest a relationship between variables X and Y.

If the relationship between two variables is linear, it can be positive or negative. For linear relationships, scatter plots that slant upward from left to right indicate positive linear relationships. In **positive linear relationships,** above-average values of one variable tend to be associated with above-average values of the other, and below-average values of the two variables also tend to be associated. Scatter plots that slant downward from left to right indicate negative linear relationships. In **negative linear relationships,** above-average values of one variable tend to be associated with below-average values of the other, and the reverse is true.

Here is a practice problem.

Problem: Describe the scatter plots below as having positive or negative linear relationships.

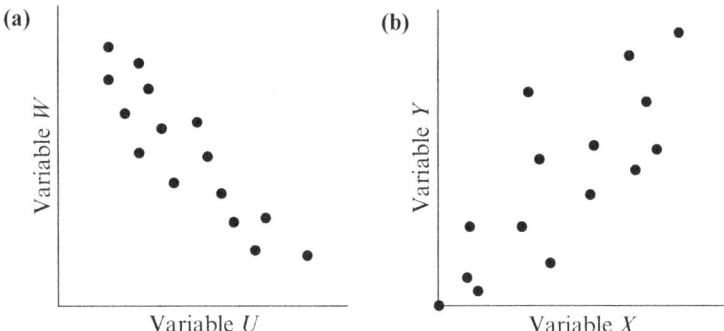

Solution: The scatter plot in **(a)** suggests a negative linear relationship between U and W. The scatter plot in **(b)** suggests a positive linear relationship between X and Y.

The closer the data points in a scatter plot cluster around an imagined line passing through the points, the stronger the linear relationship is between the two variables. Here is a practice problem.

Problem: Which scatter plot below suggests the stronger linear relationship between the two variables?

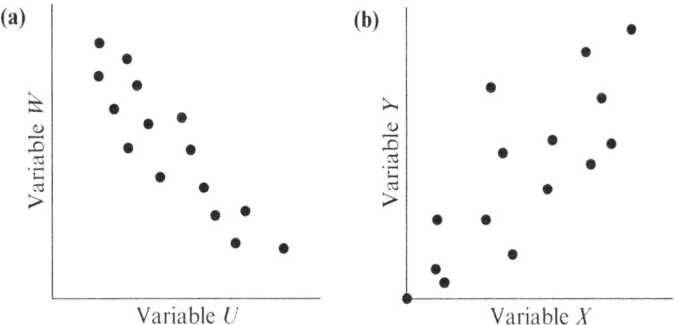

Solution: Both scatter plots indicate a linear relationship. The relationship between U and W is stronger than the relationship between X and Y because the data points in the scatter plot in **(a)** are clustered closer around an imagined line passing through the points than are the data points in the scatter plot in **(b)**.

In a scatter plot, an **outlier** is a data point that is relatively far away from the rest of the points in the scatter plot. For example, in the scatter plot shown below, the data point marked with an asterisk is a noticeable outlier.

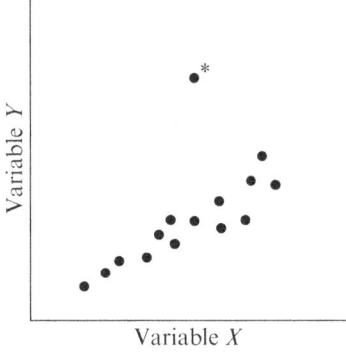

If you have *believable* information that an outlier doesn't belong with the other data points (perhaps it's the result of an error in collecting the data), you can exclude it when assessing linearity of the scatter plot.

241

Line of Best Fit and Simple Linear Regression

If the scatter plot seems approximately linear, the **line of best fit** (or **regression line**) is a straight line that best represents the data. It might pass through some of the points, none of the points, or even all of the points. It will always pass through the point whose coordinates are the means of the two variables.

If X and Y are the two variables under consideration, the equation of the line of best fit is given by the **simple linear regression equation** $\hat{Y} = a + bX$, where $\hat{Y}$ (read as "Y-hat") is the predicted value of the response variable, Y, a is a constant (corresponding to $X = 0$), and b is the regression coefficient. For statistical reasons, to be safe, you should predict only within the range of the predictor variable. When you predict within the range of the plotted data, you are **interpolating.**

The coefficient b is the **slope** of the regression line. The interpretation of the slope, b, is that if the X variable increases by 1 unit, it is predicted that the Y variable will change by b units. The interpretation of the **intercept,** a, is that when the X variable is zero, the Y variable is a units. However, if values for the X variable near zero would not make sense, then typically the interpretation of the intercept will seem unrealistic in the real world. Nevertheless, the coefficient a is a necessary part of the equation of the line of best fit.

The **residuals** are the differences between the actual Y values in the scatter plot and the $\hat{Y}$ values predicted by the regression equation. Visually, they are the vertical distances of the data points from the regression line. A **residual plot** shows the residuals on the vertical axis and the independent variable on the horizontal axis. You can use the residual plot to determine whether a linear model is appropriate for the data. A residual plot in which the points are randomly dispersed around the horizontal axis (as shown in the following graph) indicates that a linear model is appropriate for the data; otherwise, a linear model is not a good fit for the data.

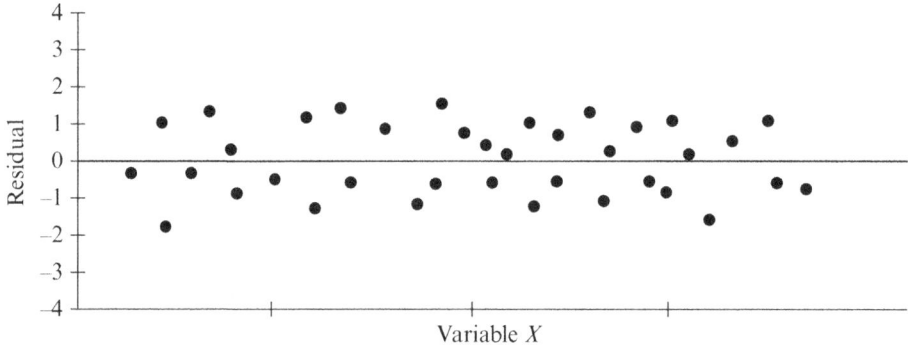

The line of best fit minimizes the sum of the squares of the residuals and is the **least-squares regression line.** The closer the plotted data points are to the regression line, the smaller the residual sum of squares. Thus, in a practical sense, the relationship between two numerical variables is strong if the data are tightly clustered around the line of best fit, and is weak if the data are loosely spread around the line. Here is a detailed example to clarify your understanding of simple linear regression.

The following table contains 10 bivariate data points for the variables X and Y.

X	10	8	13	9	11	14	6	4	12	5
Y	8.1	6.9	7.5	8.8	8.3	9.9	7.2	4.3	10.8	5.7

The scatter plot and line of best fit are shown below.

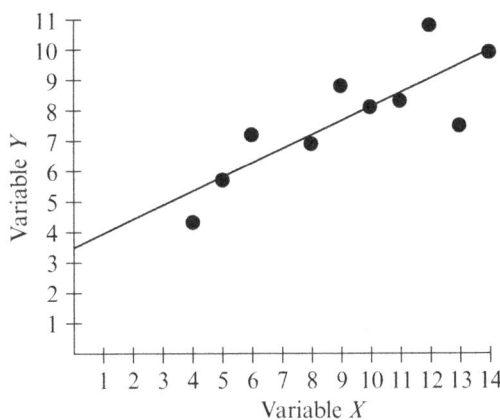

The linear regression equation of the line of best fit is $\hat{Y} = 3.5 + 0.46X$. The interpretation of the slope of 0.46 is that if the X variable increases by 1 unit, it is predicted that the Y variable will increase by 0.46 units. The interpretation of the intercept, 3.5, is that when the X variable is zero, the Y variable is 3.5 units.

The predicted Y value for $X = 12$ is $\hat{Y} = 3.5 + 0.46(12) = 9.0$. The residual for the data point (12, 10.8) is $10.8 - 9.0 = 1.8$.

The predicted Y value for $X = 7$ is $\hat{Y} = 3.5 + 0.46(7) = 6.7$. *Note:* The value 7 is within the range of the available data, so it is permissible to predict its Y value.

Tip: Regression is strongly affected by outliers. Be cautious in your interpretation of regression results if the scatter plot shows clear-cut outliers.

Tip: You can use the statistical features of your TI calculator to determine the regression equation for bivariate data. Check the calculator guidebook for instructions.

Correlation Coefficients

Scatter plots visually show the direction, shape, and strength of the relationship between two quantitative variables. If the relationship is linear, the **correlation coefficient r** is a numerical measure that describes the direction and strength of the linear relationship between the two variables.

Correlation coefficients range from –1 to +1, with –1 indicating a "perfect" negative linear relationship and +1 indicating a "perfect" positive linear relationship. The closer the correlation coefficient is to 0, the weaker the linear relationship. Conversely, the farther the correlation coefficient is from 0, the stronger the relationship. Correlation values very close to either –1 or +1 indicate very strong relationships, meaning the data points in the scatter plot lie close to a straight line. Correlations of precisely –1 or +1 occur only when the data points lie exactly along a straight line. If the two variables have *no relationship* to each other, then the correlation coefficient will be 0. (Remember, however, that you cannot have correlation coefficients below –1 or above +1.)

The existence of a recognizable correlation between two variables does *not* imply that changes in one variable cause changes in the other variable. The correlation might be a reflection of outside variables that affect both variables under study. *Tip:* For your TExES Math exam, you are expected to be able to distinguish between correlation and causation.

In simple linear regression, the correlation coefficient is a measure of the strength of the linear relationship between the predictor variable and the response variable of the linear regression equation. Therefore, it can be used to assess the regression line's "goodness of fit." The closer $|r|$ is to 1, the more perfect the linear relationship is between X and Y, and therefore, the better the regression line represents the data points. If r is close to 0, there is little or no linear relationship, so the line is not a good fit for the data. For example, for the bivariate data shown previously in "Line of Best Fit and Simple Linear Regression," the correlation coefficient is 0.82, indicating a somewhat strong linear relationship between the variables X and Y. This result suggests that the regression line is a good fit for the data.

Tip: The correlation coefficient and the slope of the regression equation are not the same measure; however, their signs are always the same.

Part 2

Part 2 of this chapter is for candidates who plan to take the TExES Math 7–12. This review material goes beyond the standards for the TExES Math 4–8.

Types of Statistical Studies

For this topic, you must demonstrate an understanding of the purposes and differences among survey, experimental, and observational studies.

Survey Studies

In **survey studies,** the purpose is to gather information from a representative sample in order to estimate or make decisions about parameters of populations. Specifying a well-defined, fixed population, using an appropriate method for randomly selecting a sample of adequate size, and ensuring accurate "measurement" of the variable of interest (for example, making sure questions are fair and unbiased) are essential components of a survey study.

Tip: In designing survey studies, you use random sampling to avoid bias, and you manage variability by selecting samples of adequate size.

Examples of this type of study include opinion surveys, fact-finding surveys, questionnaires, and interview studies. Results are summarized and reported. Keep in mind that you cannot infer causality from survey studies; and, furthermore, generalization of the survey results to the population is appropriate only when the sample has been randomly chosen from the population. (See "Random Samples" in Part 1 of this chapter for a discussion of this topic.)

Experimental Studies

In **experimental studies,** the purpose is to investigate possible cause-and-effect relationships by exposing an experimental group to a **treatment** condition (the **independent variable**) and comparing the results to a control group not receiving the treatment. Such studies are **controlled experiments.** The study is set up in such a way that one group of **experimental units** (for example, people, animals, plants) gets the treatment (the **experimental group**) and another group (the **control group**) does not, and then comparisons are made to see whether the treatment had an effect on the variable of interest (the **dependent variable**). For such comparisons to be valid, **random assignment** of subjects to either the experimental or control group is essential. Random assignment allows researchers to infer cause-and-effect relationships between variables by minimizing (or possibly eliminating) the role of confounding variables. A **confounding variable** is one that influences both the dependent and independent variable, causing a spurious association. Other sources of variation (such as extraneous variables) must be controlled as well. An **extraneous variable** influences the outcome of an experiment, but is not accounted for in the study design. Hallmarks of rigorous experimental studies are well-defined treatments, suitable experimental units, a sound plan for random assignment of the treatment, and accurate measurement of the experiment's results.

Examples of such studies include investigating the effectiveness of a new method of teaching reading on reading ability, the effect of a new drug on cancer patients, and the effect of a new type of fertilizer on plant growth. In a well-designed experimental study, experimental units are randomly assigned to either the treatment or control group to ensure that groups are similar in all respects *except* for the treatment. Therefore, any difference in the two groups can be attributed to the treatment. Only through well-designed experimental studies are cause-and-effect conclusions valid and generalizable. It should be noted that generalizing from a controlled experiment to a larger population is problematic if the subjects in the experiment do not constitute a random sample from that population.

Tip: Do not confuse random assignment (using a random process to assign subjects to experimental groups) with random sampling (selecting entities randomly from a population). These two terms are distinctly different concepts.

Note: Experimental studies can involve comparisons of multiple treatments.

Observational Studies

Observational studies involve collecting and analyzing data without changing existing conditions. Observational studies are conducted when it is not feasible (or, perhaps, not ethical) to randomly assign experimental units to some treatment condition (for example, being a smoker). Such studies are conducted in a setting that does not permit the investigator to manipulate or control all relevant variables. The main shortcoming of observational studies is that the experimenter cannot randomize a treatment condition to experimental units. The nonrandomness in sampling and the constraint imposed by observing a predetermined condition limit drawing cause-and-effect conclusions. There is a possibility that results are due to one or more variables other than the variables being studied.

Examples of observational studies include exploring the relationship between gum disease and smoking, between SAT scores and college grade point average, or between geographic location and family size. In observational studies, estimating population parameters or making statements about differences among treatments is not recommended. Nevertheless, the results of observational studies can point to patterns in data and relationships between variables.

Well-Designed Studies

Well-designed studies follow the process of **scientific inquiry.** Scientists use scientific inquiry to obtain reliable and valid information about variables of interest. In statistical studies, scientific inquiry has five main steps:

1. **Define the problem:** Pose a statistical question about a topic or variable of interest that can be answered with data.
2. **Formulate a hypothesis:** Make an educated guess about an aspect of the topic or variable.
3. **Gather evidence:** Design and perform a study to test the hypothesis; collect data about the hypothesis.
4. **Analyze the data:** Using appropriate statistical techniques, analyze the data collected.
5. **Draw conclusions:** Interpret the results and decide whether the hypothesis is supported or not supported by the results.

To provide results worthy of consideration, carefully plan well-designed studies, investigate issues that are clear and unambiguous, clearly identify populations of study, use randomization and select samples of adequate size, use well-defined variables of interest, avoid bias, and control for outside factors, such as extraneous variables, that could jeopardize the validity of conclusions. Only when investigators use well-designed studies can reliable and valid conclusions be drawn.

More about Inferential Statistics

For this topic, you must demonstrate a basic understanding of the concepts and techniques of hypothesis testing, a powerful tool of inferential statistics that is used extensively in the real world.

The Logic of Hypothesis Testing

A **hypothesis** is an assertion about the value of a population parameter. **Hypothesis testing** is a procedure for using sample data to make a decision between two competing hypotheses about a population parameter. The two hypotheses are the **null hypothesis** (for example, $\mu \leq 100$) and the **alternative hypothesis** (for example, $\mu > 100$).

In a test of hypothesis, you follow a set of commonly accepted guidelines to decide whether data from a sample provide convincing evidence against the null hypothesis, which is so called because, in most scenarios, it is the hypothesis that you, as the person conducting the test of hypothesis, are attempting to nullify. Nevertheless, it is the hypothesis you must hold true until you have sufficient evidence against it. However, if the evidence from the sample contradicts the null hypothesis to the extent that it is very unlikely to have occurred by chance if the null hypothesis were true, then you reject the null hypothesis in favor of the alternative hypothesis. At this point, you can see that the logic of a test of hypothesis is an argument by contradiction, designed to show that believing the null hypothesis is true leads to an absurd result and therefore must be rejected.

So how should you quantify the vague "very unlikely" of the previous paragraph? To be honest, the value is arbitrary. In practice, 0.05 is a common cut-off point (and so are 0.10 and 0.01). To maintain the integrity of the hypothesis testing process, you must decide on this cut-off value *before* you collect your data. This value is the **significance level,** denoted α, of your test. Thus, the argument becomes that if the sample provides evidence that has no more than a 0.05 probability to have occurred by chance if the null hypothesis were true, then you reject the null hypothesis in favor of the alternative hypothesis.

Statistical techniques allow you to calculate a *p*-**value,** which is the probability that the evidence from the sample occurred by chance if the null hypothesis were true. You compare your *p*-value to your level of significance to make a decision about your belief in the null hypothesis. If the *p*-value is less than or equal to α, you **reject** the null hypothesis in favor of its alternative; otherwise, you **fail to reject** the null hypothesis. In simple terms, the decision to reject the null hypothesis occurs because the sample data is inconsistent with what you would expect to observe if the null hypothesis were true. For example, if α is 0.05 and the calculated *p*-value is 0.03, then because $0.03 \leq 0.05$ you would reject the null hypothesis ($\mu \leq 100$) and accept the alternative hypothesis that $\mu > 100$.

Type I and Type II Errors

The aim of a hypothesis test is to make the correct decision about whether or not to reject the null hypothesis in favor of the alternative hypothesis. Unfortunately, because the conclusion of a test of hypothesis is based on probability, there is always a risk of error. Statisticians describe two types of errors that can occur when making a decision in hypothesis testing:

> A **Type I error** is the error of rejecting the null hypothesis when in fact the null hypothesis is true.
>
> A **Type II error** is the error of accepting the null hypothesis when in fact the null hypothesis is false.

Chapter 5
Mathematical Processes and Perspectives

This chapter is for all candidates who plan to take a TExES Math exam. It provides a review of mathematical processes and perspectives including basic set theory, equivalence relations, logic, basic proof techniques, and inductive and deductive reasoning.

Basic Set Theory

This topic presents basic concepts of set theory, including terminology, unions, intersections, and Venn diagrams.

Set Terminology

A **set** is a collection of objects or things. Commonly, uppercase letters, such as A and B, are used to name sets. The objects in a set A are its **elements** (or **members**). To show that x is an element of A, write $x \in A$ (read "x is an element of set A"). If y is *not* an element of A, write $y \notin A$. (Note that a diagonal slash through a symbol negates the original meaning of the symbol.)

A set is defined by means of braces in which you describe the members of the set by roster (that is, a list of the elements separated by commas), a verbal description, or mathematical symbolism. For example, the set D of digits used in the base-ten place value system can be defined in the following ways: $D = \{0, 1, 2, 3, 4, 5, 6, 7, 8, 9\}$, $D = \{\text{digits used in the base-ten place value system}\}$, or $D = \{x \in \text{Integers} \mid 0 \le x < 10\}$. You can read the third way as "The set of all x that are elements of the integers such that x is greater than or equal to zero and less than ten." The vertical line, |, is read "such that." This latter way of describing a set is **set builder notation**. The set that contains no objects is the **empty set** and is designated by the symbol $\emptyset$ or { }.

Tip: The symbol for the empty set is $\emptyset$, not $\{\emptyset\}$. The set $\{\emptyset\}$ is not an empty set; it has one element, namely $\emptyset$.

Sets should be **well-defined**. This term means that if you are given a set, you can tell which objects belong in the set and which objects do not belong in the set. For example, the set $I = \{\text{important people}\}$ is *not* well-defined because you are not given enough information to know who qualifies as an "important person." On the other hand, the set $P = \{\text{Presidents of the United States who served before 2020}\}$ is well-defined because you can decide whether a given individual does or does not belong in set P.

Two sets A and B are **equal**, written $A = B$, if and only if they contain *exactly* the same elements, without regard to the order in which the elements are listed in the two sets or whether elements are repeated. For example, $\{1, 4, 8\} = \{1, 8, 4\} = \{4, 1, 8\} = \{4, 8, 1\} = \{8, 1, 4\} = \{8, 4, 1\}$ and $\{1, 4, 8\} = \{1, 1, 4, 4, 8, 8\}$.

A set A is a **subset** of set B, denoted $A \subseteq B$, if every element of A is an element of B.

Here is a practice problem.

> Problem: Is it true that $\{1, 4\} \subseteq \{1, 4, 8\}$? Justify your answer.
> Solution: Yes, $\{1, 4\} \subseteq \{1, 4, 8\}$ because every element of $\{1, 4\}$ is an element of $\{1, 4, 8\}$.

Additionally, if B contains at least one element that is not in A, then A is a **proper subset** of B, denoted $A \subset B$. Thus, $\{1, 4\} \subset \{1, 4, 8\}$.

You can show two sets A and B are equal by showing that $A \subseteq B$ and $B \subseteq A$. In a discussion, all the sets under consideration are subsets of a **universal set** (commonly denoted U), and the empty set is a subset of every set.

Tip: Do not confuse the relationship "is an element of" with the relationship "is a subset of." For example, $4 \in \{1, 4, 8\}$, but $\{4\} \notin \{1, 4, 8\}$; on the other hand, $\{4\} \subseteq \{1, 4, 8\}$, but $4 \not\subset \{1, 4, 8\}$.

The number of distinct elements in a set A is the **cardinality** (or cardinal number) of A, denoted $|A|$ (read as "the cardinality of set A"). *Note:* Other notations for the cardinality of a set are $n(A)$ and $\#A$. The cardinality of a set can be **finite,** meaning the set has a definite number of elements that can be counted, or **infinite,** meaning the set has an unlimited number of elements. Throughout this book, the cardinality of a finite set A will be denoted $|A|$.

Here is a practice problem.

>Problem: What is the cardinality of the set $A = \{1, 4, 8\}$?
>Solution: Given $A = \{1, 4, 8\}$, then $|A| = 3$.

Set Operations and Venn Diagrams

If in a discussion all the sets under consideration are subsets of a given set U, then U is the universal set of discourse, or simply, the universal set. In this section, assume that all sets under consideration are subsets of a given universal set U.

The three basic operations for sets are union, intersection, and complement.

The **union** of two sets A and B, denoted $A \cup B$, is the set of all elements that are in A or in B or in both. In set-builder notation, $A \cup B = \{x \mid x \in A \text{ or } x \in B\}$.

Here is a practice problem.

>Problem: Given $A = \{2, 4, 6, 8\}$ and $B = \{1, 2, 4, 5, 6\}$, determine $A \cup B$.
>Solution: Given $A = \{2, 4, 6, 8\}$ and $B = \{1, 2, 4, 5, 6\}$, then $A \cup B = \{1, 2, 4, 5, 6, 8\}$.

Tip: When you form the union of two sets, do not list an element more than once because it is unnecessary to do so. Note that the word *or* is used in the *inclusive* sense; that is, *or* means "one or the other, or possibly both at the same time."

The **intersection** of two sets A and B, denoted $A \cap B$, is the set of all elements that are in both A and B. That is, the intersection of two sets is the set of elements that are common to both sets. In set-builder notation, $A \cap B = \{x \mid x \in A \text{ and } x \in B\}$.

Here is a practice problem.

>Problem: Given $A = \{2, 4, 6, 8\}$ and $B = \{1, 2, 4, 5, 6\}$, determine, $A \cap B$.
>Solution: Given $A = \{2, 4, 6, 8\}$ and $B = \{1, 2, 4, 5, 6\}$, then $A \cap B = \{2, 4, 6\}$.

When two sets have no elements in common, their intersection is the empty set, and the sets are said to be **disjoint.**

Here is a practice problem.

>Problem: Given $A = \{2, 4, 6, 8\}$ and $C = \{1, 3, 5\}$, determine, $A \cap C$.
>Solution: Given $A = \{2, 4, 6, 8\}$ and $C = \{1, 3, 5\}$, then $A \cap C = \emptyset$; so A and C are disjoint.

The **complement** of a set A, denoted A^C, is the set of all elements in the universal set U that are *not* in A. In set-builder notation, $A^C = \{x \mid x \in U, x \notin A\}$.

Here is a practice problem.

>Problem: Given $U = \{x \in \text{Integers} \mid 0 \leq x < 10\}$ and $A = \{2, 4, 6, 8\}$, determine A^C.
>Solution: Given $U = \{x \in \text{Integers} \mid 0 \leq x < 10\}$ and $A = \{2, 4, 6, 8\}$, then $A^C = \{0, 1, 3, 5, 7, 9\}$.

A **Venn diagram** is a visual depiction of a set operation or relationship. In a Venn diagram, the universal set is usually represented by a rectangular region, which encloses everything else in the diagram. The sets in U are represented by circles. Shading depicts relationships or the results of a set operation. Here are examples of Venn diagrams.

Verbal Description	Symbolism	Venn Diagram
x is an element of A	$x \in A$	
C is a proper subset of A	$C \subset A$	
A and B are disjoint	$A \cap B = \emptyset$	
The union of A and B	$A \cup B$	
The intersection of A and B	$A \cap B$	
The complement of A	A^C	

Note: An x in a diagram means the region in which it is located is not empty.

Equivalence Relations

The **Cartesian product** of two sets A and B, denoted $A \times B$, is the set of all ordered pairs (x, y) such that $x \in A$ and $y \in B$.

A **binary relation** (also called simply relation) from a set A to a set B is a subset of $A \times B$. If $A = B$, then we say the relation is on A. That is, a relation on the set A is a subset of $A \times A$.

For a relation $\Re$, the notation $x \Re y$ (read "x is related to y") is used to denote that the ordered pair $(x, y) \in \Re$.

A relation $\Re$ on a set S is

- reflexive if $x \Re x$ for all $x \in S$;
- symmetric if $x \Re y$ implies $y \Re x$ for all $x, y \in S$;
- transitive if $(x \Re y$ and $y \Re z)$ implies $x \Re z$ for all $x, y, z \in S$; or
- antisymmetric if $(x \Re y$ and $y \Re x)$ implies $x = y$ for all $x, y \in S$.

An **equivalence relation** is a reflexive, symmetric, and transitive relation. For example, if birthday is defined as "the anniversary of one's birth," then the relation "has the same birthday as" is an equivalence relation. That is, if x, y, and z are any three people, then the relation is

- reflexive because "x has the same birthday as x" for all x;
- symmetric because "x has the same birthday as y" implies "y has the same birthday as x" for all x, y; and
- transitive because ("x has the same birthday as y") and ("y has the same birthday as z") implies "x has the same birthday as z" for all x, y, z.

The relation "is taller than" is not an equivalence relation because it is not reflexive or symmetric. For example, if x and y are any two people, then the statement "x is taller than x" is not true, and the statement "x is taller than y" implies "y is taller than x," which is also not true.

Logic

For this topic, you are expected to understand basic terminology and symbols of logic, evaluate the truth of statements, and recognize and prove conditional statements.

Basic Concepts of Logic

A **statement** (or **proposition**) is a declarative sentence that can be meaningfully assigned a **truth value** of either true or false. For example, "The sum of 1 and 2 is 3" is a statement whose truth value is true, but "The sum of 1 and 2 is 5" is a statement whose truth value is false. Other examples of statements are "It is raining," "The moon is made of green cheese," and "The number $\frac{1}{2}$ is a fraction." The following examples are *not* statements because their truth values cannot be determined without further specification: "She is married," "The number x is irrational," and "The set A is a subset of the set B." Sentences that are questions ("What is your name?") or commands ("Come here.") are *not* statements because they cannot be classified as either true or false. Commonly, single letters (either lower- or uppercase) are used to designate statements.

Simple statements are statements that are simple declarative sentences. Five basic **logical connectives** can be used to construct **compound statements** from simple statements. The resulting compound statements have special names. Given the simple statements P and Q, the following table summarizes compound statements constructed from P and Q.

Compound Statements

Logical Connective	Compound Statement	Name	This compound statement is true ...	This compound statement is false ...
not	not P	negation	if and only if P is false.	if and only if P is true.
or	P or Q	disjunction	if either P is true, or Q is true, or both are true.	only if both P and Q are false.
and	P and Q	conjunction	only if both P and Q are true.	if either P is false, or Q is false, or both are false.
If ..., then ...	If P, then Q	conditional	if either both P and Q are true, or if P is false (regardless of the truth value of Q).	only when P is true and Q is false.
if and only if	P if and only if Q	biconditional	only when P and Q are either both true or are both false.	only when P and Q have opposite truth values.

Here is a practice problem.

Problem: Given P = "1 + 2 = 3," Q = "4 is an even number," R = "1 + 2 = 5," and S = "4 is an odd number," classify each of the following compound statements as true or false.

a. P and Q.
b. Not R.
c. P or S.
d. If R, then Q.
e. R or S.
f. If P, then S.
g. P and S.
h. (Not P) or Q.

Solution:

True	False	Statement
✓		(a) P and Q. Answer: P is true, and Q is true, so "P and Q" is true.
✓		(b) Not R. Answer: R is false, so "Not R" is true.
✓		(c) P or S. Answer: P is true, and S is false, so "P or S" is true.
✓		(d) If R, then Q. Answer: R is false, so "If R, then Q" is true.
	✓	(e) R or S. Answer: R is false, and S is false, so "R or S" is false.
	✓	(f) If P, then S. Answer: P is true, and S is false, so "If P, then S" is false.
	✓	(g) P and S. Answer: P is true, and S is false, so "P and S" is false.
✓		(h) (Not P) or Q. Answer: "Not P" is false, and Q is true, so "(Not P) or Q" is true.

A **tautology** is a compound statement that is always true regardless of the truth-value combinations of the simple statements from which it is constructed. A **contradiction** is a compound statement that is always false regardless of the truth-value combinations of the simple statements from which it is constructed. For example, the statement "P or not P" is a tautology, but the statement "P and not P" is a contradiction.

Tautologies that are biconditional statements are **logical equivalences.** That is to say, when a biconditional statement is a tautology, the statement on the left of "if and only if" is logically equivalent to the statement on the right of "if and only if." From a logical standpoint, the two statements have exactly the same meaning.

Statements Associated with a Conditional Statement

Associated with any conditional statement, "If P, then Q," are three other conditional statements: the converse, the inverse, and the contrapositive. The **converse** is the statement "If Q, then P." The **inverse** is the statement "If not P, then not Q." The **contrapositive** is the statement "If not Q, then not P." A conditional statement is *not* logically equivalent to either its converse or to its inverse. However, a conditional statement and its contrapositive *are* logically equivalent. That is, a contrapositive and the conditional from which it is derived have exactly the same meaning.

Here is a practice problem.

> Problem: Given the conditional statement "If a geometric shape is a square, then it is a polygon," **(a)** write an explanation of its truth value and **(b)** write its converse, inverse, and contrapositive, along with an explanation of the truth value of each.
>
> Solution: **(a)** The statement "If a geometric shape is a square, then it is a polygon" is true because all squares are polygons. The answers for part **(b)** are shown below.
>
> > Converse: "If a geometric shape is a polygon, then it is a square" is false, because the shape could be a polygon that is not a square, such as a trapezoid, hexagon, and so on.
> >
> > Inverse: "If a geometric shape is not a square, then it is not a polygon" is false, because there are geometric shapes (for example, triangles) that are not squares but are polygons.
> >
> > Contrapositive: "If a geometric shape is not a polygon, then it is not a square" is true, because there are no squares that are not polygons.

Conditional statements are used extensively in mathematics. Some ways you can express that the statement "If P, then Q" is true are the following:

> If P is true, then Q is also true.
>
> Q is true, if P is true.
>
> P is true implies Q is true.
>
> Q is true whenever P is true.
>
> P is true only if Q is also true.
>
> For Q to be true, it is sufficient that P is true.
>
> For P to be true, it is necessary that Q is true.

Symbolism Associated with a Conditional Statement

The following table shows the symbolism for the conditional statement "If P, then Q" and the symbolism for its converse, inverse, and contrapositive.

Statement Description	Verbal Statement	Symbolism
Conditional	If P, then Q.	$P \Rightarrow Q$
Converse	If Q, then P.	$Q \Rightarrow P$
Inverse	If not P, then not Q.	$\sim P \Rightarrow \sim Q$
Contrapositive	If not Q, then not P.	$\sim Q \Rightarrow \sim P$

Note: The symbol for "not" is "$\sim$."

Three Basic Proof Techniques for Conditional Statements

Three basic proof techniques for conditional statements are direct proof, proof by contradiction (or indirect proof), and proof by contrapositive.

Direct Proof

For a direct proof of $P \Rightarrow Q$, do the following:

1. Assume P is true.

2. Show that Q must follow from P.

Here is a practice problem.

> Problem: Suppose n is an integer. Using a direct proof, prove the conditional statement "If $7n + 9$ is even, then n is odd."
>
> Solution:
> 1. Assume $7n + 9$ is even.
> 2. Given $7n + 9$ is even, then, by the definition of even integer, $7n + 9 = 2k$, for some integer k. Subtracting $6n + 9$ from both sides yields $7n + 9 - (6n + 9) = 2k - (6n + 9)$. Thus, $n = 2k - 6n - 9 = 2k - 6n - 10 + 1 = 2(k - 3n - 5) + 1 = 2a + 1$, where $a = k - 3n - 5$, an integer.
>
> Therefore, n is odd by the definition of odd integer.

Proof by Contradiction (Indirect Proof)

For a proof by contradiction of $P \Rightarrow Q$, do the following:

1. Assume P is true.

2. Assume (temporarily) $\sim Q$ is true.

3. Deduce a contradiction.

Here is a practice problem.

> Problem: Suppose n is an integer. Using a proof by contradiction, prove the conditional statement "If $7n + 9$ is even, then n is odd."
>
> Solution:
> 1. Assume $7n + 9$ is even.
> 2. Assume n is not odd.
> 3. Given n is not odd, then n is even. Thus, by the definition of even integer, $n = 2k$, for some integer k. Then $7n + 9 = 7(2k) + 9 = 14k + 9 = 14k + 8 + 1 = 2(7k + 4) + 1 = 2b + 1$, where $b = 7k + 4$, an integer. Thus, by the definition of odd integer, $7n + 9$ is odd, which is a contradiction because $7n + 9$ cannot be both even and odd.
>
> Therefore, the assumption that n is not odd must be false, leading to the conclusion that n is odd must be true.

Proof by Contrapositive

Recall from "Statements Associated with a Conditional Statement" earlier in this chapter that a conditional statement and its contrapositive are logically equivalent. Therefore, you can prove $P \Rightarrow Q$ by proving $\sim Q \Rightarrow \sim P$.

For a proof by contrapositive of $P \Rightarrow Q$, do the following:

1. Assume $\sim Q$ is true.

2. Show that $\sim P$ must follow from $\sim Q$.

3. Conclude that $P \Rightarrow Q$ because it is logically equivalent to its contrapositive.

253

Here is a practice problem.

> Problem: Suppose n is an integer. Using a proof by contrapositive, prove the conditional statement "If $7n + 9$ is even, then n is odd."
>
> Solution:
>
> 1. Assume n is not odd.
> 2. Given n is not odd, then n is even. Thus, by the definition of even integer, $n = 2k$, for some integer k. Then $7n + 9 = 7(2k) + 9 = 14k + 9 = 14k + 8 + 1 = 2(7k + 4) + 1 = 2b + 1$, where $b = 7k + 4$, an integer. Thus, by the definition of odd integer, $7n + 9$ is odd. Consequently, $7n + 9$ is not even. Thus, proving $\sim Q \Rightarrow \sim P$, which is logically equivalent to $P \Rightarrow Q$.
>
> Therefore, "If $7n + 9$ is even, then n is odd" is proven by contrapositive.

Quantifiers and Negation

Quantifiers are phrases that include words such as *all, every, no, some, at least one, there exists,* and *there is at least one*. Quantifiers are used in statements to clarify the generality or existence of the objects in the statements relative to the universe of discourse. For example, if the universe of discourse is the set of polygons, P, then the quantifier, *All,* in the statement "All squares are rectangles" signifies that, for the statement to be true, it must be true for each and every square $\in P$, no exceptions. In contrast, the quantifier, *Some,* in the statement "Some rectangles are squares" signifies that, for the statement to be true, there must be at least one rectangle $\in P$ that is a square.

When a quantifier signals that for a statement to be true, *all* objects in the universe of discourse must make the statement true, the quantifier is a **universal quantifier,** symbolized by $\forall$. When a quantifier signals that for a statement to be true, there must *exist at least one* object in the universe of discourse that makes the statement true, the quantifier is an **existential quantifier,** symbolized by $\exists$.

Tip: To help you remember the symbols for the quantifiers, notice that the symbol $\forall$ looks like an inverted uppercase A (for *all*), and the symbol $\exists$ looks like a backward uppercase E (for *exists*).

The following table classifies common phrases as universal or existential quantifiers.

Quantifiers

Universal Quantifiers, Symbolized by $\forall$	Existential Quantifiers, Symbolized by $\exists$
all, for all, every, for every, each, for each, everything, no, nothing, not any, not all, none of these	some, for some, at least one, there exists at least one, there is at least one, there is, there are, something

For example:

> All flowers are plants. (universal)
>
> Some flowers are roses. (existential)

It is common for statements to omit quantifiers when the meaning is clear and the universal set is obvious. For example, the statement "Triangles are polygons" means "All triangles are polygons." Also, a quantifier might be disguised as another phrase. For example, the phrases "If x" and "whenever x" are denoted symbolically as $\forall x$. Be on the alert for such hidden quantifiers.

Negating statements involving quantifiers can be a challenge. Use the following conventions:

- To negate a statement that involves a universal quantifier, use an existential quantifier in a statement that contradicts the original statement.
- To negate a statement that involves an existential quantifier, use a universal quantifier in a statement that contradicts the original statement.

Four important forms involving quantifiers that you should be able to negate, with an example of each, are shown below.

Important Statement Forms

Statement Form	Negation of Statement Form	Example Statement	Negation of Example Statement
All As are Bs.	Some As are not Bs.	All polygons are squares.	Some polygons are not squares.
Some As are Bs.	No As are Bs.	Some triangles are right triangles.	No triangles are right triangles.
No As are Bs.	Some As are Bs	No real numbers are rational.	Some real numbers are rational.
Some As are not Bs.	All As are Bs.	Some primes are not odd.	All primes are odd.

The four statement forms are illustrated in the following Venn diagrams.

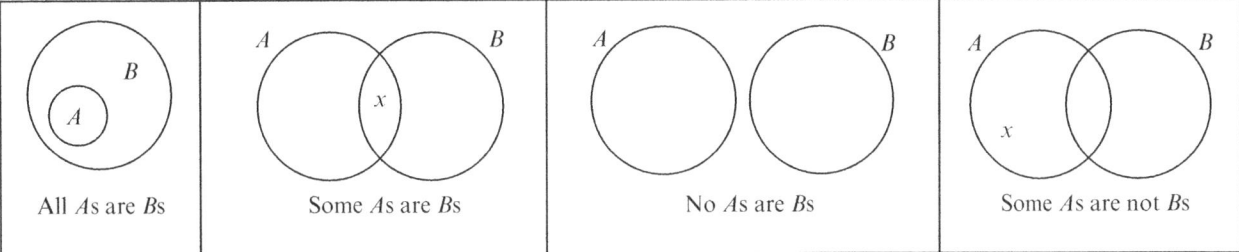

All As are Bs   Some As are Bs   No As are Bs   Some As are not Bs

Note: An x in a diagram means the region in which it is located is not empty.

Logical Reasoning

Logical reasoning involves the higher-level thinking processes that are used to make decisions or draw conclusions. Two major ways of reasoning to reach conclusions are inductive reasoning and deductive reasoning.

Inductive reasoning is the process of drawing a general conclusion based on partial information. When using inductive reasoning, you look at specific examples and try to identify a pattern or trend that fits the given examples in order to determine a general rule. For example, you might observe the coldness of a number of ice cubes and conclude (through inference) that all ice cubes are cold.

In contrast, **deductive reasoning** is the process of using an accepted rule to draw a conclusion about a specific example. When using deductive reasoning, you apply a general rule to a specific case. For example, you might start by knowing that all rectangles are parallelograms and conclude (through implication) that a square is a parallelogram because a square is a rectangle.

Syllogistic reasoning (for example, "All rectangles are parallelograms. A square is a rectangle. Therefore, a square is a parallelogram.") and **conditional reasoning** (for example, "If a figure is a rectangle, then the figure is a parallelogram. A square is a rectangle; therefore, a square is a parallelogram.") are types of deductive reasoning.

Knowing the difference between inductive and deductive reasoning is essential to evaluating arguments. An **argument** is a course of reasoning offered in support of a position. When inductive reasoning is used in an argument, inferences are used to support the position of the person making the argument. When deductive reasoning is used, accepted truths or generalizations are applied to support the favored position.

Because inductive arguments are based on observations and examples, the validity of their conclusions is always open to question. When you are evaluating inductive arguments, you should consider the reliability of the evidence, whether generalizations are adequately supported, and whether the inferences made are honest and reasonable. **Hasty generalization** (generalizing from a few atypical examples), **faulty analogy** (assuming that because two things are alike in some respects, they are alike in all respects), and **false cause** (assuming that a first thing caused a second thing because the first thing preceded the second thing in time) are examples of faulty reasoning to be watchful for when evaluating inductive arguments.

Deductive arguments use assumed generalizations or premises to logically arrive at conclusions. If the premises are true and the logic is sound, then the conclusion of the argument is valid. When you are evaluating deductive arguments, you should consider the credibility and reasonableness of the premises and the soundness of the logic used. Be on the alert for premises that are based on half-truths, exaggerated claims, or propaganda.

Also, two well-known illogical pitfalls are affirming the consequent and denying the antecedent. **Affirming the consequent** refers to assuming the first part of a conditional statement must be true when the second part is true. Here is an example: "If a person smokes, then he or she will have breathing difficulties. Tara has breathing difficulties; therefore, Tara is a smoker." This line of reasoning is illogical because Tara's breathing difficulties might be unrelated to smoking; in fact, Tara might not be a smoker at all. **Denying the antecedent** refers to assuming that when the first part of a conditional statement is not true, then the second part of the statement must also be false. Here is an example: "If a person smokes, then he or she will have breathing difficulties. Tara does not smoke; therefore, Tara does not have breathing difficulties." This reasoning is illogical because Tara might have breathing difficulties that are caused by something unrelated to smoking.

Chapter 6
Mathematical Learning, Instruction, and Assessment

This chapter is for all candidates who plan to take a TExES Math exam. It provides a review of mathematical learning, instruction, and assessment.

Mathematical Learning

For this topic, you must have an understanding of how children learn and be able to apply that understanding to mathematical instruction.

Developmentally Appropriate Practice

Effective mathematics teachers have a strong understanding of developmentally appropriate practice, and they apply this knowledge to create learning environments in which students engage in active, purposeful, and meaningful learning. They understand that as students mature, they progress through typical cognitive, social, physical, and emotional developmental stages. Moreover, effective teachers recognize that students' developmental characteristics affect their mathematics performance. Therefore, astute teachers design instruction to accommodate different learning needs and developmental levels.

Jean Piaget (in Slavin, 2008) proposed that learning involves three basic processes: *assimilation, accommodation,* and *equilibration*. **Assimilation** involves fitting new information into existing mental structures, which Piaget called **schemas. Accommodation** requires modifying current schemas or creating new schemas in order to take the new data or information into account. When children encounter new data or information, they experience **disequilibrium,** a cognitive conflict, so to speak, until they can either assimilate or accommodate it and, thus, achieve equilibrium. **Equilibrium** is present when a child's schemas can be relied on to help the child explain or understand the information being encountered. **Disequilibrium** is a result of insufficient schemas for explaining or making sense of current information. Piaget believed that disequilibrium is an unnatural state and, therefore, all learners seek equilibrium through either assimilation or accommodation when disequilibrium occurs. The process of reaching equilibrium is **equilibration.** Piaget saw the construction of meaning inherent in equilibration as the essence of learning.

Piaget concluded that children do not think like adults, nor do they see the world as adults do. According to Piaget, **cognition,** or thinking, is an active and interactive process that develops in stages. The stages of cognitive development are predictable, but the ages of children entering each stage may vary. The last two stages given below (concrete operational and formal operational) pertain to grades 4 to 12.

During the **preoperational** stage, from ages 2 to 6, children are highly imaginative, and they enjoy games of pretend. They see the world from their own points of view **(egocentric)**, focus on one aspect of a situation **(centration)**, are rapidly developing language, and are beginning to acquire some reasoning ability, although they do not infer beyond what they see. Of particular significance is the development of **symbolic thought**—the ability to mentally represent objects, events, and actions—as evidenced through the use of language and make-believe play. This period is also characterized by what children lack—**reversibility,** the ability to mentally reverse an operation, and **conservation,** the ability to recognize that number, length, quantity, area, mass, weight, and volume of objects has not necessarily changed even though the appearance of these objects might have changed. They also have difficulty distinguishing appearances from reality.

In the **concrete operational** stage, ages 7 to 11, children develop the ability to take another's point of view **(decenter)** and no longer have problems with centration, conservation, reversibility, and distinguishing appearances from reality. They can sort objects into multiple categories and, based on more than one aspect, can think of the whole and its parts simultaneously **(class inclusion)**, and can arrange objects in sequential order **(seriation)**.

They can reason logically to solve concrete problems, can reason and make inferences about reality, and can infer beyond what they see. They are able to logically reason that if *A* is related to *B* and *B* is related to *C*, then *A* is related to *C* **(transitivity)**. They acquire the ability to think about and solve problems mentally but still need concrete experiences and physical actions to make mental connections. They can think about their own thinking **(metacognition)** and use metacognitive strategies. Even though they can reason logically (for example, from cause to effect) with concrete objects, they have difficulty with abstract reasoning and hypothetical thinking.

The last stage of development, **formal operational,** begins at about age 12 and continues to adulthood. Adolescents who reach this stage begin to think more easily about **abstract concepts,** things they cannot touch or see. They can develop hypotheses, organize information, test hypotheses, and solve problems. They also can reason both deductively and inductively, make generalizations, and critically analyze the thinking of others. However, for most young adolescents, Piaget's concrete operational stage is predominant, although frequently an adolescent functions at the concrete operational stage for some topics (such as mathematical problem solving) and the formal operational stage for other topics (such as evaluating numerical expressions). Teachers should not assume that all adolescents are at the same stage developmentally or that an individual student functions at the same level in all situations. Whether all people achieve formal operational thinking at this or any other stage is still a major question to which researchers have not provided a definitive answer.

Like Piaget, Jerome Bruner (in Reinhartz and Beach, 1997) viewed learning as a process of constructing meaning by building on prior understandings. He proposed three modes through which children can learn based on their level of cognitive development:

- Up to about age 6, children primarily learn through the **enactive mode,** which involves interacting with objects in their environment.
- Elementary children (ages 6 through 11) can learn through the **iconic mode,** which involves the use of images or graphic illustrations to convey concepts.
- Older students and adults (ages 11 and above) can learn through the **symbolic mode,** which involves using symbols and words to represent concepts.

According to Bruner, when a concept is first introduced to students, teachers should structure the presentation of the concept so that it proceeds from enactive to iconic to symbolic mode. For example, in mathematics, students might first work with fraction strips, next draw pictures of fraction strips, and finally, write the symbolic representation of fractions.

Mathematical Instruction

For this topic, you must demonstrate your ability to plan and implement mathematical instruction.

Planning Mathematical Instruction

Piaget's ideas are reflected in Glenda Anthony and Margaret Walshaw's (2009) recommendations for mathematical instruction. They advised that when planning for mathematical learning, teachers should put students' current knowledge and interests at the center of their instructional decision making. Instead of trying to force concepts that are incompatible with students' cognitive development, teachers should plan learning experiences that allow students to build on their existing proficiencies, learning needs, and interests. Such teaching is responsive both to students and to the discipline of mathematics.

Effective mathematics teaching is learner-centered and emphasizes teaching for conceptual understanding, predicated on the insight that students construct knowledge by making connections between present learning experiences and the existing knowledge they already possess. It takes student competencies as starting points for planning and, also, for moment-by-moment decision making. Existing competencies, including a student's ability to cope with complexity and the student's level of mathematical reasoning, become resources to build on.

Worthwhile Mathematical Tasks

Anthony and Walshaw (2009) suggested that presenting meaningful mathematical tasks to students helps them to discover that they are capable of making sense of mathematics and can become proficient doers of mathematics. Tasks should be based on sound and significant mathematics and should be designed to provide opportunities for students to cognitively engage with important mathematical ideas.

By being aware of the thinking that goes on when their students are engaged in tasks, effective mathematics teachers are able to pose new questions or design new tasks that will challenge and extend thinking. Consider this problem: *It takes a butterfly about 2 seconds to fly 10 yards. How long should it take it to fly 110 yards?* Having observed in the past that students have solved this problem using additive thinking, a teacher might modify the task so that it is more likely to encourage multiplicative reasoning: *How long should it take the butterfly to fly 1,100 yards?* or *How long should it take a butterfly to fly 110 yards if it flies about 5 yards in 1 second?*

The ability to make connections between apparently different mathematical ideas is crucial for conceptual understanding. An elementary teacher might, for example, introduce doubles as a strategy for multiplying by 2. An algebra teacher might encourage students to generalize their knowledge of adding numerical fractions to the new context of adding algebraic fractions. Also, while students might think of fractions, decimals, and percentages as separate topics, it is important for them to recognize the interconnectedness of these numbers by exploring differing representations of the same number (for example, $\frac{1}{4} = 0.25 = 25\%$).

Additionally, effective mathematics teaching incorporates relatable real-world tasks into instruction to enhance motivation and advance student understanding. When students can envisage the situations or events in which a problem is embedded, they can use their own experiences and knowledge as a basis for developing context-related strategies that later can expand into generalized strategies. For example, young children trying to work out how to share three cookies among four children will typically use informal methods that preempt formal division procedures.

Students should do more than practice algorithms they have just been taught; rather, they should be given tasks that require them to use algorithms in ways that connect to concepts, understandings, and meaning. Nevertheless, students do need opportunities to practice what they are learning, whether it be to improve their computational fluency, problem-solving skills, or conceptual understanding. Reviewing and refining skills can often be integrated into "doing" mathematics. For example, learning addition of fractions provides opportunities for students to reinforce their understanding of factors and multiples. Real-world projects such as making mathematical-themed board games can hone skills and develop automaticity.

Mathematical Communication

Anthony and Walshaw (2009) pointed out that students need to be taught how to communicate mathematically, give sound mathematical explanations, and justify their solutions. Effective mathematics teachers model for their students how to communicate mathematical ideas orally, in writing, and by using a variety of representations. With teachers' guidance, students learn how to use mathematical ideas, language, and methods to make sense of mathematics. As a result, students focus less on finding answers and more on the mathematical thinking that leads to the answers.

Effective mathematics teachers create classroom climates in which students feel respected and valued. By ensuring safety, teachers allow students to feel comfortable thinking for themselves, asking questions, and taking intellectual risks. Students are encouraged to explain and justify their mathematical solutions against other students who might take and defend contrary positions.

Cooperative Learning in Mathematics Instruction

To acquire mathematical understandings, students need opportunities to work alone, and with partners and in small groups. Pairs and small groups allow students to develop interpersonal and small-group social skills. Paired students can help one another with both commonplace practice types of activities and also with more conceptual-based endeavors. Group learning in the form of cooperative learning instruction allows students to assume responsibility for their own learning as they work together to complete a project or activity.

Cooperative learning involves student-led small-group activities in which students work together on a collective task that has been clearly defined and explained. Students are expected to help each other learn, rather than to depend solely on the teacher. For maximum effectiveness, groups should be small—no more than four or five members—and of mixed ability. When groups include students of varying mathematical achievement, contributions come at different levels and enhance overall understandings.

Although there are variations in the application of the cooperative learning concept, according to David Johnson and Roger Johnson (2008), the five critical attributes of cooperative learning are the following:

- **Positive interdependence:** Everyone's success depends on the success of everyone else in the group.
- **Individual accountability:** Everyone in the group has to contribute and learn.
- **Group processing of social skills:** Group functioning is frequently monitored and adjusted to improve group effectiveness.
- **Face-to-face promotive interaction:** Group members facilitate and help each other by committing personal resources, encouragement, and assistance to others to achieve group goals.
- **Effective interpersonal interaction:** Group members regularly use interpersonal skills such as using appropriate tone, voice level, and turn-taking to show respect for others.

The main purpose underlying cooperative learning methods is to encourage students to help each other learn. Group members take responsibility for their own learning and for one another's learning. Teachers intervene only when necessary. The positive interdependence that is an essential component of cooperative learning is a strong motivating factor for students. Students perceive that the group "sinks or swims" together. The group incentive structure allows all students—even those who have a history of limited academic success—an opportunity to succeed, which can be highly motivating to students. Commonly, group membership should extend over a period of time to allow for intergroup responsibility and collaboration to build, although group membership should not be permanent for the entire year. Cooperative learning group activities are learner-centered, with the teacher functioning as both a facilitator to promote effective group functioning and as an academic resource.

Numerous research studies support the positive outcomes for all students when cooperative learning is used. Specifically, Marzano et al. (2000) identified cooperative learning as a high-yield instructional strategy. However, adequate training for teachers and students is necessary in order for cooperative learning to be implemented successfully. Mathematics teachers who want to use cooperative learning groups should do the following:

- Arrange the classroom furniture to support group interaction.
- Assign students to groups to ensure a mix of gender, ethnicity, linguistic level, and academic ability.
- Select tasks that students will find interesting, meaningful, and challenging and that genuinely require group effort to accomplish.
- Determine group size based on the tasks and goals for the group. For most activities, particularly problem-solving activities, groups of two to four work best.
- Present objectives as group objectives and communicate expectations clearly.
- Assign each group member a job or role.
- Make expectations of group behavior clear.
- Teach socials skills necessary for working with others (before and during activities).
- Make sure everyone understands what he or she is expected to do to make the group function well.
- Monitor group processes during activities.
- Monitor individual social skills during activities.
- Reward the group for successful completion of the task.
- Assess both group and individual performance.
- Assess group participation and cooperation using self-assessment, peer assessment, and teacher assessment.
- Always incorporate group goals and insist on individual accountability.
- Apply cooperative learning in a consistent and systematic manner but do not overuse it.

Mathematical Representations and Tools

According to Anthony and Walshaw (2009), effective mathematics teachers use a variety of mathematical representations and tools to support their students' mathematical learning. These tools include the number system itself, algebraic symbolism, graphs, diagrams, models, equations, notations, images, analogies, metaphors, stories, textbooks, and technology (including virtual manipulatives). These tools are conduits for representation, communication, reflection, and argumentation. Tools, both representations and virtual manipulatives, are helpful for communicating mathematical concepts that could otherwise be difficult to describe, talk about, or write about. They are most effective when they become integral parts of students' mathematical sense-making and reasoning. As students use tools to communicate their ideas, they develop and clarify their own thinking while providing their teachers with insight into that thinking.

Mathematics teachers must ensure that the tools they select are appropriate and used effectively. For example, Catherine Bruce et al. (2013) described circular representations of fractions as "problematic because partitioning circles equally is more difficult for odd or large numbers" (p. 11). However, with the help of appropriate tools, students can think through problems or test mathematical ideas. For example, a number line can be used to help students visualize number relationships (e.g., how far $\frac{1}{3}$ is from $\frac{1}{2}$) and ten-frame activities can show how a number can be partitioned (e.g., the part-part-whole of the number 10). Effective teachers take care when using tools, particularly predesigned physical materials such as number lines or ten-frames, to ensure that all students make the intended mathematical sense of them. They do this by modeling how the tool is used, how it represents the ideas under discussion, and how it links to operations, concepts, and symbolic representations.

An increasing array of technological tools is available for use in mathematics classrooms. These dynamic graphical, numerical, and visual applications include calculators and computers, presentation technologies such as the interactive whiteboard, mobile technologies such as clickers and data loggers, and the Internet. Used appropriately, technology can support independent inquiry and shared knowledge building. When used for mathematical investigations, technological tools can link students with the real world, making mathematics more accessible and relevant.

General Guidelines for Mathematical Instruction

When planning and implementing lessons to engage students in mathematical learning, teachers should do the following:

- Use developmentally appropriate activities and strategies.
- Routinely involve students in choosing and planning their own learning activities.
- Activate students' prior knowledge related to the concepts to be learned.
- Provide challenging experiences that actively engage students.
- Use a variety of materials and/or technologies.
- Provide meaningful experiences that reflect students' own interests and experiences.
- Routinely use hands-on, minds-on activities.
- Use activities that address students' individual needs and abilities.
- Provide opportunities for whole-group, small-group, and individual work.
- Allow opportunities for students to talk and discuss their learning among themselves and with the teacher.
- Make the learning student-centered, not teacher-focused.
- Avoid relying solely on the textbook when planning or providing limited options for students.
- Avoid using worksheets or workbooks; meaningless drills; or excessive, quiet seatwork.
- Make sure that students with special needs—for example, students receiving special education services or English language learners—participate in the lesson to the fullest extent possible.
- Offer learning activities congruent with the cultural and individual learning preferences and strengths of students.

Mathematical Assessment

Assessment is a process in which information about students' progress toward learning outcomes and performance standards is collected. Mathematical assessment should be systematic and ongoing in the classroom in both formal and informal ways.

Purpose of Mathematical Assessment

The purpose of mathematical assessment is to promote students' mathematical learning and development. Effective mathematics teachers know that assessment is most useful when it aims to help students by identifying their unique strengths and needs so as to inform teacher planning and instruction.

As mathematics teachers devise methods of assessment to measure students' mathematical knowledge and skills, they need to keep the following four major purposes of assessment in mind:

- To help students improve their performance by providing constructive feedback
- To provide students with specific criteria for success, time to respond to feedback and the quality of their work, and opportunities to self-assess and reflect on their learning
- To inform instruction by providing teachers with opportunities to align their instruction to the curriculum, reflect on the variety of learning experiences needed as they devise TEKS-based assessments, and continually adapt instruction to improve student performance based on assessment results
- To report student achievement to stakeholders interested in monitoring student performance or measuring academic accountability

(Source: Adapted from Social Studies Center for Educator Development (1999))

The most effective mathematics classroom assessments are those that are aligned directly with classroom instruction and the state mathematics curriculum and focus on student learning. Skillful mathematics teachers use a variety of assessment methods, such as observations, checklists, documentation of students' talk, interviews, anecdotal notes, collections of students' work over time, traditional teacher-made tests, self-assessment, peer assessment, and appropriate performance tasks and projects to find out how well students know, understand, and are able to apply the state curriculum. Key questions to ask about any mathematical assessment are

- Does the assessment constitute developmentally appropriate measures?
- Does the assessment align with the Mathematics TEKS and meet grade-level standards?
- Does the assessment provide multiple and varied ways for students to demonstrate understanding?
- Does the assessment provide sufficient data/information for differentiating instruction and/or providing interventions?
- Does the assessment provide sufficient data/information to determine whether instruction or interventions are effective?
- Does the assessment reflect the instructional program, the teaching resources, and the instructional method?

Three broad categories of mathematical assessment are diagnostic, formative, and summative. **Diagnostic assessment** occurs before instruction. It is used to gather information about what students already know about the topic to be taught. **Formative assessment** occurs during instruction. It provides feedback that is critical to teachers' instructional decision making. **Summative assessment** occurs after instruction has taken place at the end of an instructional unit, regular grading period, or school year.

Effective teachers are aware that careful, thoughtful, and age-appropriate assessment is important for all students. Furthermore, students assume that if something is assessed, it is important. Teachers use information collected through assessment to make decisions about students' learning strengths and needs.

Traditional Mathematical Assessments

Traditional mathematical assessments are mathematical tests composed of true-false, multiple-choice, matching, fill-in-the-blank, or constructed-response questions. Traditional mathematical assessments can provide valuable information about students' grasp of rules, facts, information, and concepts.

The key to preparing good teacher-made traditional mathematical tests is ensuring that they accurately reflect what has been taught. Mathematics teachers should try to make sure that mathematical content that was given more emphasis in class is given more weight on the test. Research on the effectiveness of testing has consistently found that tests promote learning (Slavin, 2008). This is especially true if what is to be learned is tested soon after it is introduced. The most effective tests are those given frequently and at consistent intervals. Furthermore, frequent cumulative tests result in more learning than infrequent tests or tests given only on content covered since the last test.

Planned review and practice activities before testing also are important. These activities might include games, role-playing, simulations, computer-based exercises, hands-on practice assignments, self-checks, or quizzes. Review activities and materials should be logical extensions of instruction and should involve frequent feedback from the teacher. Most of the time, reviews should be done in pairs or groups to encourage active engagement and communication among students. Frequent short reviews, spaced over time, are more effective than concentrated practice. Moreover, weekly or monthly reviews of previously learned material will help students' retention.

When designing a mathematics test, teachers must decide what form the test questions will take. In selecting a format for the test, teachers need to consider the degree of objectivity of the test questions. **Objective** questions depend less on teacher judgment when grading, and **subjective** questions require more teacher judgment in the scoring process. In general, multiple-choice, matching, fill-in-the-blank, and true-false questions are considered objective. Constructed-response questions fall into the subjective category. To reduce inconsistency in grading, teachers should try to design tests so that subjectivity in grading is minimized.

Alternative Mathematical Assessments

Effective teachers integrate assessment into everyday classroom practice and real contexts. Alternative assessments employ multiple measures, including more authentic classroom assessments of students such as performance observations (in person, by videotape, and/or audiotape); work samples (tests, papers, and projects); process observations and products; interviews; and portfolios. **Authentic mathematical assessment** incorporates real-life mathematical application tasks and enables the teacher to directly assess meaningful and complex educational performances. In theory, authentic mathematical assessment is more likely to possess validity than traditional assessment methods because it allows the teacher to directly observe what the student has learned. Following are some commonly used alternative classroom assessment methods.

Instructionally embedded mathematical assessment (also called **teacher observation**) uses systematic observational methods along with checklists, interviews, and questioning while students are engaged in mathematical learning activities.

A mathematics **portfolio** is a meaningful collection of a student's mathematics work. It provides various and comprehensive summaries of the student's mathematical performance in particular contexts. Portfolio assessment requires students to collect and reflect on examples of their mathematics work and provide documentation of what they can do. Teachers also can select pieces of a student's mathematics work to include in the portfolio. Keeping a mathematics portfolio is one of the best ways for students to engage in assessing their mathematics progress over time.

Projects or **products** include drawings, models, audio recordings, videos, PowerPoint presentations, and other mechanisms that allow students to demonstrate their acquisition of mathematical knowledge and skills.

A **checklist** of mathematical skills is an assessment tool that can be used by teachers or students to monitor learning.

Conferences and **interviews** provide an opportunity for the teacher to discuss and question a student about what the student knows and is able to do with respect to a specific mathematics topic. These methods also can be used between students.

Mathematics journals and **notebooks** provide a way for students to respond in writing to a prompt by the teacher and to reflect on their own mathematical learning.

Two other mathematical assessment methods used by teachers are student self-assessment and peer-assessment. **Student self-assessment** is performed by the student. Students can assess themselves in many ways, such as grading their own papers, group participation, and portfolio assessment. **Peer assessment** is assessment by students of their classmates' mathematics work. Generally, student self-assessment and peer assessment lack validity due to factors such as the assessor's immaturity and lack of expertise. Nevertheless, students benefit from involvement in mathematical self-assessment and peer assessment because these forms of assessment give students opportunities to develop their critical thinking and evaluation-level thinking skills.

Mathematics Homework

Another way for mathematics teachers to find out what students have learned is through homework assignments. Homework is a research-based, high-yield instructional strategy (Marzano et al., 2000). Studies indicate that carefully prepared and implemented homework assignments positively impact student achievement. In the elementary and middle school grades, students should be given mathematics homework to help them develop good study habits, develop positive attitudes toward school, and realize that learning is something that happens not only at school but also at home. By the time students reach high school, the purpose of giving mathematics homework is primarily to improve their academic achievement in mathematics. Further, homework is a valuable tool that allows parents to monitor their child's learning activities.

When mathematics homework is given as independent practice, it should

- be viewed as an integral part of mathematical instruction.
- be appropriate for the ability and maturity level of the students.
- be closely tied to what was taught in class.
- have a clearly articulated purpose.
- be worthwhile (not meaningless worksheets).
- be coordinated with what the students' other teachers are requiring them to do.
- be given immediately after presentation of the mathematical topic.
- be given frequently as a means of extending learning beyond the classroom.
- be carefully prepared and accompanied by concise written instructions, if needed.
- be clearly understood by the students before they leave class.
- be frequently checked orally in class.
- be checked and returned to students in a timely manner, when collected.
- be returned with feedback that informs the students about what they are doing correctly and what they still need to work on.
- be successfully completed by most of the students.
- *never* be given as punishment.

Regardless of grade level, teachers should have written homework policies (that might be obtained from the school or district). Students and parents should be provided copies of a teacher's homework policy, and the parent should be asked to return a signed acknowledgment of receipt of the policy. For students in elementary and middle school, the mathematics teachers should provide parents information about assignments and elicit their support to encourage completion of mathematics homework and monitor their child's study time. When a student consistently fails to complete mathematics homework assignments, parental contact is essential, and an appropriate plan to remediate the problem should be developed in consultation with the student, parent, and teacher. This plan should be appropriate to the student's needs and home environment.

Students' Errors

Effective mathematics teachers view students' errors as learning opportunities. Anthony and Walshaw (2009) explained that students make mistakes for many reasons, including insufficient time or carelessness. But errors also can arise from students' attempts to negotiate meaning from misconceptions of mathematical ideas. Rather than dismiss such attempts as "wrong-headed," perceptive mathematics teachers view them as a natural and often necessary stage in learners' conceptual development. For example, young children often transfer the result that multiplying by a whole number makes something larger to their initial attempts to understand multiplication by a unit fraction. Effective teachers take such misconceptions and use them as building blocks for developing deeper understandings.

There are many ways in which teachers can provide opportunities for students to learn from their errors. One way is to facilitate whole-class discussions that focus students' attention on difficulties that have surfaced or simply on possible errors that some students are likely to make. Another is to ask students to share their solution strategies so that they can compare and critique their own thinking. Of course, it's taken for granted that a classroom culture of openness and trust is essential for these activities.

At the same time, for students to learn, they need to know whether what they are doing is correct. Validating students' correct responses with appropriate reinforcement such as simple acknowledgment, class agreement, or specific, preferably private, praise makes students aware of their own understanding. Teachers should provide timely, specific feedback based on clear and appropriate criteria. Feedback informs the students about what they are doing correctly and what they still need to work on. Moreover, teachers know how to help students use feedback to manage and direct their own learning.

When students respond incorrectly, the teacher uses a variety of strategies such as probing, restating or rephrasing the question, or asking a leading question to encourage students to take chances and keep trying. When possible, the teacher should try to find something positive to point out about the student's response prior to pointing out errors, even if it is simply to commend the student for trying.

To correct student errors, teachers use strategies that include constructive feedback, modeling, providing an explanation of additional information, or probing by asking additional questions. Corrections often provide the opportunity to discuss common errors associated with the situation. For some teachers, it is not easy to criticize students; however, teachers can be honest without humiliating or disparaging students. Providing criticism is important so that students do not internalize misinformation or become perplexed about key concepts. Often probing, prompting, asking a follow-up question, or revoicing (that is, stating in the teacher's own words) the student's response can result in the student self-correcting his or her own error, thereby taking responsibility for correction from the teacher and allowing the student the opportunity to experience success.

References

Anthony, G., and Walshaw, M. (2009). *Effective Pedagogy in Mathematics*. Retrieved from http://www.ibe.unesco.org/fileadmin/user_upload/Publications/Educational_Practices/EdPractices_19.pdf.

Bruce, C., Chang, D., Flynn, T., and Yearley, S. (2013). *Foundations to Learning and Teaching Fractions: Addition and Subtraction*. Retrieved from http://www.edugains.ca/resources/ProfessionalLearning/FoundationstoLearningandTeachingFractions.pdf.

Johnson, D., and Johnson, R. (2008). *An Overview of Cooperative Learning*. Retrieved from https://www.ioe-rdnetwork.com/uploads/2/1/6/3/21631832/johnson_and_johnson_an_overview_of_cooperative_learning.pdf.

Marzano, R., Gaddy, B., and Dean, C. (2000). *What Works in Classroom Instruction.* Retrieved from www.sinc.stonybrook.edu/Class/est572td/whatworks/whatworks.pdf.

Reinhartz, J., and Beach, D. (1997). *Teaching and Learning in the Elementary School: Focus on Curriculum.* Upper Saddle River, NJ: Merrill.

Slavin, R. (2008). *Educational Psychology*, 9th Edition. Boston: Allyn and Bacon.

Social Studies Center for Educator Development. (1999). *Texas Social Studies Framework: Kindergarten-Grade 12.* Austin, TX: Texas Education Agency.

Definitions and Formulas

CALCULUS

First Derivative: $f'(x) = \dfrac{dy}{dx}$

Second Derivative: $f''(x) = \dfrac{d^2 y}{dx^2}$

PROBABILITY

$P(A \text{ or } B) = P(A) + P(B) - P(A \text{ and } B)$
$P(A \text{ and } B) = P(A)P(B|A) = P(B)P(A|B)$

ALGEBRA

$i \qquad i^2 = -1$

$A^{-1} \qquad$ inverse of matrix A

$A = P\left(1 + \dfrac{r}{n}\right)^{nt} \qquad$ Compound interest, where A is the final value, P is the principal, r is the interest rate, t is the term, and n is the number of divisions within the term

$[x] = n \qquad$ Greatest integer function, where n is the greatest integer such that $n \leq x < n + 1$

GEOMETRY

Congruent Angles

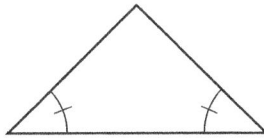

Congruent Sides

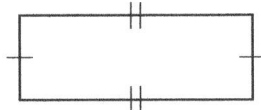

Parallel Sides

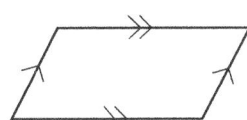

Circumference of a Circle
$C = 2\pi r$

VOLUME

Cylinder: (area of base) × height

Cone: $\dfrac{1}{3}$(area of base) × height

Sphere: $\dfrac{4}{3}\pi r^3$

Prism: (area of base) × height

AREA

Triangle: $\dfrac{1}{2}(\text{base} \times \text{height})$

Rhombus: $\dfrac{1}{2}(\text{diagonal}_1 \times \text{diagonal}_2)$

Trapezoid: $\dfrac{1}{2}\text{height}(\text{base}_1 + \text{base}_2)$

Sphere: $4\pi r^2$

Circle: πr^2

Lateral surface area of cylinder: $2\pi rh$

TRIGONOMETRY

Law of Sines: $\dfrac{\sin A}{a} = \dfrac{\sin B}{b} = \dfrac{\sin C}{c}$

Law of Cosines:
$c^2 = a^2 + b^2 - 2ab \cos C$
$b^2 = a^2 + c^2 - 2ac \cos B$
$a^2 = b^2 + c^2 - 2bc \cos A$

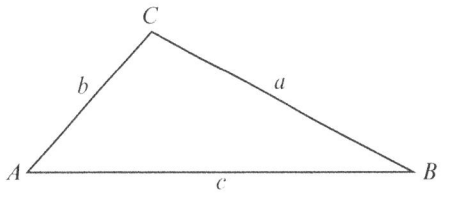

End of Definitions and Formulas

Chapter 7

TExES Math 4–8 Practice Test 1

100 Questions
Time—4 Hours 45 Minutes

Directions: Read the directions for each question carefully. For each question, select the best single answer choice unless written instructions in the question state otherwise.

---

1. Zoey and Jax both swam in the indoor pool at Gold Star Gym today. Zoey swims at Gold Star Gym every 12 days. Jax swims there every 15 days. If both continue with their regular swimming schedules at Gold Star Gym, the next time both will swim there on the same day is in how many days?

   Ⓐ 12
   Ⓑ 15
   Ⓒ 30
   Ⓓ 60

2. For which of the following expressions is $a - b$ a factor?

   Select <u>all</u> that apply.

   ☐ A $a^2 - b^2$
   ☐ B $a^2 - ab + b^2$
   ☐ C $a^3 - b^3$
   ☐ D $a^3 - 3a^2b + 3ab^2 - b^3$

Use the table below to answer question 3.

Determination of Course Grade	Percent
Average (mean) of three major exams	50%
Average (mean) of weekly quizzes	10%
Final exam score	40%

3. A student is trying to achieve an average of at least 80 to earn a grade of B in a college course. In determining the course grade, the instructor calculates a weighted average as shown in the table above. The student has scores of 72, 81, and 75 on the three major exams and an average of 92 on the weekly quizzes. What is the *lowest* score the student can make on the final exam and still receive a B in the course?

   Ⓐ 78
   Ⓑ 80
   Ⓒ 82
   Ⓓ 84

4. If $xy \neq 0$, then $\dfrac{3}{x} + \dfrac{4}{y} =$

   Ⓐ $\dfrac{12}{xy}$
   Ⓑ $\dfrac{7}{x+y}$
   Ⓒ $\dfrac{7}{xy}$
   Ⓓ $\dfrac{4x+3y}{xy}$

5. Which of the following expressions is equivalent to $\left(x^2+4\right)^{-\frac{1}{2}}$?

   Ⓐ $-\dfrac{x^2+4}{2}$
   Ⓑ $-\sqrt{x^2+4}$
   Ⓒ $\dfrac{1}{\sqrt{x^2+4}}$
   Ⓓ $\dfrac{1}{x+2}$

6. A trip of 204 miles requires 8.5 gallons of gasoline. At this rate, how many gallons of gasoline would be required for a trip of 228 miles?

   Ⓐ 9
   Ⓑ 9.5
   Ⓒ 10
   Ⓓ 10.5

7. $4^x + 12^x =$

   Ⓐ $4^x(1+3^x)$
   Ⓑ $4(5^x)$
   Ⓒ 16^x
   Ⓓ 16^{2x}

GO ON TO THE NEXT PAGE

8. If x and y are nonzero real numbers, which of the following statements must be true?

Select all that apply.

- [A] $|x| = -|-x|$
- [B] $\left|\dfrac{x}{y}\right| = \dfrac{|x|}{|y|}$
- [C] $|x| = \sqrt{(-x)^2}$
- [D] $|x + y| = |x| + |y|$

9. The whole number y is exactly three times the whole number x. The whole number z is the sum of x and y. Which of the following could be the value of z?

Select all that apply.

- [A] 314
- [B] 416
- [C] 524
- [D] 1,032

10. $2x^3y(x + 3)(3x - 1) =$

- Ⓐ $3x^2 + 8x - 3$
- Ⓑ $6x^5y - 16x^4y - 6x^3y$
- Ⓒ $6x^5y + 16x^4y - 6x^3y$
- Ⓓ $6x^6y + 16x^5y - 6x^3y$

11. Solve $2x(x - 2) = 1$.

- Ⓐ $x = \dfrac{1}{2}$ or 3
- Ⓑ $x = 1 \pm \sqrt{6}$
- Ⓒ $x = \dfrac{-2 \pm \sqrt{6}}{2}$
- Ⓓ $x = \dfrac{2 \pm \sqrt{6}}{2}$

Use the system of equations below to answer question 12.

$$3y = 2x - 16$$
$$4x + 5y = 10$$

12. What is the y value of the ordered pair that is a solution to the system shown?

- Ⓐ -5
- Ⓑ -2
- Ⓒ 2
- Ⓓ 5

13. A pharmacist measures the mass of a medical substance and uses the appropriate number of significant figures to record the mass as 10 grams, to the nearest gram. Which of the following ways most accurately expresses the range of possible values of the mass of the substance?

- Ⓐ $10 \text{ g} \pm 0.1 \text{ g}$
- Ⓑ $10 \text{ g} \pm 0.5 \text{ g}$
- Ⓒ $10 \text{ g} \pm 1.0 \text{ g}$
- Ⓓ $10 \text{ g} \pm 0.0 \text{ g}$

14. A carpenter needs to drill a hole in a triangular piece of wood so that the hole is equidistant from each side of the triangle. Which of the following constructions could the carpenter do to determine the location of the hole?

- Ⓐ Find the intersection of the bisectors of the three angles.
- Ⓑ Find the intersection of the three altitudes of the triangle.
- Ⓒ Find the intersection of the perpendicular bisectors of the three sides.
- Ⓓ Find the intersection of the three medians of the triangle.

Use the figure below to answer question 15.

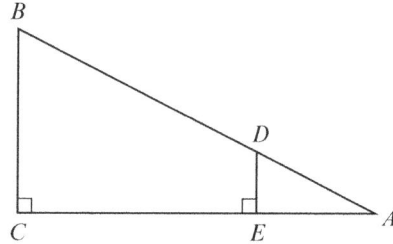

15. In the figure shown, $\overline{CE}$ has length 200 meters, $\overline{EA}$ has length 100 meters, and $\overline{DE}$ is perpendicular to $\overline{AC}$ and has length 50 meters. What is the area, in m², of $\triangle ABC$?

- Ⓐ 7,500
- Ⓑ 15,000
- Ⓒ 22,500
- Ⓓ 45,000

GO ON TO THE NEXT PAGE

Use the figure below to answer question 16.

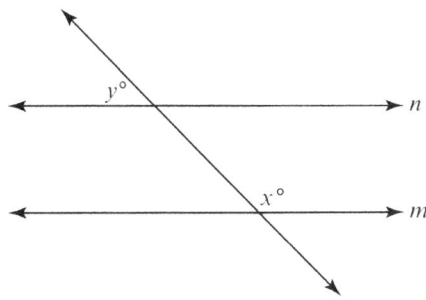

16. In the figure above, lines *m* and *n* are parallel and $x = 8y$. What is the value of *x*?

Ⓐ 10
Ⓑ 20
Ⓒ 160
Ⓓ 170

17. A length of cable is attached to the top of a 15-foot vertical pole. The cable is anchored 8 feet from the base of the pole. What is the length, in feet, of the cable?

Ⓐ 17
Ⓑ 20
Ⓒ 21
Ⓓ 23

Use the figure below to answer question 18.

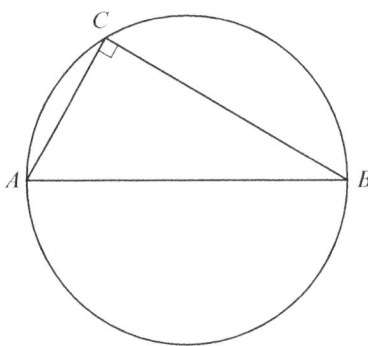

18. In the figure, the circle circumscribed about the right triangle has a radius of 5.5 centimeters. What is the length, in centimeters, of the hypotenuse of the right triangle?

Ⓐ 11
Ⓑ 5.5π
Ⓒ 11π
Ⓓ It cannot be determined from the information given.

19. A solid cube of silver has edges 4 centimeters

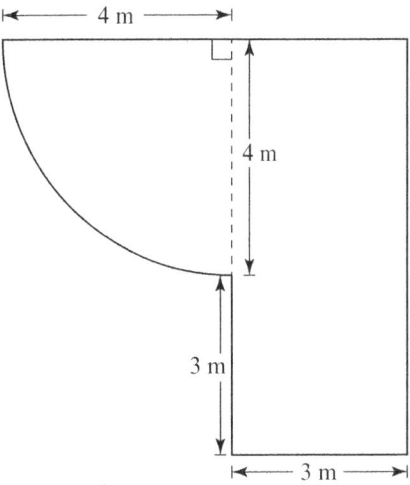

long. A metallurgist melts the cube down and uses all the molten silver to make two smaller identical solid cubes. What is the length, in centimeters, of an edge of one of the smaller cubes?

Ⓐ 2
Ⓑ $2\sqrt{2}$
Ⓒ $2\sqrt[3]{2}$
Ⓓ $2\sqrt[3]{4}$

Use the figure below to answer question 20.

20. The figure in the diagram consists of a fourth of a circle and a rectangle with the dimensions shown. What is the approximate area, in m², of the figure?

Ⓐ 21
Ⓑ 34
Ⓒ 41
Ⓓ 64

21. For disaster relief in a fire-damaged area, $1.6 billion is needed. This amount of money is approximately equivalent to spending $1 per second for how many years?

Ⓐ 10
Ⓑ 50
Ⓒ 100
Ⓓ 500

GO ON TO THE NEXT PAGE

Use the figure below to answer question 22.

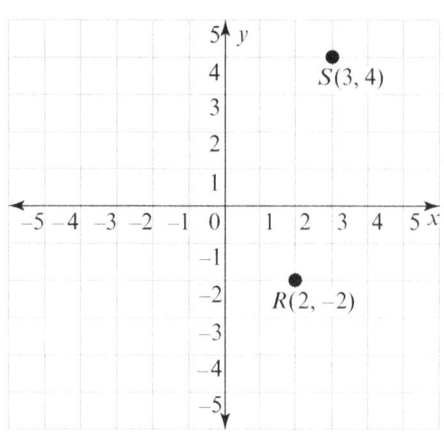

22. What is the midpoint of the line segment connecting the two points *R* and *S* shown above?

- Ⓐ (1, 6)
- Ⓑ (5, 2)
- Ⓒ (2.5, 1)
- Ⓓ (0.5, 3)

23. Which of the following sets of ordered pairs represents a function?

Select <u>all</u> that apply.

- A {(4, 5), (3, 1), (3, 10), (−2, 0)}
- B {(5, 5), (5^2, 5), (5^3, 5^3), (5^4, 5^4)}
- C {(2, 3), (4, 3), (8, 3), (16, 3)}
- D {(0, 0)}

24. Solution A contains 3×10^{-2} grams of salt. Solution B contains 6×10^2 grams of salt. The number of grams of salt in solution B is how many times the number of grams of salt in solution A?

- Ⓐ 0.0002
- Ⓑ 200
- Ⓒ 2,000
- Ⓓ 20,000

25. Determine the domain D_f and the range R_f of the function $y = \dfrac{x^2 + 40x - 500}{500}$, where *x* is a real number between 500 and 750.

- Ⓐ $D_f = \{x \mid 500 < x < 750\}$; $R_f = \{y \mid 539 < y < 1{,}184\}$
- Ⓑ $D_f = \{x \mid x \in \text{Real numbers}\}$; $R_f = \{y \mid 539 < y < 1{,}184\}$
- Ⓒ $D_f = \{y \mid 539 < y < 1{,}184\}$; $R_f = \{x \mid 500 < x < 750\}$
- Ⓓ $D_f = \{x \mid 500 < x < 750\}$; $R_f = \{y \mid y \in \text{Real numbers}\}$

26. Using data collected through experimentation, a social scientist develops a function $y = f(x)$ that relates hours of sleep *y* to age *x*. In addition to being a relation, which of the following statements MUST be true about the function?

- Ⓐ It has a smooth graph with no cusps or jagged edges.
- Ⓑ Every *y* value has one and only one *x* value.
- Ⓒ The graph of the function passes through the origin.
- Ⓓ It gives a single value for hours of sleep for each value in the age range.

27. How many different ways can four people sit in four of seven empty identical chairs that are placed in a row?

- Ⓐ 24
- Ⓑ 35
- Ⓒ 840
- Ⓓ 5,040

28. A line passes through the point (0, 5) and is perpendicular to the line that has equation $x - 3y = 10$. Which of the following equations represents the line?

- Ⓐ $x + 3y = 5$
- Ⓑ $x - 3y = 5$
- Ⓒ $3x + y = 5$
- Ⓓ $-3x + y = 5$

29. Given the cubic function $f(x) = x^3$, which of the following best describes the function $g(x) = (x-2)^3$?

- Ⓐ The same as the graph of $f(x) = x^3$ shifted up by 2 units
- Ⓑ The same as the graph of $f(x) = x^3$ shifted down by 2 units
- Ⓒ The same as the graph of $f(x) = x^3$ shifted right by 2 units
- Ⓓ The same as the graph of $f(x) = x^3$ shifted left by 2 units

30. If $f(x) = \dfrac{2x+6}{x+2}$ and $g(x) = x+2$, then $(g \circ f)(x) = g(f(x)) =$

- Ⓐ $\dfrac{4x+10}{x+2}$
- Ⓑ $\dfrac{2x+10}{x+4}$
- Ⓒ $\dfrac{4x+8}{x+2}$
- Ⓓ $\dfrac{2x+8}{x+4}$

31. Araceli has participated in eight track meets so far this season. Her running times for the 400-meter race have been 73, 63, 68, 64, 69, 61, 66, and 64 seconds. What is Araceli's median running time, in seconds, for the eight meets?

- Ⓐ 64
- Ⓑ 65
- Ⓒ 66
- Ⓓ 66.5

Use the table below to answer question 32.

Book Genre Preference

Genre	Number of Students
Biography/Historical Nonfiction	44
Historical Fiction	58
Mystery	64
Science/Nature Informational	50
Science Fiction/Fantasy	104
Total	320

32. The table shows the results of a poll of young readers regarding what genre of books they read most often. If a circle graph is constructed using the data in the table, what central angle should be used to represent the category Science Fiction/Fantasy?

- Ⓐ 100°
- Ⓑ 104°
- Ⓒ 117°
- Ⓓ 243°

Use the figure below to answer question 33.

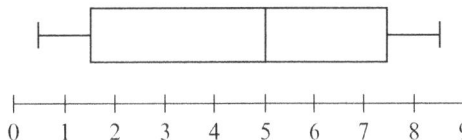

33. In the box plot shown above, the vertical line at 5 indicates that 5 is which of the following?

- Ⓐ The median
- Ⓑ The mean
- Ⓒ The first quartile
- Ⓓ The third quartile

GO ON TO THE NEXT PAGE

Use the table below to answer question 34.

Grade Level	Has a Cell Phone	Has No Cell Phone
Ninth	55	45
Tenth	70	30
Eleventh	78	22
Twelfth	95	5

34. The data in the table above show cell phone status by grade level of 400 high school students. If one of the 400 students is randomly selected, what is the probability that the student has a cell phone, given that the student is a ninth-grader?

Ⓐ $\dfrac{149}{800}$

Ⓑ $\dfrac{11}{100}$

Ⓒ $\dfrac{11}{80}$

Ⓓ $\dfrac{11}{20}$

Use the figure below to answer question 35.

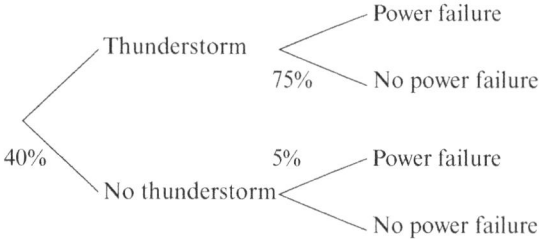

35. The partially completed probability diagram shown above represents the incidence of power failure during weather in which a thunderstorm might or might not develop. What is the probability that a thunderstorm develops and a power failure occurs?

Ⓐ 2%
Ⓑ 15%
Ⓒ 65%
Ⓓ 85%

36. Only one of 10 remote controls in a box is defective. The remote controls are tested one at a time. If the first three remote controls tested are not defective, what is the probability that the fourth remote control tested is defective?

Ⓐ $\dfrac{1}{10}$

Ⓑ $\dfrac{1}{7}$

Ⓒ $\dfrac{7}{10}$

Ⓓ $\dfrac{9}{10}$

37. What is the value of $f(3)$ for the recursive sequence defined by

$f(0) = 5$,

$f(n) = 2f(n-1) + 1$ for $n \geq 1$?

Ⓐ 11
Ⓑ 23
Ⓒ 47
Ⓓ 95

38. If both digits and letters can repeat, which of the following computations can be used to determine how many different license plate alphanumeric codes consisting of three digits followed by three uppercase letters of the English alphabet are possible?

Ⓐ $(3)(3)$
Ⓑ $(_{10}C_3)(_{26}C_3)$
Ⓒ $(10^3)(26^3)$
Ⓓ 36^6

39. A high school club has 50 members. A committee of four members is to be selected to attend a national conference. How many different committees could be formed from the 50 club members?

Ⓐ 100
Ⓑ 200
Ⓒ 230,300
Ⓓ 55,527,200

GO ON TO THE NEXT PAGE

40. A small motor uses $3\frac{1}{4}$ gallons of gasoline every 15 hours. What is the motor's rate in gallons per day?

Ⓐ 4.6
Ⓑ 5.2
Ⓒ 9.2
Ⓓ 10.4

41. Which of the following statements correctly describes the graph of the function f defined by $5x - 3y = 15$?

Select *all* that apply.

☐ A The graph has slope of $-\frac{3}{5}$.

☐ B The graph has slope of $\frac{5}{3}$.

☐ C The graph's x intercept is 3.
☐ D The graph's y intercept is 5.

42. Set A consists of all positive integers that are multiples of 4. Set B consists of all 2-digit positive integers that are less than 100 and have a units digit of 8. How many integers are in the intersection of sets A and B?

Ⓐ 2
Ⓑ 3
Ⓒ 4
Ⓓ 5

43. The sum of three consecutive odd integers is 40 less than 5 times the least of the integers. What is the value of the middle integer?

Ⓐ 21
Ⓑ 23
Ⓒ 25
Ⓓ 27

Use the figure below to answer question 44.

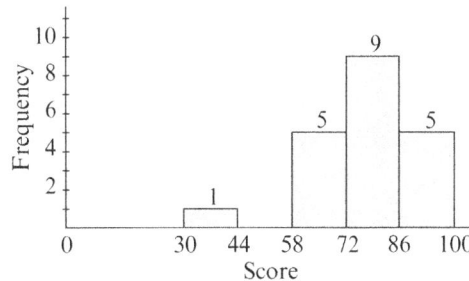

44. The histogram summarizes the scores of 20 sixth-grade students on a social studies test. Based on the histogram, which of the following statements about the social studies test scores can be determined conclusively to be correct?

Select *all* that apply.

☐ A The mean score of the 20 students is less than their median score.
☐ B The modal score of the 20 students is 79.
☐ C The lowest score on the test was 30.
☐ D The highest score on the test was 100.

Use the stem-and-leaf plot below to answer question 45.

Weights, in Pounds, of 35 Members of a Fitness Club

Stem	Leaf
12	3 8 8
13	1 3 4 4 5 6 8
14	0 0 2 4 5 5 7 7 7 8 9
15	0 1 3 3 5 6 7 8 9 9
16	1 2 2 9
Legend: 12|3 = 123	

45. The stem-and-leaf plot above displays the weights of 35 members of a fitness club. What is the median weight, in pounds, of the 35 members?

Ⓐ 137
Ⓑ 140
Ⓒ 147
Ⓓ 149

GO ON TO THE NEXT PAGE

46. The mean of six different positive integers is 73. Four of the integers are 48, 53, 61, and 82. What is the maximum possible value of the largest of the six integers?

- Ⓐ 82
- Ⓑ 83
- Ⓒ 193
- Ⓓ 194

47. According to a survey of 200 students, 75 are enrolled in an English course and 52 are enrolled in a history course. Of those surveyed, 34 are enrolled in an English course, but not in a history course. How many students are enrolled in neither an English course nor a history course?

- Ⓐ 41
- Ⓑ 73
- Ⓒ 86
- Ⓓ 114

48. Rose took a cab from the airport to her home. She gave the cab driver $38.50, which included the fare and a tip of $5. The cab company charges $3.50 for the first mile and $1.50 for each additional half-mile after that. How many miles is Rose's home from the airport?

- Ⓐ 10 miles
- Ⓑ 11 miles
- Ⓒ 20 miles
- Ⓓ 21 miles

49. Working alone at its constant rate, Machine 1 produces $40x$ electrical components in 10 hours. Working alone at its constant rate, Machine 2 produces $40x$ electrical components in 15 hours. How many hours does it take machines 1 and 2, working simultaneously at their respective constant rates, to produce $40x$ electrical components?

- Ⓐ 5 hours
- Ⓑ 6 hours
- Ⓒ $8\frac{1}{4}$ hours
- Ⓓ $12\frac{1}{2}$ hours

Use the figure below to answer question 50.

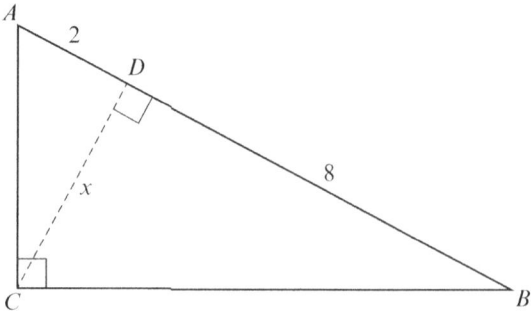

50. In the figure above, $\overline{CD}$ is an altitude of right triangle ABC, $AD = 2$, and $DB = 8$. Find the perimeter of $\triangle ABC$.

- Ⓐ $16\sqrt{5}$
- Ⓑ $10 + 6\sqrt{5}$
- Ⓒ $10 + 2\sqrt{5}$
- Ⓓ It cannot be determined from the information given.

51. In the xy-plane, the graphs defined by $f(x) = \dfrac{x^2 + x - 6}{(x+3)}$ and $g(x) = 2.5x + 2.5$ intersect in how many distinct points?

- Ⓐ 0
- Ⓑ 1
- Ⓒ 2
- Ⓓ 4

52. The enrollment at a small community college for the fall semester is 10% higher than the enrollment in the fall semester a year ago. The number of female students increased by 5% and the number of male students increased by 20%. Female students make up what fraction of the current enrollment at the community college?

- Ⓐ $\dfrac{1}{4}$
- Ⓑ $\dfrac{1}{3}$
- Ⓒ $\dfrac{7}{11}$
- Ⓓ $\dfrac{2}{3}$

53. The number 200 lies between $\frac{1}{4}x$ and $\frac{1}{3}x$.

Which of the following numbers could be values of x?

Select all that apply.

- A 550
- B 650
- C 750
- D 850

54. If $\frac{1}{3^x} = \frac{1}{3^n} + \frac{1}{3^n} + \frac{1}{3^n}$, then x expressed in terms of n is

- Ⓐ $n - 1$
- Ⓑ $n + 1$
- Ⓒ $3n$
- Ⓓ n^3

55. In the equation $y = \frac{k}{x}$, x and y are both positive and k is a constant. If y increases by $\frac{1}{2}$ of its value, then the value of x decreases by what fraction of its value?

- Ⓐ $\frac{1}{4}$
- Ⓑ $\frac{1}{3}$
- Ⓒ $\frac{1}{2}$
- Ⓓ $\frac{2}{3}$

Use the figure below to answer question 56.

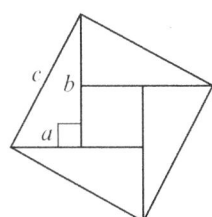

56. A teacher shares the above figure with the students during a geometry lesson. What geometric concept are the learners investigating?

- Ⓐ The Pythagorean theorem
- Ⓑ The triangle inequality
- Ⓒ Exterior angle theorem
- Ⓓ 30°-60°-90° triangle theorem

57. Which of the following figures is a net for a cube?

Select all that apply.

A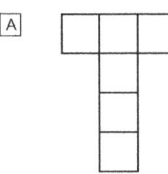

B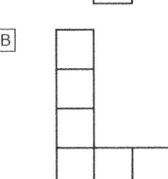

C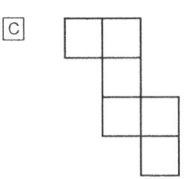

D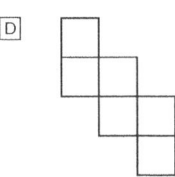

58. The number 144 has how many positive factors?

- Ⓐ 6
- Ⓑ 8
- Ⓒ 15
- Ⓓ 30

59. Using a protractor, a student measures the acute angles in a right triangle and then adds the two measurements to obtain a sum of 81°. What is the percent error of the sum?

- Ⓐ 0.10%
- Ⓑ 0.11%
- Ⓒ 10%
- Ⓓ 11%

GO ON TO THE NEXT PAGE

Use the figure below to answer question 60.

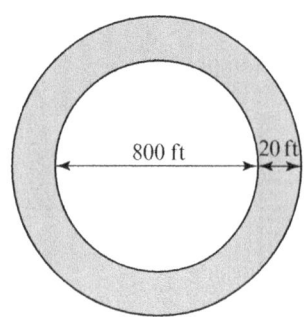

60. The figure above shows two concentric circles. Find the area, in ft², of the shaded region.

- Ⓐ $8,100\pi$
- Ⓑ $16,400\pi$
- Ⓒ $32,400\pi$
- Ⓓ $65,600\pi$

61. On a number line, line segment x has endpoints $6\frac{1}{4}$ and $6\frac{1}{2}$, and line segment y has endpoints $\frac{5}{\sqrt{8}}$ and $\frac{3}{\sqrt{2}}$. What is the ratio of the length of y to the length of x?

- Ⓐ $\frac{1}{\sqrt{2}}$
- Ⓑ $\sqrt{2}$
- Ⓒ $\frac{4}{\sqrt{2}}$
- Ⓓ $4\sqrt{2}$

62. The ratio of the volume of sphere A to the volume of sphere B is 27 to 1. What is the ratio of the surface area of sphere A to the surface area of sphere B?

- Ⓐ 3 to 1
- Ⓑ 6 to 1
- Ⓒ 9 to 1
- Ⓓ 27 to 1

63. A 40-foot cable is attached to the outside wall of a four-story building. One end of the cable is anchored 24 feet from the base of the building. How high up (in feet) on the outside wall of the building does the other end of the cable reach?

- Ⓐ 16
- Ⓑ 32
- Ⓒ 36
- Ⓓ 47

Use the figure below to answer question 64.

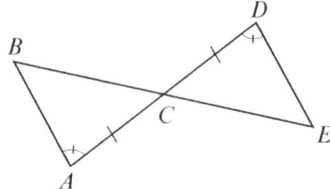

64. In the figure above, $\angle A \cong \angle D$ and $\overline{BE}$ bisects $\overline{AD}$. Of the following methods, which should be used to show $\triangle ABC$ is congruent to $\triangle DEC$?

- Ⓐ SSS
- Ⓑ SAS
- Ⓒ AAA
- Ⓓ ASA

65. If the surface area of a sphere is 144π cm², find the volume, in cm³, of the sphere.

- Ⓐ 36
- Ⓑ 288
- Ⓒ 216π
- Ⓓ 288π

66. Students in a seventh-grade mathematics class are learning to solve one-variable linear equations. Of the following methods, which is the most appropriate way for the teacher to assess the students' understanding of this procedure?

- Ⓐ Use an observational checklist.
- Ⓑ Give a short quiz.
- Ⓒ Have students complete a worksheet.
- Ⓓ Have the students complete an online homework assignment.

GO ON TO THE NEXT PAGE

67. In keeping with a desire to foster higher-order thinking and enhance problem-solving skills, which of the following strategies would be LEAST desirable for a mathematics teacher to use?

- Ⓐ Establish a highly managed classroom environment that focuses on procedural knowledge.
- Ⓑ Encourage students to take time to think before deciding on a solution strategy when they are initially given a word problem.
- Ⓒ Spend more class time on problems requiring analytical skills than on basic computational problems.
- Ⓓ Provide opportunities for students to correct their errors rather than expecting them to rely on the teacher to determine whether their work is mathematically correct.

68. Which of the following activities involving decimals in fourth grade is consistent with effective teaching practices?

Select all that apply.

- Ⓐ Working individually and with partners, students solve teacher-posed real-world problems involving decimals.
- Ⓑ As a whole class, students design a project focused on decimals.
- Ⓒ As the teacher models problem solving involving decimals, students take notes and practice with the teacher.
- Ⓓ Students copy decimal problems from the textbook and use calculators to obtain the answers.

Use the graph below to answer question 69.

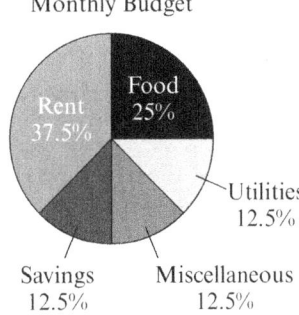

69. The graph shows a budget for a monthly salary after taxes. If the monthly salary is $2,800, how much money is budgeted for food?

- Ⓐ $105
- Ⓑ $350
- Ⓒ $700
- Ⓓ $1,050

70. How many $\frac{3}{8}$-pound hamburger patties can be made from $4\frac{1}{2}$ pounds of ground beef?

- Ⓐ $1\frac{11}{16}$
- Ⓑ 12
- Ⓒ 8
- Ⓓ 6

71. Which of the following points is the vertex of the graph of $y = 3x^2 - 6x + 5$ in the xy-plane?

- Ⓐ $(-2, 29)$
- Ⓑ $(-1, 14)$
- Ⓒ $(1, 2)$
- Ⓓ $(2, 1)$

GO ON TO THE NEXT PAGE

72. Three grandsons and two granddaughters inherit land from a grandparent's estate. The older granddaughter inherits $\frac{1}{3}$ of the land. The four other grandchildren equally share the remaining land.

What fraction of the land does the younger granddaughter inherit?

Ⓐ $\frac{1}{6}$

Ⓑ $\frac{1}{4}$

Ⓒ $\frac{1}{2}$

Ⓓ $\frac{2}{3}$

73. If a crate is packed to capacity with 81 cubes measuring 4 inches on each edge, what is the volume, in in³, of the crate?

Ⓐ 64
Ⓑ 81
Ⓒ 1,296
Ⓓ 5,184

74. For lunch at the end-of-school picnic, students can choose from four types of sandwiches: ham, turkey, tuna, or peanut butter. They can choose from two drinks: milk or juice. They can select from three types of chips: potato chips, corn chips, or tortilla chips. How many possible combinations consisting of one sandwich, one drink, and one bag of chips can the students choose from for lunch?

Ⓐ 8
Ⓑ 9
Ⓒ 11
Ⓓ 24

Use the graph below to answer question 75.

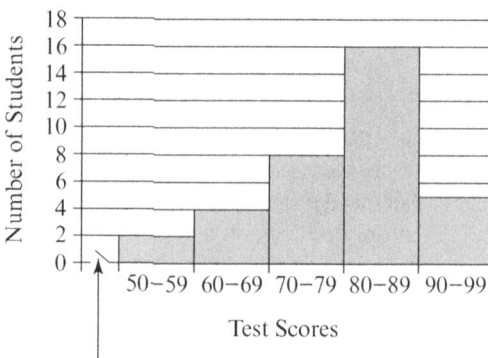

This symbol means there is a break in the horizontal scale.

75. The histogram above shows the grade distribution of 35 students on the first test in a geometry class. Using the graph, what is the probability a student randomly selected from the 35 students scored below 70?

Ⓐ $\frac{2}{35}$

Ⓑ $\frac{4}{35}$

Ⓒ $\frac{6}{35}$

Ⓓ $\frac{14}{35}$

76. Two friends drove 40 miles by car to a restaurant. Due to heavy traffic, it took them 1 hour and 20 minutes to get there. What was their average speed in miles per hour?

Ⓐ 24
Ⓑ 30
Ⓒ 32
Ⓓ 40

GO ON TO THE NEXT PAGE

77. A researcher analyzes data from a study using a simple linear regression model. Using statistical software, the researcher enters the data and runs a least-squares linear regression. In addition to providing the regression coefficients, the software output shows a correlation coefficient of 0.03. What can the researcher infer from this coefficient?

- Ⓐ The linear model is not a good fit for the data.
- Ⓑ The predictor and response variables have a strong positive correlation.
- Ⓒ The linear model has a 3% probability of fitting the data.
- Ⓓ The slope of the regression equation is 0.03.

Use the figure below to answer question 78.

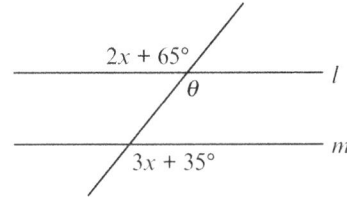

78. In the preceding figure, lines *l* and *m* are parallel. What is the measure of angle θ?

- Ⓐ 125°
- Ⓑ 97°
- Ⓒ 30°
- Ⓓ 16°

79. Suppose the distribution of the lifetimes of a certain type of disposable razor is normally distributed with a mean of 16.8 shavings and a standard deviation of 2.4 shavings. What percentage of disposable razors of this type will last more than 19.2 shavings?

- Ⓐ 2.5%
- Ⓑ 16%
- Ⓒ 34%
- Ⓓ 68%

80. Evaluate $20 - 3(-4^2) + \dfrac{8(42-18)}{12} - (-4)^2$.

- Ⓐ −28
- Ⓑ 36
- Ⓒ 68
- Ⓓ 100

81. Which system of equations has no solution?

- Ⓐ $x - 2y = 5$
  $2x - 4y = 10$
- Ⓑ $x - 2y = 5$
  $2x - 4y = 8$
- Ⓒ $x - 2y = 5$
  $2x + 4y = 10$
- Ⓓ $x + 2y = 5$
  $2x - 4y = 3$

Use the table below to answer question 82.

Volume, v (in cubic centimeters)	Weight, w (in grams)
12	32.4
20	54.0
45	121.5
74	199.8

82. The table shows a partial representation of a proportional function between volume, *v* (in cubic centimeters) and the weight, *w* (in grams), of aluminum.

Write an equation for the function represented in the table.

- Ⓐ $w = 2.7v$
- Ⓑ $w = 21.6v$
- Ⓒ $v = 2.7w$
- Ⓓ $v = 21.6w$

GO ON TO THE NEXT PAGE

Use the figure below to answer question 83.

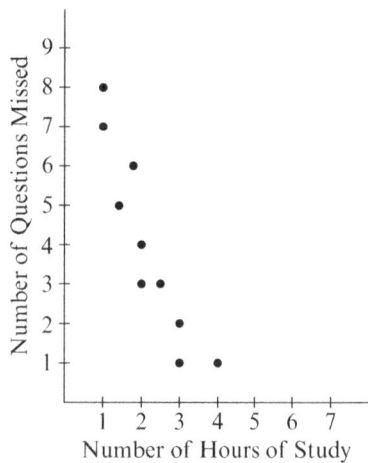

83. A scatter plot showing the linear relationship between the number of hours of study and the number of questions missed on a mathematics midterm exam by 10 eighth-graders is shown above. If you were to use the scatter plot to predict the number of questions missed based on the number of hours studied, you should limit the number of hours to between

   Ⓐ   1 and 4
   Ⓑ   1 and 5
   Ⓒ   1 and 6
   Ⓓ   1 and 7

84. Students in an eighth-grade mathematics class are being introduced to geometric probability. Which of the following activities would best help students develop insight into the concept of geometric probability?

   Ⓐ   Students design a target inside a circle so that the ratio of the target's area to the area of the whole circle fits a given ratio.
   Ⓑ   Students toss a fair die a given number of times and compute the ratio of the number of times the up face is six to the total number of tosses.
   Ⓒ   Students design a multicolored spinner for which the ratio of the number of times the spinner pointer falls on a certain color fits a given ratio.
   Ⓓ   Students flip a fair coin and compute the ratio of the number of times the up face is heads to the total number of flips.

85. A third-grade teacher begins a mathematics lesson about polygons by reading to students the book *The Greedy Triangle* by Marilyn Burns. This book tells a story about triangles and other polygons. The probable purpose for this way of beginning the lesson is to

   Ⓐ   gain students' attention.
   Ⓑ   communicate the objective for the lesson.
   Ⓒ   present the lesson content.
   Ⓓ   assess student learning.

86. Which of the following assessments is most effective in determining the extent to which students use specific problem-solving strategies in math?

   Ⓐ   Norm-referenced achievement test
   Ⓑ   Criterion-referenced skills test
   Ⓒ   Self-monitoring checklist
   Ⓓ   Holistic scoring rubric

87. A student who scores in the 80th percentile on a standardized achievement test has

   Ⓐ   scored the same as or better than 80% of a norm group.
   Ⓑ   scored better than 20% of a norm group.
   Ⓒ   correctly answered 80% of the test questions.
   Ⓓ   correctly answered 20% of the test questions.

88. Which of the following are recommended models when teaching fractions to students?

   Select <u>all</u> that apply.

   [A]   Fraction strips
   [B]   Rectangles
   [C]   Circular disks
   [D]   Number lines

89. Which of the following are common reasons students have difficulty developing a conceptual understanding of fractions?

   Select <u>all</u> that apply.

   [A]   Students view the numerator and denominator as separate numbers rather than as a unified whole.
   [B]   Unlike with whole numbers, fraction multiplication does not always result in an answer larger than the multiplicand.
   [C]   Unlike with whole numbers, fraction division does not always result in an answer smaller than the dividend.
   [D]   Students have trouble understanding that between any two fractions there are an infinite number of numbers.

90. Students in a sixth-grade class are working in groups using foldable geometric shapes to learn about nets of polyhedra. A major reason to provide students with hands-on concrete models is to

- Ⓐ promote their conceptual understanding through visual representations.
- Ⓑ activate their prior knowledge about concepts.
- Ⓒ increase their awareness of the practical use of mathematics.
- Ⓓ increase their interest in mathematical games and activities.

91. Three-fourths of the students in a math class passed their unit test. One-fifth of those who passed the test received an A. Which of the following computations describes the fraction of the class that received an A?

- Ⓐ $\dfrac{3}{4} - \dfrac{1}{5}$
- Ⓑ $\dfrac{1}{5} \times \dfrac{3}{4}$
- Ⓒ $\dfrac{3}{4} \div \dfrac{1}{5}$
- Ⓓ $1 - \dfrac{1}{5} \times \dfrac{3}{4}$

92. Which of the following number lines illustrates the solution to $\dfrac{2-x}{5} < 1$?

- Ⓐ
- Ⓑ
- Ⓒ
- Ⓓ

93. Two vehicles leave the same location at 10:45 a.m., one traveling due north at 70 miles per hour and the other due south at 60 miles per hour. If the vehicles maintain their respective speeds, at what time will they be 325 miles apart?

- Ⓐ 12:15 p.m.
- Ⓑ 1:15 p.m.
- Ⓒ 2:15 p.m.
- Ⓓ 3 p.m.

94. The square root of the product of p and q is 14, where p and q are two positive integers. Which of the following integers could be a sum for $(p+q)$?

Select all that apply.

- Ⓐ 35
- Ⓑ 54
- Ⓒ 100
- Ⓓ 197

95. Which of the following sets is closed with respect to the given operation?

Select all that apply.

- Ⓐ The set of whole numbers with respect to subtraction
- Ⓑ The set of integers with respect to division
- Ⓒ The set of prime numbers with respect to addition
- Ⓓ The set of perfect squares with respect to multiplication

Use the dot plot below to answer question 96.

Scores of 20 Students on Science Exam

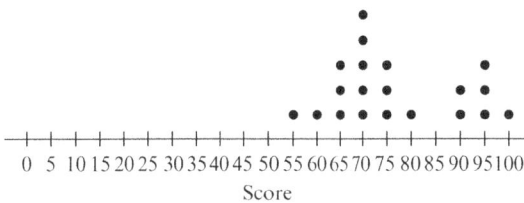

96. The preceding dot plot displays the scores of 20 students on a science exam. The standard deviation of these data is approximately 13.2. Determine the number of students whose scores are within 1 standard deviation of the mean.

- Ⓐ 11
- Ⓑ 12
- Ⓒ 13
- Ⓓ 14

Use the box plot below to answer question 97.

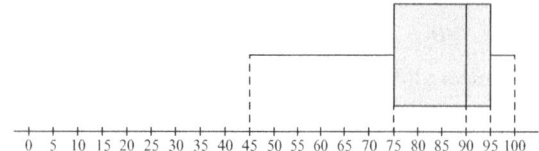

Mathematics Benchmark Assessment Scores of 100 Sixth-Graders

97. A box plot for mathematics benchmark assessment scores of 100 sixth-graders is shown above. Determine the interquartile range for the students' test scores.

- Ⓐ 20
- Ⓑ 25
- Ⓒ 30
- Ⓓ 55

Use the multiplication computation below to answer question 98.

$$\begin{array}{r} 317 \\ \times 23 \\ \hline 951 \\ 634 \\ \hline 1585 \end{array}$$

98. When performing the above multi-digit multiplication, Quinn completes the computation as shown above. Which of the following strategies would best help Quinn self-correct this error?

- Ⓐ Tell Quinn to put a zero after the 4 in the second partial product.
- Ⓑ Explain to Quinn that a zero is needed as a placeholder to keep the digits lined up in the correct column.
- Ⓒ Suggest that Quinn estimate the answer by multiplying rounded values of the multiplicand and multiplier first.
- Ⓓ Remind Quinn of the algorithm for performing the computation correctly.

Use the graph below to answer question 99.

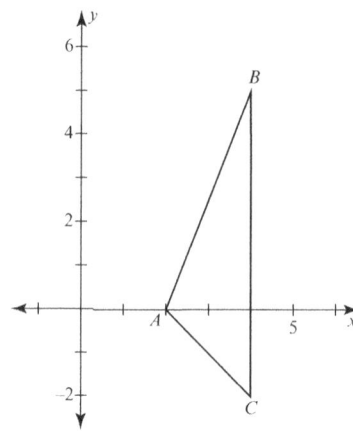

99. The triangle shown has vertices $A(2, 0)$, $B(4, 5)$, and $C(4, -2)$. Determine its area.

- Ⓐ 5
- Ⓑ 6
- Ⓒ 7
- Ⓓ 8

100. What is the product of the complex numbers $(3 - 5i)$ and $(3 + 5i)$?

- Ⓐ -16
- Ⓑ 34
- Ⓒ $9 - 25i$
- Ⓓ $9 + 25i$

Answer Key

Question Number	Correct Answer	Chapter(s)	Question Number	Correct Answer	Chapter(s)
1.	D	1, 5	26.	D	2
2.	A, C, D	2	27.	C	4
3.	C	4	28.	C	2
4.	D	2	29.	C	2
5.	C	1	30.	A	2
6.	B	1, 5	31.	B	4
7.	A	1	32.	C	4
8.	B, C	1	33.	A	4, 5
9.	B, C, D	2, 5	34.	D	4, 5
10.	C	2	35.	B	4, 5
11.	D	2	36.	B	4, 5
12.	B	2	37.	C	2
13.	B	3	38.	C	4, 5
14.	A	3	39.	C	4, 5
15.	C	3	40.	B	1, 5
16.	C	2, 3	41.	B, C	2
17.	A	3, 5	42.	C	1, 5
18.	A	3	43.	C	1, 5
19.	D	3, 5	44.	A	4
20.	B	3	45.	C	4
21.	B	3, 5	46.	C	4, 5
22.	C	2	47.	D	5
23.	B, C, D	2	48.	B	2
24.	D	1, 5	49.	B	2
25.	A	2	50.	B	3

Question Number	Correct Answer	Chapter(s)	Question Number	Correct Answer	Chapter(s)
51.	A	2	76.	B	1, 3
52.	C	1, 5	77.	A	4, 5
53.	B, C	2	78.	A	3, 5
54.	A	1, 5	79.	B	4, 5
55.	B	2	80.	C	1
56.	A	3, 6	81.	B	2, 5
57.	A, C, D	3	82.	A	2, 5
58.	C	1	83.	A	4, 5
59.	C	3	84.	A	6
60.	B	3	85.	A	6
61.	B	2, 3	86.	C	6
62.	C	3, 5	87.	A	4, 6
63.	B	3, 5	88.	A, B, D	1, 6
64.	D	3	89.	A, B, C, D	1, 6
65.	D	3	90.	A	6
66.	A	2, 6	91.	B	1
67.	A	2, 6	92.	D	2
68.	A, B, C	1, 6	93.	B	2, 6
69.	C	2, 4	94.	A, C, D	1
70.	B	1	95.	D	1
71.	C	2	96.	B	4
72.	A	1	97.	A	4
73.	D	3	98.	C	6
74.	D	4	99.	C	3, 5
75.	C	4	100.	B	1

Answer Explanations

1. **D.** The number of days until the next time is the least common multiple of 12 and 15, which is 60. It will be 60 days before Zoey and Jax both will swim at Gold Star Gym on the same day, choice D.

2. **A, C, D.** Select choice A because $a^2 - b^2 = (a + b)(a - b)$. Eliminate choice B because $a^2 - ab + b^2$ is *not* factorable over the real numbers. Select choice C because $a^3 - b^3 = (a - b)(a^2 + ab + b^2)$. Select choice D because $a^3 - 3a^2b + 3ab^2 - b^3 = (a - b)^3$.

   Tip: If you have not memorized the special products given in Chapter 2, "Patterns and Algebra," you should do so before the test.

3. **C.** The question asks: What is the *lowest* score the student can make on the final exam and still receive a B in the course? From the instructor's grading guidelines, you can see that you first must calculate the mean of the student's three major exam scores: mean $= \dfrac{72+81+75}{3} = 76$.

   Let x = the lowest score the student can make on the final exam and still have at least an 80 average.

   Solve the following equation for x.

   $$50\%(76) + 10\%(92) + 40\%(x) = 80$$
   $$0.5(76) + 0.1(92) + 0.4(x) = 80$$
   $$38 + 9.2 + 0.4x = 80$$
   $$47.2 + 0.4x = 80$$
   $$0.4x = 32.8$$
   $$x = 82$$

   The lowest score that will yield an average of at least 80 is 82, choice C.

4. **D.** $\dfrac{3}{x} + \dfrac{4}{y} = \dfrac{3y}{xy} + \dfrac{4x}{xy} = \dfrac{3y+4x}{xy} = \dfrac{4x+3y}{xy}$, choice D.

5. **C.** $\left(x^2 + 4\right)^{-\frac{1}{2}} = \dfrac{1}{\left(x^2+4\right)^{\frac{1}{2}}} = \dfrac{1}{\sqrt{x^2+4}}$, choice C.

6. **B.** The amount of gasoline needed for a 204-mile trip is 8.5 gallons. Let x = the amount, in gallons, needed for a 228-mile trip. Set up a proportion and solve for x.

   $$\dfrac{x}{228 \text{ miles}} = \dfrac{8.5 \text{ gal}}{204 \text{ miles}}$$
   $$x = \dfrac{(8.5 \text{ gal})(228 \text{ miles})}{204 \text{ miles}}$$
   $$x = 9.5 \text{ gal, choice B}$$

   Tip: Check the units to make sure that (mathematically) they work out to be the desired units for the answer.

7. **A.** $4^x + 12^x = 4^x + (3 \cdot 4)^x = 4^x + 3^x \cdot 4^x = 4^x(1 + 3^x)$, choice A.

8. **B, C.** The absolute value of a nonzero number is always positive. Eliminate choice A because for any nonzero number, $|x|$ is positive and $-|-x|$ is negative, so the statement is always false. Eliminate choice D because, for example, $|-2 + 10| = |8| = 8$, but $|-2| + |10| = 2 + 10 = 12$.

   Select choice B. If the quotient of two numbers is positive, then both numbers are positive or both numbers are negative. If the quotient is negative, then the two numbers have opposite signs. Case 1: If x and y are both positive, then $\left|\frac{x}{y}\right| = \frac{x}{y} = \frac{|x|}{|y|}$. Similarly, if x and y are both negative, then $\left|\frac{x}{y}\right| = \frac{-x}{-y} = \frac{|x|}{|y|}$. Case 2: If x and y have opposite signs, with $x < 0$, then $\left|\frac{x}{y}\right| = -\frac{x}{y} = \frac{-x}{y} = \frac{|x|}{|y|}$. If x and y have opposite signs, with $y < 0$, then $\left|\frac{x}{y}\right| = -\frac{x}{y} = \frac{x}{-y} = \frac{|x|}{|y|}$. Thus, for all nonzero real numbers x and y, choice B is true.

Select choice C. The square root of a nonzero number is always positive: $\sqrt{(-x)^2} = \sqrt{x^2} = |x|$, so choice C is always true.

Tip: Memorize the properties for absolute value given in Chapter 1, "Number Concepts," before you take the TExES Math 4–8.

9. **B, C, D.** Given that x and y are whole numbers and $z = x + y = x + 3x = 4x$, then z is a multiple of 4. Therefore, z represents a whole number that is divisible by 4. A number is divisible by 4 if and only if the last two digits form a number that is divisible by 4. Of the answer choices, only choice A fails the test for divisibility by 4—because the last two digits of 314 are 14, which is not divisible by 4. Choices B, C, and D are divisible by 4, so each could be the value of z.

10. **C.** $2x^3y(x + 3)(3x - 1) = 2x^3y(3x^2 + 8x - 3) = 6x^5y + 16x^4y - 6x^3y$, choice C.

11. **D.** Express $2x(x - 2) = 1$ in standard form.

$$2x(x-2) = 1$$
$$2x^2 - 4x = 1$$
$$2x^2 - 4x - 1 = 0$$

Using the quadratic formula, $a = 2$, $b = -4$, $c = -1$ (include the $-$ signs).

Plug into the formula.

$$x = \frac{-(-4) \pm \sqrt{(-4)^2 - 4(2)(-1)}}{2(2)} = \frac{4 \pm \sqrt{16+8}}{4} = \frac{4 \pm \sqrt{24}}{4} = \frac{4 \pm 2\sqrt{6}}{4} = \frac{2 \pm \sqrt{6}}{2}, \text{ choice D}$$

12. **B.** Solve the system by the method of elimination.

Write both equations in standard form (for convenience, the equations are numbered):

$$(1)\ 2x - 3y = 16$$
$$(2)\ 4x + 5y = 10$$

Quick check: The system has exactly one solution because $\frac{2}{4} \neq \frac{-3}{5}$.

To eliminate x, multiply equation (1) by -2 and add the result to equation (2).

$$\begin{array}{c} 2x - 3y = 16 \\ 4x + 5y = 10 \end{array} \text{ implies } \begin{array}{c} -4x + 6y = -32 \\ 4x + 5y = 10 \end{array} \text{ implies } 11y = -22 \text{ implies } y = -2, \text{ choice B}$$

13. **B.** The maximum possible error of a measurement is half the magnitude of the smallest measurement unit used to obtain the measurement. The most accurate way of expressing the measurement is as a tolerance interval. Thus, a measurement of 10 grams, to the nearest gram, should be reported as 10 g ± 0.5 g, choice B.

14. **A.** The angle bisectors of a triangle are concurrent in a point that is equidistant from the three sides, making choice A the correct response.

15. **C.** From the figure, $\triangle ABC$ is a right triangle. To find the area of a right triangle, find $\frac{1}{2}$ the product of the lengths of the two legs. To find the area of $\triangle ABC$, do three steps. First, determine CA, the length of leg $\overline{CA}$. Next, determine BC, the length of leg $\overline{BC}$. Then, find the area of $\triangle ABC$ by calculating $\frac{1}{2}bh = \frac{1}{2}(CA)(BC)$.

Step 1. Find CA by adding the lengths of the two segments, $\overline{CE}$ and $\overline{EA}$.

$$CA = 200 \text{ m} + 100 \text{ m} = 300 \text{ m}$$

Step 2. Find BC. Right triangles ABC and ADE are similar triangles because they have two congruent right angles, and they have the acute angle A in common. Determine BC by using properties of similar triangles.

$$\frac{BC}{300 \text{ m}} = \frac{50 \text{ m}}{100 \text{ m}} \text{ implies } BC = \frac{(300 \text{ m})(50)}{100} = 150 \text{ m}$$

Step 3. Find the area of $\triangle ABC$.

$$\text{area} = \frac{1}{2}bh = \frac{1}{2}(CA)(BC) = \frac{1}{2}(300 \text{ m})(150 \text{ m}) = 22\,500 \text{ m}^2, \text{ choice C}$$

16. **C.** The angles that measure $x°$ and $y°$ are angles formed when parallel lines are cut by a transversal. Use the properties of angles formed when parallel lines are cut by a transversal to find x and y. The angle that measures $y°$ and the angle adjacent to the angle that measures $x°$ are congruent because they are corresponding angles. Thus, the angles that measure $x°$ and $y°$ are supplementary angles. Recall that the sum of supplementary angles is 180°. It is given that $x = 8y$, so $x + y = 180$, which implies that $8y + y = 180$. Solve for y, and then determine $x = 8y$.

$$8y + y = 180$$
$$9y = 180$$
$$y = 20$$
$$x = 8y = 8(20) = 160, \text{ choice C}$$

Tip: Make sure you answer the question asked. This problem asks for the value of x, so after you find y, you need to keep going and find x.

17. **A.** Sketch a diagram.

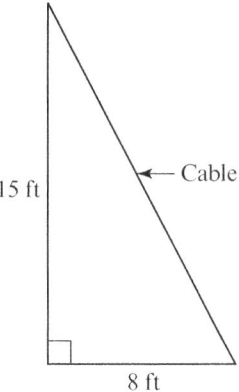

The pole, the cable, and the ground form a right triangle. From the diagram, the cable is the hypotenuse of a right triangle that has legs of 15 feet and 8 feet. Use the Pythagorean theorem to find the length, in feet, of the hypotenuse, denoted by c (omit the units for convenience).

$$c^2 = 15^2 + 8^2 = 225 + 64 = 289$$

Thus, $c = \sqrt{289} = 17$, choice A. The length of the cable is 17 feet.

Note: The number -17 is also a solution, but it is rejected because length is nonnegative.

18. **A.** From the figure, right angle ACB is an inscribed angle. The measure of an inscribed angle is half the degree measure of its intercepted arc. Thus, the degree measure of arc $\overset{\frown}{AB}$ is 180°, making the chord $\overline{AB}$, which is the hypotenuse of right triangle ABC, a diameter of the circle. To find the length of the hypotenuse, multiply the radius by 2. The length of the hypotenuse = 2(5.5 cm) = 11 cm, choice A.

19. **D.** The volume V of a cube with edge e is given by $V = e^3$. The volume of the original cube will equal the sum of the volumes of the two smaller cubes. To find the length of an edge of one of the smaller cubes, do three steps: First, find the volume of the original cube. Next, find the volume of one of the smaller cubes. Finally, find the length of an edge of one of the smaller cubes.

    Step 1. Find the volume V_o of the original cube: $V_o = (4 \text{ cm})^3 = 64 \text{ cm}^3$.

    Step 2. Find the volume V_s of one of the smaller cubes: $V_s + V_s = V_o = 64 \text{ cm}^3$ implies that $2V_s = 64 \text{ cm}^3$. Thus, the volume of one of the smaller cubes is 32 cm^3.

    Step 3. Find the length, call it e_s, of an edge of one of the smaller cubes.

    $$e_s^3 = 32 \text{ cm}^3 \text{ implies}$$
    $$e_s = \sqrt[3]{32 \text{ cm}^3} = \sqrt[3]{(8 \text{ cm}^3)(4)} = 2\sqrt[3]{4} \text{ cm, choice D}$$

20. **B.** The area of the figure is the sum of the area of the fourth of the circle and the area of the rectangle. The formula for the area of a circle is πr^2 and the formula for the area of a rectangle is lw. From the diagram, you can determine that the radius of the fourth of the circle is 4 m and that the length of the rectangle is 4 m + 3 m = 7 m. Hence, the area of the figure equals

    $$\frac{1}{4}\pi r^2 + lw = \frac{1}{4}\pi(4 \text{ m})^2 + (7\text{m})(3 \text{ m}) = \frac{1}{4}\pi(16 \text{ m}^2) + (21 \text{ m}^2) \approx 34 \text{ m}^2 \text{, choice B.}$$

21. **B.** You want to know how many years it would take to spend $1.6 billion at the rate of $1 per second $\left(\frac{\$1}{1 \text{ s}}\right)$.

    To determine the answer, use dimensional analysis. Write $1.6 billion as a fraction with denominator 1 and let unit analysis tell you which conversion fractions to multiply by, keeping in mind that you want years as your final answer.

    $$\frac{\$1,600,000,000}{1} \times \frac{1 \text{ s}}{\$1} \times \frac{1 \text{ min}}{60 \text{ s}} \times \frac{1 \text{ h}}{60 \text{ min}} \times \frac{1 \text{ d}}{24 \text{ h}} \times \frac{1 \text{ yr}}{365 \text{ d}} \approx 50 \text{ years, choice B}$$

22. **C.** Plug into the midpoint formula to find the midpoint between $(2, -2)$ and $(3, 4)$.

    $$\left(\frac{x_1 + x_2}{2}, \frac{y_1 + y_2}{2}\right) = \left(\frac{2+3}{2}, \frac{-2+4}{2}\right) = (2.5, 1), \text{ choice C.}$$

23. **B, C, D.** A function is a relation in which each first component is paired with *one and only one* second component. No two distinct ordered pairs have the same first components and different second components. Only the relation in choice A does not satisfy this requirement because the ordered pairs (3, 1) and (3, 10) have the same first component, 3, but different second components, 1 and 10. The sets of ordered pairs in choices B, C, and D represent functions.

24. **D.** Divide 6×10^2 grams by 3×10^{-2} grams.

    $$\frac{6 \times 10^2 \text{ g}}{3 \times 10^{-2} \text{ g}} = \frac{\overset{2}{\cancel{6}} \times 10^2 \cancel{\text{g}}}{\underset{1}{\cancel{3}} \times 10^{-2} \cancel{\text{g}}} = 2 \times 10^{2-(-2)} = 2 \times 10^{2+2} = 2 \times 10^4 = 20{,}000$$

    The number of grams of salt in solution B is 20,000 times the number of grams of salt in solution A, choice D.

25. **A.** The function $y = \dfrac{x^2 + 40x - 500}{500}$ has no excluded values, so its domain is the set consisting of all its possible x values; that is, $D_f = \{x \mid 500 < x < 750\}$.

    The range of $y = \dfrac{x^2 + 40x - 500}{500}$ is the set consisting of all its possible y values. That is,

    $$R_f = \left\{y \;\Big|\; \frac{500^2 + 40(500) - 500}{500} < y < \frac{750^2 + 40(750) - 500}{500}\right\},$$

    which implies $R_f = \{y \mid 539 < y < 1{,}184\}$. Thus, choice A is the correct response.

26. **D.** The problem states that the relation is a function. Therefore, by definition, each first component (age value) is paired with one and only one second component (hours value). Thus, only the statement given in choice D will always be true about the social scientist's function. None of the other statements are guaranteed to be true about the social scientist's function.

27. **C.** There are two overall tasks to be accomplished. The first overall task is to select four of the seven chairs. Noting that different orderings of the chairs do not produce different arrangements, the number of ways to select four of seven chairs is $_7C_4$. The second overall task is to arrange the four people in the four chairs. Noting that different orderings of the people result in different arrangements, the number of different ways to seat four people in four chairs is $(4)(3)(2)(1) = 4!$ This is true because there are four ways to seat someone in the first chair, three ways to seat someone in the second chair, and so on. Therefore, by the fundamental counting principle, the total number of ways to seat four people in four of seven empty identical chairs is

$$_7C_4 \cdot 4! = \frac{7!}{4!3!} \cdot 4! = 35 \cdot 24 = 840, \text{ choice C}$$

28. **C.** Determine the equation of the line that passes through (0, 5) and is perpendicular to the line that has equation $x - 3y = 10$. When two lines are perpendicular, their slopes are negative reciprocals of each other. Use the slope-intercept form to write the desired equation. The equation has intercept 5 because (0, 5) is the y-intercept of the line. You need two steps. First, find the slope of the desired equation by writing the equation $x - 3y = 10$ in slope-intercept form, and determine the negative reciprocal of its slope. Next, write the desired equation in slope-intercept form and then put it in standard form (because the answer choices are in standard form).

Step 1. Find the slope for the desired equation. Write $x - 3y = 10$ in slope-intercept form.

$$x - 3y = 10$$
$$-3y = -x + 10$$
$$y = \frac{1}{3}x - \frac{10}{3}$$

The slope of $x - 3y = 10$ is $\frac{1}{3}$, so the desired equation has slope -3.

Step 2. Write the desired equation and put it in standard form: $y = -3x + 5$ implies $3x + y = 5$, choice C.

29. **C.** Subtracting a positive constant h from x will result in a horizontal shift of h units to the right. The graph of $g(x) = (x - 2)^3$ is the same as the graph of $f(x) = x^3$ shifted right by 2 units, choice C.

30. **A.** $(g \circ f)(x) = g(f(x)) = g\left(\frac{2x+6}{x+2}\right) = \frac{2x+6}{x+2} + 2 = \frac{2x+6}{x+2} + \frac{2(x+2)}{x+2} = \frac{2x+6}{x+2} + \frac{2x+4}{x+2} = \frac{4x+10}{x+2}$, choice A.

31. **B.** In an ordered set of numbers, the median is the middle number if there is a middle number; otherwise, the median is the arithmetic average of the pair of middle numbers. First, put the running times in order from smallest to largest: 61, 63, 64, 64, 66, 68, 69, 73. Since there is no middle number, average the two running times that are the middle pair in the list, 64 and 66.

$$\frac{64 + 66}{2} = \frac{130}{2} = 65, \text{ choice B}$$

32. **C.** A circle graph is made by dividing the 360 degrees of the circle that makes the graph into portions that correspond to the proportion for each category. The central angle that should be used to represent the category Science Fiction/Fantasy is $\frac{104}{320}(360°) = 117°$, choice C.

33. **A.** A box plot graphically summarizes a data set by showing five numbers in the following order: the minimum value, the first quartile, the median, the third quartile, and the maximum value. Thus, the vertical line at 5 indicates that 5 is the median, choice A.

34. **D.** First, fill in the row and column totals for the table.

Grade Level	Has a Cell Phone	Has No Cell Phone	Row Total
Ninth	55	45	100
Tenth	70	30	100
Eleventh	78	22	100
Twelfth	95	5	100
Column Total	**298**	**102**	**400**

This question requires that you find a conditional probability; that is, you are to find the probability when you already know that the student is a ninth-grader. Thus, when computing the probability, the number of possible students under consideration is no longer 400, but is reduced to the total number of ninth-graders, which is 100. According to the table, 55 of the 100 ninth-graders have a cell phone.

Thus, P(the student has a cell phone given that the student is a ninth-grader) $= \frac{55}{100} = \frac{11}{20}$, choice D.

35. B. Fill in the missing probabilities.

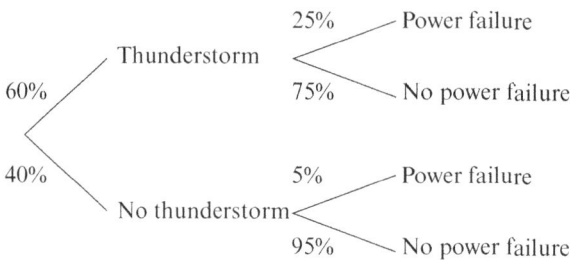

This problem requires an application of the multiplication rule, which states that $P(A \text{ and } B) = P(A)P(B|A)$. P(thunderstorm and power failure) $= P$(thunderstorm) $\times P$(power failure given a thunderstorm has developed) $= (60\%)(25\%) = 15\%$, choice B.

36. B. After three nondefective remote controls have been drawn, there are only seven remote controls left in the box, one of which is defective. Therefore, the probability that the next remote control is defective $= \frac{1}{7}$, choice B.

37. C. For the recursive formula given in the problem, you will need to find $f(1)$ and $f(2)$ before you can find $f(3)$. The problem tells you that $f(0) = 5$ and that $f(n) = 2f(n-1) + 1$ for $n \geq 1$. Thus,

$f(1) = 2f(0) + 1 = 2(5) + 1 = 10 + 1 = 11$

$f(2) = 2f(1) + 1 = 2(11) + 1 = 22 + 1 = 23$

$f(3) = 2f(2) + 1 = 2(23) + 1 = 46 + 1 = 47$

The value of $f(3)$ is 47, choice C.

38. C. Use the fundamental counting principle to work this problem. There are six slots to be filled, so to speak, on a license plate. There are 10 possibilities for each of the three digits and 26 possible values for each of the three letters, which means the total number of possible license plates is $10 \cdot 10 \cdot 10 \cdot 26 \cdot 26 \cdot 26 = (10^3)(26^3)$, choice C.

39. C. Noting that the order in which committee members are chosen does not make a difference regarding the composition of the committee, the number of different four-member committees that can be selected from the 50 members is the number of combinations of 50 things taken 4 at a time, which is $_{50}C_4 = 230,300$, choice C.

Tip: Use the nCr option under the (prb) key menu of the on-screen calculator to calculate the answer.

40. B. First, change 15 hours to days.

$$15 \text{ hr} \times \frac{1 \text{ day}}{24 \text{ hr}} = \frac{\cancel{15}^5 \text{ hr}}{1} \times \frac{1 \text{ day}}{\cancel{24}^8 \text{ hr}} = \frac{5}{8} \text{ day}$$

The rate in gallons per day is $\dfrac{3\frac{1}{4} \text{ gal}}{\frac{5}{8} \text{ day}} = \dfrac{\frac{13}{4} \text{ gal}}{\frac{5}{8} \text{ day}} = \dfrac{8\left(\frac{13}{4}\right) \text{ gal}}{8\left(\frac{5}{8}\right) \text{ day}} = \dfrac{26 \text{ gal}}{5 \text{ day}} = 5.2 \text{ gal/day}$, choice B.

41. **B, C.** Write the equation in slope-intercept form.

$$5x - 3y = 15$$
$$-3y = -5x + 15$$
$$y = \frac{5}{3}x - 5$$

The graph has slope of $\frac{5}{3}$ and y intercept of -5. Thus, select choice B and eliminate choices A and D. To find the x intercept, let $y = 0$ and solve for x in the original equation.

$$5x - 3y = 15$$
$$5x - 3(0) = 15$$
$$5x = 15$$
$$x = 3$$

Therefore, the x intercept is 3, so select choice C.

42. **C.** The elements in set A are 4, 8, 12, 16, 20, 24, 28, and so on. The elements in set B are 18, 28, 38, 48, 58, 68, 78, 88, and 98. Of the numbers in set B, 28, 48, 68, and 88 are multiples of 4 and therefore in set A as well. Thus, 4 integers are in the intersection of sets A and B, choice C.

43. **C.** Let n, $n + 2$, and $n + 4$ be the three consecutive odd integers. Solve the following equation for $n + 2$, the middle integer.

$$n + (n + 2) + (n + 4) = 5n - 40$$
$$n + n + 2 + n + 4 = 5n - 40$$
$$3n + 6 = 5n - 40$$
$$-2n = -46$$
$$n = 23$$
$$n + 2 = 25$$

The middle integer is 25, choice C.

44. **A.** Because of the grouping of data into intervals, the exact data values are not displayed in a histogram. Thus, histograms do not provide high levels of specific information about data values. For example, you know there is one data value in the interval "30 to less than 44," but without further information, you cannot determine its exact value (eliminate choice C). For the same reason, the maximum value and the mode cannot be identified (eliminate choices D and B). However, the histogram does give information about the shape of the distribution. The distribution has a tail to the left, indicating negative skewness. Therefore, the mean score of the data lies to the left of the median score (select choice A).

45. **C.** In an ordered set of data values, the median is the $\left(\frac{n+1}{2}\right)$ data value. There are 35 data values, so the median is the $\frac{35+1}{2} = \frac{36}{2} = 18$th data value. Counting from the least weight, the 18th weight in the stem-and-leaf plot is 147 pounds, choice C.

46. **C.** Let x and y be the two positive integers whose values you are not given and, for convenience, let $x < y$. Given that 73 is the mean of the six numbers, $\dfrac{48 + 53 + 61 + 82 + x + y}{6} = 73$. Solve this equation for $x + y$.

$$\frac{48+53+61+82+x+y}{6} = 73$$
$$48+53+61+82+x+y = (6)(73)$$
$$244+x+y = 438$$
$$x+y = 194$$

Because x and y are positive integers, the least that x can be is 1. Therefore, the greatest that y can be is 193, choice C.

47. D. Of the 75 students who are enrolled in an English course, 34 are not enrolled in a history course. Thus, $75 - 34 = 41$ students are enrolled in both English and history. Of the 52 students who are enrolled in history, $52 - 41 = 11$ are enrolled in history only. Sketch a Venn diagram to illustrate the information.

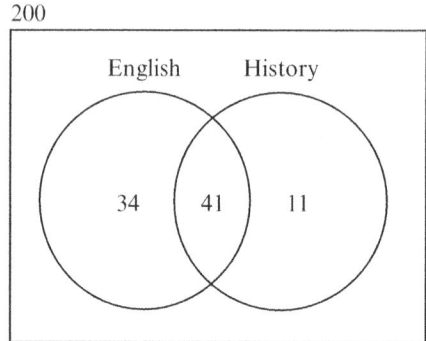

The entire rectangle represents the 200 students. The region that is outside the two intersecting circles represents the students who are enrolled in neither an English course nor a history course. From the diagram, the number of students who are enrolled in neither an English course nor a history course is $200 - (34 + 41 + 11) = 200 - 86 = 114$, choice D.

48. B. The fare is $3.50 for the first mile plus $1.50 for each additional half-mile.

To solve the problem, break the distance into a 1-mile portion plus a portion composed of half-mile segments. Then write and solve an equation that models the situation.

Let $n =$ the number of half-mile segments.

Distance from the airport to Rose's home = 1 mile + n half-miles

$$\text{Fare} = \$3.50 \text{ (for the first mile)} + n \cdot \frac{\$1.50}{\text{half-mile}}$$

Write an equation that represents the facts given.

$$\text{Fare} + \text{Tip} = \$38.50$$
$$\left(\$3.50 + n \cdot \frac{\$1.50}{\text{half-mile}}\right) + \$5 \text{ (tip)} = \$38.50$$

Solve the equation, omitting the units for convenience.

$$(3.50 + n \cdot 1.50) + 5 = 38.50$$
$$3.50 + 1.5n + 5 = 38.50$$
$$1.5n = 30$$
$$n = 20 \text{ half-mile segments}$$

Distance from the airport to Rose's home = 1 mile + 20 half-miles = 1 mile + 10 miles = 11 miles, choice B.

49. B. You have two "workers" (in this problem, the two machines) that can do the same job (in this problem, produce $40x$ electrical components), so use the quick solution method. Multiply their individual times, then divide this product by the sum of their individual times. Omitting the units, calculate $\frac{(10)(15)}{10+15} = \frac{150}{25} = 6$.

The time it takes machines 1 and 2, working simultaneously at their respective constant rates, to produce $40x$ electrical components is 6 hours, choice B.

Tip: You should eliminate choice D at the outset because the time for the two machines working together should be less than either of their times working alone.

50. B. The perimeter of $\triangle ABC = \left(\text{length of } \overline{AB}\right) + \left(\text{length of } \overline{BC}\right) + \left(\text{length of } \overline{AC}\right) = AB + BC + AC$.

From the information given, $AB = AD + DB = 2 + 8 = 10$. Now, determine BC and AC to find the perimeter.

The altitude to the hypotenuse of a right triangle is the geometric mean of the lengths of the two segments into which it separates the hypotenuse. Therefore, $\dfrac{AD}{x} = \dfrac{x}{DB}$. Substitute $AD = 2$ and $DB = 8$ and solve for x.

$$\frac{2}{x} = \frac{x}{8}$$
$$x^2 = 16$$
$$x = 4$$

Tip: The number -4 is also a solution, but it is rejected because length is nonnegative.

Use the Pythagorean theorem to solve for BC and AC.

$$BC = \sqrt{4^2 + 8^2} = \sqrt{80} = 4\sqrt{5} \text{ and } AC = \sqrt{4^2 + 2^2} = \sqrt{20} = 2\sqrt{5}$$

Thus, the perimeter of $\triangle ABC = 10 + 4\sqrt{5} + 2\sqrt{5} = 10 + 6\sqrt{5}$, choice B.

51. A. The rational function f defined by $f(x) = \dfrac{x^2 + x - 6}{(x+3)} = \dfrac{(x+3)(x-2)}{(x+3)}$ is undefined when $x = -3$.

Simplified, $f(x) = \dfrac{(x+3)(x-2)}{(x+3)} = x - 2$, so the graph of f is the line whose equation is $y = x - 2$, but with a "hole" at the point $(-3, -5)$. The graph of the linear function g defined by $g(x) = 2.5x + 2.5$ is the line $y = 2.5x + 2.5$ that intersects the line $y = x - 2$ at $(-3, -5)$. That is, $(-3, -5)$ satisfies both $y = x - 2$ and $y = 2.5x + 2.5$. However, -3 is not in the domain of f, so the graphs of f and g do not intersect, choice A.

52. C. Let f be the number of female students enrolled in the fall semester a year ago. Then, $f + 0.05f = 1.05f$ equals the number of female students currently enrolled.

Let m be the number of male students enrolled in the fall semester a year ago. Then, $m + 0.20m = 1.20m$ equals the number of male students currently enrolled.

You know that $f + m$ equals the total enrollment in the fall semester a year ago, so $(f + m) + 0.10(f + m) = 1.10(f + m)$ equals the current enrollment at the community college.

The current enrollment also equals $1.05f + 1.20m$.

Therefore, $1.05f + 1.20m = 1.10(f + m)$, from which you have $0.10m = 0.05f$, or equivalently, $2m = f$. This result tells you that in the fall semester a year ago, there were twice as many female students as male students. Pick convenient values for m and f that satisfy this relationship. For example, let $m = 100$ and $f = 200$. With these values, the total enrollment a year ago is 300. *Tip:* You can check that $1.20(100) + 1.05(200) = 120 + 210 = 330$, which is the same as $1.10(300)$.

Thus, the fraction of the current enrollment at the community college that is female students is

$$\frac{1.05(200)}{1.10(300)} = \frac{210}{330} = \frac{7}{11}, \text{ choice C.}$$

Chapter 7: TExES Math 4–8 Practice Test 1

Tip: When you work with ratios (fractions), proportions, and percents, you often can pick convenient numbers to work with. Just make sure the numbers you pick satisfy all the conditions of the problem.

53. B, C. First, eliminate fractions by multiplying through by 12:

$\frac{1}{4}x < 200 < \frac{1}{3}x$ implies that $12\left(\frac{1}{4}x\right) < 12(200) < 12\left(\frac{1}{3}x\right)$, which is equivalent to $3x < 2{,}400 < 4x$. Check the answer choices for numbers that satisfy this double inequality.

Check A: $3(550) = 1{,}650$ and $4(550) = 2{,}200$, so reject choice A because 550 is too low.

Check B: $3(650) = 1{,}950$ and $4(650) = 2{,}600$, so select choice B because $x = 650$ satisfies the double inequality.

Check C: $3(750) = 2{,}250$ and $4(750) = 3{,}000$, so select choice C because $x = 750$ satisfies the double inequality.

Check D: $3(850) = 2{,}550$, so reject choice D because $x = 850$ is too high.

Tip: Eliminating fractions at the outset simplifies the calculations for this problem.

54. A. Simplify the equation and then solve for x.

$$\frac{1}{3^x} = \frac{1}{3^n} + \frac{1}{3^n} + \frac{1}{3^n}$$

$$\frac{1}{3^x} = \frac{3}{3^n}$$

$$\frac{1}{3^x} = \frac{1}{3^{n-1}}, \text{ from which you have } x = n - 1, \text{ choice A}$$

55. B. Given that $y = \frac{k}{x}$, then $xy = k$, where k is a constant. If y is increased by $\frac{1}{2}$ of its value to $\frac{3}{2}y$, then x must be decreased to $\frac{2}{3}x$ so that the product $\left(\frac{2}{3}x\right)\left(\frac{3}{2}y\right) = xy = k$ remains constant. Thus, if y is increased by $\frac{1}{2}$ of its value, then x is decreased by $\frac{1}{3}$ of its value, choice B.

56. A. The figure can be used to prove the Pythagorean theorem, choice A. Here's how:

The large square has sides each of length c. Its area of c^2 equals $4 \times \frac{1}{2}ab = 2ab$ (the area of the four outer right triangles with legs of lengths a and b) plus $(b - a)^2$ (the area of the small square with sides each of length $(b - a)$ in the center).

Thus, $c^2 = 2ab + (b - a)^2 = 2ab + b^2 - 2ab + a^2 = a^2 + b^2$.

The figure would not be useful for proving any of the theorems given in the other answer choices.

57. A, C, D. A net is a two-dimensional shape that can be folded into a three-dimensional object. Only choice B will not fold into a cube. One of the squares of this two-dimensional shape will overlap another square, resulting in a hole in the resulting figure.

58. C. The prime factorization of 144 is $2^4 \times 3^2$. Therefore, the number 144 has $(4 + 1)(2 + 1) = (5)(3) = 15$ positive factors, choice C.

59. C. The sum of the acute angles of a right triangle is 90°. To find the percent error of the student's sum, do two steps. First, find the absolute error by finding the difference between 90° and the student's sum. Next, find the percent error by dividing the difference by 90° and expressing the result as a percent.

Step 1. The absolute error is $90° - 81° = 9°$.

Step 2. The percent error is $\frac{9°}{90°} = 0.10 = 10\%$, choice C.

60. B. The shaded region is the difference between the area of the larger circle and the area of the smaller circle. The formula for the area of a circle is πr^2. Calculate the two areas and subtract. From the figure, you have the diameter of the larger circle is 800 ft + 2(20 ft) = 840 ft, and the diameter of the smaller circle is 800 ft. Thus, the radius of the larger circle is $\frac{1}{2}(840 \text{ ft}) = 420 \text{ ft}$, and the radius of the smaller circle is $\frac{1}{2}(800 \text{ ft}) = 400 \text{ ft}$.

The area of the shaded region is $\pi(420 \text{ ft})^2 - \pi(400 \text{ ft})^2 = 16{,}400\pi \text{ ft}^2$, choice B.

61. B. You are given the endpoints of segments x and y, so you can find their lengths by subtracting endpoints. To find the ratio of the length of y to the length of x, do two steps. First, find the lengths of each of the line segments. Next, find the ratio of the length of y to the length of x.

Step 1. The length of segment x is $6\frac{1}{2} - 6\frac{1}{4} = \frac{1}{4}$; the length of segment y is

$$\frac{3}{\sqrt{2}} - \frac{5}{\sqrt{8}} = \frac{3}{\sqrt{2}} - \frac{5}{\sqrt{4 \cdot 2}} = \frac{3}{\sqrt{2}} - \frac{5}{2\sqrt{2}} = \frac{6}{2\sqrt{2}} - \frac{5}{2\sqrt{2}} = \frac{1}{2\sqrt{2}} = \frac{1 \cdot \sqrt{2}}{2\sqrt{2}\sqrt{2}} = \frac{\sqrt{2}}{4}.$$

Step 2. $\dfrac{y}{x} = \dfrac{\frac{\sqrt{2}}{4}}{\frac{1}{4}} = \dfrac{4\left(\frac{\sqrt{2}}{4}\right)}{4\left(\frac{1}{4}\right)} = \dfrac{\sqrt{2}}{1} = \sqrt{2}$, choice B.

62. C. Upon first reading, you might think this problem will take some time to work out. However, recall that when the dimensions of a solid figure are multiplied by a scale factor, the surface area and volume are multiplied by the scale factor raised to the second power and third power, respectively. To find the ratio of the surface areas of the spheres, do two steps. First, using the ratio of the volumes, determine the scale factor. Next, find the ratio of the surface areas by squaring the scale factor.

Step 1. The ratio of the volumes is $\dfrac{27}{1}$, which implies (scale factor)^3 = 27. Thus, the scale factor is 3.

Step 2. The ratio of the surface areas is 3^2 to 1, which is 9 to 1, choice C.

Tip: Knowing how scale factors impact area and volume can be very helpful to you on the test.

63. B. Make a sketch.

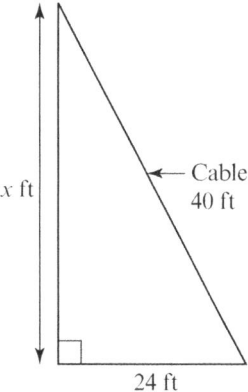

The building, the cable, and the ground form a right triangle. From the sketch, the length of the cable, 40 feet, is the length of the hypotenuse of a right triangle that has legs of 24 feet and x feet. Use the Pythagorean theorem to find the missing leg, x.

Method 1. Omitting the units, use the Pythagorean theorem to solve for x.

$$x^2 = 40^2 - 24^2 = 1{,}600 - 576 = 1{,}024$$

Thus, $x = \sqrt{1{,}024} = 32$, choice B

The cable reaches 32 feet up the wall.

Tip: The number −32 is also a solution, but it is rejected because length is nonnegative.

Method 2. The Pythagorean triple (3, 4, 5) and its multiples (6, 8, 10), (9, 12, 15), …, (24, 32, 40), and so on, satisfy the Pythagorean theorem. The length of the hypotenuse is 40 and one of the legs has length of 24. Therefore, you know that the length of the third leg of the right triangle must be 32. Thus, $x = 32$, choice B.

64. **D.** Eliminate choice C because AAA is not a method for proving congruence. Looking at the figure, you have $\angle ACB \cong \angle DCE$ because they are vertical angles. You know that $\overline{AC} \cong \overline{DC}$ because $\overline{BE}$ bisects $\overline{AD}$. You are given that $\angle A \cong \angle D$. Thus, you have two angles and the included side of $\triangle ABC$ congruent to two angles and the included side of $\triangle DEC$. Therefore, ASA, choice D, is the correct response.

65. **D.** The formula for the surface area of a sphere is $S.A. = 4\pi r^2$. The formula for the volume, V, of a sphere is $\frac{4}{3}\pi r^3$. To find the volume of the sphere, do two steps. First, find the radius of the sphere using the formula for surface area. Next, use the radius to find the volume.

    Step 1. $S.A. = 4\pi r^2 = 144\pi$, from which you have $r^2 = 36$. Thus, $r = 6$.

    Step 2. $V = \frac{4}{3}\pi r^3 = \frac{4}{3}\pi(6)^3 = \frac{4}{3}\pi(216) = 288\pi$, choice D.

    Tip: Be sure to memorize the basic geometry formulas for area and volume given in Chapter 3 before taking the test.

66. **A.** Directly observing the students working to solve one-variable linear equations and using a checklist to record their implementation of the procedure, choice A, is a powerful way to find out what the students know and understand about the process. This method is more likely to yield valid and reliable information about the students' learning than the methods given in choices B, C, and D.

67. **A.** Notice that you must select the choice that is *least* desirable. Eliminate choices B, C, and D because these are desirable strategies. When students are encouraged to take time to think before deciding on a solution strategy for a problem (choice B), they spend more time thinking about and analyzing the problem. Allowing more time for problems requiring analytical skills than basic computational problems (choice C) would be more conducive to higher-order thinking and problem solving. When students rely on themselves to determine whether their work is mathematically correct (choice D), they engage in critical thinking in order to clarify their mathematical thinking. Procedural knowledge is knowledge of the rules and procedures that are used to carry out routine mathematical tasks and of the symbolism that is used to represent mathematical concepts. A highly managed classroom environment focused on procedural knowledge likely would result in less risk taking and less higher-level thinking from students. Thus, choice A is the correct response.

68. **A, B, C.** Select choices A, B, and C because these answer choices are consistent with effective teaching practices. Choice D is a textbook-centered approach. Copying textbook problems and using calculators to obtain the answers would likely discourage active inquiry and result in less risk taking and less higher-level thinking from the students. Thus, eliminate choice D.

69. **C.** From the graph, you can see 25% of the monthly salary is budgeted for food. To answer the question, you must find 25% of $2,800. Change 25% to a decimal fraction and multiply: 25% of $2,800 = (0.25) ($2,800) = $700, choice C.

70. **B.** Divide $4\frac{1}{2}$ pounds into equal $\frac{3}{8}$-pound patties. Carry the units along in your computation, so you can see the units of the answer work out to be patties.

    $$4\frac{1}{2} \text{ pounds} \div \frac{3 \text{ pounds}}{8 \text{ patties}} = \frac{9}{2} \text{ pounds} \times \frac{8 \text{ patties}}{3 \text{ pounds}} = \frac{\cancel{9}^3}{\cancel{2}_1} \text{ pounds} \times \frac{\cancel{8}^4 \text{ patties}}{\cancel{3}_1 \text{ pounds}} = \frac{12 \text{ patties}}{1} = 12 \text{ patties}$$

    As you can see, the pounds "cancel out" when you multiply.

    12 hamburger patties can be made, choice B.

71. **C.** The standard form of the graph of a parabola is $y = a(x - h)^2 + k$ ($a \neq 0$), where the parabola's vertex has coordinates (h, k). Using the technique of completing the square, the equation $y = 3x^2 - 6x + 5 = 3(x^2 - 2x) + 5 = 3(x^2 - 2x + 1) + 5 - 3 = 3(x - 1)^2 + 2$, indicating the vertex is $(1, 2)$, choice C.

72. **A.** To solve the problem, do two steps. First, subtract the older granddaughter's part from the whole. Then, divide what remains into four equal parts.

Step 1. The older granddaughter inherits $\frac{1}{3}$ of the land. Subtract to find the remaining part of the land.

$$1 - \frac{1}{3} = \frac{2}{3}$$

Step 2. The younger granddaughter and her three brothers equally share the remaining part of the land. Use division to separate $\frac{2}{3}$ into four equal parts.

$$\frac{2}{3} \div 4 = \frac{2}{3} \div \frac{4}{1} = \frac{2}{3} \cdot \frac{1}{4} = \frac{\cancel{2}^1}{3} \cdot \frac{1}{\cancel{4}_2} = \frac{1}{6}$$

Thus, the younger granddaughter inherits $\frac{1}{6}$ of the land, choice A.

73. **D.** To solve the problem, do two steps. First, find the volume of one 4-inch cube. Then, find the volume of the crate by multiplying the volume of one 4-inch cube by 81.

Step 1. Find the volume of one 4-inch cube.

The volume of a 4-inch cube is $V_{cube} = e^3 = (4 \text{ in})^3 = 64 \text{ in}^3$

Tip: You will find it helpful to memorize that the volume of a cube is $V = e^3$, where e is the length of an edge of the cube.

Step 2. Find the volume of the crate.

It takes 81 cubes to fill the crate, so the volume of the crate is $V_{crate} = 81(V_{cube}) = 81(64 \text{ in}^3) = 5{,}184 \text{ in}^3$, choice D.

74. **D.** Use the fundamental counting principle to work this problem. The students have three tasks to perform. The first task is to choose a sandwich. After that task, the second task is to select a drink. After that, the third task is to make a chip selection. The number of ways each task can occur does not depend on the outcome of the other tasks. To find the possible combinations for the three tasks, multiply the number of ways the first task can occur by the number of ways the second task can occur by the number of ways the third task can occur.

Total number of possible combinations = (number of ways to select a sandwich) × (number of ways to select a drink) × (number of ways to make a chip selection) = 4 × 2 × 3 = 24 ways.

Thus, the students can select from 24 different combinations consisting of one sandwich, one drink, and one bag of chips for lunch, choice D.

75. **C.** The scale on the vertical axis shows the number of students who achieved the grade. The scale is marked in multiples of 2. The top of the bars for the intervals 50–59 and 60–69 are at 2 and 4, respectively. Thus, 2 + 4 = 6 students scored below 70. Therefore, the probability a student randomly selected from the 35 students scored below 70 is $\frac{6}{35}$, choice C.

76. **B.** Average speed is distance divided by time. One hour and 20 minutes is $1\frac{1}{3}$ hours, so the average speed was $40 \text{ miles} \div 1\frac{1}{3} \text{ hours} = 40 \text{ miles} \div \frac{4 \text{ hours}}{3} = \cancel{40}^{10} \text{ miles} \times \frac{3}{\cancel{4}_1 \text{ hours}} = 30 \frac{\text{miles}}{\text{hours}}$, choice B.

77. A. Because the correlation coefficient measures the linear relationship between the predictor and response variables of the simple-linear regression model, it can be used as an estimate of the "goodness of fit" of the regression model. The closer the correlation coefficient is to 0, the weaker the linear relationship. Given the value 0.03 of the correlation coefficient is near 0, it fails to support a linear relationship between the variables of the linear regression, indicating that the linear model is not a good fit for the data, choice A.

78. A. The measure of angle θ equals $2x + 65°$ because vertical angles have the same measure. The measure of angle θ equals $3x + 35°$ because corresponding angles of parallel lines have the same measure.

Thus, $2x + 65°$ and $3x + 35°$ are equal. Solve the following equation for x.

$$3x + 35° = 2x + 65°$$
$$x = 30°$$

Substituting this value for x into $2x + 65°$ (or into $3x + 35°$, if you prefer) yields the measure of angle θ, which is $2x + 65° = 2(30°) + 65° = 125°$, choice A.

79. B. According to the 68-95-99.7 rule, approximately 68% of the values of a normal distribution fall within one standard deviation of the mean, about 95% fall within two standard deviations of the mean, and about 99.7% fall within three standard deviations of the mean. The mean number of shavings for the razors is 16.8, with a standard deviation of 2.4 shavings.

The z-score for $19.2 = \dfrac{\text{data value} - \text{mean}}{\text{standard deviation}} = \dfrac{19.2 - 16.8}{2.4} = 1$. Therefore, 19.2 is one standard deviation above the mean.

Find the percentage of the normal distribution that is one standard deviation above the mean.

By the 68-95-99.7 rule, 68% of the distribution is within one standard deviation of the mean. Since the normal curve is symmetric, about $\dfrac{1}{2}$ of 68% = 34% of the distribution is between the mean and one standard deviation. Make a sketch to illustrate the problem.

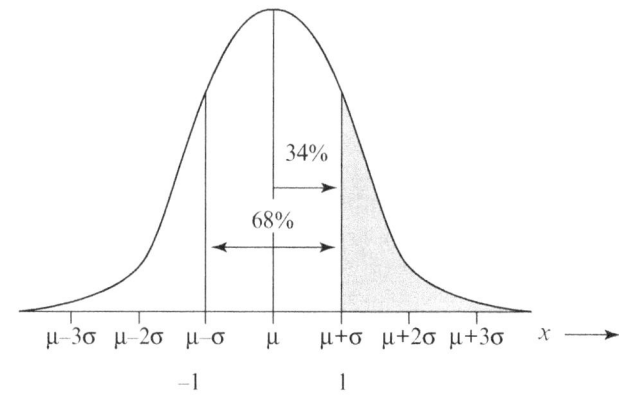

Again, due to symmetry, 50% of the distribution is above the mean. Thus, approximately 50% − 34% = 16% of the distribution is above one standard deviation above the mean. Thus, about 16% of the razors will last more than 19.2 shavings, choice B.

80. C. Follow the order of operations.

$$20 - 3(-4^2) + \dfrac{8(42-18)}{12} - (-4)^2 = 20 - 3(-4^2) + \dfrac{8(24)}{12} - (-4)^2$$
$$= 20 - 3(-16) + \dfrac{8(24)}{12} - (16)$$
$$= 20 + 48 + \dfrac{8(\cancel{24}^2)}{\cancel{12}} - 16 = 20 + 48 + 16 - 16 = 68, \text{ choice C}$$

81. B. Check the answer choices by comparing the ratios of the coefficients of the two equations.

Check A: $\frac{1}{2}, \frac{-2}{-4}$, and $\frac{5}{10}$ are equivalent ratios; the system $\begin{array}{l} x - 2y = 5 \\ 2x - 4y = 10 \end{array}$ has infinitely many solutions.

Check B: $\frac{1}{2} = \frac{-2}{-4} \neq \frac{5}{8}$; the system $\begin{array}{l} x - 2y = 5 \\ 2x - 4y = 8 \end{array}$ has no solution. ✓ Choice B is correct.

In a test situation, you should move on to the next question. For your information, the systems $\begin{array}{l} x - 2y = 5 \\ 2x + 4y = 10 \end{array}$ (choice C) and $\begin{array}{l} x + 2y = 5 \\ 2x - 4y = 3 \end{array}$ (choice D) each have exactly one solution.

82. A. The input-output ordered pairs are (12, 32.4), (20, 54.0), (45, 121.5), and (74, 199.8). A proportional function has the form $y = mx$, where m is the function's rate of change. Using the ordered pairs (12, 32.4) and (20, 54.0), the constant of proportionality (rate of change) is $\frac{54.0 - 32.4}{20 - 12} = \frac{21.6}{8} = 2.7$. Therefore, the function has equation $w = 2.7v$, choice A.

83. A. For statistical reasons, you should predict only within the range of the predictor variable, which is the number of hours in this case. The minimum number of hours studied is 1 and the maximum number is 4. You should restrict the number of hours to between 1 and 4, choice A.

84. A. The ratios of the areas of parts of a figure and the whole figure determine geometric probability. Therefore, the activity described in choice A would best help students develop insight into the concept of geometric probability because the activity involves the ratio of the area of a portion of a circle and the area of the whole circle. The activities in the other answer choices do not involve a ratio of areas.

85. A. The probable purpose for beginning the introduction by reading the book is to activate student interest and motivate students to engage in learning—in other words, to gain students' attention, choice A. Eliminate choices C and D because these purposes occur at a later point in the lesson, after the introduction. Eliminate choice B because although a teacher should communicate the objective in the introduction of the lesson, there is no evidence to indicate that the book *The Greedy Triangle* will communicate the objective for the lesson.

86. C. A self-monitoring checklist, choice C, can be used to cue students to use specific strategies while problem solving. The student checks off each step (such as "I read the problem and underlined key information") as it is completed. The student turns in the checklist along with the solved problem to the teacher. Eliminate choices A and B because these are standardized instruments to assess skills, not strategies. Eliminate choice D because a holistic scoring rubric assigns a single score to all components considered as a whole, not individually.

87. A. For standardized tests, percentile scores are scores that reflect a student's standing relative to a norm group. The 80th percentile is the same as or better than 80% of the scores of the norm group, choice A. The other answer choices are incorrect interpretations of a percentile score.

88. A, B, D. Fraction strips (choice A), rectangles (choice B), and number lines (choice D) are appropriate and recommended models for teaching fractions. Circular disks (choice C; e.g., pizza models) are poor models because they are difficult to divide into equal parts, especially for children; another reason is that unlike, for example, rectangles, they are not useful for modeling fraction multiplication.

89. A, B, C, D. According to Bruce et al. (2013), the average student never gains a conceptual understanding of fractions. The reasons given in the four answer choices are associated with the difficulty that students have dealing with the reality that many properties of whole numbers do not generalize to fractions.

90. A. A major reason to provide students with hands-on concrete models is to promote their conceptual understanding through visual representations, choice A. Eliminate choice B because activating prior knowledge should occur before a lesson activity begins. Eliminate choices C and D because, while these outcomes might occur, neither is a major reason for providing students with hands-on concrete models.

91. **B.** You have that $\frac{1}{5}$ of $\frac{3}{4} = \frac{1}{5} \times \frac{3}{4}$ (choice B) is the fraction of the class that received an A.

92. **D.** Solve the inequality.
$$\frac{2-x}{5} < 1$$
$$2 - x < 5$$
$$-x < 3$$
$$x > -3$$

The graph for this inequality is a ray extending to the right from the point -3 with an open dot at the point -3, choice D. You can eliminate choices A and B at the outset because the inequality is strictly less than, so a solid dot would not be used in the graph of the solution.

Tip: Remember to reverse the direction of the inequality when you multiply (or divide) both sides by a negative quantity.

93. **B.** Recall that distance = (rate)(time). The key idea in problems involving the distance formula is that a given distance is determined by a uniform rate and the time traveled at that rate. For the situation in this problem, the two vehicles simultaneously will travel the same amount of time. To determine the time at which the two vehicles will be 325 miles apart, do two steps. First, let t be the time traveled by the two vehicles. Write an equation and solve for t. Next, determine the time of day by adding the time traveled to the time of departure.

Step 1. Let t = the time (in hours) it will take for the two vehicles to be 325 miles apart.

Given that the two vehicles are traveling in opposite directions, they are moving away from each other at the rate of their combined speed, which is $70 \frac{\text{miles}}{\text{hr}} + 60 \frac{\text{miles}}{\text{hr}} = 130 \frac{\text{miles}}{\text{hr}}$.

The total distance covered by the two vehicles in t hours is $\left(130 \frac{\text{miles}}{\text{hr}}\right)(t)$. Thus,

$$130 \frac{\text{miles}}{\text{hr}} t = 325 \text{ miles}$$

Solve for t (omitting the units for convenience).

$$130t = 325$$
$$t = 2.5$$

The time it will take for the two vehicles to be 325 miles apart is 2.5 hours or 2 hours 30 minutes.

Step 2. The clock time is 10:45 a.m. + 2 hours 30 minutes = 1:15 p.m., choice B.

94. **A, C, D.** $\sqrt{pq} = 14$ implies $pq = 196$. The positive factors of 196 are 1, 2, 4, 7, 14, 28, 49, 98, and 196. The possible two-factor combinations for p and q are 1 and 196, 2 and 98, 4 and 49, 7 and 28, and 14 and 14. The possible sums for these two-factor combinations are 197 (select choice D), 100 (select choice C), 53, 35 (select choice A), and 28. Choice B is not a possible sum.

95. **D.** A set is closed with respect to an operation if the result of performing the operation with any pair of elements in the set yields an element contained in the set. Choice D is the only correct response. To show that the set of perfect squares is closed with respect to multiplication, let a^2 and b^2 be any two perfect squares. Then $(a^2)(b^2) = (ab)^2$, which is also a perfect square.

Eliminate the other answer choices by determining they are not closed with respect to the given operation by selecting arbitrary pairs of values and testing them. A set is not closed with respect to the operation if you can find just *one* pair of elements that does not yield an element in the set when the operation is performed with that pair of elements. Eliminate choice A because 5 and 9 are whole numbers, but $5 - 9 = -4$ is not.

Eliminate choice B because 1 and 2 are integers, but $\frac{1}{2}$ is not. Eliminate choice C because 3 and 5 are prime numbers, but $3 + 5 = 8$ is not.

96. **B.** Examine the dot plot.

The mean of the scores is $\dfrac{55+60+3(65)+5(70)+3(75)+80+2(90)+3(95)+100}{20} = \dfrac{1{,}530}{20} = 76.5$.

One standard deviation below the mean is 76.5 − 13.2 = 63.3, and one standard deviation above the mean is 76.5 + 13.2 = 89.7. Exactly 12 scores fall between these two values, meaning 12 scores are within one standard deviation of the mean, choice B.

97. **A.** The interquartile range (IQR) is the difference between the upper and lower quartiles of the students' test scores. The box plot shows the upper quartile is 95 and the lower quartile is 75. Thus, IQR = 95 − 75 = 20, choice A.

98. **C.** Eliminate choices A, B, and D because these teacher-centered strategies do not allow Quinn the opportunity to figure out why the answer is incorrect and to correct it. By estimating (choice C), Quinn likely will recognize that there must be an error in the computation. The teacher should give Quinn time to think about why the answer is much smaller than the estimate and how to fix the answer. If Quinn asks for assistance, the teacher can scaffold the situation by asking questions such as "What is the place value of the number 2 in the multiplier?"

99. **C.** Enclose the triangle in a rectangle and determine the coordinates of all vertices.

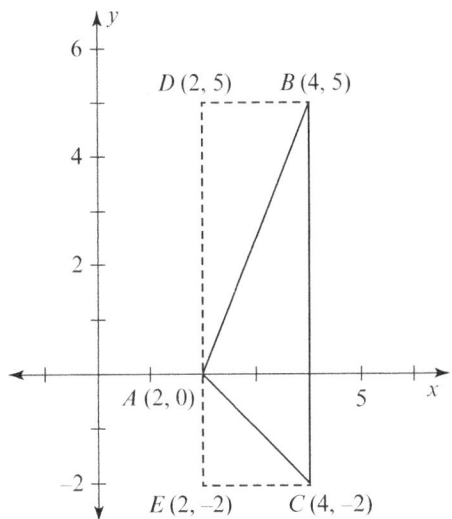

The area, A, of triangle ABC is the area of rectangle $DBCE$ minus the areas of right triangles ADB and AEC. In the figure, D has coordinates (2, 5) and E has coordinates (2, −2). Thus, $DB = EC = 4 - 2 = 2$, $DE = BC = 5 - (-2) = 7$, $DA = 5 - (0) = 5$, and $AE = 0 - (-2) = 2$. Thus,

$A = (DE)(DB) - \dfrac{1}{2}(DA)(DB) - \dfrac{1}{2}(AE)(EC) = (7)(2) - \dfrac{1}{2}(5)(2) - \dfrac{1}{2}(2)(2) = 14 - 5 - 2 = 7$, choice C.

100. **B.** Perform the multiplication, following the rules for multiplying complex numbers.

$(3 - 5i)(3 + 5i) = 9 + 15i - 15i - 25i^2 = 9 - 25i^2 = 9 - 25(-1) = 9 + 25 = 34$, choice B.

Tip: Remember that $i^2 = -1$.

Chapter 8

TExES Math 4–8 Practice Test 2

100 Questions

Time—4 Hours 45 Minutes

Directions: Read the directions for each question carefully. For each question, select the best single answer choice unless written instructions in the question state otherwise.

---

1. Which of the following equations defines y as a function of x?

   Ⓐ $9x - 16y^2 = 9$
   Ⓑ $x^2 + y^2 = 100$
   Ⓒ $5y - 125x^2 = 10$
   Ⓓ $x = |y|$

Use the figure below to answer question 2.

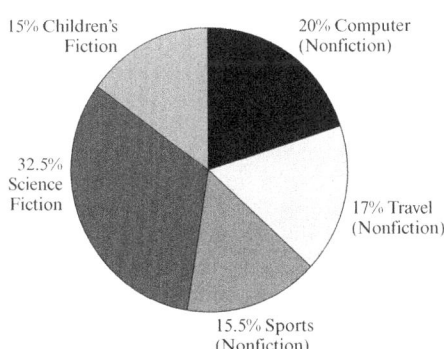

Categories of 1,200 Books Sold at The World of Books in December

15% Children's Fiction
20% Computer (Nonfiction)
32.5% Science Fiction
17% Travel (Nonfiction)
15.5% Sports (Nonfiction)

2. The circle graph displays the categories, by percentages, of 1,200 books sold at The World of Books bookstore. According to the information in the graph, how many fiction books were sold in December?

   Ⓐ 180
   Ⓑ 390
   Ⓒ 570
   Ⓓ 630

3. A student solved a word problem and correctly gave the numerical part of the solution as 6.3. Which of the following questions could have been asked in the word problem?

   Select all that apply.

   Ⓐ How many buses are needed to transport the students?
   Ⓑ What is the average time, in minutes, that customers spent waiting in line?
   Ⓒ What is the length, in centimeters, of each piece of ribbon?
   Ⓓ How many possible ways can the three different letters be arranged?

Use the measurement equivalents below to answer question 4.

$$1 \text{ cup} = 16 \text{ tablespoons (T)}$$
$$1 \text{ tablespoon} = 3 \text{ teaspoons (tsp)}$$

4. A punch recipe calls for $2\frac{3}{4}$ cups of cranberry juice, $1\frac{1}{2}$ cups of orange juice, $\frac{3}{4}$ cup of water, 1 teaspoon of cinnamon, and 3 tablespoons of sugar. What is the ratio of the total amount of fruit juice to the total amount of cinnamon and sugar called for in the recipe?

   Ⓐ 1 to 20
   Ⓑ 68 to 1
   Ⓒ 102 to 5
   Ⓓ 227 to 1

GO ON TO THE NEXT PAGE

5. Maria withdrew 25% of her money from her savings account. Later she withdrew another $150, leaving a balance of $975. How much money was in Maria's account originally if no other transactions were posted to her account?

- Ⓐ $1,125.00
- Ⓑ $1,500.00
- Ⓒ $1,968.75
- Ⓓ $4,500.00

Use the figure below to answer question 6.

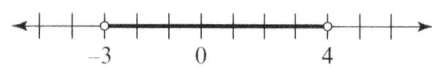

6. The graph on the number line shown represents the set of values of x satisfying which of the following inequalities?

- Ⓐ $\left|x - \frac{1}{2}\right| < \frac{7}{2}$
- Ⓑ $\left|x - \frac{1}{2}\right| > \frac{7}{2}$
- Ⓒ $\left|x - \frac{1}{2}\right| \leq \frac{7}{2}$
- Ⓓ $\left|x - \frac{1}{2}\right| \geq \frac{7}{2}$

Use the table below to answer question 7.

n	1	2	3	4	...
m	0	1	4	9	...

7. If the pattern shown in the table continues indefinitely, which of the following expressions should be used to find m for a given value of n?

- Ⓐ $\sqrt{n}$
- Ⓑ n^2
- Ⓒ $n^2 - 1$
- Ⓓ $(n - 1)^2$

8. Given: $\frac{a}{b} = 10$ and $\frac{b}{c} = 5$, where $bc \neq 0$. What is the value of $\frac{a}{b+c}$?

- Ⓐ $\frac{25}{6}$
- Ⓑ $\frac{25}{3}$
- Ⓒ $\frac{5}{3}$
- Ⓓ 12

Use the figure below to answer question 9.

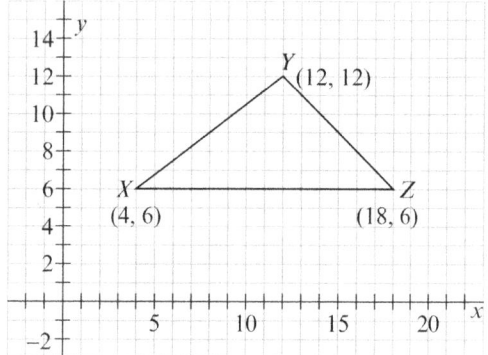

9. Which of the following properties associated with $\triangle XYZ$ is a rational quantity?

Select all that apply.

- Ⓐ perimeter of $\triangle XYZ$
- Ⓑ area of $\triangle XYZ$
- Ⓒ length of side $\overline{XY}$
- Ⓓ midpoint of side $\overline{XZ}$

GO ON TO THE NEXT PAGE

Use the figure below to answer question 10.

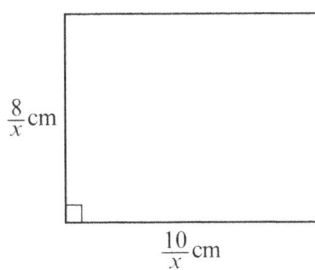

10. If the perimeter of the rectangle shown is 18 centimeters, what is the area of the rectangle, in cm²?

- Ⓐ 20
- Ⓑ 40
- Ⓒ 60
- Ⓓ 80

11. $(3 - 2i)(3 + 4i) =$

- Ⓐ $17 + 6i$
- Ⓑ $17 - 6i$
- Ⓒ $1 + 6i$
- Ⓓ $1 - 6i$

12. To estimate the population of fish in a lake, a parks and recreation team captures and tags 500 fish and then releases the tagged fish back into the lake. One month later, the team returns and captures 100 fish from the lake, 20 of which bear tags that identify them as being among the previously captured fish. If all the tagged fish are still active in the lake when the second group of fish is captured, what is the best estimate of the fish population in the lake based on the information obtained through this capture-recapture strategy?

- Ⓐ 100
- Ⓑ 1,500
- Ⓒ 2,500
- Ⓓ 3,000

Use the figure below to answer question 13.

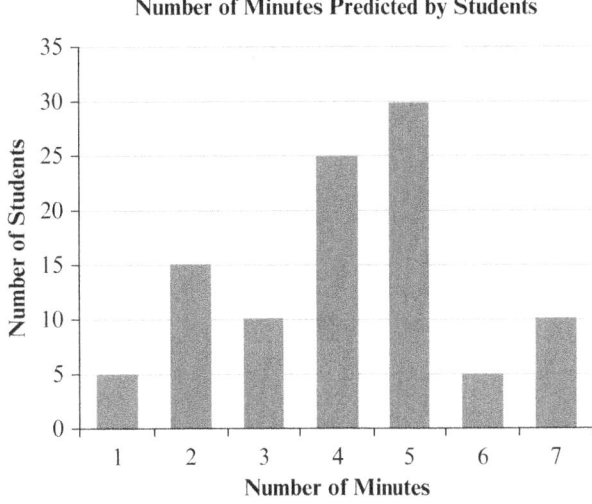

13. A science teacher asked 100 students to predict the number of minutes it would take a chemical reaction to reach completion. The graph shown displays the students' responses. To the nearest tenth, what is the mean (arithmetic average) number of minutes predicted by the students?

- Ⓐ 4.0
- Ⓑ 4.2
- Ⓒ 4.8
- Ⓓ 5.0

Use the figure below to answer question 14.

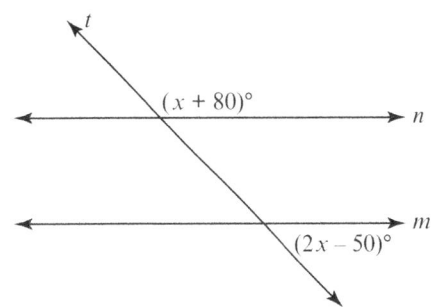

14. In the figure, line t is a transversal of lines m and n. For what value of x will lines m and n be parallel?

- Ⓐ $16\frac{2}{3}$
- Ⓑ 50
- Ⓒ 100
- Ⓓ 130

GO ON TO THE NEXT PAGE

15. A length of cable is attached to the top of a 12-foot vertical pole. The cable is anchored 5 feet from the base of the pole. What is the length of the cable, in feet?

- Ⓐ 7
- Ⓑ 13
- Ⓒ 17
- Ⓓ 169

Use the figure below to answer question 16.

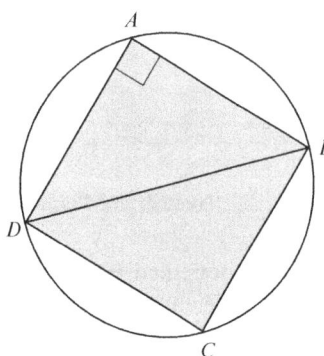

16. In the figure, the circle circumscribed about the square $ABCD$ has a circumference of 8π. Find the area of the square $ABCD$.

- Ⓐ $4\sqrt{2}$
- Ⓑ 32
- Ⓒ 32π
- Ⓓ It cannot be determined from the information given.

17. The density of silver is 10.5 grams per cubic centimeter. What is the mass, in grams, of a cube of silver that measures 2 centimeters on an edge?

- Ⓐ 21
- Ⓑ 42
- Ⓒ 84
- Ⓓ 168

18. Priya bought a precious stone pendant in 2010 for $500. By 2015, the pendant had lost 10% of its value. In 2017, it was worth 10% more than in 2015. By 2020 it had lost 20% of its value from 3 years previously. What was the pendant worth in 2020?

- Ⓐ $324
- Ⓑ $396
- Ⓒ $400
- Ⓓ $495

19. A national health study estimates that 35% of the people over the age of 65 in the United States will get flu shots this year. According to the study, of the people who get flu shots, an estimated 2% will have some sort of adverse reaction. If N represents the number of people over the age of 65 in the United States, estimate how many people over age 65 will have an adverse reaction after getting flu shots this year.

- Ⓐ $0.007N$
- Ⓑ $0.02N$
- Ⓒ $0.35N$
- Ⓓ $0.37N$

20. For what value of $k > 0$ will the function defined by $y = 16x^2 - kx + 25$ have exactly one real zero?

- Ⓐ 4
- Ⓑ 8
- Ⓒ 20
- Ⓓ 40

21. Which two of the following functions have the same domain and the same range?

Select <u>the two</u> that apply.

- ☐ A {(0, 0), (1, 1), (2, 4), (3, 9), (4, 16)}
- ☐ B $\{(x, y) \mid y = x^2\}$
- ☐ C {(0, 0), (1, 1), (2, 4), (3, 9), (4, 16), …}
- ☐ D $\{(x, y) \mid y = |x|\}$

22. A team of biologists introduces a herd of 100 deer onto an uninhabited island. If the deer population doubles every 8 years, which of the following functions models the growth of the deer population on the island if t is the time in years?

- Ⓐ $(100)^{0.125t}$
- Ⓑ $(100)2^{0.125t}$
- Ⓒ $(100)^{8t}$
- Ⓓ $(100)2^{8t}$

23. What is the equation of the line that is perpendicular to the line whose equation is $5x - 6y = 4$ and passes through the point (3, 1)?

- Ⓐ $5x - 6y = 9$
- Ⓑ $-6x + 5y = -13$
- Ⓒ $6x + 5y = 23$
- Ⓓ $6x + 5y = 21$

24. The exterior of a spherical tank with radius 12 feet is to be painted with one coat of paint. The paint sells for $24.50 per gallon and can be purchased in 1-gallon cans only. If a can of paint will cover approximately 400 square feet, what is the cost of the paint needed to paint the exterior of the tank?

- Ⓐ $24.50
- Ⓑ $98.00
- Ⓒ $110.25
- Ⓓ $122.50

25. An experiment consists of flipping a coin five times and observing the up face of the coin. Which of the following expressions gives the number of different outcomes in the sample space for this experiment?

- Ⓐ 2^5
- Ⓑ $_5P_2$
- Ⓒ 5^2
- Ⓓ $_5C_2$

Use the table below to answer question 26.

⊗	a	b
a	a	b
b	b	b

26. The table shown defines an operation ⊗ on the set $S = \{a, b\}$. Which of the following statements about set S with respect to ⊗ are true?

Select all that apply.

- ☐ A Set S is closed.
- ☐ B Set S is commutative.
- ☐ C Set S contains an identity element.
- ☐ D Set S contains inverses for all elements in set S.

27. A teacher is facilitating a whole-class discussion of various graphical representations. Of the following graphical representations, which would the students likely select as the one that is most convenient for determining the median, range, and quartiles of a data set?

- Ⓐ Dot plot
- Ⓑ Box-and-whisker plot
- Ⓒ Bar graph
- Ⓓ Histogram

Use the graph below to answer question 28.

Weights (in pounds) of the 36 Members of a Middle School Track Team

Stem	Leaf					
10	0	3	3	7	8	
11	1	1	1	4	7	8
12	2	6	8	8	9	
13	2	6	6	8		
14	1	2	4			
15	3	4	7	7	7	
16	3	7	8			
17	2	4	8			
18	3	6				

28. The graph shown is a stem-and-leaf plot of the weights of 36 students who make up the membership of a middle school track team. What percentage of the students on the track team weigh less than 115 pounds?

- Ⓐ 10%
- Ⓑ 15%
- Ⓒ 25%
- Ⓓ 30%

29. At a grand-opening sale of an appliance store, 152 customers bought a washer or a dryer. Looking at the inventory, the store manager found that 94 washers and 80 dryers were sold. Of the 152 customers, how many bought only a washer?

- Ⓐ 22
- Ⓑ 58
- Ⓒ 72
- Ⓓ 130

GO ON TO THE NEXT PAGE

30. $\dfrac{a}{a^2-b^2} - \dfrac{b}{a^2+ab} =$

Ⓐ $\dfrac{a-b}{b(a+b)}$

Ⓑ $\dfrac{a-b}{a(a+b)}$

Ⓒ $\dfrac{a^2-ab+b^2}{a(a+b)(a-b)}$

Ⓓ $\dfrac{a^2-ab-b^2}{a(a+b)(a-b)}$

31. What are the units of the quantity $Y = \dfrac{Adv}{t}$, where A is measured in square centimeters (cm^2), d is expressed in grams per cm^3 $\left(\dfrac{g}{cm^3}\right)$, v is expressed in centimeters per second $\left(\dfrac{cm}{s}\right)$, and t is given in seconds (s)?

Ⓐ g

Ⓑ $\dfrac{g}{s^2}$

Ⓒ $\dfrac{g\cdot cm}{s}$

Ⓓ $\dfrac{g\cdot cm}{s^2}$

Use the table below to answer question 32.

Resident Status of Second-Year Students
(n = 500)

	On Campus	Off Campus
Male	114	135
Female	156	95

32. The table shows the resident status, by gender, of 500 second-year students at a small community college. If one of the 500 students is randomly selected, what is the probability that the student resides off-campus given that the student is a female?

Ⓐ $\dfrac{86}{125}$

Ⓑ $\dfrac{95}{251}$

Ⓒ $\dfrac{19}{100}$

Ⓓ $\dfrac{4{,}769}{50{,}000}$

33. What is the approximate volume, in in^3, of a right triangular prism that is 20 inches in height and whose bases are equilateral triangles that are 4 inches on a side?

Ⓐ 7
Ⓑ 46
Ⓒ 80
Ⓓ 139

34. A collection of dimes and quarters has a value of $22.50. Ten times as many dimes as quarters are in the collection of coins. How many dimes are in the collection?

Ⓐ 18
Ⓑ 60
Ⓒ 90
Ⓓ 180

35. In a coordinate plane, $\triangle ABC$ has vertices $A(2, 1)$, $B(2, 5)$, and $C(5, 2)$. $\triangle A'B'C'$ is the image of $\triangle ABC$ after a reflection over the y-axis followed by a translation of 4 units to the right and 6 units down. What are the coordinates of B'?

Ⓐ $(-2, 5)$
Ⓑ $(2, -1)$
Ⓒ $(6, -1)$
Ⓓ $(6, 1)$

36. The lengths of two sides of a triangle are 7 and 19. Which of the following could be the length of the third side?

Select <u>all</u> that apply.

☐ A 11
☐ B 13
☐ C 25
☐ D 27

GO ON TO THE NEXT PAGE

37. The probability is $\frac{1}{6}$ that a number cube, with faces numbered 1 to 6, will show the number 3 on the up face in one toss of the cube. In three tosses of the number cube, what is the probability that the number 3 will appear on the up face in at least one of the tosses?

Ⓐ $\frac{91}{216}$

Ⓑ $\frac{125}{216}$

Ⓒ $\frac{5}{6}$

Ⓓ $\frac{17}{18}$

38. Which of the following scenarios has the greatest number of possible outcomes?

Ⓐ The number of ways three different prizes can be awarded among 10 people if no one person can receive more than one prize

Ⓑ The number of different three-letter arrangements of the 10 uppercase letters, A through J, if no letter can repeat

Ⓒ The number of different committees of three people that can be formed from among a group of 10 people

Ⓓ The number of different three-digit passcodes that can be formed using the 10 digits 0 through 9, if digits can repeat

39. The ratio of x to y is 20 to 11, and the ratio of y to z is 3 to 5. What is the ratio of x to z?

Ⓐ $\frac{5}{12}$

Ⓑ $\frac{11}{12}$

Ⓒ $\frac{12}{11}$

Ⓓ $\frac{12}{5}$

Use the equation below to answer question 40.

$$y = 4(x + 3) + 5$$

40. If the value of x in the equation above is increased by 1, the value of y will increase by

Ⓐ 4

Ⓑ 5

Ⓒ 17

Ⓓ 21

Use the figure below to answer question 41.

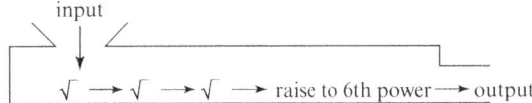

41. If a positive number x is used as the input for the function machine shown, which of the following expressions is equivalent to the output?

Ⓐ $x^{\frac{1}{24}}$

Ⓑ $x^{\frac{3}{4}}$

Ⓒ x

Ⓓ $x^{\frac{3}{2}}$

42. The operation $\oplus$ is defined on the set R of real numbers by $x \oplus y = 3x + xy$, where x and y are real numbers and the operations on the right side of the equal sign denote the standard operations for the real number system. A student should ask which of the following questions to decide whether the operation $\oplus$ is commutative?

Ⓐ Does $x + y = y + x$ for all real numbers x and y?

Ⓑ Does $3x + xy = 3x + yx$ for all real numbers x and y?

Ⓒ Does $3x + x^2 = 3y + y^2$ for all real numbers x and y?

Ⓓ Does $3x + xy = 3y + yx$ for all real numbers x and y?

GO ON TO THE NEXT PAGE

43. The original price of a sofa was 30% less than the sofa's suggested retail price of $500. The price at which the sofa was sold was 30% more than the original price. What is the price at which the sofa was sold?

Ⓐ $350
Ⓑ $400
Ⓒ $455
Ⓓ $500

Use the figure below to answer question 44.

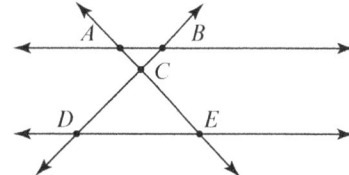

44. In the figure shown above, $\overline{AB} \parallel \overline{DE}$, which of the following geometric theorems most likely would be used in a proof that $\triangle ABC \sim \triangle EDC$?

Select all that apply.

Ⓐ Vertical angles of intersecting lines are congruent.
Ⓑ If two parallel lines are cut by a transversal, then any pair of alternate interior angles are congruent.
Ⓒ If two angles of one triangle are congruent to two corresponding angles of another triangle, then the triangles are similar.
Ⓓ The measure of an exterior angle of a triangle equals the sum of the measures of the remote interior angles.

Use the equation below to answer question 45.

$$2x = \sqrt{3x+1}$$

45. A teacher introduces students to solving radical equations by presenting the equation shown above. After some discussion, the students suggest that squaring both sides of the equation will remove the radical from the equation. By allowing the students to proceed with this strategy, the teacher likely is intending for the students to discover that squaring both sides of the equation $2x = \sqrt{3x+1}$ and then solving for x gives rise to what extraneous solution?

Ⓐ -1
Ⓑ $-\dfrac{1}{4}$
Ⓒ $\dfrac{1}{4}$
Ⓓ 1

46. If a prime number p is a factor of both $(14n + 13)$ and $(7n + 1)$, what is the value of p?

Ⓐ 7
Ⓑ 11
Ⓒ 13
Ⓓ It cannot be determined from the information given.

47. What is the third term in the binomial expansion of $(x + 2y)^5$?

Ⓐ $10x^2y^3$
Ⓑ $10x^3y^2$
Ⓒ $40x^3y^2$
Ⓓ $80x^2y^3$

48. $2\sqrt{5}(\sqrt{2} + \sqrt{5}) =$

Ⓐ $2\sqrt{10} + \sqrt{5}$
Ⓑ $2\sqrt{7} + 2\sqrt{10}$
Ⓒ $2\sqrt{35}$
Ⓓ $2\sqrt{10} + 10$

49. Given $x^2 + kx + c = (x + h)^2$, where c, k, and h are real numbers, if $k = 6$, what is the value of c?

Ⓐ -9
Ⓑ -3
Ⓒ 3
Ⓓ 9

50. Students are playing a simulation game in which players must acquire treasure coins. The treasure coins in the game are distributed among five locations in the ratio 1:2:3:4:5. To win the game, a player must acquire at least half of the number of coins in at least three of the five locations. To win, a player must acquire what minimum percent of the total coins?

Ⓐ 10%
Ⓑ 15%
Ⓒ 20%
Ⓓ 25%

51. If f is a real-valued function, which of the following values are NOT in the domain of f, where $f(x) = \dfrac{\sqrt{x+2}}{2x^3 + x^2 - 2x - 1}$?

Select all that apply.

Ⓐ -3
Ⓑ -1
Ⓒ $-\dfrac{1}{2}$
Ⓓ 1

GO ON TO THE NEXT PAGE

52. A family on vacation in an RV leaves home at 9 a.m., travels at an average speed of 50 miles per hour, and arrives at the vacation destination at 2 p.m., with no stops along the way. At approximately what time would the family have arrived if the average speed of the trip had been 65 miles per hour?

- Ⓐ   12:24 p.m.
- Ⓑ   12:51 p.m.
- Ⓒ   1:24 p.m.
- Ⓓ   1:51 p.m.

Use the figure below to answer question 53.

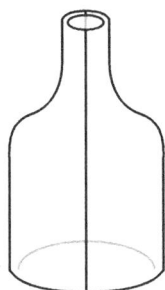

53. Water is poured at a constant rate into the container shown in the diagram. Which of the following graphs best represents the height of the water in the container as a function of time?

Ⓐ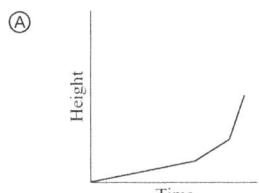

Ⓑ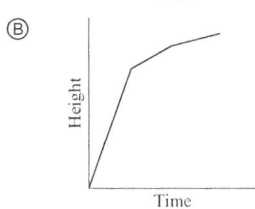

Ⓒ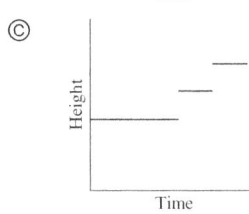

Ⓓ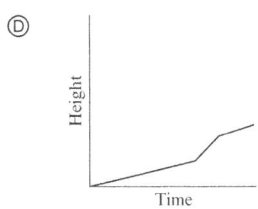

54. For a school fundraiser, the parents of a child pledge to donate $3.75 for the first 50-yard lap their 6-year-old child runs and $0.55 for each additional lap. Suppose that the total amount donated by the parents to the fundraiser for their child's run is $11.45. For how many laps did their child run?

- Ⓐ   12
- Ⓑ   13
- Ⓒ   14
- Ⓓ   15

55. What is the least positive integer k such that $\dfrac{1}{4^k} < 0.001$?

- Ⓐ   2
- Ⓑ   3
- Ⓒ   4
- Ⓓ   5

56. Viralyn runs the same distance each morning before going to work. For 10 days, she records her running times for her target distance. Her recorded running times are 21 minutes, 35 minutes, 34 minutes, 30 minutes, 32 minutes, 36 minutes, 24 minutes, 35 minutes, 28 minutes, and 35 minutes. What is the difference, in minutes, between Viralyn's median running time and her mean running time for the 10 days?

- Ⓐ   0
- Ⓑ   2
- Ⓒ   3
- Ⓓ   4

57. $(a^{-1} + b^{-1})^{-1} =$

- Ⓐ $a + b$
- Ⓑ $\dfrac{1}{a} + \dfrac{1}{b}$
- Ⓒ $\dfrac{ab}{a+b}$
- Ⓓ $\dfrac{2}{a+b}$

58. In a mixture, the ratio of cornmeal to wheat bran, by weight, is 2 to 3. Find the amount, in ounces, of the mixture if it contains 30 ounces of cornmeal.

- Ⓐ   30
- Ⓑ   40
- Ⓒ   50
- Ⓓ   75

GO ON TO THE NEXT PAGE

59. $(2x^2 - 3x - 2)^{-1}(2x^2 + 7x + 3)(x^2 - x - 2)(x^2 - 9)^{-1} =$

Ⓐ $\dfrac{x+1}{x-3}$

Ⓑ $\dfrac{x-1}{x+3}$

Ⓒ $\dfrac{(x+7)(x+1)}{(x+3)(x-3)}$

Ⓓ $-\dfrac{1}{3}$

60. $\dfrac{ab - b^2}{ab - a^2} - \dfrac{a^2b - b^2}{ab} =$

Ⓐ $-\dfrac{1}{a}$

Ⓑ $-a$

Ⓒ a

Ⓓ $-\dfrac{a^2 + 2b}{a}$

Use the figure below to answer question 61.

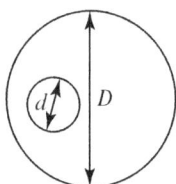

61. When presented with the picture shown above and the information that the diameter, D, of the larger circle is four times the diameter, d, of the smaller circle, students commonly speculate that the area of the larger circle is four times bigger than the area of the smaller circle. In reality, the ratio of the area of the smaller circle to the area of the larger circle is which of the following ratios?

Ⓐ $\dfrac{1}{16}$

Ⓑ $\dfrac{1}{8}$

Ⓒ $\dfrac{1}{4}$

Ⓓ $\dfrac{1}{2}$

62. Two identical machines can do a job in 10 days. How many days will it take five such machines to do the same job?

Ⓐ 4
Ⓑ 5
Ⓒ 20
Ⓓ 25

63. A gardener wants to divide a rectangular field that measures 24 feet by 36 feet into equal square plots with no land left over. What is the greatest length, in feet, for each side of the square plots?

Ⓐ 6
Ⓑ 9
Ⓒ 12
Ⓓ 18

Use the graph below to answer question 64.

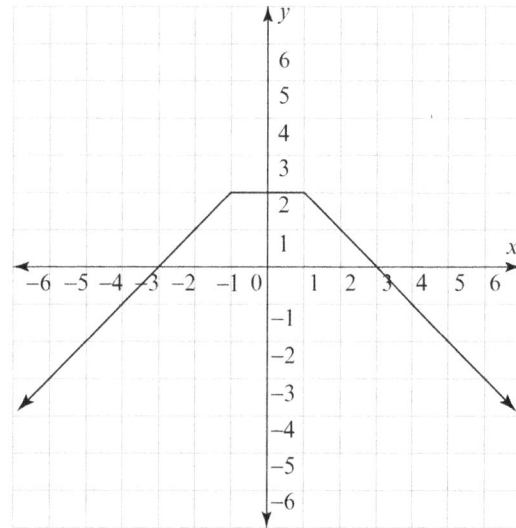

64. Which of the following sets is the range of the function shown above?

Ⓐ $\{y \mid y \text{ is a real number}\}$
Ⓑ $\{y \mid y \text{ is a real number}, y \leq 2\}$
Ⓒ $\{y \mid y \text{ is a real number}, -3 \leq y \leq 3\}$
Ⓓ $\{y \mid y \text{ is a real number}, -6 \leq y \leq 6\}$

GO ON TO THE NEXT PAGE

65. Which of the following polynomial functions have zeros at -4, -1, $\frac{1}{2}$, and 2?

Select all that apply.

- [A] $P(x) = x(x+4)\left(x-\frac{1}{2}\right)(x-2)(x+1)$
- [B] $P(x) = (x-4)(2x+1)(x+2)(x-1)$
- [C] $P(x) = (x+4)(2x-1)(x-2)(x+1)$
- [D] $P(x) = 2x(x+4)\left(x-\frac{1}{2}\right)(x-2)(x+1)$

66. A candy store owner mixes candy that normally sells for \$5.00 per pound and candy that normally sells for \$7.50 per pound to make a 90-pound mixture to sell at \$6.00 per pound. To make sure that \$6.00 per pound is a fair price, how many pounds of the \$5.00 candy should the owner use?

- Ⓐ 36
- Ⓑ 42
- Ⓒ 50
- Ⓓ 54

Use the figure below to answer question 67.

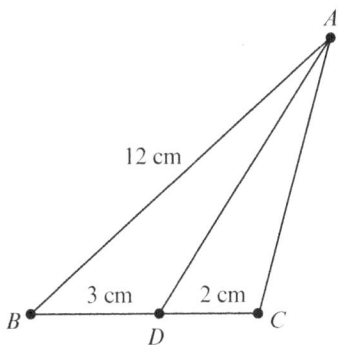

67. In $\triangle ABC$, $\angle DAB \cong \angle DAC$. What is the length of $\overline{AC}$, in centimeters?

- Ⓐ 6
- Ⓑ 7
- Ⓒ 8
- Ⓓ It cannot be determined from the information given.

68. Parents meet with a teacher to discuss their child Kandice's percentile score on a standardized multiple-choice exam. Kandice scored at the 85th percentile. The best interpretation of this information to tell the parents is that

- Ⓐ Kandice answered 85 percent of the questions on the test correctly.
- Ⓑ only 15 percent of the other students did worse on the test than Kandice.
- Ⓒ Kandice answered 85 questions correctly.
- Ⓓ Kandice did as well or better than 85 percent of the students who took the exam.

69. A water tank can be filled in 6 hours when the input valve is open and the outlet valve is closed. When the input valve is closed and the outlet valve is open, the same tank can be emptied in 10 hours. If a tank is filled with both valves open, how many hours will it take to fill the tank?

- Ⓐ 4
- Ⓑ $7\frac{1}{2}$
- Ⓒ 15
- Ⓓ 16

70. Given the cubic function $f(x) = x^3$, which of the following best describes the function $g(x) = (x-5)^3 + 2$?

- Ⓐ The same as the graph of $f(x) = x^3$ shifted right by 5 units and up by 2 units
- Ⓑ The same as the graph of $f(x) = x^3$ shifted left by 5 units and up by 2 units
- Ⓒ The same as the graph of $f(x) = x^3$ shifted right by 5 units and down by 2 units
- Ⓓ The same as the graph of $f(x) = x^3$ shifted left by 5 units and down by 2 units

GO ON TO THE NEXT PAGE

71. A Realtor who is selling houses located in an upscale housing development has determined the following probabilities for two neighboring houses, one of which is a model home: The probability that the model home will be sold is 0.50, the probability that the house next door will be sold is 0.40, and the probability that at least one of the two houses will be sold is 0.80. Find the probability that the house next door will be sold given that the model home has already been sold.

Ⓐ 10%
Ⓑ 20%
Ⓒ 30%
Ⓓ 40%

72. First prize for a television show's promotional drawing is a 24 × 16 × 8-inch rectangular box stuffed to capacity with U.S. $20 bills. On average, U.S. $20 bills measure 6.14 inches long and 2.61 inches wide, and a stack of one hundred $20 bills is about 0.43 inch thick. What is the approximate total value of money in the first-prize box of $20 bills?

Ⓐ $45,000
Ⓑ $890,000
Ⓒ $1,160,000
Ⓓ $8,920,000

73. A couple establishes a savings account for their child with an investment of $10,000, at an annual interest rate of 3% compounded monthly. Assuming no withdrawals and no additional deposits are made, which of the following amounts is closest to the balance in the account after 20 years?

Ⓐ $18,207.55
Ⓑ $18,061.11
Ⓒ $16,000.00
Ⓓ $10,512.06

74. The formula for the distance from point (x_1, y_1) to line $Ax + By + C = 0$ is given by $d = \dfrac{|Ax_1 + By_1 + C|}{\sqrt{A^2 + B^2}}$. What is the distance from the point $(-3, 7)$ to the line that has equation $4x + 3y = -5$?

Ⓐ 0.6
Ⓑ 0.8
Ⓒ 2.0
Ⓓ 2.8

Use the table below to answer question 75.

Library Users by Gender (N = 200)

	Female	Male
Former Student	25	5
Current Student	93	77

75. The data in the table show the student status, by gender, of 200 library users at a small college for a given day. If one of the 200 students is randomly selected, what is the probability that the student is a male former student?

Ⓐ $\dfrac{1}{40}$
Ⓑ $\dfrac{1}{8}$
Ⓒ $\dfrac{5}{8}$
Ⓓ $\dfrac{5}{6}$

Use the figure below to answer question 76.

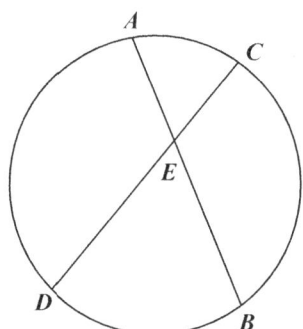

76. In the circle shown, chords $\overline{AB}$ and $\overline{CD}$ intersect at point E such that the length of $\overline{AE}$ is one-half the length of $\overline{EB}$. If the length of $\overline{CE}$ is 2 centimeters and the length of $\overline{ED}$ is 6 centimeters, find the length, in centimeters, of chord $\overline{AB}$.

Ⓐ $\sqrt{6}$
Ⓑ 4
Ⓒ $2\sqrt{6}$
Ⓓ $3\sqrt{6}$

77. Which equation has both −4 and 4 in the solution set?

Ⓐ $x = \sqrt[3]{64}$
Ⓑ $x = \sqrt{16}$
Ⓒ $x^2 = 16$
Ⓓ $x^3 = 64$

GO ON TO THE NEXT PAGE

78. A small town has one area code and four prefixes available—560, 562, 564, and 569—for the ten-digit telephone numbers in the town. Which of the following computations will yield the number of different telephone numbers that are possible if all four prefixes are used?

Ⓐ $4(_{10}C_4)$
Ⓑ $4(10^4)$
Ⓒ 10^8
Ⓓ 10^{16}

79. If $f(x) = -16x^{-4}$, then $f(-2)$ is

Ⓐ -1
Ⓑ 1
Ⓒ 128
Ⓓ 256

80. A box contains 25 wooden tiles of identical size and shape, which are numbered 1 through 25. If one tile is drawn at random from the box, what is the probability that the number on the tile is a prime number?

Ⓐ $\dfrac{1}{25}$
Ⓑ $\dfrac{9}{25}$
Ⓒ $\dfrac{2}{5}$
Ⓓ $\dfrac{12}{25}$

81. If $x^2 - 13 = 12x$, what is the value of $|x - 6|$?

Ⓐ 1
Ⓑ 6
Ⓒ 7
Ⓓ 13

82. If $p(x) = (2x - 3)(x + k)$ and $p(1) = -3$, what is the value of k?

Ⓐ -6
Ⓑ -3
Ⓒ 2
Ⓓ 6

Use the table below to answer question 83.

Mean Score	65
Median Score	73
Modal Score	77
Range	52
Mean Absolute Deviation	15
Number of Students	50

83. The data in the table summarize the scores of 50 students on a social studies exam. Which of the following statements best describes the distribution of the scores?

Ⓐ The distribution is positively skewed.
Ⓑ The distribution is negatively skewed.
Ⓒ The distribution is symmetric.
Ⓓ The distribution is bimodal.

84. What is the inverse of the function defined by $y = x^5 - 3$?

Ⓐ $y = \dfrac{1}{\sqrt[5]{x-3}}$
Ⓑ $y = \dfrac{1}{x^5 - 3}$
Ⓒ $y = \sqrt[5]{x} + 3$
Ⓓ $y = \sqrt[5]{x + 3}$

GO ON TO THE NEXT PAGE

Use the figure below to answer question 85.

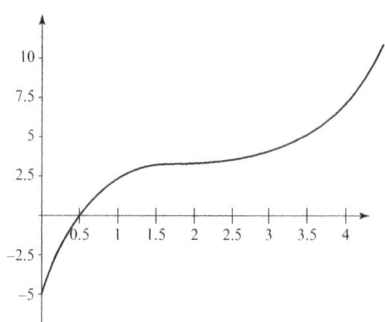

85. The graph shown is the graph of $y = x^3 - 6x^2 + 12x - 5$. The rate of change of a curve at a point is described by the slope of the tangent to the curve at the point. Which of the following statements is true about the rate of change of y with respect to x?

Ⓐ The rate of change is constant between 0 and 0.5.
Ⓑ The rate of change is increasing between 0.5 and 1.5.
Ⓒ The rate of change is decreasing between 2 and 3.
Ⓓ The rate of change is increasing between 3 and 3.5.

86. Which of the following sets is the solution to $2x^2 - x < 1$?

Ⓐ $\{x \in \text{reals}, x < -1 \text{ or } x > \frac{1}{2}\}$
Ⓑ $\{x \in \text{reals}, x < \frac{1}{2} \text{ or } x > 1\}$
Ⓒ $\{x \in \text{reals}, -\frac{1}{2} < x < 1\}$
Ⓓ $\{x \in \text{reals}, -1 < x < \frac{1}{2}\}$

87. A bag contains 10 blue marbles, 7 red marbles, 5 green marbles, and 3 yellow marbles. If two marbles are randomly drawn from the bag, one after the other, without replacement after the first draw, what is the probability that both marbles will be yellow?

Ⓐ $\frac{9}{625}$

Ⓑ $\frac{1}{100}$

Ⓒ $\frac{3}{25}$

Ⓓ $\frac{2}{24}$

Use the figure below to answer question 88.

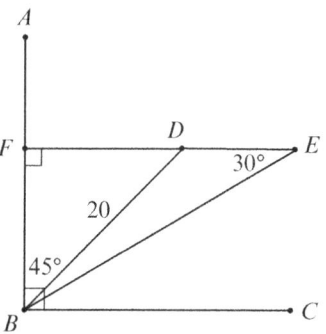

88. In the figure shown, $\overline{AB} \perp \overline{BC}$, $\overline{AB} \perp \overline{EF}$, and $BD = 20$. What is the perimeter of $\triangle DBE$?

Ⓐ $10(2 + \sqrt{2} + 3)$
Ⓑ $10(2 + \sqrt{2} + \sqrt{6})$
Ⓒ $20(2 + \sqrt{2} + \sqrt{3})$
Ⓓ $20(2 + 2\sqrt{2})$

GO ON TO THE NEXT PAGE

Use the figure below to answer question 89.

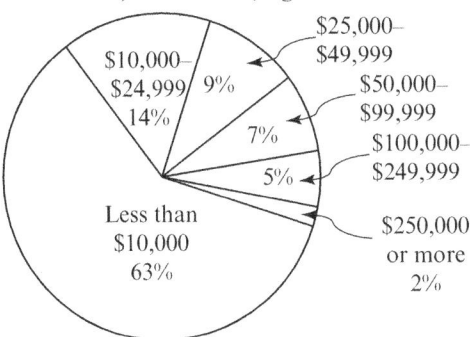

89. The circle graph above shows the distribution of 3,000 workers, ages 30 to 50, according to their total savings and investments. According to the graph, the number of workers who have less than $10,000 in savings and investments is what percent of the number of workers who have $100,000 or more in savings and investments?

   Ⓐ 7%
   Ⓑ 9%
   Ⓒ 700%
   Ⓓ 900%

90. Suppose $a = \dfrac{x}{4} + \dfrac{y}{4^2} + \dfrac{z}{4^3}$, where x, y, and z are each either 0 or 1. Which of the following fractions are possible values of a?

   Select all that apply.

   A $\dfrac{5}{64}$
   B $\dfrac{13}{64}$
   C $\dfrac{3}{16}$
   D $\dfrac{5}{16}$

91. Given $3x + 2y + 6z = 50$ and $7x + 8y + 4z = 70$, what is the arithmetic average of x, y, and z?

   Ⓐ 4
   Ⓑ 10
   Ⓒ 12
   Ⓓ It cannot be determined from the information given.

92. One of the interior angles of a regular polygon measures 140°. What is the sum of the measures of the polygon's interior angles?

   Ⓐ 360°
   Ⓑ 720°
   Ⓒ 1,260°
   Ⓓ 1,620°

93. Two boxes each contain four tiles, numbered 1, 2, 3, and 4. The tiles are identical in shape and size. A student randomly draws one tile from each box and calculates the product of the two numbers on the tiles. Which of the following products is most likely to occur?

   Ⓐ 2
   Ⓑ 4
   Ⓒ 6
   Ⓓ 8

94. The graph of the function f defined by $f(x) = 3^x$ is reflected over the x-axis and translated 5 units to the right to become the function g. Which of the following equations defines g?

   Ⓐ $g(x) = -3^{x-5}$
   Ⓑ $g(x) = -3^x - 5$
   Ⓒ $g(x) = 3^{-(x+5)}$
   Ⓓ $g(x) = 3^{-x} - 5$

95. A camper leaves camp and jogs 3 miles to a river, rests for a while, and then jogs 4 more miles. At this point which of the following could be the jogger's distance, in miles, from camp?

   Select all that apply.

   A 1
   B 5
   C 7
   D 9

GO ON TO THE NEXT PAGE

96. A teacher has assigned students to cooperative learning groups. The teacher provides each group of students with 36 identical square tiles, and gives the students the challenge to determine the maximum number of different rectangles they can form using the tiles, with no tiles left over and where a $p \times q$ rectangle is counted as different from a $q \times p$ rectangle. The teacher has students repeat the challenge several times, using a different number of tiles each time. This activity directly contributes to students' understanding of which of the following concepts?

Select all that apply.

- [A] Greatest common factor
- [B] Least common multiple
- [C] Factor pairs
- [D] Prime numbers

Use the figure below to answer question 97.

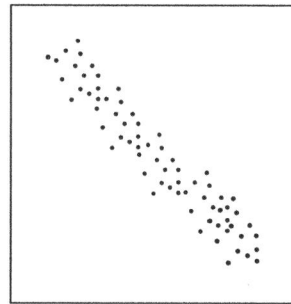

97. The preceding graph is a scatter plot for a set of bivariate data, paired values of data from two variables. What does the shape of the scatter plot most strongly suggest about the relationship between the two variables?

- Ⓐ There is little relationship between the two variables.
- Ⓑ There is a negative linear relationship between the two variables.
- Ⓒ There is a positive linear relationship between the two variables.
- Ⓓ There is an exponential relationship between the two variables.

98. The greatest common factor of m and 108 is 12, and the least common multiple of m and 108 is 756. What is m?

- Ⓐ 72
- Ⓑ 84
- Ⓒ 168
- Ⓓ 216

99. A ball is dropped from a height of 120 feet. If each rebound is $\frac{3}{4}$ the height of the previous bounce, which of the following functions would best model the ball's height as a function of rebound number n?

- Ⓐ Quadratic
- Ⓑ Polynomial
- Ⓒ Linear
- Ⓓ Exponential

100. Which of the following statements follows logically from the statement "If it is Monday, then I will go to work"?

- Ⓐ It is not Monday, so I am not going to work.
- Ⓑ It is Monday, so I am going to work.
- Ⓒ I am going to work, so it must be Monday.
- Ⓓ I am not going to work, so it is not Monday.

Answer Key

Question Number	Correct Answer	Chapter(s)	Question Number	Correct Answer	Chapter(s)
1.	C	2	26.	A, B, C	2
2.	C	1, 4	27.	B	4, 6
3.	B, C	6	28.	C	1, 4, 5
4.	C	1, 3	29.	C	5
5.	B	1, 2	30.	C	2
6.	A	2	31.	B	3
7.	D	2	32.	B	4
8.	B	1, 2	33.	D	3, 5
9.	B, C, D	3	34.	D	2, 5
10.	A	2, 3	35.	B	3
11.	A	1	36.	B, C	3
12.	C	1	37.	A	4
13.	B	4	38.	D	4, 5
14.	B	3	39.	C	1, 5
15.	B	3	40.	A	2
16.	B	3	41.	B	1
17.	C	3, 5	42.	D	1, 6
18.	B	1, 5	43.	C	1, 5
19.	A	1, 5	44.	A, B, C	3, 5
20.	D	2	45.	B	2, 6
21.	B, D	2	46.	B	1, 5
22.	B	2, 5	47.	C	2
23.	C	2	48.	D	1
24.	D	1, 3, 5	49.	D	2, 5
25.	A	4	50.	C	1, 5, 6

Question Number	Correct Answer	Chapter(s)	Question Number	Correct Answer	Chapter(s)
51.	A, B, C, D	2	76.	D	3
52.	B	1, 5	77.	C	2
53.	A	2	78.	B	4
54.	D	2, 5	79.	A	2
55.	D	1	80.	B	1, 4
56.	B	4	81.	C	2
57.	C	1, 2	82.	C	2
58.	D	2, 5	83.	B	4
59.	A	2	84.	D	2
60.	B	2	85.	D	2
61.	A	3, 6	86.	C	2
62.	A	2, 5, 6	87.	B	4, 5
63.	C	1, 5	88.	B	3, 5
64.	B	2	89.	D	1, 4
65.	A, C, D	2	90.	A, D	1, 2
66.	D	2, 5	91.	A	2, 4
67.	C	3, 5	92.	C	3
68.	D	4, 6	93.	B	4
69.	C	2, 5	94.	A	2
70.	A	2	95.	A, B, C	1, 2
71.	B	4, 5	96.	C, D	1, 6
72.	B	1, 5	97.	B	4
73.	A	1	98.	B	1, 5
74.	D	2	99.	D	1, 2, 5
75.	A	4	100.	D	5

Chapter 8: TExES Math 4–8 Practice Test 2

Answer Explanations

1. **C.** Recall that a function is a set of ordered pairs in which each first component is paired with *one and only one* second component; that is, each x value is paired with one and only one y value. First, eliminate choices with equations that contain y^2 because when y is squared, the equation will *not* define a function. Hence, eliminate choices A and B. Next, eliminate choice D because both (2, 2) and (2, –2) satisfy the equation, demonstrating that the equation yields an x value that is paired with two different y values. Thus, choice C is the correct response. You should go on to the next question; but just so you know, the equation in choice C, which can be written as $y = 25x^2 + 2$, yields exactly one value of y for every x value.

2. **C.** The graph shows the percentage of children's fiction books and the percentage of science fiction books sold in December. To find how many fiction books were sold, do two steps. First, find the total percentage of fiction books sold. Next, find the total number of fiction books sold.

   Step 1. 15% + 32.5% = 47.5%

   Step 2. 47.5% of 1,200 books = (0.475)(1,200 books) = 570 books, choice C

3. **B, C.** Eliminate choice A because the number of buses must be a whole number. Select choice B because the average time could be 6.3 minutes. Select choice C because the length of each piece of ribbon could be 6.3 centimeters. Eliminate choice D because the number of possible ways must be a whole number.

4. **C.** To compare the total amount of fruit juice to the total amount of cinnamon and sugar, both amounts need to be in the same units. To answer the question, do three steps. First, find the total amount of fruit juice in cups; then, using the measurement equivalents, convert the answer to tablespoons. Next, using the measurement equivalents, convert the amount of cinnamon into tablespoons. Then find the total amount of cinnamon and sugar in tablespoons. Finally, find the ratio of the total amount of fruit juice to the total amount of cinnamon and sugar.

   Step 1. $2\frac{3}{4}$ c + $1\frac{1}{2}$ c = $4\frac{1}{4}$ c; $4\frac{1}{4}$ c × $\frac{16\,T}{c}$ = 68 T fruit juice

   Step 2. 1 tsp cinnamon = $\frac{1}{3}$ T cinnamon; $\frac{1}{3}$ T cinnamon + 3 T sugar = $3\frac{1}{3}$ T cinnamon and sugar

   Step 3. The ratio of the total amount of fruit juice to the total amount of cinnamon and sugar is

   $\dfrac{68\,T}{3\frac{1}{3}\,T} = \dfrac{68\,\cancel{T}}{\frac{10}{3}\,\cancel{T}} = \dfrac{3(68)}{\cancel{3}\left(\frac{10}{\cancel{3}}\right)} = \dfrac{204}{10} = \dfrac{102}{5}$, choice C.

   Tip: Notice that the amount of water in the recipe was information that you did not need in order to answer the question.

5. **B.** Let x = the original amount in Maria's account. Write an equation that represents the transactions and solve for x.

   $$x - 0.25x - \$150 = \$975$$
   $$0.75x = \$975 + \$150$$
   $$0.75x = \$1{,}125$$
   $$x = \$1{,}500$$

   The original amount in Maria's account was $1,500, choice B.

6. **A.** From your knowledge of solving inequalities, you know the open circles at –3 and 4 mean that –3 and 4 are not included in the solution set. Thus, the inequality symbol in the answer must be either < or >, so eliminate choices C and D.

   Method 1. Test a number from the interval shown in the graph in each of the inequalities given in choices A and B. For convenience and ease of calculation, select 0 as your test number. Select choice A because when

323

$x = 0$, $\left|x - \frac{1}{2}\right| = \left|0 - \frac{1}{2}\right| = \left|-\frac{1}{2}\right| = \frac{1}{2} < \frac{7}{2}$, which is true. You have determined that choice A is the correct response, so go on to the next problem. However, you can easily see that $x = 0$ does not satisfy the inequality in choice B because $\frac{1}{2} > \frac{7}{2}$ is false.

Tip: You also can use this method for testing a number in inequalities that contain the symbols ≤ or ≥. When you test a number from a given interval in these inequalities, do not select one of the endpoints of the interval as your test number because doing so might lead you to make a wrong decision about which inequality is the correct answer.

Method 2. Another approach is to solve the inequalities given in choices A and B. Select choice A because $\left|x - \frac{1}{2}\right| < \frac{7}{2}$ yields the solution $-3 < x < 4$, which is the inequality illustrated in the graph shown. You have determined that choice A is the correct response, so go on to the next problem. However, for your information, the solution to the inequality in choice B is $x < -3$ or $x > 4$, which is not the inequality illustrated in the graph shown.

7. **D.** Check the formulas given in the answer choices using the values in the table.

   Check A: When $n = 1$, $\sqrt{n} = \sqrt{1} = 1$, not 0; eliminate choice A.

   Check B: When $n = 1$, $n^2 = 1^2 = 1$, not 0; eliminate choice B.

   Check C: When $n = 1$, $n^2 - 1 = 1^2 - 1 = 0$ ✓; when $n = 2$, $n^2 - 1 = 2^2 - 1 = 3$, not 1; eliminate choice C. Therefore, you know that choice D is the correct response. You should go on to the next problem.

   For your information, here is the check for choice D: When $n = 1$, $(n - 1)^2 = (1 - 1)^2 = 0$ ✓; when $n = 2$, $(n - 1)^2 = (2 - 1)^2 = 1$ ✓; when $n = 3$, $(n - 1)^2 = (3 - 1)^2 = 4$ ✓; and when $n = 4$, $(n - 1)^2 = (4 - 1)^2 = 9$ ✓.

   Tip: When simple math is involved, do the checks mentally to save time.

8. **B. Method 1.** Substitute numerical values for a, b, and c that satisfy the conditions given, and then work with your substituted numbers.

   Let $a = 100$, $b = 10$, and $c = 2$. Then $\frac{a}{b} = \frac{100}{10} = 10$ ✓, $\frac{10}{2} = 5$ ✓, and $\frac{a}{b+c} = \frac{100}{10+2} = \frac{100}{12} = \frac{25}{3}$, choice B.

   Tip: As shown above, when you substitute numerical values for the variables, always check to make sure the values satisfy the conditions given in the problem.

   Method 2. Another approach is to express $\frac{a}{b+c}$ in terms of $\frac{a}{b}$ and $\frac{b}{c}$ by dividing each term in its numerator and denominator by b, and then simplifying the result to obtain $\frac{25}{3}$, choice B.

9. **B, C, D.** Make a sketch. Draw the altitude from vertex Y to side $\overline{XZ}$ and label the point of intersection P as shown here.

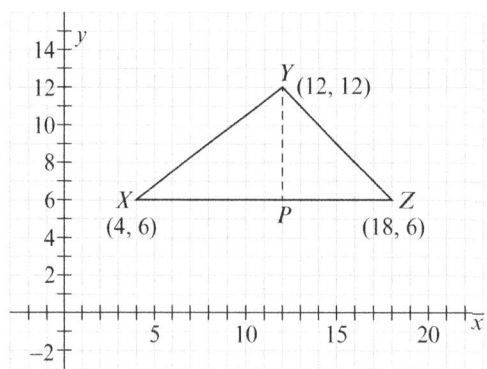

From the figure, you can determine that the length of side $\overline{XZ}$ is 14 and that the altitude of $\triangle XYZ$, from the vertex Y to side $\overline{XZ}$, is 6. The line segment $\overline{YP}$ creates two right triangles: $\triangle XPY$ and $\triangle ZPY$. Use the information given and the properties of right triangles to check the answer choices. Start by selecting answer choices that are obviously rational quantities.

Select choice B because the area of $\triangle XYZ$ is $\frac{1}{2}(XZ)(YP) = \frac{1}{2}(14)(6)$, which is a rational quantity. Select choice C because $\overline{XY}$ is the hypotenuse of a right triangle whose legs are 8 and 6; thus, the length of $\overline{XY}$ is 10, a rational quantity. Select choice D because the length of $\overline{XZ}$ is 14, a rational quantity, so its midpoint is a rational quantity as well. Eliminate choice A. The perimeter of $\triangle XYZ$ is irrational because it has a portion, namely $\overline{YZ}$, that is the hypotenuse of a right triangle whose legs are each 6; thus, the length of $\overline{YZ} = \sqrt{6^2 + 6^2} = \sqrt{72}$, an irrational quantity.

10. **A.** In terms of x, the dimensions of the rectangle are $\frac{8}{x}$ cm by $\frac{10}{x}$ cm. Write an equation that represents the facts given.

$$2\left(\frac{8}{x} \text{ cm}\right) + 2\left(\frac{10}{x} \text{ cm}\right) = 18 \text{ cm}$$

Solve the equation for x (omitting the units for convenience) and then compute $\frac{8}{x}$ cm and $\frac{10}{x}$ cm.

$$2\left(\frac{8}{x}\right) + 2\left(\frac{10}{x}\right) = 18$$
$$x\left(\frac{16}{x}\right) + x\left(\frac{20}{x}\right) = x(18)$$
$$16 + 20 = 18x$$
$$36 = 18x$$
$$2 = x$$

Thus, $\frac{8}{x}$ cm = $\frac{8}{2}$ cm = 4 cm and $\frac{10}{x}$ cm = $\frac{10}{2}$ cm = 5 cm.

The dimensions of the rectangle are 4 cm by 5 cm, so it has area (4 cm)(5 cm) = 20 cm², choice A.

11. **A.** Multiply as indicated: $(3 - 2i)(3 + 4i) = 9 + 12i - 6i - 8i^2 = 9 + 12i - 6i + 8 = 17 + 6i$, choice A.

12. **C.** If all the tagged fish are still active in the lake when the second group of fish is captured, the proportion of tagged fish in the second group should equal the proportion of tagged fish in the whole population, P, of fish in the lake. Set up a proportion and solve for P.

$$\frac{20}{100} = \frac{500}{P} \text{ implies } P = \frac{(100)(500)}{20} = 2{,}500$$

The best estimate of the fish population is 2,500 fish, choice C.

13. **B.** To find the mean, multiply each of the number of minutes by the number of students who predicted that many minutes and divide the result by 100 (the total number of students).

$$\text{mean} = \frac{5(1) + 15(2) + 10(3) + 25(4) + 30(5) + 5(6) + 10(7)}{100} = \frac{415}{100} = 4.15 \approx 4.2, \text{ choice B}$$

14. **B.** From the properties of parallel lines cut by a transversal, the lines m and n will be parallel if two corresponding angles created by the transversal t are congruent. In the figure, the angle that measures $(x + 80)°$ corresponds to the angle above line m that is supplementary to the angle that measures $(2x - 50)°$. Therefore, lines m and n are parallel when $(x + 80)° = 180° - (2x - 50)°$. Solve for x (omitting the units for convenience).

$$(x + 80) = 180 - (2x - 50)$$
$$x + 80 = 180 - 2x + 50$$
$$3x = 150$$
$$x = 50, \text{ choice B}$$

15. B. Make a sketch.

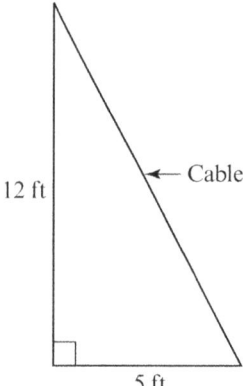

The pole, the cable, and the ground form a right triangle. From the sketch, the cable is the hypotenuse of a right triangle that has legs of 12 feet and 5 feet. Use the Pythagorean theorem to find the length of the hypotenuse, denoted by c (omit the units for convenience).

$c^2 = (12)^2 + (5)^2 = 144 + 25 = 169$

Thus, $c = \sqrt{169} = 13$. The length of the cable is 13 feet, choice B.

Tip: The number -13 is also a solution, but is rejected because length is nonnegative.

16. B. From the figure, right angle DAB is an inscribed angle. The measure of an inscribed angle is half the degree measure of its intercepted arc. Thus, the degree measure of arc $\overset{\frown}{DB}$ is 180°. Therefore, chord $\overline{DB}$ is a diameter of the circle that has circumference 8π. Also, chord $\overline{DB}$ is the diagonal of the square $ABCD$ and the hypotenuse of right triangle DAB. The area of square $ABCD$ is $x \cdot x = x^2$. To find the area of square $ABCD$, do two steps. First, use the formula for the circumference of a circle to find the length of chord $\overline{DB}$, which is the same as d, the diameter of the circle. Next, use the Pythagorean theorem to find x^2, the area of the square.

Step 1. Using $C = \pi d$, solve for the length of chord $DB = d$.

$$C = \pi d$$
$$\pi d = 8\pi$$
$$d = 8 = \text{the length of chord } \overline{DB}$$

Step 2. Apply the Pythagorean theorem in right triangle DAB to find x^2, the area of the square.

$$x^2 + x^2 = (8)^2$$
$$2x^2 = 64$$
$$x^2 = 32$$

Thus, the area of square $ABCD$ is 32, choice B.

Tip: In an isosceles right triangle, the square of the length of the hypotenuse is always twice the square of the length of a leg of the triangle.

17. C. You are to find the mass, in grams, of the cube. The units for density are grams per cubic centimeter $\left(\dfrac{g}{cm^3}\right)$, so dimensional analysis tells you that if you want to have grams as the units of the answer, then you will need to "cancel" cm^3 from the denominator of the density quantity. Cubic centimeters are units of volume. To find the mass of the silver cube, do two steps. First, find the volume of the cube, and then multiply by the density of silver.

Step 1. Volume of cube $= (2 \text{ cm})^3 = 8 \text{ cm}^3$

Step 2. Mass of cube = $(8 \text{ cm}^3)\left(\dfrac{10.5 \text{ g}}{\text{cm}^3}\right) = 84$ g

The mass of the cube is 84 grams, choice C.

18. **B.** Systematically calculate the percent increases and decreases from year to year.

    In 2010, the value is $500. In 2015, the value is $500 − 10%($500) = 90%($500) = 0.90($500) = $450. In 2017, the value is $450 + 10%($450) = $450 + 0.10($450) = $495. In 2020, the value is $495 − 20%($495) = 80%($495) = 0.80($495) = $396, choice B.

19. **A.** The number of people over age 65 who get a flu shot is $35\%N = 0.35N$. Of this number, 2 percent will have an adverse reaction. Thus, the estimated number of people over age 65 who will have an adverse reaction after getting flu shots is $(0.02)(0.35)N = 0.007N$, choice A.

20. **D.** The quadratic function defined by $y = 16x^2 - kx + 25$ will have exactly one real zero when the discriminant of $16x^2 - kx + 25 = 0$ is zero. The coefficients for $16x^2 - kx + 25 = 0$ are $a = 16$, $b = -k$, and $c = 25$. Set the discriminant equal to zero and solve for k: $b^2 - 4ac = (-k)^2 - 4(16)(25) = k^2 - 1{,}600 = 0$, which implies the positive value $k = \sqrt{1{,}600} = 40$, choice D.

21. **B, D.** The function given in choice A is a finite function. None of the other functions are finite, so eliminate choice A. Compare the domains of the functions, and then compare the ranges. The domain of each of the functions given in choices B and D is the set of real numbers; however, the domain in choice C is the set of whole numbers, so eliminate choice C. The range of each of the functions in choices B and D is the nonnegative real numbers, so the two correct choices are B and D.

22. **B.** Make a chart that shows the growth of the deer population as a function of time, t, at 8-year intervals.

Time in years	$t = 0$	$t = 8$	$t = 16$	$t = 24$	...
Deer population	100	(100)2	$(100)2^2$	$(100)2^3$	...

    Let $y = f(t)$ be the function that models the growth of the population. From your table, you can see that the initial population is 100 with a growth factor of 2, indicating that $y = (100)2^{kt}$. Because the population doubles every 8 years, time must be measured in periods of 8 years. Therefore, $k = \dfrac{1}{8} = 0.125$ and $y = (100)2^{0.125t}$, choice B.

23. **C.** When two lines are perpendicular, their slopes are negative reciprocals of each other. You can write the equation of a line when you know the slope of the line and a point on the line. To find the equation of the line that is perpendicular to the line whose equation is $5x - 6y = 4$ and passes through the point $(3, 1)$, do three steps. First, find the slope, m, of the line whose equation is $5x - 6y = 4$. Next, find the negative reciprocal of m, which is $-\dfrac{1}{m}$. Then use the point-slope form to determine the equation of the line with slope $-\dfrac{1}{m}$ that passes through the point $(3, 1)$.

    Step 1. Rewrite $5x - 6y = 4$ as $y = \dfrac{5}{6}x - \dfrac{2}{3}$, which shows the slope of this line is $\dfrac{5}{6}$.

    Step 2. The negative reciprocal of $\dfrac{5}{6}$ is $-\dfrac{6}{5}$.

    Step 3. Use the point-slope form to write the equation of the line.

    $$y - 1 = -\dfrac{6}{5}(x - 3)$$

    $$y = -\dfrac{6}{5}x + \dfrac{18}{5} + 1$$

    $$5(y) = 5\left(-\dfrac{6}{5}x + \dfrac{23}{5}\right)$$

    $$5y = -6x + 23$$

    $$6x + 5y = 23, \text{ choice C}$$

24. **D.** To determine the cost of the paint, do three steps. First, find the surface area (S.A.) of the sphere. Next, find the number of gallons of paint needed. Then find the cost of the paint.

    Step 1. S.A. $= 4\pi r^2 = 4\pi(12 \text{ ft})^2 = 1{,}809.5575\ldots$ ft^2 (Don't round this answer.)

    Step 2. Number of gallons needed $= 1{,}809.5575\ldots \text{ ft}^2 \times \dfrac{1 \text{ gal}}{400 \text{ ft}^2} \approx 4.5$ gal, so 5 gallons will need to be purchased (because the paint is sold in gallon containers only).

    Step 3. Cost of 5 gallons of paint $= 5 \text{ gal} \times \dfrac{\$24.50}{1 \text{ gal}} = \$122.50$, choice D.

    Tip: The formula for the surface area of a sphere is available during the exam in the on-screen "Definitions and Formulas" reference material.

25. **A.** The coin is flipped five times, so use the fundamental counting principle to work this problem. There are two possibilities for each of the five coin flips, which means the total number of possible outcomes in the sample space is $2 \cdot 2 \cdot 2 \cdot 2 \cdot 2 = 2^5$, choice A.

26. **A, B, C.** Using the table, list the possible "products" and check for the properties given in the answer choices.

    From the table, you have $a \otimes a = a$, $a \otimes b = b$, $b \otimes a = b$, and $b \otimes b = b$.

    Select choice A: Set S is closed with respect to $\otimes$ because when $\otimes$ is performed on any two elements in set S, the result is an element in set S. Select choice B: Because $a \otimes b = b$ and $b \otimes a = b$, set S is commutative with respect to $\otimes$. Select choice C: Given that $a \otimes a = a$, $a \otimes b = b$, and $b \otimes a = b$, set S contains an identity element, namely a, with respect to the operation of $\otimes$. Eliminate choice D: Set S does not contain an inverse for every element in set S. In particular, the element b does not have an inverse because there is no element in set S such that $b \otimes$ (that element) $= a$ (the identity element).

27. **B.** The students likely would select the box-and-whisker plot as most convenient for determining the median, range, and quartiles of a data set. A box-and-whisker plot displays five measures from a data set: the minimum value, the first quartile, the median, the third quartile, and the maximum value. The median, range, and quartiles are easily determined from this information. None of the graphical representations in the other choices provides the level of convenience for determining these measures as does the box-and-whisker plot.

28. **C.** According to the stem-and-leaf plot, there are nine weights that are less than 115 pounds (100, 103, 103, 107, 108, 111, 111, 111, and 114). Therefore, the percentage of the 36 students who weigh less than 115 pounds is $\dfrac{9}{36} = 25\%$, choice C.

29. **C.** Let $W =$ the set of customers who bought washers and $D =$ the set of customers who bought dryers. Using the notation $|X|$ to represent the number of elements in a set, you have $|W| = 94$ and $|D| = 80$. Because $|W| + |D| = 94 + 80 = 174$, which is greater than 152, the total number of customers, you logically can conclude that $174 - 152 = 22$ customers bought both a washer and a dryer. Therefore, the number of customers who bought only a washer is $94 - 22 = 72$, choice C.

30. **C.** Simplify:

$$\dfrac{a}{a^2-b^2} - \dfrac{b}{a^2+ab} = \dfrac{a}{(a+b)(a-b)} - \dfrac{b}{a(a+b)}$$

$$= \dfrac{a \cdot a}{a(a+b)(a-b)} - \dfrac{b(a-b)}{a(a+b)(a-b)}$$

$$= \dfrac{a^2}{a(a+b)(a-b)} - \dfrac{ab-b^2}{a(a+b)(a-b)}$$

$$= \dfrac{a^2 - ab + b^2}{a(a+b)(a-b)}, \text{ choice C}$$

Tip: Watch your signs! A minus sign before a fraction applies to the entire numerator, not just to the first term.

31. B. Plug the units into the formula and simplify as you would for variable quantities.

$$Y = \frac{Adv}{t} = \frac{(cm^2)\left(\frac{g}{cm^3}\right)\left(\frac{cm}{s}\right)}{s} = \frac{\frac{g}{s}}{s} = \frac{g}{s^2}, \text{ choice B}$$

32. B. The question requires that you find a conditional probability. That is, you determine the probability when you already know the student is female. Thus, when computing the probability, the number of possible students under consideration is no longer 500, but is reduced to the total number of female students. Specifically, once you know that the selected person is a female student, you are dealing only with the students in the second row of the table. First, find the total number of female students. Next, among those, determine the number who reside off-campus, and then compute the conditional probability.

The total number of female students is $156 + 95 = 251$. Among these 251 female students, 95 reside off-campus. Thus, $P(\text{resides off-campus} \mid \text{given student is female}) = \frac{95}{251}$, choice B.

33. D. The volume of a right prism is given by $V = Bh$. To find the volume of the right triangular prism, do two steps. First, find the area, B, of one of the equilateral triangular bases. Next, find the volume by multiplying B by 20 inches, the height (h) of the prism.

Step 1. The area of an equilateral triangle with sides of 4 inches is $\frac{\sqrt{3}}{4}s^2 = \frac{\sqrt{3}}{4}(4 \text{ in})^2 = 4\sqrt{3} \text{ in}^2$.

Tip: You can derive this result by using the Pythagorean theorem to determine the height (altitude) of the triangle, and then using area $= \frac{1}{2}bh$ to find the area of the equilateral triangle.

Step 2. Volume $= (4\sqrt{3} \text{ in}^2)(20 \text{ in}) \approx 139 \text{ in}^3$, choice D.

34. D. Let q = the number of quarters and $10q$ = the number of dimes.

Make a table to organize the coin information.

Denomination	Dimes	Quarters	Total
Face Value per Coin	$0.10	$0.25	N/A
Number of Coins	$10q$	q	Not given
Value of Coins	$0.10(10q)$	$0.25q$	$22.50

Using the table information, write an equation that represents the facts.

$0.10(10q) + 0.25q = 22.50$

Solve the equation for q, the number of quarters, omitting the units for convenience. Then compute $10q$, the number of dimes.

$$0.10(10q) + 0.25q = 22.50$$
$$q + 0.25q = 22.50$$
$$1.25q = 22.50$$
$$q = 18$$
$$10q = 10(18) = 180$$

There are 180 dimes in the collection, choice D.

Tip: Be sure to answer the question asked. After you determine the number of quarters, use the result to determine the number of dimes.

35. **B.** Under a reflection over the y-axis, $(2, 5) \to (-2, 5)$. Under a translation of 4 units right and 6 units down, $(-2, 5) \to (-2 + 4, 5 - 6) = (2, -1)$. The coordinates of B' are $(2, -1)$, choice B.

36. **B, C.** The sum of the lengths of any two sides of a triangle must be greater than the third side. It follows that given two sides of lengths x and y, where $x > y$, the length of the third side, call it z, satisfies the inequality $(x - y) < z < (x + y)$. Thus, if two sides have lengths of 7 and 19, then the length of the third side must be greater than $19 - 7 = 12$ and less than $19 + 7 = 26$. Select choices B and C because 13 and 25 fall between 12 and 26. Choice A is too short, and choice D is too long.

37. **A.** The probability of at least one 3 appearing on the up face in three tosses of the number cube is 1 minus the probability of no 3s appearing in three tosses. The probability of no 3 in one toss of the number cube is $1 - \frac{1}{6} = \frac{5}{6}$. The probability of no 3s in three tosses is $\frac{5}{6} \cdot \frac{5}{6} \cdot \frac{5}{6} = \frac{125}{216}$. Therefore, the probability of at least one 3 in three tosses of the number cube is $1 - \frac{125}{216} = \frac{91}{216}$, choice A.

38. **D.** Calculate the result in each scenario. For choice A, using the fundamental counting principle (FCP), the number of ways to award the three prizes is $(10)(9)(8) = 720$. For choice B, using the FCP, the number of arrangements is $(10)(9)(8) = 720$. Eliminate choices A and B because these two scenarios result in an equal number of outcomes, so neither can be the correct answer. For choice C, the number of different committees is ${}_{10}C_3 = \frac{10!}{3!7!} = 120$. Eliminate choice C because the result is less than choice A or B, so choice C cannot be the correct answer. Therefore, you know that choice D is the correct response. You should go on to the next problem. For your information, using the FCP, the number of different passcodes is $(10)(10)(10) = 1,000$, which is greater than any of the results in the other answer choices.

39. **C.** The ratio of x to y is 20 to 11, so $\frac{x}{y} = \frac{20}{11}$. The ratio of y to z is 3 to 5, $\frac{y}{z} = \frac{3}{5}$. The product of $\frac{x}{y}$ and $\frac{y}{z}$ is $\frac{x}{y} \cdot \frac{y}{z} = \frac{x}{\cancel{y}} \cdot \frac{\cancel{y}}{z} = \frac{x}{z}$, which is the ratio of x to z. Therefore, the ratio of x to z is $\frac{x}{y} \cdot \frac{y}{z} = \frac{\cancel{20}^4}{11} \cdot \frac{3}{\cancel{5}^1} = \frac{12}{11}$, choice C.

40. **A.** The equation $y = 4(x + 3) + 5$ is equivalent to $y = 4x + 17$. The rate of change for this equation is 4. Therefore, for every 1-unit change in x, there is a 4-unit change in y, choice A.

41. **B.** The answer choices are given as exponential expressions, so a logical way to work this problem is to perform on x the sequence of operations indicated by the function machine, using the exponential form for the operation.

$$\left(\left(\left((x)^{\frac{1}{2}}\right)^{\frac{1}{2}}\right)^{\frac{1}{2}}\right)^6 = x^{\frac{1}{2} \cdot \frac{1}{2} \cdot \frac{1}{2} \cdot 6} = x^{\frac{6}{8}} = x^{\frac{3}{4}}, \text{ choice B}$$

42. **D.** The operation $\oplus$ is commutative on the set R of real numbers if $x \oplus y = y \oplus x$ for all real numbers x and y. By the definition of the operation, $x \oplus y = 3x + xy$ and $y \oplus x = 3y + yx$, so the question that tests commutativity is "Does $3x + xy = 3y + yx$ for all real numbers x and y?", choice D.

43. **C.** The sofa's original price was 70% of $500, which is $0.7(\$500) = \$350$. The sofa's selling price was 130% of $350, which is $1.3(\$350) = \$455$, choice C.

44. **A, B, C.** Considering the theorems given in the answer options, only choice D would be eliminated from the proof. A simple way to show that two triangles are similar is to show that two angles of one triangle are congruent to two corresponding angles of the other triangle (select choice C). You could proceed by showing that $\angle ACB$ is congruent to $\angle ECD$ because these angles are vertical angles of intersecting lines (select choice A), and then showing $\angle ABC$ is congruent to $\angle EDC$ because these angles form a pair of alternate-interior angles of two parallel lines cut by a transversal (select choice B).

45. **B.** Squaring both sides of the equation $2x = \sqrt{3x + 1}$ and solving for x yields

$$(2x)^2 = \left(\sqrt{3x+1}\right)^2$$
$$4x^2 = 3x + 1$$
$$4x^2 - 3x - 1 = 0$$
$$(4x+1)(x-1) = 0$$
$$x = -\frac{1}{4} \text{(extraneous) or } x = 1$$

Note that $-\frac{1}{4}$, choice B, is an extraneous solution because it makes the left side of the original equation negative, so it cannot equal $\sqrt{3x+1}$, which is always nonnegative. The other solution, $x = 1$ (choice D), is not an extraneous solution because it satisfies the original equation as shown below.

$$2(1) \stackrel{?}{=} \sqrt{3(1)+1}$$
$$2 \stackrel{?}{=} \sqrt{4}$$
$$2 = 2$$

Tip: Remember to answer the question posed. The question asks about the extraneous solution.

46. B. If an integer is a factor of both of the integers x and y, then it is a factor of $ax + by$, for any integers a and b. Let $x = (14n + 13)$ and $y = (7n + 1)$. Because p is a factor of both $x = (14n + 13)$ and $y = (7n + 1)$, then p is a factor of $1 \cdot x - 2y = (1)(14n + 13) - 2(7n + 1) = 14n + 13 - 14n - 2 = 11$. The only positive factors of 11 are 1 and 11. Given that p is prime, it follows that p equals 11, choice B.

47. C. Use the binomial theorem, $(x+y)^n = \sum_{k=0}^{n}\binom{n}{k}x^{n-k}y^k$. For this problem, $(x+2y)^5 = \sum_{k=0}^{5}\binom{5}{k}x^{5-k}(2y)^k$.

The third term is $\binom{5}{2}x^{5-2}(2y)^2 = 10(x^3)(2y)^2 = 10(x^3)(4y^2) = 40x^3y^2$, choice C.

Tip: You can use the nCr option under the prb key menu of the on-screen calculator to compute $\binom{5}{2} = {_5}C_2$. Keying in 5 nCr 2 returns 10.

48. D. Compute as indicated: $2\sqrt{5}(\sqrt{2} + \sqrt{5}) = 2\sqrt{5} \cdot \sqrt{2} + 2\sqrt{5} \cdot \sqrt{5} = 2\sqrt{10} + 2(5) = 2\sqrt{10} + 10$, choice D.

49. D. Given $x^2 + 6x + c = (x+h)^2$, or equivalently $x^2 + 6x + c = x^2 + 2xh + h^2$, then $6 = 2h$ and $c = h^2$ (because corresponding coefficients are equal). Thus, $h = 3$ and $c = 3^2 = 9$, choice D.

50. C. For convenience, designate the locations L1, L2, L3, L4, and L5, with treasure coins in the ratio 1:2:3:4:5, respectively. Let n = the number of coins in L1, then L1, L2, L3, L4, and L5 have n, $2n$, $3n$, $4n$, and $5n$ coins, respectively. The minimum number of coins needed to win is half of the combined number of coins in L1, L2, and L3 (because these locations have the fewest number of coins). This minimum number is $\frac{1}{2}(n + 2n + 3n) = \frac{1}{2}(6n) = 3n$. The total number of coins is $n + 2n + 3n + 4n + 5n = 15n$. The minimum percent to win is $\frac{3n}{15n} = \frac{1}{5} = 20\%$, choice C.

Tip: Notice that you do not need to know the actual number of coins at any of the locations or the actual total number of coins. Instead, you can work with the ratio relationships to answer the question.

51. A, B, C, D. Any value of x for which $f(x) = \frac{\sqrt{x+2}}{2x^3 + x^2 - 2x - 1}$ is undefined over the real numbers is not in the domain of f. Therefore, you must exclude from the domain values for which $(x + 2) < 0$ (or equivalently $x < -2$) and values for which the denominator evaluates to zero.

First, check the answer choices for values less than –2. Only –3 (choice A) is less than –2, so –3 is not in the domain of f. Select choice A.

Next, check whether any of the values given in choices B, C, or D is a value for which the denominator evaluates to zero.

Method 1. Factor $2x^3 + x^2 - 2x - 1$ to obtain $2x^3 + x^2 - 2x - 1 = x^2(2x + 1) - (2x + 1) = (2x +1)(x^2 - 1) = (2x +1)(x + 1)(x - 1)$, which implies $-\frac{1}{2}$ (select choice C), –1 (select choice B), and 1 (select choice D) are values for which the denominator evaluates to zero.

Method 2. Another approach is to evaluate $f(x) = 2x^3 + x^2 - 2x - 1$ at each of the values given in choices B, C, and D. Proceeding in this manner $f(-1) = 0$ (select choice B), $f\left(-\frac{1}{2}\right) = 0$ (select choice C), and $f(1) = 0$ (select choice D).

52. B. At 50 miles per hour, it took the family 5 hours (9 a.m. to 2 p.m.) to reach their destination. The distance traveled is $(5 \text{ hr})\left(50 \frac{\text{miles}}{\text{hr}}\right) = 250$ miles. At an average speed of 65 miles per hour, the trip would have taken $\frac{250 \text{ miles}}{65 \frac{\text{miles}}{\text{hr}}} \approx 3.85$ hours = 3 hours 51 minutes. Therefore, if the family left at 9 a.m. and traveled at an average speed of 65 miles per hour, they would have arrived at (approximately) 9 a.m. plus 3 hours 51 minutes, which is 12:51 p.m., choice B.

53. A. Analyze the figure. As water is poured into the container at a constant rate, the height of the water rises at a constant rate until it reaches the point near the top where the bottle narrows. At that point, the water rises at a faster (but still constant) rate until it reaches the bottle's neck, where it rises at an even faster rate. The graph that corresponds to this analysis is given in choice A.

Choice B is incorrect because it indicates that the rate at which the water rises slows down as the water reaches the top of the bottle. Choice C is incorrect because it indicates that the height of the water in the bottle is constant at first, then suddenly leaps to a higher level and remains constant at that level for a while and, finally, leaps to an even higher level, where it remains constant. Choice D is incorrect because it indicates that the rate at which the water rises initially is the same as the rate at which it rises when it reaches the bottle's neck.

54. D. Suppose x is the total number of laps that the child ran. Then x is the sum of the first lap and the total number of laps after the first lap, which is $x - 1$. The donation for the first lap, $3.75, plus the donation for the additional laps, $0.55(x - 1)$, equals the total donation to the fundraiser, $11.45. Write an equation to represent the facts and solve for x (omitting the units for convenience).

$$3.75 + 0.55(x - 1) = 11.45$$
$$3.75 + 0.55x - 0.55 = 11.45$$
$$0.55x = 8.25$$
$$x = 15$$

The child ran 15 laps, choice D.

55. D. The inequality $\frac{1}{4^k} < 0.001$ implies that $4^k > 1{,}000$. Substitute possible values of k until you obtain one that satisfies this inequality: $4^1 = 4$, $4^2 = 16$, $4^3 = 64$, $4^4 = 256$, $4^5 = 1{,}024$. Thus, $k = 5$ is the least integer that satisfies the inequality, choice D.

56. B. To find the difference between the median and the mean, do three steps. First, calculate the mean. Next, calculate the median. Then compute the difference, median – mean.

Step 1. Omitting the units for convenience, the mean is $\frac{21+24+28+30+32+34+35+35+35+36}{10} = 31$.

Step 2. Omitting the units, first, put the times in order: 21, 24, 28, 30, 32, 34, 35, 35, 35, 36. Next, average the middle pair: $\frac{32+34}{2} = 33$.

Step 3. The difference is 33 minutes – 31 minutes = 2 minutes, choice B.

57. C. Simplify: $\left(a^{-1}+b^{-1}\right)^{-1} = \frac{1}{\left(a^{-1}+b^{-1}\right)} = \frac{1}{\left(\frac{1}{a}+\frac{1}{b}\right)} = \frac{ab \cdot 1}{ab\left(\frac{1}{a}+\frac{1}{b}\right)} = \frac{ab}{b+a} = \frac{ab}{a+b}$, choice C

58. D. The amount (in ounces) in the mixture is the sum of the amount (in ounces) of cornmeal in the mixture and the amount (in ounces) of wheat bran in the mixture. You are given that the amount of cornmeal in the mixture is 30 ounces. Let x equal the amount, in ounces, of wheat bran in the mixture. To find the total number of ounces in the mixture, do two steps. First, set up a proportion and determine x. Next, find the total amount (in ounces) of the mixture.

Step 1. Omitting the units, solve the following proportion as shown:

$\frac{30}{x} = \frac{2}{3}$ implies $x = \frac{(30)(3)}{2} = 45$

Thus, the amount of wheat bran in the mixture is 45 ounces.

Step 2. The total amount of the mixture is 30 ounces + 45 ounces = 75 ounces, choice D.

59. A. Simplify:

$$(2x^2 - 3x - 2)^{-1}(2x^2 + 7x + 3)(x^2 - x - 2)(x^2 - 9)^{-1} = \frac{(2x^2 + 7x + 3)(x^2 - x - 2)}{(2x^2 - 3x - 2)(x^2 - 9)}$$

$$= \frac{(2x+1)(x+3)(x+1)(x-2)}{(2x+1)(x-2)(x+3)(x-3)}$$

$$= \frac{\cancel{(2x+1)}\cancel{(x+3)}(x+1)\cancel{(x-2)}}{\cancel{(2x+1)}\cancel{(x-2)}\cancel{(x+3)}(x-3)}$$

$$= \frac{x+1}{x-3}, \text{ choice A}$$

60. B. Simplify:

$$\frac{ab-b^2}{ab-a^2} - \frac{a^2b-b^2}{ab} = \frac{b(a-b)}{a(b-a)} - \frac{b(a^2-b)}{ab} = \frac{-b}{a} - \frac{(a^2-b)}{a} = \frac{-b-a^2+b}{a} = \frac{-a^2}{a} = -a, \text{ choice B}$$

Tip: Watch your signs! A minus sign before a fraction applies to all terms in the numerator, not just to the first term.

61. A. The diameter, D, of the larger circle is four times the diameter, d, of the smaller circle. One way to work the problem is to use the formula $A = \pi r^2$ to find the areas of the two circles in terms of D, and then find the ratio of the area of the smaller circle to the larger circle. However, you should remember that when the dimensions of a two-dimensional figure are multiplied by a scale factor, s, the area of the figure produced is s^2 times the area of the original figure. Therefore, the area of the larger circle in the diagram is $4^2 = 16$ times the area of the smaller circle. Hence, the ratio of the area of the smaller circle to the larger circle is $\frac{1}{16}$, choice A.

Tip: Knowing how scale factors impact area and volume can save you time on the test.

62. A. Use logical reasoning to reach the solution. The machines are identical, so if two machines can do the job in 10 days, then it should take twice as long for one machine to do the same job. So, one machine can do the job in 20 days. If five such machines do the job together, they should take $\frac{1}{5}$ as long as it takes for one machine. Therefore, five machines can do the same job in $\frac{1}{5}(20 \text{ days}) = 4$ days, choice A.

63. C. The greatest length for each side of the square plots is the greatest common factor of 24 and 36. Because $24 = 2^3 \cdot 3$ and $36 = 2^2 \cdot 3^2$, the gcf $(24, 36) = 2^2 \cdot 3 = 12$. Therefore, the greatest length for each side of the square plots is 12 feet, choice C.

64. B. The range of a function is the set of possible second components of the ordered pairs that compose the function. From the graph, the values of y are less than or equal to 2. Thus, choice B is the correct response.

65. A, C, D. If $x - r$ is a factor of $P(x)$, then the number r is a zero of $P(x)$. By inspection, choices A and D have the desired zeros plus an additional zero of 0. Choice C also has the desired zeros because the factor $(2x - 1)$ would yield a zero of $\frac{1}{2}$. Select choices A, C, and D. Eliminate choice B because this function does not have the desired zeros.

66. D. Let $x =$ the number of pounds of the candy priced at \$5.00 per pound needed. Then $90 - x =$ the number of pounds of the candy priced at \$7.50 per pound needed. Make a table to organize the information given.

When	Price per Pound	Number of Pounds	Value
Before mixing	\$5.00	x	\$5.00x
	\$7.50	$90 - x$	\$7.50$(90 - x)$
After mixing	\$6.00	90	\$6.00(90)

The value of the candy before it is mixed should equal the value after it is mixed. Using the information in the table, write an equation that represents the facts given (omitting "pounds" and "per pound" because these units cancel each other).

$$\$5.00x + \$7.50(90 - x) = \$6.00(90)$$

Solve the equation, omitting the units for convenience.

$$5.00x + 7.50(90 - x) = 6.00(90)$$
$$5.00x + 675 - 7.50x = 540$$
$$-2.50x = -135$$
$$x = 54$$

The owner should use 54 pounds of the \$5.00 candy, choice D.

Tip: Use logical reasoning when you are problem solving. If the owner used half of each type of candy, then the price should be the average of \$5.00 and \$7.50, which is \$6.25. So, you know that to bring the price down to \$6.00 per pound will require more than 45 pounds (half) of the lower-priced candy. Therefore, eliminate choices A and B at the start.

67. C. $\angle DAB \cong \angle DAC$; therefore, $\overline{AD}$ bisects $\angle A$. Recall that the angle bisector of an angle of a triangle divides the opposite side in the ratio of the sides that form the angle bisected. Thus, $\frac{BD}{DC} = \frac{AB}{AC}$. Substitute the values given into this proportion and solve for AC.

$$\frac{3 \text{ cm}}{2 \text{ cm}} = \frac{12 \text{ cm}}{AC} \text{ implies } AC = \frac{(2)(12 \text{ cm})}{3} = 8 \text{ cm, choice C}$$

68. D. The 85th percentile is a value at or below which 85% of the data fall. Therefore, the best interpretation of Kandice's score is that she did as well or better than 85% of the students who took the exam, choice D.

69. C. This problem is best analyzed as a "work problem." The key idea in a work problem is that the rate at which work is done equals the amount of work accomplished divided by the amount of time worked:

$$\text{rate} = \frac{\text{amount of work done}}{\text{time worked}}.$$ For the situation in this problem, the work to be done is to fill the tank.

However, only the input valve works to fill the tank. The outlet valve works counter to the input valve because it works to empty the tank. Let $t =$ the time (in hours) it will take to fill the tank with both valves open.

To find t, do two steps. First, determine the rate, R, at which the tank can be filled when the input valve is open and the outlet valve is closed, and the rate, r, at which the tank can be emptied when the input valve is closed and the outlet valve is open. Next, write an equation and solve for t.

Step 1. The rate for filling the tank is $R = \dfrac{1 \text{ full tank}}{6 \text{ hr}} = \dfrac{1}{6}$ tank per hr. The rate for emptying the tank is $r = \dfrac{1 \text{ full tank}}{10 \text{ hr}} = \dfrac{1}{10}$ tank per hr.

Step 2. $\left(\dfrac{1}{6} \text{ tank per hr}\right)(t) - \left(\dfrac{1}{10} \text{ tank per hr}\right)(t) = 1$ full tank

Omit the units and solve for t.

$$\left(\dfrac{1}{6}\right)(t) - \left(\dfrac{1}{10}\right)(t) = 1$$

$$30\left(\dfrac{1}{6}\right)(t) - 30\left(\dfrac{1}{10}\right)(t) = 30(1)$$

$$5t - 3t = 30$$

$$2t = 30$$

$$t = 15$$

With both valves open, it will take 15 hours to fill the tank, choice C.

70. **A.** Subtracting 5 from x will result in a horizontal shift of 5 units to the right. Adding 2 to $f(x)$ will result in a vertical shift of 2 units up. Thus, the graph of $g(x) = (x - 5)^3 + 2$ is the same as the graph of $f(x) = x^3$ shifted right by 5 units and up by 2 units, choice A.

71. **B.** The problem asks: Find the probability that the house next door will be sold given that the model home has already been sold. This probability is a conditional probability. If A is the event that the model home will be sold and B is the event that the house next door will be sold, then find $P(B|A) = \dfrac{P(A \cap B)}{P(A)}$.

Looking at the formula, you see that you are given $P(A) = 0.50$, but you are not given $P(A \cap B)$, which is the probability that both houses are sold. The problem states "the probability that at least one of the two houses will be sold is 0.80." The probability that at least one of the two houses will be sold is $P(A \cup B)$. Recall that $P(A \cup B) = P(A) + P(B) - P(A \cap B)$. Thus, given $P(A) = 0.50$, $P(B) = 0.40$, and $P(A \cup B) = 0.80$, you can determine $P(A \cap B)$.

To find $P(B|A)$, do two steps. First, determine $P(A \cap B)$. Next, use the information obtained and information given in the problem to calculate $P(B|A)$.

Step 1. $P(A \cup B) = P(A) + P(B) - P(A \cap B)$ implies $0.80 = 0.50 + 0.40 - P(A \cap B)$. Thus, $P(A \cap B) = 0.90 - 0.80 = 0.10$.

Step 2. $P(B|A) = \dfrac{P(A \cap B)}{P(A)} = \dfrac{0.10}{0.50} = 0.20 = 20\%$, choice B.

72. **B.** The capacity of the box is its volume, which equals (24 in)(16 in)(8 in). The thickness of a single U.S. $20 bill is $\dfrac{0.43 \text{ in}}{100} = 0.0043$ in, and the dimensions of a U.S. $20 bill are 6.14 × 2.61 × 0.0043 inches. Thus, the approximate total value of money in the first-prize box of $20 bills is

$$\dfrac{(24 \text{ in})(16 \text{ in})(8 \text{ in})}{(6.14 \text{ in})(2.61 \text{ in})(0.0043 \text{ in})} \cdot \$20 = \dfrac{3{,}072 \text{ in}^3}{0.06890922 \text{ in}^3} \cdot \$20 = \$891{,}607.83 \approx \$890{,}000, \text{ choice B.}$$

73. **A.** The compound interest formula is $A = P\left(1 + \dfrac{r}{n}\right)^{nt}$, where P is the initial investment, r is the interest rate, compounded n times per year, and A is the final value after t years. (*Note:* This formula is available during the exam in the on-screen "Definitions and Formulas" reference material.) From the question information,

A is unknown, P is \$10,000, r is 3%, n is 12, and t is 20 years. Substituting into the formula yields

$$A = P\left(1+\frac{r}{n}\right)^{nt} = \$10{,}000\left(1+\frac{0.03}{12}\right)^{12 \cdot 20} = \$10{,}000(1.0025)^{240} \approx \$18{,}207.55, \text{ choice A.}$$

74. **D.** First, rewrite $4x + 3y = -5$ as $4x + 3y + 5 = 0$, and then apply the formula using the point $(-3, 7)$.

$$d = \frac{|Ax_1 + By_1 + C|}{\sqrt{A^2 + B^2}} = \frac{|4(-3) + 3(7) + 5|}{\sqrt{4^2 + 3^2}} = \frac{|-12 + 21 + 5|}{\sqrt{25}} = \frac{|14|}{5} = \frac{14}{5} \text{ or } 2.8, \text{ choice D.}$$

75. **A.** From the table, you can determine that of the 200 students, 5 are male former students. Thus, P(male former student) $= \frac{5}{200} = \frac{1}{40}$, choice A.

76. **D.** Recall that if two chords intersect within a circle, the product of the lengths of the segments of one chord equals the product of the lengths of the segments of the other. Therefore, $(AE)(EB) = (CE)(ED)$. Let $x = AE$. Then $2x = EB$. To determine AB, do two steps. First, use $(AE)(EB) = (CE)(ED)$ to determine AE and EB. Next, add AE and EB.

Step 1. Solve for x and $2x$.

$$(x)(2x) = (2)(6)$$
$$2x^2 = 12$$
$$x^2 = 6$$
$$x = \sqrt{6}$$
$$2x = 2\sqrt{6}$$

Thus, $AE = \sqrt{6}$ and $EB = 2\sqrt{6}$.

Step 2. The length of chord $\overline{AB}$ is $\sqrt{6} + 2\sqrt{6} = 3\sqrt{6}$, choice D.

Tip: Make sure you answer the question asked.

77. **C.** Eliminate choice A because the solution set of $x = \sqrt[3]{64}$ is $\{4\}$. Eliminate choice B because the solution set of $x = \sqrt{16}$ is $\{4\}$. *Tip:* The square root radical symbol $(\sqrt{})$ always returns the principal square root, which is nonnegative. Select choice C because the solution set of $x^2 = 16$ is $\{-4, 4\}$. In a test situation, you should move on to the next question. For your information, the solution set of $x^3 = 64$ (choice D) is $\{4\}$.

78. **B.** Use the fundamental counting principle to determine the number of possible telephone numbers for each prefix. After the prefix, there are four slots to fill. For each slot, 10 digits are available, which means the number of possible telephone numbers for each prefix is $10 \cdot 10 \cdot 10 \cdot 10 = 10^4$. By the addition principle, the total number of possible telephone numbers if all four prefixes are used is $10^4 + 10^4 + 10^4 + 10^4 = 4(10^4)$, choice B.

79. **A.** Evaluate the function when $x = -2$: $f(-2) = -16(-2)^{-4} = -16\frac{1}{(-2)^4} = \frac{-16}{16} = -1$, choice A.

80. **B.** First, count how many numbers between 1 and 25 are prime. Next, divide this answer by 25. The primes between 1 and 25 are 2, 3, 5, 7, 11, 13, 17, 19, and 23, giving a total of 9 primes. (Remember, the number 1 is neither prime nor composite.) Therefore, the probability that the number drawn is prime is $\frac{9}{25}$, choice B.

81. **C.** First, rearrange the terms so that only x terms are on the left side of the equation. Next, complete the square for the x terms. Then take the square root of both sides of the equation. Remember, $\sqrt{(x)^2} = |x|$.

$$x^2 - 13 = 12x$$
$$x^2 - 12x = 13$$
$$x^2 - 12x + 36 = 13 + 36$$
$$(x - 6)^2 = 49$$
$$|x - 6| = 7, \text{ choice C}$$

82. **C.** Given: $p(1) = -3$. Substitute into $p(x)$ and solve for k.
$$p(x) = (2x-3)(x+k)$$
$$p(1) = (2(1)-3)((1)+k)$$
$$-3 = (-1)(1+k)$$
$$-3 = -1-k$$
$$k = 2, \text{ choice C}$$

83. **B.** If the data were represented using a histogram, the mean would lie to the left of both the median and the mode on the horizontal axis, indicating that the data are skewed, with a tail on the left. Thus, the distribution is negatively skewed, choice B.

84. **D.** Interchange x and y in $y = x^5 - 3$, and then solve for y.
$$x = y^5 - 3$$
$$x + 3 = y^5$$
$$\sqrt[5]{x+3} = y$$
$$y = \sqrt[5]{x+3}, \text{ choice D}$$

85. **D.** Check each statement against the behavior of the graph of the function. Choice A is incorrect because the slope of the tangent line is decreasing between 0 and 0.5, not constant. Choice B is incorrect because the slope of the tangent line is decreasing between 0.5 and 1.5. Choice C is incorrect because the slope of the tangent line is increasing between 2 and 3. Choice D is correct because the slope of the tangent line is increasing between 3 and 3.5.

86. **C.** Rewrite $2x^2 - x < 1$ as $2x^2 - x - 1 < 0$.

    Factor the left side of the inequality to obtain $(2x + 1)(x - 1) < 0$. Now determine when the product $(2x + 1)(x - 1)$ is negative. First, find the values for x at which the factors change sign; that is, find the zero for each factor.

    Set each factor equal to 0 and solve for x.

    $2x + 1 = 0$ yields $x = -\dfrac{1}{2}$ and $x - 1 = 0$ yields $x = 1$.

    The two values $-\dfrac{1}{2}$ and 1 divide the number line into three intervals: $\left(-\infty, -\dfrac{1}{2}\right)$, $\left(-\dfrac{1}{2}, 1\right)$, and $(1, \infty)$.

    Next, determine in which interval(s) the product of the two factors is negative.

    Make an organized table to determine the sign of $(2x + 1)(x - 1)$ for each of these intervals.

Interval	Sign of $(2x + 1)$	Sign of $(x - 1)$	Sign of $(2x + 1)(x - 1)$
$\left(-\infty, -\dfrac{1}{2}\right)$	negative	negative	positive
$\left(-\dfrac{1}{2}, 1\right)$	positive	negative	negative
$(1, \infty)$	positive	positive	positive

   Thus, $(2x + 1)(x - 1)$ is negative only in the interval $\left(-\dfrac{1}{2}, 1\right)$, choice C.

87. **B.** By the multiplication rule, $P(A \cap B) = P(A)P(B|A)$. The probability that a yellow marble is drawn on the first draw is
$$P(\text{yellow on first draw}) = \frac{\text{Number of yellow marbles in bag}}{\text{Total number of marbles}} = \frac{3}{25}$$

After this event occurs, since the yellow marble drawn first is not put back in the bag, the probability that a yellow marble will be drawn on the second draw is

$$P(\text{yellow on second draw given first draw is yellow}) = \frac{2}{24} = \frac{1}{12}$$

Hence, the probability that both marbles will be yellow when two marbles are randomly drawn from the bag without replacement is

$$\frac{3}{25} \cdot \frac{1}{12} = \frac{1}{100}, \text{ choice B}$$

88. **B.** The perimeter of $\triangle DBE$ is $DB + BE + ED = 20 + BE + ED$. You need $BE + ED$. First, find BF and DF, the lengths of the legs of the 45°-45°-90° right triangle DFB, which has hypotenuse of length 20. Use BF to find BE, which is the length of the hypotenuse of the 30°-60°-90° right triangle EFB. Next, use BF to find EF, which is the length of the side opposite the 60° angle in the 30°-60°-90° right triangle EFB. Use EF and DF to find ED, which is $EF - DF$. Then, find the perimeter.

Step 1. Find BF and DF.

The lengths of the sides of a 45°-45°-90° right triangle are in the ratio $\frac{1}{\sqrt{2}} : \frac{1}{\sqrt{2}} : 1$. Hence,
$BF = DF = 20\left(\frac{1}{\sqrt{2}}\right) = \frac{20}{\sqrt{2}} = 10\sqrt{2}$.

Step 2. Use BF to find BE.

In the 30°-60°-90° right triangle EFB, BF is the side opposite the 30° angle and BE is the hypotenuse. The lengths of the sides of a 30°-60°-90° right triangle are in the ratio $1 : \sqrt{3} : 2$. So $BE = (BF)(2) = (10\sqrt{2})(2) = 20\sqrt{2}$.

Step 3. Use BF to find EF.

In the 30°-60°-90° right triangle EFB, EF is the length of the side opposite the 60° angle and BF is the length of the other leg. The lengths of the sides of a 30°-60°-90° right triangle are in the ratio $1 : \sqrt{3} : 2$. So $EF = (BF)(\sqrt{3}) = (10\sqrt{2})(\sqrt{3}) = 10\sqrt{6}$.

Step 4. Use EF and DF to find ED.

$ED = EF - DF = 10\sqrt{6} - 10\sqrt{2}$

Step 5. Find the perimeter.

Perimeter $= 20 + BE + ED = 20 + 20\sqrt{2} + 10\sqrt{6} - 10\sqrt{2} = 20 + 10\sqrt{2} + 10\sqrt{6} = 10(2 + \sqrt{2} + \sqrt{6})$, choice B

Tip: When a figure has angles of 30° and 45°, think about the ratios of the sides in 30°-60°-90° and 45°-45°-90° right triangles.

Note: The explanation for this question might seem lengthy (and, perhaps, complicated) to you. Actually, because of the two special right triangles, the computations are straightforward and can be done without a calculator.

89. **D.** All of the percentages in the circle graph have the same base (3,000 workers), so work with the percentages rather than the actual number of workers. The percent of workers who have less than $10,000 in savings and investments is 63%. The percent of workers who have $100,000 or more in savings and investments is 5% + 2% = 7%. To answer the question, determine what percent 63% is of 7% as follows:

$$\frac{63\%}{7\%} = 9 = 900\%, \text{ choice D}.$$

90. **A, D.** There are eight possibilities for x, y, and z. Written as ordered triples, the eight possibilities are (0, 0, 0), which yields $a = 0$; (0, 0, 1), which yields $a = \frac{1}{4^3} = \frac{1}{64}$; (0, 1, 0), which yields $a = \frac{1}{4^2} = \frac{1}{16}$; (0, 1, 1), which yields $a = \frac{1}{4^2} + \frac{1}{4^3} = \frac{1}{16} + \frac{1}{64} = \frac{5}{64}$ (select choice A); (1, 0, 0), which yields $a = \frac{1}{4}$; (1, 0, 1), which yields $a = \frac{1}{4} + \frac{1}{4^3} = \frac{1}{4} + \frac{1}{64} = \frac{17}{64}$; (1, 1, 0), which yields $a = \frac{1}{4} + \frac{1}{4^2} = \frac{1}{4} + \frac{1}{16} = \frac{5}{16}$ (select choice D); and (1, 1, 1), which yields $a = \frac{1}{4} + \frac{1}{4^2} + \frac{1}{4^3} = \frac{1}{4} + \frac{1}{16} + \frac{1}{64} = \frac{21}{64}$. The fractions in choices B and C are not possible values of a. Only the fractions in choices A and D are possible values of a.

91. A. The average is $\frac{x+y+z}{3}$. You have three variables and only two equations, so finding specific values for x, y, and z is problematic. Notice that if you can determine the sum $x + y + z$, you can answer the question. Observe that corresponding coefficients in the two equations add to 10. Add the two equations and solve for $(x + y + z)$.

$$\begin{aligned} 3x + 2y + 6z &= 50 \\ 7x + 8y + 4z &= 70 \\ \hline 10x + 10y + 10z &= 120 \\ 10(x + y + z) &= 120 \\ (x + y + z) &= 12 \end{aligned}$$

Thus, the average is $\frac{12}{3} = 4$, choice A.

92. C. The measure of an exterior angle of the regular polygon is 180° – 140° = 40°. The sum of the measures of the exterior angles of a polygon is 360°, no matter how many sides the polygon has. Because the polygon is a regular polygon, its number of sides is $\frac{360°}{40°} = 9$. The polygon has 9 sides and 9 congruent interior angles. The sum of the measures of the interior angles is (9)(140°) = 1,260°, choice C.

93. B. Show the sample space in a table.

		Box 1			
		1	2	3	4
Box 2	1	1	2	3	4
	2	2	4	6	8
	3	3	6	9	12
	4	4	8	12	16

The possible products and their frequencies are 1 (1 time), 2 (2 times), 3 (2 times), 4 (3 times), 6 (2 times), 8 (2 times), 9 (1 time), 12 (2 times), and 16 (1 time). The product 4 (choice B) occurs three times, and, thus, is most likely to occur.

94. A. The transformation $-f(x)$ is a reflection of $f(x)$ over the x-axis, and the transformation $f(x - 5)$ is a horizontal shift of 5 units to the right. Applying both of these transformations to f defined by $f(x) = 3^x$ results in the new function g defined by $g(x) = -3^{x-5}$, choice A.

95. A, B, C. Do not assume that the jogger went in a straight line in one direction. Let x be the jogger's distance from camp. Make a sketch. Show the camp and river as 3 miles apart. Construct a circle at the river with radius 4 miles.

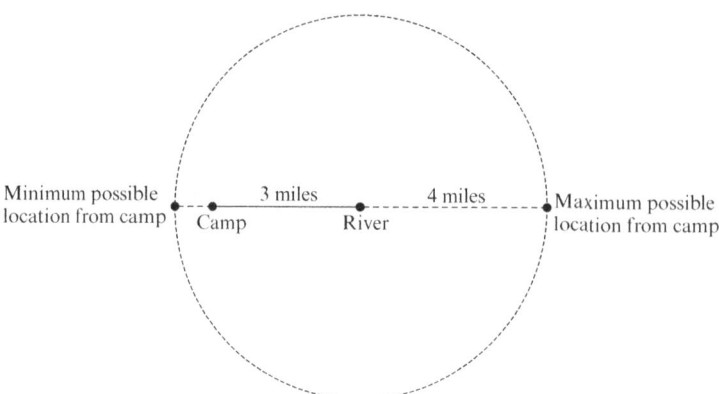

From the sketch, you can determine that $1 \le x \le 7$. Select choices A, B, and C because each falls in this interval. Eliminate choice D because it is too far.

96. **C, D.** Arranging n tiles in the shape of rectangles allows the students to find two positive integer factors that multiply to give n. For example, using 36 tiles, the possible rectangles are 1×36, 2×18, 3×12, 4×9, 6×6, 9×4, 12×3, 18×2, and 36×1. From these arrangements, they can determine the factor pairs of 36 (select choice C). When n is a prime number (for example, 11 or 13), the students will discover that only $1 \times n$ and $n \times 1$ rectangles can be created, leading them to the inductive conclusion that the factors of a prime number are itself and the number 1 (select choice D). Understanding of the concepts given in choices A and B is not directly related to the activity.

97. **B.** Examine the scatter plot. It appears that a linear relationship exists between the two variables, so you can delete choices A and D. Since the line of best fit would slant downward from left to right, the relationship is negative. Thus, choice B is the correct response.

98. **B.** The least common multiple (lcm) of two positive integers is their product divided by their greatest common factor (gcf). Use this fact about the relationship between least common multiple and greatest common factor to write an equation and solve for m.

$$\frac{(108)(m)}{\text{gcf}(m, 108)} = \text{lcm}(m, 108)$$

$$\frac{108m}{12} = 756$$

$$9m = 756$$

$$m = 84, \text{ choice B}$$

99. **D.** Make a table showing the height of the ball as a function of rebound number.

Height of Ball (in feet)	120	$120\left(\dfrac{3}{4}\right)$	$120\left(\dfrac{3}{4}\right)\left(\dfrac{3}{4}\right)$	$120\left(\dfrac{3}{4}\right)\left(\dfrac{3}{4}\right)\left(\dfrac{3}{4}\right)$	...
Rebound Number n	0	1	2	3	...

Examination of the table leads to a general term for the nth bounce: $120\left(\dfrac{3}{4}\right)^n$, where $n = 0, 1, 2, \ldots$. Thus, an exponential function (choice D) would best model the height of the ball as a function of rebound number n. None of the functions in the other answer choices works as well as an exponential model.

100. **D.** The statement "If it is Monday, then I will go to work" is a conditional statement. It has the logical form "If P, then Q," where P is the statement "it is Monday" and Q is the statement "I will go to work." In logic, the logical equivalent of "If P, then Q" is its contrapositive, which is stated like so: "If not Q, then not P." The contrapositive for the statement given is "If I will not go to work, then it is not Monday." Only choice D is compatible with this statement.

Chapter 9

TExES Math 7–12 Practice Test 1

100 questions

Time—4 Hours 45 Minutes

Directions: Read the directions for each question carefully. For each question, select the best single answer choice unless written instructions in the question state otherwise.

1. Rose drove 50 miles in 1 hour, and then drove for an additional 40 minutes. If her average speed for the entire trip was 54 miles per hour, what was her average speed, in miles per hour, for the last 40 minutes of the trip?

   Ⓐ 45
   Ⓑ 50
   Ⓒ 55
   Ⓓ 60

2. The whole number y is exactly six times the whole number x. The whole number z is the sum of $2x$ and y. Which of the following could be the value of z?

   Select all that apply.

   ☐ A 121,006,233,314
   ☐ B 422,986,033,016
   ☐ C 815,985,237,824
   ☐ D 721,914,536,032

3. The arithmetic average of 20 numbers is X. Ten of these numbers have an arithmetic average of 15. In terms of X, what is the arithmetic average of the other 10 of these numbers?

   Ⓐ $X - 7.5$
   Ⓑ $2X - 15$
   Ⓒ $3X - 15$
   Ⓓ $20X - 150$

4. Which of the following true statements can be proven using the principle of mathematical induction?

   Ⓐ $\sin^2\theta + \cos^2\theta = 1$, where θ is a real number
   Ⓑ $\lim_{x \to 0} \dfrac{\sin x}{x} = 1$, where x is a real number
   Ⓒ $\sum_{k=1}^{n} k = \dfrac{n(n+1)}{2}$, where n is a natural number
   Ⓓ $\int_{a}^{b} f(x)\,dx = F(b) - F(a)$, where $F'(x) = f(x)$ and a, b are real numbers

5. Which of the following numbers is the multiplicative inverse of the complex number $-4 + 3i$?

   Ⓐ $4 - 3i$
   Ⓑ $-\dfrac{1}{4} + \dfrac{1}{3}i$
   Ⓒ $-0.16 - .12i$
   Ⓓ $-0.16 + .12i$

6. Each edge of a solid cube of brass measures 8 centimeters. A metallurgist melts the cube and uses all the molten brass to make two smaller identical solid cubes. What is the length of an edge, in centimeters, of one of the smaller cubes?

   Ⓐ 4
   Ⓑ $4\sqrt{2}$
   Ⓒ $2\sqrt[3]{4}$
   Ⓓ $4\sqrt[3]{4}$

GO ON TO THE NEXT PAGE

Use the figure below to answer question 7.

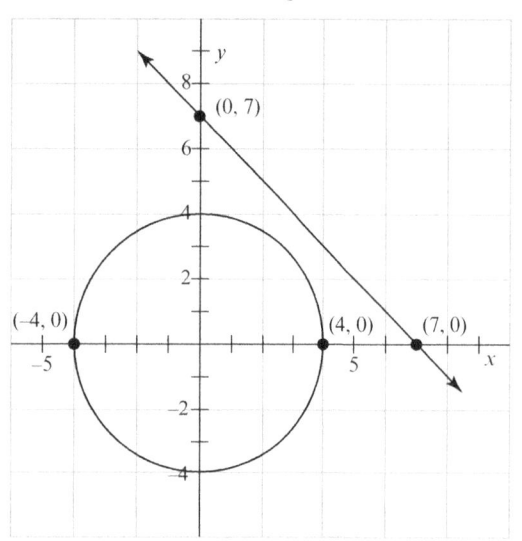

7. Which of the following statements is true about the solution set of the system of equations represented by the graphs of the circle and line shown above?

Ⓐ The system of equations has no solution because the two graphs do not intersect.
Ⓑ The solution set is {–4, 4, 7}.
Ⓒ An x-value that satisfies the system is $\dfrac{7}{2} + i\dfrac{\sqrt{41}}{2}$.
Ⓓ An x-value that satisfies the system is $\dfrac{7}{2} - i\dfrac{\sqrt{17}}{2}$.

8. A line l passes through the point (0, 5) and is perpendicular to the line that has equation $x - 3y = 10$. Which of the following equations represents the line l?

Ⓐ $x + 3y = 5$
Ⓑ $x - 3y = 5$
Ⓒ $3x + y = 5$
Ⓓ $-3x + y = 5$

9. In the xy plane, what is the center of the circle that has equation $x^2 + 6x + y^2 - 8y = 24$?

Ⓐ (–3, 4)
Ⓑ (3, –4)
Ⓒ (–6, 8)
Ⓓ (3, –4)

10. Josie and Gigi both swam in the indoor pool at Stay-Fit Gym today. Josie swims at Stay-Fit Gym every 12 days. Gigi swims there every 15 days. If both continue with their regular swimming schedule at Stay-Fit Gym, the next time both will swim there on the same day is in how many days?

Ⓐ 12
Ⓑ 15
Ⓒ 30
Ⓓ 60

11. For disaster relief in a hurricane-damaged area, $0.8 billion is needed. This amount of money is approximately equivalent to spending $1 per second for how many years?

Ⓐ 25
Ⓑ 50
Ⓒ 100
Ⓓ 500

12. A teacher introduces a geometry activity with a story about a carpenter who needs to drill a hole in a triangular piece of wood so that the center of the hole is equidistant from each side of the triangle. The teacher asks the students to discuss with a partner how the carpenter might find the correct spot to drill. Based on this introduction, which of the following geometric concepts is likely the focus of the teacher's geometry activity?

Ⓐ The intersection of the bisectors of the three angles of a triangle
Ⓑ The intersection of the three altitudes of a triangle
Ⓒ The intersection of the perpendicular bisectors of the three sides of a triangle
Ⓓ The intersection of the three medians of a triangle

GO ON TO THE NEXT PAGE

Use the figure below to answer question 13.

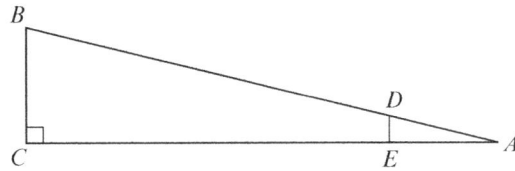

13. In △ABC shown above, $\overline{CE}$ has length 10, $\overline{EA}$ has length 5, and $\overline{DE}$ is perpendicular to $\overline{AC}$ and has length 2. What is the area of △ABC?

Ⓐ 15
Ⓑ 45
Ⓒ 90
Ⓓ 180

Use the figure below to answer question 14.

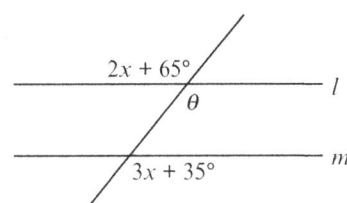

14. In the preceding figure, lines *l* and *m* are parallel. What is the measure of angle θ?

Ⓐ 125°
Ⓑ 97°
Ⓒ 30°
Ⓓ 16°

Use the figure below to answer question 15.

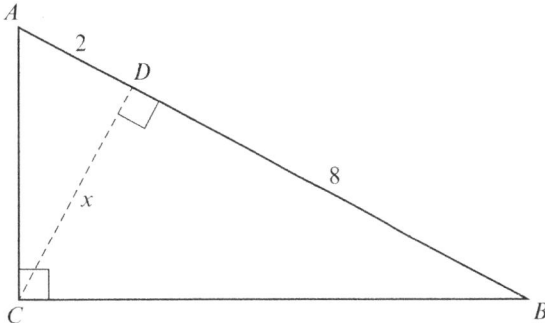

15. In the figure above, $\overline{CD}$ is an altitude of right triangle *ABC*, *AD* = 2, and *DB* = 8. Find *x*, the length of $\overline{CD}$.

Ⓐ $\sqrt{10}$
Ⓑ 4
Ⓒ 16
Ⓓ It cannot be determined from the information given.

16. In the *xy* plane, point *K* lies on *l* and has coordinates (–3, 5). If *l* is rotated counterclockwise 90° about the origin and then translated 4 units right and 7 units down, what will be the coordinates of *K′*, the image of *K*, under this series of transformations?

Ⓐ (–1, –12)
Ⓑ (–1, –10)
Ⓒ (–1, –7)
Ⓓ (–1, –4)

GO ON TO THE NEXT PAGE

Use the figure below to answer question 17.

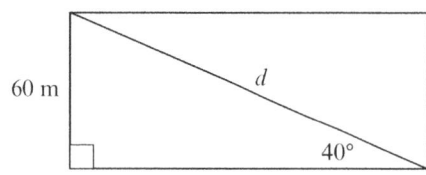

17. In the rectangle shown above, what is the length of the diagonal, d, to the nearest tenth of a meter?

- Ⓐ 71.5
- Ⓑ 78.3
- Ⓒ 80.5
- Ⓓ 93.3

18. Which of the following is an identity for the trigonometric expression $10\sin(4\theta)\cos(-4\theta)$?

- Ⓐ $5\sin(4\theta)$
- Ⓑ $5\sin(8\theta)$
- Ⓒ $10\sin(8\theta)$
- Ⓓ $-5\sin(4\theta)$

Use the figure below to answer question 19.

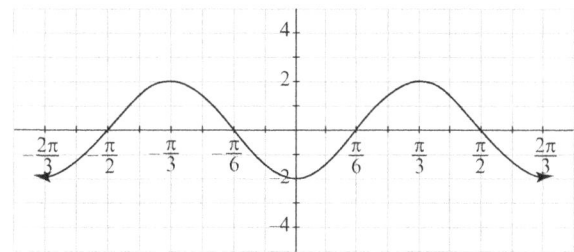

19. The graph above shows a representation of a sound wave on an oscilloscope. Describe the function that best models the curve.

- Ⓐ Sine function with amplitude = 2, period = 2π, and phase shift = $\frac{\pi}{3}$ to the right of the origin
- Ⓑ Cosine function with amplitude = 2, period = 2π, and phase shift = $\frac{\pi}{3}$ to the right of the origin
- Ⓒ Sine function with amplitude = 2, period = $\frac{2\pi}{3}$, and phase shift = $\frac{\pi}{6}$ to the right of the origin
- Ⓓ Cosine function with amplitude = 2, period = $\frac{2\pi}{3}$, and phase shift = $\frac{\pi}{6}$ to the right of the origin

Use the figure below to answer question 20.

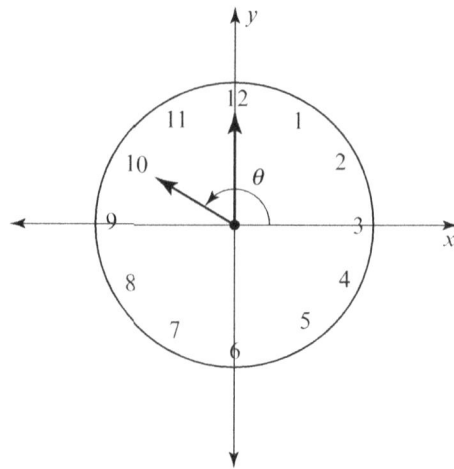

20. The diagram above shows a clock on an xy plane with the center of the clock at the origin. If the hour hand has a length of 5 centimeters, what are the coordinates of the tip of the hour hand at 10:00?

- Ⓐ $\left(5\cos\frac{\pi}{6}, 5\sin\frac{\pi}{6}\right)$
- Ⓑ $\left(5\cos\frac{5\pi}{6}, 5\sin\frac{5\pi}{6}\right)$
- Ⓒ $\left(5\sin\frac{\pi}{6}, 5\cos\frac{\pi}{6}\right)$
- Ⓓ $\left(5\sin\frac{5\pi}{6}, 5\cos\frac{5\pi}{6}\right)$

GO ON TO THE NEXT PAGE

Use the figure below to answer question 21.

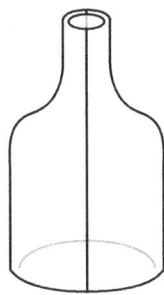

21. Water is poured at a constant rate into the container shown in the figure above. Which of the following graphs best represents the height of the water in the container as a function of time?

Ⓐ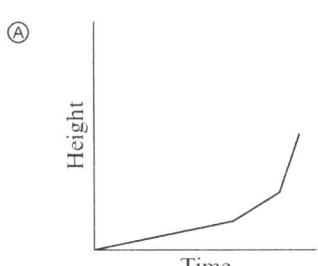

Ⓑ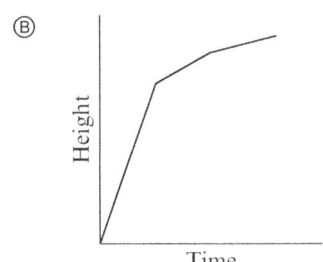

Ⓒ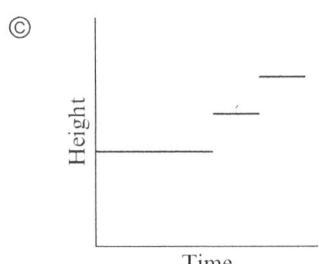

Ⓓ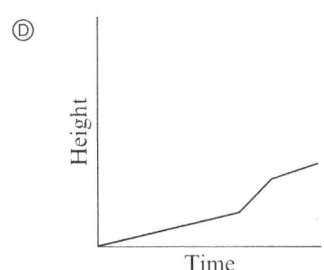

22. Given $f(x) = \dfrac{3x+4}{x+3}$ and $g(x) = x + 2$, find $f(g(a))$.

Ⓐ $\dfrac{3a+6}{a+2}$

Ⓑ $\dfrac{3a+4}{a+3}$

Ⓒ $\dfrac{3a+6}{a+3}$

Ⓓ $\dfrac{3a+10}{a+5}$

Use the statement below to answer question 23.

> Some books are entertaining.

23. To facilitate students' understanding of the logical concept of negation, a teacher asks students to think on their own for at least 10 seconds, then discuss their thinking with a partner to produce a negation of the above statement that they will share with the whole class. Which of the following are likely benefits of this think-pair-share strategy?

Select **all** that apply.

- Ⓐ Giving students think time improves the quality of their responses.
- Ⓑ Most students find it less intimidating to discuss their thinking with a partner before speaking out to the whole class.
- Ⓒ It frees up time for the teacher to attend to other classroom concerns.
- Ⓓ It allows students to build on the ideas of others.

24. Using data collected through experimentation, an electrical engineer develops a function that relates the electric current that passes through a material to the temperature of the material in a given temperature range. In addition to being a relation, which of the following statements must be true about the function?

- Ⓐ It has a smooth graph with no cusps or jagged edges.
- Ⓑ It is continuous and takes on values at all points in the temperature range.
- Ⓒ It is differentiable at all points in the temperature range.
- Ⓓ It gives a single value for the current at each point in the temperature range.

GO ON TO THE NEXT PAGE

Use the figure below to answer question 25.

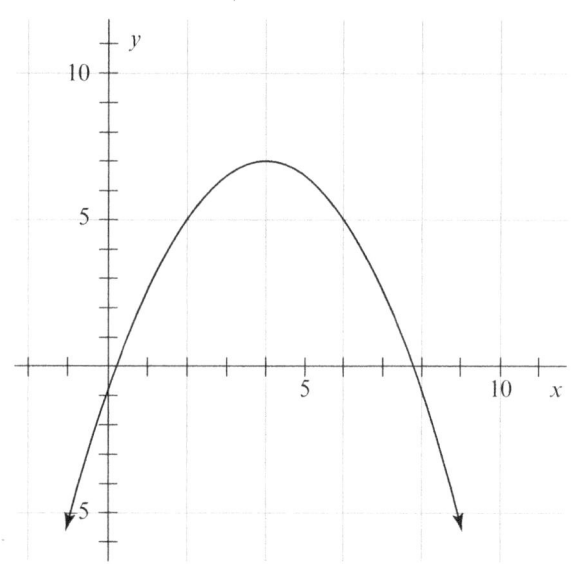

25. A quadratic function $f(x) = ax^2 + bx + c$ has the graph shown above. Which of the statements about the discriminant of $f(x) = 0$ is true?

- Ⓐ $b^2 - 4ac < 0$
- Ⓑ $b^2 - 4ac = 0$
- Ⓒ $b^2 - 4ac > 0$
- Ⓓ $b^2 - 4ac$ is undefined

26. Given the cubic function $f(x) = x^3$, which of the following best describes the function $g(x) = (x - 3)^3 + 8$?

- Ⓐ The same as the graph of $f(x) = x^3$ shifted right by 3 units and up by 8 units
- Ⓑ The same as the graph of $f(x) = x^3$ shifted left by 3 units and up by 8 units
- Ⓒ The same as the graph of $f(x) = x^3$ shifted right by 3 units and down by 8 units
- Ⓓ The same as the graph of $f(x) = x^3$ shifted left by 3 units and down by 8 units

27. In the xy plane, the graphs defined by $y = \dfrac{x^2 + x - 6}{(x + 3)}$ and $5x - 2y = -5$ intersect in how many distinct points?

- Ⓐ 0
- Ⓑ 1
- Ⓒ 2
- Ⓓ 4

Use the table below to answer question 28.

x	$f(x)$	$g(x)$
1	3	3
2	1	4
3	4	2
4	2	1

28. Selected values of the functions f and g are given in the table shown above. What is the value of $g(f(3))$?

- Ⓐ 1
- Ⓑ 2
- Ⓒ 3
- Ⓓ 4

29. A quality control engineer has determined that a machine can produce $Q(d)$ units per day after d days in operation, where $Q(d) = \dfrac{5(6d + 14)}{d + 7}$. Assuming the machine continues to work efficiently, approximately how many components is the machine able to produce per day after being in operation for an extended period of time?

- Ⓐ 6 components
- Ⓑ 10 components
- Ⓒ 14 components
- Ⓓ 30 components

30. The value of the first derivative for the graph of an acceleration curve $a(t)$ at times $t_1, t_2, t_3,$ and t_4 is as follows:

$a'(t_1) = -0.8$

$a'(t_2) = -0.35$

$a'(t_3) = 0.5$

$a'(t_4) = 0.72$

At which time is the acceleration changing most rapidly?

- Ⓐ t_1
- Ⓑ t_2
- Ⓒ t_3
- Ⓓ t_4

GO ON TO THE NEXT PAGE

31. Find the area, in unit², of the region in the *xy* plane bounded by the curve $y = \dfrac{x^2}{2}$ and the line $y = 2$.

Ⓐ $\dfrac{8}{3}$ Ⓑ $\dfrac{16}{3}$ Ⓒ $\dfrac{24}{3}$ Ⓓ $\dfrac{40}{3}$

Use the figure below to answer question 32.

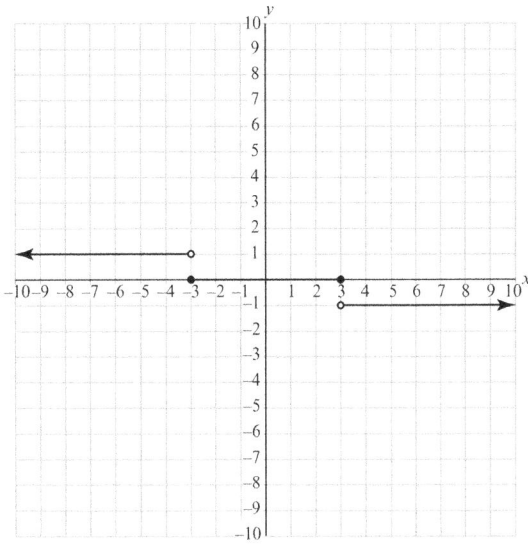

32. The figure above is a graph of $y = f'(x)$. Which of the following graphs is a possible representation of f?

Ⓐ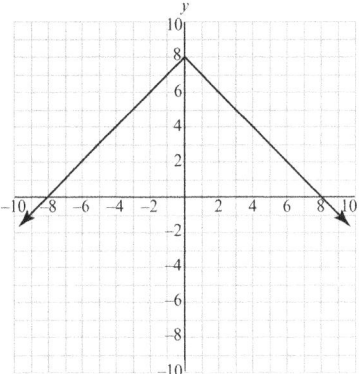

Ⓑ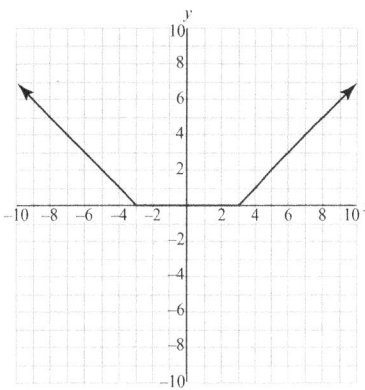

Ⓒ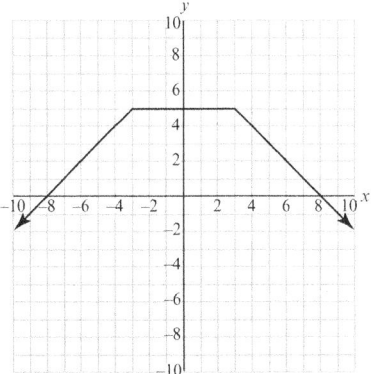

Ⓓ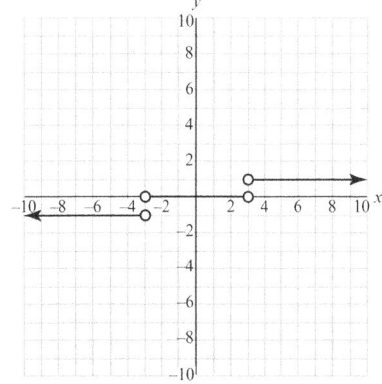

GO ON TO THE NEXT PAGE

347

33. The velocity, in feet per second, of a car during the first 10 seconds of a test run is given by $v(t) = 0.9t^2$. What is the distance, in feet, the car has traveled after 10 seconds?

- Ⓐ 90
- Ⓑ 300
- Ⓒ 600
- Ⓓ 900

34. A rectangular pen is to be adjacent to a brick wall and is to have fencing on three sides, with the side on the brick wall requiring no fencing. If 550 yards of fencing is available, find the length, in yards, of the portion of the fence that is parallel to the wall of the pen that has the largest area.

- Ⓐ 110
- Ⓑ 137.5
- Ⓒ 183.3
- Ⓓ 275

Use the information below to answer question 35.

Scaled Scores of 35 Students on a Mathematics Test

Stem	Leaf
12	3 8 8
13	1 3 4 4 5 6 8
14	0 0 2 4 5 5 7 7 7 8 9
15	0 1 3 3 5 6 7 8 9 9
16	1 2 2 9
Legend: 12|3 = 123	

35. The stem-and-leaf plot above displays the scaled scores of 35 students on a standardized mathematics test. What is the median scaled score of the 35 students?

- Ⓐ 137
- Ⓑ 140
- Ⓒ 147
- Ⓓ 149

Use the information below to answer question 36.

Book Genre Preference

Genre	Number of Students
Adventure/Fantasy	104
Biography/Historical Nonfiction	44
Mystery	64
Science Fiction	58
Science/Nature Informational	50
Total	320

36. The preceding table shows the results of a poll of young adult readers who were asked what genre of books they read most often. If a circle graph is constructed using the data in the table, what is the measure of the central angle that should be used to represent the Mystery category?

- Ⓐ 64°
- Ⓑ 72°
- Ⓒ 84°
- Ⓓ 144°

Use the information below to answer question 37.

Group	Mean	Standard Deviation
A	30 cm	5 cm
B	30 cm	8 cm
C	25 cm	10 cm
D	25 cm	9 cm

37. The data in the preceding table are based on five repetitions of the same experiment performed by four different groups of students: Group A, Group B, Group C, and Group D. The data of which group are most reliable?

- Ⓐ Group A
- Ⓑ Group B
- Ⓒ Group C
- Ⓓ Group D

38. The distribution of the lifetimes of a certain type of disposable razor follows a normal distribution with a mean of 16.8 shavings and a standard deviation of 2.4 shavings. What percentage of disposable razors of this type will last more than 19.2 shavings?

- Ⓐ 2.5%
- Ⓑ 16%
- Ⓒ 34%
- Ⓓ 68%

GO ON TO THE NEXT PAGE

39. A researcher analyzes data from a study using a simple linear regression model. Using statistical software, the researcher enters the data and runs a least-squares linear regression. In addition to providing the regression coefficients, the software output shows a correlation coefficient of 0.03. What can the researcher infer from this coefficient?

- Ⓐ The linear model is not a good fit for the data.
- Ⓑ The predictor and response variables have a strong positive correlation.
- Ⓒ The linear model has a 3% probability of fitting the data.
- Ⓓ The slope of the regression equation is 0.03.

Use the information below to answer question 40.

Grade Level	Owns a Graphing Calculator	Does Not Own a Graphing Calculator
Ninth	110	90
Tenth	140	60
Eleventh	156	44
Twelfth	190	10

40. The data in the preceding table show graphing calculator ownership status by grade level of 800 high school students. If 1 of the 800 students is randomly selected, what is the probability that the student owns a graphing calculator given that the student is a ninth-grader?

- Ⓐ $\dfrac{149}{800}$
- Ⓑ $\dfrac{11}{100}$
- Ⓒ $\dfrac{11}{80}$
- Ⓓ $\dfrac{11}{20}$

Use the figure below to answer question 41.

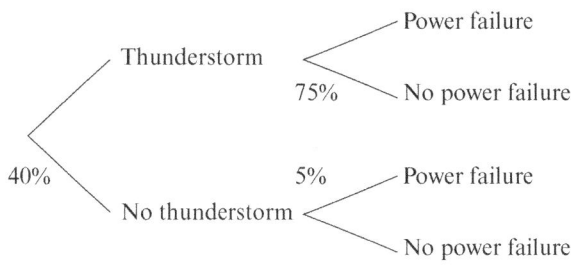

41. The partially completed probability diagram shown above represents the incidence of power failure during weather in which a thunderstorm might or might not develop. What is the probability that a thunderstorm develops and no power failure occurs?

- Ⓐ 2%
- Ⓑ 15%
- Ⓒ 45%
- Ⓓ 75%

Use the data below to answer question 42.

250	375	406	440	455	470
325	375	411	440	456	570
335	395	425	445	458	
355	400	427	448	465	
370	403	435	449	467	

42. The data above are scaled scores for 27 students on a standardized exam. What is the interquartile range of this data set?

- Ⓐ 80
- Ⓑ 85
- Ⓒ 90
- Ⓓ 95

GO ON TO THE NEXT PAGE

43. The mean of seven different positive integers is 75. Five of the integers are 30, 45, 50, 60, and 85. What is the maximum possible value of the largest of the seven integers?

- Ⓐ 85
- Ⓑ 250
- Ⓒ 254
- Ⓓ 255

44. Given $\triangle ABC$ with vertices $A(0, 0)$, $B(3, 0)$, and $C(0, 4)$ in the xy plane, which of the following matrix transformations represents a dilation of $\triangle ABC$ with center $(0, 0)$ and scale factor 3?

- Ⓐ $\begin{bmatrix} 0 & 3 \\ 0 & 3 \end{bmatrix} \begin{bmatrix} 0 & 3 & 0 \\ 0 & 0 & 4 \end{bmatrix}$
- Ⓑ $\begin{bmatrix} 3 & 3 \\ 0 & 0 \end{bmatrix} \begin{bmatrix} 0 & 3 & 0 \\ 0 & 0 & 4 \end{bmatrix}$
- Ⓒ $\begin{bmatrix} 3 & 3 \\ 3 & 3 \end{bmatrix} \begin{bmatrix} 0 & 3 & 0 \\ 0 & 0 & 4 \end{bmatrix}$
- Ⓓ $\begin{bmatrix} 3 & 0 \\ 0 & 3 \end{bmatrix} \begin{bmatrix} 0 & 3 & 0 \\ 0 & 0 & 4 \end{bmatrix}$

45. Under which of the following transformations will the lengths of the sides of a triangle be unchanged?

Select all that apply.

- A A rotation of $\theta°$ about the origin
- B A translation of h units to the right and k units up
- C A dilation with center at the origin by a scale factor of m
- D A reflection over the y-axis

Use the matrix below to answer question 46.

$$\begin{bmatrix} 5 & 1.5 \\ 2 & d \end{bmatrix}$$

46. For what value of d is the 2×2 matrix shown above NOT invertible?

- Ⓐ -0.6
- Ⓑ 0
- Ⓒ 0.6
- Ⓓ 3

47. Given the recursive function defined by

$$f(0) = 3 \text{ and}$$
$$f(n) = 2f(n - 1) + 3 \text{ for } n \geq 1,$$

what is the value of $f(3)$?

- Ⓐ 9
- Ⓑ 21
- Ⓒ 45
- Ⓓ 93

48. A box contains 400 marbles, of which 45% are red and the rest are green. If 20 marbles are randomly selected, what is the expected number of green marbles in the selection?

- Ⓐ 8
- Ⓑ 9
- Ⓒ 11
- Ⓓ 13

49. How many different ways can five people be seated in five of seven empty identical chairs that are placed in a row?

- Ⓐ 120
- Ⓑ 840
- Ⓒ 1,260
- Ⓓ 2,520

50. The relation "is a subset of" satisfies which of the following properties?

Select all that apply.

- A Reflexive
- B Symmetric
- C Transitive
- D Antisymmetric

GO ON TO THE NEXT PAGE

Use the figure below to answer question 51.

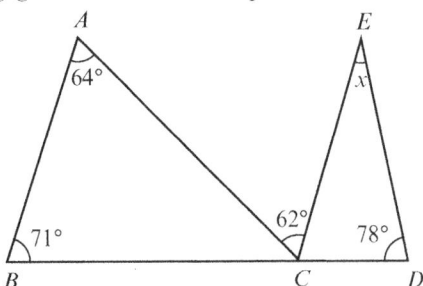

51. In the diagram with the measures of the angles as shown above, what is the measure of angle E?

- Ⓐ 12°
- Ⓑ 29°
- Ⓒ 31°
- Ⓓ 45°

52. If $x = \left(1 + \left(1 + 2^{-1}\right)^{-1}\right)^{-1}$, then $50x =$

- Ⓐ 30
- Ⓑ $\dfrac{75}{2}$
- Ⓒ 60
- Ⓓ $\dfrac{200}{3}$

53. Which of the following expressions is equivalent to $3^x + 12^x$?

- Ⓐ $3^x(1 + 4^x)$
- Ⓑ $3(5^x)$
- Ⓒ 15^x
- Ⓓ 15^{2x}

54. Which of the following equations shows a correct solution to $\dfrac{1}{4^x} = 0.001$?

Select all that apply.

- A $x = \dfrac{\log_{10} 4}{3}$
- B $x = \dfrac{3}{\log_{10} 4}$
- C $x = \dfrac{\ln(1{,}000)}{\ln 4}$
- D $x = \dfrac{3\ln 10}{2\ln 2}$

55. The number 288 has how many positive factors?

- Ⓐ 6
- Ⓑ 7
- Ⓒ 15
- Ⓓ 18

Use the figure below to answer question 56.

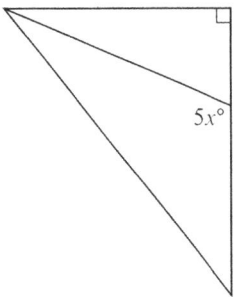

56. In the figure shown above, which of the following numbers could be values of x?

Select all that apply.

- A 10
- B 20
- C 30
- D 40

57. If $\dfrac{1}{4^x} = \dfrac{1}{4^n} + \dfrac{1}{4^n} + \dfrac{1}{4^n} + \dfrac{1}{4^n}$, then x expressed in terms of n is

- Ⓐ $n - 1$
- Ⓑ $n + 1$
- Ⓒ $4n$
- Ⓓ n^4

58. Two sides of a triangle have measures 8 and 15. Which of the following could be the approximate area, in unit², of the triangle.

Select all that apply.

- A 30
- B 42
- C 52
- D 65

59. If $\log_{(2x+3)}(125) = 3$, $x > 0$, what is the value of x?

- Ⓐ 1
- Ⓑ 2
- Ⓒ 3
- Ⓓ 4

GO ON TO THE NEXT PAGE

60. When $-4 - i$ is multiplied by its conjugate, the result is

Ⓐ -17
Ⓑ -15
Ⓒ 15
Ⓓ 17

61. The greatest common factor of n and 168 is 12, and the least common multiple of n and 168 is 1,512. What is n?

Ⓐ   54
Ⓑ   108
Ⓒ   168
Ⓓ   252

Use the table below to answer question 62.

⊗	a	b
a	a	b
b	b	b

62. The preceding table defines an operation ⊗ on the set $S = \{a, b\}$. Which of the following statements about S with respect to ⊗ are true?

Select all that apply.

Ⓐ S is closed.
Ⓑ S is commutative.
Ⓒ S contains an identity element.
Ⓓ S contains inverses for all elements in S.

Use the information below to answer question 63.

First Quarter XYZ Stock Performance

Month	Beginning-of-Month Price per Share
January	$50.00
February	$54.00
March	$58.32

63. According to the table shown above, the price per share of XYZ stock increased geometrically over the first quarter of the year. What is the common ratio of this increase?

Ⓐ   4%
Ⓑ   8%
Ⓒ   16%
Ⓓ   108%

64. If two identical machines can do a job in 10 days, how many days will it take five such machines to do the same job?

Ⓐ   4 days
Ⓑ   5 days
Ⓒ   8 days
Ⓓ   25 days

65. If $y = e^{x+1}$, then $x =$

Ⓐ $\ln(y-1)$
Ⓑ $\ln y - 1$
Ⓒ $\dfrac{y-1}{e}$
Ⓓ $\dfrac{y}{e} - 1$

66. Two bicycle riders are 42 miles apart on the same east-west path. Rider A is traveling due east, and Rider B is traveling due west. Rider A is traveling at a speed of 9 miles per hour and Rider B is traveling at a speed of 12 miles per hour. If the two bicyclists maintain their respective speeds, how long, in hours, will it take them to reach each other?

Ⓐ $1\dfrac{1}{2}$ hours
Ⓑ   2 hours
Ⓒ $2\dfrac{1}{2}$ hours
Ⓓ   3 hours

67. In a student election, Jaxon received $\dfrac{1}{3}$ more votes than his opponent. Which of the following could be the total number of votes cast for the two candidates?

Ⓐ   275
Ⓑ   280
Ⓒ   285
Ⓓ   290

GO ON TO THE NEXT PAGE

Use the figure below to answer question 68.

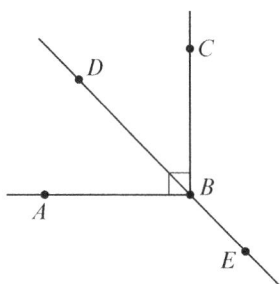

68. In the figure shown, if D and E lie on the angle bisector of $\angle ABC$, what is the measure of $\angle CBE$?
  Ⓐ 120°
  Ⓑ 125°
  Ⓒ 130°
  Ⓓ 135°

Use the figure below to answer question 69.

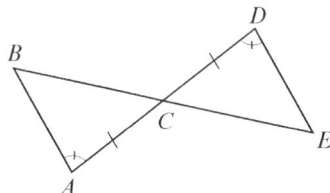

69. In the preceding figure, $\overline{BE}$ bisects $\overline{AD}$ and $\angle A \cong \angle D = 75°$. If AB is 10 and AD is 12, what is the approximate total area, in unit², of the figure shown?
  Ⓐ 29
  Ⓑ 58
  Ⓒ 60
  Ⓓ 116

70. A student scored at the 75th percentile on a multiple-choice algebra exam. The student's parents meet with the teacher for clarification about the percentile score. In response to the parents' concerns, the teacher can explain that their child's percentile score indicates the child
  Ⓐ answered 75 questions correctly.
  Ⓑ answered 75% of the exam questions correctly.
  Ⓒ did as well or better than 25% of the students who took the exam.
  Ⓓ did as well or better than 75% of the students who took the exam.

71. If $\sin\theta = -\dfrac{5}{13}$ and $\pi < \theta < \dfrac{3\pi}{2}$, then $\tan\theta$ is
  Ⓐ $-\dfrac{12}{5}$
  Ⓑ $-\dfrac{5}{12}$
  Ⓒ $\dfrac{12}{5}$
  Ⓓ $\dfrac{5}{12}$

72. If $x^2 - 17 = 16x$, what is the value of $|x - 8|$?
  Ⓐ 8
  Ⓑ 9
  Ⓒ 10
  Ⓓ 11

73. If $y = \left|\sin x - \dfrac{1}{4}\right|$, what is the maximum value of y?
  Ⓐ $\dfrac{1}{4}$
  Ⓑ $\dfrac{3}{4}$
  Ⓒ 1
  Ⓓ $\dfrac{5}{4}$

74. Which of the following expressions is an identity for $\dfrac{\tan\theta + \cot\theta}{\sec\theta\csc\theta}$?
  Ⓐ $\sin^2\theta + \cos^2\theta$
  Ⓑ $2\cos^2\theta$
  Ⓒ $2\sin\theta\cos\theta$
  Ⓓ $1 - 2\sin^2\theta$

75. If $p(x) = (2x - 3)(x + k)$, and -3 is the remainder when $p(x)$ is divided by $(x - 1)$, what is the value of k?
  Ⓐ -6
  Ⓑ -3
  Ⓒ 2
  Ⓓ 6

GO ON TO THE NEXT PAGE

76. Determine k so that the function f defined by $f(x) = x + \dfrac{k}{x}$ has a relative minimum at $x = 2$ and a relative maximum at $x = -2$.

- Ⓐ -4
- Ⓑ -2
- Ⓒ 2
- Ⓓ 4

77. For a classroom activity, an algebra 1 teacher allows student pairs to choose 5 problems to work together. Each pair must choose 3 problems from among a set of 5 different quadratic function problems and 2 problems from among a set of 6 different exponential function problems. What is the total number of different problem combinations that a student pair can choose?

- Ⓐ 16
- Ⓑ 150
- Ⓒ 180
- Ⓓ 720

78. A real estate agent selling houses located in an upscale housing development has determined the following probabilities for two neighboring houses, one of which is a model home: The probability that the model home will be sold is 0.50, the probability that the house next door will be sold is 0.40, and the probability that at least one of the two houses will be sold is 0.80. Find the probability that the house next door will be sold given that the model home has already been sold.

- Ⓐ 10%
- Ⓑ 20%
- Ⓒ 30%
- Ⓓ 40%

79. $i^{218} =$

- Ⓐ -1
- Ⓑ $-i$
- Ⓒ 1
- Ⓓ i

80. What is the inverse of the function defined by $y = x^3 - 8$?

- Ⓐ $y = \dfrac{1}{\sqrt[3]{x-8}}$
- Ⓑ $y = \dfrac{1}{x-2}$
- Ⓒ $y = \sqrt[3]{x} + 8$
- Ⓓ $y = \sqrt[3]{x+8}$

81. Which of the following expressions is equivalent to the expression $\log_{10}\left(\dfrac{x^3}{20}\right)$?

- Ⓐ $(\log_{10} x)^3 - 2$
- Ⓑ $3\log_{10} x - 2$
- Ⓒ $(\log_{10} x)^3 - \log_{10} 20$
- Ⓓ $3\log_{10} x - \log_{10} 2 - 1$

82. Which of the following matrices are nonsingular? Select all that apply.

- A $\begin{bmatrix} -3 & 5 \\ -6 & 10 \end{bmatrix}$
- B $\begin{bmatrix} 4 & 0 \\ 0 & 4 \end{bmatrix}$
- C $\begin{bmatrix} 2 & -5 & 3 \\ 6 & 1 & -4 \\ 0 & 0 & 0 \end{bmatrix}$
- D $\begin{bmatrix} 1 & 0 & 0 \\ 0 & 1 & 0 \\ 0 & 0 & 1 \end{bmatrix}$

83. A water tank can be filled in 6 hours when the input valve is open and the outlet valve is closed. When the input valve is closed and the outlet valve is open, the same tank can be emptied in 10 hours. If a tank is filled with both valves open, how many hours will it take to fill the tank? If t is the time, in hours, to fill the tank, which of the following equations correctly models the situation?

- Ⓐ $\dfrac{1}{6}t - \dfrac{1}{10}t = 1$
- Ⓑ $\dfrac{1}{6}t + \dfrac{1}{10}t = 1$
- Ⓒ $\dfrac{1}{10}t - \dfrac{1}{6}t = 1$
- Ⓓ $6t - 10t = 1$

GO ON TO THE NEXT PAGE

Use the figure below to answer question 84.

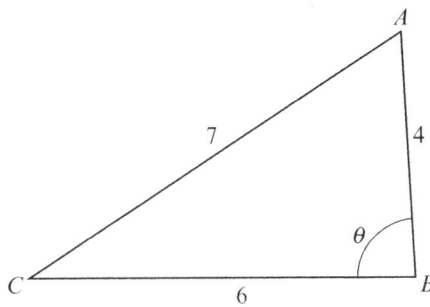

84. In △ABC shown above, cos θ =

Ⓐ $\dfrac{1}{16}$

Ⓑ $\dfrac{29}{56}$

Ⓒ $\dfrac{2}{3}$

Ⓓ $\dfrac{6}{7}$

85. If $f(x) = -16x^{-4}$, then $f'(2)$ is

Ⓐ -2

Ⓑ $-\dfrac{1}{2}$

Ⓒ $\dfrac{1}{2}$

Ⓓ 2

86. Using a statistical software program, a student produced a graph of a scatter plot showing the line of best fit for a set of paired data from two variables X and Y. The student's teacher suggests that the student create a residual plot of the data. The best reason for creating the residual plot is to

Ⓐ check whether all the data points are shown in the scatter plot.

Ⓑ calculate the medians of the observed data values associated with each variable.

Ⓒ assess how well the line of best fit models the data.

Ⓓ calculate the correlation coefficient between variables X and Y.

87. Given $A = \begin{bmatrix} 0 & 2 \\ 1 & 3 \end{bmatrix}$ and $B = \begin{bmatrix} -2 & 3 \\ 2 & 0 \end{bmatrix}$, then $(BA)^{-1}$ is

Ⓐ $\begin{bmatrix} 3 & 5 \\ 0 & 4 \end{bmatrix}$

Ⓑ $\begin{bmatrix} \dfrac{1}{3} & -\dfrac{5}{12} \\ 0 & \dfrac{1}{4} \end{bmatrix}$

Ⓒ $\begin{bmatrix} 4 & 0 \\ 4 & 3 \end{bmatrix}$

Ⓓ $\begin{bmatrix} \dfrac{1}{4} & 0 \\ -\dfrac{1}{3} & \dfrac{1}{3} \end{bmatrix}$

88. If $f(x) = x^2 - 4$ and $g(x) = 3x + 2$, then $(f \circ g)(x) = f(g(x)) =$

Ⓐ $(x^2 - 4)(3x + 2)$

Ⓑ $9x^2$

Ⓒ $3x(3x + 4)$

Ⓓ $3x^2 - 10$

89. Which of the following situations is an example of inverse variation?

Ⓐ The number of hours to paint a house depends on the number of painters.

Ⓑ The cost of a taxi fare depends on the distance traveled.

Ⓒ The perimeter of a square depends on the length of a side of the square.

Ⓓ The amount of a weekly paycheck depends on the number of hours worked.

90. Suppose that the parents of a newborn child establish a savings account for the child with an initial investment of $10,000. Assuming no withdrawals and no additional deposits are made, approximately what interest rate compounded annually is needed to double the investment in 20 years?

Ⓐ 3.5%

Ⓑ 5.5%

Ⓒ 10.0%

Ⓓ 103.5%

GO ON TO THE NEXT PAGE

Use the statement below to answer question 91.

> Given $A \subseteq B$, if $x \notin B$, then $x \notin A$.

91. In a unit on logic, a teacher challenges the students in the class to prove the above statement is true by proving its contrapositive is true. Which of the following procedures should the students follow in order to use this method of proof?

    Ⓐ Given $A \subseteq B$, assume $x \notin B$ and then deduce $x \notin A$.
    Ⓑ Given $A \subseteq B$, assume $x \in B$ and then deduce $x \in A$.
    Ⓒ Given $A \subseteq B$, assume $x \notin A$ and then deduce $x \in B$.
    Ⓓ Given $A \subseteq B$, assume $x \in A$ and then deduce $x \in B$.

92. Students in an algebra 1 class are learning to solve quadratic equations. Which of the following methods is the most appropriate way for the teacher to assess the students' understanding of this procedure?

    Ⓐ Use an observational checklist.
    Ⓑ Give a short quiz.
    Ⓒ Have students complete a worksheet.
    Ⓓ Have the students complete an online homework assignment.

93. Students in a geometry class are learning about the properties of quadrilaterals. The teacher asks, "If the diagonals of a quadrilateral are perpendicular bisectors of each other, what kind of quadrilateral must it be?" A correct response to this question is

    Select all that apply.

    A rectangle.
    B square.
    C rhombus.
    D parallelogram.

Use the statement below to answer question 94.

> Some books are entertaining.

94. Which of the following statements is a negation of the above statement?

    Ⓐ Some books are not entertaining.
    Ⓑ All books are entertaining.
    Ⓒ No books are entertaining.
    Ⓓ No books are not entertaining.

95. A bicyclist is traveling at the speed of 10 miles per hour. The front wheel of the bicycle has a diameter of 26 inches. Approximately how fast is the front wheel spinning in revolutions per minute (rpm)?

    Ⓐ 20
    Ⓑ 65
    Ⓒ 129
    Ⓓ 406

96. Find $\lim\limits_{x \to -2} \dfrac{x^2 + 6x + 8}{x^2 - x - 6}$.

    Ⓐ $-\dfrac{4}{3}$
    Ⓑ $-\dfrac{2}{5}$
    Ⓒ 0
    Ⓓ undefined

Use the equation below to answer question 97.

$$x^2 - y^2 + 6x - 8y = 0$$

97. Referring students to the preceding equation, a teacher hints that inspection of the coefficients of the equation's squared terms can be quite helpful in determining which conic section is represented by the equation. Using the teacher's hint, determine which of the following conic sections is represented by the equation.

    Ⓐ a circle
    Ⓑ an ellipse
    Ⓒ a hyperbola
    Ⓓ a parabola

GO ON TO THE NEXT PAGE

98. An algebra 2 teacher computed a mean of 73 and a standard deviation of 8 for the scores on a multiple-choice unit test. Disappointed with this result, the teacher looked over the questions that were missed by most of the students. This analysis revealed that a 10-point question had been scored incorrectly because the answer key was wrong. In fact, all of the students had marked the correct answer. The teacher immediately added 10 points to each student's score. What will be the mean and standard deviation of the revised scores?

- Ⓐ mean = 73, standard deviation = 8
- Ⓑ mean = 73, standard deviation = 18
- Ⓒ mean = 83, standard deviation = 8
- Ⓓ mean = 83, standard deviation = 18

99. A precalculus teacher has a classroom set of graphing calculators. Students can use the graphing feature of these calculators to graph one or more functions on the same coordinate grid. They also can use the trace feature to track the coordinates of the cursor as it is moved along any one of the graphs. Students will find these two features most useful for determining the

- Ⓐ derivative of a function.
- Ⓑ solution to a two-variable system of two linear equations.
- Ⓒ complex zeros of a polynomial function.
- Ⓓ inverse of a matrix.

Use the task given below to answer question 100.

> Use what you know about adding two fractions in arithmetic to write out a plan for adding two algebraic fractions.

100. A high school algebra 1 teacher gives students the preceding task. In giving the students this task, the teacher is most likely promoting students' use of

- Ⓐ generalization.
- Ⓑ logical argument.
- Ⓒ deductive reasoning.
- Ⓓ inductive reasoning.

Answer Key

Question Number	Correct Answer	Chapter(s)	Question Number	Correct Answer	Chapter(s)
1.	D	1, 5	26.	A	3
2.	B, C, D	1	27.	A	2
3.	B	4, 5	28.	A	2
4.	C	1, 5	29.	D	2
5.	C	1	30.	A	2
6.	D	3, 5	31.	B	2
7.	D	2, 5	32.	C	2
8.	C	2	33.	B	2
9.	A	3	34.	D	2, 3
10.	D	1, 5	35.	C	4
11.	A	3	36.	B	3
12.	A	3, 6	37.	A	4
13.	B	3, 5	38.	B	4, 5
14.	A	3	39.	A	4
15.	B	3, 5	40.	D	4
16.	B	3	41.	C	4
17.	D	2, 3	42.	A	4
18.	B	2	43.	C	4, 5
19.	C	2, 3	44.	D	3
20.	B	2	45.	A, B, D	3
21.	A	2	46.	C	1
22.	D	2	47.	C	2
23.	A, B, D	6	48.	C	4
24.	D	2	49.	D	4, 5
25.	C	2	50.	A, C, D	5

Question Number	Correct Answer	Chapter(s)	Question Number	Correct Answer	Chapter(s)
51.	B	3	76.	D	3
52.	A	1	77.	B	4, 6
53.	A	1	78.	B	4
54.	B, C, D	2	79.	A	1
55.	D	1	80.	D	2
56.	B, C	3	81.	D	2
57.	A	1	82.	B, D	2
58.	A, B, C	2, 3	83.	A	2, 5
59.	A	2	84.	A	2
60.	D	1	85.	D	2
61.	B	1, 2	86.	C	4, 6
62.	A, B, C	1	87.	B	4, 5
63.	B	2	88.	C	2
64.	A	5	89.	A	2, 5
65.	B	2	90.	A	2
66.	B	2, 5	91.	D	5, 6
67.	B	1, 5	92.	A	6
68.	D	3	93.	B, C	3, 6
69.	B	3	94.	C	5
70.	D	4, 6	95.	C	3
71.	D	2	96.	B	2
72.	B	2	97.	C	3, 6
73.	D	2	98.	C	4, 6
74.	A	2	99.	B	6
75.	C	2	100.	A	6

Answer Explanations

1. **D.** Let x = the average speed (in miles per hour) for the last 40 minutes $\left(=\frac{2}{3} \text{ hour}\right)$ of the trip. Because the average speed for the entire trip was 54 miles per hour (mph), the total distance traveled is $(54 \text{ mph})\left(1\frac{2}{3} \text{ h}\right) = 90$ miles. Rose drove 50 miles in the first hour, so she drove 90 miles – 50 miles = 40 miles in the last $\frac{2}{3}$ hour of the trip.

   Write an equation that represents the facts.

   $$x \cdot \frac{2}{3} \text{ hour} = 40 \text{ miles}$$

   Solve the equation, omitting the units for convenience.

   $$\frac{2}{3}x = 40$$

   $$\frac{3}{2} \cdot \frac{2}{3}x = \frac{3}{2} \cdot 40$$

   $$x = 60, \text{ choice D}$$

2. **B, C, D.** Given that x and y are whole numbers and $z = 2x + y = 2x + 6x = 8x$, then z is a multiple of 8. Therefore, z represents a whole number that is divisible by 8. A number is divisible by 8 only if the last 3 digits form a number that is divisible by 8. Of the answer choices, only choice A fails the test for divisibility by 8—because the last 3 digits of 121,006,233,314 are 314, which is not divisible by 8. Choices B, C, and D are divisible by 8, so each could be the value of z.

3. **B.** Let S = the sum of the 20 numbers. Then $\frac{S}{20} = X$, which implies $S = 20X$. The sum of the 10 numbers whose arithmetic average is 15 is $(10)(15) = 150$. Thus, the sum of the remaining 10 numbers is $S - 150 = 20X - 150$.

   Hence, the arithmetic average of the remaining 10 numbers is $\frac{20X - 150}{10} = 2X - 15$, choice B.

4. **C.** The principle of mathematical induction states that any set of counting numbers that contains the number 1 and also contains $(k + 1)$ whenever it contains the counting number k contains all the counting numbers. Eliminate choices A, B, and D, which are statements about the real numbers. Choice C is a statement about the sum of the first n natural numbers. The natural numbers is another name for the counting numbers, so the statement in choice C can be proven using the principle of mathematical induction. Choice A can be proven using trigonometric concepts and the Pythagorean theorem. Choices B and D can be proven using techniques from calculus.

5. **C.** The multiplicative inverse of a complex number $x + yi$ is the complex number $\left(\frac{x}{x^2 + y^2}\right) + \left(\frac{-y}{x^2 + y^2}\right)i$.

   Thus, the multiplicative inverse of the complex number $4 + 3i$ is $\left(\frac{-4}{(-4)^2 + 3^2}\right) + \left(\frac{-3}{(-4)^2 + 3^2}\right)i =$
   $\frac{-4}{16+9} + \frac{-3}{16+9}i = \frac{-4}{25} + \frac{-3}{25}i = -0.16 - 0.12i$, choice C.

6. **D.** The volume V of a cube with edge e is given by $V = e^3$. The volume of the original cube will equal the sum of the volumes of the two smaller cubes.

   The volume V_o of the original cube is $V_o = (8 \text{ cm})^3 = 512 \text{ cm}^3$.

   The volume V_s of one of the smaller cubes = $\frac{1}{2}V_o = \frac{1}{2} \cdot 512 \text{ cm}^3 = 256 \text{ cm}^3$.

Let e = the length of an edge of one of the smaller cubes. Then $e^3 = 256$ cm^3, so $e = \sqrt[3]{256 \text{ cm}^3} = \sqrt[3]{64 \text{ cm}^3 \cdot 4} = 4\sqrt[3]{4}$ centimeters, choice D.

7. **D.** The figure shows a circle centered at 0 with radius 4 units and a line that passes through the points (0, 7) and (7, 0). Write equations that represent each of the graphs shown, and then find the simultaneous solution of the two equations.

   The equation of a circle centered at 0 with radius 4 is $x^2 + y^2 = 16$.

   The slope of the line that passes through the points (0, 7) and (7, 0) is $m = \dfrac{0-7}{7-0} = \dfrac{-7}{7} = -1$. The y-intercept b is 7. The equation of the line is $y = -x + 7$.

   The system of two equations is $\begin{array}{l} x^2 + y^2 = 16 \\ y = -x + 7 \end{array}$.

   Caution: When an equation or a system of equations has real solutions, you can use features of your graphing calculator to find a solution. This method will not work when the graphs do not intersect, as in this problem.

   Substitute $y = -x + 7$ into the equation $x^2 + y^2 = 16$ to obtain

   $$x^2 + (-x+7)^2 = 16$$
   $$x^2 + x^2 - 14x + 49 = 16$$
   $$2x^2 - 14x + 33 = 0$$

   Using the quadratic formula,

   $$a = 2, b = -14, c = 33$$

   $$x = \dfrac{-(-14) \pm \sqrt{(-14)^2 - 4(2)(33)}}{2(2)} = \dfrac{14 \pm \sqrt{196-264}}{4} = \dfrac{14 \pm \sqrt{-68}}{4} = \dfrac{14 \pm 2i\sqrt{17}}{4} = \dfrac{7}{2} \pm i\dfrac{\sqrt{17}}{2}$$

   Thus, $\dfrac{7}{2} - i\dfrac{\sqrt{17}}{2}$ is an x-value that satisfies the system, choice D.

8. **C.** When two lines are perpendicular, their slopes are negative reciprocals of each other.
   Solve $x - 3y = 10$ for y to find its slope.

   $$x - 3y = 10$$
   $$-3y = -x + 10$$
   $$y = \dfrac{1}{3}x - \dfrac{10}{3}$$

   The slope of $x - 3y = 10$ is $\dfrac{1}{3}$, so the desired equation has slope -3. The line passes through (0, 5), so 5 is the y-intercept. In slope-intercept form, the desired equation is $y = -3x + 5$. In standard form the equation is $3x + y = 5$, choice C.

9. **A.** Put the equation in standard form $(x - h)^2 + (y - k)^2 = r^2$ by completing the square for the terms involving x and completing the square for the terms involving y.

   $$x^2 + 6x + y^2 - 8y = 24$$
   $$(x^2 + 6x + 9) + (y^2 - 8y + 16) = 24 + 25$$
   $$(x+3)^2 + (y-4)^2 = 49$$

   Therefore, the circle's center is $(-3, 4)$, choice A.

10. D. The number of days until the next time is the least common multiple of 12 and 15, which is 60. It will be 60 days before Josie and Gigi both will swim at Stay-Fit Gym on the same day, choice D.

Tip: Use your TI graphing calculator to compute the lcm of two numbers. The lcm feature is under the NUM menu of the MATH key.

11. A. Perform the following calculation to determine how many years it would take to spend $0.8 billion at the rate of $1 per second.

$$\frac{\$800{,}000{,}000}{1} \cdot \frac{1 \text{ sec}}{\$1} \cdot \frac{1 \text{ min}}{60 \text{ sec}} \cdot \frac{1 \text{ hr}}{60 \text{ min}} \cdot \frac{1 \text{ day}}{24 \text{ hr}} \cdot \frac{1 \text{ yr}}{365 \text{ days}} \approx 25 \text{ years, choice A}$$

12. A. The angle bisectors of a triangle are concurrent in a point that is equidistant from the three sides, which means choice A is likely the focus of the teacher's geometry activity. Choice B is incorrect because the altitudes of a triangle are concurrent in a point; but, in general, the point of concurrency is not equidistant from the three sides. Choice C is incorrect because the perpendicular bisectors of a triangle are concurrent in a point that is equidistant from the vertices of the triangle; but, in general, the point of concurrency is not equidistant from the three sides. Choice D is incorrect because the medians of a triangle are concurrent in a point; but, in general, the point of concurrency is not equidistant from the three sides.

13. B. Triangles *ABC* and *ADE* are similar right triangles because they share the common angle *A*. The area of $\triangle ABC = \frac{1}{2}(\text{length of } \overline{CA})(\text{length of } \overline{BC}) = \frac{1}{2}(CA)(BC)$. To find the area, determine *CA* and *BC*.

$$CA = CE + EA = 10 + 5 = 15$$

Let *x* = *BC*. Set up a proportion based on corresponding sides of similar triangles. Solve for *x*, omitting the units for convenience.

$$\frac{x}{15} = \frac{2}{5} \text{ implies } x = \frac{(15)(2)}{5} = 6$$

Thus, the area of $\triangle ABC = \frac{1}{2}(15)(6) = 45$, choice B.

14. A. The measure of angle θ equals $2x + 65°$ because vertical angles have the same measure. The measure of angle θ equals $3x + 35°$ because corresponding angles of parallel lines have the same measure.

Thus, $2x + 65°$ and $3x + 35°$ are equal. Solve the following equation for *x*.

$$3x + 35° = 2x + 65°$$
$$x = 30°$$

Substituting this value for *x* into $2x + 65°$ yields the measure of angle $\theta = 2x + 65° = 2(30°) + 65° = 125°$, choice A.

15. B. The altitude to the hypotenuse of a right triangle is the geometric mean of the lengths of the two segments into which it separates the hypotenuse. Therefore, $\frac{AD}{x} = \frac{x}{DB}$. Substitute *AD* = 2 and *DB* = 8 and solve for *x*.

$$\frac{2}{x} = \frac{x}{8} \text{ implies } x^2 = 16$$

Hence, *x* = 4.

Thus, the length of $\overline{CD}$ is 4, choice B.

Tip: The number –4 is also a solution of $x^2 = 16$, but it is rejected because length is nonnegative.

16. B. The image of (–3, 5) under a counterclockwise rotation of 90° about the origin is (–5, –3). The image of (–5, –3) under a translation of 4 units right and 7 units down is (–1, –10). Therefore, the image *K'* of *K* under the series of transformations is (–1, –10), choice B.

17. D. The diagonal divides the rectangle into two right triangles. In the lower right triangle, the side 60 m is opposite the angle 40°. To find *d*, use the definition of the sine function, and then solve.

$$\sin 40° = \frac{\text{length of side opposite } 40° \text{ angle}}{\text{length of hypotenuse}} = \frac{60 \text{ m}}{d}$$

Thus, $d = \dfrac{60 \text{ m}}{\sin 40°} \approx 93.3 \text{ m}$ (rounded to the nearest tenth of a meter), choice D.

Tip: Be sure to check that your graphing calculator is in degree mode when the angle given is in degrees.

18. **B.** The cosine is an even function, so $10 \sin(4\theta)\cos(-4\theta) = 10 \sin(4\theta)\cos(4\theta)$.

    Rewrite $10 \sin(4\theta)\cos(4\theta)$ as $5 \cdot 2 \sin(4\theta)\cos(4\theta)$. The expression $2 \sin(4\theta)\cos(4\theta)$ has the form of the double-angle formula $\sin(2x) = 2 \sin(x)\cos(x)$, where $x = 4\theta$ and $2x = 8\theta$; therefore, $5 \cdot 2 \sin(4\theta)\cos(4\theta) = 5 \cdot \sin(8\theta) = 5 \sin(8\theta)$, choice B.

19. **C.** The graph's shape suggests either a sine or a cosine function is an appropriate model. Regardless whether you view the graph as a sine or a cosine function, the graph has amplitude 2, period $= \dfrac{2\pi}{3}$, and no vertical shift. Eliminate choices A and B because the period in these choices is 2π. If you view the graph as a sine function, the graph has a phase shift of $\dfrac{\pi}{6}$ units to the right of the origin, making choice C the correct response. Choice D is incorrect because if you view the graph as a cosine function, the phase shift is $\dfrac{\pi}{3}$ units, not $\dfrac{\pi}{6}$ units, to the right of the origin.

20. **B.** The hour hand is at 10:00. The angle θ from the positive x-axis to the hour hand is $120° = \dfrac{5\pi}{6}$. The length of the hour hand is 5 centimeters. Using trigonometry, the tip of the hour hand has coordinates $x = r \cos \theta$ and $y = r \sin \theta$. Substituting $r = 5$ and $\theta = \dfrac{5\pi}{6}$, the coordinates of the tip of the hour hand are $\left(5\cos\dfrac{5\pi}{6}, 5\sin\dfrac{5\pi}{6}\right)$, choice B.

21. **A.** Analyze the figure. As water is poured into the container at a constant rate, the height of the water rises at a constant rate until it reaches the point near the top where the bottle narrows. At that point, the water rises at a faster (but still constant) rate until it reaches the bottle's neck, where it rises at an even faster rate. The graph that corresponds to this analysis is given in choice A.

    Choice B is incorrect because it indicates that the rate at which the water rises slows down as the water reaches the top of the bottle. Choice C is incorrect because it indicates that the height of the water in the bottle is constant at first, then suddenly leaps to a higher level and remains constant at that level for a while and, finally, leaps to an even higher level, where it remains constant. Choice D is incorrect because it indicates that the rate at which the water rises initially is the same as the rate at which it rises when it reaches the bottle's neck.

22. **D.** $f(g(a)) = f(a+2) = \dfrac{3(a+2)+4}{(a+2)+3} = \dfrac{3a+6+4}{a+2+3} = \dfrac{3a+10}{a+5}$, choice D

23. **A, B, D.** Think-pair-share is a proven strategy for engaging students in learning. The statements given in choices A, B, and D are benefits that occur when the strategy is implemented appropriately. Choice C is incorrect because the teacher should monitor the discussions between student pairs and listen for common misconceptions that can be addressed with the whole class.

24. **D.** Only the statement given in choice D will always be true about the engineer's function. By definition, each first component (temperature value) is paired with one and only one second component (current value). None of the other statements are guaranteed to be true about the engineer's function.

25. **C.** Examine the graph. The graph intersects the real axis at two distinct points, indicating the function has two distinct real zeros. Therefore, $b^2 - 4ac > 0$, choice C.

26. **A.** Subtracting 3 from x will result in a horizontal shift of 3 units to the right. Adding 8 to $f(x)$ will result in a vertical shift of 8 units up. Thus, the graph of $g(x) = (x-3)^3 + 8$ is the same as the graph of $f(x) = x^3$ shifted right by 3 units and up by 8 units, choice A.

    Tip: If you are unsure whether a shift is to the right or left (or up or down), graph the functions using your graphing calculator to check.

27. **A.** The rational function f defined by $y = \dfrac{x^2 + x - 6}{(x+3)} = \dfrac{(x+3)(x-2)}{(x+3)}$ is undefined when $x = -3$. Simplified, $y = \dfrac{(x+3)(x-2)}{(x+3)} = x - 2$, so the graph of f is the line whose equation is $y = x - 2$, but with a "hole" at the point $(-3, -5)$. The graph of the linear function g defined by $5x - 2y = -5$ intersects the line $y = x - 2$ at $(-3, -5)$. That is, $(-3, -5)$ satisfies both $y = x - 2$ and $5x - 2y = -5$. However, since -3 is not in the domain of f, the graphs of f and g do not intersect. Therefore, the graphs intersect at 0 distinct points, choice A.

Caution: Using your graphing calculator for problems involving holes in graphs can lead to incorrect answers.

28. **A.** According to the table, $f(3) = 4$ and $g(4) = 1$. Therefore, $g(f(3)) = g(4) = 1$, choice A.

29. **D.** The phrase "an extended period of time" is a clue that this is a calculus problem involving the limit of a function as the variable approaches infinity. To answer the question, find the limit of the function $Q(d) = \dfrac{5(6d + 14)}{d + 7}$ as d approaches infinity: $\lim_{d \to \infty} \dfrac{5(6d+14)}{d+7} = \lim_{d \to \infty} \dfrac{30d+70}{d+7} = \lim_{d \to \infty} \dfrac{30d+70}{d+7} = \lim_{d \to \infty} \dfrac{30 + \dfrac{70}{d}}{1 + \dfrac{7}{d}} = \dfrac{30 + 0}{1 + 0} = \dfrac{30}{1} = 30$.

Thus, after being in operation for an extended period of time, the machine is able to produce 30 components per day, choice D.

30. **A.** The value of the first derivative at each time t_1, t_2, t_3, and t_4 is the instantaneous rate of change of the acceleration curve at that time. The acceleration is changing most rapidly at the time t_1 because the magnitude of the change is greatest at this time, choice A.

Tip: To avoid making a careless mistake, add 0s to make the number of decimal places in each value the same before making a comparison: $a'(t_1) = -0.80$, $a'(t_2) = -0.35$, $a'(t_3) = 0.50$, $a'(t_4) = 0.72$.

31. **B.** Make a quick sketch and shade the area bounded by $y = \dfrac{x^2}{2}$ and $y = 2$.

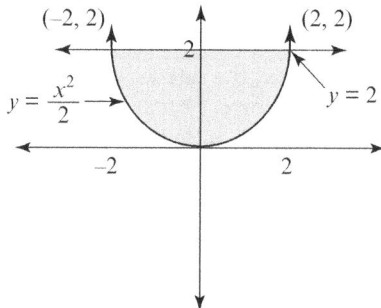

The curve and the line intersect at the points $(-2, 2)$ and $(2, 2)$, and $y = 2$ lies above $y = \dfrac{x^2}{2}$ between $x = -2$ and $x = 2$. To find the area of the shaded region, evaluate the integral $\int_{-2}^{2} \left(2 - \dfrac{x^2}{2}\right) dx$.

$$\int_{-2}^{2}\left(2 - \dfrac{x^2}{2}\right)dx = \left(2x - \dfrac{x^3}{6}\right)\Big|_{-2}^{2} = \left(2(2) - \dfrac{(2)^3}{6}\right) - \left(2(-2) - \dfrac{(-2)^3}{6}\right)$$

$$= \left(4 - \dfrac{8}{6}\right) - \left(-4 - \dfrac{-8}{6}\right)$$

$$= 4 - \dfrac{4}{3} + 4 - \dfrac{4}{3}$$

$$= 8 - \dfrac{8}{3}$$

$$= \dfrac{24}{3} - \dfrac{8}{3}$$

$$= \dfrac{16}{3}, \text{ choice B}$$

32. C. Analyze the graph of f'. Recall that the first derivative of a function at a point is equal to the slope of the graph of the function at that point. If $f'(x) > 0$ in an interval, f is increasing on that interval. If $f'(x) < 0$ in an interval, f is decreasing on that interval. And if $f'(x) = 0$ in an interval, f is constant on that interval. By inspecting the graph of f', you can see that to the left of -3 the slope of the graph of f is a constant value of positive 1, indicating that to the left of -3 the graph of f is a straight line slanting upward from left to right with slope of 1. Eliminate choices B and D because the graphs in these answer choices do not meet this condition.

Between -3 and 3, according to the graph of f', the slope of the graph of f is a constant value of 0, indicating that between -3 and 3 the graph of f is a horizontal line. Eliminate choice A because the graph in this answer choice does not have a horizontal component. Therefore, choice C is the correct response. The graph in choice C is the only graph shown in the answer choices that is consistent with the behavior of f'.

33. B. Recall that the first derivative of a position function is the velocity function. To find the distance traveled after 10 seconds, find the numerical integral of the velocity function between 0 and 10 seconds. That is, evaluate the integral $\int_0^{10} 0.9t^2\, dt$.

$\int_0^{10} 0.9t^2\, dt = \dfrac{0.9t^3}{3}\Big|_0^{10} = 0.3t^3\Big|_0^{10} = 0.3(10)^3 - 0.3(0)^3 = 0.3(1{,}000) - 0.3(0) = 300 - 0 = 300$. Therefore, the distance the car has traveled after 10 seconds is 300 feet, choice B.

34. D. Let the two sides of the pen that are perpendicular to the brick wall each have length of x yards. The side parallel to the wall has length 550 yards $-2x$ because the sum of the three sides is 550 yards. Sketch a diagram to illustrate the problem.

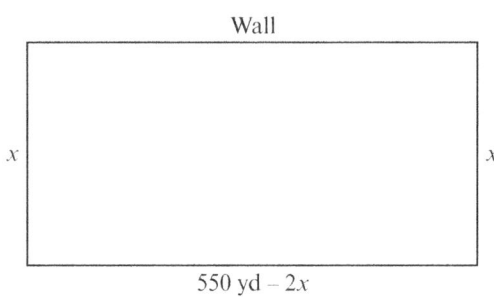

The area of the pen is width times length and is given by the function f, where $f(x) = x(550 - 2x) = 550x - 2x^2$. The pen will have maximum area when $f(x)$ is the maximum value of f. To find the length of the pen with largest area, first solve $f'(x) = 0$ to find the critical number(s) for f.

$f(x) = 550x - 2x^2$
$f'(x) = 550 - 4x = 0$
$x = 137.5$ is a critical number of f.
Then check $f''(137.5)$ to determine whether $f(137.5)$ is a maximum.
$$f''(x) = -4$$
Therefore, $f''(137.5) = -4 < 0$
By the second derivative test, $f(137.5)$ is the maximum area of the pen. The length of the pen that encloses the maximum area is 550 yards $- 2(137.5$ yards$) = 275$ yards, choice D.

35. C. In an ordered set of data values, the median is the value in the $\left(\dfrac{n+1}{2}\right)$ position. There are 35 data values, so the median is the $\dfrac{35+1}{2} = \dfrac{36}{2} = 18$th data value. Counting from the least score, the 18th score in the stem-and-leaf plot is 147, choice C.

36. B. A circle graph is made by dividing the 360 degrees of the circle to partition the graph into portions that correspond to the proportion for each category.

The measure of the central angle that should be used to represent the Mystery category is $\dfrac{64}{320}(360°) = 72°$, choice B.

37. A. Analyze the information in the table. The standard deviation for the data obtained by Group A is less than the standard deviations of the data from the other groups. This result means the data from Group A have less variability and are, therefore, more reliable. Thus, choice A is the correct response.

38. B. According to the 68-95-99.7 rule, approximately 68% of the values of a normal distribution fall within one standard deviation of the mean, about 95% fall within two standard deviations of the mean, and about 99.7% fall within three standard deviations of the mean. The mean number of shavings for the razors is 16.8, with a standard deviation of 2.4 shavings.

The z-score for $19.2 = \dfrac{\text{data value} - \text{mean}}{\text{standard deviation}} = \dfrac{19.2 - 16.8}{2.4} = 1$. Therefore, 19.2 is one standard deviation above the mean.

Find the percentage of the normal distribution that is one standard deviation above the mean.

By the 68-95-99.7 rule, 68% of the distribution is within one standard deviation of the mean. Since the normal curve is symmetric, about $\dfrac{1}{2}$ of 68% = 34% of the distribution is between the mean and one standard deviation. Make a sketch to illustrate the problem.

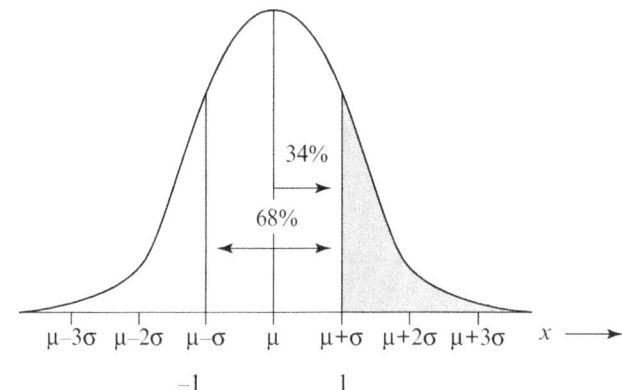

Again, due to symmetry, 50% of the distribution is above the mean. Thus, approximately 50% − 34% = 16% of the distribution is above one standard deviation above the mean. Thus, about 16% of the razors will last more than 19.2 shavings, choice B.

39. A. Because the correlation coefficient measures the linear relationship between the predictor and response variables of the simple-linear regression model, it can be used as an estimate of the "goodness of fit" of the regression model. The closer the correlation coefficient is to 0, the weaker the linear relationship. Given the value 0.03 of the correlation coefficient is near 0, it fails to support a linear relationship between the variables of the linear regression, indicating that the linear model is not a good fit for the data, choice A.

40. D. Add an additional row and column. Then fill in the row and column totals for the table.

Grade Level	Owns a Graphing Calculator	Does Not Own a Graphing Calculator	Total
Ninth	110	90	200
Tenth	140	60	200
Eleventh	156	44	200
Twelfth	190	10	200
Total	596	204	800

This question requires that you find a conditional probability; that is, you are to find the probability when you already know that the student is a ninth-grader. Thus, when computing the probability, the number of possible students under consideration is no longer 800, but is reduced to the total number of ninth-graders, which is 200. According to the table, 110 of the 200 ninth-graders own a graphing calculator.

Therefore, P(the student owns a graphing calculator given that the student is a ninth-grader) is $\dfrac{110}{200} = \dfrac{11}{20}$, choice D.

41. C. Fill in the missing probabilities.

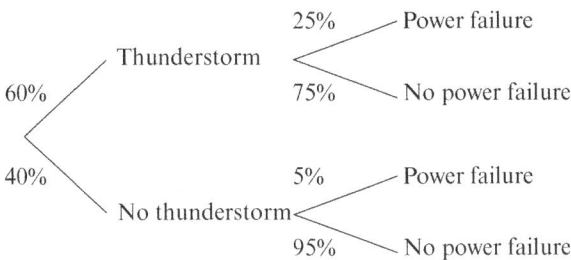

This problem requires an application of the multiplication rule, which states that $P(A \text{ and } B) = P(A)P(B|A)$. $P(\text{thunderstorm and no power failure}) = P(\text{thunderstorm}) \cdot P(\text{no power failure given a thunderstorm has developed}) = 60\% \cdot 75\% = 45\%$, choice C.

42. A. The interquartile range is the difference between the third quartile and the first quartile. First, find the median, which is 427, the middle number in the ordered data set. There are 13 scores below the median and 13 scores above the median. The median of the lower 13 scores is the first quartile, which is 375; and the median of the upper 13 scores is the third quartile, which is 455. Hence, the interquartile range is $455 - 375 = 80$, choice A.

43. C. Let x and y be the two positive integers whose values you are not given and, for convenience and without loss of generality, let $x < y$. Given that 75 is the mean of the seven numbers, $\dfrac{30 + 45 + 50 + 60 + 85 + x + y}{7} = 75$. Solve this equation for $x + y$.

$$\dfrac{30 + 45 + 50 + 60 + 85 + x + y}{7} = 75$$
$$30 + 45 + 50 + 60 + 85 + x + y = (7)(75)$$
$$270 + x + y = 525$$
$$x + y = 255$$

Because x and y are positive integers, the least that x can be is 1. Therefore, the greatest that y can be is 254, choice C.

44. D. You can represent $\triangle ABC$ with vertices $A(0, 0)$, $B(3, 0)$, and $C(0, 4)$ using a 2×3 matrix, with each column $\begin{bmatrix} x \\ y \end{bmatrix}$ representing a vertex: $\begin{bmatrix} 0 & 3 & 0 \\ 0 & 0 & 4 \end{bmatrix}$. The dilation of $\triangle ABC$, using a scale factor of 3, is represented by the matrix $\begin{bmatrix} 0 & 9 & 0 \\ 0 & 0 & 12 \end{bmatrix}$. Look at the answer choices and select the 2×2 matrix that will multiply times $\begin{bmatrix} 0 & 3 & 0 \\ 0 & 0 & 4 \end{bmatrix}$ to give $\begin{bmatrix} 0 & 9 & 0 \\ 0 & 0 & 12 \end{bmatrix}$. A quick way to work this problem is to check the answer choices.

Check A: $\begin{bmatrix} 0 & 3 \\ 0 & 3 \end{bmatrix} \begin{bmatrix} 0 & 3 & 0 \\ 0 & 0 & 4 \end{bmatrix} = \begin{bmatrix} 0 & 0 & \\ & & \end{bmatrix}$; eliminate choice A because the element in the first row second column is not 9. There is no need to complete the multiplication.

Check B: $\begin{bmatrix} 3 & 3 \\ 0 & 0 \end{bmatrix} \begin{bmatrix} 0 & 3 & 0 \\ 0 & 0 & 4 \end{bmatrix} = \begin{bmatrix} 0 & 9 & 12 \\ & & \end{bmatrix}$; eliminate choice B because the element in the first row third column is not 0. There is no need to complete the multiplication.

Check C: $\begin{bmatrix} 3 & 3 \\ 3 & 3 \end{bmatrix} \begin{bmatrix} 0 & 3 & 0 \\ 0 & 0 & 4 \end{bmatrix} = \begin{bmatrix} 0 & 9 & 12 \\ & & \end{bmatrix}$; eliminate choice C because the element in the first row third column is not 0. There is no need to complete the multiplication.

Thus, choice D is the correct response since you've eliminated choices A, B, and C. You should move on to the next question, but just so you know: $\begin{bmatrix} 3 & 0 \\ 0 & 3 \end{bmatrix} \begin{bmatrix} 0 & 3 & 0 \\ 0 & 0 & 4 \end{bmatrix} = \begin{bmatrix} 0 & 9 & 0 \\ 0 & 0 & 12 \end{bmatrix}$.

45. **A, B, D.** Length is preserved only under rotations (select choice A), translations (select choice B), and reflections (select choice D). Length is not preserved under dilations (eliminate choice C).

46. **C.** The matrix $\begin{bmatrix} 5 & 1.5 \\ 2 & d \end{bmatrix}$ is not invertible if its determinant is equal to 0. Set the determinant of the matrix equal to 0 and solve for d.

$$5d - (2)(1.5) = 5d - 3 = 0$$

Thus, $d = \dfrac{3}{5} = 0.6$, choice C.

47. **C.** For the recursive formula given in the problem, you will need to find $f(2)$ and $f(1)$ before you can find $f(3)$. Given $f(0) = 3$ and $f(n) = 2f(n-1) + 3$ for $n \geq 1$, then

$f(1) = 2f(0) + 3 = 2(3) + 3 = 6 + 3 = 9$

$f(2) = 2f(1) + 3 = 2(9) + 3 = 18 + 3 = 21$

$f(3) = 2f(2) + 3 = 2(21) + 3 = 42 + 3 = 45$, choice C.

48. **C.** Given 45% of the marbles are red, then 55% are green. Thus, in the random sample of 20 marbles, the expected number of green marbles is $0.55(20) = 11$, choice C.

49. **D.** There are two tasks to be accomplished. The first task is to select 5 of the 7 chairs. Noting that different ordering of the chairs does not produce different arrangements, the number of ways to select 5 of 7 identical chairs is $_7C_5$. The second task is to arrange the 5 people in the 5 chairs. Since different orderings of the people result in different arrangements, the number of ways to seat 5 people in 5 chairs is $(5)(4)(3)(2)(1) = 5!$ because there are 5 ways to seat someone in the first chair, 4 ways to seat someone in the second chair, and so on. Therefore, by the fundamental counting principle, the total number of ways to seat 5 people in 5 of 7 empty identical chairs is $_7C_5 \cdot 5! = \dfrac{7!}{5!2!} \cdot 5! = (21)(120) = 2{,}520$, choice D.

50. **A, C, D.** A relation $\mathfrak{R}$ on a set S is reflexive if $x \mathfrak{R} x$ for all $x \in S$; symmetric if $x \mathfrak{R} y$ implies $y \mathfrak{R} x$ for all $x, y \in S$; transitive if $(x \mathfrak{R} y$ and $y \mathfrak{R} z)$ implies $x \mathfrak{R} z$ for all $x, y, z \in S$; or antisymmetric if $(x \mathfrak{R} y$ and $y \mathfrak{R} x)$ implies $x = y$ for all $x, y \in S$.

Recall that set A is a subset of set B, written $A \subseteq B$, if and only if $x \in A$ implies that $x \in B$, for every $x \in A$.

The relation "is a subset of" is reflexive (select choice A) because every set is a subset of itself; that is, $A \subseteq A$. The relation "is a subset of" is not symmetric (eliminate choice B) because, for example, $\{1, 3\} \subseteq$ Integers, but Integers $\not\subseteq \{1, 3\}$. The relation "is a subset of" is transitive (select choice C) because if $A \subseteq B$ and $B \subseteq C$, then $A \subseteq C$. The relation "is a subset of" is antisymmetric (select choice D) because if $A \subseteq B$ and $B \subseteq A$, then $A = B$.

51. **B.** Start with the angles for which you can find the measure by using the given information. As you determine the measure of each angle, you will gain enough information to find the solution.

$m\angle ACB = 180° - 64° - 71° = 45°$ (because the sum of the measures of the interior angles of a triangle is 180°)

$m\angle BCE = 45° + 62° = 107°$

The measure of an exterior angle of a triangle equals the sum of the measures of the nonadjacent interior angles. Thus, $m\angle BCE = 107° = 78° + x$; hence, $x = 107° - 78° = 29°$; $m\angle E = 29°$, choice B.

52. **A.** Substitute the given value of x, and use your knowledge of exponents to solve for $50x$.

$$50x = 50\left(1+\left(1+2^{-1}\right)^{-1}\right)^{-1}$$

$$= 50\left(1+\left(1+\frac{1}{2}\right)^{-1}\right)^{-1} = 50\left(1+\left(\frac{3}{2}\right)^{-1}\right)^{-1} = 50\left(1+\frac{2}{3}\right)^{-1} = 50\left(\frac{5}{3}\right)^{-1} = \cancel{50}^{10}\left(\frac{3}{\cancel{5}}\right) = 30, \text{ choice A}$$

53. **A.** Follow the rules for exponents.

$$3^x + 12^x = 3^x + (3 \cdot 4)^x = 3^x + 3^x 4^x = 3^x(1 + 4^x), \text{ choice A}$$

54. **B, C, D.** The equation $\frac{1}{4^x} = 0.001$ implies that $4^x = 1{,}000$. Solve $4^x = 1{,}000$ for x.
You can solve this equation in two different ways; however, all the solutions are equivalent expressions for x.

Method 1. Take the logarithm (base 10) of both sides of the equation, simplify, and solve for x.

$$4^x = 1{,}000$$
$$\log_{10}(4^x) = \log_{10}(1{,}000)$$
$$x \log_{10} 4 = 3$$
$$x = \frac{3}{\log_{10} 4}, \text{ choice B}$$

Method 2. Take the logarithm (base e) of both sides of the equation, simplify, and solve for x. *Note:* $\log_e a$ is denoted $\ln a$.

$$4^x = 1{,}000$$
$$\ln(4^x) = \ln(1{,}000)$$
$$x \ln 4 = \ln(1{,}000)$$
$$x = \frac{\ln(1{,}000)}{\ln 4}, \text{ choice C}$$

or

$$x = \frac{\ln(1{,}000)}{\ln 4} = \frac{\ln 10^3}{\ln 2^2} = \frac{3 \ln 10}{2 \ln 2}, \text{ choice D}$$

55. **D.** The prime factorization of 288 is $2^5 \cdot 3^2$. Therefore, the number 288 has $(5 + 1)(2 + 1) = (6)(3) = 18$ positive factors, choice D.

56. **B, C.** From the figure you have $5x° < 180°$ (because it is an interior angle of a triangle) and $5x° > 90°$ (because the measure of an exterior angle of a triangle is greater than the measure of either nonadjacent interior angles). Thus, $90 < 5x < 180$, which yields $18 < x < 36$. Only choices B and C satisfy this inequality.

57. **A.** Simplify the equation, and then determine the value of x.

$$\frac{1}{4^x} = \frac{1}{4^n} + \frac{1}{4^n} + \frac{1}{4^n} + \frac{1}{4^n}$$

$$\frac{1}{4^x} = \frac{4}{4^n}$$

$$\frac{1}{4^x} = \frac{1}{4^{n-1}}, \text{ which implies}$$

$$x = n - 1, \text{ choice A}$$

58. **A, B, C.** Using the trigonometric formula for the area of a triangle, the area equals $\frac{1}{2}(8)(15)\sin\theta$, where θ is the angle between the two given sides such that $0° < \theta < 180°$. From your knowledge of the sine function, you know that between $0°$ and $180°$, it has a maximum value of 1 at $90°$. So, the triangle has maximum area when it is a right triangle with 8 and 15 as the legs. Therefore, its maximum area is $\frac{1}{2}(8)(15) = 60$. Thus, $0 < \text{area} \leq 60$. Choices A, B, and C satisfy this inequality.

59. **A.** The equation $\log_{(2x+3)}(125) = 3$ is equivalent to $(2x+3)^3 = 125$. Solve this equation by taking the cube root of both sides to obtain $2x + 3 = 5$, which yields $x = 1$, choice A.

Tip: You also can work this problem by checking the answer choices. Only choice A satisfies the original equation because $\log_{(2 \cdot 1 + 3)}(125) = \log_{(5)}(125) = 3$.

60. **D.** The conjugate of $-4 - i$ is $-4 + i$. The product is $(-4 - i)(-4 + i) = (-4)^2 - (i)^2 = 16 - (-1) = 16 + 1 = 17$, choice D.

61. **B.** The least common multiple (lcm) of two positive integers is their product divided by their greatest common factor (gcf). Use this fact about the relationship between least common multiple and greatest common factor to write an equation and solve for n.

$$\frac{(168)(n)}{\gcf(n,168)} = \lcm(n,168)$$

$$\frac{168n}{12} = 1{,}512$$

$$14n = 1{,}512$$

$$n = 108, \text{ choice B}$$

62. **A, B, C.** Determine which of the given properties hold for $S = \{a, b\}$ with respect to $\otimes$.

Using the given table, list the possible "products" and check for the properties given in the answer choices.

$a \otimes a = a$, $a \otimes b = b$, $b \otimes a = b$, and $b \otimes b = b$

Check A: S is closed with respect to $\otimes$ because when $\otimes$ is performed using any two elements in S, the result is an element in S. Select choice A.

Check B: Because $a \otimes b = b$ and $b \otimes a = b$, S is commutative with respect to $\otimes$. Select choice B.

Check C: Because $a \otimes a = a$ and $a \otimes b = b \otimes a = b$, S contains an identity element, namely a, with respect to $\otimes$. Select choice C.

Check D: S does not contain an inverse for every element in S. In particular, the element b does not have an inverse because there is no element in S such that $b \otimes$ (that element) $= a$, the identity element. Eliminate choice D.

63. **B.** The question states specifically that you are looking for a common ratio of this geometric sequence. Knowing this information, you need only calculate the common ratio of any two consecutive entries in the table and express the result as a percentage increase. For example, the difference between January and February is $4.00. Dividing $4.00 by $50.00 yields 0.08, which equals 8%, choice B.

64. **A.** Use logical reasoning to reach the solution. The machines are identical, so if two machines can do the job in 10 days, then it should take twice as long for one machine to do the same job. Therefore, one machine can do the job in 20 days. If five such machines do the job together, they should take $\frac{1}{5}$ as long as it takes for one machine. Therefore, five machines can do the same job in $\frac{1}{5}(20 \text{ days}) = 4$ days, choice A.

65. **B.** Recall that $\ln a$ is the natural logarithm and is used to represent $\log_e a$. Take the natural log of both sides of the equation, and then solve for x.

$$y = e^{x+1}$$

$$\ln y = \ln(e^{x+1})$$

$$\ln y = (x+1)\ln(e)$$

$$\ln y = x + 1$$

$$\ln y - 1 = x, \text{ choice B}$$

66. **B.** Let t = the time, in hours, it will take the two bicyclists to reach other. They are getting closer to each other at a combined speed of 9 mph + 12 mph = 21 mph. Therefore, (21 mph)(t) = 42 miles. Solving this equation for t yields $t = \frac{42 \text{ miles}}{21 \text{ mph}} = 2$ hours, choice B.

67. B. Let N = the total number of votes cast and n = the number of votes Jaxon's opponent received. Then Jaxon received $\frac{4}{3}n$ votes. N, n, and $\frac{4}{3}n$ must be whole numbers with $N = n + \frac{4}{3}n = \frac{7}{3}n$, which implies that $\frac{3}{7}N = n$. Given that n is a whole number, then N must be divisible by 7. Of the choices given, only 280 (choice B) is divisible by 7.

68. D. Given that D lies on the angle bisector of $\angle ABC$, then $\angle DBC$ has measure of $\frac{1}{2}(90°) = 45°$. Points D, B, and E are collinear, so the sum of $\angle DBC$ and $\angle CBE$ is 180°. Therefore, the measure of $\angle CBE$ equals $180° - 45° = 135°$, choice D.

69. B. Using ASA, you can show that $\triangle ACB$ and $\triangle DCE$ are congruent as follows: $\angle ACB \cong \angle DCE$ because they are vertical angles. $\overline{AC} \cong \overline{DC}$ because $\overline{BE}$ bisects $\overline{AD}$. You are given that $\angle A \cong \angle D = 75°$. Thus, you have two angles and the included side of $\triangle ABC$ congruent to two angles and the included side of $\triangle DCE$, so the two triangles are congruent. Therefore, the total area of the figure shown is twice the area of either of the two triangles. For convenience, determine twice the area of $\triangle ABC$. Given that AD is 12, then because $\overline{BE}$ bisects $\overline{AD}$, AC is 6. Thus, twice the area of $\triangle ABC$ equals $2\left(\frac{1}{2}\right)(10)(6)\sin 75° \approx 58$, choice B.

70. D. The 75th percentile is a value at or below which 75% of the data fall. Therefore, the best interpretation of the student's percentile score is that the student did as well or better than 75% of the students who took the exam, choice D.

71. D. Make a sketch to illustrate the problem.

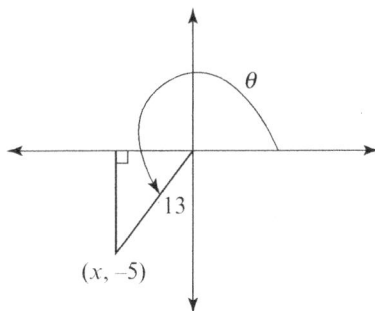

Method 1. Eliminate answer choices based on the information provided. The sketch shows that $\tan\theta = \frac{y}{x} = \frac{-5}{x}$ and that $x < 0$. Therefore, $\tan\theta > 0$ because it is the quotient of two negative numbers. Eliminate choices A and B because these answer choices contain negative values. Of the two remaining answer choices, only choice D has a 5 in the numerator for the tangent, meaning that choice D must be the correct response.

Method 2. Use the formulas $r^2 = x^2 + y^2$ and $\tan\theta = \frac{y}{x}$ to determine that $x = \sqrt{13^2 - (-5)^2} = \sqrt{144} = \pm 12$. Because x is to the left of the origin, $x = -12$. Thus, $\tan\theta = \frac{y}{x} = \frac{-5}{-12} = \frac{5}{12}$, choice D.

72. B. First, rearrange the terms so that only x terms are on the left side of the equation. Next, complete the square for the x terms. Then take the square root of both sides of the equation. **Tip:** Remember, $\sqrt{(x)^2} = |x|$.

$$x^2 - 17 = 16x$$
$$x^2 - 16x = 17$$
$$x^2 - 16x + 64 = 17 + 64$$
$$(x-8)^2 = 81$$
$$|x-8| = 9, \text{ choice B}$$

73. D. You know that $|\sin x| \leq 1$. Using this fact yields the following:

$$-1 \leq \sin x \leq 1$$
$$-1 - \frac{1}{4} \leq \sin x - \frac{1}{4} \leq 1 - \frac{1}{4}$$
$$-\frac{5}{4} \leq \sin x - \frac{1}{4} \leq \frac{3}{4}$$

Thus, the maximum value of y is $\left|-\frac{5}{4}\right| = \frac{5}{4}$, choice D.

74. A. Method 1. Since all the answer choices are given in terms of sine and cosine, rewrite $\dfrac{\tan\theta + \cot\theta}{\sec\theta \csc\theta}$ as

$$\frac{\dfrac{\sin\theta}{\cos\theta} + \dfrac{\cos\theta}{\sin\theta}}{\dfrac{1}{\cos\theta} \cdot \dfrac{1}{\sin\theta}} = \frac{\dfrac{\sin^2\theta + \cos^2\theta}{\cos\theta\sin\theta}}{\dfrac{1}{\cos\theta\sin\theta}} = \sin^2\theta + \cos^2\theta \text{, choice A.}$$

Method 2. Rewrite $\dfrac{\tan\theta + \cot\theta}{\sec\theta \csc\theta}$ as $\dfrac{\tan\theta + \dfrac{1}{\tan\theta}}{\dfrac{1}{\cos\theta} \cdot \dfrac{1}{\sin\theta}}$, so that you can use the trig function keys on your graphing calculator to evaluate the expression for a convenient value of θ, say 30°. *Note:* Make sure your calculator is set to degree mode. When you evaluate $\dfrac{\tan 30° + \dfrac{1}{\tan 30°}}{\dfrac{1}{\cos 30°} \cdot \dfrac{1}{\sin 30°}}$, you get 1 for an answer. You should recognize that $\sin^2\theta + \cos^2\theta$ (choice A) is an identity that equals 1 for all values of θ.

In a test situation, you should go on to the next question since you have found the correct answer. You would not have to check the other answer choices; but for your information, when $\theta = 30°$, choice B yields 1.5, choice C yields 0.8660. . ., and choice D yields 0.5.

75. C. By the remainder theorem, $p(1) = -3$. Substitute into $p(x)$ and solve for k.

$$p(x) = (2x - 3)(x + k)$$
$$p(1) = (2(1) - 3)((1) + k)$$
$$-3 = (-1)(1 + k)$$
$$-3 = -1 - k$$
$$k = 2, \text{ choice C}$$

76. D. Find $f'(x)$ and then solve $f'(2) = 0$ and $f'(-2) = 0$ for k.

$$f(x) = x + \frac{k}{x} = x + kx^{-1}$$
$$f'(x) = 1 - kx^{-2} = 1 - \frac{k}{x^2}$$
$$f'(2) = 1 - \frac{k}{(2)^2} = 1 - \frac{k}{4} \text{ and } f'(-2) = 1 - \frac{k}{(-2)^2} = 1 - \frac{k}{4}$$

Now, setting $1 - \dfrac{k}{4} = 0$ and solving for k yields

$$1 - \frac{k}{4} = 0$$
$$4 - k = 0$$
$$k = 4, \text{ choice D}$$

When $k = 4$, $f'(x) = 1 - \frac{4}{x^2} = 1 - 4x^{-2}$, which implies $f''(x) = 8x^{-3}$. Thus, $f''(2) = 8(2)^{-3} = 1 > 0$ and $f''(-2) = 8(-2)^{-3} = -1 < 0$. This result verifies that f has a relative minimum at $x = 2$ and a relative maximum at $x = -2$.

Tip: Use your graphing calculator to graph $f(x) = x + \frac{4}{x}$ to verify your results.

77. **B.** The total number of different problem combinations is $(_5C_3)(_6C_2) = \left(\frac{5!}{3!2!}\right)\left(\frac{6!}{2!4!}\right) = (10)(15) = 150$, choice B.

    Tip: Use your TI graphing calculator to compute $(_5C_3)(_6C_2)$ by using the $_nC_r$ option under the PRB menu of the MATH key.

78. **B.** The problem requires that you find the probability that the house next door will be sold given that the model home has already been sold. This probability is a conditional probability. If A is the event that the model home will be sold and B is the event that the house next door will be sold, then you need to find $P(B \mid A) = \frac{P(A \cap B)}{P(A)}$. You are given $P(A) = 0.50$, but you are not given $P(A \cap B)$, which is the probability that both houses are sold. The problem states "the probability that at least one of the two houses will be sold is 0.80." For this problem situation, the probability that at least one of the two houses will be sold is $P(A \cup B)$. Recall that $P(A \cup B) = P(A) + P(B) - P(A \cap B)$. Thus, given $P(A) = 0.50$, $P(B) = 0.40$, and $P(A \cup B) = 0.80$, you can determine $P(A \cap B)$. To find $P(B|A)$, first determine $P(A \cap B)$. Next, use the information found and information given in the problem to calculate $P(B|A)$.

$$P(A \cup B) = P(A) + P(B) - P(A \cap B)$$
$$0.80 = 0.50 + 0.40 - P(A \cap B)$$
$$P(A \cap B) = 0.90 - 0.80$$
$$P(A \cap B) = 0.10$$

Thus, $P(B \mid A) = \frac{P(A \cap B)}{P(A)} = \frac{0.10}{0.50} = 0.20 = 20\%$, choice B.

79. **A.** The powers of the complex unit i are cyclic. That is, $i = i$, $i^2 = -1$, $i^3 = -i$, $i^4 = 1$, $i^5 = i$, $i^6 = -1$, $i^7 = -i$, $i^8 = 1$, $i^9 = i$, and so on. The pattern of $i, -1, -i, 1$ repeats consecutively. In general, $i^{4k+1} = i$, $i^{4k+2} = i^2 = -1$, $i^{4k+3} = i^3 = w - i$, and $i^{4k+4} = i^4 = 1$.

    Therefore, to evaluate a power of i, divide its exponent by 4 and use the remainder as the exponent for i. Thus, $i^{218} = i^{4(54)+2} = i^2 = -1$, choice A.

80. **D.** Interchange x and y in $y = x^3 - 8$, and then solve for y.

$$x = y^3 - 8$$
$$x + 8 = y^3$$
$$\sqrt[3]{x+8} = y, \text{ choice D}$$

81. **D.** Use the properties of logarithms to rewrite the expression.

$$\log_{10}\left(\frac{x^3}{20}\right) = \log_{10} x^3 - \log_{10} 20$$
$$= 3\log_{10} x - \log_{10}(2 \cdot 10)$$
$$= 3\log_{10} x - (\log_{10} 2 + \log_{10} 10)$$
$$= 3\log_{10} x - \log_{10} 2 - \log_{10} 10$$
$$= 3\log_{10} x - \log_{10} 2 - 1, \text{ choice D}$$

82. **B, D.** A matrix that has an inverse is nonsingular. A matrix has an inverse if and only if its determinant does *not* equal 0. Therefore, to determine which of the matrices are nonsingular, compute the determinant for each. If the determinant is *not* equal to 0, the matrix is nonsingular. Check the answer choices.

Check A: $\begin{vmatrix} -3 & 5 \\ -6 & 10 \end{vmatrix} = (-3)(10) - (5)(-6) = -30 - (-30) = -30 + 30 = 0$, so $\begin{bmatrix} -3 & 5 \\ -6 & 10 \end{bmatrix}$ is *not* a nonsingular matrix. Eliminate choice A.

Check B: $\begin{vmatrix} 4 & 0 \\ 0 & 4 \end{vmatrix} = (4)(4) - (0)(0) = 16 \ne 0$, so $\begin{bmatrix} 4 & 0 \\ 0 & 4 \end{bmatrix}$ is a nonsingular matrix. Select choice B.

Check C: The matrix $\begin{bmatrix} 2 & -5 & 3 \\ 6 & 1 & -4 \\ 0 & 0 & 0 \end{bmatrix}$ has a row of 0s. If a square matrix has a row or column consisting of only 0s, the determinant of the matrix equals 0. Therefore, $\begin{bmatrix} 2 & -5 & 3 \\ 6 & 1 & -4 \\ 0 & 0 & 0 \end{bmatrix}$ is *not* a nonsingular matrix. Eliminate choice C.

Check D: $\begin{bmatrix} 1 & 0 & 0 \\ 0 & 1 & 0 \\ 0 & 0 & 1 \end{bmatrix} = (1)\begin{vmatrix} 1 & 0 \\ 0 & 1 \end{vmatrix} - (0)\begin{vmatrix} 0 & 0 \\ 0 & 1 \end{vmatrix} + (0)\begin{vmatrix} 0 & 1 \\ 0 & 0 \end{vmatrix} = 1 - 0 + 0 = 1 \ne 0$, so $\begin{bmatrix} 1 & 0 & 0 \\ 0 & 1 & 0 \\ 0 & 0 & 1 \end{bmatrix}$ is a nonsingular matrix. Select choice D.

83. **A.** This problem is best analyzed as a "work problem." The key idea in a work problem is that the rate at which work is done equals the amount of work accomplished divided by the amount of time worked: rate = $\dfrac{\text{amount of work done}}{\text{time worked}}$. For the situation in this problem, the work to be done is to fill the tank.

However, only the input valve works to fill the tank. The outlet valve works counter to the input valve because it works to empty the tank. Let t = time it will take to fill the tank with both valves open. To find t, first determine the rate, r_{fill}, at which the tank can be filled when the input valve is open and the outlet valve is closed, and the rate r_{empty}, at which the tank can be emptied when the input valve is closed and the outlet valve is open. Next, write an equation and solve for t.

The rate for filling the tank is $r_{fill} = \dfrac{1 \text{ full tank}}{6 \text{ hr}} = \dfrac{1}{6}$ tank/hr.

The rate for emptying the tank is $r_{empty} = \dfrac{1 \text{ full tank}}{10 \text{ hr}} = \dfrac{1}{10}$ tank/hr.

Thus, when both valves are open, $\left(\dfrac{1}{6} \text{ tank/hr}\right)t - \left(\dfrac{1}{10} \text{ tank/hr}\right)t = 1 \text{ full tank}$.

Thus, omitting the units, the equation that correctly models the situation is $\dfrac{1}{6}t - \dfrac{1}{10}t = 1$, choice A.

84. **A.** Apply the law of cosines and solve for $\cos\theta$.

$$7^2 = 6^2 + 4^2 - 2(6)(4)\cos\theta$$
$$49 = 36 + 16 - 48\cos\theta$$
$$48\cos\theta = 3$$
$$\cos\theta = \dfrac{3}{48} = \dfrac{1}{16}, \text{ choice A}$$

85. **D.** First, find $f'(x)$, then determine $f'(2)$.

$f(x) = -16x^{-4}$ implies $f'(x) = 64x^{-5}$

$f'(2) = 64(2)^{-5} = 64\left(\dfrac{1}{32}\right) = 2$, choice D

86. **C.** The residuals are the differences between the actual y values and their predicted values based on the equation of the line of best fit. A residual plot shows the residuals on the vertical axis and the corresponding x values on the horizontal axis. A positive value for a residual (on the y-axis) means the predicted value was too low, and a negative value means the predicted value was too high; a value of zero for a residual means the predicted value was exactly correct. If the residuals are randomly scattered around the horizontal line at 0, it is reasonable to assume that the relationship between X and Y is linear and the line of best fit is a satisfactory model for the data. Thus, choice C is the correct response.

87. **B.** Use the definition for matrix multiplication to compute the product BA, then determine $(BA)^{-1}$.

$$BA = \begin{bmatrix} -2 & 3 \\ 2 & 0 \end{bmatrix}\begin{bmatrix} 0 & 2 \\ 1 & 3 \end{bmatrix} = \begin{bmatrix} -2(0)+3(1) & -2(2)+3(3) \\ 2(0)+0(1) & 2(2)+0(3) \end{bmatrix} = \begin{bmatrix} 3 & 5 \\ 0 & 4 \end{bmatrix}$$

The determinant of $BA = (3)(4) - (5)(0) = 12$.

$$(BA)^{-1} = \begin{bmatrix} 3 & 5 \\ 0 & 4 \end{bmatrix}^{-1} = \frac{1}{\det(BA)}\begin{bmatrix} 4 & -5 \\ 0 & 3 \end{bmatrix} = \frac{1}{12}\begin{bmatrix} 4 & -5 \\ 0 & 3 \end{bmatrix} = \begin{bmatrix} \frac{1}{3} & -\frac{5}{12} \\ 0 & \frac{1}{4} \end{bmatrix},\text{ choice B}$$

Tip: Your TI graphing calculator has matrix features that you might want to use during your TExES Math exam. Check your calculator guidebook for information.

88. **C.** $(f \circ g)(x) = f(g(x)) = f(3x + 2) = (3x + 2)^2 - 4 = 9x^2 + 12x + 4 - 4 = 9x^2 + 12x = 3x(3x + 4)$, choice C

89. **A.** With inverse variation, as one variable increases, the other variable decreases, and conversely. Choice A is an example of inverse variation because as the number of painters increases, the number of hours to paint the house decreases; and as the number of painters decreases, the number of hours to paint the house increases. The situations in choices B, C, and D are examples of direct variation because as one variable increases, the other variable increases as well; and as one variable decreases, the other variable also decreases.

90. **A.** The compound interest formula is $A = P\left(1 + \frac{r}{n}\right)^{nt}$, where P is the initial investment, r is the interest rate, compounded n times per year, and A is the final value after t years. (*Note:* This formula is available during the exam in the on-screen "Definitions and Formulas" reference material.) You need to find the rate, compounded annually, that will double an initial investment of $10,000 in 20 years. In other words, you need to find the rate, compounded annually, that will yield a value of $20,000 for A in 20 years when $P = \$10,000$. Given that the interest is compounded annually, n is 1 and t is 20 years.

Substitute into the formula (omitting the units for convenience) and solve for r.

$$A = P(1+r)^t$$
$$20,000 = 10,000(1+r)^{20}$$
$$2 = (1+r)^{20}$$
$$\ln 2 = \ln(1+r)^{20}$$
$$\ln 2 = 20\ln(1+r)$$
$$\frac{\ln 2}{20} = \ln(1+r) \text{ implies}$$
$$1+r = e^{\frac{\ln 2}{20}}$$
$$r = e^{\frac{\ln 2}{20}} - 1 \approx .035 \text{ or } 3.5\%, \text{ choice A}$$

91. **D.** The contrapositive of an if-then statement such as "If P, then Q" is "If not Q, then not P." In the given statement, "P" is "$x \notin B$" and "Q" is "$x \notin A$." So, "not P" is "$x \in B$" and "not Q" is "$x \in A$." Therefore, the contrapositive of "if $x \notin B$, then $x \notin A$" is "if $x \in A$, then $x \in B$." Thus, the students must assume $x \in A$ and then deduce $x \in B$, choice D.

92. **A.** Directly observing the students working to solve quadratic equations and using a checklist to record their implementation of the procedure is a powerful way to find out what the students know and understand about the process, choice A. This method is more likely to yield valid and reliable information about the students' learning than the methods given in choices B, C, and D.

93. **B, C.** If the diagonals of a quadrilateral are perpendicular bisectors of each other, the quadrilateral must be a square (select choice B) or a rhombus (select choice C). The diagonals of rectangles (choice A) and parallelograms (choice D) bisect each other, but they are not always perpendicular to each other.

94. **C.** In logic, the negation of a statement is a statement that has the opposite truth value. That is, when the given statement is true, its negation is false, and when the given statement is false, its negation is true. The given statement "Some books are entertaining" contains the existential quantifier "Some." You can eliminate choice A because the negation of a statement that contains an existential quantifier is a statement that contains a universal quantifier (such as "All," "No," and "None"). The statement "Some books are entertaining" has the logical form "Some b are e." The negation has the form "No b are e." Therefore, the negation of "Some books are entertaining" is "No books are entertaining," choice C.

95. **C.** Given that 1 mile (mi) = 5,280 feet (ft), 1 ft = 12 inches (in), 1 hour (hr) = 60 minutes (min), and 1 revolution = 26π in, use dimensional analysis to convert the speed of 10 miles per hour to rpm as follows:

$$\frac{10 \text{ mi}}{1 \text{ hr}} \times \frac{5{,}280 \text{ ft}}{1 \text{ mi}} \times \frac{12 \text{ in}}{1 \text{ ft}} \times \frac{1 \text{ hr}}{60 \text{ min}} \times \frac{1 \text{ revolution}}{26\pi \text{ in}} \approx 129 \text{ rpm, choice C}$$

96. **B.** As x approaches -2 in the given expression, both the numerator and denominator approach zero. However, as shown below, you can overcome this problem by factoring both the numerator and denominator and dividing out a common nonzero factor of $x + 2$, and then evaluating the limit.

$$\lim_{x \to -2} \frac{x^2 + 6x + 8}{x^2 - x - 6} = \lim_{x \to -2} \frac{(x+4)(x+2)}{(x-3)(x+2)} = \lim_{x \to -2} \frac{x+4}{x-3} = \frac{-2+4}{-2-3} = -\frac{2}{5}, \text{ choice B}$$

Tip: You know $x + 2$ is nonzero because x is approaching -2, meaning $x + 2$ is approaching zero, but not reaching that value.

97. **C.** Eliminate choice D because a parabola has either an x^2 term or a y^2 term, but not both. Now, examining the coefficients of x^2 and y^2 reveals that their coefficients have different signs, indicating that the equation represents a hyperbola, choice C. Eliminate choice A because the coefficients of x^2 and y^2 are identical in the equation of a circle. Eliminate choice B because in the equation of an ellipse, the coefficients of x^2 and y^2 have identical signs, but different absolute values.

98. **C.** If the data values of a data set are uniformly increased by a given amount, measures of central tendency (mean, median, and mode) will increase by that amount. Adding the same given amount to each data value does not change the distances between values, so measures of variability (standard deviation, variance, and range) will remain unchanged. Therefore, the revised scores have a mean of 83 and a standard deviation of 8, choice C.

99. **B.** Students will find these two features most useful for determining the solution to a two-variable system of two linear equations, choice B. When the two equations are graphed on the same coordinate grid, the solution (to a consistent system) will be the point where the graphs intersect. The trace feature can be used to trace along the graphs to the point of intersection. Eliminate choices A and D because the trace feature is not useful in determining the derivative of a function (choice A) or the inverse of a matrix (choice D). Eliminate choice C because it refers to complex zeros, which are not shown on graphing calculators. These calculators show only real zeros of a function.

100. **A.** The teacher wants the students to take a skill previously acquired in one setting and apply it in a new, but related context. The ability to start with something simple and familiar and then move toward the more general underlying foundations is *generalization* (also known as *transfer of learning*), choice A, an indispensable skill in mathematics. The other answer choices do not apply as well to the task as choice A.

Chapter 10

TExES Math 7–12 Practice Test 2

100 Questions

Time—4 Hours 45 Minutes

Directions: Read the directions for each question carefully. For each question, select the best single answer choice unless written instructions in the question state otherwise.

1. In the xy plane, which of the following points lies inside the circular region of radius 4 centered at $(-2, 3)$?

    Ⓐ $(-6, 3)$
    Ⓑ $(-2, -1)$
    Ⓒ $(1, 5)$
    Ⓓ $(2, 3)$

2. Suppose k is an integer such that $1 < k^2 < 50$. If the units digit of k^2 is 6 and the units digit of $(k-1)^2$ is 5, what is the units digit of $(k+1)^2$?

    Ⓐ 1
    Ⓑ 4
    Ⓒ 6
    Ⓓ 9

Use the sequence below to answer question 3.

$2 + 2, 4 + 4 + 4, 8 + 8 + 8 + 8, \ldots$

3. Given the sequence of sums shown above, if the pattern continues, which of the following expressions can be used to find the nth sum of the sequence?

    Ⓐ $n(2^n)$
    Ⓑ $n(2^{n-1})$
    Ⓒ $(n+1)(2^n)$
    Ⓓ $(n+1)(2^{n-1})$

Use the statement below to answer question 4.

> The variable z equals the quotient of twice the square root of the sum of x and y and the fourth power of the product of $2x$ and y.

4. As a culmination of a lesson on translating words into algebraic symbolism, a teacher writes the statement above on the whiteboard and asks students to express it as an algebraic equation. Which of the following equations correctly represents the statement?

    Ⓐ $z = \dfrac{2\sqrt{x+y}}{(2xy)^4}$

    Ⓑ $z = \dfrac{\sqrt{2(x+y)}}{(2xy)^4}$

    Ⓒ $z = \dfrac{2\sqrt{x+y}}{2xy^4}$

    Ⓓ $z = 2\sqrt{\dfrac{x+y}{(2xy)^4}}$

5. Definition: The *normal line* to the curve $y = f(x)$ at the point T is the line perpendicular to the tangent line to the curve at T. If an equation of the normal line to the graph of the function defined by $y = f(x)$ at the point $(3, 1)$ is $y = \dfrac{5}{6}x - \dfrac{3}{2}$, find the equation of the tangent line at $(3, 1)$.

    Ⓐ $5x - 6y = 9$
    Ⓑ $-6x + 5y = -13$
    Ⓒ $6x + 5y = 23$
    Ⓓ $6x + 5y = 21$

GO ON TO THE NEXT PAGE

6. Given $f(x) = -x^2 + 12\sqrt{x}$, find the slope of the tangent line to the graph of f at $x = 4$.

   Ⓐ −5
   Ⓑ 5
   Ⓒ 8
   Ⓓ 32

7. Given that a, b, c, and d are digits such that $a < b < c < d$, which of the following numbers is greatest?

   Ⓐ $0.4abc\overline{d}$
   Ⓑ $0.4ab\overline{cd}$
   Ⓒ $0.4a\overline{bcd}$
   Ⓓ $0.4\overline{abcd}$

8. Right triangle ABC is similar to right triangle DEF. $\triangle ABC$ has a height of 8, a base of x, and an area of 48. If $\triangle DEF$ has an area of 24, what is the length of y, the base of $\triangle DEF$?

   Ⓐ $3\sqrt{2}$
   Ⓑ 6
   Ⓒ $6\sqrt{2}$
   Ⓓ 12

Use the problem below to answer question 9.

> A pen on a farm contains only ducks and goats. If there are 36 legs and 13 heads in the pen, how many ducks and how many goats does it contain?

9. For the problem above, if d is the number of ducks and g is the number of goats, which of the following matrix equations will yield a correct solution?

   Ⓐ $\begin{bmatrix} 1 & 1 \\ 2 & 4 \end{bmatrix} \begin{bmatrix} 13 \\ 36 \end{bmatrix} = \begin{bmatrix} d \\ g \end{bmatrix}$

   Ⓑ $\begin{bmatrix} 1 & 1 \\ 2 & 4 \end{bmatrix} \begin{bmatrix} g \\ d \end{bmatrix} = \begin{bmatrix} 36 \\ 13 \end{bmatrix}$

   Ⓒ $\begin{bmatrix} 1 & 1 \\ 2 & 4 \end{bmatrix} \begin{bmatrix} 36 \\ 13 \end{bmatrix} = \begin{bmatrix} g \\ d \end{bmatrix}$

   Ⓓ $\begin{bmatrix} 1 & 1 \\ 2 & 4 \end{bmatrix} \begin{bmatrix} d \\ g \end{bmatrix} = \begin{bmatrix} 13 \\ 36 \end{bmatrix}$

10. To estimate the population of turtles in a lake, a parks and recreation team captures and tags 25 turtles and then releases the tagged turtles back into the lake. One month later, the team returns and captures 50 turtles from the lake, 2 of which have tags that identify them as being among the previously captured turtles. If all the tagged turtles are still active in the lake when the second group of turtles is captured, what is the best estimate of the turtle population in the lake based on the information obtained through this capture-tag-release-recapture strategy?

   Ⓐ 10
   Ⓑ 15
   Ⓒ 250
   Ⓓ 625

11. Which of the following statements follows logically from the statement "If it is a holiday, then I do not go to work"?

   Ⓐ It is not a holiday, so I do go to work.
   Ⓑ It is a holiday, so I do go to work.
   Ⓒ I do go to work, so it is not a holiday.
   Ⓓ I do not go to work, so it is a holiday.

12. Given $\dfrac{p}{q} = 20$ and $\dfrac{q}{r} = 10$, with $qr \neq 0$, what is the value of $\dfrac{p}{q+r}$?

   Ⓐ $\dfrac{200}{11}$
   Ⓑ $\dfrac{100}{11}$
   Ⓒ $\dfrac{11}{100}$
   Ⓓ $\dfrac{11}{200}$

13. $(2\cos 10° + 2i \sin 10°)^3 =$

   Ⓐ $4\sqrt{3} + 4i$
   Ⓑ $4 + 4\sqrt{3}i$
   Ⓒ $8\cos 1{,}000° + 8i \sin 1{,}000°$
   Ⓓ $8\sin 1{,}000° + 8i \cos 1{,}000°$

GO ON TO THE NEXT PAGE

14. A mixture weighs 78 grams. It consists of ingredients A, B, and C in the ratio of 6:5:2, respectively, by weight. What is the difference, in grams, in the weights of ingredient A and ingredient C in the mixture?

Ⓐ 8
Ⓑ 12
Ⓒ 18
Ⓓ 24

15. $\triangle ABC$ has vertices (2, 1), (−3, 4), and (5, −3). Which of the following matrix multiplications would result in a reflection of $\triangle ABC$ over the x-axis?

Ⓐ $\begin{bmatrix} -1 & 0 \\ 0 & 1 \end{bmatrix} \begin{bmatrix} 2 & -3 & 5 \\ 1 & 4 & -3 \end{bmatrix}$

Ⓑ $\begin{bmatrix} 0 & 1 \\ -1 & 0 \end{bmatrix} \begin{bmatrix} 2 & -3 & 5 \\ 1 & 4 & -3 \end{bmatrix}$

Ⓒ $\begin{bmatrix} 1 & 0 \\ 0 & -1 \end{bmatrix} \begin{bmatrix} 2 & -3 & 5 \\ 1 & 4 & -3 \end{bmatrix}$

Ⓓ $\begin{bmatrix} 0 & 1 \\ 1 & 0 \end{bmatrix} \begin{bmatrix} 2 & -3 & 5 \\ 1 & 4 & -3 \end{bmatrix}$

16. In right triangle ABC with right angle C, the length of one leg is x, and the length of the other leg is 7 units longer. What is the length, c, of the hypotenuse?

Ⓐ $\sqrt{x^2 + 49}$
Ⓑ $\sqrt{2x^2 + 49}$
Ⓒ $\sqrt{x^2 + 14x + 49}$
Ⓓ $\sqrt{2x^2 + 14x + 49}$

17. For which of the following data sets is the median clearly a preferred alternative to the mean as a measure of central tendency?

Ⓐ The data set contains some extremely high, without corresponding extremely low, data values.
Ⓑ The data set has a somewhat symmetrical distribution.
Ⓒ The data set is very large in number and has no mode.
Ⓓ The data set is very small in number and has no mode.

18. At the end of the week, as a quick review, an algebra 1 teacher has the practice of giving a short quiz consisting of five multiple-choice questions. Each question has four possible answer choices, one of which is the correct response. Suppose that an unprepared student does not read the question, but instead makes a random selection for each question. What is the probability that the student will choose correctly on at least one question?

Ⓐ $\dfrac{1}{1,024}$
Ⓑ $\dfrac{1,023}{1,024}$
Ⓒ $\dfrac{781}{1,024}$
Ⓓ $\dfrac{5}{4}$

19. To find the distance across the lake between two houses separated by the lake, a surveyor measures the angle between the houses from a distant point, X, on dry land. The surveyor then measures the straight-line distance on dry land from X to each of the two houses. The distance from X to the first house is 60 feet and from X to the second house is 75 feet. If the angle measured at point X between the two houses is 60°, approximately how far apart, in feet, are the two houses?

Ⓐ 39
Ⓑ 69
Ⓒ 96
Ⓓ 135

20. The density of lead is 11.3 grams per cubic centimeter. What is the mass (to the nearest tenth of a gram) of a lead cube that measures 1.5 centimeters on an edge?

Ⓐ 3.3
Ⓑ 17.0
Ⓒ 25.4
Ⓓ 38.1

GO ON TO THE NEXT PAGE

21. The original price of a suit was 30% less than the suit's suggested retail price of $500. The price at which the suit was sold was 30% more than the original price. What is the price at which the suit was sold?

Ⓐ $350
Ⓑ $425
Ⓒ $455
Ⓓ $500

22. Given the functions $f = \{(-2, -8), (-1, 3), (0, 1), (1, 4), (2, 8)\}$ and $g = \{(-2, -7), (-1, 4), (0, -2), (1, 2), (2, 0), (3, 8)\}$, find $g \circ f$, where $(g \circ f)(x) = g(f(x))$.

Ⓐ $\{(0, -8), (1, 8), (2, 1)\}$
Ⓑ $\{(-1, 8), (0, 2)\}$
Ⓒ $\{(-2, 56), (-1, -12), (0, -2), (1, 8), (2, 0)\}$
Ⓓ $\{(-2, -15), (-1, -1), (0, -1), (1, 6), (2, 8)\}$

23. A team of biologists introduces a herd of 250 deer onto an uninhabited island. If the deer population doubles every 8 years, which of the following functions models the growth of the deer population on the island if t is the time in years?

Ⓐ $(250)^{0.125t}$
Ⓑ $(250)2^{0.125t}$
Ⓒ $(250)^{8t}$
Ⓓ $(250)2^{8t}$

24. For what values of x in the interval $0 \leq x \leq 2\pi$ does $\sin^2 x - 5 \sin x + 4 = 0$?

Select all that apply.

Ⓐ 1, 4
Ⓑ π
Ⓒ $\dfrac{\pi}{2}$
Ⓓ $\dfrac{3\pi}{2}$

25. If $f(x) = -x^{-2}$, then $f''(2)$ is

Ⓐ -1
Ⓑ $-\dfrac{1}{4}$
Ⓒ $\dfrac{1}{4}$
Ⓓ 1

Use the table below to answer question 26.

Correlation Table for Variables A, B, C, and D

	A	B	C	D
A	1			
B	−0.88	1		
C	0.65	0.15	1	
D	−0.59	0.50	0.78	1

26. The preceding correlation table shows the correlations between pairs of variables from among the four variables A, B, C, and D. The correlation coefficient between which of the following pairs of variables shows the strongest relationship?

Ⓐ A and B
Ⓑ A and C
Ⓒ A and D
Ⓓ C and D

27. In general, with respect to matrix multiplication on the set of $n \times n$ matrices whose elements are real numbers only, which of the following properties hold?

Select all that apply.

Ⓐ Closure
Ⓑ Commutativity
Ⓒ Associativity
Ⓓ Distributive property

28. If x is a positive integer such that $x \equiv 1 \pmod{3}$ and $x \equiv 5 \pmod{8}$, which of the following integers is a possible value of x?

Ⓐ 7
Ⓑ 13
Ⓒ 17
Ⓓ 21

Use the sequence below to answer question 29.

$$1, 2, 4, 7, 11, 16, \ldots$$

29. A middle-school mathematics teacher gives students the sequence above and asks them to look for a pattern, and then determine the next term. The teacher observes that several students are struggling to find a pattern and are getting frustrated. Which of the following questions could the teacher ask to scaffold the task for these students?

- Ⓐ   Have you tried looking at the differences between successive terms?
- Ⓑ   Have you tried dividing each term by the previous term?
- Ⓒ   Have you tried adding the two previous terms?
- Ⓓ   Have you tried determining the prime factors of each term?

Use the figure below to answer question 30.

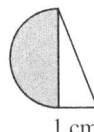

1 cm

30. The figure above consists of a semicircle with radius of 1 centimeter and an attached right triangle with one leg equal to the radius of the semicircle as shown. What is the figure's perimeter to the nearest tenth of a centimeter?

- Ⓐ   5.4
- Ⓑ   5.9
- Ⓒ   6.4
- Ⓓ   9.5

31. A father, who is 38 years old, and his daughter, who is 10 years old, share the same birthday month and day. In how many years will the father be twice as old as his daughter?

- Ⓐ   10
- Ⓑ   18
- Ⓒ   20
- Ⓓ   28

32. What is the value of $\lim\limits_{x \to 3} \dfrac{2x - 6}{x^2 - 9}$?

- Ⓐ   The limit does not exist.
- Ⓑ $\dfrac{1}{6}$
- Ⓒ $\dfrac{1}{3}$
- Ⓓ   1

33. The velocity function for a particle moving in a straight line is given by $v(t) = 1.8t^2$. How far does the particle move between time $t = 0$ and $t = 5$?

- Ⓐ   15
- Ⓑ   45
- Ⓒ   75
- Ⓓ   225

34. Find a, b, c, and d if

$$\begin{bmatrix} a & 5 \\ 4b & d \end{bmatrix} - \begin{bmatrix} 3a & 2c \\ -6 & -2d \end{bmatrix} = \begin{bmatrix} -8 & 7 \\ b & 9 \end{bmatrix}.$$

- Ⓐ $a = -4, b = 2, c = -1, d = 3$
- Ⓑ $a = 4, b = -2, c = -1, d = 3$
- Ⓒ $a = 4, b = -2, c = 1, d = -3$
- Ⓓ $a = -4, b = 2, c = 1, d = 3$

35. At an electronic superstore's grand-opening sale, 304 customers bought a computer or a printer. Looking at the inventory, the store manager found that 188 computers and 160 printers were sold. Of the 304 customers, how many bought only a computer?

- Ⓐ   44
- Ⓑ   116
- Ⓒ   144
- Ⓓ   260

36. The equation of the line tangent to the graph of $y = 2x^3 - x + 3$ at the point where $x = 1$ is given by

- Ⓐ $6x - y = 2$
- Ⓑ $5x - y = 1$
- Ⓒ $5x - y = 5$
- Ⓓ $5x - y = -1$

GO ON TO THE NEXT PAGE

37. What is the area, in unit², of the region bounded by the graph of $f(x) = 3x^2 + 1$ and the x-axis over the closed interval [1, 3]?

- Ⓐ 26
- Ⓑ 28
- Ⓒ 30
- Ⓓ 32

38. The distribution of the heights of a certain type of indoor plant follows a normal distribution with a mean of 24 inches and a standard deviation of 3.5 inches. What is the approximate probability a plant of this type chosen at random will be between 20.5 inches and 27.5 inches tall?

- Ⓐ 16%
- Ⓑ 34%
- Ⓒ 68%
- Ⓓ 84%

39. While summing a series, a student observes the following pattern:

$1 + 3 = 4 = 2^2$

$1 + 3 + 5 = 9 = 3^2$

$1 + 3 + 5 + 7 = 16 = 4^2$

The student conjectures that the sum of the first n consecutive odd integers equals n^2. The student's conjecture is a result of

- Ⓐ proof by contradiction.
- Ⓑ proof by contrapositive.
- Ⓒ inductive reasoning.
- Ⓓ deductive reasoning.

Use the table below to answer question 40.

	Exam 1	Exam 2	Exam 3	Exam 4
Student's Grade	65	87	92	70
Class Mean	55	88	86	60
Class Standard Deviation	5	2	4	10

40. The data in the preceding table show a student's grades on four exams in a college statistics class along with the means and standard deviations of the grades for all the students in the class of 50 students. On which of the exams did the student perform best relative to the mean performance of all the students?

- Ⓐ Exam 1
- Ⓑ Exam 2
- Ⓒ Exam 3
- Ⓓ Exam 4

41. Which of the following number lines illustrates the solution to $2 - 4x < 5 - 3x$?

Ⓐ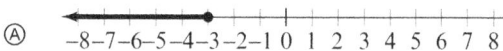
 −8−7−6−5−4−3−2−1 0 1 2 3 4 5 6 7 8

Ⓑ
 −8−7−6−5−4−3−2−1 0 1 2 3 4 5 6 7 8

Ⓒ
 −8−7−6−5−4−3−2−1 0 1 2 3 4 5 6 7 8

Ⓓ
 −8−7−6−5−4−3−2−1 0 1 2 3 4 5 6 7 8

GO ON TO THE NEXT PAGE

42. If a and b are prime numbers such that $\dfrac{10}{a^4} = \dfrac{b^2}{40}$, what is the sum of a and b?

- Ⓐ 5
- Ⓑ 7
- Ⓒ 9
- Ⓓ 11

43. Which of the following functions is the factored form of the polynomial of lowest degree with real coefficients and leading coefficient 1 that has zeros at 0, $2 - i$, 4, and -3?

- Ⓐ $P(x) = x(x - 2 + i)(x - 4)(x + 3)$
- Ⓑ $P(x) = x(x + 2 - i)(x + 4)(x - 3)$
- Ⓒ $P(x) = x(x - 2 - i)(x - 2 + i)(x + 4)(x - 3)$
- Ⓓ $P(x) = x(x - 2 + i)(x - 2 - i)(x - 4)(x + 3)$

44. What is the value of k such that $x - i$ is a factor of the polynomial $P(x) = k^2 x^4 - 8kx^2 + 16$?

- Ⓐ -8
- Ⓑ -4
- Ⓒ 4
- Ⓓ 8

Use the figure below to answer question 45.

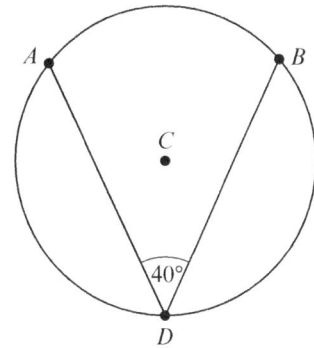

45. The circle with center C shown above has a radius of 4 inches. What is the length, in inches, of minor arc $\overline{AB}$?

- Ⓐ $\dfrac{4\pi}{9}$
- Ⓑ $\dfrac{8\pi}{9}$
- Ⓒ $\dfrac{16\pi}{9}$
- Ⓓ $\dfrac{32\pi}{9}$

46. In the xy plane, $\triangle ABC$ has vertices (0, 0), (8, 0), and (0, 15). A dilation of $\triangle ABC$ with center (0, 0) and scale factor 5 is achieved by premultiplying the vertex matrix $\begin{bmatrix} x_i \\ y_i \end{bmatrix}$ by which of the following transformation matrices?

- Ⓐ $\begin{bmatrix} 5 & 5 \\ 5 & 5 \end{bmatrix}$
- Ⓑ $\begin{bmatrix} 5 & 0 \\ 5 & 0 \end{bmatrix}$
- Ⓒ $\begin{bmatrix} 5 & 0 \\ 0 & 5 \end{bmatrix}$
- Ⓓ $\begin{bmatrix} 0 & 5 \\ 0 & 5 \end{bmatrix}$

47. What is the approximate volume, in cm³, of a right hexagonal prism that is 30 centimeters in height and whose bases are regular hexagons that are 6 centimeters on a side?

- Ⓐ 468
- Ⓑ 1,080
- Ⓒ 2,806
- Ⓓ 3,240

Use the equation below to answer question 48.

$$x = \sqrt{\dfrac{9x + 2}{5}}$$

48. A teacher introduces students to solving radical equations by presenting the equation shown above. After some discussion, the students suggest that squaring both sides of the equation will remove the radical from the equation. By allowing the students to proceed with this strategy, the teacher likely is intending for the students to discover that squaring both sides of the equation $x = \sqrt{\dfrac{9x + 2}{5}}$, and then solving for x, gives rise to what extraneous solution?

- Ⓐ -2
- Ⓑ $-\dfrac{1}{5}$
- Ⓒ $\dfrac{1}{5}$
- Ⓓ 2

GO ON TO THE NEXT PAGE

49. Find the area, in unit², enclosed by the curve $y = 2x - x^2$ and the line $y = 2x - 4$.

- Ⓐ $\dfrac{16}{3}$
- Ⓑ $\dfrac{32}{3}$
- Ⓒ 16
- Ⓓ $\dfrac{64}{3}$

Use the table below to answer question 50.

Age	On-Campus	Off-Campus
Younger Than 21	114	135
21 or Older	156	95

50. The preceding table shows the resident status, by age category, of 500 second-year students at a community college. If 1 of the 500 students is randomly selected, what is the probability that the student resides off-campus, given that the student selected is younger than 21?

- Ⓐ $\dfrac{135}{500}$
- Ⓑ $\dfrac{95}{500}$
- Ⓒ $\dfrac{135}{249}$
- Ⓓ $\dfrac{95}{251}$

51. If a prime number p is a factor of both $(10n + 9)$ and $(5n - 1)$, what is the value of p?

- Ⓐ 7
- Ⓑ 11
- Ⓒ 13
- Ⓓ It cannot be determined from the information given.

52. What is the fourth term in the binomial expansion of $(x - 2y)^5$?

- Ⓐ $-80x^2y^3$
- Ⓑ $80x^2y^3$
- Ⓒ $-80x^4y$
- Ⓓ $80xy^4$

53. Given the function defined by $f(x) = 5x + 7$, then $f^{-1}(x)$ is defined by which of the following equations?

- Ⓐ $f^{-1}(x) = -5x - 7$
- Ⓑ $f^{-1}(x) = \dfrac{1}{5x+7},\ x \neq -\dfrac{7}{5}$
- Ⓒ $f^{-1}(x) = \dfrac{x}{5} - 7$
- Ⓓ $f^{-1}(x) = \dfrac{x-7}{5}$

Use the dot plot below to answer question 54.

Scores of 20 Students on Biology Exam

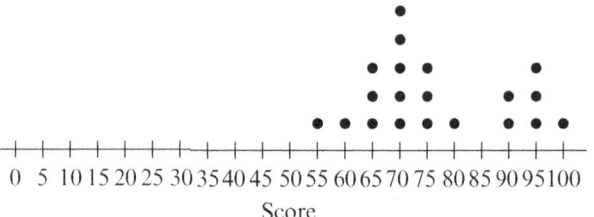

54. The preceding dot plot displays the scores of 20 students on a biology exam. The standard deviation of these data is approximately 13.2. Determine the number of students whose scores are more than one standard deviation above the mean.

- Ⓐ 0
- Ⓑ 4
- Ⓒ 5
- Ⓓ 6

55. To investigate the effect of Fertilizer X on plant growth, a researcher decides to conduct an experimental study with 80 identical plant seedlings (a plant seedling is a young plant) and two plots of identical soil. The seedlings are randomly assigned to either the treatment plot or the control plot (40 plants in each plot). The plant seedlings in the treatment plot will be those that

- Ⓐ have plant growth.
- Ⓑ do not have plant growth.
- Ⓒ receive applications of Fertilizer X.
- Ⓓ do not receive applications of Fertilizer X.

GO ON TO THE NEXT PAGE

56. Given $x^2 + kx + c = (x + h)^2$, where c, k, and h are real numbers, if $k = 14$, what is the value of c?

- Ⓐ 7
- Ⓑ 14
- Ⓒ 49
- Ⓓ 98

57. Treasure coins in a video game are distributed among five locations in the ratio 1:2:3:4:5. To win the game, a player must acquire at least 50% of the coins in each of three or more of the five locations. To win, a player must acquire what minimum percent of the total coins?

- Ⓐ 10%
- Ⓑ 15%
- Ⓒ 20%
- Ⓓ 25%

58. If f is a real-valued function, which of the following values are NOT in the domain of f, where $f(x) = \dfrac{\sqrt{x+3}}{2x^3 + x^2 - 2x - 1}$? Select all that apply.

- A -3
- B -1
- C $-\dfrac{1}{2}$
- D 1

59. Find $\lim\limits_{h \to 0} \dfrac{\left(\dfrac{1}{2}+h\right)^8 - \left(\dfrac{1}{2}\right)^8}{h}$.

- Ⓐ 0
- Ⓑ $\dfrac{1}{2}$
- Ⓒ $\dfrac{1}{16}$
- Ⓓ The limit does not exist.

60. If f is a function such that, for all x, $f'(x) > 0$ and $f''(x) < 0$, which of the following could be a portion of the graph of f?

Ⓐ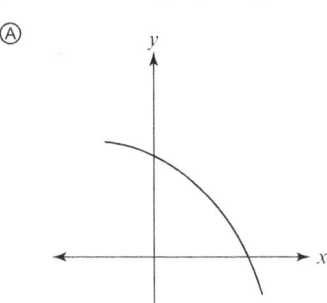

Ⓑ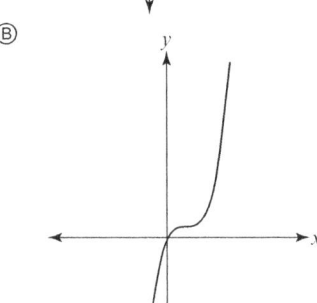

Ⓒ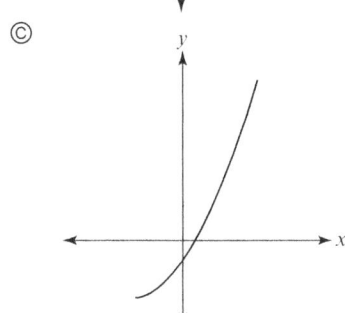

Ⓓ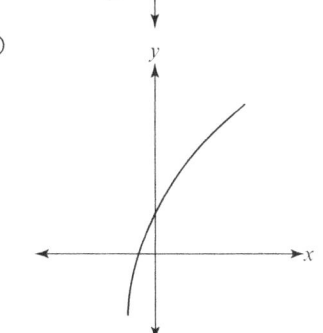

GO ON TO THE NEXT PAGE

Use the figure below to answer question 61.

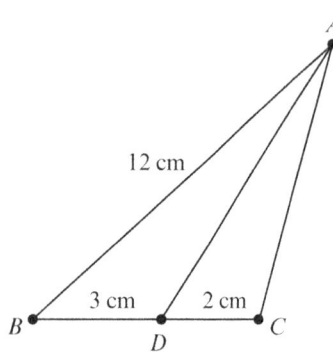

61. In $\triangle ABC$ above, $\angle DAB \cong \angle DAC$. What is the perimeter, in centimeters, of $\triangle ABC$?

Ⓐ 23
Ⓑ 24
Ⓒ 25
Ⓓ It cannot be determined from the information given.

62. A manufacturing company purchases a robotic machine that can produce $Q(h)$ components per hour, where $Q(h) = \dfrac{10(4h+25)}{2h+5}$. Assuming the machine continues to work efficiently, approximately how many components is the machine able to produce per hour after being in operation for an extended period of time?

Ⓐ 5
Ⓑ 20
Ⓒ 40
Ⓓ 50

63. Water is running into a right cylindrical tank, which has a radius of 5 feet, at a constant rate of 30 cubic feet per minute $\left(\dfrac{\text{ft}^3}{\text{min}}\right)$. What is the instantaneous rate of change of the water's height, in feet per minute $\left(\dfrac{\text{ft}}{\text{min}}\right)$, after the water starts running?

Ⓐ 0.38
Ⓑ 0.95
Ⓒ 1.05
Ⓓ 2.60

64. A student organization has 60 members, 36 boys and 24 girls. For a community activity, the organization's faculty sponsor uniformly divides the boys and girls into x groups so that each group has the same number of boys and the same number of girls as the other groups and no one is left out. What is the greatest number that x could be?

Ⓐ 5
Ⓑ 6
Ⓒ 10
Ⓓ 12

65. In a certain small town, all the phone numbers have the same area code, and all of the last 7 digits of the phone numbers begin with either 560, 564, or 569 (called prefixes). Which of the following computations will yield the number of different phone numbers that are possible if all three prefixes are used?

Ⓐ $(3)(_{10}C_4)$
Ⓑ $(3)(10^4)$
Ⓒ 10^4
Ⓓ 10^7

Use the graph below to answer question 66.

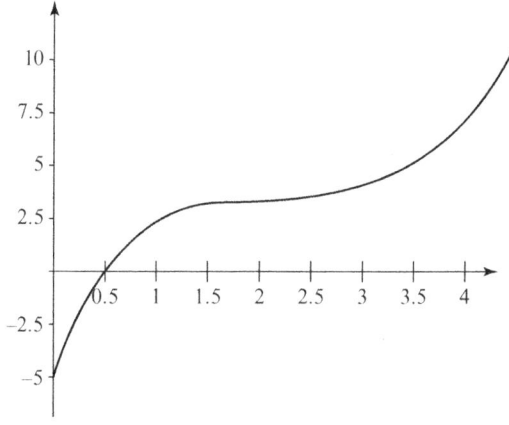

66. The graph of $y = x^3 - 6x^2 + 12x - 5$ is shown above. Which of the following statements is true about the rate of change of y with respect to x?

Select all that apply.

Ⓐ The rate of change is decreasing between 0 and 0.5.
Ⓑ The rate of change is increasing between 0.5 and 1.5.
Ⓒ The rate of change is decreasing between 2 and 3.
Ⓓ The rate of change is increasing between 3 and 3.5.

GO ON TO THE NEXT PAGE

Use the graph below to answer question 67.

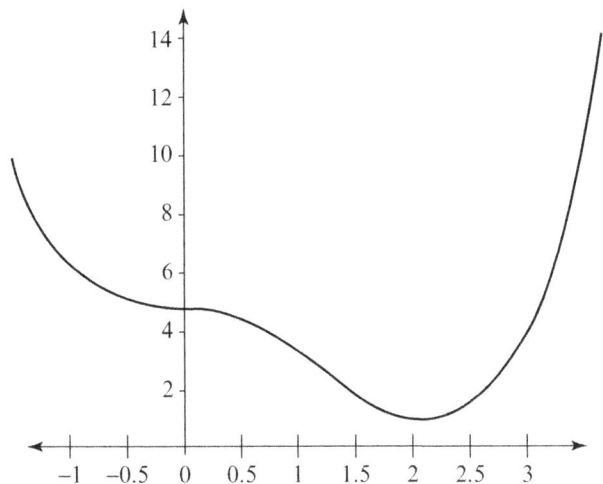

67. The function f defined by $f(x) = x^4 - 3x^3 + x^2 + 5$ has the graph shown above. What is the area, in unit^2, of the region bounded by the graph of f and the x-axis over the closed interval $[0, 2]$?

Ⓐ 1
Ⓑ 5
Ⓒ $\dfrac{32}{5}$
Ⓓ $\dfrac{106}{15}$

68. The gas mileage in miles per gallon (mpg) for automobiles of a certain luxury model is normally distributed with a mean of 29 mpg and a standard deviation of 4 mpg. What is the approximate probability that an automobile of this type chosen at random has gas mileage less than 25 mpg?

Ⓐ 16%
Ⓑ 34%
Ⓒ 68%
Ⓓ 84%

69. For the point $(-2, -8)$ on the graph of f defined by $f(x) = x^3$, give the coordinates of the corresponding point on the graph of g defined by $g(x) = f(2x)$.

Ⓐ $(-1, -8)$
Ⓑ $(-4, -8)$
Ⓒ $(-2, -16)$
Ⓓ $(-2, -4{,}096)$

70. For which of the following studies could the results validly establish a cause-effect relationship?

Ⓐ An experimental study investigating the effect of a new type of fertilizer on plant growth
Ⓑ A survey of teachers' opinions about standardized testing of students
Ⓒ An observational study investigating factors related to prosocial behavior of adolescents
Ⓓ An observational study investigating the relationship between college GPA and birth order

71. Which of the following sets is the solution to $3x^2 - 2x < 1$?

Ⓐ $\left\{x \in \text{reals}, x < -1 \text{ or } x > \dfrac{1}{3}\right\}$
Ⓑ $\left\{x \in \text{reals}, x < \dfrac{1}{3} \text{ or } x > 1\right\}$
Ⓒ $\left\{x \in \text{reals}, -\dfrac{1}{3} < x < 1\right\}$
Ⓓ $\left\{x \in \text{reals}, -1 < x < \dfrac{1}{3}\right\}$

Use the table below to answer question 72.

Time (in years)	Population
0	500
5	1,500

72. The preceding table gives the population of a deer herd at two different times in years. The population's growth is modeled by the function $P(t) = P_0 e^{xt}$, where t is in years. Based on this information, what is the value of x?

Ⓐ $\dfrac{\ln 3}{5}$
Ⓑ $\ln 3$
Ⓒ $\ln 3 - \ln 5$
Ⓓ $\ln\left(\dfrac{3}{5}\right)$

GO ON TO THE NEXT PAGE

73. A ball is dropped from a height of 60 feet. If each rebound is $\frac{3}{5}$ the height of the previous bounce, which of the following functions would best model the ball's height as a function of rebound number n?

- Ⓐ Quadratic
- Ⓑ Polynomial
- Ⓒ Linear
- Ⓓ Exponential

74. The graph of $y = \frac{x^4 - 81}{x^2 + x - 12}$ has how many asymptotes?

- Ⓐ 0
- Ⓑ 1
- Ⓒ 2
- Ⓓ 3

75. Given $f(x) = 3x$ and $g(x) = \frac{4}{x-1}$, what is the solution of $f(g(x)) = g(f(x))$?

- Ⓐ -2
- Ⓑ $-\frac{1}{4}$
- Ⓒ $\frac{1}{4}$
- Ⓓ 2

76. A sequence is defined recursively by

$a_1 = 1$

$a_n = a_{n-1} + 2n + 3$ for $n \geq 2$.

A polynomial model for the nth term of the sequence is best described as

- Ⓐ linear.
- Ⓑ quadratic.
- Ⓒ cubic.
- Ⓓ quartic.

77. On a trip from city A to city B, a vehicle is traveling at a constant rate of speed. At 10 a.m., the vehicle is $\frac{1}{4}$ of the distance between the two cities. At 4 p.m., it is $\frac{7}{10}$ of the distance between the two cities. At what fraction of the distance between the two cities was the vehicle at 2 p.m.?

- Ⓐ $\frac{3}{10}$
- Ⓑ $\frac{11}{20}$
- Ⓒ $\frac{3}{5}$
- Ⓓ $\frac{13}{20}$

78. An experiment consists of flipping a coin and noting the up face six times. Which of the following computations will yield the number of different outcomes in the sample space for this experiment?

- Ⓐ 6^2
- Ⓑ 2^6
- Ⓒ $6!$
- Ⓓ 6^6

79. Find the area, in unit², enclosed by the curves $y = \frac{1}{4}x^2$ and $y = x^2 + 3x - 9$.

- Ⓐ 64
- Ⓑ 118
- Ⓒ 172
- Ⓓ It cannot be determined from the information given.

80. Two consecutives angles of a parallelogram have measures $(x + 43°)$ and $(2x - 73°)$. Which of the following could be measures of the parallelogram's angles?

Select all that apply.

- ☐ A   67°
- ☐ B   70°
- ☐ C   110°
- ☐ D   113°

GO ON TO THE NEXT PAGE

81. Which of the following conditions for a quadrilateral is alone sufficient to prove that it is a parallelogram?

Select all that apply.

- [A] It is equilateral.
- [B] Its diagonals are congruent and perpendicular to each other.
- [C] Three of its angles are right angles.
- [D] Its diagonals bisect each other.

82. An algebra 1 teacher's students are using their graphing calculators to compare the graphs of pairs of functions that have the forms $f(x) = ax^2 + b$ and $g(x) = -ax^2 - b$. The teacher's likely purpose for engaging students in this activity is to enhance their understanding of which of the following concepts from transformational geometry?

- Ⓐ Reflection
- Ⓑ Rotation
- Ⓒ Translation
- Ⓓ Dilation

Use the matrix below to answer question 83.

$$A = \begin{bmatrix} a_{11} & a_{12} & a_{13} \\ a_{21} & a_{22} & a_{23} \\ a_{31} & a_{32} & a_{33} \end{bmatrix}$$

83. In matrix A shown above, if the second row of A is multiplied by -5 and added to its first row, describe the effect of this single elementary row operation on the determinant of A.

- Ⓐ The determinant is unchanged.
- Ⓑ The determinant is multiplied by -5.
- Ⓒ The determinant changes signs.
- Ⓓ The determinant is multiplied by $-\frac{1}{5}$.

84. How many different ways can the five digits 2, 4, 4, 6, 8 be arranged into a 5-digit number so that the two occurrences of the digit 4 are separated by at least one other digit?

- Ⓐ 18
- Ⓑ 24
- Ⓒ 36
- Ⓓ 48

85. For the past 3 weeks, students in a personal financial literacy class have been role playing as online shoppers. As the activity began, the teacher provided a suggested weekly limit for simulated purchases. In the third week of the activity, Dev, a student in the class, spent 20% more mock money than he did in the second week. In the second week, he spent 30% more than he did in the first week. In the first week, he spent 10% of the suggested weekly limit. If Dev spent $460 in the third week, approximately what amount of funds was the suggested limit?

- Ⓐ $270
- Ⓑ $330
- Ⓒ $380
- Ⓓ $450

Use the computation below to answer question 86.

$$-2 + 7^2 = 5^2 = 25$$

86. The above computation by a student was observed by a seventh-grade mathematics teacher during guided practice. Before the student works out additional computations, a discussion of which of the following concepts would best address the student's error?

- Ⓐ Addition of integers
- Ⓑ Order of operations
- Ⓒ Meaning of whole-number exponents
- Ⓓ Associative property

GO ON TO THE NEXT PAGE

Use the information below to answer question 87.

Solve:

$$x - 2y = 6$$
$$2x - 3y = 4$$

Solution:

$$x - 2y = 6$$
$$2x - 3y = 4$$

$$x - 2y = 6$$
$$x = 2y + 6$$

$$(2y + 6) - 2y = 6$$
$$2y + 6 - 2y = 6$$
$$6 = 6$$

87. A student's solution to a problem involving systems of linear equations is shown above. Which of the following is an accurate analysis of the student's work?

- Ⓐ The student's work is correct. The final equation of "6 = 6" indicates the system has no solution.
- Ⓑ The student's work is correct. The final equation of "6 = 6" indicates the system has an infinite number of solutions.
- Ⓒ The student's work is incorrect. The student should have solved the first equation for y instead of x.
- Ⓓ The student's work is incorrect. After solving for x, the student should have substituted the result into the other equation.

Use the system of linear equations below to answer question 88.

$$3x + 2y = 4$$
$$x - 2y = 3$$

88. Given the system of linear equations shown above, determine the value of the product xy.

- Ⓐ $-\dfrac{9}{8}$
- Ⓑ $-\dfrac{35}{32}$
- Ⓒ $\dfrac{35}{32}$
- Ⓓ $\dfrac{9}{8}$

Use the information below to answer question 89.

Let $x = 5$

$$x^2 = 5x$$
$$x^2 - 25 = 5x - 25$$
$$(x+5)(x-5) = 5(x-5)$$
$$\frac{(x+5)\cancel{(x-5)}}{\cancel{(x-5)}} = \frac{5\cancel{(x-5)}}{\cancel{(x-5)}}$$
$$x + 5 = 5$$
$$5 + 5 = 5$$
$$10 = 5$$

89. Which of the following is the reason that the fallacy above results?

- Ⓐ Substituted incorrectly
- Ⓑ Factored incorrectly
- Ⓒ Failed to follow the order of operations
- Ⓓ Divided by zero

GO ON TO THE NEXT PAGE

Use the scatter plot below to answer question 90.

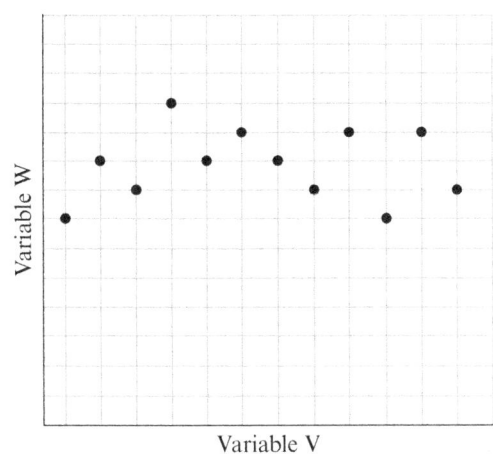

Variable W

Variable V

90. A student produces the above scatter plot of 12 paired data points from variables V and W. Which of the following conclusions should the student draw about the relationship between variables V and W?

- Ⓐ Variable W is directly proportional to variable V.
- Ⓑ Variable W is inversely proportional to variable V.
- Ⓒ Variables V and W are linearly correlated.
- Ⓓ Variables V and W are not linearly correlated.

Use the figure below to answer question 91.

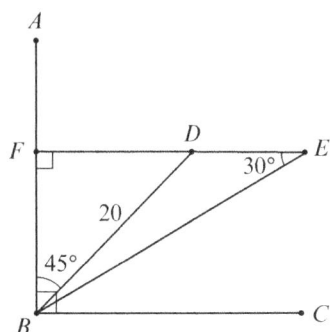

91. In the figure shown above, $\overline{AB} \perp \overline{BC}$, $\overline{AB} \perp \overline{EF}$, and $BD = 20$. What is the perimeter of $\triangle DBE$?

- Ⓐ $10(2+\sqrt{2}+3)$
- Ⓑ $10(2+\sqrt{2}+\sqrt{6})$
- Ⓒ $20(2+\sqrt{2}+\sqrt{3})$
- Ⓓ $20(2+2\sqrt{2})$

92. The amounts of 10,000 donations to a certain charity are approximately normally distributed with a mean of $650. If 30% of the donations are less than $625, what is the probability that a randomly chosen donation will be between $625 and $675?

- Ⓐ 30%
- Ⓑ 40%
- Ⓒ 50%
- Ⓓ 60%

93. A particle moves horizontally in a straight line with velocity $v(t) = 6t^2$. How far does the particle move between times $t = 1$ and $t = 2$?

- Ⓐ 2
- Ⓑ 14
- Ⓒ 18
- Ⓓ 42

94. Given that m and n are both positive integers greater than 1, which of the following expressions must represent a rational number?

Select all that apply.

- A $\dfrac{m^n}{n^m}$
- B $\dfrac{m!}{n!}$
- C $\sqrt{mn}$
- D $(mn)^{\frac{m}{n}}$

95. Given $4x + 5y - 2z = 60$ and $2x + y + 8z = 84$, what is the arithmetic average of x, y, and z?

- Ⓐ 6
- Ⓑ 8
- Ⓒ 24
- Ⓓ It cannot be determined from the information given.

GO ON TO THE NEXT PAGE

96. A shipping box is made in the shape of a right rectangular prism. If its dimensions are length = $120 - 4x$ and width = height = x, where $x > 0$, what value of x will maximize the volume of the shipping box?

- Ⓐ $\sqrt{10}$
- Ⓑ $\sqrt{30}$
- Ⓒ 20
- Ⓓ 30

97. Suppose f and g are differentiable functions such that

$$f(0) = 1 \qquad g(0) = 1$$
$$f'(0) = 3 \qquad g'(0) = -3$$
$$f'(1) = -4 \qquad g'(1) = -5$$

If $h(x) = f(g(x))$, what is the value of $h'(0)$?

- Ⓐ -15
- Ⓑ 0
- Ⓒ 12
- Ⓓ 15

98. A geometry teacher uses a variety of informal and formal assessment methods, such as observations, interviews, anecdotal records, test scores, and samples of daily work throughout each instructional unit. The primary benefit of this approach is that it is likely to

- Ⓐ encourage students to self-assess their acquisition of knowledge and skills.
- Ⓑ decrease students' uncertainty with regard to the grading process.
- Ⓒ provide the teacher ample assessment data for assigning grades to students.
- Ⓓ provide the teacher fair and accurate data for monitoring students' progress.

99. A seventh-grade teacher meets with a student's parents. The student's grade equivalent score on a standardized mathematics exam is 8.5. Based on this result, the parents want to know whether their child can spend part of the day receiving mathematics instruction with an eighth-grade class. Which of the following responses would be most appropriate for the teacher to make?

- Ⓐ Explain that the student's score indicates the student is ready for content that is typically taught to eighth-graders during the fifth month of school.
- Ⓑ Clarify that the student's score indicates the student's level of performance on seventh-grade level, not eighth-grade level, mathematics.
- Ⓒ Suggest that the child attend after-school eighth-grade mathematics tutorials.
- Ⓓ Agree to arrange for the child to attend an eighth-grade mathematics class.

100. To foster higher-order thinking and enhance problem-solving skills of students, which of the following strategies would be desirable for an algebra 1 teacher to use?

Select all that apply.

- Ⓐ Establish a highly managed classroom environment that focuses on procedural knowledge.
- Ⓑ Encourage students to take time to think before deciding on a solution strategy when they are initially given a multi-step problem.
- Ⓒ Spend more class time on problems requiring analytical skills than on basic computational problems.
- Ⓓ Provide opportunities for students to correct their errors rather than expect them to rely on the teacher to determine whether their work is mathematically correct.

Answer Key

Question Number	Correct Answer	Chapter(s)	Question Number	Correct Answer	Chapter(s)
1.	C	3	26.	A	2
2.	D	1	27.	A, C, D	1
3.	C	2	28.	B	1
4.	A	2, 6	29.	A	2, 6
5.	C	2	30.	C	3
6.	A	2, 5	31.	B	2, 5
7.	A	2, 5	32.	C	2
8.	C	1	33.	C	2
9.	D	2	34.	B	1
10.	D	2, 5	35.	C	5
11.	C	5	36.	B	2
12.	A	1	37.	B	2
13.	A	2	38.	C	2
14.	D	2, 5	39.	C	5
15.	C	3	40.	A	2
16.	D	3	41.	D	2
17.	A	2	42.	B	1
18.	C	2, 6	43.	D	1, 2
19.	B	2, 5	44.	B	1, 2
20.	D	3	45.	C	3
21.	C	1, 5	46.	C	3
22.	B	2	47.	C	3
23.	B	2	48.	B	2, 6
24.	C	2	49.	B	2
25.	C	2	50.	C	2

Question Number	Correct Answer	Chapter(s)	Question Number	Correct Answer	Chapter(s)
51.	B	1	76.	B	2
52.	A	2, 5	77.	B	1, 5
53.	D	2	78.	B	2
54.	D	2	79.	A	2
55.	C	2	80.	A, D	3
56.	C	2	81.	A, C, D	3
57.	C	1, 2	82.	A	2, 3, 6
58.	B, C, D	2	83.	A	1, 2
59.	C	2	84.	C	2
60.	D	2	85.	B	1
61.	C	3	86.	B	1, 6
62.	B	2	87.	D	2, 6
63.	A	2	88.	B	2
64.	D	1	89.	D	2, 5
65.	B	2	90.	D	2, 6
66.	A, D	2	91.	B	3
67.	D	2	92.	B	2
68.	A	2	93.	B	2
69.	A	2, 3	94.	A, B	1
70.	A	2	95.	B	2, 4
71.	C	2	96.	C	2, 3
72.	A	2	97.	C	2
73.	D	2, 6	98.	D	6
74.	B	2	99.	B	4, 6
75.	C	2	100.	B, C, D	6

Answer Explanations

1. **C.** Make a sketch of the circle and plot the points given in the answer choices.

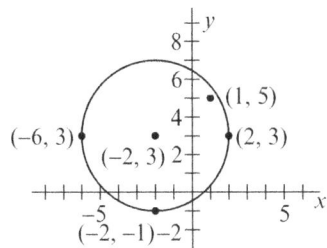

   The center of the circle is at (−2, 3) with radius 4, so its equation is $(x + 2)^2 + (y − 3)^2 = 16$. Eliminate choices A, B, and D because the points (−6, 3), (−2, −1), and (2, 3) given in these answer choices lie on the circle. When you substitute their coordinates into the equation of the circle, they satisfy the equation as shown below:

   $((−6) + 2)^2 + ((3) − 3)^2 = (−4)^2 + (0)^2 = 16 + 0 = 16$

   $((−2) + 2)^2 + ((−1) − 3)^2 = (0)^2 + (−4)^2 = 0 + 16 = 16$

   $((2) + 2)^2 + ((3) − 3)^2 = (4)^2 + (0)^2 = 16 + 0 = 16$

   Because $((1) + 2)^2 + ((5) − 3)^2 = (3)^2 + (2)^2 = 9 + 4 = 13 < 16$, only (1, 5) clearly lies within the interior of the circle. Thus, choice C is the correct response.

2. **D.** The squares between 1 and 50 that have units digit 6 are 16 and 36, so k is either 4 or 6. Suppose k is 4, then 9 is the units digit of $(k − 1)^2 = (4 − 1)^2 = 3^2 = 9$, which shows k cannot be 4. If k is 6, then 5 is the units digit of $(k − 1)^2 = (6 − 1)^2 = 5^2 = 25$. This computation verifies that k is 6. The units digit of $(k + 1)^2$ is 7 because $(k + 1)^2 = (6 + 1)^2 = 7^2 = 49$, which has units digit 9, choice D.

3. **C.** The sums of the numbers in the sequence are (2)(2), (3)(4), (4)(8), and so on. These sums can be expressed as $(2)(2^1)$, $(3)(2^2)$, $(4)(2^3)$, and so on. In each case, the multiplier on the left is one more than the sequence number, and the exponent of 2 in the second factor is the same as the sequence number. Thus, the nth sum of the sequence is $(n + 1)(2^n)$, choice C.

4. **A.** Only choice A correctly represents the statement. The equations in the other answer choices are incorrect representations.

5. **C.** Because the normal line is perpendicular to the tangent line at (3, 1), the slope of the tangent line through the point (3, 1) is the negative reciprocal of the slope of the normal line. The slope of the normal line $y = \frac{5}{6}x − \frac{3}{2}$ is $\frac{5}{6}$. Therefore, the tangent line at (3, 1) has slope $-\frac{6}{5}$.
   Use the point-slope form to determine the equation of the tangent line at (3, 1).

   $$y − 1 = -\frac{6}{5}(x − 3)$$
   $$5y − 5 = −6x + 18$$
   $$6x + 5y = 23, \text{ choice C}$$

6. **A.** The slope of the tangent line to the graph of f at $x = 4$ is $f'(4)$. $f(x) = -x^2 + 12\sqrt{x} = -x^2 + 12x^{\frac{1}{2}}$. Then $f'(x) = -2x + \left(\frac{1}{2}\right)(12)x^{-\frac{1}{2}} = -2x + 6x^{-\frac{1}{2}}$ and $f'(4) = -2(4) + 6(4)^{-\frac{1}{2}} = -8 + \frac{6}{\sqrt{4}} = -8 + 3 = -5$, choice A.

7. **A.** In the decimal representation of a number, the placement of a bar over a sequence of one or more adjacent digits indicates that those digits repeat indefinitely. In choice A, d is the repeating digit beginning in the 10-thousandths decimal place and continuing indefinitely, meaning d is the digit in the 100-thousandth decimal place. In choice B, c is the digit in the 100-thousandths decimal place. In choice C,

Chapter 10: TExES Math 7–12 Practice Test 2

b is the digit in the 100-thousandths decimal place. And in choice D, a is the digit in the 100-thousandths decimal place. Because d is the greatest of the four given digits, $0.4abc\overline{d}$, choice A, is the greatest of the numbers in the answer choices.

8. **C.** The area of $\triangle ABC$ is $\frac{1}{2}(\text{base})(\text{height}) = \frac{1}{2}(x)(8) = 4x = 48$, which implies $x = 12$. Therefore, in $\triangle ABC$, the ratio of the height to the base is 8 to 12, meaning $\text{height} = \frac{2}{3} \text{base}$. Because the two triangles are similar, this ratio also applies to the height and base of $\triangle DEF$. Thus, the area of $\triangle DEF$ is $\frac{1}{2}(\text{base})(\text{height}) = \frac{1}{2}(y)\left(\frac{2}{3}y\right) = \frac{y^2}{3} = 24$, which implies $y^2 = 72$. Solving for y yields $y = \sqrt{72} = 6\sqrt{2}$, choice C.

9. **D.** Given d = the number of ducks and g = the number of goats, because both ducks and goats each have one head, $1d + 1g = 13$. Likewise, because ducks have two legs and goats have four, $2d + 4g = 36$. Thus, you have the following system of equations: $\begin{array}{l} 1d + 1g = 13 \\ 2d + 4g = 36 \end{array}$. This system of equations is equivalent to the matrix equation $\begin{bmatrix} 1 & 1 \\ 2 & 4 \end{bmatrix} \begin{bmatrix} d \\ g \end{bmatrix} = \begin{bmatrix} 13 \\ 36 \end{bmatrix}$, choice D, because when the left side is multiplied,

$\begin{bmatrix} 1 & 1 \\ 2 & 4 \end{bmatrix} \begin{bmatrix} d \\ g \end{bmatrix} = \begin{bmatrix} 36 \\ 13 \end{bmatrix}$ yields $\begin{bmatrix} 1d + 1g \\ 2d + 4g \end{bmatrix} = \begin{bmatrix} 13 \\ 36 \end{bmatrix}$.

10. **D.** If all the tagged turtles are still active in the lake when the second group of turtles is captured, the proportion of tagged turtles in the second group should be equal to the proportion of tagged turtles in the whole population, P, of turtles in the lake. Set up a proportion and solve for P.

$\frac{2}{50} = \frac{25}{P}$ implies $\frac{1}{25} = \frac{25}{P}$, which yields $P = (25)(25) = 625$

Thus, the best estimate of the turtle population in the lake is 625 turtles, choice D.

11. **C.** The statement "If it is a holiday, then I do not go to work" is a conditional statement. It has the logical form "If P, then Q," where P is the statement "it is a holiday" and Q is the statement "I do not go to work." In logic, the equivalent of "If P, then Q" is its contrapositive, which is stated "If not Q, then not P." The contrapositive for the statement given is "If I do go to work, then it is not a holiday." Only choice C is compatible with this statement.

12. **A. Method 1.** Substitute numerical values for p, q, and r that satisfy the conditions given, and then work with your substituted numbers as shown below.

Let $p = 200$, $q = 10$, and $r = 1$. Then $\frac{p}{q} = \frac{200}{10} = 20$ ✓, $\frac{q}{r} = \frac{10}{1} = 10$ ✓, and $\frac{p}{q+r} = \frac{200}{10+1} = \frac{200}{11}$, choice A.

Tip: As shown above, when you substitute numerical values for the variables, always check to make sure the values satisfy the conditions given in the problem.

Method 2. Another approach is to express $\frac{p}{q+r}$ in terms of $\frac{p}{q}$ and $\frac{q}{r}$ by dividing each term in the numerator and denominator by q and then simplifying the result to obtain $\frac{200}{11}$, choice A.

13. **A.** Using De Moivre's theorem, $(2 \cos 10° + 2i \sin 10°)^3 = 2^3[\cos(3 \cdot 10°) + i \sin(3 \cdot 10°)] = 8(\cos 30° + i \sin 30°)$. Evaluating the second factor of this product yields $8(\cos 30° + i \sin 30°) = 8\left(\frac{\sqrt{3}}{2} + i\frac{1}{2}\right) = 4\sqrt{3} + 4i$, choice A.

14. D. Let $6x$, $5x$, and $2x$ equal the weights (in grams) of ingredients A, B, and C, respectively. Then the difference in the weights of ingredient A and ingredient C is $6x - 2x = 4x$. First, solve $6x + 5x + 2x = 78$ for x. Then determine $4x$.

$$6x + 5x + 2x = 78$$
$$13x = 78$$
$$x = 6$$
$$4x = 24, \text{ choice D}$$

15. C. $\triangle ABC$ with vertices (2, 1), (−3, 4), and (5, −3) can be represented by the 2 × 3 (vertex) matrix $\begin{bmatrix} 2 & -3 & 5 \\ 1 & 4 & -3 \end{bmatrix}$, where the x-coordinates are in the first row and their corresponding y-coordinates are in the second row. In a reflection over the x-axis, the x-coordinates of the image will be the same as the x-coordinates of the preimage, and the y-coordinates of the image will be the negatives of the y-coordinates of the preimage. Thus, you are looking for a matrix multiplication that will yield the product matrix $\begin{bmatrix} 2 & -3 & 5 \\ -1 & -4 & 3 \end{bmatrix}$.

A quick way to work this problem is to check the answer choices.

Mentally multiply the matrices.

Check A: $\begin{bmatrix} -1 & 0 \\ 0 & 1 \end{bmatrix} \begin{bmatrix} 2 & -3 & 5 \\ 1 & 4 & -3 \end{bmatrix} = \begin{bmatrix} -2 & & \\ & & \end{bmatrix}$. Eliminate choice A because the element in the first row first column is not 2. There is no need to complete the multiplication.

Check B: $\begin{bmatrix} 0 & 1 \\ -1 & 0 \end{bmatrix} \begin{bmatrix} 2 & -3 & 5 \\ 1 & 4 & -3 \end{bmatrix} = \begin{bmatrix} 1 & & \\ & & \end{bmatrix}$. Eliminate choice B because the element in the first row first column is not 2. There is no need to complete the multiplication.

Check C: $\begin{bmatrix} 1 & 0 \\ 0 & -1 \end{bmatrix} \begin{bmatrix} 2 & -3 & 5 \\ 1 & 4 & -3 \end{bmatrix} = \begin{bmatrix} 2 & -3 & 5 \\ -1 & -4 & 3 \end{bmatrix}$. The product is the desired matrix, so choice C is the correct response. Go on to the next question.

16. D. Given x = the length of one leg, then let $x + 7$ = the length of the other leg. Using the Pythagorean theorem, $c^2 = x^2 + (x+7)^2 = x^2 + x^2 + 14x + 49 = 2x^2 + 14x + 49$ which implies $c = \sqrt{2x^2 + 14x + 49}$. Thus, the length of the hypotenuse is $\sqrt{2x^2 + 14x + 49}$, choice D.

17. A. When a data set contains some extremely high values that are not balanced by corresponding extremely low values, the mean for the data set will be misleadingly high as an indication of a "typical" or "central" value for the data set. The median, which is not strongly influenced by extreme values, is the preferred alternative to the mean when the situation of unbalanced extremely high values occurs in a data set, choice A. Since the data set in choice B is somewhat symmetrical, there would be no particular reason to prefer the median over the mean as a measure of central tendency. For the data sets given in choices C and D, there is not enough information to "clearly" prefer the median over the mean.

18. C. Eliminate choice D because probabilities fall between 0 and 1, inclusive. For a given question, the probability that the student will choose correctly is $\frac{1}{4}$, and the probability the student will choose incorrectly is $1 - \frac{1}{4} = \frac{3}{4}$. Given that the student is selecting randomly, the selections are independent of each other. Therefore, the probability that the student chooses incorrectly for all five questions is $\frac{3}{4} \cdot \frac{3}{4} \cdot \frac{3}{4} \cdot \frac{3}{4} \cdot \frac{3}{4} = \frac{243}{1,024}$. Thus, the probability that the student will choose correctly on at least one question is $1 - \frac{243}{1,024} = \frac{781}{1,024}$, choice C.

19. B. Sketch a diagram, letting d = the distance between the two houses.

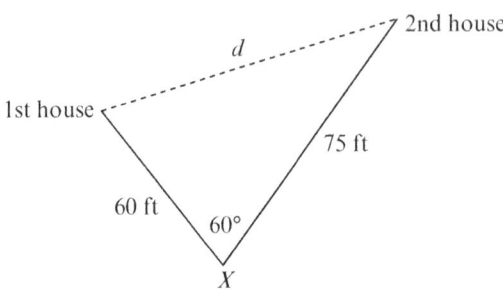

Looking at the sketch, you can see that you are given the measures of two sides and the included angle of an oblique triangle. To find the distance between the two houses, substitute the given information into the law of cosines and solve for d.

$$c^2 = a^2 + b^2 - 2ab \cos C$$

Tip: The formula for the law of cosines is available during the exam in the on-screen "Definitions and Formulas" reference material.

The side d corresponds to c, $a = 60$ ft, and $b = 75$ ft. Substitute into the formula and solve for d, omitting the units for convenience.

$$d^2 = (60)^2 + (75)^2 - 2(60)(75)(\cos 60°)$$
$$d^2 = 3,600 + 5,625 - 9,000\left(\frac{1}{2}\right)$$
$$d^2 = 4,725$$
$$d = \sqrt{4,725} \approx 69$$

The distance between the two houses is approximately 69 feet, choice B.

Tip: Be sure to check that your calculator is in degree mode when the angle given is in degrees.

20. D. You are to find the mass, in grams, of the cube. The units for density are grams per cubic centimeter $\left(\frac{g}{cm^3}\right)$, so dimensional analysis tells you that if you want to have grams as the units of your answer, then you will need to cancel cm^3 from the denominator of the density quantity. Cubic centimeters are units of volume. Therefore, find the volume of the cube, and then multiply by the density of lead.

Volume of cube = $(1.5 \text{ cm})^3 = 3.375 \text{ cm}^3$

Multiply the volume of the cube by the density of lead.

$$\left(3.375 \, \cancel{cm^3}\right)\left(\frac{11.3 \text{ g}}{\cancel{cm^3}}\right) \approx 38.1 \text{ g}$$

The mass of the lead cube is approximately 38.1 grams, choice D.

21. **C.** The suit's original price was 70% of $500, which is 0.7($500) = $350. The suit's selling price was 130% of $350, which is 1.3($350) = $455, choice C.
22. **B.** The domain of $g \circ f$ is the set of elements x in the domain of f for which $f(x)$, the image of x, is in the domain of g. Only the elements -1 and 0 have images that are in the domain of g. The images of -1 and 0 under $g \circ f$ are $(g \circ f)(-1) = g(f(-1)) = g(3) = 8$ and $(g \circ f)(0) = g(f(0)) = g(1) = 2$. Thus, $g \circ f = \{(-1, 8), (0, 2)\}$, choice B.
23. **B**. Make a table showing the growth of the deer population as a function of time, t.

Time in Years	$t = 0$	$t = 8$	$t = 16$	$t = 24$	...
Deer Population	250	$(250)2^1$	$(250)2^2$	$(250)2^3$	...

Let $y = f(t)$ be the function that models the growth of the population. From your table, you can see that the initial population is 250 with a growth factor of 2, indicating that $y = (250)2^{kt}$. Because the population doubles every 8 years, time must be measured in periods of 8 years. Therefore, $k = \frac{1}{8} = 0.125$ and $y = (250)2^{0.125t}$, choice B.

24. **C.** Solve the trigonometric equation $\sin^2 x - 5 \sin x + 4 = 0$.

$$\sin^2 x - 5\sin x + 4 = 0$$
$$(\sin x - 1)(\sin x - 4) = 0$$
$$\sin x = 1 \text{ or } \sin x = 4 \text{ (no solution)}$$
$$x = \sin^{-1}(1)$$
$$x = \frac{\pi}{2}$$

Therefore, $\frac{\pi}{2}$ is the only solution in the interval $0 \leq x \leq 2\pi$, choice C.

25. **C.** Find the numerical derivative using methods of calculus.

Given $f(x) = -x^{-2}$, then $f'(x) = 2x^{-3}$ and $f'(2) = 2(2)^{-3} = 2\left(\frac{1}{8}\right) = \frac{1}{4}$, choice C.

26. **A.** Examine the table. Correlation values very close to either -1 or $+1$ indicate very *strong* correlations. The closer $|r|$ is to 1, the stronger the relationship. Thus, the correlation coefficient between A and B (choice A) indicates the strongest relationship because $|-0.88|$ is greater than the absolute values of the correlation coefficients for the pairs of variables in the other answer choices.
27. **A, C, D.** On the set of $n \times n$ matrices whose elements are real numbers, matrix multiplication is closed (select choice A) and associative (select choice C), and the distributive property holds (select choice D); but, in general, matrix multiplication is not commutative (eliminate choice B).
28. **B.** Of the integers given in the answer choices, only 13, choice B, satisfies both conditions of the problem; that is, $13 \equiv 1 \pmod 3$ because $13 = (3)(4) + 1$ and $13 \equiv 5 \pmod 8$ because $13 = (8)(1) + 5$. None of the integers given in the other answer choices satisfies both conditions.
29. **A.** The teacher is using a question to make a suggestion. Suggesting that the students look at the differences between successive terms, choice A, would allow them to see that the differences between the successive terms listed are 1, 2, 3, 4, and 5. This leads them to predict that the difference between 16 and the next term is 6, making the next term 22. This approach is a good way to scaffold the task for the students because it provides assistance that allows them to experience a measure of success with the task. The suggestions in the other answer choices lead to dead ends, so they would not be helpful.
30. **C.** Examine the figure. The perimeter around the figure can be broken into three portions: (one-half the circumference of a circle with radius 1 cm) plus (the hypotenuse of a right triangle with legs of 1 cm and 2 cm) plus (a horizontal segment of length 1 cm).

Find one-half the circumference of a circle with radius 1 cm.

$$\frac{1}{2}(2\pi r) = \frac{1}{\cancel{2}}\left(\cancel{2}\pi(1 \text{ cm})\right) = \pi \text{ cm} \quad \text{(Don't evaluate yet.)}$$

Find the length of the hypotenuse of a right triangle with legs of 1 cm and 2 cm.

$$c^2 = 1^2 + 2^2 = 5, \text{ which implies } c = \sqrt{5}$$

The hypotenuse of the right triangle has length of $\sqrt{5}$ cm. (Don't evaluate yet.)

Find the perimeter: Perimeter $= 1 \text{ cm} + \pi \text{ cm} + \sqrt{5} \text{ cm} \approx 6.4$ cm, choice C.

31. **B.** Use logical reasoning to determine the solution. The difference (in years) between the father's age and the daughter's age is $38 - 10 = 28$. Therefore, when the daughter is 28 years old, the father will be 2(28 years) = 56 years old. The daughter is 10 years old, so in 18 years (because $28 - 10 = 18$), she will be 28 years old and her father will be 56 years old, twice her age. Thus, choice B is the correct response.

32. **C.** Substituting 3 into the numerator and denominator yields the indeterminate form $\frac{0}{0}$.

    Method 1. $\lim_{x \to 3} \frac{2x-6}{x^2-9} = \lim_{x \to 3} \frac{2(x-3)}{(x+3)(x-3)} = \lim_{x \to 3} \frac{2}{(x+3)} = \frac{2}{6} = \frac{1}{3}$, choice C.

    Method 2. Because $\lim_{x \to 3}(2x - 6) = 0$ and $\lim_{x \to 3}(x^2 - 9) = 0$, you can use L'Hôpital's rule to evaluate the limit by taking the derivatives of the numerator and denominator before evaluating the limit.

    Thus, you have $\lim_{x \to 3} \frac{2x-6}{x^2-9} = \lim_{x \to 3} \frac{2}{2x} = \frac{2}{6} = \frac{1}{3}$, choice C.

33. **C.** The particle does not change direction because the velocity function $v(t) = 1.8t^2$ is always positive. Recall that the first derivative of a position function is the velocity function. To find the distance traveled between $t = 0$ and $t = 5$, evaluate the following definite integral: $\int_0^5 1.8t^2 \, dt$.

    Integrate the function using methods of calculus.

    $\int_0^5 1.8t^2 \, dt = \frac{1.8t^3}{3}\Big|_0^5 = 0.6t^3\Big|_0^5 = 0.6(5)^3 - 0.6(0)^3 = 0.6(125) - 0.6(0) = 75 - 0 = 75$. Therefore, the distance traveled is 75, choice C.

34. **B.** Using the rules for matrix subtraction, you can write four equations: $a - 3a = -8$, $4b + 6 = b$, $5 - 2c = 7$, and $d + 2d = 9$.

    Solving $a - 3a = -8$ yields $a = 4$; eliminate choices A and D because these answer choices have $a = -4$. Since both of the remaining answer choices have $b = -2$, go on to the next equation. You have $5 - 2c = 7$, so $c = -1$; eliminate choice C. Thus, choice B is the correct response.

35. **C.** Let C = the set of customers who bought computers and P = the set of customers who bought printers. Using the notation $|X|$ to represent the number of elements in a set, you have $|C| = 188$ and $|P| = 160$. Because $|C| + |P| = 188 + 160 = 348$, which is greater than 304, the total number of customers, you can conclude that $348 - 304 = 44$ customers bought both a computer and a printer. Therefore, the number of customers who bought only a computer equals $188 - 44 = 144$, choice C.

    Note: The notation $|X|$ is read "the cardinality of set X." The *cardinality* of a set is the number of elements in the set.

36. **B.** Given: $y = f(x) = 2x^3 - x + 3$. The y-value at the point where $x = 1$ is $f(1) = 2(1)^3 - (1) + 3 = 4$. The slope, m, of the tangent line at the point $(1, f(1))$ is given by $f'(1)$.

    $f(x) = 2x^3 - x + 3$ implies $f'(x) = 6x^2 - 1$. Thus, $m = f'(1) = 6(1)^2 - 1 = 5$ when $x = 1$.

    Use the point-slope form to find the equation of the tangent line at the point (1, 4).

    $$y - 4 = 5(x - 1)$$
    $$y - 4 = 5x - 5$$
    $$1 = 5x - y \text{ or } 5x - y = 1, \text{ choice B}$$

37. B. Make a sketch and shade the area of interest.

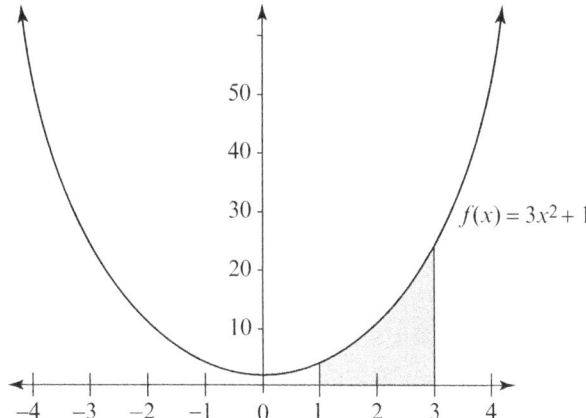

The area of the region bounded by the graph of $f(x) = 3x^2 + 1$, the x-axis, and the vertical lines $x = 1$ and $x = 3$ is given by Area $= \int_1^3 (3x^2 + 1)dx$.

Evaluate the definite integral using methods of calculus.

$$\int_1^3 (3x^2 + 1)dx = (x^3 + x)\Big|_1^3 = (3^3 + 3) - (1^3 + 1) = 30 - 2 = 28, \text{ choice B}$$

38. C. According to the 68-95-99.7 rule, approximately 68% of the data in a normal distribution fall within one standard deviation of the mean, about 95% fall within two standard deviations of the mean, and about 99.7% fall within three standard deviations of the mean. You want to find the approximate probability that a randomly chosen plant from a distribution with mean of 24 inches and standard deviation of 3.5 inches will be between 20.5 inches and 27.5 inches tall.

To find the approximate probability, first determine the z-scores for 20.5 inches and 27.5 inches, and then find the percentage of the normal distribution that is between those two z-scores.

Find the z-scores for 20.5 inches and 27.5 inches.

z-score $= \dfrac{\text{data value} - \text{mean}}{\text{standard deviation}} = \dfrac{20.5 - 24}{3.5} = -1$. Therefore, 20.5 is one standard deviation below the mean.

z-score $= \dfrac{\text{data value} - \text{mean}}{\text{standard deviation}} = \dfrac{27.5 - 24}{3.5} = 1$. Therefore, 27.5 is one standard deviation above the mean.

Now find the percentage of the normal distribution that is between the z-scores -1 and 1.

According to the 68-95-99.7 rule, about 68%, choice C, of the distribution is within one standard deviation of the mean.

39. C. The student looked at specific examples, identified a pattern that fit the given examples, and conjectured a general rule based on the examples. This type of reasoning is inductive reasoning, choice C. Eliminate choices A and B because the student did not engage in a proof. Eliminate choice D because deductive reasoning is the process of using an accepted rule to draw a conclusion about a specific example.

40. A. To compare the student's performance on the four exams relative to the mean performance of all the students, compute the student's z-score for each of the four exams.

Exam 1: z-score $= \dfrac{\text{data value} - \text{mean}}{\text{standard deviation}} = \dfrac{65 - 55}{5} = 2$. Therefore, the student scored 2 standard deviations above the mean on Exam 1.

Exam 2: z-score $= \dfrac{\text{data value} - \text{mean}}{\text{standard deviation}} = \dfrac{87 - 88}{2} = -0.5$. Therefore, the student scored 0.5 standard deviation below the mean on Exam 2.

Exam 3: z-score = $\dfrac{\text{data value} - \text{mean}}{\text{standard deviation}} = \dfrac{92-86}{4} = 1.5$. Therefore, the student scored 1.5 standard deviations above the mean on Exam 3.

Exam 4: z-score = $\dfrac{\text{data value} - \text{mean}}{\text{standard deviation}} = \dfrac{70-60}{10} = 1$. Therefore, the student scored 1 standard deviation above the mean on Exam 4.

Because the student's z-score for Exam 1 is greater than any of the z-scores for the other exams, the student's best performance relative to the mean performance of all the students was on Exam 1 (choice A).

41. **D.** Solve the inequality.

$$2 - 4x < 5 - 3x$$
$$2 - x < 5$$
$$-x < 3$$
$$x > -3$$

The graph for this inequality is a ray extending to the right from the point -3 with an open dot at the point -3, choice D.

Tip: Remember to reverse the direction of the inequality when you multiply both sides by a negative quantity.

42. **B.** Multiplying both sides of $\dfrac{10}{a^4} = \dfrac{b^2}{40}$ by $40a^4$ yields $a^4 b^2 = 400 = 2^4 5^2$. Given that a and b are both prime, then $a^4 b^2 = 2^4 5^2$ implies that $a = 2$ and $b = 5$. So, $a + b = 2 + 5 = 7$, choice B.

43. **D.** You are given that $P(x)$ has zeros 0, $2 - i$, 4, and -3. Because $P(x)$ has real coefficients, the complex conjugate, $2 + i$, of $2 - i$ is also a zero. Hence, $P(x)$ has five zeros (eliminate choices A and B). By the factor theorem, if r is a zero of a polynomial, $P(x)$, then $x - r$ is a factor of $P(x)$; so $P(x) = (x - 0)[x - (2 - i)][x - (2 + i)](x - 4)[x - (-3)] = x(x - 2 + i)(x - 2 - i)(x - 4)(x + 3)$, choice D. Choice C is eliminated because its last two factors are incorrect.

44. **B.** By the factor theorem, $x - i$ is a factor of $P(x)$ if $P(i) = 0$. First, determine $P(i)$. Next, solve $P(i) = 0$ for k.

Determine $P(i)$.

$$P(i) = k^2(i)^4 - 8k(i)^2 + 16 = k^2(1) - 8k(-1) + 16 = k^2 + 8k + 16$$

Solve $P(i) = 0$ for k.

$$k^2 + 8k + 16 = 0$$
$$(k + 4)^2 = 0$$
$$k = -4, \text{ choice B}$$

45. **C.** On the figure, construct the central angle subtended by $\overset{\frown}{AB}$.

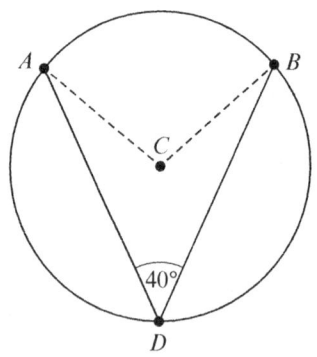

The length of $\overset{\frown}{AB}$ is $r\theta$, where r is the radius of the circle and θ is the central angle (in radians) subtended by $\overset{\frown}{AB}$. The central angle subtended by $\overset{\frown}{AB}$ has measure $(2)(40°) = 80°$. This is true because the measure of the inscribed $\angle ADB$ is half the measure of central $\angle ACB$. In terms of radians, $80° = 80° \times \dfrac{\pi}{180°} = \dfrac{4\pi}{9}$. Hence, the length of $\overset{\frown}{AB}$ is $r\theta = (4)\left(\dfrac{4\pi}{9}\right) = \dfrac{16\pi}{9}$, choice C.

46. **C.** From the 2×2 matrices in the answer choices, you want the one that premultiplies the vertex matrix $\begin{bmatrix} x_i \\ y_i \end{bmatrix}$ to yield $\begin{bmatrix} 5x_i \\ 5y_i \end{bmatrix}$, where $i = 1, 2, 3$. Check the answer choices.

Check A: $\begin{bmatrix} 5 & 5 \\ 5 & 5 \end{bmatrix} \begin{bmatrix} x_i \\ y_i \end{bmatrix} = \begin{bmatrix} 5x_i + 5y_i \\ 5x_i + 5y_i \end{bmatrix}$; eliminate choice A.

Check B: $\begin{bmatrix} 5 & 0 \\ 5 & 0 \end{bmatrix} \begin{bmatrix} x_i \\ y_i \end{bmatrix} = \begin{bmatrix} 5x_i \\ 5x_i \end{bmatrix}$; eliminate choice B.

Check C: $\begin{bmatrix} 5 & 0 \\ 0 & 5 \end{bmatrix} \begin{bmatrix} x_i \\ y_i \end{bmatrix} = \begin{bmatrix} 5x_i \\ 5y_i \end{bmatrix}$; thus, choice C is the correct response. Go on to the next question.

47. **C.** The volume of a right prism is $V = Bh$. To find the volume of the right hexagonal prism, first find the area, B, of one of the regular hexagonal bases, and then find the volume by multiplying B by the height of the prism, h.

Find the area of one of the regular hexagonal bases.

Sketch a diagram.

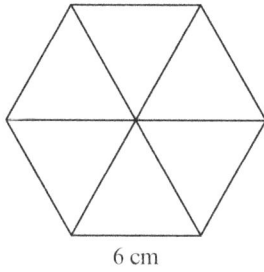

6 cm

A regular hexagon with side 6 cm can be divided into 6 equilateral triangles with each side equal to 6 cm and angles of 60°. Using the trigonometric formula for the area of a triangle, the area of one of the equilateral triangles is $\dfrac{1}{2}(6 \text{ cm})(6 \text{ cm})\sin 60° = 18 \text{ cm}^2 \cdot \dfrac{\sqrt{3}}{2} = 9\sqrt{3} \text{ cm}^2$.

Thus, the area of the regular hexagonal base of the prism is $B = 6(9\sqrt{3} \text{ cm}^2) = 54\sqrt{3} \text{ cm}^2$.

Therefore, the volume of the prism is $Bh = (54\sqrt{3} \text{ cm}^2)(30 \text{ cm}) \approx 2{,}806 \text{ cm}^3$, choice C.

48. **B.** Square both sides of the equation $x = \sqrt{\dfrac{9x+2}{5}}$ and solve for x.

$$x^2 = \dfrac{9x+2}{5}$$
$$5x^2 = 9x + 2$$
$$5x^2 - 9x - 2 = 0$$
$$(5x+1)(x-2) = 0$$
$$x = -\dfrac{1}{5} \text{ (extraneous) or } x = 2$$

$-\frac{1}{5}$ (choice B) is an extraneous solution because it makes the left side of the original equation negative, so it cannot equal $\sqrt{\frac{9x+2}{5}}$, which is always nonnegative. The other solution, $x = 2$ (choice D), is not an extraneous solution because it satisfies the original equation as shown below.

$$2 \overset{?}{=} \sqrt{\frac{9(2)+2}{5}}$$

$$2 \overset{?}{=} \sqrt{4}$$

$$2 \overset{\checkmark}{=} 2$$

Tip: Remember to answer the question posed. The question asks for the extraneous solution.

49. **B.** Make a sketch and shade the area of interest.

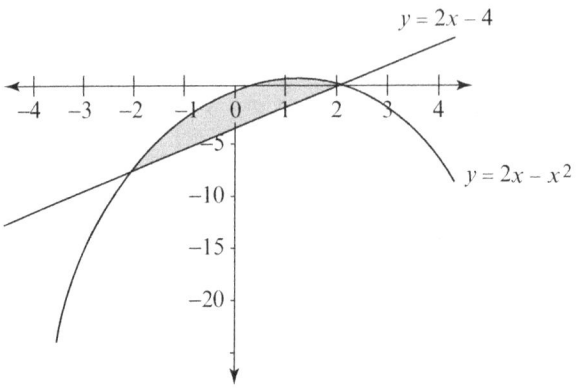

Use your graphing calculator to determine that the two graphs intersect at two points and the graph of $y = 2x - x^2$ lies above $y = 2x - 4$ between the points of intersection. To find the area of the region bounded by the two graphs, first find the x values for the points of intersection of the two graphs. Next, find the difference between the two functions, being sure to subtract the equation of the lower graph from the equation of the upper graph, and then evaluate the definite integral of the difference of the two graphs between the two x values of their points of intersection.

Find the x values for the points of intersection of the two graphs.

Using substitution,

$$2x - x^2 = 2x - 4$$
$$-x^2 = -4$$
$$x^2 = 4$$
$$x = \pm 2$$

Tip: You also can use features of your graphing calculator to determine the x values of the points of intersection.

Find the difference between the two functions.

Difference = $(2x - x^2) - (2x - 4) = 2x - x^2 - 2x + 4 = -x^2 + 4$

Evaluate the definite integral $\int_{-2}^{2} (-x^2 + 4) dx$.

Integrate the integral using methods of calculus.

$$\int_{-2}^{2}(-x^2+4)dx = \left(-\frac{x^3}{3}+4x\right)\Big|_{-2}^{2} = \left(-\frac{(2)^3}{3}+4(2)\right)-\left(-\frac{(-2)^3}{3}+4(-2)\right)$$

$$=\left(-\frac{8}{3}+8\right)-\left(\frac{8}{3}-8\right) = -\frac{8}{3}+8-\frac{8}{3}+8 = 16-\frac{16}{3} = \frac{32}{3}, \text{ choice B}$$

50. **C.** Fill in the row and column totals for the table.

Resident Status of Second-Year Students ($n = 500$)

Age	On-Campus	Off-Campus	Row Total
Younger Than 21	114	135	249
21 or Older	156	95	251
Column Total	270	230	500

Find the probability when you already know that the student is younger than 21. Thus, when computing the probability, the number of possible students under consideration is no longer 500 but is reduced to the total number of students who are under 21. So, you are dealing only with the students in the first row of the table. To find the probability, first find the total number of students who are younger than 21. Next, among those, determine the number who reside off-campus, and then compute the conditional probability.

Among the 249 students who are under 21, 135 reside off-campus. Thus,

P(resides off-campus given the student is under 21) = $\frac{135}{249}$, choice C.

51. **B.** If an integer is a factor of both of the integers x and y, then it is a factor of $ax + by$, for any integers a and b. Let $x = (10n + 9)$ and $y = (5n - 1)$. Because p is a factor of both $x = (10n + 9)$ and $y = (5n - 1)$, then p is a factor of $1x - 2y = (1)(10n + 9) - 2(5n - 1) = 10n + 9 - 10n + 2 = 11$. The only positive factors of 11 are 1 and 11. Given that p is prime, it follows that p equals 11, choice B.

52. **A.** Use the binomial theorem, $(x+y)^n = \sum_{k=0}^{n}\binom{n}{k}x^{n-k}y^k$. For this problem, $(x-2y)^5 = \sum_{k=0}^{5}\binom{5}{k}x^{5-k}(-2y)^k$.

For the fourth term, $k = 3$ yielding $\binom{5}{3}x^{5-3}(-2y)^3 = 10x^2(-2y)^3 = 10x^2(-8y^3) = -80x^2y^3$, choice A.

Tip: You can use your graphing calculator to compute $\binom{5}{3} = {}_5C_3$. Keying in $_nC_r(5,3)$ returns 10.

53. **D.** Let $y = f(x) = 5x + 7$. Interchange x and y in $y = f(x)$, and then solve for y.

$$x = 5y + 7$$
$$x - 7 = 5y$$
$$\frac{x-7}{5} = y$$
$$f^{-1}(x) = \frac{x-7}{5}, \text{ choice D}$$

54. **D.** Examine the dot plot.

The mean of the scores is $\frac{55+60+3(65)+5(70)+3(75)+80+2(90)+3(95)+100}{20} = \frac{1{,}530}{20} = 76.5$. One standard deviation above the mean is $76.5 + 13.2 = 89.7$. Exactly 6 scores fall above this value, meaning 6 scores are more than one standard deviation above the mean, choice D.

55. **C.** In this study, Fertilizer X (independent variable) is the treatment and plant growth (dependent variable) is the variable of interest. In an experimental study, the treatment group receives the treatment, so the plant seedlings in the treatment plot will receive applications of Fertilizer X, choice C. Choices A and B are

incorrect because these choices are related to the variable of interest, which is not manipulated by the researcher. The seedlings in the treatment plot might or might not have plant growth. The outcome depends on the effectiveness of Fertilizer X, which is what the researcher is investigating. Choice D is incorrect because the plant seedlings in the control plot, not the treatment plot, will not receive applications of Fertilizer X.

56. **C.** Given $x^2 + 14x + c = (x + h)^2$ or equivalently $x^2 + 14x + c = x^2 + 2xh + h^2$, then $14 = 2h$ and $c = h^2$ (because corresponding coefficients are equal). Therefore, $h = 7$ and $c = 7^2 = 49$, choice C.

57. **C.** For convenience, designate the locations L1, L2, L3, L4, and L5 with treasure coins in the ratio 1:2:3:4:5, respectively. Let n = the number of coins in L1, then L1, L2, L3, L4, and L5 have n, $2n$, $3n$, $4n$, and $5n$ coins, respectively. The minimum number of coins needed to win is 50% of the combined number of coins in L1, L2, and L3 (because these locations have the fewest number of coins). This minimum number is $50\%(n + 2n + 3n) = 0.5(6n) = 3n$. The total number of coins is $n + 2n + 3n + 4n + 5n = 15n$. The minimum percent to win is $\frac{3n}{15n} = \frac{1}{5} = 20\%$, choice C.

58. **B, C, D.** Any value of x, for which $f(x) = \frac{\sqrt{x+3}}{2x^3 + x^2 - 2x - 1}$ is undefined over the real numbers, is not in the domain of f. Exclude from the domain any value for which $(x + 3) < 0$ (or equivalently $x < -3$). Eliminate choice A because -3 is in the domain given that $\sqrt{-3+3} = \sqrt{0} = 0$, which is a real number. Exclude values for which the denominator evaluates to zero. Factor the denominator to identify such excluded values.
$$f(x) = \frac{\sqrt{x+2}}{2x^3 + x^2 - 2x - 1} = \frac{\sqrt{x+2}}{x^2(2x+1) - (2x+1)} = \frac{\sqrt{x+2}}{(2x+1)(x^2-1)} = \frac{\sqrt{x+2}}{(2x+1)(x+1)(x-1)}.$$ The denominator is zero when x is -1 (select choice B), $-\frac{1}{2}$ (select choice C), or 1 (select choice D), so these values are excluded.

Tip: You also could work this problem by substituting the values in the answer choices into f(x) to check which values yield an undefined expression.

59. **C.** Recall that the derivative of f is defined as $f'(x) = \lim_{h \to 0} \frac{f(x+h) - f(x)}{h}$ and the derivative of f at $x = x_0$ equals $f'(x_0) = \lim_{h \to 0} \frac{f(x_0+h) - f(x_0)}{h}$. For this problem, $\lim_{h \to 0} \frac{\left(\frac{1}{2}+h\right)^8 - \left(\frac{1}{2}\right)^8}{h}$ is the derivative of the function f defined by $f(x) = x^8$ at $x = \frac{1}{2}$. Thus, $f'(x) = 8x^7$ and $f'\left(\frac{1}{2}\right) = 8\left(\frac{1}{2}\right)^7 = 2^3\left(\frac{1}{2^7}\right) = \frac{1}{2^4} = \frac{1}{16}$, choice C.

60. **D.** If $f'(x) > 0$ for all x, then f is increasing, and if $f''(x) < 0$ for all f, f is concave downward. Eliminate choice A because f is decreasing, not increasing. Eliminate choice B because f is not concave down for all x. Eliminate choice C because f is concave up, not concave down. Only choice D meets both conditions given.

Tip: The tangent lines lie below the curve when a function is concave up and lie above the curve when the function is concave down.

61. **C.** The perimeter of $\triangle ABC$ = 12 cm + 3 cm + 2 cm + AC.
First, determine AC, then calculate the perimeter. Given $\angle DAB \cong \angle DAC$, then $\overline{AD}$ bisects $\angle A$. An angle bisector of an angle of a triangle divides the opposite side in the ratio of the sides that form the angle bisected. Thus, $\frac{BD}{DC} = \frac{AB}{AC}$. Substitute values from the figure into this proportion and solve for AC (omitting the units for convenience).
$$\frac{3}{2} = \frac{12}{AC} \text{ implies } AC = \frac{(2)(12)}{3} = 8$$
Thus, the perimeter of $\triangle ABC$ = 12 cm + 3 cm + 2 cm + AC = 12 cm + 3 cm + 2 cm + 8 cm = 25 cm, choice C.

62. B. The phrase "an extended period of time" is a clue that this is a calculus problem in which you need to find the limit of a function as the variable approaches infinity. To answer the question, find the limit of the function $Q(h) = \dfrac{10(4h+25)}{2h+5}$ as h approaches infinity:

$$\lim_{h\to\infty}\frac{10(4h+25)}{2h+5} = \lim_{h\to\infty}\frac{40h+250}{2h+5} = \lim_{h\to\infty}\frac{40+\dfrac{250}{h}}{2+\dfrac{5}{h}} = \frac{40+0}{2+0} = \frac{40}{2} = 20 \text{ components, choice B}$$

63. A. At any time t after the water starts running, let $h(t)$ be the height of the water in the tank. The instantaneous rate of change of the water's height is $h'(t)$. Express $h(t)$ in terms of t, then find $h'(t)$.

The volume of water at any time t is $30\dfrac{\text{ft}^3}{\text{min}}t$. Substitute into the formula for the volume of a right cylinder and then solve for $h(t)$, omitting the units for convenience.

$$V = \pi r^2 [h(t)]$$
$$30t = \pi(5)^2[h(t)]$$
$$30t = 25\pi[h(t)]$$
$$h(t) = \frac{30t}{25\pi} \text{ implies}$$
$$h'(t) = \frac{30}{25\pi} \approx 0.38$$

The instantaneous rate of change of the height of the water at any time t is approximately $0.38\ \dfrac{\text{ft}}{\text{min}}$, choice A.

64. D. The greatest number that x can be is the greatest common factor of 36 and 24, which is 12, choice D. In each of the 12 groups there are 5 students: 3 boys (36 boys ÷ 12) and 2 girls (24 girls ÷ 12). *Tip:* Notice that $5 \times 12 = 60$, which is the total number of students.

65. B. Use the fundamental counting principle to determine the number of possible telephone numbers for each prefix as follows. After the prefix, there are four slots, so to speak, to fill. For each slot, 10 digits are available, which means the number of possible telephone numbers for each prefix is $10 \cdot 10 \cdot 10 \cdot 10 = 10^4$. By the addition principle, the total number of possible telephone numbers if all three prefixes are used is $10^4 + 10^4 + 10^4 = 3 \cdot 10^4$ or $(3)(10^4)$, choice B.

66. A, D. The rate of change of a curve at a point is described by the slope of the tangent to the curve at the point. Check each statement against the behavior of the graph of the function.

Select choice A because the slope of the tangent line is decreasing between 0 and 0.5. Eliminate choice B because the slope of the tangent line is decreasing between 0.5 and 1.5. Eliminate choice C because the slope of the tangent line is increasing between 2 and 3. Select choice D because the slope of the tangent line is increasing between 3 and 3.5.

67. D. The area of the region bounded by the graph of $f(x) = x^4 - 3x^3 + x^2 + 5$, the x-axis, and the vertical lines $x = 0$ (y-axis) and $x = 2$ is $\int_0^2 (x^4 - 3x^3 + x^2 + 5)dx$. Evaluate this definite integral using methods of calculus.

$$\int_0^2 (x^4 - 3x^3 + x^2 + 5)dx = \left(\frac{x^5}{5} - \frac{3x^4}{4} + \frac{x^3}{3} + 5x\right)\Big|_0^2$$
$$= \left(\frac{(2)^5}{5} - \frac{3(2)^4}{4} + \frac{(2)^3}{3} + 5(2)\right) - \left(\frac{(0)^5}{5} - \frac{3(0)^4}{4} + \frac{(0)^3}{3} + 5(0)\right) = \frac{32}{5} - \frac{48}{4} + \frac{8}{3} + 10 = \frac{106}{15}, \text{ choice D}$$

68. A. According to the 68-95-99.7 rule, approximately 68% of the data in a normal distribution fall within one standard deviation of the mean, about 95% fall within two standard deviations of the mean, and about 99.7% fall within three standard deviations of the mean. The mean miles per gallon of the automobiles is 29 mpg with standard deviation of 4 mpg.

To find the approximate probability that a randomly chosen automobile will have gas mileage less than 25 mpg, first determine the z-score for 25 mpg, and then find the percentage of the normal distribution that is below this z-score.

$$z\text{-score} = \frac{\text{data value} - \text{mean}}{\text{standard deviation}} = \frac{25 - 29}{4} = -1.$$ Therefore, 25 is one standard deviation below the mean.

Find the percentage of the normal distribution that is below a z-score of −1.

About 68% of the distribution is within one standard deviation of the mean. Make a sketch to illustrate the problem.

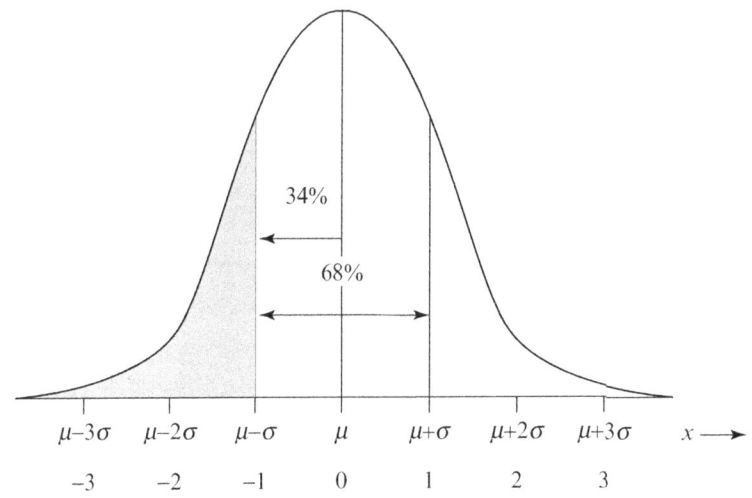

The normal curve is symmetric, so about 34% $\left(\frac{1}{2} \text{ of } 68\%\right)$ of the distribution is between the mean and a z-score of −1. Again, due to symmetry, 50% of the total distribution is to the left of the mean. Thus, approximately 50% − 34% = 16% of the distribution is below a z-score of −1. The approximate probability that an automobile of this type chosen at random has gas mileage less than 25 mpg is 16%, choice A.

69. A. When $b > 1$, the graph defined by $g(x) = f(bx)$ is a horizontal compression toward the y-axis of the graph defined by $y = f(x)$. If (x, y) is on the graph defined by $y = f(x)$, then $\left(\frac{x}{b}, y\right)$ is on the graph defined by $g(x) = f(bx)$. Thus, if $(−2, −8)$ is on the graph of f defined by $f(x) = x^3$, then the corresponding point on the graph of g defined by $g(x) = f(2x)$ is $\left(\frac{-2}{2}, -8\right) = (-1, -8)$, choice A.

70. A. Only through well-designed experimental studies can investigators validly establish cause-and-effect relationships, so choice A is the correct response. Choice B is incorrect because cause-effect relationships are not established with survey studies. Choices C and D are incorrect because establishing cause-effect relationships in observational studies is problematic given that the investigators are unable to manipulate variables of interest.

71. C. Rewrite $3x^2 - 2x < 1$ as $3x^2 - 2x - 1 < 0$.

Factor the left side of the inequality to obtain $(3x + 1)(x - 1) < 0$. Next, determine when the product $(3x + 1)(x - 1)$ is negative. First, find the values for x at which the factors change sign; that is, find the zero for each factor.

Set each factor equal to 0 and solve for x.

$3x + 1 = 0$ implies $x = -\frac{1}{3}$ and $x - 1 = 0$ implies $x = 1$.

The two values $-\frac{1}{3}$ and 1 divide the number line into three intervals: $\left(-\infty, -\frac{1}{3}\right)$, $\left(-\frac{1}{3}, 1\right)$, and $(1, \infty)$. Next, determine in which interval(s) the product of the two factors is negative.

Method 1. Make an organized table to determine the sign of $(3x + 1)(x - 1)$ for each of these intervals.

Interval	Sign of $(3x + 1)$	Sign of $(x - 1)$	Sign of $(3x + 1)(x - 1)$
$\left(-\infty, -\frac{1}{3}\right)$	negative	negative	positive
$\left(-\frac{1}{3}, 1\right)$	positive	negative	negative
$(1, \infty)$	positive	positive	positive

Thus, $(3x + 1)(x - 1)$ is negative only in the interval $\left(-\frac{1}{3}, 1\right)$, choice C.

Method 2. Use your graphing calculator to graph $y = 3x^2 - 2x - 1$.

The graph intersects the x-axis at $x = -\frac{1}{3}$ and $x = 1$. You can see that the graph is below the x-axis (and, therefore, negative) between these two points and above the x-axis otherwise. Thus, $3x^2 - 2x - 1$ is negative only in the interval $\left(-\frac{1}{3}, 1\right)$, choice C.

72. **A.** You are given two points $(0, 500)$ and $(5, 1{,}500)$ that satisfy the function $P(t) = P_0 e^{xt}$. First, substitute the values for the two points into $P(t) = P_0 e^{xt}$ and then solve the resulting system of equations for x.

$$500 = P_0 e^{x(0)} = P_0 e^0 = P_0(1) = P_0$$

$1{,}500 = P_0 e^{x(5)} = P_0 e^{5x} = 500 e^{5x}$ (using the results from the first equation). Solve for x.

$$1{,}500 = 500 e^{5x}, \text{ which implies } 3 = e^{5x}$$

Taking the natural logarithm of both sides of the equation $3 = e^{5x}$ yields $\ln 3 = \ln e^{5x} = 5x \ln e = 5x(1) = 5x$, which implies $\frac{\ln 3}{5} = x$, choice A.

73. **D.** Make a table showing the height of the ball as a function of rebound number.

Height of Ball (in feet)	60	$60\left(\frac{3}{5}\right)$	$60\left(\frac{3}{5}\right)\left(\frac{3}{5}\right)$	$60\left(\frac{3}{5}\right)\left(\frac{3}{5}\right)\left(\frac{3}{5}\right)$	...
Rebound Number n	0	1	2	3	...

Examination of the table leads to a general term for the nth bounce: $60\left(\frac{3}{5}\right)^n$, where $n = 0, 1, 2, \ldots$. Thus, an exponential function (choice D) would best model the height of the ball as a function of rebound number n. None of the functions in the other answer choices works as well as an exponential model.

74. **B.** The degree of the numerator polynomial exceeds the degree of the denominator polynomial by 2, so the graph has no horizontal or oblique asymptotes. To find vertical asymptotes, first simplify $y = \frac{x^4 - 81}{x^2 + x - 12}$, then find all values of x that make the denominator equal to zero.

$$y = \frac{x^4 - 81}{x^2 + x - 12} = \frac{(x^2 + 9)(x^2 - 9)}{(x + 4)(x - 3)} = \frac{(x^2 + 9)(x + 3)\cancel{(x - 3)}}{(x + 4)\cancel{(x - 3)}} = \frac{(x^2 + 9)(x + 3)}{(x + 4)}$$

When $x = -4$, the denominator of the simplified function is zero. So, the graph has one asymptote at $x = -4$. Thus, choice B is the correct response. *Tip:* The graph does not have an asymptote at $x = 3$. The graph has a "hole" at $x = 3$ because the function is undefined at that point.

75. **C.** Solve $f(g(x)) = g(f(x))$ for x.

$$f(g(x)) = g(f(x))$$
$$3\left(\frac{4}{x-1}\right) = \frac{4}{(3x)-1}$$
$$\frac{12}{x-1} = \frac{4}{3x-1}$$
$$12(3x-1) = 4(x-1)$$
$$3(3x-1) = (x-1)$$
$$9x - 3 = x - 1$$
$$8x = 2$$
$$x = \frac{1}{4}, \text{ choice C}$$

76. **B.** To determine a polynomial model for the nth term of the sequence requires looking for a pattern in the first-order, second-order, and so on differences of the terms of the sequence. If the first differences are equal, the polynomial model is linear; if the second differences are equal, the polynomial model is quadratic; if the third differences are equal, the polynomial model is cubic; and so on. Make a table to look for a pattern in consecutive differences.

n	a_n	1st Difference	2nd Difference
1	1	8 − 1 = 7	
2	8	17 − 8 = 9	9 − 7 = 2
3	17	28 − 17 = 11	11 − 9 = 2
4	28		13 − 11 = 2
5	41	41 − 28 = 13	15 − 13 = 2
6	56	56 − 41 = 15	

The preceding table shows that the second differences are equal. When the second differences are equal, the polynomial model for the nth term of the sequence is quadratic, choice B.

77. **B.** Let D = the distance between the two cities. After 6 hours (10 a.m. to 4 p.m.), the vehicle has traveled $\frac{7}{10} - \frac{1}{4} = \frac{14}{20} - \frac{5}{20} = \frac{9}{20}$ of D. Therefore, each hour the vehicle travels $\frac{1}{6} \cdot \frac{9}{20} = \frac{3}{40}$ of D. Thus, in the 4 hours from 10 a.m. to 2 p.m., the vehicle travels $4 \cdot \frac{3}{40} = \frac{3}{10}$ of D. Hence, at 2 p.m., the vehicle is $\frac{1}{4} + \frac{3}{10} = \frac{5}{20} + \frac{6}{20} = \frac{11}{20}$ of the distance between the two cities, choice B.

78. **B.** Given the coin is to be flipped six times, work this problem using the fundamental counting principle. There are two possibilities for each of the six coin flips, which means the total number of possible outcomes in the sample space is $2 \cdot 2 \cdot 2 \cdot 2 \cdot 2 \cdot 2 = 2^6$, choice B.

79. A. Make a sketch of the two curves and shade the area of interest.

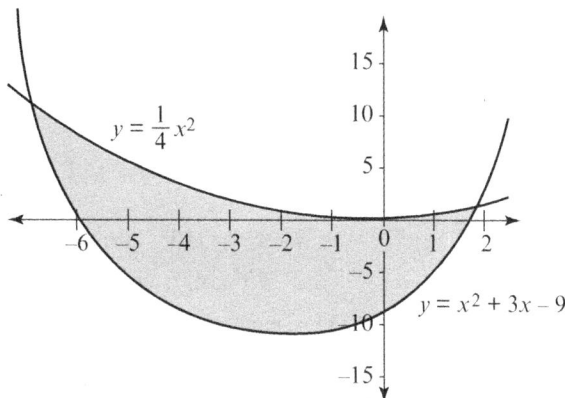

The two curves intersect at two points and $y = \frac{1}{4}x^2$ lies above $y = x^2 + 3x - 9$ between the points of intersection. First, find the x values for the points of intersection of the two curves. Next, find the difference between the two functions, being sure to subtract the equation of the lower curve from the equation of the upper curve. Then evaluate the definite integral of the difference, between the two x values of their intersection.

Step 1. Find the x values for the points of intersection of the two curves.

Use substitution and then solve for x.

$$\frac{1}{4}x^2 = x^2 + 3x - 9$$

$$0 = \frac{3}{4}x^2 + 3x - 9$$

$$0 = 3x^2 + 12x - 36$$

$$0 = x^2 + 4x - 12$$

$$0 = (x+6)(x-2)$$

$$x = -6 \text{ or } x = 2$$

Step 2. Find the difference between the two curves.

$$\text{Difference} = \left(\frac{1}{4}x^2\right) - (x^2 + 3x - 9) = \frac{1}{4}x^2 - x^2 - 3x + 9 = -\frac{3}{4}x^2 - 3x + 9$$

Step 3. Evaluate the definite integral $\int_{-6}^{2}\left(-\frac{3}{4}x^2 - 3x + 9\right)dx$ using methods of calculus.

$$\int_{-6}^{2}\left(-\frac{3}{4}x^2 - 3x + 9\right)dx = \left(-\frac{x^3}{4} - \frac{3x^2}{2} + 9x\right)\Bigg|_{-6}^{2} = \left(-\frac{(2)^3}{4} - \frac{3(2)^2}{2} + 9(2)\right) - \left(-\frac{(-6)^3}{4} - \frac{3(-6)^2}{2} + 9(-6)\right)$$

$$= (-2 - 6 + 18) - (54 - 54 - 54) = 10 + 54 = 64, \text{ choice A}$$

80. **A, D.** Consecutive angles of a parallelogram are supplementary. Solve $(x + 43°) + (2x − 73°) = 180°$ for x. Then evaluate $(x + 43°)$ and $(2x − 73°)$ to determine the measures of the parallelogram's angles.

$$(x + 43°) + (2x − 73°) = 180°$$
$$3x − 30° = 180°$$
$$3x = 210°$$
$$x = 70°$$

$$x + 43° = 113°, \text{ choice D}$$
$$2x − 73° = 67°, \text{ choice A}$$

81. **A, C, D.** The statements in choices A, C, and D are each alone sufficient to prove a quadrilateral is a parallelogram. A quadrilateral that is equilateral (select choice A) is a rhombus; consequently, it's a parallelogram. If a quadrilateral has three right angles (select choice C), then the fourth angle is also a right angle. Thus, the quadrilateral is a rectangle; ergo it's a parallelogram. If the diagonals of a quadrilateral bisect each other (select choice D), the quadrilateral is a parallelogram. The statement in choice B is not sufficient to guarantee that the quadrilateral is a parallelogram.

82. **A.** The function $g(x) = −ax^2 − b$ equals $−f(x)$. Making the output negative results in a reflection over the x axis. Therefore, the graph of $g(x)$ is a reflection of the graph of $f(x)$ over the x axis. In simple terms, a reflection is a geometric transformation that results in a "flip" of a figure. The teacher's likely purpose for engaging students in this activity is to enhance their understanding of reflection, choice A.

83. **A.** Adding a multiple of one row to another row of a square matrix does not change the value of its determinant. Thus, choice A is the correct response. Choice B will result if a row is multiplied by $−5$. Choice C will result if two rows are interchanged. And choice D will result if a row is multiplied by $−\frac{1}{5}$.

84. **C.** In a 5-digit number there are five place values to fill. If there were no restrictions on the placement of the two 4s, the number of ways to select two locations for the two 4s from the five place value slots is the combination of 5 things taken 2 at a time. This number is $_5C_2 = \frac{5!}{2!3!} = \frac{5 \cdot 4 \cdot 3 \cdot 2 \cdot 1}{(2 \cdot 1)(3 \cdot 2 \cdot 1)} = \frac{5 \cdot \cancel{4}^2 \cdot \cancel{3} \cdot \cancel{2} \cdot \cancel{1}}{\cancel{2} \cdot 1 \cdot \cancel{3} \cdot \cancel{2} \cdot \cancel{1}} = 10$.

However, you must remove from this number the number of ways for the two 4s to be adjacent to each other. There are four ways for the two 4s to be adjacent to each other as illustrated here, with x marking a place for each of the other three digits: 44xxx, x44xx, xx44x, and xxx44. Therefore, the number of ways to select the location for the two 4s is the number of ways to select two of the five place value locations minus the four ways in which the two selected locations would be adjacent. This number is $10 − 4 = 6$. Now, for each of these 6 ways, there are $3 × 2 × 1 = 6$ ways to arrange the other three digits. Therefore, there are $6 × 6 = 36$ ways (choice C) to arrange the given digits into a 5-digit number so that the two occurrences of the digit 4 are separated by at least one other digit.

85. **B.** Let L = the suggested weekly limit. The first week, Dev spent $(100\% − 10\%)$ of $L = 90\%$ of L. The second week, he spent $(100\% + 30\%)$ of 90% of $L = 130\%$ of 90% of L. The third week, he spent $(100\% + 20\%)$ of 130% of 90% of $L = 120\%$ of 130% of 90% of L. Given that Dev spent $460 in the third week, solve the following equation for L:

$$(120\%)(130\%)(90\%)L = \$460$$
$$(1.2)(1.3)(0.9)L = \$460$$
$$1.404L = \$460$$
$$L \approx \$330$$

Thus, the suggested weekly limit was approximately $330, choice B.

86. **B.** The student failed to follow the order of operations. The correct computation is $−2 + 7^2 = −2 + 49 = 47$. A discussion of the order of operations that clarifies that the student should perform the exponentiation in the problem first, and then do addition, would best address the student's error. Thus, choice B is the correct response. The error in the student's work does not indicate a need for a discussion of the concepts given in choices A, C, or D.

87. **D.** The student's work is incorrect. After solving for x, the student should have substituted the result into the other equation. Thus, choice D is the correct response. None of the other answer choices contains an accurate analysis of the student's work.

88. **B.** Add the two equations to eliminate y, and then solve for x. Substitute the result into either of the two equations and solve for y. Then compute x times y.

$$\begin{array}{l} 3x+2y=4 \\ \underline{x-2y=3} \\ 4x\quad\;\;=7 \\ x=\dfrac{7}{4} \end{array} \qquad \begin{array}{l} 3x+2y=4 \\ 3\left(\dfrac{7}{4}\right)+2y=4 \\ \dfrac{21}{4}+2y=4 \\ 2y=4-\dfrac{21}{4} \\ 2y=-\dfrac{5}{4} \\ y=-\dfrac{5}{8} \end{array} \qquad xy=\dfrac{7}{4}\cdot-\dfrac{5}{8}=-\dfrac{35}{32}, \text{choice B}$$

89. **D.** Because $x = 5$, then $x - 5 = 0$. Therefore, when both sides of the equation are divided by $(x - 5)$, division by zero occurs, resulting in the false statement $10 = 5$. Thus, choice D is the correct response.

90. **D.** As the values of V increase, the values of W vary, but not in a predictable manner. The scatter plot shows no unmistakable linear pattern. Thus, the student should conclude that variables V and W are not linearly correlated, choice D.

91. **B.** Examine the figure. The perimeter of $\triangle DBE$ is $DB + BE + ED = 20 + BE + ED$. You need $BE + ED$. First, find BF and DF, the lengths of the legs of 45°-45°-90° right $\triangle DFB$, which has hypotenuse of length 20. Use BF to find BE, which is the length of the hypotenuse of 30°-60°-90° right $\triangle EFB$. Next, use BF to find EF, which is the length of the side opposite the 60° angle in 30°-60°-90° right $\triangle EFB$. Use EF and DF to find ED, which is $EF - DF$. Then, find the perimeter.

Find BF and DF.

The length of the sides of a 45°-45°-90° right triangle are in the ratio $\dfrac{1}{\sqrt{2}}:\dfrac{1}{\sqrt{2}}:1$. Hence, $BF = DF = 20\left(\dfrac{1}{\sqrt{2}}\right) = \dfrac{20}{\sqrt{2}} = 10\sqrt{2}$.

Use BF to find BE.

In 30°-60°-90° right $\triangle EFB$, BF is the side opposite the 30° angle and BE is the hypotenuse. The lengths of the sides of a 30°-60°-90° right triangle are in the ratio $1:\sqrt{3}:2$. So $BE = (BF)(2) = (10\sqrt{2})(2) = 20\sqrt{2}$.

Use BF to find EF.

In 30°-60°-90° right $\triangle EFB$, EF is the length of the side opposite the 60° angle and BF is the length of the other leg. The lengths of the sides of a 30°-60°-90° right triangle are in the ratio $1:\sqrt{3}:2$. Therefore, $EF = (BF)(\sqrt{3}) = (10\sqrt{2})(\sqrt{3}) = 10\sqrt{6}$.

Use EF and DF to find ED.

$$ED = EF - DF = 10\sqrt{6} - 10\sqrt{2}$$

Find the perimeter.

Perimeter $= 20 + BE + ED = 20 + 20\sqrt{2} + 10\sqrt{6} - 10\sqrt{2} = 20 + 10\sqrt{2} + 10\sqrt{6} = 10(2 + \sqrt{2} + \sqrt{6})$, choice B

This explanation might seem lengthy (and, perhaps, complicated) to you. Actually, using what you know about the ratios of the sides in the special right triangles, the computations are straightforward and can be done without a calculator.

Tip: When a figure has angles of 30° and/or 45°, recall the ratios of the sides of 30°-60°-90° and/or 45°-45°-90° right triangles.

92. **B.** A normal distribution is symmetric about its mean. Thus, if 30% of the donations are less than $625 (which is $25 below the mean), then 30% of the donations are greater than $675 (which is $25 above the mean). Thus, 100% − (30% + 30%) = 40% is the probability that a randomly chosen donation will be between $625 and $675, choice B.

93. **B.** Let $s(t)$ be the position of the particle at time t. The velocity of the particle is $s'(t) = v(t) = 6t^2$. The velocity is nonnegative, so the distance the particle moves between $t = 1$ and $t = 2$ is

$$\int_1^2 v(t)\,dt = \int_1^2 6t^2\,dt = 6\int_1^2 t^2\,dt = 6\left(\frac{t^3}{3}\bigg|_1^2\right) = \left(\frac{6}{3}\right)\left(t^3\bigg|_1^2\right) = 2\left(t^3\bigg|_1^2\right) = 2(2^3 - 1^3) = 2(7) = 14,\text{ choice B}$$

Tip: The total distance traveled over the time interval a to b is $\int_a^b |v(t)|\,dt$. In this problem, the velocity is nonnegative, so the absolute value bars are not needed.

94. **A, B.** A rational number is the quotient of two integers, excluding division by zero. Given that m and n are positive integers, m^n and n^m are positive integers because each is a product of positive integers. Therefore, $\dfrac{m^n}{n^m}$ (select choice A) is always a rational number because it is the quotient of two positive integers. Given that m and n are positive integers, $m!$ and $n!$ are positive integers because each is a product of consecutive positive integers. Therefore, $\dfrac{m!}{n!}$ (select choice B) is always a rational number because it is the quotient of two positive integers. The expressions in the other two answer choices can be either rational or irrational numbers, depending on the values of m and n. So, eliminate choices C and D.

95. **B.** The average is $\dfrac{x+y+z}{3}$. You have three variables and only two equations, so finding specific values for x, y, and z is problematic. However, if you can determine the sum $x + y + z$, you can answer the question. Observe that corresponding coefficients in the two equations add to 6. Add the two equations and solve for $(x + y + z)$.

$$4x + 5y - 2z = 60$$
$$2x + y + 8z = 84$$
$$\overline{6x + 6y + 6z = 144}$$
$$6(x + y + z) = 144$$
$$(x + y + z) = 24$$

Thus, the average is $\dfrac{24}{3} = 8$, choice B.

96. **C.** The volume of a right rectangular prism is $V = lwh$. Therefore, $V(x) = (120 − 4x)(x)(x) = 120x^2 − 4x^3$. To find local extrema, set the first derivative of the function V equal to zero and then solve for x. $V(x) = 120x^2 − 4x^3$ implies $V'(x) = 240x − 12x^2$. Then $240x − 12x^2 = 0$ implies $12x(20 − x) = 0$, which yields $x = 0$ (reject) or $x = 20$. $V(20) = 120x^2 − 4x^3 = 120(20)^2 − 4(20)^3 = 16{,}000 > 0$. Because $V''(x) = 240 − 24x$ indicates that $V''(20) = 240 − 24(20) = −240 < 0$, by the second derivative test, the volume is a maximum when $x = 20$, choice C.

97. **C.** Use the chain rule, $h'(x) = f'(g(x))g'(x)$.
$$h'(0) = f'(g(0))g'(0) = f'(1)g'(0) = (-4)(-3) = 12,\text{ choice C}$$

98. **D.** Of the choices given, the primary benefit of using various types of assessment throughout instructional units is to provide multiple ways to determine students' progress toward achieving the knowledge and skills that have been taught, choice D. Such ongoing progress monitoring provides data that the teacher can use to make decisions about classroom instruction. The other answer choices would not be considered primary benefits.

99. **B.** Grade equivalent scores can easily be misinterpreted, especially by parents. The teacher should clarify that the score indicates the student's level of performance on seventh-grade level, not eighth-grade level, mathematics. Thus, choice B is the correct response. The responses in the other answer choices would be inappropriate because these responses reflect incorrect interpretations of the student's grade equivalent score.

100. **B, C, D.** Procedural knowledge is knowledge of the rules and procedures that are used to carry out routine mathematical tasks and of the symbolism that is used to represent mathematical concepts. A highly managed classroom environment focused on procedural knowledge likely would result in less risk taking and less higher-level thinking from students. Thus, eliminate choice A. Select choices B, C, and D because these are effective teacher strategies. When students are encouraged to take time to think before deciding on a solution strategy for a multi-step problem (choice B), they spend more time thinking about and analyzing the problem. Allowing more time for problems requiring analytical skills than for basic computational problems (choice C) would be more conducive to higher-order thinking and problem solving. When students rely on themselves to determine whether their work is mathematically correct (choice D), they engage in critical thinking in order to clarify their mathematical understandings.

Appendix A

Simplifying Radicals

A radical is simplified when

- the radicand contains no variable factor raised to a power equal to or greater than the index of the radical;
- the radicand contains no constant factor that can be expressed as a power equal to or greater than the index of the radical;
- the radicand contains no fractions;
- no fractions contain radicals in the denominator;
- and the index of the radical is reduced to its lowest value.

Here are examples.

$\sqrt[3]{24a^5b^6} = \left(\sqrt[3]{8a^3b^6}\right)\left(\sqrt[3]{3a^2}\right) = 2ab^2\left(\sqrt[3]{3a^2}\right)$ is simplified.

$\sqrt{12} = \left(\sqrt{4}\right)\left(\sqrt{3}\right) = 2\sqrt{3}$ is simplified.

$\dfrac{\sqrt{54}}{\sqrt{6}} = \sqrt{9} = 3$ is simplified.

$\dfrac{1}{\sqrt{2}} = \left(\dfrac{1}{\sqrt{2}}\right)\left(\dfrac{\sqrt{2}}{\sqrt{2}}\right) = \dfrac{\sqrt{2}}{2}$ is simplified.

$\sqrt[4]{5^2} = \sqrt{5}$ is simplified.

Because square roots occur so frequently, the remainder of the examples will use only square root radicals.

Radicals that have the same index and the same radicand are called *like radicals*. To add or subtract like radicals, combine their coefficients and write the result as the coefficient of the common radical factor. Indicate the sum or difference of unlike radicals.

$$5\sqrt{3} + 2\sqrt{3} = 7\sqrt{3}$$

You may have to simplify the radical expressions before combining them.

$$5\sqrt{3} + \sqrt{12} = 5\sqrt{3} + \sqrt{4 \cdot 3} = 5\sqrt{3} + 2\sqrt{3} = 7\sqrt{3}$$

To multiply radicals that have the same index, multiply their coefficients to find the coefficient of the product. Multiply the radicands to find the radicand of the product. Simplify the results.

$$5\sqrt{3} \cdot 2\sqrt{3} = 10 \cdot 3 = 30$$

For a sum or difference, treat the factors as you would binomials, being sure to simplify radicals after you multiply.

$$\begin{aligned}\left(2\sqrt{3} + 5\sqrt{7}\right)\left(\sqrt{3} - 3\sqrt{6}\right) &= 2\sqrt{9} - 6\sqrt{18} + 5\sqrt{21} - 15\sqrt{42} \\ &= 2(3) - 6\sqrt{9 \cdot 2} + 5\sqrt{21} - 15\sqrt{42} \\ &= 6 - 18\sqrt{2} + 5\sqrt{21} - 15\sqrt{42}\end{aligned}$$

$$\begin{aligned}\left(1 - \sqrt{3}\right)\left(1 + \sqrt{3}\right) &= 1 + \sqrt{3} - \sqrt{3} - 3 \\ &= 1 - 3 \\ &= -2\end{aligned}$$

Appendix A: Simplifying Radicals

The technique of rationalizing is used to remove radicals from the denominator (or numerator) of a fraction. For square root radicals, if the denominator (numerator) contains a single term, multiply the numerator and denominator by the smallest radical that will produce a perfect square in the denominator (numerator). Here is an example.

$$\frac{5}{\sqrt{3}} = \frac{5}{\sqrt{3}} \cdot \frac{\sqrt{3}}{\sqrt{3}} = \frac{5\sqrt{3}}{3}$$

If the denominator (numerator) contains a sum or difference of two terms involving square roots, multiply the numerator and denominator by the conjugate, which is obtained by changing the sign between the two terms. This action causes the middle terms to sum to 0 when you multiply. Here is an example.

$$\frac{5}{1-\sqrt{3}} = \frac{5\left(1+\sqrt{3}\right)}{\left(1-\sqrt{3}\right)\left(1+\sqrt{3}\right)} = \frac{5\left(1+\sqrt{3}\right)}{1-3} = -\frac{5+5\sqrt{3}}{2}$$

Appendix B

Long Division of Polynomials

Here is an example of long division of polynomials.

$$\frac{4x^3 + 8x - 6x^2 + 1}{2x - 1} =$$

$2x - 1 \overline{\smash{\big)}\, 4x^3 - 6x^2 + 8x + 1}$	1. Arrange the terms of both the dividend and divisor in descending powers of the variable x.
$\begin{array}{r} 2x^2 \\ 2x - 1 \overline{\smash{\big)}\, 4x^3 - 6x^2 + 8x + 1} \end{array}$	2. Divide the first term of the dividend by the first term of the divisor, and write the answer as the first term of the quotient.
$\begin{array}{r} 2x^2 \\ 2x - 1 \overline{\smash{\big)}\, 4x^3 - 6x^2 + 8x + 1} \\ 4x^3 - 2x^2 \end{array}$	3. Multiply $2x^2$ by $2x - 1$ and enter the product under the dividend.
$\begin{array}{r} 2x^2 \\ 2x - 1 \overline{\smash{\big)}\, 4x^3 - 6x^2 + 8x + 1} \\ 4x^3 - 2x^2 \\ \hline -4x^2 \end{array}$	4. Subtract $4x^3 - 2x^2$ from the dividend, being sure to mentally change the signs of both terms.
$\begin{array}{r} 2x^2 - 2x \\ 2x - 1 \overline{\smash{\big)}\, 4x^3 - 6x^2 + 8x + 1} \\ 4x^3 - 2x^2 \\ \hline -4x^2 + 8x \\ -4x^2 + 2x \\ \hline 6x \end{array}$	5. Bring down $8x$, the next term of the dividend, and repeat Steps 2–4.
$\begin{array}{r} 2x^2 - 2x + 3 \\ 2x - 1 \overline{\smash{\big)}\, 4x^3 - 6x^2 + 8x + 1} \\ 4x^3 - 2x^2 \\ \hline -4x^2 + 8x \\ -4x^2 + 2x \\ \hline 6x + 1 \\ 6x - 3 \\ \hline 4 \end{array}$	6. Bring down 1, the last term of the dividend, and repeat Steps 2–4.
$\dfrac{4x^3 + 8x - 6x^2 + 1}{2x - 1} = 2x^2 - 2x + 3 + \dfrac{4}{2x - 1}$	7. Write the answer as quotient $+ \dfrac{\text{remainder}}{\text{divisor}}$.

Appendix C

Measurement Units and Conversions

U.S. Customary Units	Conversion
Length	
Inch (in)	$1 \text{ in} = \frac{1}{12} \text{ ft}$
Foot (ft)	$1 \text{ ft} = 12 \text{ in}$ $1 \text{ ft} = \frac{1}{3} \text{ yd}$
Yard (yd)	$1 \text{ yd} = 36 \text{ in}$ $1 \text{ yd} = 3 \text{ ft}$
Mile (mi)	$1 \text{ mi} = 5{,}280 \text{ ft}$ $1 \text{ mi} = 1{,}760 \text{ yd}$
Weight	
Pound (lb)	$1 \text{ lb} = 16 \text{ oz}$
Ton (T)	$1 \text{ T} = 2{,}000 \text{ lb}$
Capacity	
Fluid ounce (fl oz)	$1 \text{ fl oz} = \frac{1}{8} \text{ c}$
Cup (c)	$1 \text{ c} = 8 \text{ fl oz}$
Pint (pt)	$1 \text{ pt} = 2 \text{ c}$
Quart (qt)	$1 \text{ qt} = 32 \text{ fl oz}$ $1 \text{ qt} = 4 \text{ c}$ $1 \text{ qt} = 2 \text{ pt}$ $1 \text{ qt} = \frac{1}{4} \text{ gal}$
Gallon (gal)	$1 \text{ gal} = 128 \text{ fl oz}$ $1 \text{ gal} = 16 \text{ c}$ $1 \text{ gal} = 8 \text{ pt}$ $1 \text{ gal} = 4 \text{ qt}$

Metric Units	Conversion
Length	
Millimeter (mm)	$1 \text{ mm} = 0.1 \text{ cm} = \frac{1}{10} \text{ cm}$ $1 \text{ mm} = 0.001 \text{ m} = \frac{1}{1000} \text{ m}$
Centimeter (cm)	$1 \text{ cm} = 10 \text{ mm}$ $1 \text{ cm} = 0.01 \text{ m} = \frac{1}{100} \text{ m}$

Appendix C: Measurement Units and Conversions

Metric Units	Conversion
Meter (m)	1 m = 1000 mm 1 m = 100 cm 1 m = 0.001 km = $\frac{1}{1000}$ km
Kilometer (km)	1 km = 1000 m
Mass	
Milligram (mg)	1 mg = 0.001 g = $\frac{1}{1000}$ g
Gram (g)	1 g = 1000 mg 1 g = 0.001 kg = $\frac{1}{1000}$ kg
Kilogram (kg)	1 kg = 1000 g
Capacity	
Milliliter (mL)	1 mL = 0.001 L = $\frac{1}{1000}$ L
Liter (L)	1 L = 1000 mL

Time	Conversion
Second (s)	1 s = $\frac{1}{60}$ min 1 s = $\frac{1}{3,600}$ hr
Minute (min)	1 min = 60 s 1 min = $\frac{1}{60}$ hr
Hour (hr)	1 hr = 3,600 s 1 hr = 60 min 1 hr = $\frac{1}{24}$ d
Day (d)	1 d = 24 hr
Week (wk)	1 wk = 7 d
Year (yr)	1 yr = 365 d 1 yr = 52 wk

Approximate Equivalents

English to Metric	Metric to English
1 in = 2.54 cm (exactly)	1 cm ≈ 0.3937 in
1 ft ≈ 30.48 cm	1 m ≈ 39.37 in ≈ 1.094 yd
1 yd ≈ 0.914 m	1 km ≈ 0.621 mi
1 mi ≈ 1.609 km	
1 oz ≈ 28.35 g	1 g ≈ 0.035 oz
1 lb ≈ 0.454 kg	1 kg ≈ 2.205 lb
1 ton ≈ 907.18 kg	1000 kg ≈ 1.1 tons
1 fl oz ≈ 29.574 mL (cc)	
1 c ≈ 237 mL (cc)	
1 qt ≈ 0.946 L	1 L ≈ 1.057 qt

Made in the USA
Monee, IL
03 May 2026